Forms of Poetry

Edited by

JAMES L. CALDERWOOD

and

HAROLD E. TOLIVER

University of California, Irvine

PRENTICE-HALL, INC., *Englewood Cliffs, New Jersey*

to Robert B. Heilman and Arnold Stein

PRENTICE-HALL INTERNATIONAL, INC., *London*
PRENTICE-HALL OF AUSTRALIA, PTY. LTD., *Sydney*
PRENTICE-HALL OF CANADA, LTD., *Toronto*
PRENTICE-HALL OF INDIA PRIVATE LTD., *New Delhi*
PRENTICE-HALL OF JAPAN, INC., *Tokyo*

Prentice-Hall English Literature Series

MAYNARD MACK,   *Editor*

Library of Congress Catalog Card Number: 68-10110

Printed in the United States of America

Current Printing (last digit):
10 9 8 7 6 5 4 3 2 1

Preface

Forms of Poetry, like its forthcoming companion volumes *Forms of Drama* and *Forms of Fiction,* is designed to assist students to an informed and organized analysis of literature. We stress generic principles of organization on the assumption that most students will benefit from a stronger framework than that provided by either chronology or a progression from easy to difficult works, both arrangements being usually somewhat arbitrary. The opening section explains why *genre,* and the closing section on critical views puts formal analysis itself in a larger context—as one of many ways of looking at literary blackbirds. We make this critical material available because at certain points some students, even in the introduction to literature courses for which this text is primarily intended, will want to consider the nature of criticism itself.

The selections are designed to give the instructor enough options to apply the text to his own purposes, using the arrangements and commentaries as points of departure as he wishes. We have tried to avoid the impression that poetry and literary history are made up of short lyrics. Heroic, narrative, dramatic, and satiric works are amply represented. Within each genre, selections from all periods of the historical spectrum are presented chronologically so that the student can examine a range of strategies, forms, historical contexts, and later responses to earlier form (responses ranging from acquiescence to rejection and parody). In so doing, he may gradually realize some of the important *interactions* of history and form.

Contents

Ode and Hymn

Elegy

Reflective, Religious, and Meditative Lyrics

Dramatic Monologue

PASTORAL

HEROIC MODES

ROMANCE

SATIRE

Chronological
Table of Contents

The Study
of
Literary Genres

I.   Three Approaches: Historical, Objective, Generic   The approach to literature (poetry) in this book is through genres, or the 'kinds," modes, forms, or categories of writing into which writers past and present have transformed experience in order to express it. In their broadest form, the genres available to the writer are expository writing, fiction, drama, and poetry; but over the long run of literature, many variations and subspecies of these genres have developed, such as lyric, pastoral, epic, romance, tragedy, comedy, short story, novel, and so on. Each of these recurrent modes offers the writer certain conventional attitudes, strategies, structures, tones, and moods, in terms of which he selects and organizes his material. To "justify the ways of God to men," as Milton knew in writing *Paradise Lost,* requires a genre of considerable scope—hardly the theme for a sonnet. Tragedy does not lend itself to the expression of sunrise-feelings, nor is the heroic mode fit for the depiction of a bourgeois social order. Moreover, as writers sit down not just to "write" but to write a particular kind of work, readers often read by genre too, looking for the poetry, fiction, or drama section of the library, turning to the television guide for "drama" or "situational comedy" or perhaps "cartoons" and debating whether to see a "war film" or a "musical."

The student who is aware of the method implicit in given forms is obviously better prepared to appraise them than one who is not, and from the standpoint of critical reading he will also be better prepared to use what he has learned from the reading of one work as assistance in reading others. When he sees, for instance, that pastoral elegies make certain connections between biological nature and the dead "shepherd," he is more likely to understand why Milton turns from nature to the supernatural in the Christian elegy "Lycidas." Not every sea creature is exactly like all of his kin, but some notion of, say, "spongeness" is valuable to those to whom sea-distinctions are important; and a skin diver may understandably prefer to react to a particular dorsal-finned fish in terms of "sharkness" without waiting to explore individual variations in the species. The aim of this book is to help students of poetry to make distinctions of the right kind among certain literary forms to which man, the symbol-using animal, resorts when he has something important to say and wants the saying of it to be memorable.

There are, to be sure, other ways of approaching literature, the most common being the *historical* and the *objective,* or "new-critical." (The latter is so called because its method of close textual analysis has received new emphasis among contemporary critics.) The historical approach assumes that the "times" in general and the "moment" in particular from which a poem issues provide the best context for its study. The objective approach, on the other hand, minimizes a poem's historical (and generic) connections with other works and stresses its unique identity. We suggest, however, that often a better way to understand both historical movements in literature and the special integrity of particular poems is to begin with the normative expectations aroused by recurrent form. There is much truth in Yeats's claim that "works of art are always begotten by previous works of art." And there is truth, too, in the notion that however a work is *begotten,* an analysis of it requires a critical framework that neither the isolated poem nor history provides.

But these are polemic issues that need to be looked at more closely. In asking the student to consider matters of literary form, we do not mean that he should ignore other approaches, for ideally they all complement one another, each having special value. History provides us with a "dictionary" of the past in which we try to search out the meanings of a poem's words, concepts, themes, topical allusions, and so on; the objective view offers a set of analytic tools by which the structure, statement, and tone of individual poems may be examined closely; and the approach by forms or genres uses both of the other approaches as tools to provide a full "grammar" of forms. We stress the approach by forms, especially for an introduction to poetry, because we believe that it comes closer to encompassing the other two than they to encompassing it (or each other).

Perhaps the chief advantage of a generic approach as opposed to a strictly historical emphasis is that a "grammar" of forms may be sought primarily within literature itself and can include (quite literally) grammatical elements of language. We shall note in other places, for instance, that recurrent grammatical moods and tenses distinguish certain forms, as pastoral tends to deal in subjunctives of unfulfilled (idyllic) desire (yearnings for a Golden Age) and as satire tends to imply some such imperative as "alter your ways, transgressor!" Equally important, knowing what linguistic form does to reality is necessary not only for literary analysis but for all accurate communication. Aristotle remarks that history is concerned with individual cases, with "fact," whereas literature interprets fact, by which he seems to mean that facts may come to us unscreened in some forms of communication. We are now more aware than Aristotle that any written document transforms the nonverbal stuff to which it refers by imposing formal order upon it. Hence even when we think we are reading pure "history," we need to bear in mind the generic laws of the medium. A newspaper account of a peace march, for instance, selects certain details and publishes certain photographs in keeping with the generic demands of reporting, the bias of the paper, and the current mood of society. A ballad, an epic, an elegy, a novel, or a satire dealing with the same peace march would each give us quite a different view. Similarly, a social historian, likely to be concerned with accuracy, would handle the "facts" differently than would a Freudian psychoanalyst or a politician. Thus all verbal accounts are translations with built-in perspectives. The literary analyst as opposed to the historian concentrates on the *translating medium* and what it has done to the viable stuff of events, putting dinosaurs into one bin, mice into another, and so on with other inhabitants of the literary zoo. As a naturalist avoids thinking of a kangaroo as an enlarged rabbit-mouse with a vest pocket, so the literary analyst avoids thinking of Shakespeare and Spenser as similar "Elizabethans": not so much overlapping dates and common environment as the nature of drama and allegory gives him a framework within which to examine the individual allegorist and dramatist.

We shall return to another aspect of the drawbacks of an exclusively historical approach in a moment. Here we should note that strictly objective analysis also has shortcomings unless supplemented by historical and generic considerations. Most beginning students of literature when attempting to analyze an isolated poem become studies in trial-and-error behavior, which someone has called "the random movements of a baffled organism." But a student who works back and forth from genus to differentia in studying, say, Pope's *The Dunciad,* brings to the poem a set of critical expectations developed from his study of satire. He does not encounter simply "a" poem but a particular "kind" of poem. Merely the act of trying to determine why it is this kind of poem rather than something else is a critical engagement involving the student in a consideration of plot, tone, imagery, theme, structure, historical content, and so on. Likewise, a student who considers heroic journeys and virtues from the Old English epic *Beowulf* through Wordsworth's personal narrative *The Prelude* is more likely to be aware of recurrent ways of transforming daily reality into heroic myth than one who tries to swallow an entire period in one intellectual gulp or slice it into single poem portions.

We suggest, then, that because form "defines" (gives boundaries to) the *trans*formed materials of poetry it is the most natural basis of comparison in literary matters. As we pursue each genre and try to describe its formative laws, it becomes evident that poets use decorum—that is, their sense of what is suitable to a given genre—as a filtering and organizing device and that without such filtering and organizing there would be no art. Similar screening processes govern pragmatic as well as "creative" activities. A salesman, for instance, whether Hellenic Greek or modern European, filters out incoming customers by categorizing them—perhaps as "quality minded," "economy minded," and "prestige minded"—and the categories shape, in turn, the salesman's own responses, which assume the form of quality, economy, and prestige "sales pitches." On the basis of his experience and training, he thus develops a rudimentary "grammar" of selling, emphasizing, let us say, a judicious mixture of the indicative, interrogative, and imperative moods in describing the product, helping the customer see it in a certain way (by planting leading questions in his mind), and urging him to buy it. The salesman approaches his victim and overcomes his reluctance in a trained, institutionalized fashion, just as any decorum—of the courtroom, the legislature, the classroom—formalizes the "cases" fed into it. There is a decorum of the dinner table, the subway, the entering of doors, the courtship of wives, the killing of enemies, and the writing of letters, each with its own "stylistic" variants.

Literary modes are no different in principle but are forms not of pragmatic action but of indirect symbolic reflection or imitation; they belong to the fine rather than the practical arts and are ends instead of means. What we hope the student will discover eventually is that each set of conventions—those pertaining to tragedy, comedy, hymn, pastoral, epic, and so on—has its own transformational principles by which reality is formulated. Whereas the salesman sometimes meets customers who do not fit his "grammar" and is forced to ring up the no-sale sign, the artist who uses the form intelligently can always translate the material to fit it: he "lets in" only what he wants and can create new molds to fit material he finds important.

II. The Approaches Applied   Assuming that formal analysis has the potentials we have been discussing, we still need to clarify the respective functions of the various approaches to literature. In reading the following sonnet by Shakespeare let us consider what formal analysis has to offer that other approaches to the poem might overlook:

> When I consider everything that grows
> Holds in perfection but a little moment,
> That this huge stage presenteth nought but shows
> Whereon the stars in secret influence comment;
> When I perceive that men as plants increase,
> Cheered and check'd even by the self-same sky,
> Vaunt in their youthful sap, at height decrease,
> And wear their brave state out of memory;
> Then the conceit of this inconstant stay
> Sets you most rich in youth before my sight,
> Where wasteful Time debateth with Decay
> To change your day of youth to sullied night;
> > And all in war with Time for love of you,
> > As he takes from you, I engraft you new.

It would be foolish to consider this poem "timeless" when one of the significant facts about it is that it was written by Shakespeare and published as part of an interrelated series of sonnets. An awareness of history, not only here but in general, can help prevent certain fundamental misinterpretations—as in reading Chaucer, for instance, we must know something about the fourteenth-century church and the deportment of nuns to know whether the Prioress is innocently orthodox or culpably worldly. Such issues are not resolved merely by amassing facts about the past: we need to put on historical spectacles, to acquire a *feel* for earlier ways of thought.

A historical approach, then, tells us that in this sonnet Shakespeare addresses a young man whose identity is something of a mystery and that the meanings of various words differ from those in modern usage. "Conceit," for instance, means essentially "thought," although a dictionary paraphrase should be reinforced by reading in Elizabethan literature to recapture something of the full flavor and variety of the word. (*The Oxford English Dictionary* is usually a good place to begin.) A history of Renaissance astrology will enrich the significance of the "stars" and their "secret influence." And beyond that, we can call upon the history of ideas to explain the intellectual background of the poem, and upon Shakespeare's other works, used as reference material for this one, to articulate the poem's concern with "time" and "shows," both of which are recurrent Shakespearean themes, and the use of "love" in addressing a male friend. Finally, the poem should be placed in its proper sequence in the series because the meaning of a given poem can be vitally affected by the poems preceding and following it. From these and other considerations, it becomes clear that the poem demands an effort of historical research and imagination to translate its sense of the past into terms that we can understand.

Yet even as we realize this, we are implicitly treating the foreignness or historical dimension of the poem as part of a basic context of meanings that have remained unchanged since Shakespeare's times. Even if much more in the poem required translation than is the case, we would discover that Shakespeare was in part merely using different words to describe familiar experiences and ideas. Indeed, has not Shakespeare himself in the sonnet arrived at the specific, historical "you" from a consideration of "everything that grows," moving from a truth generally experienced to a specific instance? It is partly that generality—the fact that we too have experienced the truth of Time's destructiveness—that justifies his assertion that he is "engrafting" the subject into art, for the poem is a verbal mode of conversion of transient substance into permanent form, part of which is thematic statement. Other relatively permanent elements in this case are the musical interplay of vowels and consonants; patterns of rhyme, rhythm, and image; and the sonnet structure as a whole—all of which compose the poem's special mode of transformation. (We shall comment further on this in a moment.) Thus, the poem has special qualities present in no other poem and, at the same time, has typical qualities of the sonnet and lyric. These verbal elements replace the young man whom Shakespeare addresses somewhat as marble replaces a sculptor's model.

The formal organization of all poems implicitly argues the same thing that Shakespeare has asserted in the sonnet: not men but statements about them, and primarily statements having literary value, endure (*vita brevis, ars longa est*; "life is short, art long"). Form as such is as much outside time as the mathematical equation $8 + 6 = 14$. It is true that a poem is composed of words, that words refer to real objects in the external world, and that because words change their meanings and sounds, a poem can never approach pure form. Yet Shakespeare's intent was obviously to "abstract" the subject. He substitutes art for life without offering even the basic resemblance a sculptor or painter might have given us. The subject suffers a sea-change like that of Ferdinand's father in *The Tempest*:

> Full fathom five thy father lies;
> Of his bones are coral made;

> Those are pearls that were his eyes:
> Nothing of him that doth fade
> But doth suffer a sea-change
> Into something rich and strange.

Whatever Shakespeare may have felt as a man about his young friend, then, as a poet he is primarily interested in him as a means of bringing time and art into literary focus. "You" is not definable as the historical friend but as the part of him that can become a second-person pronoun capable of being addressed as a grammatical object, arousing certain feelings and suggesting certain values—in short, as a symbol of what time and art do to a historical object.

The formal question raised by our example is how Shakespeare has transformed the outer world to which the poem refers into sonnet-shaped coral and pearl. Only if we are convinced that the sonnet form was indeed the right one and is answerable to the experience can we find the poem a successful artifact. In this case, even a brief glance will show that the logic of the argument is beautifully suited to the poetic structure, which in Shakespearean sonnets is divided into three quatrains and a couplet. Each quatrain is stopped with a semicolon and rounded into a precise unit of thought, signaled not only by the punctuation but by the grammatical construction of "When I consider," "When I perceive," and "Then." Thus grammar and thought are molded to the sonnet's preconceived rhyme scheme, which is the same for all Shakespearean sonnets.

In other words, as critics of form we are describing the "mirror" itself, including what is "reflected" in it—a structured, reordering sort of mirror. Whatever we finally decide about the relevance of Elizabethan ideas or Shakespeare himself to this sonnet, these historical factors must be expressed as adjectival qualifiers of the primary literary substance: not "this is Elizabethan or Shakespearean thought made sonnet-like" but "this is an Elizabethan, Shakespearean sonnet" ("Those *are* pearls that *were* his eyes" rather than "Those are eyes made into pearls").

III.   Toward Total Analysis   The study of literary types is most meaningful when the various forms are described in a manner sufficiently general to cover the range of the field but sufficiently precise—by means of adjectival qualifiers mainly—to be relevant to particular works, their periods, their authors, and their audiences. Naturally, the choice of bins and name-tags is crucial and the selection of occupants often difficult: literature, like nature, has its share of duckbilled platypi for which the only accurate genre may be Polonius' "tragical-comical-historical-pastoral." Using various aspects of subject matter as criteria, we could group works according to setting (sea stories, novels of the road, etc.), time (historical, topical, and futuristic works), character (works featuring aristocrats, villains, women, etc.), theme (stories of love, success, betrayal, parenthood), and so on. Or using purely formal criteria, we could group works according to such elements as meter, rhyme scheme, and length. The number of bins is as endless as one's capacity for perceiving resemblances, however trivial. But such groupings would enable us to compare works only at the most superficial level. The traditional categories we have elected to use—tragedy, comedy, lyric, epic, romance, and so on—are based on qualities considerably more elusive and complex than those mentioned above. But in electing to use them both here and in the other two volumes of this series (on drama and fiction), we are trying to stay reasonably close to common language and to encourage the student to work gradually toward complete analysis, not to feel satisfied when he has found a convenient handle such as a thematic pattern or a historical allusion.

It should be clear, however, that we are not attempting to revive neoclassical conceptions of genre, which were heavily prescriptive and generally based on a hierarchy of form, with the epigram at the bottom and epic and tragedy at the top. It is impractical to lay down rigid rules in this manner, either for the creation or the assessment of poems. Such rule-making was founded on the belief, held with varying degrees of confidence from the sixteenth through the eighteenth centuries, that all genres were known and unalterable. But as the evolution of the novel from romance would indicate, literary forms are not Platonic universals eternally fixed in the heavens to guide wandering writers. Though relatively stable as a "grammar" of forms by comparison with rapid changes in referential content, they come into existence gradually and historically, and they flourish only as long as they remain relevant to central human concerns, which is to say, only as long as they provide satisfying means of shaping, intensifying, and rendering meaningful the flux of human experience.

Hence, whereas we have accepted genres largely according to tradition, we have also re-examined them in terms of their modern availability. We have generally put individual poems into genres that we think offer the greatest critical return. For instance, we classify Keats's "Ode to a Nightingale" as pastoral, not because it is not an ode, but because perhaps more can be said about it as pastoral (that is, as odic pastoral rather than pastoral ode). For this reason, both the instructor and the student will probably want to make comparisons and contrasts that are impossible to indicate merely by situating poems next to each other.

Finally, a study of literary genres may cast light eventually not only on the individuality of poems but also on "literature" as a whole, promoting freer imaginative traffic between the isolated work and the surrounding literary community. An awareness of literary forms may even lead to an awareness of the form of literature, the student gradually realizing that literature is not merely an interminable number of discrete works strung out on the abacus-wire of chronology but a total imaginative structure transcending time, however he arranges the parts. From this perspective he may see that although Milton had no historical influence on Virgil, *Paradise Lost* has a critical and formal influence on one's reading of *The Aeneid;* that although he would never think of putting Hopkins and Wyatt together in a biographical work, he might very well want to put their lyrics side by side in a critical study. When the student perceives that a heightening of the opposition in pastoral between rustic simplicity and urban sophistication moves that genre to the borders of satire, that a gentling of satiric irony moves satire in the direction of comedy, and that a transformation of tone and a displacement of emphasis in comic form may lead to romance, then the student may begin to get some sense of the world, not that literature mirrors, but that it creates and is.

Lyric

Introduction

Although all poetry is like music in patterning sound in time, the associations of the lyric with music are especially close. The term "lyric" is from the Greek *lyrikos*, which in turn comes from *lyra* or *lyre*, the instrument used to accompany the singing of such poems. Perhaps the greatest of the Greek lyric poets, Pindar (518?–438? B.C.), united the talents of poet, singer, musical composer, and instrumentalist. In the same tradition were the twelfth- and thirteenth-century troubadours of Provence, who wrote poems like the *canso* (love song) and the *alba* (dawn song), designed to be sung publicly by either the troubadour himself or a professional entertainer. The proliferation of airs, songs, and madrigals in Renaissance England testifies to a continuing connection between the lyric and music; and in the title of Wyatt's "Blame Not My Lute" we have merely one example indicating that the lyricist remains a performing musician as well as a poet. Today, of course, the lyric is no longer distinguished by instrumental accompaniment, and most popular songs are no longer distinguished by literary merit. However, in its stress on complex rhythmic variations and on such sound-associations as rhyme, pun, alliteration, and assonance, the lyric still reveals an impulse toward song and chant that reflects its musical traditions.

This tendency of the lyric to move into song or chant, that is, toward the forms of public utterance in which the poet's role is that of performer, is counterbalanced in some forms of lyric by a tendency to move *inward*, toward a purely private utterance in which the poet's role is that of self-analyst. Stephen Daedalus says in Joyce's *Portrait of the Artist* that the lyric poet presents his image (poem) in immediate relation to himself, as opposed to the dramatist, who presents his image (play) in immediate relation to an audience, he himself withdrawing entirely. In line with this view, most definitions of the lyric stress its subjectivity.

The popular definition of the lyric as a brief expression of personal, subjective feeling or thought—the usual emphasis being on feeling—derives partly from the English romantics, Blake, Shelley, Keats, Wordsworth, and Coleridge, and partly from the German idealists who preceded and influenced them. In poetry the romantics sought to assert the importance of interior experience in a world in which science had created a sharp cleavage between the self and the not-self. Thus Wordsworth speaks of poetry as "the spontaneous overflow of powerful feelings," and Keats endows the imagination with the power of attaining unique knowledge: "What the Imagination seizes as Beauty must be truth." At the same time the romantics sought to bridge the gap between self and not-self, to re-establish rapport between man and nature. In the Renaissance, "nature" (the external world) was important to the poet both in itself and as a subject for imitation. To the romantics, not so much nature for its own sake as the poet's relation to nature was significant. Hegel, one philosopher of romanticism, regarded the lyric poet as one who takes all nature into himself, making it internal and personal. In the same vein, Wordsworth's "wise passiveness" describes the spiritual precondition enabling the poet to assimilate nature "in the living soul" rather than through the senses. Keats also stresses the poet's relation to nature, but he does not regard it as one of assimilation; rather he hopes to unite himself with nature through identification and empathy. Thus he sees the poet as having "no Identity—he is continually informing— and filling some other body," that is, projecting himself imaginatively into nature.

This view of the lyric as an expression of personal feeling or imaginative insight is in accord with what the romantic poets considered themselves to be doing. Only with certain qualifications, however, will this view account for what they actually did, and it will not account for lyrics of other periods. Turning from the romantic to the Elizabethan lyric, for instance, we can hardly fail to be impressed by the comparative anonymity of the latter. Whereas we can easily enough distinguish a sonnet by Wordsworth from one by Keats, we would have some difficulty attributing four unidentified love sonnets of the sixteenth century to, say, Drayton, Sidney, Ralegh, and Daniel. The early Elizabethan lyric issues from a "poet," a poet fashioning a particular kind of poem—sonnet, ode, hymn, and so on—consciously, with concern for decorum, expressing not merely his own private emotions but the emotions that poems of this kind *can* express, and whose tone is therefore less personal than conventional.

This suggests that whereas the lyric as a whole exhibits greater subjectivity than drama, epic, romance, satire, and so on, poems *within* the lyric genre may range between the extremes of public formality and private subjectivity. On the whole, the latter extreme is the province of the romantic lyric; the former that of the medieval, Renaissance, and Augustan lyric. Even, however, in the most subjective of lyric poems, romantic or other, we will find a struggle between form and personal feeling, because like all literature the lyric is an ordering or "forming" of experience (actual or imaginative) within the medium of language. No poetry—despite Wordsworth's "spontaneous overflow of powerful feeling" or Shelley's skylark pouring forth its "full heart / In profuse strains of *unpremeditated* art"—is truly spontaneous. The very act of writing—of transposing thought and feeling into received forms—precludes spontaneity. Only laughs, groans, or shouts are truly spontaneous, and these as symptoms rather than symbols of emotion lie outside the boundaries of poetry.

This is not to deny that the lyric poet subjectifies the external world but merely to round out this observation with the companion idea that the lyric poet, like any other, also objectifies the internal world of personal thoughts and feelings in formal language. A painter works with oils and canvas, a sculptor with stone, a poet with words. Because words are intangible, their meanings being more important than they themselves, we often fail to see that the poet uses them as objects, as material that he molds into the shape of a poem—for as a consideration of metrics reveals, words have certain phonetic shapes dependent upon their stressed and unstressed syllables. An iamb (as in *agáin*), for instance, is an "object," the first part of which is small (or horizontal or thin or low) and the second part large (or vertical or thick or high). A trochee (*lówly*) is just the reverse. An anapest (*on the wáy*) climbs "upward," a dactyl (*glímmering*) falls away, and so on. By extending the pattern to include a line of poetry, we get the shape or form of a line: iambic tetrameter or four stress lines ("This coyness lady were no crime"); trochaic trimeter or three stress lines ("Merry, merry sparrow"); and so down to monometers and dimeters or up to pentameters and hexameters (one, two, five, and six stress lines). The older terms *measure* and *number* indicate perhaps more clearly still that we are treating this aspect of poetry as one would treat an object that is measurable, countable, and divisible into quantitative units. Again, when we speak of rhyme, assonance (repeated vowel sounds), and alliteration (repeated initial consonants) we are thinking of words as phonic objects and emphasizing relations between words that have nothing to do with their meaning. By the same token, a sight-rhyme such as "wear/gear" asserts a purely visual relation between two words regardless of their sound or sense. We associate *things* by means of *words* on the basis of the sound properties of words; hogs and frogs that have nothing to do with each other in the natural world may lie down together on the written page. The *associational* powers of sound thus have a "grammatical" function as surely as the verb and the preposition; they, too, chart relations of things on verbal maps of the artist's making.

If we expand the scope of our attention to stanzas and whole units, we may even speak of the "poem" as a single "shape"—of prescribed length, meter, and rhyme scheme. So with the sonnet, the ode, and such things as the rhyme royal stanza, the quatrain, and so forth, all of which are "grammatical" units of enlarged organizational scope. Even when a poet lets his poem find its own rhyme scheme, the very fact that a "scheme" is involved, however original, implies a limitation on the free play of expression.

Forms of the Lyric   The friction between inner expressive impulse and outer poetic form inevitably becomes part of the creative process and as such contributes its share to the final product, the created poem. The poet's attempt to find an articulate form for his insight transforms that insight into something different. Each traditional lyric convention exerts its own characteristic pressure on the poet's original impulse. (It would be a mistake, for instance, to celebrate an important historical event in a limerick.) Hence the reader approaching poetry with formal considerations in mind should consider the potential of each lyric type separately. The following descriptions of particular forms are meant to suggest rather than to define that potential.

Ballad

The ballad is a mixed form, sharing the communal nature and sometimes the heroes of epic (though its narratives are not extensively detailed); although the best ballads can be enjoyed without music, it suggests song in its emphasis on verse regularity and performable music; it is often elegiac, tragic, or romantic in mood; it resembles the history chronicle in its occasional adaptation of actual historical events; it sometimes suggests the humorous fabliau in treating domestic events; and in later variations composed by professional or semi-professional poets ("broadside" ballads), it contains a large admixture of satire and propaganda. The satirist and propagandist undoubtedly turn to the ballad partly because of its folk aspects in order to exploit the simplicity and popularity of the form.

It is the folk element that seems to be central to the ballad in all its variations. Although a first-person narrator is sometimes assumed to be the presenter of the tale, the ballad traditionally grows out of the anonymous people rather than from the singular emotions of the "I" who sings it or of a particular composer. Like the song, it routes emotion *through* a predominantly impersonal medium.

Its methods of doing so are not complicated for the most part, although they are highly variable. Despite the ballad's overtones of class struggle, which may cause individual listeners to identify with a specific economic or social cause, it is traditionally more often romantic or austerely tragic than political. Perhaps because highly unusual events enable one to forget serfdom or life in the coal mines (or if not to forget them, to cope with them), ballads are predominantly concerned with heroic acts, violence, ghostly visitations, adventures, and love. Lord Randal, for example, is poisoned by his "true" love, a grisly but romantic fate; Edward murders his father at his mother's insistence; Sir Patrick Spens dies a heroic death in the service of a king whom he replaces as the center of the community at the bottom of the sea. Love affairs like Barbara Allen's are intense, once-in-a-lifetime affairs, tragically beautiful and frequently supernatural in the uncanny communications between lovers or in the interwoven rose bushes that grow out of the lovers' graves.

Although the subject matter of the ballad is thus elevated, the perspective is usually from below, from the common man looking up at a life beyond his everyday existence and indulging in an unrestricted dream of heroic fulfillment—or at least of a heroic and highly significant death. If the ballad often echoes the epic "I sing of arms and the man," it is cast in the lower key of folk groups, "Let me tell you a tale. . . ." Because of this folk-perspective, the ballad is not seriously intellectual, and it seldom generalizes. Even its concern with class problems tends to be immediate and "human" rather than abstractly humanitarian, as its concern with religious experience is spontaneous rather than rational or moral. The end of "Lamkin," for instance, is a bare statement of fact where we might expect the ballad to declare some sympathy for Lord Wearie, whose wife and son have been murdered by Lamkin and a nurse because of the Lord's failure to pay Lamkin for his work:

> "And wha's blood is this," he says,
>   "That lies in my ha?"
> "It is your young son's heart's blood;
>   'T is the clearest ava."
>
> O sweetly sang the black-bird
>   That sat upon the tree;
> But sairer grat Lamkin,
>   When he was condemnd to die.
>
> And bonny sang the mavis
>   Out o the thorny brake;
> But sairer grat the nourice,
>   When she was tied to the stake.

It is true that a moral commentary is implied in the ironic statement that though the birds called out loudly they were not nearly so loud as Lamkin and the nurse (hanged and burned respectively), who have been vocal critics of certain social and economic injustices. But the tone is far from moralistic. It is a tough-minded, austere irony that comes of the juxtaposition of birds' song and human grating; there is no implication that if all servants were loyal they would find better rewards.

Likewise, the protest of ballads that refer to social conditions more directly, such as the modern protest against nuclear bombs, "What Have They Done to the Rain," is not the sort to cause their listeners to storm the barricades. On the contrary, the tone of the genuine protest ballad, as opposed to ballads composed purposely to unite people in a specific cause, is usually one of resignation and elegiac lament. As in other forms of song, the formalizing of emotion takes the place of action and gives the poet and his listeners a way of raising and purging emotions.

In external form and structure, the ballad is normally either dramatic, like "Lord Randal," or narrative in general framework but including a series of dramatic scenes that as a ballad historian once wrote, have a "lingering and leaping" effect. Refrains and incremental repetition (repetition with variations), like the formal elements of other songs, tend to shift the emphasis from personal emotion to performance. (Note the effect of the ritualized form of "Lamkin" and of the "O" that begins many of the stanzas.)

Professionally composed ballads or imitations of ballad form such as the "Rime of the Ancient Mariner" generally borrow some of the external characteristics of the form without attempting to capture the compressed, dramatic nature of folk art. The "Rime of the Ancient Mariner," however, does emphasize the supernatural flavor of many traditional ballads and the loose, paratactic syntax with which the ballad brings together elements of the narrative:

> It is an ancient Mariner,
>   And he stoppeth one of three.

"By thy long gray beard and glittering eye,
    Now wherefore stopp'st me?"

The connective "and" (along with the Mariner's glittering eye and sudden materialization in "it is...") implies that something extra-rational is under way. Why this one out of three? Why three? Where has he come from? These are questions a ballad would also normally leave hanging, for the ballad, like the folk-riddle, allows the reader to discover the connections for himself; it avoids logic and explicit commentary, making the narrative carry its own weight and imply its own meaning.

FINE FLOWERS IN THE VALLEY

The compassion of the ballad, like its moralistic judgment, is normally understated. The refrain of "Fine Flowers in the Valley" carries much of the burden of a highly condensed narrative by turning in several ways an indirect, elusive metaphor for the mother's feeling.

ANONYMOUS

She sat down below a thorn,
    Fine flowers in the valley,
And there she has her sweet babe born,
    And the green leaves they grow rarely.

"Smile na sae sweet, my bonny babe,   5
    Fine flowers in the valley,
And ye smile sae sweet, ye'll smile me dead,"
    And the green leaves they grow rarely.

She's ta'en out her little pen-knife,
    Fine flowers in the valley,   10
And twinnd the sweet babe o' its life,
    And the green leaves they grow rarely.

She's howket a grave by the light o' the moon,
    Fine flowers in the valley,
And there she's buried her sweet babe in,   15
    And the green leaves they grow rarely.

As she was going to the church,
    Fine flowers in the valley,
She saw a sweet babe in the porch,
    And the green leaves they grow rarely.   20

"O sweet babe, and thou were mine,
    Fine flowers in the valley,
I wad cleed thee in the silk so fine,"
    And the green leaves they grow rarely.

---

11 *twinnd*: robbed.   13 *howket*: dug.   23 *cleed*: clothe.

> "O mother dear, when I was thine,
>> *Fine flowers in the valley.*
> You did na prove to me sae kind,"
>> *And the green leaves they grow rarely.*

25

EDWARD AND LORD RANDAL

Discovery and recognition in both "Edward" and "Lord Randal" grow out of the common ballad technique of question and response, which in this case involves the complex relations of mother and son as well as the recent events that make up the narrative element. The crucial moment in each is the revelation of a current, dramatic reaction to the murders just committed. The refrain in both ballads reinforces the dramatic ironies appearing in the interplay of past and present and in "Lord Randal" sets up a critical shift in tone in the concluding lines.

EDWARD

ANONYMOUS

> "Why dois your brand sae drap wi bluid,
>> Edward, Edward,
> Why dois your brand sae drap wi bluid,
>> And why sae sad gang yee O?"
> "O I hae killed my hauke sae guid,
>> Mither, mither,
> O I hae killed my hauke sae guid,
>> And I had nae mair bot hee O."

> "Your haukis bluid was nevir sae reid,
>> Edward, Edward,
> Your haukis bluid was nevir sae reid,
>> My deir son I tell thee O."
> "O I hae killed my reid-roan steid,
>> Mither, mither,
> O I hae killed my reid-roan steid,
>> That erst was sae fair and frie O."

> "Your steid was auld, and ye hae gat mair,
>> Edward, Edward,
> Your steid was auld, and ye hae gat mair,
>> Sum other dule ye drie O."
> "O I hae killed my fadir deir,
>> Mither, mither,
> O I hae killed my fadir deir,
>> Alas, and wae is mee O!"

> "And whatten penance wul ye drie for that,
>> Edward, Edward,
> And whatten penance wul ye drie for that?
>> My deir son, now tell me O."

5

10

15

20

25

---

20 *dule*: sorrow; *drie*: suffer.

"Ile set my feit in yonder boat,
                Mither, mither,   30
Ile set my feit in yonder boat,
   And Ile fare ovir the sea O."
"And what wul ye doe wi your towirs and your ha,
                Edward, Edward?
And what wul ye doe wi your towirs and your ha,   35
   That were sae fair to see O?"
"Ile let thame stand tul they doun fa,
                Mither, mither,
Ile let thame stand tul they doun fa,
   For here nevir mair maun I bee O."   40

"And what wul ye leive to your bairns and your wife,
                Edward, Edward,
And what wul ye leive to your bairns and your wife,
   Whan ye gang ovir the sea O?"
"The warldis room, late them beg thrae life,   45
                Mither, mither,
The warldis room, late them beg thrae life,
   For thame nevir mair wul I see O."

"And what wul ye leive to your ain mither deir,
                Edward, Edward?   50
And what wul ye leive to your ain mither deir?
   My deir son, now tell me O."
"The curse of hell frae me sall ye beir,
                Mither, mither,
The curse of hell frae me sall ye beir,   55
   Sic counseils ye gave to me O."

LORD RANDAL

ANONYMOUS

"O where ha you been, Lord Randal, my son?
And where ha you been, my handsome young man?"
"I ha been at the greenwood; mother, mak my bed soon,
For I'm wearied wi hunting, and fain wad lie down."

"An wha met ye there, Lord Randal, my son?   5
An wha met you there, my handsome young man?"
"O I met wi my true-love; mother, mak my bed soon,
For I'm wearied wi hunting, and fain wad lie down."

"And what did she give you, Lord Randal, my son?
And what did she give you, my handsome young man?"   10
"Eels fried in a pan; mother, mak my bed soon,
For I'm wearied wi huntin, and fain wad lie down."

"An wha gat your leavins, Lord Randal, my son?
And wha gat your leavins, my handsome young man?"
"My hawks and my hounds; mother, mak my bed soon,   15
For I'm wearied wi huntin, and fain wad lie down."

"And what becam of them, Lord Randal, my son?
And what becam of them, my handsome young man?"
"They stretched their legs out and died; mother, mak my bed soon,
For I'm wearied wi huntin, and fain wad lie down." 20

"O I fear you are poisoned, Lord Randal, my son!
I fear you are poisoned, my handsome young man!"
"O yes, I am poisoned; mother, mak my bed soon,
For I'm sick at the heart, and I fain wad lie down." 25

LAMKIN AND THE TWA CORBIES

Even songs of protest sometimes make their best points indirectly. In modern times, such songs are apt to take the form of "blues" or union songs, only marginally ballads. In all times, frustration and indignation often appear tragically inevitable in folk art—whether a coal-mining company, an unjust father or mother, a rambling lover, or perhaps the universe itself is to blame. In "Lamkin," everyone loses; the protest of one class against another is subordinated to the violence of crime and retaliation. In "The Twa Corbies," everything except the hungry ravens proves indifferent to one who has made the mistake of dying out of the common way, where not even hypocrisy matters.

LAMKIN

ANONYMOUS

It's Lamkin was a mason good
　　As ever built wi stane;
He built Lord Wearie's castle,
　　But payment got he nane.

"O pay me, Lord Wearie, 5
　　Come, pay me my fee:"
"I canna pay you, Lamkin,
　　For I maun gang oer the sea."

"O pay me now, Lord Wearie,
　　Come, pay me out o hand:" 10
"I canna pay you, Lamkin,
　　Unless I sell my land."

"O gin ye winna pay me,
　　I here sall mak a vow,
Before that ye come hame again, 15
　　Ye sall hae cause to rue."

Lord Wearie got a bonny ship,
　　To sail the saut sea faem;
Bade his lady weel the castle keep,
　　Ay till he should come hame. 20

8 *maun*: must. 13 *gin*: it; *winna*: will not. 21 *nourice*: nurse; *limmer*: rascal.

But the nourice was a fause limmer
  As eer hung on a tree;
She laid a plot wi Lamkin,
  Whan her lord was oer the sea.

She laid a plot wi Lamkin,   25
  Whan the servants were awa,
Loot him in at a little shot-window,
  And brought him to the ha.

"O whare's a' the men o this house,
  That ca me Lamkin?"   30
"They're at the barn-well thrashing;
  'Twill be lang ere they come in."

"And whare's the women o this house,
  That ca me Lamkin?"
"They're at the far well washing;   35
  'Twill be lang ere they come in."

"And whare's the bairns o this house,
  That ca me Lamkin?"
"They're at the school reading;
  'Twill be night or they come hame."   40

"O whare's the lady o this house,
  That ca's me Lamkin?"
"She's up in her bower sewing,
  But we soon can bring her down."

Then Lamkin's tane a sharp knife,   45
  That hang down by his gaire,
And he has gien the bonny babe
  A deep wound and a sair.

Then Lamkin he rocked,
  And the fause nourice sang,
Till frae ilkae bore o the cradle   50
  The red blood out sprang.

Then out it spak the lady,
  As she stood on the stair:
"What ails my bairn, nourice,   55
  That he's greeting sae sair?

"O still my bairn, nourice,
  O still him wi the pap!"
"He winna still, lady,
  For this nor for that."   60

"O still my bairn, nourice,
  O still him wi the wand!"
"He winna still, lady,
  For a' his father's land."

---

27 *shot-window*: hinged window. 46 *gaire*: gore. 51 *frae ilkae bore*: from the hole.
56 *greeting*: crying.

"O still my bairn, nourice,   65
    O still him wi the bell!"
"He winna still, lady,
    Till ye come down yoursel."

O the firsten step she steppit,
    She steppit on a stane;   70
But the neisten step she steppit,
    She met him Lamkin.

"O mercy, mercy, Lamkin,
    Hae mercy upon me!
Though you've taen my young son's life,   75
    Ye may let mysel be."

"O sall I kill her, nourice,
    Or sall I lat her be?"
"O kill her, kill her, Lamkin,
    For she neer was good to me."   80

"O scour the bason, nourice,
    And mak it fair and clean,
For to keep this lady's heart's blood,
    For she's come o noble kin."

"There need nae bason, Lamkin,   85
    Lat it run through the floor;
What better is the heart's blood
    O the rich than o the poor?"

But ere three months were at an end,
    Lord Wearie came again;
But dowie, dowie was his heart   90
    When first he came hame.

"O wha's blood is this,." he says,
    "That lies in the chamer?"
"It is your lady's heart's blood;   95
    'Tis as clear as the lamer."

"And wha's blood is this," he says,
    "That lies in my ha?"
"It is your young son's heart's blood;
    'Tis the clearest ava."   100

O sweetly sang the black-bird
    That sat upon the tree;
But sairer grat Lamkin,
    When he was condemned to die.

And bonny sang the mavis,   105
    Out o the thorny brake;
But sairer grat the nourice,
    When she was tied to the stake.

---

90 *dowie*: dismal. 96 *lamer*: amber. 103 *grat*: wept. 105 *mavis*: thrush.

THE TWA CORBIES

ANONYMOUS

As I was walking all alane,
I heard twa corbies making a mane;
The tane unto the t' other say,
"Where sall we gang and dine to-day?"

"In behint yon auld fail dyke,   5
I wot there lies a new-slain knight;
And naebody kens that he lies there,
But his hawk, his hound, and lady fair.

"His hound is to the hunting gane,
His hawk to fetch the wild-fowl hame,   10
His lady's ta'en another mate,
So we may mak our dinner sweet.

"Ye'll sit on his white hause-bane,
And I'll pike out his bonny blue een;
Wi'ae lock o' his gowden hair   15
We'll theek our nest when it grows bare.

"Mony a one for him makes mane,
But nane sall ken where he is gane;
O'er his white banes, when they are bare,
The wind sall blaw for evermair."   20

SIR PATRICK SPENS

Unrecognized superiority to their official masters characterizes many folk heroes, but it is seldom implied with such fine irony and compassion as in "Sir Patrick Spens," Sir Patrick's own noble qualities unfortunately being appreciated only in the court at the bottom of the sea.

ANONYMOUS

The king sits in Dunfermline toune,
    Drinking the blude-red wine:
"O whar will I get a guid sailor,
    To sail this schip of mine?"

Up and spak an eldern knicht,   5
    Sat at the kings richt kne:
"Sir Patrick Spens is the best sailor
    That sails upon the sea."

The king has written a braid letter,
    And signd it wi' his hand,   10
And sent it to Sir Patrick Spens,
    Was walking on the sand.

---

2 *corbies*: ravens; *mane*: moan. 5 *fail*: sod. 6 *wot*: know. 7 *kens*: knows. 13 *hause-bane*: neck bone. 16 *theek*: thatch.
9 *braid*: clear.

The first line that Sir Patrick red,
    A loud lauch lauched he:
The next line that Sir Patrick red,   15
    The teir blinded his ee.

"O wha is this has don this deid,
    This ill deid don to me,
To send me out this time o' the yeir,
    To sail upon the se!   20

"Mak hast, mak haste, my mirry men all,
    Our guid schip sails the morne":
"O say na sae, my master deir,
    For I feir a deadlie storme.

"Late late yestreen I saw the new moone,   25
    Wi' the auld moone in hir arme;
And I feir, I feir, my deir master,
    That we will come to harme."

O our Scots nobles wer richt laith
    To weet their cork-heild schoone;   30
But lang owre a' the play wer playd,
    Thair hats they swam aboone.

O lang, lang may their ladies sit,
    Wi' thair fans into their hand,
Or eir they see Sir Patrick Spens   35
    Cum sailing to the land.

O lang, lang may the ladies stand
    Wi' their gold kems in their hair,
Waiting for thair ain deir lords,
    For they'll se them na mair.   40

Haf owre, haf owre to Aberdour,
    It's fiftie fadom deip,
And thair lies guid Sir Patrick Spens,
    Wi' the Scots lords at his feit.

WILLIAM BLAKE *(1757–1827)*

The strange events of ballads are easily converted into the kind of conscious symbol and allegory that appealed to the romantics. Thus Fairyland for Blake becomes a magic cabinet of art through which the poet sees reality in a different light. Yet Blake suggests, too, that if the poet presses too hard in trying to grasp the secret of the magic of that strange vision, its capacity to transform is reversed, like that of magic wands, which in good hands metamorphose people into princes and princesses, and in evil hands, into beasts. Falling through dream to nightmare, the speaker becomes an abandoned child surrounded by alien objects. Although the initial impression of the narrative is that of a past-tense story, it develops into a symbolic medium of more than balladlike complexity.

---

41 *haf owre*: half way.

THE CRYSTAL CABINET

The Maiden caught me in the Wild,
Where I was dancing merrily;
She put me into her Cabinet
And Lock'd me up with a golden Key.

This Cabinet is form'd of Gold   5
And Pearl & Crystal shining bright,
And within it opens into a World
And a little lovely Moony Night.

Another England there I saw,
Another London with its Tower,   10
Another Thames & other Hills,
And another•pleasant Surrey Bower,

Another Maiden like herself,
Translucent, lovely, shining clear,
Threefold each in the other clos'd—   15
O, what a pleasant trembling fear!

O, what a smile! a threefold Smile
Fill'd me, that like a flame I burn'd;
I bent to Kiss the lovely Maid,
And found a Threefold Kiss return'd.   20

I strove to sieze the inmost Form
With ardor fierce & hands of flame,
But burst the Crystal Cabinet,
And like a Weeping Babe became—

A weeping Babe upon the wild,   25
And Weeping Woman pale reclin'd,
And in the outward air again
I fill'd with woes the passing Wind.

JOHN KEATS *(1795–1821)*

The mad ride away from safe ground into the unknown is a common folk
theme. Romance, allegory, and ballad cross in Keats's version of it, which
makes it the vehicle of the same programmed voyage to a land beyond ordinary
life and disillusioned return that much of Keats's other poetry concerns. (See
the headnotes to Keats's treatment of similar concerns in Romance and
Pastoral.)

LA BELLE DAME SANS MERCI

O what can ail thee, Knight at arms,
  Alone and palely loitering?
The sedge has withered from the Lake
  And no birds sing!

O what can ail thee, Knight at arms,   5
  So haggard, and so woe begone?

The Squirrel's granary is full
    And the harvest's done.

I see a lily on thy brow
    With anguish moist and fever dew,   10
And on thy cheeks a fading rose
    Fast withereth too—

I met a Lady in the Meads,
    Full beautiful, a faery's child
Her hair was long, her foot was light   15
    And her eyes were wild—

I made a Garland for her head,
    And bracelets too, and fragrant Zone
She look'd at me as she did love
    And made sweet moan—   20

I set her on my pacing steed
    And nothing else saw all day long
For sidelong would she bend and sing
    A faery's song—

She found me roots of relish sweet   25
    And honey wild and manna dew
And sure in language strange she said
    I love thee true—

She took me to her elfin grot
    And there she wept and sigh'd full sore,   30
And there I shut her wild wild eyes
    With kisses four.

And there she lulled me asleep
    And there I dream'd, Ah Woe betide!
The latest dream I ever dreamt   35
    On the cold hill side.

I saw pale Kings and Princes too,
    Pale warriors, death-pale were they all;
They cried—"La belle Dame sans Merci
    Thee hath in thrall!"   40

I saw their starved lips in the gloam
    With horrid warning gapéd wide,
And I awoke and found me here
    On the cold hill's side.

And this is why I sojourn here   45
    Alone and palely loitering,
Though the sedge is wither'd from the Lake
    And no birds sing.

EZRA POUND *(1885–   )*

Unlike the passive and feminine Christ of some portraits, Pound's Christ is a masculine folk hero associated with the open sea and hearty fellowship. The seeming incongruity of this and the orthodox view is cheerfully dismissed in the vigorous rhythm of the ballad and in the speaker's sly glimpse at other literary genres, especially scripture, which he predicts will never house so great a spirit. The ballad is saved from a kind of breezy bravado by the seriousness of the subject and by Pound's awareness of the ballad's reckless capacity to rollick into apocalyptic vision.

BALLAD OF THE GOODLY FERE*
Simon Zelotes Speaketh It Somewhile After the Crucifixion

Ha' we lost the goodliest fere o' all
For the priests and the gallows tree?
Aye lover he was of brawny men,
O' ships and the open sea.

When they came wi' a host to take Our Man   5
His smile was good to see,
"First let these go!" quo' our Goodly Fere,
"Or I'll see ye damned," says he.

Aye he sent us out through the crossed high spears
And the scorn of his laugh rang free,   10
"Why took ye not me when I walked about
Alone in the town?" says he.

Oh we drunk his "Hale" in the good red wine
When we last made company
No capon priest was the Goodly Fere   15
But a man o' men was he.

I ha' seen him drive a hundred men
Wi' a bundle o' cords swung free,
That they took the high and holy house
For their pawn and treasury.   20

They'll no' get him a' in a book I think
Though they write it cunningly;
No mouse of the scrolls was the Goodly Fere
But aye loved the open sea.

If they think they ha' snared our Goodly Fere   25
They are fools to the last degree.
"I'll go to the feast," quo' our Goodly Fere,
"Though I go to the gallows tree."

"Ye ha' seen me heal the lame and blind,
And wake the dead," says he,   30
"Ye shall see one thing to master all:
'Tis how a brave man dies on the tree."

A son of God was the Goodly Fere
That bade us his brothers be.
I ha' seen him cow a thousand men.   35
I have seen him upon the tree.

He cried no cry when they drave the nails
And the blood gushed hot and free,
The hounds of the crimson sky gave tongue
But never a cry cried he.   40

I ha' seen him cow a thousand men
On the hills o' Galilee,
They whined as he walked out calm between,
Wi' his eyes like the grey o' the sea,

Like the sea that brooks no voyaging   45
With the winds unleashed and free,
Like the sea that he cowed at Genseret
Wi' twey words spoke' suddently.

A master of men was the Goodly Fere,
A mate of the wind and sea,   50
If they think they ha' slain our Goodly Fere
They are fools eternally.

I ha' seen him eat o' the honey-comb
Sin' they nailed him to the tree.

JOHN CROWE RANSOM *(1888–   )*

This poem goes beyond Keats's "La Belle Dame" in contrasting a balladic narrative with the sophisticated uses to which it is put. The interplay between the heroic expectations of the form and the bizarre achievements of Ransom's hero is continuous and subtle. The past is deftly used to define an ambivalent and typically modern attitude toward a latter-day Don Quixote.

CAPTAIN CARPENTER*

Captain Carpenter rose up in his prime
Put on his pistols and went riding out
But had got wellnigh nowhere at that time
Till he fell in with ladies in a rout.

It was a pretty lady and all her train   5
That played with him so sweetly but before
An hour she'd taken a sword with all her main
And twined him of his nose for evermore.

---

* From *Poems and Essays* by John Crowe Ransom. Copyright 1924 by Alfred A. Knopf, Inc. Renewed, 1952, by John Crowe Ransom. Reprinted by permission of Alfred A. Knopf, Inc.

Captain Carpenter mounted up one day
And rode straightway into a stranger rogue   10
That looked unchristian but be that as may
The Captain did not wait upon prologue.

But drew upon him out of his great heart
The other swing against him with a club
And cracked his two legs at the shinny part   15
And let him roll and stick like any tub.

Captain Carpenter rode many a time
From male and female took he sundry harms
He met the wife of Satan crying "I'm
The she-wolf bids you shall bear no more arms."   20

Their strokes and counters whistled in the wind
I wish he had delivered half his blows
But where she could have made off like a hind
The bitch bit off his arms at the elbows.

And Captain Carpenter parted with his ears   25
To a black devil that used him in this wise
O Jesus ere his threescore and ten years
Another had plucked out his sweet blue eyes.

Captain Carpenter got up on his roan
And sallied from the gate in hell's despite   30
I heard him asking in the grimmest tone
If any enemy yet there was to fight?

"To any adversary it is fame
If he risk to be wounded by my tongue
Or burnt in two beneath my red heart's flame   35
Such are the perils he is cast among.

"But if he can he has a pretty choice
From an anatomy with little to lose
Whether he cut my tongue and take my voice
Or whether it be my round red heart he choose."   40

It was the neatest knave that ever was seen
Stepping in perfume from his lady's bower
Who at this word put in his merry mien
And fell on Captain Carpenter like a tower.

I would not knock old fellows in the dust   45
But there lay Captain Carpenter on his back
His weapons were the old heart in his bust
And a blade shook between rotten teeth alack.

The rogue in scarlet and grey soon knew his mind
He wished to get his trophy and depart   50
With gentle apology and touch refined
He pierced him and produced the Captain's heart.

God's mercy rest on Captain Carpenter now
I thought him Sirs an honest gentleman

Citizen husband soldier and scholar enow   55
Let jangling kites eat of him if they can.

But God's deep curses follow after those
That shore him of his goodly nose and ears
His legs and strong arms at the two elbows
And eyes that had not watered seventy years.   60

The curse of hell upon the sleek upstart
Who got the Captain finally on his back
And took the red red vitals of his heart
And made the kites to whet their beaks clack clack.

Song

Drink to me only with thine eyes,
And I will pledge with mine;
Or leave a kiss but in the cup,
And I'll not look for wine.
The thirst that from the soul doth rise
Doth ask a drink divine;
But might I of Jove's nectar sup,
I would not change for thine.

It is the nature of a song to be *impersonally* personal. The singer may appear to be overwhelmed with emotion—exaltation in drinking songs, love in love songs, chauvinistic emotion in patriotic songs, and so forth—yet he is, after all, singing and not speaking. (A singer who mistakes the performer for the real self does not disprove the assumption.) The singer's emotion is not exactly falsified, but neither is it "sincere" in any common sense. He puts himself *into a conventional situation,* which maintains its independence at the same time that he borrows its exterior. It belongs intrinsically to the owners of convention and common language, that is, to all who understand the words and gestures. The "personal" emotion of the form is thus, almost by definition, common property also. Songs emphasize conventional images and metaphors—for example, the eyes, lips, wine cups, and idealistic aspects of romance. They tend to have a prominent and regular metrical structure, not only because music is temporally structured by a regular beat and melody line but also because in the compromise between outer form and inner emotion, emotion loses its individual, irregular stamp. Although songs are commonly cast in a mood of beseeching—note the imperative mood in Jonson's song above—the *tension of expectation* is resolved in the *regularity of form*: even as the singer asks that a kiss be given, the stanzaic music rounds off to a final close. Only in musical comedy would Celia be naive enough to take the singer literally. His passion is sufficiently exaggerated to appear more polite flattery than desperate thirst.

The song in light moments such as this demands little of us except passive listening and perhaps applause for a finished performance. This is no less true of a seemingly disturbing song, a song of betrayed love or unfulfilled yearning. The man who revenges his betrayal is not the same as the man who sings about it. Formal articulation takes the place of action. Exceptions to this rule are often illuminating simply because, as variations of a common pattern, they enable us to see the characteristics of pure song more clearly. "The Love Song of J. Alfred Prufrock," for example, at first appears to reject everything that we have defined as songlike but on closer examination reinforces our expectations. Eliot's title is ironic insofar as Prufrock, unlike ordinary singers of love songs, is afraid to declare his love publicly. He cannot step outside himself as performer and thus use convention to create a public mask capable of communicating his passion to the lady. Consequently, his "song" remains a nondramatic monologue in which he tells everything to a private listener, probably his own alter ego. As the epigraph to the poem reveals, he cannot bring himself to trust his message to someone who will tell all. Usually, however, in straightforward songs we are concerned primarily with musical qualities rather than irony, complexity of imagery and voice, and tonal shading. For practice in the kind of analysis demanded by songs, consider "The Blossom" from Blake's *Songs of Innocence*:

> Merry, Merry Sparrow!
> Under leaves so green
> A happy Blossom
> Sees you swift as arrow
> Seek your cradle narrow   5
> Near my Bosom.
>
> Pretty, Pretty Robin!
> Under leaves so green
> A happy Blossom
> Hears you sobbing, sobbing
> Pretty, Pretty Robin,   10
> Near my Bosom.

Our first concern is the kind of grammar or order created by the individual line, the stanza pattern, and ultimately the cross-referencing of the two six-line units. Notice initially the establishing and varying of a basic trochaic pattern:

> Merry, Merry Sparrow!
> Under leaves so green

Blake accomplishes a sense of completed musical phrase at "green" by varying the metrical pattern slightly. Each foot except the last is a single word stressed on the first syllable; the ending of the first line is "weak" or "feminine" (unstressed). So symmetrical is the pattern (with its ritual three "rr" sounds and balanced pair of lines) and so distinct the "green" that as we pause, we listen for a matching line.

When the student has grasped this movement, he will have gone some of the way toward explaining the musical phrasing of the poem, which is readily distinguishable from the phrasing of spoken cadences or reflective meditations. At the same time, noting the symmetry and balance of these musical qualities is only a first step in describing the poem's effect, which is not that simply of an uncomplicated idyll about the completed home-seeking of birds. Both the meaning and the metrical structure of the poem have raw edges. Because lines four and five compose an obvious pair, for instance, we anticipate a concluding line as partner to the third; when three and six also make a pair, we anticipate still more strongly a pairing of some sort for line two, with a rhyme for "green." But the second anticipation is altogether disappointed and the first partly so. "Bosom," a weak half rhyme, rings dissonantly and prevents the total relaxation that a musical stanza normally gives us.

These musically unbalanced elements are slight, as befits a song, but they are in keeping with the second stanza, in which the disquiet becomes more pronounced. The comfortable proximity of the sparrow gives way to the disturbing closeness of the sobbing (rather than singing) robin. All told, the poem's uneasiness is a hint that something is not yet accounted for, something that the other songs of the related series concern. The "disturbed symmetry" of the musical structure reflects in the matter of form the situation of the world of "innocence" in the trying world of "experience."

Yet the poem takes these dissonant qualities in stride. It does not convert them into the kind of disquiet that characterizes Blake's songs of experience. The happy arrival at the green tree and the unhappy noise of the robin exactly balance each other, and the speaker offers no personal comment. Despite the lengthened syllables in "sobbing, sobbing" (achieved by the singable duration of *o*), the tone and the perspective remain neutral. We are not led to question the causes of the robin's sorrow, merely to acknowledge it. The second "Pretty, Pretty Robin" comes as if after a mere ripple on the surface of the poem's calm.

The student may wish to think of such songs as something besides musical structures, but no complete account of them can overlook their interplay of sound and sense. He should find in the following selections (1) an imitation if not precisely of the singing voice at least of the rhythmic movement of song, with its stress on symmetry, metrical regularity, and harmonious phonetic combinations; (2) relative anonymity (the speaker, as in "The Blossom," is generally unobtrusive); (3) stylistic uniformity, songs being less subject to historical influences than, say, to the voice of Frost or the style of Hopkins; together with (4) enough variation to reward a close look at a given poet's influence on the form.

THE WIFE'S LAMENT

This poem by an unknown Anglo-Saxon author is a lament on that most constant of poetic subjects, inconstancy. The wife sings elegiacally of her departed husband from whom she has been separated by the unexplained enmity of his relatives. Although the accents of personal grief are apparent, it is a formulated grief. "I sing for my sorrow," she says, and that reminds us that sorrow itself may wail or cry but cannot sing; it needs an artist-singer, an "I" somewhat detached from the suffering lover, to give it voice and eloquence and to set personal suffering in a wider context, as in the final lines. Much of the eloquence of this particular sorrow is owing to the form of Anglo-Saxon alliterative verse: the four-beat line with a variable number of unstressed syllables, the sharp *caesura*, or pause, in the middle, and the alliterative inter-stitching (somewhat less prominent here than in the original Anglo-Saxon, but note, for instance, the recurrent *s* of the opening line) that keeps the caesura from breaking the line in two.

ANONYMOUS *(Translated by John F. Adams)**

This song of lament   I sing for my sorrow,
My life's sad days.   There is no doubt
No hardship or misery,   none in my life
Recent or past,   no, none equaled these.
I've suffered all torments,   each misery and pain.   5
     All began when my master   went away from his people,
Crossed the wild ocean;   then tears fell each morning
For the uncertain day: what sea would he sail?
Joyless and wretched   each long day I wandered,
Sought for companions   to comfort my loss.   10
     My man's own kinsmen   made spiteful plans,
Laid their dark schemes   to our mutual division,
Sewed seeds of difference   that none in the world
Should we hate as each other;   but my love-longing grew.
     My master in parting   said I should remain,   15
Though few were my loved ones,   few friends to serve me,
Here in this place.   So now my heart saddens:
Now he is changed,   my own perfect mate,
Grown heavy-hearted   pondering his misery;
Deceived and imposed on,   dissembles his feelings.   20
When our company was joyous   we often vowed
Nothing could part us,   saving death only;
Nothing but death.   Now that's all changed—
Now it might seem   there never had been
Any friendship between us.   Wherever I go   25
I must endure for my lover   venom and spite.
     I was driven to dwell   in a wooded grove,
To live in a sod hut   under an oak.
My earth house is ancient,   a pest house to me;
Dark valleys below,   and above, the high mountains;   30
Hard by this dwelling,   this home lacking joy,
Grow thickets of briar.   Often pains seize me,
Recalling his leaving.   There are still friends on earth,
Lovers alive somewhere,   who lie by each other;
I arise from solitude   to go out at dawn,   35
Alone from my dirt tomb   under the oak tree.
Here I must sit   through the long summer day,
Here I must weep   for my own wretched life,
My many misfortunes;   I'll never find comfort,
No peace or rest: there is none for heart-sickness,   40

---

* Reprinted by permission of John F. Adams.

None for this sorrow   life pours over me.
   Each young man must finally   reject his heart's dictates,
Become heavy-hearted,   think sternly of love:
Though care fill his breast   be outwardly pleasant;
On his wide wanderings   an army of troubles   45
Follows him always,   and no zest in living
So far from his home.   Even thus sits my loved one,
By a cliff's scant shelter,   freezing in blizzards;
My sad-hearted friend   soaked by the weather
In like dreary quarter.   My dearest endures   50
Heartbreak eternal;   too often remembers
His happier home.   Miserable are those
Filled with vain longing   for loved ones away.

BACK AND SIDE GO BARE, GO BARE

Some ideas are attractive enough not only to sing lustily about but to repeat
in numerous variations in verse after verse. So it is with the drinking song
"Back and Side Go Bare, Go Bare," which gives ample opportunity in the
singing to put its message into practice. As the rhetorical amplification of a
simple theme, it allows the spirit to swell and the mind to rest.

ANONYMOUS

Back and side go bare, go bare,
  Both hand and foot go cold,
But belly, God send thee good ale enough
  Whether it be new or old!

But if that I may have truly   5
  Good ale my belly full,
I shall look like one, by sweet Saint John,
  Were shorn against the wool.

Though I go bare, take you no care,
  I am nothing a-cold,   10
I stuff my skin so full within
  Of jolly good ale and old.

I cannot eat but little meat,
  My stomach is not good;
But sure I think that I could drink   15
  With him that weareth an hood.
Drink is my life; although my wife
  Some time do chide and scold,
Yet spare I not to ply the pot
  Of jolly good ale and old.   20

I love no roast but a brown toast,
  Or a crab in the fire;
A little bread shall do me stead;

Much bread I never desire.
Nor frost, nor snow, nor wind I trow,   25
  Can hurt me if it would,
I am so wrapped within and lapped
  With jolly good ale and old.

I care right nought, I take no thought
  For clothes to keep me warm;   30
Have I good drink, I surely think
  Nothing can do me harm:
For truly than I fear no man,
  Be he never so bold,
When I am armed and throughly warmed   35
  With jolly good ale and cold.

But now and then I curse and ban,
  They make their ale so small;
God give them care and evil to fare!
  They stry the malt and all.   40
Such peevish pew, I tell you true,
  Not for a crown of gold,
There cometh one sip within my lip,
  Whether it be new or old.

Good ale and strong maketh me among   45
  Full jocund and full light,
That oft I sleep and take no keep
  From morning until night.
Then start I up and flee to the cup;
  The right way on I hold;   50
My thirst to staunch, I fill my paunch
  With jolly good ale and old.

And Kit my wife, that as her life
  Loveth well good ale to seek,
Full oft drinketh she, that ye may see   55
  The tears run down her cheek.
Then doth she troll to me the bowl,
  As a good malt-worm should,
And say "Sweet-heart, I have take my part
  Of jolly good ale and old."   60

They that do drink till they nod and wink,
  Even as good fellows should do,
They shall not miss to have the bliss,
  That good ale hath brought them to.
And all poor souls that scour black bowls,   65
  And them hath lustily trolled,
God save the lives of them and their wives,
  Whether they be young or old!

---

40 *stry*: destroy. 41 *peevish pew*: thin stuff.

SIR THOMAS WYATT *(1503?–1542)*

Wyatt inherited the light grace of medieval songs but complicated it with irony and a sense of moral outrage. With him for perhaps the first time in the English lyric the rhythms of poetry are made to accommodate the accents of the speaking voice. Except for its irony and sense of personal injury, however, "Blame Not My Lute" is predominantly songlike.

BLAME NOT MY LUTE

Blame not my lute! for he must sound
  Of these and that as liketh me;
  For lack of wit the lute is bound
  To give such tunes as pleaseth me.
  Though my songs be somewhat strange,   5
  And speaks such words as touch thy change,
    Blame not my lute!

My lute, alas, doth not offend,
  Though that perforce he must agree
  To sound such tunes as I intend   10
  To sing to them that heareth me;
  Then though my songs be somewhat plain,
  And toucheth some that use to feign,
    Blame not my lute!

My lute and strings may not deny,   15
  But as I strike they must obey;
  Break not them then so wrongfully,
  But wreak thyself some wiser way;
  And though the songs which I indite
  Do quit thy change with rightful spite,   20
    Blame not my lute!

Spite asketh spite, and changing change,
  And falsèd faith must needs be known;
  The fault so great, the case so strange,
  Of right it must abroad be blown;   25
  Then since that by thine own desert
  My songs do tell how true thou art,
    Blame not my lute!

Blame but thyself that hast misdone
  And well deservèd to have blame;   30
  Change thou thy way, so evil begone,
  And then my lute shall sound that same;
  But if till then my fingers play
  By thy desert their wonted way,
    Blame not my lute!   35

Farewell, unknown! for though thou break
  My strings in spite with great disdain,
  Yet have I found out, for thy sake,

Strings for to string my lute again.
And if, perchance, this silly rhyme   40
Do make thee blush at any time,
    Blame not my lute!

DANIEL, SHAKESPEARE, CAMPION, JONSON

Typical Elizabethan songs, as those of Daniel, Shakespeare, Campion, and
Jonson here illustrate, continue the metrical grace of the English song tradition but tend to stress specific thematic concerns and proper names like
"Celia" rather than allowing both poet and subject to remain generalized.
Shakespeare's songs were sung as part of the performances of certain plays
and hence take added meaning from their dramatic context. Isolated, their musical qualities tend to outweigh their considerable thematic and metaphoric
richness.

LOVE IS A SICKNESS

SAMUEL DANIEL *(1562–1619)*

Love is a sickness full of woes,
    All remedies refusing;
A plant that with most cutting grows,
    Most barren with best using.
        Why so?   5
More we enjoy it, more it dies;
If not enjoyed, it sighing cries—
        Heigh ho!

Love is a torment of the mind,
    A tempest everlasting;   10
And Jove hath made it of a kind
    Not well, nor full nor fasting.
        Why so?
More we enjoy it, more it dies;
If not enjoyed, it sighing cries—   15
        Heigh ho!

SONG FROM *CYMBELINE*

WILLIAM SHAKESPEARE *(1564–1616)*

Fear no more the heat o' the sun
    Nor the furious winter's rages;
Thou thy worldly task hast done,
    Home art gone and ta'en thy wages;
Golden lads and girls all must,   5
As chimney-sweepers, come to dust.

Fear no more the frown o' the great,
    Thou art past the tyrant's stroke;
Care no more to clothe and eat;
    To thee the reed is as the oak: 10

The sceptre, learning, physic, must
All follow this, and come to dust.

Fear no more the lightning-flash
    Nor the all-dreaded thunder-stone;
Fear not slander, censure rash;   15
    Thou hast finish'd joy and moan;
Consign to thee, and come to dust.

SONG FROM *THE TEMPEST*

WILLIAM SHAKESPEARE

Full fathom five thy father lies:
    Of his bones are coral made;
Those are pearls that were his eyes:
    Nothing of him that doth fade
But doth suffer a sea-change   5
Into something rich and strange.
Sea-nymphs hourly ring his knell:
Hark! now I hear them,—
    Ding, dong, bell.

ROSE-CHEEKED LAURA, COME

THOMAS CAMPION *(1567–1620)*

Rose-cheeked Laura, come;
Sing thou smoothly with thy beauty's
Silent music, either other
    Sweetly gracing.

Lovely forms do flow   5
From concent divinely framed;
Heaven is music, and thy beauty's
    Birth is heavenly.

These dull notes we sing
Discords need for helps to grace them;   10
Only beauty purely loving
    Knows no discord;

But still moves delight,
Like clear springs renewed by flowing,
Ever perfect, ever in them-   15
    selves eternal.

COME, MY CELIA, LET US PROVE

BEN JONSON *(1573?–1637)*

Come, my Celia, let us prove,
While we can, the sports of love;
Time will not be ours for ever,
He, at length, our good will sever.
Spend not then his gifts in vain: 5

Suns that set may rise again;
But if once we lose this light,
'Tis with us perpetual night.
Why should we defer our joys?
Fame and rumour are but toys.   10
Cannot we delude the eyes
Of a few poor household spies?
Or his easier ears beguile,
Thus removëd by our wile?
'Tis no sin love's fruits to steal,   15
But the sweet thefts to reveal;
To be taken, to be seen.
These have crimes accounted been.

JOHN DONNE *(1573–1631)*

Most modern students of Donne are more aware of his overturning of conventions in the interests of wit and satire than of his capacity to hold an exacting measure. In the following poem, he achieves a harmonious fusion of light wit, satiric keenness, and formal excellence.

SONG: GO AND CATCH A FALLING STAR

Go, and catch a falling star,
  Get with child a mandrake root,
Tell me, where all past years are,
  Or who cleft the devil's foot,
Teach me to hear mermaids' singing,   5
  Or to keep off envy's stinging,
          And find
          What wind
Serves to advance an honest mind.

If thou be'st born to strange sights,   10
  Things invisible to see,
Ride ten thousand days and nights,
  Till age snow white hairs on thee;
Thou, when thou return'st, will tell me
All strange wonders that befell thee,   15
          And swear
          No where
Lives a woman true, and fair.

If thou find'st one, let me know;
  Such a pilgrimage were sweet,   20
Yet do not, I would not go,
  Though at next door we might meet.
Though she were true, when you met her,
And last, till you write your letter,
          Yet she   25
          Will be
False, ere I come, to two, or three.

TOM O'BEDLAM'S SONG

Like the nonsense poems of *Alice in Wonderland,* Tom O' Bedlam's illogical verse has a way of insinuating contact with a world better left undescribed. The random sequence of images allows the poet to depart from sense in order to swoop down at will upon Tom's pathetic poverty. Tom perhaps speaks better than he knows in claiming knowledge superior to Apollo's (or reason's) because his kind of nighttime dream is not revealed to those who never deviate from well-marked paths.

ANONYMOUS

From the hag and hungry goblin
  That into rags would rend ye.
And the spirit that stands by the naked man
  In the book of moons, defend ye,
That of your five sound senses   5
  You never be forsaken,
Nor wander from yourselves with Tom,
  Abroad to beg your bacon.
    While I do sing: Any food,
      Any feeding, drink, or clothing?   10
    Come, dame or maid, be not afraid,
      Poor Tom will injure nothing.

Of thirty bare years have I
  Twice twenty been enragèd,
And of forty been three times fifteen   15
  In durance soundly cagèd
On the lordly lofts of Bedlam,
  With stubble soft and dainty,
Brave bracelets strong, sweet whips, ding-dong
  With wholesome hunger plenty.   20
    And now I sing: Any food,
      Any feeding, drink, or clothing?
    Come, dame or maid, be not afraid,
      Poor Tom will injure nothing.

With a thought I took for Maudlin,   25
  And a cruse of cockle pottage,
With a thing thus tall, sky bless you all,
  I befell into this dotage.
I slept not since the Conquest,
  Till then I never wakèd,   30
Till the roguish boy of love where I lay
  Me found and stripped me naked.
    And now I sing: Any food,
      Any feeding, drink, or clothing?

---

17 *Bedlam*: Bethlehem Hospital (for the insane). 31 *roguish boy*: Cupid.

Come, dame or maid, be not afraid,   35
    Poor Tom will injure nothing.

When I short have shorn my sour-face,
    And swigged my horny barrel,
In an oaken inn I pound my skin,
    As a suit of gilt apparel.   40
The moon's my constant mistress,
    And the lowly owl my morrow;
The flaming drake and the night-crow make
    Me music to my sorrow.
      While I do sing: Any food,
        Any feeding, drink, or clothing   45
      Come, dame or maid, be not afraid,
      Poor Tom will injure nothing.

The palsy plagues my pulses
    When I prig your pigs or pullen,   50
Your culvers take, or matchless make
    Your chanticleer or sullen.
When I want provant, with Humphrey
    I sup, and when benighted,
I repose in Powles with waking souls,   55
    Yet never am affrighted.
      But I do sing: Any food,
        Any feeding, drink, or clothing?
      Come, dame or maid, be not afraid,
      Poor Tom will injure nothing.   60

I know more than Apollo,
    For oft when he lies sleeping,
I see the stars at bloody wars
    In the wounded welkin weeping,
The moon embrace her shepherd,   65
    And the queen of love her warrior,
While the first doth horn the star of morn,
    And the next the heavenly Farrier.
      While I do sing: Any food,
        Any feeding, drink, or clothing?   70
      Come, dame or maid, be not afraid,
      Poor Tom will injure nothing.

The gipsy Snap and Pedro
    Are none of Tom's comradoes,
The punk I scorn, and the cutpurse sworn,   75
    And the roaring boys' bravadoes.

---

50 *prig*: steal; *pullen*: poultry.   51 *culvers*: doves or pigeons; *matchless make*: i.e., castrate. 53–54 *Humphrey...sup*: to dine with Duke Humphrey = to go hungry.   55 *Powles*: St. Paul's churchyard.   64 *welkin*: sky.   65 *her Shepherd*: Endymion.   66 *queen of love*: Venus.   67 *horn*: cuckold.   68 *Farrier*: Vulcan, husband of Venus.   75 *punk*: whore. 76 *roaring boys*: gangs of young toughs.

The meek, the white, the gentle,
  Me handle, touch, and spare not;
But those that cross Tom Rhinoceros
  Do what the panther dare not.   80
    Although I sing: Any food,
      Any feeding, drink, or clothing?
    Come, dame or maid, be not afraid,
      Poor Tom will injure nothing.

With an host of furious fancies   85
  Whereof I am commander,
With a burning spear and a horse of air
  To the wilderness I wander.
By a knight of ghosts and shadows
  I summoned am to tourney   90
Ten leagues beyond the wide world's end.
  Methinks it is no journey.
    Yet will I sing: Any food,
      Any feeding, drink, or clothing?
    Come, dame or maid, be not afraid,   95
      Poor Tom will injure nothing.

HERRICK, CAREW, WALLER, SUCKLING

In later Renaissance and seventeenth-century lyrics, especially where Donne's influence prevails, songs tend to assume some of the characteristics of "metaphysical" verse, which Dr. Johnson later accused of yoking unlike things by violence at the cost of "judgment" and smooth "numbers." They become more intricately metaphoric and dramatic in, say, the speaker-mistress relation. But although complexity of theme and the cadence of speech are evident in the songs of Greville, Carew, Suckling, Waller, and especially Herrick, these poets normally stress the musical ingredients of the lyric.

THE NIGHT-PIECE: TO JULIA

ROBERT HERRICK *(1591–1664)*

Her eyes the glow worm lend thee;
The shooting stars attend thee;
  And the elves also,
  Whose little eyes glow,
Like the sparks of fire, befriend thee.   5

No will-o'-the-wisp mislight thee;
Nor snake, or slow worm bite thee.
  But on, on thy way,
  Not making a stay,
Since ghost there's none to affright thee.   10

Let not the dark thee cumber;
What though the moon does slumber?

The stars of the night
Will lend thee their light,
Like tapers clear without number.   15

Then, Julia, let me woo thee,
Thus, thus to come unto me.
    And when I shall meet
    Thy silvery feet,
My soul I'll pour into thee.   20

SONG

THOMAS CAREW *(1595–1639)*

Ask me no more where Jove bestows,
When June is past, the fading rose;
For in your beauty's orient deep
These flowers, as in their causes, sleep.

Ask me no more whither doth stray   5
The golden atoms of the day;
For in pure love heaven did prepare
Those powders to enrich your hair.

Ask me no more whither doth haste
The nightingale when May is past;   10
For in your sweet dividing throat
She winters, and keeps warm her note.

Ask me no more where those stars light
That downwards fall in dead of night;
For in your eyes they sit, and there   15
Fixèd become as in their sphere.

Ask me no more if east or west
The phoenix builds her spicy nest;
For unto you at last she flies,
And in your fragrant bosom dies.   20

PERSUASIONS TO ENJOY: A SONG

THOMAS CAREW

If the quick spirits in your eye
Now languish and anon must die;
If every sweet and every grace
Must fly from that forsaken face;
    Then, Celia, let us reap our joys   5
    Ere Time such goodly fruit destroys.

Or if that golden fleece must grow
For ever free from agèd snow;
If those bright suns must know no shade,
Nor your fresh beauties ever fade;   10

Then fear not, Celia, to bestow
What, still being gather'd, still must grow.

Thus either Time his sickle brings
In vain, or else in vain his wings.

GO, LOVELY ROSE

EDMUND WALLER *(1606–1687)*

Go, lovely Rose—
Tell her that wastes her time and me
  That now she knows,
When I resemble her to thee,
How sweet and fair she seems to be.   5

  Tell her that's young,
And shuns to have her graces spied,
  That hadst thou sprung
In deserts where no men abide,
Thou must have uncommended died.   10

  Small is the worth
Of beauty from the light retired:
  Bid her come forth,
Suffer herself to be desired,
And not blush so to be admired.   15

  Then die—that she
The common fate of all things rare
  May read in thee:
How small a part of time they share
That are so wondrous sweet and fair.   20

SONG: OUT UPON IT

SIR JOHN SUCKLING *(1609–1642)*

Out upon it, I have loved
  Three whole days together!
And am like to love three more,
  If it prove fair weather.

Time shall moult away his wings,   5
  Ere he shall discover
In the whole wide world again
  Such a constant lover.

But the spite on't is, no praise
  Is due at all to me: 10
Love with me had made no stays,
  Had it any been but she.

Had it any been but she,
  And that very face,
There had been at least ere this   15
  A dozen dozen in her place.

BLAKE, BURNS, ROSSETTI

Among romantics and Victorians, "song" (apart from folk songs, which stand outside the history of literary movements) meant essentially "love song," as today "ballad" popularly means "love ballad" unless the singer is a cowboy. But Blake's songs are exceptions to the rule. Although he considered them songs and although they seem simple and musical, they are sometimes dense in texture, metaphorically complex, and (especially in *Songs of Innocence* and *Songs of Experience*) interconnected like several voices in antiphonal relationships. Hence most of his songs will be found under other rubrics, and "How Sweet I Roam'd" should not be read as though it were exactly the same kind of verse as the songs by Burns and Rossetti.

INTRODUCTION [FROM *SONGS OF INNOCENCE*]

WILLIAM BLAKE *(1757–1827)*

Piping down the valleys wild,
Piping songs of pleasant glee,
On a cloud I saw a child,
And he laughing said to me:

"Pipe a song about a Lamb!"   5
So I piped with merry chear.
"Piper, pipe that song again;"
So I piped: he wept to hear.

"Drop thy pipe, thy happy pipe;
Sing thy songs of happy chear:"   10
So I sung the same again,
While he wept with joy to hear.

"Piper, sit thee down and write
In a book that all may read."
So he vanish'd from my sight,   15
And I pluck'd a hollow reed,

And I made a rural pen,
And I stain'd the water clear,
And I wrote my happy songs
Every child may joy to hear.   20

MAD SONG

WILLIAM BLAKE

The wild winds weep,
And the night is a-cold;
Come hither, Sleep,
And my griefs unfold:
But lo! the morning peeps   5
Over the eastern steeps,
And the rustling beds of dawn
The earth do scorn.

Lo! to the vault
Of paved heaven,   10
With sorrow fraught
My notes are driven:
They strike the ear of night,
Make weep the eyes of day;
They make mad the roaring winds,   15
And with tempests play.

Like a fiend in a cloud,
With howling woe
After night I do crowd,
And with night will go;   20
I turn my back to the east
From whence comforts have increased;
For light doth seize my brain
With frantic pain.

O MY LUVE'S LIKE A RED, RED ROSE

ROBERT BURNS *(1759–1796)*

O my Luve's like a red, red rose
That's newly sprung in June:
O my Luve's like the melodie
That's sweetly play'd in tune.

As fair art thou, my bonnie lass,   5
So deep in luve am I:
And I will luve thee still, my dear,
Till a' the seas gang dry:

Till a' the seas gang dry, my dear,
And the rocks melt wi' the sun;   10
I will luve thee still, my dear,
While the sands o' life shall run.

And fare thee weel, my only Luve!
And fare thee weel a while!
And I will come again, my Luve,   15
Tho' it were ten thousand mile.

SONG: WHEN I AM DEAD, MY DEAREST

CHRISTINA ROSSETTI *(1830–1894)*

When I am dead, my dearest,
Sing no sad songs for me;
Plant thou no roses at my head,
Nor shady cypress tree.
Be the green grass above me   5
With showers and dewdrops wet;
And if thou wilt, remember,
And if thou wilt, forget.
I shall not see the shadows,
I shall not feel the rain;   10

I shall not hear the nightingale
   Sing on as if in pain.
And dreaming through the twilight
   That doth not rise nor set,
Haply I may remember,   15
   And haply may forget.

WILLIAM BUTLER YEATS *(1865–1939)*

Probably the best writer of songs among modern lyric poets, Yeats suggests at various times the Renaissance lyric, Blake, and the native Irish tradition. Intense, intellectual, and riddling, his songs could easily be considered metaphysical and reflective lyrics even when he labels them songs. Passionate and visionary as his poems often are, however, nothing is allowed to disrupt their finely chiseled surfaces.

TWO SONGS FROM A PLAY*

1

I saw a staring virgin stand
Where holy Dionysus died,
And tear the heart out of his side,
And lay the heart upon her hand
And bear that beating heart away;   5
And then did all the Muses sing
Of Magnus Annus at the spring,
As though God's death were but a play.

Another Troy must rise and set,
Another lineage feed the crow,   10
Another Argo's painted prow
Drive to a flashier bauble yet.
The Roman Empire stood appalled:
It dropped the reigns of peace and war
When that fierce virgin and her Star   15
Out of the fabulous darkness called.

2

In pity for man's darkening thought
He walked that room and issued thence
In Galilean turbulence;
The Babylonian starlight brought
A fabulous, formless darkness in;   5
Odour of blood when Christ was slain
Made all Platonic tolerance vain
And vain all Doric discipline.

---

* Reprinted with permission of the publisher from *The Collected Poems of W. B. Yeats* by William Butler Yeats. Copyright 1928 by The Macmillan Company, renewed 1956 by Georgie Yeats.

---

1 *staring virgin*: Athena. 7 *Magnus Annus*: the great year, or the Platonic Year, is one complete cycle in Yeats's theory of history. 11 *argo*: Jason's ship; the "bauble" of line 12 is "flashier" than the Golden Fleece.

Everything that man esteems
Endures a moment or a day.   10
Love's pleasure drives his love away,
The painter's brush consumes his dreams;
The herald's cry, the soldier's tread
Exhaust his glory and his might:
Whatever flames upon the night   15
Man's own resinous heart has fed.

Sonnet

Like the song, the sonnet stresses formal regularity. Whether "Shakespearean" in form with three quatrains and a couplet (rhymed *abab, cdcd, efef, gg*) or "Petrarchan" with an octave (*abba, abba*) and a sestet (rhymed variously), it modulates and organizes emotion in an essentially impersonal medium. Or so it did traditionally. Renaissance versions of the form tend to be more conventional than modern versions, which are frequently merely another stanzaic form. The average Renaissance sonneteer adhered not only to standard metrical and rhyme schemes but also by and large to conventional rhetorical patterns and themes. The ostensible sources of the poet's emotion were Cupid and the lady's resistance, both more or less beyond his control and both part of an accepted public manner in writing love verse.

The conventions were seldom accepted without modification by the best of the sonneteers, however, who used them rather for points of departure than for maps. Shakespeare, for instance, in describing the "dark lady" of his sonnets inverts the conventional catalogue of superlatives:

My mistress' eyes are nothing like the sun;
Coral is far more red than her lips' red;
If snow be white, why then her breasts are dun;
If hairs be wires, black wires grow on her head.

Sir Philip Sidney thinks of the conventions as a discipline forcing the poet to rise above personal feeling, a kind of idealizing form of culture capable of transforming and ceremonializing sensual crudeness. As the first sonnet of *Astrophel and Stella* illustrates, the tension between form and emotion was for Sidney a central and explicit concern:

Loving in truth, and fain in verse my love to show,
That She, dear She, might take some pleasure of my pain:
Pleasure might cause her read, reading might make her know,
Knowledge might pity win, and pity grace obtain,
I sought fit words to paint the blackest face of woe,
Studying inventions fine, her wits to entertain:
Oft turning others' leaves, to see if thence would flow
Some fresh and fruitful showers upon my sunburned brain.

But words came halting forth, wanting Invention's stay,
Invention, Nature's child, fled step-dame Study's blows,
And others' feet still seemed but strangers in my way.
Thus great with child to speak, and helpless in my throes,
Biting my truant pen, beating myself for spite,
"Fool," said my Muse to me, "look in thy heart and write."

Desiring to make his pain public—at least to the "dear She"—the poet casts about in standard rhetorical figures and conventional themes for "fit words." But nature proves incompatible with "study" and the path "others' feet" have taken. Lacerating himself for being so foolish, the poet looks into the truth-saying, spontaneous heart for words. Yet, paradoxically, the sonnet (like the others in the collection) finds those words coming in regular forms and traditional images. (In fact, it is conventional for a sonneteer to pretend to be unconventional.) Rejecting the shopworn methods of previous sonneteers is thus only a preliminary step toward reconceiving them in less mechanical ways, toward making them more responsible to the inner debates that plague the lover.

After Sidney and Shakespeare, poets expanded the range of themes treated in sonnet form so considerably that in reading them we tend to forget that the sonnet arouses certain formal expectations beside the structural divisions indicated by the rhyme scheme. Milton, for instance, writes of a massacre at Piedmont, his wife's death, and his blindness. Although he maintains many of the regular formal features of the sonnet such as the Petrarchan twofold division, he modulates the break between octave and sestet. By Keats's time, nearly any subject was fair game for the sonneteer, although Keats himself, apparently to gain additional freedom, gradually shifted to the looser form of the ode. In the twentieth century, poets have tended to avoid conventional formality almost entirely. But in sonnets, as in songs, modern variations of the form are sometimes more meaningful if we know that they *are* variations.

SIR THOMAS WYATT *(1503?–1542)*

Wyatt and Surrey are credited with initiating the sonnet vogue in England. Although he translated and borrowed from Italian sonneteers, Wyatt adapted the Italian sonnet to his own themes and moods. "Whoso List to Hunt" is a good example of his capacity to meet the sonnet's strict movements and yet make them seem appropriate for a personal, caustic statement.

WHOSO LIST TO HUNT

Whoso list to hunt, I know where is an hind,
  But as for me—alas, I may no more.
  The vain travail hath wearied me so sore,
  I am of them that farthest cometh behind.
  Yet may I, by no means, my wearied mind   5

---

1 *list*: desires; *hind*: deer, doe.

Draw from the deer; but as she fleeth afore
Fainting I follow. I leave off therefore,
Since in a net I seek to hold the wind.
Who list her hunt, I put him out of doubt,
    As well as I, may spend his time in vain.   10
    And graven with diamonds in letters plain
There is written, her fair neck round about:
Noli me tangere, for Caesar's I am,
And wild for to hold, though I seem tame.

SIR WALTER RALEGH *(1552?–1618)*

"Three Things There Be" combines the teasing enigmas of the riddle, the normal divisions of the Shakespearean sonnet, and the gradual unfolding of a dramatic lyric. All three yield their best in the speaker's delivery of an effectively pointed piece of gnomic advice to a "pretty knave."

THREE THINGS THERE BE THAT PROSPER UP APACE
(Sometimes Attributed to Ralegh)

Three things there be that prosper up apace
And flourish, whilst they grow asunder far,
But on a day, they meet all in one place,
And when they meet, they one another mar;
    And they be these: the wood, the weed, the wag.   5
The wood is that which makes the Gallow tree,
The weed is that which strings the Hangman's bag,
The wag, my pretty knave, betokeneth thee.
Mark well, dear boy, whilst these assemble not,
    Green spring the tree, hemp grows, the wag is wild,   10
But when they meet, it makes the timber rot,
If frets the halter, and it chokes the child.
    Then bless thee, and beware, and let us pray,
    We part not with thee at this meeting day.

SIR PHILIP SIDNEY *(1554–1586)*

By Sidney's time, the writing of sonnet sequences was nearing the peak of its vogue. Because his own sonnets are part of a collection (*Astrophel and Stella*), it is difficult to grasp their specific functions out of context. However, the sonnets included here illustrate something of Sidney's thought concerning love— the main subject of all Renaissance sonneteers—and the problems of writing in the current conventions.

WHEN FAR SPENT NIGHT

When far spent night persuades each mortal eye,
    To whom nor art nor nature granteth light,

---

13 *Noli me tangere*: touch me not; *Caesar's*: possibly refers to Henry VIII, as the "hind" may refer to Anne Boleyn, who may have been Wyatt's mistress before becoming Henry's queen.

To lay his then mark-wanting shafts of sight,
Clos'd with their quivers in sleep's armory;
With windows ope then most my mind doth lie,   5
   Viewing the shape of darkness and delight,
   Takes in that sad hue, which with th' inward night
Of his mazed powers keeps perfect harmony:
But when birds charm, and that sweet air, which is
   Morn's messenger, with rose enamled skies   10
Calls each wight to salute the flower of bliss;
   In tomb of lids, then buried are mine eyes,
      Forced by their Lord, who is asham'd to find
      Such light in sense, with such a darkened mind.

THOU BLIND MAN'S MARK

Thou blind man's mark, thou fool's self-chosen snare,
   Fond fancy's scum, and dregs of scattered thought,
Band of all evils, cradle of causeless care,
   Thou web of will, whose end is never wrought;
Desire, desire I have too dearly bought   5
   With price of mangled mind thy worthless ware,
Too long, too long asleep thou hast me brought,
   Who should my mind to higher things prepare.
But yet in vain thou hast my ruin sought,
   In vain thou madest me to vain things aspire,   10
   In vain thou kindlest all thy smoky fire;
For virtue hath this better lesson taught,
   Within my self to seek my only hire:
   Desiring naught but how to kill desire.

MICHAEL DRAYTON *(1563–1631)*

Drayton's "Since There's No Help" combines English and Italian forms, breaking into three quatrains and a couplet and dividing firmly at the end of the second quatrain. It also combines the sense of immediate, spoken drama with the even rhythmic structure of the "sugared" style (for which Shakespeare and Spenser are noted).

SINCE THERE'S NO HELP, COME LET US KISS AND PART

Since there's no help, come let us kiss and part.
   Nay, I have done; you get no more of me,
And I am glad, yea, glad with all my heart,
   That thus so cleanly I myself can free
Shake hands for ever, cancel all our vows,   5
   And when we meet at any time again,
Be it not seen in either of our brows
   That we one jot of former love retain.
Now at the last gasp of Love's latest breath,
   When, his pulse failing, Passion speechless lies,   10
When Faith is kneeling by his bed of death,

And Innocence is closing up his eyes,
   Now if thou wouldst, when all have given him over,
From death to life thou mightst him yet recover.

WILLIAM SHAKESPEARE *(1564–1616)*

The Shakespearean or English form of the sonnet (rhymed *abab cdcd efef gg*)
generally stresses metaphoric units of four lines each, rather than the "thesis
and response" movement of the Petrarchan or Italian form (which divides
into an octet and a sestet). The advantages of the former to Shakespeare, who
handles metaphor so effectively, are obvious; but the strain on the final
couplet is occasionally quite extreme. The last two lines may summarize,
take up a new direction difficult to develop in a short space, or counterbalance
the preceding twelve lines. Whatever the effectiveness of the couplet, Shakespeare's sonnets at their best combine metaphoric brilliance, structural control,
and musical grace.

THAT TIME OF YEAR

That time of year thou mayst in me behold
When yellow leaves, or none, or few, do hang
Upon those boughs which shake against the cold,
Bare ruin'd choirs, where late the sweet birds sang.
In me thou see'st the twilight of such day   5
As after sunset fadeth in the west,
Which by and by black night doth take away,
Death's second self, that seals up all in rest.
In me thou see'st the glowing of such fire,
That on the ashes of his youth doth lie,   10
As the death-bed whereon it must expire,
Consum'd with that which it was nourish'd by.
   This thou perceiv'st, which makes thy love more strong,
   To love that well which thou must leave ere long.

THEY THAT HAVE POW'R TO HURT

They that have pow'r to hurt and will do none,
That do not do the thing they most do show,
Who, moving others, are themselves as stone,
Unmoved, cold, and to temptation slow,
They rightly do inherit heaven's graces   5
And husband nature's riches from expense;
They are the lords and owners of their faces,
Others but stewards of their excellence.
The summer's flow'r is to the summer sweet
Though to itself it only live and die,   10
But if that flow'r with base infection meet,
The basest weed outbraves his dignity:
   For sweetest things turn sourest by their deeds;
   Lilies that fester smell far worse than weeds.

LET ME NOT TO THE MARRIAGE OF TRUE MINDS

Let me not to the marriage of true minds
Admit impediments. Love is not love
Which alters when it alteration finds,
Or bends with the remover to remove.
O, no! it is an ever-fixèd mark   5
That looks on tempests and is never shaken;
It is the star to every wand'ring bark,
Whose worth's unknown, although his height be taken.
Love's not Time's fool, though rosy lips and cheeks
Within his bending sickle's compass come;   10
Love alters not with his brief hours and weeks,
But bears it out even to the edge of doom.
   If this be error, and upon me proved,
   I never writ, nor no man ever loved.

TH' EXPENSE OF SPIRIT IN A WASTE OF SHAME

Th' expense of spirit in a waste of shame
Is lust in action; and till action, lust
Is perjur'd, murd'rous, bloody, full of blame,
Savage, extreme, rude, cruel, not to trust:
Enjoy'd no sooner but despisèd straight;   5
Past reason hunted, and no sooner had,
Past reason hated, as a swallowed bait
On purpose laid to make the taker mad:
Mad in pursuit and in possession so;
Had, having, and in quest to have, extreme;   10
A bliss in proof, and prov'd, a very woe;
Before, a joy propos'd; behind, a dream.
   All this the world well knows; yet none knows well
   To shun the heaven that leads men to this hell.

JOHN DONNE *(1573–1631)*

One of the ironies in Donne's stock is his transfer of techniques from his love songs and sonnets (themselves often inversions of or ironic reflections on conventions of the day) to appeals to God. He suggests through an implicit running comparison of secular to divine love that language falls short of the subject but that man and God may nonetheless be reconciled. He accommodates the structural units of the sonnet to the flow of religious debate and meditation.

HOLY SONNETS

7

At the round earth's imagin'd corners, blow
Your trumpets, angels, and arise, arise
From death, you numberless infinities
Of souls, and to your scattred bodies go,
All whom the flood did, and fire shall o'er throw,   5

All whom war, dearth, age, agues, tyrannies,
Despair, law, chance, hath slain, and you whose eyes,
Shall behold God, and never taste death's woe.
But let them sleep, Lord, and me mourn a space,
For, if above all these, my sins abound,   10
'Tis late to ask abundance of thy grace,
When we are there; here on this lowly ground,
Teach me how to repent; for that's as good
As if thou'hadst seal'd my pardon, with thy blood.

14

Batter my heart, three person'd God; for, you
As yet but knock, breathe, shine, and seek to mend;
That I may rise, and stand, o'erthrow me,'and bend
Your force, to break, blow, burn and make me new.
I, like an usurpt town, to'another due,   5
Labour to'admit you, but Oh, to no end,
Reason your viceroy in me, me should defend,
But is captiv'd, and proves weak or untrue,
Yet dearly' I love you, and would be lovèd fain,
But am betroth'd unto your enemy,   10
Divorce me,'untie, or break that knot again,
Take me to you, imprison me, for I
Except you'enthrall me, never shall be free,
Nor ever chaste, except you ravish me.

MILTON AND WORDSWORTH

Milton's remodeling of the sonnet to accommodate expanded subject matter
entailed some loosening of line units to gain flexibility. The sonnet tends to
become two short paragraphs, or perhaps one paragraph that shifts direction
at about line 9, rather than a carefully measured and balanced grouping of
end-stopped lines. Wordsworth takes Milton's variations of the form as a
model in making the line unit less prominent (through the use of frequent
"run-on" lines and extended sentences) than it normally is and in using the
contrast of octave and sestet to reinforce modulations of feeling rather than
logical or rhetorical divisions. "It Is a Beauteous Evening" breaks decisively at
the customary place, not in order to shift to new ground but as a sign of
the poet's increasingly intense involvement in the child he addresses.

ON HIS BLINDNESS

JOHN MILTON *(1608–1674)*

When I consider how my light is spent
Ere half my days in this dark world and wide,
And that one talent which is death to hide
Lodged with me useless, though my soul more bent
To serve therewith my Maker, and present   5
My true account, lest he returning chide,
"Doth God exact day-labor, light denied?"

I fondly ask. But Patience, to prevent
That murmur, soon replies, "God doth not need
Either man's work or his own gifts. Who best   10
Bear his mild yoke, they serve him best. His state
Is kingly: thousands at his bidding speed,
And post o'er land and ocean without rest;
They also serve who only stand and wait."

IT IS A BEAUTEOUS EVENING

WILLIAM WORDSWORTH *(1770–1850)*

It is a beauteous evening, calm and free;
The holy time is quiet as a nun
Breathless with adoration; the broad sun
Is sinking down in its tranquility;
The gentleness of heaven broods o'er the sea: 5
Listen! the mighty Being is awake,
And doth with his eternal motion make
A sound like thunder—everlastingly.
Dear child! dear girl! that walkest with me here,
If thou appear untouched by solemn thought,   10
Thy nature is not therefore less divine:
Thou liest in Abraham's bosom all the year,
And worship'st at the Temple's inner shrine,
God being with thee when we know it not.

JOHN KEATS *(1795–1821)*

Although as a rule Keats preferred the ode to the sonnet, "Chapman's Homer"
skillfully exploits the potentials of the latter. Unlike Milton and Wordsworth,
he stays strictly within the normal boundaries, making image and statement
conform to the musical signals of a regular rhyme pattern.

ON FIRST LOOKING INTO CHAPMAN'S HOMER

Much have I travell'd in the realms of gold
And many goodly states and kingdoms seen;
Round many western islands have I been
Which bards in fealty to Apollo hold.
Oft of one wide expanse had I been told   5
That deep-brow'd Homer ruled as his demesne;
Yet did I never breathe its pure serene
Till I heard Chapman speak out loud and bold:
Then felt I like some watcher of the skies
When a new planet swims into his ken;   10
Or like stout Cortez, when with eagle eyes
He stared at the Pacific—and all his men
Look'd at each other with a wild surmise—
Silent, upon a peak in Darien.

GEORGE MEREDITH *(1828–1909)*

The sonnets Meredith wrote in *Modern Love* on the argument of a husband and wife are composed of sixteen lines each. The psychological orientation and the meditative movement of the series fit well with the expanded length, which frees the poet of what for his purposes would be an overly precise and musical form.

MARK WHERE THE PRESSING WIND

Mark where the pressing wind shoots javelin-like
Its skeleton shadow on the broad-backed wave!
Here is a fitting spot to dig love's grave;
Here where the ponderous breakers plunge and strike,
And dart their hissing tongues high up the sand: 5
In hearing of the ocean, and in sight
Of those ribbed wind-streaks running into white.
If I the death of love had deeply planned,
I never could have made it half so sure,
As by the unblest kisses which upbraid   10
The full-waked sense; or failing that, degrade!
'Tis morning: but no morning can restore
What we have forfeited. I see no sin:
The wrong is mixed. In tragic life, God wot
No villain need be! Passions spin the plot: 15
We are betrayed by what is false within.

DANTE GABRIEL ROSSETTI *(1828–1882)*

As Rossetti's title suggests, the sonnet "Winter" describes a season, or typical scenes of a season; and as description it bypasses the logical development of theme and rhetorical statement. Still, the sonnet develops through the sequence of scenes, and hence has a recognizable architecture. It is composed not of one panel but three—the last one lifting the perspective in the final lines to a scene beyond those immediately visible.

WINTER

How large that thrush looks on the bare thorn-tree!
  A swarm of such, three little months ago,
  Had hidden in the leaves and let none know
Save by the outburst of their minstrelsy.
A white flake here and there—a snow lily   5
  Of last night's frost—our naked flower-beds hold;
  And for a rose-flower on the darkling mould
The hungry redbreast gleams. No bloom, no bee.

The current shudders to its ice-bound sedge:
  Nipped in their bath, the stark reeds one by one   10
  Flash each its clinging diamond in the sun:
'Neath winds which for this winter's sovereign pledge
Shall curb great king-masts to the ocean's edge
  And leave memorial forest-king's o'erthrown.

GERARD MANLEY HOPKINS *(1845–1889)*

If Shakespeare liked the combination of three quatrains and a summary statement encouraged by the English sonnet form, Hopkins preferred the dialectical possibilities of the Italian form. "God's Grandeur" reveals some of the reasons for this preference: the universe itself for Hopkins is engaged in a dialectic between the natural and the supernatural (see also "The Windhover"). Thus the shift from octet into sestet is a graduation from wasted potential to realization, from man's natural "smudge" to the emergent clarity of God's spring. If we are conscious of the expectations of the Italian form, we anticipate Hopkins' structure and are led to look for interconnections and contrasts between the two parts.

GOD'S GRANDEUR

The world is charged with the grandeur of God.
  It will flame out, like shining from shook foil;
  It gathers to a greatness, like the ooze of oil
Crushed. Why do men then now not reck his rod?
Generations have trod, have trod, have trod;   5
  And all is seared with trade; bleared, smeared with toil;
  And wears man's smudge and shares man's smell: the soil
Is bare now, nor can foot feel, being shod.

And for all this, nature is never spent;
  There lives the dearest freshness deep down things;   10
And though the last lights off the black West went
  Oh, morning, at the brown brink eastward, springs—
Because the Holy Ghost over the bent
  World broods with warm breast and with ah! bright wings.

WILLIAM BUTLER YEATS *(1865–1939)*

The movement of Yeats's sonnet "Leda and the Swan" progresses straight through the fourteen lines rather than breaking into the normal sonnet units, beginning with a description of the swan's power and proceeding to the rhetorical questions of the second quatrain, the apocalyptic vision of the next two lines and a half, and the genuine question of the final three lines and a half. This sense of continuous, irresolvable movement is reinforced by the disguising of traditionally placed rhymes and the weakening of the final rhyme and accords with the poem's intellectual expansion through time and space until it encompasses the mythic history of an empire's founding. The final question, whether or not Leda puts on divine knowledge with power, is a basic cosmic and psychological question: are human destiny and personality governed by order or unrestrained violence? Does the cycle of history here set in motion have a meaning available to those caught up in it?

LEDA AND THE SWAN*

A sudden blow: the great wings beating still
Above the staggering girl, her thighs caressed

By the dark webs, her nape caught in his bill,
He holds her helpless breast upon his breast.

How can those terrified vague fingers push   5
The feathered glory from her loosening thighs?
And how can body, laid in that white rush,
But feel the strange heart beating where it lies?

A shudder in the loins engenders there
The broken wall, the burning roof and tower   10
And Agamemnon dead.
               Being so caught up,
So mastered by the brute blood of the air,
Did she put on his knowledge with his power
Before the indifferent beak could let her drop?   15

ELINOR WYLIE *(1885–1928)*

Elinor Wylie's "August" uses the customary shape of the sonnet to point up a simple contrast of moods.

AUGUST*

Why should this Negro insolently stride
Down the red noonday on such noiseless feet?
Piled in his barrow, tawnier than wheat,
Lie heaps of smoldering daisies, somber-eyed,
Their copper petals shriveled up with pride,   5
Hot with a superfluity of heat,
Like a great brazier borne along the street
By captive leopards, black and burning-pied.

Are there no water-lilies, smooth as cream,
With long stems dripping crystal? Are there none   10
Like those white lilies, luminous and cool,
Plucked from some hemlock-darkened northern stream
By fair-haired swimmers, diving where the sun
Scarce warms the surface of the deepest pool?

JOHN CROWE RANSOM *(1888–   )*

Ransom strengthens the normal interweaving of the two main sections of the Petrarchan form with a number of contrasts signaled by the change of speakers. Youth and age, life and death, romance and realism stand opposed—but not as equals, both the old man and the poet imply, and not for much longer.

PIAZZA PIECE†

—I am a gentleman in a dustcoat trying
To make you hear. Your ears are soft and small

---

* Reprinted by permission of AAK, Inc. from *Collected Poems* by Elinor Wylie. "August" copyright 1921 by AAK, Inc. Renewed, 1949, by William Rose Benet.
† Reprinted by permission of AAK, Inc. from *Poems and Essays* by John Crowe Ransom. Copyright 1927 AAK, Inc. and renewed 1955 by John Crowe Ransom.

And listen to an old man not at all;
They want the young men's whispering and sighing.
But see the roses on your trellis dying   5
And hear the spectral singing of the moon—
For I must have my lovely lady soon.
I am a gentleman in a dustcoat trying.

—I am a lady young in beauty waiting
Until my truelove comes, and then we kiss.   10
But what gray man among the vines is this
Whose words are dry and faint as in a dream?
Back from my trellis, sir, before I scream!
I am a lady young in beauty waiting.

WILFRED OWEN *(1893–1918)*

Owen's "Anthem" is an ironic denial that songs, especially of the patriotic
sort, have any relevance for men at war. Owen therefore offers a new music
suitable to the times—the sound of rifles stuttering out their hasty "orisons."

ANTHEM FOR DOOMED YOUTH*

What passing-bells for these who die as cattle?
Only the monstrous anger of the guns.
Only the stuttering rifles' rapid rattle
Can patter out their hasty orisons.
No mockeries for them; no prayers nor bells,   5
Nor any voice of mourning save the choirs,—
The shrill, demented choirs of wailing shells;
And bugles calling for them from sad shires.
What candles may be held to speed them all?
Not in the hands of boys, but in their eyes   10
Shall shine the holy glimmers of good-byes.
The pallor of girls' brows shall be their pall;
Their flowers the tenderness of patient minds,
And each slow dusk a drawing-down of blinds.

Ode and Hymn

The ode and the hymn present a special problem in formal analysis because
of a curious inversion in the emotion-form ratio. Instead of channeling and
articulating emotion through regularized form and convention, they purport
to heighten it by apparent irregularity. For example, in the "Pindaric" ode,
popularized primarily by Abraham Cowley in the seventeenth century, irregular

* From *Collected Poems of Wilfred Owen* by Wilfred Owen. Reprinted by permission of
New Directions. Reprinted for Canadian Circulation by permission of Chatto & Windus,
Ltd. and Mr. Harold Owen.

lines and stanzas are used to suggest a rhapsodic emotion too great to be contained in regular units. The odes of Pindar himself (the fifth-century B.C. Greek poet) were commonly composed of three parts—strophe, antistrophe, and epode—but each part was loose and irregular in itself. And as his odes reveal, the emotional, almost religious fervor generated in odic celebrations sometimes derives from subjects one would not normally respond to in this way—athletic contests in Pindar's case and the Royal Society, coronations, and nightingales in the case of English poets. One way of approaching the ode, then, is as a lyric that transfers personal emotion to a subject through stylistic means. In the Renaissance and eighteenth century, for instance, odes celebrated public occasions, political figures, institutions, and historic events. Among the romantics, despite a shift of emphasis from public to personal subjects, the ode was still used to celebrate things *in a public manner;* the voice that speaks the ode has full resonance even though it may only address a Grecian urn. It is both a progressive dramatic form, in which the speaker's relation to the object changes, and a proclamation—a kind of meditation declaimed. We generally need to ask what well-spring of enthusiasm the poet is tapping and what cause he is diverting it to. The "Ode on a Grecian Urn" ends with an assertion that sounds much like a public credo: "Beauty is truth, truth beauty." This proposition is supported by the evidence of the urn, whose "art" transcends the burning foreheads and parching tongues of the mortals whom it pictures and to whom it speaks. Likewise, Shelley in the "Ode to the West Wind" transfers the energy and creativity of his symbol, the wind, to the poet-as-prophet. The ode is not addressed to the wind as much as to the power of poetry:

> Drive my dead thoughts over the universe
> Like withered leaves to quicken a new birth!
> And, by the incantation of this verse,
> Scatter, as from an unextinguished hearth
> Ashes and sparks, *my words* among mankind!
> Be *through my lips* to unawakened earth
> The trumpet of a prophecy! (Our italics.)

Shelley's odes to liberty and to Naples are still more obviously public and reformatory. The public element in the quasi-ode "To a Skylark" is reduced somewhat, but the connection between skylark, poet, and society is revealed in the concluding lines:

> Teach me half the gladness
> That thy brain must know,
> Such harmonious madness
> From my lips would flow,
> The world should listen then, as I am listening now.

In writing an ode, then, the poet sets out in a less intimate, more oratorical key than the writer of a reflective lyric and with less tight formal restrictions than the writer of a sonnet or song. The form tends to preclude both song-like impersonality and the conversational tones and subtle nuances that characterize forms more answerable to the flux of thought and emotion. In at least one corner of his mind, the writer of an ode is aware of his audience and his stance before it.

Nearly everything that we have said of the ode can also be said of the hymn, the chief difference being that the hymn, as its name suggests, tends to evoke religious veneration for its subject; it is more liturgical than oratorical, and its subject is likely to be thought of as transcendent enough to require imploring or beseeching. But the relation between the speaker and the addressee remains essentially an I-Thou relation. Whereas Renaissance and eighteenth-century poets usually addressed hymns to religious subjects and odes to secular subjects, the romantics made no real distinction between them. (Shelley's "Hymn to Intellectual Beauty" could easily have been called an ode, for instance.) Both are normally *high* lyric modes, but notice Jonson's and Donne's variations.

EDMUND SPENSER (1552?–1599)

Like his earlier "Epithalamion," Spenser's "Prothalamion" is a marriage hymn. It combines mythological allusions, elaborate descriptive passages, and stately stanzaic movement in an ornamental form appropriate to the elaborate aristocratic weddings it commemorates. The subtitle gives some idea both of the formality of the occasion and of Spenser's concept of the poem's commemorative function: "A spousal verse...in honor of the double marriage of the two honorable and vertuous ladies, the Lady Elizabeth and the Lady Katherine Somerset, daughters to the right honorable Earl of Worcester and espoused to the two worthy gentlemen Master Henry Gilford, and Master William Peter." As both the subtitle and the high ratio of superlatives in the poem indicate, "high" lyric modes of this kind share with orations a tendency to tell posterity of the incomparable glory of the subject, neither weddings nor party rallies being occasions for plain speaking.

PROTHALAMION

Calm was the day, and through the trembling air
  Sweet-breathing Zephyrus did softly play,
  A gentle spirit, that lightly did delay
Hot Titan's beams, which then did glister fair:
    When I, whose sullen care,   5
Through discontent of my long fruitless stay
  In princes' court, and expectation vain
Of idle hopes, which still do fly away
  Like empty shadows, did afflict my brain,
    Walk'd forth to ease my pain   10
Along the shore of silver-streaming Thames,
Whose rutty bank, the which his river hems,
  Was painted all with variable flowers,
And all the meads adorn'd with dainty gems
    Fit to deck maidens' bowers,   15
    And crown their paramours
Against the bridal day, which is not long:
Sweet Thames, run softly, till I end my song.

There, in a meadow, by the river's side
   A flock of nymphs I chancéd to espy,   20
   All lovely daughters of the flood thereby,
With goodly greenish locks all loose untied,
     As each had been a bride;
And each one had a little wicker basket,
   Made of fine twigs, entailéd curiously,   25
In which they gather'd flowers to fill their flasket;
   And with fine fingers cropt full feateously
     The tender stalks on high.
Of every sort, which in that meadow grew,
They gather'd some; the violet pallid blue,   30
   The little daisy, that at evening closes,
The virgin lily and the primrose true,
     With store of vermeil roses,
     To deck their bridegrooms' posies
Against the bridal day, which was not long: 35
Sweet Thames, run softly, till I end my song.

With that I saw two swans of goodly hue
   Come softly swimming down along the lee;
   Two fairer birds I yet did never see.
The snow which doth the top of Pindus strow   40
     Did never whiter show,
Nor Jove himself, when he a swan would be
   For love of Leda, whiter did appear:
Yet Leda was, they say, as white as he,
   Yet not so white as these, nor nothing near;   45
     So purely white they were,
That even the gentle stream, the which them bare,
Seem'd foul to them, and bade his billows spare
   To wet their silken feathers, lest they might
Soil their fair plumes with water not so fair,   50
     And mar their beauties bright,
     That shone as heaven's light,
Against their bridal day, which was not long:
Sweet Thames, run softly, till I end my song.

Eftsoons the nymphs, which now had flowers their fill,   55
   Ran all in haste to see that silver brood
   As they came floating on the crystal flood;
Whom when they saw, they stood amazéd still,
     Their wondering eyes to fill.
Them seem'd they never saw a sight so fair,   60
   Of fowls so lovely, that they sure did deem
Them heavenly born, or to be that same pair
   Which through the sky draw Venus' silver team;
     For sure they did not seem
     To be begot of any earthly seed,   65

---

40 *Pindus*: Greek mountain.   55 *Eftsoons*: immediately.

But rather angels or of angels' breed:
  Yet were they bred of summer's-heat, they say,
In sweetest season, when each flower and weed
    The earth did fresh array;
    So fresh they seem'd as day,   70
Even as their bridal day, which was not long:
Sweet Thames, run softly, till I end my song.

Then forth they all out of their baskets drew
  Great store of flowers, the honour of the field,
  That to the sense did fragrant odours yield,   75
All which upon those goodly birds they threw,
    And all the waves did strew,
That like old Peneus' waters they did seem,
  When down along by pleasant Tempe's shore,
Scatter'd with flowers, through Thessaly they stream, 80
    That they appear, through lilies' plenteous store,
      Like a bride's chamber-floor.
Two of those nymphs, meanwhile, two garlands bound
Of freshest flowers which in that mead they found,
  The which presenting all in trim array,   85
Their snowy foreheads therewithal they crown'd,
    Whilst one did sing this lay,
    Prepared against that day,
Against their bridal day, which was not long:
Sweet Thames, run softly, till I end my song.   90

"Ye gentle birds, the world's fair ornament,
  And heaven's glory, whom this happy hour
  Doth lead unto your lovers' blissful bower,
Joy may you have, and gentle heart's content
    Of your love's couplement: 95
And let fair Venus, that is Queen of Love,
  With her heart-quelling son upon you smile,
Whose smile, they say, hath virtue to remove
  All love's dislike, and friendship's faulty guile
    For ever to assoil.   100
Let endless peace your steadfast hearts accord,
And blessed plenty wait upon your board;
  And let your bed with pleasures chaste abound,
That fruitful issue may to you afford,
    Which may your foes confound,   105
    And make your joys redound,
Upon your bridal day, which is not long:
Sweet Thames, run softly, till I end my song."

So ended she; and all the rest around
  To her redoubled that her undersong,   110
    Which said, their bridal day should not be long.

---

67 *summer's-heat*: play on Somerset's name. 78 *Peneus*: river of Thessaly that flows from Mount Pindus through the plains of Tempe.

And gentle Echo from the neighbour ground
 Their accents did resound.
So forth those joyous birds did pass along,
 Adown the lee that to them murmur'd low,   115
As he would speak, but that he lack'd a tongue,
 Yet did by signs his glad affection show,
  Making his stream run slow.
And all the fowl which in his flood did dwell
'Gan flock about these twain, that did excel   120
 The rest, so far, as Cynthia doth shend
The lesser stars. So they enrangéd well,
  Did on those two attend,
  And their best service lend
Against their wedding day, which was not long: 125
Sweet Thames, run softly, till I end my song.

At length they all to merry London came,
 To merry London, my most kindly nurse,
 That to me gave this life's first native source,
Though from another place I take my name,   130
  An house of ancient fame:
There when they came, whereas those bricky towers,
 The which on Thames' broad aged back do ride,
Where now the studious lawyers have their bowers,
 There whilome wont the Templar-knights to bide,   135
  Till they decay'd through pride:
Next whereunto there stands a stately place,
Where oft I gainéd gifts and goodly grace,
 Of that great Lord, which therein wont to dwell,
Whose want too well now feels my friendless case: 140
  But ah! here fits not well
  Old woes but joys to tell
Against the bridal day, which is not long:
Sweet Thames, run softly, till I end my song.

Yet therein now doth lodge a noble Peer,   145
 Great England's glory and the world's wide wonder,
 Whose dreadful name late through all Spain did thunder,
And Hercules' two pillars standing near,
  Did make to quake and fear:
Fair branch of honour, flower of chivalry!   150
 That fillest England with thy triumphs' fame,
Joy have thou of thy noble victory,
 And endless happiness of thine own name
  That promiseth the same:

---

121 *shend*: put to shame. 122 *enrangéd*: arranged in a row. 132 *whereas*: where. 135
Templar-knights: The Temple compound, which lay between the Strand and the Thames,
was the home of legal students in Elizabethan times. The Templar Knights owned it in
the fourteenth century. 139 *that great lord*: Earl of Leicester. 145 *a noble Peer*: Robert
Devereux, Earl of Essex. 147 Essex helped capture Cadiz in 1596. 153 *thine own name*:
Devereux = ever heureux (happy).

That through thy prowess and victorious arms,   155
　　And great Eliza's glorious name may ring
Through all the world, fill'd with thy wide alarms.
　　　　Which some brave muse may sing
　　　　To ages following,   160
Upon the bridal day, which is not long:
Sweet Thames, run softly, till I end my song.

From those high towers, this noble lord issúing,
　　Like radiant Hesper when his golden hair
　　In th' ocean billows he hath bathéd fair,   165
Descended to the river's open viewing,
　　　　With a great train ensuing.
Above the rest were goodly to be seen
Beseeming well the bower of any queen,   170
　　With gifts of wit and ornaments of nature,
　　　　Fit for so goodly stature:
That like the twins of Jove they seem'd in sight,
Which deck the baldric of the heavens bright;
　　They two forth pacing to the river's side,   175
Received those two fair bridges, their love's delight,
　　　　Which at th' appointed tide,
　　　　Each one did make his bride,
Against their bridal day, which is not long:
Sweet Thames, run softly, till I end my song.   180

SIDNEY AND NASHE

A litany is a solemn, responsive form of prayer that as Nashe's poem on the plague reveals, can be used for special secular purposes. Sidney uses its inherent sacredness ironically, to castigate what the speaker supposes is the deceit and hypocrisy of the "devotions" that lovers offer to their mistresses—who deserve something less than religious "services." But once his exasperation is purged in the mock-litany, the speaker returns to the fold, chastised and solemn, and the litany ends in genuine prayer.

A LITANY

SIR PHILIP SIDNEY *(1554–1586)*

Ring out your bells! Let mourning shows be spread!
For Love is dead.
　　All love is dead, infected
　　With plague of deep disdain;
　　Worth, as nought worth, rejected;   5
　　And faith, fair scorn doth gain.
　　　　From so ungrateful fancy,
　　　　From such a female franzy,
　　　　From them that use men thus,
　　　　Good Lord, deliver us!   10

---

173 *twins of Jove*: Castor and Pollux.

Weep! neighbours, weep! Do you not hear it said
That Love is dead?
    His deathbed, peacock's folly;
    His winding-sheet is shame;
    His will, false-seeming holy;   15
    His sole exec'tor, blame.
        From so ungrateful fancy,
        From such a female franzy,
        From them that use men thus,
        Good Lord, deliver us!   20

Let dirge be sung, and trentals rightly read!
For Love is dead.
    Sir Wrong his tomb ordaineth
    My mistress' marble heart;
    Which epitaph containeth—   25
    'Her eyes were once his dart.'
        From so ungrateful fancy,
        From such a female franzy,
        From them that use men thus,
        Good Lord, deliver us!   30

Alas, I lie: rage hath this error bred;
Love is not dead.
    Love is not dead, but sleepeth
    In her unmatchèd mind,
    Where she his counsel keepeth,   35
    Till due desert she find.
        Therefore, from so vile fancy,
        To call such wit a franzy,
        Who love can temper thus,
        Good Lord, deliver us!   40

A LITANY IN PLAGUE TIME

THOMAS NASHE *(1567–1601)*

Adieu, farewell earth's bliss,
This world uncertain is;
Fond are life's lustful joys,
Death proves them all but toys,
None from his darts can fly.   5
I am sick, I must die.
    Lord, have mercy on us!

Rich men, trust not in wealth,
Gold cannot buy you health;
Physic himself must fade,   10
All things to end are made,
The plague full swift goes by;
I am sick, I must die.
    Lord, have mercy on us!

Beauty is but a flower   15
Which wrinkles will devour:
Brightness falls from the air,
Queens have died young and fair,
Dust hath closed Helen's eye.
I am sick, I must die.   20
  Lord, have mercy on us!

Strength stoops unto the grave,
Worms feed on Hector brave,
Swords may not fight with fate.
Earth still holds ope her gate;   25
Come! come! the bells do cry.
I am sick, I must die.
  Lord, have mercy on us!

Wit with his wantonness
Tasteth death's bitterness;   30
Hell's executioner
Hath no ears for to hear
What vain art can reply.
I am sick, I must die.
  Lord, have mercy on us!   35

Haste, therefore, each degree,
To welcome destiny.
Heaven is our heritage,
Earth but a player's stage;
Mount we unto the sky.   40
I am sick, I must die.
  Lord, have mercy on us!

JONSON AND DONNE

The hymns of both Jonson and Donne are varieties of songlike prayer, more familiar than exalted in tone and more nimble than "accumulative" in movement. Jonson's manner is that of an honest man addressing a human superior and asking only to be chastised. Because the distance between speaker and listener is not great, the voice can speak quietly and respond to reason as well as emotion. Donne's hymn also practices wit and familiarity in the exercise of repentance. The puns on "done" are not merely ingenious, however. In summing up all that he is—in "having done"—he leaves no hidden corner for which he might be reproached later. He "undoes" himself now so that the merciful Son might have Donne before the Father has him.

A HYMN TO GOD THE FATHER

BEN JONSON *(1572?–1637)*

Hear me, O God!
  A broken heart
  Is my best part:

Use still thy rod
    That I may prove   5
    Therein, thy Love.

If thou hadst not
    Been stern to me.
    But left me free,
I had forgot   10
    Myself and thee.

For sin's so sweet,
    As minds ill bent
    Rarely repent,
Until they meet   15
    Their punishment.

Who more can crave
    Than thou hast done:
    That gav'st a Son
To free a slave?   20
    First made of nought;
    With All since bought.

Sin, Death, and Hell,
    His glorious Name
    Quite overcame,   25
Yet I rebel
    And slight the same.

But, I'll come in,
    Before my loss
    Me farther toss,   30
As sure to win,
    Under his Cross.

A HYMN TO GOD THE FATHER

JOHN DONNE *(1573–1631)*

Wilt thou forgive that sin where I begun,
    Which was my sin, though it were done before?
Wilt thou forgive those sinnes through which I run,
    And do run still; though still I do deplore?
        When thou hast done, thou hast not done,   5
           For I have more.

Wilt thou forgive that sin which I have won
    Others to sin, and made my sin their door?
Wilt thou forgive that sin which I did shun
    A year or two; but wallowed in a score?   10
        When thou hast done, thou hast not done,
           For I have more.

I have a sin of fear, that, when I have spun
    My last thread, I shall perish on the shore;

Swear by thyself that at my death the Son   15
  Shall shine as he shines now, and heretofore;
      And, having done that, thou hast done,
          I fear no more.

ANDREW MARVELL *(1621–1678)*

As a practiced, sensitive, and shrewd public man, well grounded in the conventions of rhetoric, Marvell knew that no simply eulogistic celebration of Cromwell could be adequate in the political climate of his times. Within a precise stanzaic form and with the urbanity characteristic of Horace, "An Horatian Ode" condenses an unusual amount of feeling for what has been lost in Cromwell's rise. It renders high tribute to both sides, only one of which, however, has the sanction of destiny.

AN HORATIAN ODE UPON CROMWELL'S RETURN FROM IRELAND

The forward youth that would appear,
Must now forsake his muses dear,
    Nor in the shadows sing
    His numbers languishing.

'Tis time to leave the books in dust,   5
And oil th' unuséd armour's rust,
    Removing from the wall
    The corslet of the hall.

So restless Cromwell could not cease
In the inglorious arts of peace,   10
    But through adventurous war
    Urged his active star:

And, like the three-fork'd lightning, first
Breaking the clouds where it was nurst,
    Did thorough his own side   15
    His fiery way divide:

(For 'tis all one to courage high
The emulous, or enemy;
    And with such, to enclose
    Is more than to oppose;)   20

Then burning through the air he went
And palaces and temples rent;
    And Caesar's head at last
    Did through his laurels blast.

'Tis madness to resist or blame   25
The force of angry heaven's flame;
    And, if we would speak true,
    Much to the man is due.

Who, from his private gardens, where
He lived reservéd and austere   30

(As if his highest plot
To plant the bergamot),

Could by industrious valour climb
To ruin the great work of time,
    And cast the kingdoms old   35
    Into another mould;

Though justice against fate complain,
And plead the ancient rights in vain:
    But those do hold or break
    As men are strong or weak.   40

Nature, that hateth emptiness,
Allows of penetration less,
    And therefore must make room
    Where greater spirits come.

What field of all the Civil Wars   45
Where his were not the deepest scars?
    And Hampton shows what part
    He had of wiser art;

Where, twining subtle fears with hope,
He wove a net of such a scope   50
    That Charles himself might chase
    To Carisbrook's narrow case;

That thence the royal actor borne
The tragic scaffold might adorn:
    While round the arméd bands   55
    Did clap their bloody hands;

He nothing common did or mean
Upon that memorable scene,
    But with his keener eye
    The axe's edge did try;   60

Nor call'd the gods, with vulgar spite,
To vindicate his helpless right;
    But bow'd his comely head
    Down, as upon a bed.

—This was that memorable hour   65
Which first assured the forcéd power.
    So when they did design
    The capitol's first line,

A bleeding head, where they begun,
Did fright the architects to run;   70
    And yet in that the state
    Foresaw its happy fate!

---

69 *bleeding head*: workmen digging foundations for the temple of Jupiter were said to have found a head, which has taken for a good omen.

And now the Irish are ashamed
To see themselves in one year tamed:
    So much one man can do   75
    That does both act and know.

They can affirm his praises best,
And have, though overcome, confest
    How good he is, how just
    And fit for highest trust;   80

Nor yet grown stiffer with command,
But still in the republic's hand:
    How fit he is to sway
    That can so well obey!

He to the commons' feet presents   85
A kingdom for his first year's rents,
    And (what he may) forbears
    His fame, to make it theirs:

And has his sword and spoils ungirt
To lay them at the public's skirt.   90
    So when the falcon high
    Falls heavy from the sky,

She, having kill'd, no more does search
But on the next green bough to perch,
    Where, when he first does lure,   95
    The falconer has her sure.

—What may not then our isle presume
While victory his crest does plume?
    What may not others fear
    If thus he crown each year?   100

As Caesar he, ere long, to Gaul,
To Italy an Hannibal,
    And to all states not free
    Shall climacteric be.

The Pict no shelter now shall find   105
Within his parti-colour'd mind,
    But from this valour sad,
    Shrink underneath the plaid—

Happy, if in the tufted brake
The English hunter him mistake,   110
    Nor lay his hounds in near
    The Caledonian deer.

But thou, the war's and fortune's son,
March indefatigably on;
    And for the last effect   115
    Still keep the sword erect:

---

105 *Pict*: Scot. 107 *sad*: steadfast. 112 *Caledonian*: Scottish.

Besides the force it has to fright
The spirits of the shady night,
  The same arts that did gain
  A power must it maintain.   120

JOHN DRYDEN *(1631–1700)*

Many poets in Dryden's day wrote hymns to St. Cecilia, the saint of music, but Dryden's stands distinctively above the others in its imitative sound effects, which give special point to the traditional connection of music with the making, the temporal history, and the unmaking of the world.

A SONG FOR ST. CECILIA'S DAY

1

From harmony, from heavenly harmony
  This universal frame began:
  When Nature underneath a heap
    Of jarring atoms lay,
  And could not heave her head,   5
The tuneful voice was heard from high:
  "Arise, ye more than dead."
Then cold, and hot, and moist, and dry,
In order to their stations leap,
    And Music's power obey.   10
From harmony, from heavenly harmony
  This universal frame began:
  From harmony to harmony
Through all the compass of the notes it ran,
The diapason closing full in man.   15

2

What passion cannot Music raise and quell!
    When Jubal struck the corded shell,
    His listening brethren stood around,
    And, wondering, on their faces fell
    To worship that celestial sound.   20
Less than a god they thought there could not dwell
    Within the hollow of that shell
    That spoke so sweetly and so well.
What passion cannot Music raise and quell!

3

The trumpet's loud clangor   25
    Excites us to arms,
  With shrill notes of anger,
    And mortal alarms.
  The double double double beat
    Of the thund'ring drum   30
Cries, "Hark! the foes come;
Charge, charge, 'tis too late to retreat."

4

The soft complaining flute
In dying notes discovers
The woes of hopeless lovers,   35
Whose dirge is whispered by the warbling lute.

5

Sharp violins proclaim
Their jealous pangs and desperation,
Fury, frantic indignation,
Depth of pains, and height of passion   40
For the fair, disdainful dame.

6

But oh! what art can teach,
What human voice can reach
The sacred organs' praise?
Notes inspiring holy love,   45
Notes that wing their heav'nly ways
To mend the choirs above.

7

Orpheus could lead the savage race;
And trees unrooted left their place,
Sequacious of the lyre;   50
But bright Cecilia raised the wonder higher:
When to her organ vocal breath was giv'n,
An angel heard, and straight appeared,
Mistaking earth for heav'n.

GRAND CHORUS

As from the pow'r of sacred lays   55
The spheres began to move,
And sung the great Creator's praise
To all the blest above;
So, when the last and dreadful hour
This crumbling pageant shall devour,   60
The trumpet shall be heard on high,
The dead shall live, the living die,
And Music shall untune the sky.

[*1687*]

GRAY, COLLINS, COWPER

Because of its traditional enthusiasm, the ode was something of a counterforce in eighteenth-century poetry. Along with the sublime prospect-painting of many topographical poems, often written in Miltonic blank verse, it preserved a poetry of sympathy and imagination as opposed to poetry of judgment and wit. It is not surprising, then, to find many of the odes of Gray, Collins, and Cowper addressed to nature's prospects and to a spirit of poetry regarded as majestic, sublime, full of "tender notes" and freedom.

ODE ON A DISTANT PROSPECT OF ETON COLLEGE

THOMAS GRAY *(1716–1771)*

Ye distant spires, ye antique towers
   That crown the watery glade,
Where grateful Science still adores
   Her Henry's holy shade;
And ye, that from the stately brow   5
Of Windsor's heights th' expanse below
   Of grove, of lawn, of mead survey,
Whose turf, whose shade, whose flowers among
Wanders the hoary Thames along
   His silver-winding way: 10

Ah happy hills! ah pleasing shade!
   Ah fields beloved in vain!
Where once my careless childhood stray'd,
   A stranger yet to pain!
I feel the gales that from ye blow   15
A momentary bliss bestow,
   As waving fresh their gladsome wing
My weary soul they seem to soothe,
And, redolent of joy and youth,
   To breathe a second spring.   20

Say, Father Thames, for thou hast seen
   Full many a sprightly race
Disporting on thy margent green
   The paths of pleasure trace;
Who foremost now delight to cleave   25
With pliant arm, thy glassy wave?
   The captive linnet which enthral?
What idle progeny succeed
To chase the rolling circle's speed
   Or urge the flying ball?   30

While some on earnest business bent
   Their murmuring labours ply
'Gainst graver hours, that bring constraint
   To sweeten liberty:
Some bold adventurers disdain   35
The limits of their little reign
   And unknown regions dare descry:
Still as they run they look behind,
They hear a voice in every wind,
   And snatch a fearful joy.   40

Gay hope is theirs by fancy fed,
   Less pleasing when possest;
The tear forgot as soon as shed,
   The sunshine of the breast:
Theirs buxom health, of rosy hue,   45

Wild wit, invention ever new,
   And lively cheer, of vigour born;
The thoughtless day, the easy night,
The spirits pure, the slumbers light
   That fly th' approach of morn.   50

Alas! regardless of their doom
   The little victims play!
No sense have they of ills to come
   Nor care beyond to-day:
Yet see how all around them wait   55
The ministers of human fate
   And black misfortune's baleful train!
Ah show them where in ambush stand
To seize their prey, the murderous band!
   Ah, tell them they are men!   60

These shall the fury passions tear,
   The vultures of the mind,
Disdainful anger, pallid fear,
   And shame that skulks behind;
Or pining love shall waste their youth,   65
Or jealousy with rankling tooth
   That inly gnaws the secret heart,
And envy wan, and faded care,
Grim-visaged comfortless despair,
   And sorrow's piercing dart.   70

Ambition this shall tempt to rise,
   Then whirl the wretch from high,
To bitter scorn a sacrifice
   And grinning infamy.
The stings of falsehood those shall try,   75
And hard unkindness' alter'd eye,
   That mocks the tear it forced to flow;
And keen remorse with blood defiled,
And moody madness laughing wild
   Amid severest woe.   80

Lo, in the vale of years beneath
   A griesly troop are seen,
The painful family of death,
   More hideous than their queen:
This racks the joints, this fires the veins,   85
That every labouring sinew strains,
   Those in the deeper vitals rage:
Lo, poverty, to fill the band,
That numbs the soul with icy hand,
   And slow-consuming age.   90

To each his sufferings: all are men,
   Condemn'd alike to groan;
The tender for another's pain,

Th' unfeeling for his own.
Yet, ah! why should they know their fate,   95
Since sorrow never comes too late,
   And happiness too swiftly flies?
Thought would destroy their paradise.
No more;—where ignorance is bliss,
   'Tis folly to be wise.   100

ODE TO EVENING

WILLIAM COLLINS *(1721?–1759)*

If aught of oaten stop, or pastoral song,
May hope, chaste Eve, to soothe thy modest ear,
   Like thy own solemn springs,
   Thy springs and dying gales,

O nymph reserved, while now the bright-haired sun   5
Sits in yon western tent, whose cloudy skirts,
   With brede ethereal wove,
   O'erhang his wavy bed:

Now air is hushed, save where the weak-eyed bat,
With short shrill shriek, flits by on leathern wing,   10
   Or where the beetle winds
   His small but sullen horn,

As oft he rises 'midst the twilight path,
Against the pilgrim borne in heedless hum:
   Now teach me, maid composed,   15
   To breathe some softened strain,

Whose numbers, stealing through thy dark'ning vale,
May not unseemly with its stillness suit,
   As, musing slow, I hail
   Thy genial loved return!   20

For when thy folding-star arising shows
His paly circlet at his warning lamp
   The fragrant hours, and elves
   Who slept in flowers the day,

And many a nymph who wreaths her brows with sedge,   25
And sheds the fresh'ning dew, and, lovelier still,
   The pensive pleasures sweet,
   Prepare thy shadowy car.

Then lead, calm vot'ress, where some sheety lake
Cheers the lone heath, or some time-hallowed pile   30
   Or upland fallows gray
   Reflect its last cool gleam.

But when chill blust'ring winds, or driving rain,
Forbid my willing feet, be mine the hut
   That from the mountain's side   35
   Views wilds, and swelling floods,

And hamlets brown, and dim-discovered spires,
And hears their simple bell, and marks o'er all
   Thy dewy fingers draw
   The gradual dusky veil.   40

While Spring shall pour his show'rs, as oft he wont,
And bathe thy breathing tresses, meekest Eve;
   While Summer loves to sport
   Beneath thy ling'ring light;

While sallow Autumn fills thy lap with leaves;   45
Or Winter, yelling through the troublous air,
   Affrights thy shrinking train,
   And rudely rends thy robes;

So long, sure-found beneath the sylvan shed,
Shall fancy, friendship, science, rose-lipped health,   50
   Thy gentlest influence own,
   And hymn thy fav'rite name!

AN ODE: SECUNDUM ARTEM

WILLIAM COWPER *(1731–1800)*

1

Shall I begin with *Ah,* or *Oh?*
Be sad? *Oh!* yes. Be glad? *Ah!* no.
Light subjects suit not grave Pindaric ode,
Which walks in metre down the Strophic road.
   But let the sober matron wear   5
   Her own mechanic sober air:
Ah me! ill suits, *alas!* the sprightly jig,
Long robes of ermine, or Sir Cloudsley's wig.
   Come, placid Dullness, gently come,
   And all my faculties benumb,   10
Let thought turn exile, while the vacant mind
To trickie words and pretty phrase confin'd,
   Pumping for trim description's art,
   To win the ear, neglects the heart.
So shall thy sister Taste's peculiar sons,   15
Lineal descendants from the Goths and Huns,
   Struck with the true and grand sublime
   Of *rhythm* converted into *Rime,*
Court the quaint Muse; and con her lessons o'er,
When sleep the sluggish waves by Granta's shore: 20
   There shall each poet pare and trim,
   Stretch, cramp, or lop the verse's limb,
While rebel Wit beholds them with disdain,
And Fancy flies aloft, nor heeds their servile chain.

2

Oh Fancy, bright aerial maid!   25
Where have thy vagrant footsteps stray'd?

For *ah!* I miss thee midst thy wonted haunt,
Since silent now th' enthusiastic chaunt,
   Which erst like frenzy roll'd along,
   Driv'n by th' impetuous tide of song,   30
Rushing secure where native genius bore,
Not cautious coasting by the shelving shore.
   Hail to the sons of modern rime,
   Mechanic dealers in sublime,
Whose lady Muse full wantonly is dress'd,   35
In light expressions quaint, and tinsel vest,
   Where swelling epithets are laid
   (Art's ineffectual parade)
As varnish on the cheek of Harlot light;
The rest thin sown with profit or delight,   40
   But ill compares with ancient song,
   Where Genius pour'd its flood along;
Yet such is Art's presumptuous idle claim,
She marshals out the way to modern fame;
   From Grecian fables' pompous lore,   45
   Description's studied, glittering store,
Smooth, soothing sounds, and sweet alternate rime,
Clinking like change of bells, in tingle tangle chime.

3

   The lark shall soar in ev'ry ode,
   With flow'rs of light description strew'd,   50
And sweetly, warbling Philomel, shall flow
Thy soothing sadness in mechanic woe.
   Trim epithets shall spread their gloss,
   While ev'ry cell's o'ergrown with moss:
Here oaks shall rise in chains of ivy bound,   55
There smould'ring stones o'er-spread the rugged ground.
   Here forests brown, and azure hills,
   There babbling fonts, and prattling rills;
Here some gay river floats in crisped streams,
While the bright sun now gilds his morning beams,   60
   Or sinking to his Thetis' breast,
   Drives in description down the west.
—Oh let me boast, with pride becoming skill,
I crown the summit of Parnassus' Hill:
   While Taste with Genius shall dispense,   65
   And sound shall triumph over sense;
O'er the gay mead with curious steps I'll stray;
And, like the bee, steal all its sweets away,
   Extract its beauty, and its pow'r,
   From every new poetic flow'r,   70
Whose sweets collected may a wreath compose,
To bind the poet's brow, or please the critic's nose.

WILLIAM WORDSWORTH *(1770–1850)*

Although Wordsworth's nature-wanderers are typically joyful, they may also realize sadly that "there hath passed away a glory from the earth." The Intimations Ode first juxtaposes joy and sorrow in alternation and then fuses them in a single ambivalent mood, appropriate not to *achieved* visions of immortality or even the close proximity to the "glory and the dream" that the speaker remembers from his youth, but to *intimations* of that glory. The celebrative hymn is thus modulated with elegiac tones in the last two stanzas and with the deliberative modulations of a "philosophic mind" that has "kept watch o'er man's mortality."

ODE: INTIMATIONS OF IMMORTALITY FROM RECOLLECTIONS OF EARLY CHILDHOOD

The Child is father of the Man,
And I could wish my days to be
Bound each to each by natural piety.

1

There was a time when meadow, grove, and stream,
The earth, and every common sight,
    To me did seem
    Apparelled in celestial light,
The glory and the freshness of a dream.   5
It is not now as it hath been of yore;—
    Turn wheresoe'er I may,
      By night or day,
The things which I have seen I now can see no more.

2

    The Rainbow comes and goes,   10
    And lovely is the Rose;
    The Moon doth with delight
Look round her when the heavens are bare;
    Waters on a starry night
    Are beautiful and fair;   15
    The sunshine is a glorious birth;
    But yet I know, where'er I go,
That there hath past away a glory from the earth.

3

Now, while the birds thus sing a joyous song,
    And while the young lambs bound   20
      As to the tabor's sound,
To me alone there came a thought of grief:
A timely utterance gave that thought relief,
    And I again am strong:
The cataracts blow their trumpets from the steep;   25

No more shall grief of mine the season wrong;
I hear the Echoes through the mountains throng,
The Winds come to me from the fields of sleep,
    And all the earth is gay;
        Land and sea   30
    Give themselves up to jollity,
        And with the heart of May
    Doth every Beast keep holiday;—
        Thou Child of Joy,
Shout round me, let me hear thy shouts, thou   35
    happy Shepherd-boy!

4

Ye blessed Creatures, I have heard the call
    Ye to each other make; I see
The heavens laugh with you in your jubilee;
    My heart is at your festival,   40
    My head hath its coronal,
The fulness of your bliss, I feel—I feel it all.
        Oh evil day! if I were sullen
        While Earth herself is adorning,
          This sweet May-morning,   45
    And the Children are culling
        On every side,
    In a thousand valleys far and wide,
    Fresh flowers; while the sun shines warm,
And the Babe leaps up on his Mother's arm:—   50
    I hear, I hear, with joy I hear!
    —But there's a Tree, of many, one,
A single Field which I have looked upon,
Both of them speak of something that is gone;
    The Pansy at my feet   55
    Doth the same tale repeat:
Whither is fled the visionary gleam?
Where is it now, the glory and the dream?

5

Our birth is but a sleep and a forgetting:
The Soul that rises with us, our life's Star,   60
    Hath had elsewhere its setting,
        And cometh from afar:
    Not in entire forgetfulness,
    And not in utter nakedness,
But trailing clouds of glory do we come   65
    From God, who is our home:
Heaven lies about us in our infancy!
Shades of the prison-house begin to close
    Upon the growing Boy,
But he beholds the light, and whence it flows,   70
    He sees it in his joy;

The Youth, who daily farther from the east
    Must travel, still is Nature's Priest,
    And by the vision splendid
    Is on his way attended;   75
At length the Man perceives it die away,
And fade into the light of common day.

6

Earth fills her lap with pleasures of her own;
Yearnings she hath in her own natural kind,
And, even with something of a Mother's mind,   80
    And no unworthy aim,
    The homely Nurse doth all she can
To make her Foster-child, her Inmate Man,
    Forget the glories he hath known,
And that imperial palace whence he came.   85

7

Behold the Child among his new-born blisses,
A six years' Darling of a pigmy size!
See, where 'mid work of his own hand he lies,
Fretted by sallies of his mother's kisses,
With light upon him from his father's eyes!   90
See, at his feet, some little plan or chart,
Some fragment from his dream of human life,
Shaped by himself with newly-learned art;
    A wedding or a festival,
    A mourning or a funeral;   95
     And this hath now his heart,
    And unto this he frames his song:
    Then will he fit his tongue
To dialogues of business, love or strife;
    But it will not be long   100
    Ere this be thrown aside,
    And with new joy and pride
The little Actor cons another part;
Filling from time to time his "humorous stage"
With all the Persons, down to palsied Age,   105
That Life brings with her in her equipage;
    As if his whole vocation
    Were endless imitation.

8

Thou, whose exterior semblance doth belie
    Thy Soul's immensity;   110
Thou best Philosopher, who yet does keep
Thy heritage, thou Eye among the blind,
That, deaf and silent, read'st the eternal deep,
Haunted for ever by the eternal mind,—
    Mighty Prophet! Seer blest!   115
    On whom those truths do rest,

Which we are toiling all our lives to find,
In darkness lost, the darkness of the grave;
Thou, over whom thy Immortality
Broods like the Day, a Master o'er a Slave, 120
A Presence which is not to be put by;
   To whom the grave
Is but a lonely bed without the sense or sight
   Of day or the warm light,
A place of thought where we in waiting lie; 125
Thou little Child, yet glorious in the might
Of heaven-born freedom on thy being's height,
Why with such earnest pains dost thou provoke
The years to bring the inevitable yoke,
Thus blindly with thy blessedness at strife? 130
Full soon thy Soul shall have her earthly freight,
And custom lie upon thee with a weight,
Heavy as frost, and deep almost as life!

       9

   O joy! that in our embers
   Is something that doth live, 135
   That nature yet remembers
   What was so fugitive!
The thought of our past years in me doth breed
Perpetual benediction: not indeed
For that which is most worthy to be blest; 140
Delight and liberty, the simple creed
Of childhood, whether busy or at rest,
With new-fledged hope still fluttering in his breast:—
   Not for these I raise
   The song of thanks and praise; 145
   But for those obstinate questionings
   Of sense and outward things,
   Fallings from us, vanishings;
   Blank misgivings of a Creature
Moving about in worlds not realized, 150
High instincts before which our mortal nature
Did tremble like a guilty thing surprised:
   But for those first affections,
   Those shadowy recollections,
   Which, be they what they may, 155
Are yet the fountain-light of all our day,
Are yet a master-light of all our seeing;
   Uphold us, cherish, and have power to make
Our noisy years seem moments in the being
Of the Eternal Silence: truths that wake, 160
   To perish never:
Which neither listlessness, nor mad endeavor,
   Nor man nor boy,

Nor all that is at enmity with joy,
Can utterly abolish or destroy!   165
    Hence in a season of calm weather
    Though inland far we be,
Our souls have sight of that immortal sea
    Which brought us hither,
    Can in a moment travel thither,   170
And see the children sport upon the shore,
And hear the mighty waters rolling evermore.

10

Then sing, ye Birds, sing, sing a joyous song!
    And let the young Lambs bound
    As to the tabor's sound!   175
We in thought will join your throng,
    Ye that pipe and ye that play,
    Ye that through your hearts to-day
    Feel the gladness of the May!
What though the radiance which was once so bright   180
Be now forever taken from my sight,
    Though nothing can bring back the hour
Of splendor in the grass, of glory in the flower;
    We will grieve not, rather find
    Strength in what remains behind;   185
    In the primal sympathy
    Which having been must ever be;
    In the soothing thoughts that spring
    Out of human suffering;
    In the faith that looks through death,   190
In years that bring the philosophic mind.

11

And O, ye Fountains, Meadows, Hills, and Groves,
Forebode not any severing of our loves!
Yet in my heart of hearts I feel your might;
I only have relinquished one delight   195
To live beneath your more habitual sway.
I love the Brooks which down their channels fret,
Even more than when I tripped lightly as they;
The innocent brightness of a new-born Day
    Is lovely yet;   200
The Clouds that gather round the setting sun
Do take a sober coloring from an eye
That hath kept watch o'er man's mortality;
Another race hath been, and other palms are won.
Thanks to the human heart by which we live,   205
Thanks to its tenderness, its joys, and fears,
To me the meanest flower that blows can give
Thoughts that do often lie too deep for tears.

PERCY BYSSHE SHELLEY *(1792–1822)*

Because Shelley's west wind is a transcendent force, his poem combines odic
transport with hymnal prayer. Perhaps more than any other single poem, it
demonstrates why the romantic poets tended to think of the ode as the form
most answerable to the high purposes of poetry.

ODE TO THE WEST WIND

1

O wild West Wind, thou breath of Autumn's being,
Thou, from whose unseen presence the leaves dead
Are driven, like ghosts from an enchanter fleeing,

Yellow, and black, and pale, and hectic red,
Pestilence-stricken multitudes: O thou,   5
Who chariotest to their dark wintry bed

The wingèd seeds, where they lie cold and low,
Each like a corpse within its grave, until
Thine azure sister of the Spring shall blow

Her clarion o'er the dreaming earth, and fill   10
(Driving sweet buds like flocks to feed in air)
With living hues and odors plain and hill:

Wild Spirit, which art moving everywhere;
Destroyer and preserver; hear! oh, hear!

2

Thou on whose stream, mid the steep sky's commotion,   15
Loose clouds like earth's decaying leaves are shed,
Shook from the tangled boughs of Heaven and Ocean,

Angels of rain and lightning: there are spread
On the blue surface of thine airy surge,
Like the bright hair uplifted from the head   20

Of some fierce Mænad, even from the dim verge
Of the horizon to the zenith's height,
The locks of the approaching storm. Thou dirge

Of the dying year, to which this closing night
Will be the dome of a vast sepulcher,   25
Vaulted with all thy congregated might

Of vapors, from whose solid atmosphere
Black rain, and fire, and hail will burst: oh, hear!

3

Thou who didst waken from his summer dreams
The blue Mediterranean, where he lay,   30
Lulled by the coil of his crystàlline streams,

Beside a pumice isle in Baiæ's bay,
And saw in sleep old palaces and towers
Quivering within the wave's intenser day,

All overgrown with azure moss and flowers   35
So sweet, the sense faints picturing them! thou
For whose path the Atlantic's level powers

Cleave themselves into chasms, while far below
The sea-blooms and the oozy woods which wear
The sapless foliage of the ocean, know   40

Thy voice, and suddenly grow gray with fear,
And tremble and despoil themselves: oh, hear!

4

If I were a dead leaf thou mightest bear;
If I were a swift cloud to fly with thee;
A wave to pant beneath thy power, and share

The impulse of thy strength, only less free
Than thou, O uncontrollable! If even
I were as in my boyhood, and could be

The comrade of thy wanderings over heaven,
As then, when to outstrip thy skiey speed   50
Scarce seemed a vision; I would ne'er have striven

As thus with thee in prayer in my sore need.
Oh lift me as a wave, a leaf, a cloud!
I fall upon the thorns of life! I bleed!

A heavy weight of hours has chained and bowed   55
One too like thee: tameless, and swift, and proud.

5

Make me thy lyre, even as the forest is:
What if my leaves are falling like its own!
The tumult of thy mighty harmonies

Will take from both a deep, autumnal tone,   60
Sweet though in sadness. Be thou, spirit fierce,
My spirit! Be thou me, impetuous one!

Drive my dead thoughts over the universe
Like withered leaves to quicken a new birth!
And, by the incantation of this verse,   65

Scatter, as from an unextinguished hearth
Ashes and sparks, my words among mankind!
Be through my lips to unawakened earth

The trumpet of a prophecy! Oh, wind,
If Winter comes, can Spring be far behind?   70

Elegy

The function of the elegy is chiefly to celebrate, but in a manner different from the ode. A funeral celebration is obviously not a festive occasion in the same way that a public anniversary or achievement is. Rather than transfer emotion to a cause of some sort, the elegist seeks to convert sorrow to consolation, ordinarily sorrow for human mortality but also at times for things like universal injustice or a hostile universe. If the world has neither "joy, nor love, nor light / Nor certitude, nor peace, nor help for pain," Arnold writes to his "love," the two of them can at least be "true / To one another," which is some consolation. Milton's Lycidas, though sunk "beneath the watery floor," is resurrected and returns as a guardian spirit "To all that wander" in the "perilous flood."

Philosophic and religious consolations of the latter kind may be reinforced by explicit doctrine, as they are in Tennyson's *In Memoriam*. If in the ode and hymn self-analysis and ideas are normally made to serve a governing rhetorical purpose, in the elegy they are an intrinsic part of the search for consolation. When the elegist asks why certain things should be as they are, intellectual and religious concepts are apt to provide the answers, which makes a natural alliance between elegiac attitudes and meditational lyrics. But there are other alliances as well. Sidney uses the normal expectations of the elegy in "A Litany" to expose the lightness with which his mistress kills "love," the solemnity of the dirge and her fickleness consorting incongruously together:

> Let dirge be sung, and trentals rightly read,
> > For Love is dead:
> > > Sir Wrong his tomb ordaineth,
> > > My mistress' marble heart,
> > > Which epitaph containeth,
> > > 'Her eyes were once his dart'.
> > > > From so ungrateful fancy,
> > > > From such a female franzy,
> > > > From them that use men thus,
> > > > Good Lord deliver us.

As this suggests, elegiac attitudes can be combined with parody ("par" = "para" meaning "against" and "ody" = "ode" meaning "song"—hence mock song or mock dirge). Apparently more straightforward in elegiac strategy is Sidney's shepherd dirge in which lamentation is its own delight:

> I joy in grief, and do detest all joys:
> Despise delight, am tired with thought of ease;
> I turn my mind to all forms of annoyes, . . .
> Dwell in my ruins, feed with sucking smart,
> I think from me, not from my woes to part.

Here however, the shepherd's position is so exaggerated as to amount to another kind of parody, of an awkward elegiac stance. The shepherd has some justification, because he laments the loss of "Urania" (heavenly harmony), but he goes a step too far. Poets of the eighteenth-century "graveyard" school later make a similar funereal melancholy "pleasing" but subtract the parody, the general feeling about such poses being that they reflect a legitimately pervasive discouragement over an incurable condition.

The closing lines of Pope's *The Dunciad* reveal that such an assumption can also be combined with other elements. The account of the end of learning, order, and light in the coming reign of Dulness is cast in a mixture of melancholy and satire (which is not to say parody):

> Lo! thy dread Empire, Chaos! is restor'd;
> Light dies before thy uncreating word:
> Thy hand, great Anarch! lets the curtain fall;
> And Universal Darkness buries All.

No doubt Pope did not mean literally that the world was coming to an end, yet the exaggeration is no reflection on elegiac conventions. Rather, it represents a fusion of wit and lamentation, reinforced by cosmic images from Genesis and the weight of the epic parallels of the rest of the poem. The function of the elegiac tone is thus one of intensification: it helps cement epic and satiric elements together.

Elegiac *attitudes*, then, are adaptable to satiric, comic, tragic, and lyric forms as secondary elements.

The combination of pastoral and elegy is perhaps the most common, partly because cycles of death and rebirth, so likely to arouse elegiac sentiments, are predominantly *natural*. "Grass" and mortal "flesh" are frequently linked. Bion's "Lament for Adonis," for instance, associates the dying god with flowers: "now that he is dead let them die too, let every flower die." Adonis' death is thus made fatalistic and natural, which is a pastoral-elegiac strategy. Since dying vegetation undergoes a yearly rebirth, however, the pastoral setting is likely to contrast with this the permanence of man's dying, as in Moschus' "Lament for Bion": "And so it shall be that thou wilt lie in the earth beneath a covering of silence, albeit the little croaking frog o' the tree by ordinance of the nymphs may sing for evermore." Or if as in "Lycidas" and "Adonais" the subject proves immortal, the pastoral element helps define the nature of his transcendence by a contrast of its material to his spiritual image. The result is a form of *tragedia di lieto fin* ("tragedy with a happy ending"), in which elegiac elements are part of a movement toward hymn or ode. Whether or not a given elegy is reversed in this manner, it is likely to be stationed at the meeting point of disaster and hope, praise and ceremonial lamentation.

THE FALCON

The perennial tendency of the elegy to move through lamentation to consolation is evident in this medieval poem as the ravaging falcon leads to a vision of Christ, the redemptive falcon.

ANONYMOUS

> *Lully, lulley! lully, lulley!*
> *The faucon hath borne my make away!*
>
> He bare him up, he bare him down,
> He bare him into an orchard brown.
>
> In that orchard there was an halle,   5
> That was hangèd with purple and pall.

---

2 *make*: mate.

And in that hall there was a bed,
It was hangèd with gold so red.

And in that bed there li'th a knight,
His woundès bleeding day and night.   10

At that bed's foot there li'th a hound,
Licking the blood as it runs down.

By that bed-side kneeleth a may,
And she weepeth both night and day.

And at that bed's head standeth a stone,   15
Corpus Christi written thereon.

Lully, lulley! lully, lulley!
The faucon hath borne my make away.

HENRY HOWARD, EARL OF SURREY *(1517?–1547)*

Surrey's elegy on Wyatt may seem more shrewd than reverent, but Surrey makes praise count by making it ring true. The paradoxes of Wyatt's character —his disdain and envy, matched by virtue and "heavenly gifts," and his visage both stern and mild—are resolved in the final separation of earthly and heavenly parts. That separation enables Surrey to eulogize the subject more freely and to accept, on behalf of a world that should have received Wyatt differently, the burden of Wyatt's disdain.

ON THE DEATH OF SIR T[HOMAS] W[YATT]

W[yatt] resteth here that quick could never rest;
  Whose heavenly gifts increased by disdain,
And virtue sank the deeper in his breast;
  Such profit he by envy could obtain.

A head where wisdom mysteries did frame,   5
  Whose hammers beat still in that lively brain,
As on a stithe where that some work of fame
  Was daily wrought, to turn to Britain's gain.

A visage stern and mild: where both did grow
  Vice to contemn, in virtue to rejoice;   10
Amid great storms whom grace assured so
  To live upright, and smile at fortune's choice.

A hand that taught what might be said in rhyme;
  That reft Chaucer the glory of his wit;
A mark, the which (unperfected for time)   15
  Some may approach, but never none shall hit.

A tongue that served in foreign realms his king;
  Whose courteous talk to virtue did inflame

---

13 *may*: maid.
1 *quick*: alive. 7 *stithe*: anvil.

Each noble heart: a worthy guide to bring
  Our English youth by travail unto fame.   20

An eye whose judgment none affect could blind,
  Friends to allure and foes to reconcile,
Whose piercing look did represent a mind
  With virtue fraught reposed void of guile.

A heart where dread was never so imprest   25
  To hide the thought that might the truth advance;
In neither fortune loft, nor yet represt,
  To swell in wealth, or yield unto mischance.

A valiant corpse, where force and beauty met,
  Happy alas, too happy but for foes,   30
Lived, and ran the race that nature set;
  Of manhood's shape where she the mould did lose.

But to the heavens that simple soul is fled,
  Which left with such as covet Christ to know
Witness of faith that never shall be dead,   35
  Sent for our health, but not received so.

Thus, for our guilt, this jewel have we lost;
The earth his bones, the heavens possess his ghost!

CHIDIOCK TICHBORNE *(c. 1558–1586)*

Like any normal person, Tichborne obviously wants to get it off his chest
once and for all; but his situation in the Tower is anything but normal, and
neither is the style of his catalog of grievances. The poem is elegiac rather
than, say, satiric or contemplative partly because of its witty resignation and
universal inclusiveness. Tichborne does not have it in for society or even anyone's idea of society, but he is scarcely pleased with the way things are going—
which must have seemed to him beyond satire at the moment. The monotony
of the poem's succession of paradoxical facts, one per line, suggests the mechanism of the dirge.

TICHBORNE'S ELEGY, WRITTEN IN THE TOWER
BEFORE HIS EXECUTION, 1586

My prime of youth is but a frost of cares;
  My feast of joy is but a dish of pain;
My crop of corn is but a field of tares;
  And all my good is but vain hope of gain:
The day is past, and yet I saw no sun;   5
And now I live, and now my life is done.

My tale was heard, and yet it was not told;
  My fruit is fallen, and yet my leaves are green;
My youth is spent, and yet I am not old;
  I saw the world, and yet I was not seen: 10

---

21 *none affect*: no affection. 27 *loft*: proud.

My thread is cut, and yet it is not spun;
And now I live, and now my life is done.

I sought my death, and found it in my womb;
  I looked for life, and saw it was a shade;
I trod the earth, and knew it was my tomb;   15
  And now I die, and now I was but made:
My glass is full, and now my glass is run;
And now I live, and now my life is done.

JONSON AND CLEVELAND

Jonson's elegy to his son is a classic example of the brief lament, which condenses the expression of loss and its consolations into epitaph form. As the poem assumes an immediate confrontation of speaker and grave, the form resembles the dramatic monologue; although one party is necessarily silent, his imagined presence and the fiction that he can at least listen are perhaps as important to the consolation as the "justice" of his early loss. As Cleveland's poem demonstrates, intellectual acuteness and irony are not incompatible with sorrow.

ON MY FIRST SON (1616)

BEN JONSON *(1572?–1637)*

Farewell, thou child of my right hand, and joy!
My sin was too much hope of thee, loved boy;
Seven years thou wert lent to me, and I thee pay,
Exacted by thy fate, on the just day.
Oh, could I lose all father now! For why   5
Will man lament the state he should envy—
To have so soon 'scaped world's and flesh's rage,
And, if no other misery, yet age?
Rest in soft peace, and asked, say here doth lie
Ben Jonson his best piece of poetry: 10
For whose sake, henceforth, all his vows be such
As what he loves may never like too much.

EPITAPH ON THE EARL OF STRAFFORD

JOHN CLEVELAND *(1613–1658)*

Here lies wise and valiant dust,
Huddled up 'twixt fit and just:
Strafford, who was hurried hence
'Twixt treason and convenience.
He spent his time here in a mist,   5
A Papist, yet a Calvinist;
His Prince's nearest joy and grief:

6–7 *A Papist...grief:* as a supporter of the king and the bishops, Strafford was considered a Papist; in personal belief he was probably closer to Calvinism. As the king's strongest supporter, he was his "nearest joy"; but since precisely because of this he was the one person whose sacrificial death would most appease the parliament, he was also the king's "grief."

He had, yet wanted, all relief:
The prop and ruin of the state,
The people's violent love and hate.   10
One in extremes lov'd and abhorr'd.
Riddles lie here, or in a word,
Here lies blood, and let it lie
Speechless still, and never cry.

THOMAS GRAY *(1716–1771)*

The mood of Gray's elegy is what an eighteenth-century poet might call "sweet melancholy," which, given the universal and impersonal operations of death in most eighteenth-century "graveyard" poems, is perhaps not so contradictory as it seems—for death as Gray describes it is democratic and natural (hence pastoral and Utopian). In the inherent dignity of common things, Gray discovers adequate consolation for their final obscurity.

ELEGY WRITTEN IN A COUNTRY CHURCHYARD

The curfew tolls the knell of parting day,
  The lowing herd winds slowly o'er the lea,
The plowman homeward plods his weary way,
  And leaves the world to darkness and to me.

Now fades the glimmering landscape on the sight,   5
  And all the air a solemn stillness holds,
Save where the beetle wheels his droning flight,
  And drowsy tinklings lull the distant folds;

Save that from yonder ivy-mantled tower
  The moping owl does to the moon complain   10
Of such, as wand'ring near her secret bower,
  Molest her ancient solitary reign.

Beneath those rugged elms, that yew-tree's shade,
  Where heaves the turf in many a mold'ring heap,
Each in his narrow cell for ever laid,   15
  The rude forefathers of the hamlet sleep.

The breezy call of incense-breathing morn,
  The swallow twitt'ring from the straw-built shed,
The cock's shrill clarion, or the echoing horn,
  No more shall rouse them from their lowly bed.   20

For them no more the blazing hearth shall burn,
  Or busy housewife ply her evening care:
No children run to lisp their sire's return,
  Or climb his knees the envied kiss to share.

Oft did the harvest to their sickle yield,   25
  Their furrow oft the stubborn glebe has broke;
How jocund did they drive their team afield!
  How bowed the woods beneath their sturdy stroke!

8 *wanted*: lacked.

Let not ambition mock their useful toil,
  Their homely joys, and destiny obscure;   30
Nor grandeur hear with a disdainful smile,
  The short and simple annals of the poor.

The boast of heraldry, the pomps of power,
  And all that beauty, all that wealth e'er gave,
Await alike th' inevitable hour.   35
  The paths of glory lead but to the grave.

Nor you, ye proud, impute to these the fault,
  If memory o'er their tomb no trophies raise,
Where through the long-drawn aisle and fretted vault
  The pealing anthem swells the note of praise.   40

Can storied urn or animated bust
  Back to its mansion call the fleeting breath?
Can honor's voice provoke the silent dust,
  Or flattery soothe the dull cold ear of death?

Perhaps in this neglected spot is laid   45
  Some heart once pregnant with celestial fire;
Hands that the rod of empire might have swayed,
  Or waked to ecstasy the living lyre.

But knowledge to their eyes her ample page
  Rich with the spoils of time did ne'er unroll;   50
Chill penury repressed their noble rage,
  And froze the genial current of the soul.

Full many a gem of purest ray serene,
  The dark unfathomed caves of ocean bear:
Full many a flower is born to blush unseen,   55
  And waste its sweetness on the desert air.

Some village Hampden, that, with dauntless breast
  The little tyrant of his fields withstood;
Some mute inglorious Milton here may rest,
  Some Cromwell guiltless of his country's blood.   60

Th' applause of listening senates to command,
  The threats of pain and ruin to despise,
To scatter plenty o'er a smiling land,
  And read their history in a nation's eyes,

Their lot forbade: nor circumscribed alone   65
  Their growing virtues, but their crimes confined;
Forbade to wade through slaughter to a throne,
  And shut the gates of mercy on mankind.

The struggling pangs of conscious truth to hide,
  To quench the blushes of ingenuous shame,   70
Or heap the shrine of luxury and pride
  With incense kindled at the muse's flame.

Far from the madding crowd's ignoble strife,
  Their sober wishes never learned to stray;

Along the cool requestered vale of life   75
   They kept the noiseless tenor of their way.

Yet ev'n these bones from insult to protect
   Some frail memorial still erected nigh,
With uncouth rimes and shapeless sculpture decked,
   Implores the passing tribute of a sigh.   80

Their name, their years, spelt by th' unlettered muse,
   The place of fame and elegy supply:
And many a holy text around she strews,
   That teach the rustic moralist to die.

For who to dumb forgetfulness a prey,   85
   This pleasing anxious being e'er resigned,
Left the warm precincts of the cheerful day,
   Nor cast one longing ling'ring look behind?

On some fond breast the parting soul relies,
   Some pious drops the closing eye requires;   90
Ev'n from the tomb the voice of Nature cries,
   Ev'n in our ashes live their wonted fires.

For thee, who mindful of th' unhonored dead
   Dost in these lines their artless tale relate;
If chance, by lonely contemplation led,   95
   Some kindred Spirit shall inquire thy fate,

Haply some hoary-headed swain may say,
   "Oft have we seen him at the peep of dawn
Brushing with hasty steps the dews away
   To meet the sun upon the upland lawn.   100

"There at the foot of yonder nodding beech
   That wreathes its old fantastic roots so high,
His listless length at noontide would he stretch,
   And pore upon the brook that babbles by.

"Hard by yon wood, now smiling as in scorn,   105
   Mutt'ring his wayward fancies he would rove,
Now drooping, woeful wan, like one forlorn,
   Or crazed with care, or crossed in hopeless love.

"One morn I missed him on the customed hill,
   Along the heath and near his fav'rite tree;   110
Another came; nor yet beside the rill,
   Nor up the lawn, nor at the wood was he;

"The next with dirges due in sad array
   Slow through the church-way path we saw him borne.
Approach and read (for thou canst read) the lay   115
   Graved on the stone beneath yon agèd thorn."

The Epitaph

Here rests his head upon the lap of earth
   A youth, to fortune and to fame unknown;

Fair science frown'd not on his humble birth,
    And melancholy mark'd him for her own.   120

Large was his bounty, and his soul sincere;
    Heaven did a recompense as largely send:
He gave to misery all he had, a tear,
    He gain'd from heaven, 'twas all he wish'd, a friend.

No farther seek his merits to disclose,   125
    Or draw his frailties from their dread abode,
(There they alike in trembling hope repose,)
    The bosom of his father and his God.

WALTER SAVAGE LANDOR *(1775–1864)*

Landor's "Rose Aylmer" concerns Baron Aylmer's young daughter, who died
a few years after Landor met her. It concludes a lament for mankind in general and Rose Aylmer in particular with a vow to consecrate one night of
memories and sighs to her memory—a rather inexpensive purchase of tranquility.

ROSE AYLMER

Ah what avails the sceptred race,
    Ah what the form divine!
What every virtue, every grace!
    Rose Aylmer, all were thine.

Rose Aylmer, whom these wakeful eyes
    May weep, but never see,
A night of memories and sighs
    I consecrate to thee.

ALFRED, LORD TENNYSON *(1809–1892)*

In Memoriam encompasses a wide range of moods from despair to joy, not
all of which are elegiac. But the poem as a whole is devoted to finding consolation for the death of Tennyson's friend Arthur Hallam and hence illustrates
both the special problems confronted by a Victorian elegist whose faith has
been undermined and Tennyson's particular philosophical and religious answers.
The nostalgia of "Tears, Idle Tears" is typical of elegiac verse, but nostalgia
in this case is treated as a metaphysical problem—as the impingement of past
on present, death on life.

IN MEMORIAM [SELECTIONS]

5

I sometimes hold it half a sin
    To put in words the grief I feel;
    For words, like Nature, half reveal
And half conceal the soul within.

But, for the unquiet heart and brain,   5
    A use in measured language lies;

The sad mechanic exercise,
Like dull narcotics, numbing pain.

In words, like weeds, I'll wrap me o'er,
   Like coarsest clothes against the cold;   10
   But that large grief which these enfold
Is given in outline and no more.

7

Dark house, by which once more I stand
   Here in the long unlovely street,
   Doors, where my heart was used to beat
So quickly, waiting for a hand,

A hand that can be clasped no more—   5
   Behold me, for I cannot sleep,
   And like a guilty thing I creep
At earliest morning to the door.

He is not here; but far away
   The noise of life begins again,   10
   And ghastly through the drizzling rain
On the bald street breaks the blank day.

11

Calm is the morn without a sound,
   Calm as to suit a calmer grief,
   And only thro' the faded leaf
The chestnut pattering to the ground;

Calm and deep peace on this high wold,   5
   And on these dews that drench the furze,
   And all the silvery gossamers
That twinkle into green and gold;

Calm and still light on yon great plain
   That sweeps with all its autumn bowers,   10
   And crowded farms and lessening towers,
To mingle with the bounding main;

Calm and deep peace in this wide air,
   These leaves that redden to the fall;
   And in my heart, if calm at all,   15
If any calm, a calm despair;

Calm on the seas, and silver sleep,
   And waves that sway themselves in rest,
   And dead calm in that noble breast
Which heaves but with the heaving deep.   20

16

What words are these have fall'n from me?
   Can calm despair and wild unrest
   Be tenants of a single breast,
Or sorrow such a changeling be?

Or doth she only seem to take   5
    The touch of change in calm or storm;
    But knows no more of transient form
In her deep self, than some dead lake

That holds the shadow of a lark
    Hung in the shadow of a heaven?   10
    Or has the shock, so harshly given,
Confused me like the unhappy bark

That strikes by night a craggy shelf,
    And staggers blindly ere she sink?
    And stunned me from my power to think   15
And all my knowledge of myself;

And made me that delirious man
    Whose fancy fuses old and new,
    And flashes into false and true,
And mingles all without a plan?   20

21

I sing to him that rests below,
    And, since the grasses round me wave,
    I take the grasses of the grave,
And make them pipes whereon to blow.

The traveller hears me now and then,   5
    And sometimes harshly will he speak:
    "This fellow would make weakness weak,
And melt the waxen hearts of men."

Another answers, "Let him be,
    He loves to make parade of pain,   10
    That with his piping he may gain
The praise that comes to constancy."

A third is wroth: "Is this an hour
    For private sorrow's barren song,
    When more and more the people throng   15
The chairs and thrones of evil power?

"A time to sicken and to swoon,
    When Science reaches forth her arms
    To feel from world to world, and charms
Her secret from the latest moon?"   20

Behold, ye speak an idle thing:
    Ye never knew the sacred dust:
    I do but sing because I must,
And pipe but as the linnets sing:

And one is glad; her note is gay,   25
    For now her little ones have ranged;
    And one is sad; her note is changed,
Because her brood is stol'n away.

34

My own dim life should teach me this,
  That life shall live for evermore,
  Else earth is darkness at the core,
And dust and ashes all that is;

This round of green, this orb of flame,   5
  Fantastic beauty; such as lurks
  In some wild poet, when he works
Without a conscience or an aim.

What then were God to such as I?
  'Twere hardly worth my while to choose   10
  Of things all mortal, or to use
A little patience ere I die;

'Twere best at once to sink to peace,
  Like birds the charming serpent draws,
  To drop head-foremost in the jaws   15
Of vacant darkness and to cease.

55

The wish, that of the living whole
  No life may fail beyond the grave,
  Derives it not from what we have
The likest God within the soul?

Are God and Nature then at strife,   5
  That Nature lends such evil dreams?
  So careful of the type she seems,
So careless of the single life,

That I, considering everywhere
  Her secret meaning in her deeds,
  And finding that of fifty seeds   10
She often brings but one to bear,

I falter where I firmly trod,
  And falling with my weight of cares
  Upon the great world's altar-stairs   15
That slope thro' darkness up to God,

I stretch lame hands of faith, and grope,
  And father dust and chaff, and call
  To what I feel is Lord of all,
And faintly trust the larger hope.   20

56

"So careful of the type?" but no.
  From scarped cliff and quarried stone
  She cries, "A thousand types are gone;
I care for nothing, all shall go.

"Thou makest thine appeal to me.   5
  I bring to life, I bring to death;

The spirit does but mean the breath.
I know no more." And he, shall he,

Man, her last work, who seemed so fair,
  Such splendid purpose in his eyes,   10
  Who rolled the psalm to wintry skies,
Who built him fanes of fruitless prayer,

Who trusted God was love indeed
  And love Creation's final law—
  Though Nature, red in tooth and claw   15
With ravine, shrieked against his creed—

Who loved, who suffered countless ills,
  Who battled for the True, the Just,
  Be blown about the desert dust,
Or sealed within the iron hills?   20

No more? A monster then, a dream,
  A discord. Dragons of the prime,
  That tare each other in their slime,
Were mellow music matched with him.

O life as futile, then, as frail!   25
  O for thy voice to soothe and bless!
  What hope of answer, or redress?
Behind the veil, behind the veil.

70

I cannot see the features right,
  When on the gloom I strive to paint
  The face I know; the hues are faint
And mix with hollow masks of night;

Cloud-towers by ghostly masons wrought,   5
  A gulf that ever shuts and gapes,
  A hand that points, and palled shapes
In shadowy thoroughfares of thought;

And crowds that stream from yawning doors,
  And shoals of pucker'd faces drive;   10
  Dark bulks that tumble half alive,
And lazy lengths on boundless shores;

Till all at once beyond the will
  I hear a wizard music roll,
  And thro' a lattice on the soul   15
Looks thy fair face and makes it still.

95

By night we linger'd on the lawn,
  For underfoot the herb was dry;
  And genial warmth; and o'er the sky
The silvery haze of summer drawn;

And calm that let the tapers burn 5
 Unwavering: not a cricket chirr'd;
 The brook alone far-off was heard,
And on the board the fluttering urn.

And bats went round in fragrant skies,
 And wheel'd or lit the filmy shapes 10
 That haunt the dusk, with ermine capes
And woolly breasts and beaded eyes;

While now we sang old songs that peal'd
 From knoll to knoll, where, couch'd at ease,
 The white kine glimmer'd, and the trees 15
Laid their dark arms about the field.

But when those others, one by one,
 Withdrew themselves from me and night,
 And in the house light after light
Went out, and I was all alone, 20

A hunger seized my heart; I read
 Of that glad year which once had been,
 In those fall'n leaves which kept their green,
The noble letters of the dead.

And strangely on the silence broke 25
 The silent-speaking words, and strange
 Was love's dumb cry defying change
To test his worth; and strangely spoke

The faith, the vigor, bold to dwell
 On doubts that drive the coward back, 30
 And keen thro' wordy snares to track
Suggestion to her inmost cell.

So word by word, and line by line,
 The dead man touch'd me from the past,
 And all at once it seem'd at last 35
The living soul was flash'd on mine,

And mine in this was wound, and whirl'd
 About empyreal heights of thought,
 And came on that which is, and caught
The deep pulsations of the world, 40

Æonian music measuring out
 The steps of Time—the shocks of Chance—
 The blows of Death. At length my trance
Was cancell'd, stricken thro' with doubt.

Vague words! but ah, how hard to frame 45
 In matter-moulded forms of speech,
 Or even for intellect to reach
Thro' memory that which I became;

Till now the doubtful dusk reveal'd
  The knolls once more where, couch'd at ease,   50
  The white kine glimmer'd, and the trees
Laid their dark arms about the field;

And suck'd from out the distant gloom
  A breeze began to tremble o'er
  The large leaves of the sycamore,   55
And fluctuate all the still perfume,

And gathering freshlier overhead,
  Rock'd the full-foliaged elms, and swung
  The heavy-folded rose, and flung
The lilies to and fro, and said,   60

"The dawn, the dawn," and died away;
  And east and west, without a breath
  Mixt their dim light, like life and death,
To broaden into boundless day.

124

That which we dare invoke to bless;
  Our dearest faith; our ghastliest doubt;
  He, They, One, All; within, without;
The Power in darkness whom we guess;

I found Him not in world or sun,   5
  Or eagle's wing, or insect's eye;
  Nor thro' the questions men may try,
The petty cobwebs we have spun:

If e'er when faith had fall'n asleep,
  I heard a voice, "Believe no more"   10
  And heard an ever-breaking shore
That tumbled in the Godless deep;

A warmth within the breast would melt
  The freezing reason's colder part,
  And like a man in wrath the heart   15
Stood up and answered, "I have felt."

No, like a child in doubt and fear:
  But that blind clamor made me wise;
  Then was I as a child that cries,
But, crying, knows his father near;   20

And what I am beheld again
  What is, and no man understands;
  And out of darkness came the hands
That reach through nature, molding men.

130

Thy voice is on the rolling air;
  I hear thee where the waters run;
  Thou standest in the rising sun,
And in the setting thou art fair.

What art thou then? I cannot guess;   5
  But tho' I seem in star and flower
  To feel thee some diffusive power,
I do not therefore love thee less:

My love involves the love before;
  My love is vaster passion now;   10
  Tho' mixed with God and Nature thou,
I seem to love thee more and more.

Far off thou art, but ever nigh;
  I have thee still, and I rejoice;
  I prosper, circled with thy voice;   15
I shall not lose thee tho' I die.

TEARS, IDLE TEARS

Tears, idle tears, I know not what they mean;
Tears from the depth of some divine despair
Rise in the heart, and gather to the eyes,
In looking on the happy autumn-fields,
And thinking of the days that are no more.   5

Fresh as the first beam glittering on a sail,
That brings our friends up from the under-world,
Sad as the last which reddens over one
That sinks with all we love below the verge;
So sad, so fresh, the days that are no more.   10

Ah, sad and strange as in dark summer dawns
The earliest pipe of half-awakened birds
To dying ears, when unto dying eyes
The casement slowly grows a glimmering square;
So sad, so strange, the days that are no more.   15

Dear as remembered kisses after death,
And sweet as those by hopeless fancy feigned
On lips that are for others; deep as love,
Deep as first love, and wild with all regret;
O Death in Life, the days that are no more!   20

MATTHEW ARNOLD *(1822–1888)*

Arnold's consolation for the darkness of the world in "Dover Beach" is ostensibly reciprocal love. But the melancholy tranquility of the verse indicates that he has already adjusted to the clash of "ignorant armies" by night and stands apart from the strife that he laments. In part, the poem assesses the comforts not of philosophy but of resignation.

DOVER BEACH

The sea is calm tonight,
The tide is full, the moon lies fair
Upon the straits;—on the French coast the light

Gleams and is gone; the cliffs of England stand,
Glimmering and vast, out in the tranquil bay. 5
Come to the window, sweet is the night-air!
Only, from the long line of spray
Where the sea meets the moon-blanched land,
Listen! you hear the grating roar
Of pebbles which the waves draw back, and fling, 10
At their return, up the high strand,
Begin, and cease, and then again begin,
With tremulous cadence slow, and bring
The eternal note of sadness in.

Sophocles long ago 15
Heard it on the Ægæan, and it brought
Into his mind the turbid ebb and flow
Of human misery; we
Find also in the sound a thought,
Hearing it by this distant northern sea. 20

The Sea of Faith
Was once, too, at the full, and round earth's shore
Lay like the folds of a bright girdle furled.
But now I only hear
Its melancholy, long, withdrawing roar, 25
Retreating, to the breath
Of the night-wind, down the vast edges drear
And naked shingles of the world.

Ah, love, let us be true
To one another! for the world, which seems 30
To lie before us like a land of dreams,
So various, so beautiful, so new,
Hath really neither joy, nor love, nor light,
Nor certitude, nor peace, nor help for pain;
And we are here as on a darkling plain 35
Swept with confused alarms of struggle and flight,
Where ignorant armies clash by night.

THOMAS HARDY *(1840-1928)*

Hardy's "Neutral Tones" allows very little consolation to come between the speaker and his grief. It returns ceremonially to its initial wan images of blight with the satisfaction of the pessimist proved right by still another misfortune.

NEUTRAL TONES*

We stood by a pond that winter day,
And the sun was white, as though chidden of God,
And a few leaves lay on the starving sod;
    They had fallen from an ash, and were gray.

---

* Reprinted from *Collected Poems of Thomas Hardy* by permission of the Estate, Macmillan & Co., Ltd., London, and The Macmillan Company of Canada Limited.

Your eyes on me were as eyes that rove 5
Over tedious riddles solved years ago;
And some words played between us to and fro
    On which lost the more by our love.

The smile on your mouth was the deadest thing
Alive enough to have strength to die; 10
And a grin of bitterness swept thereby
    Like an ominous bird a-wing. . . .

Since then, keen lessons that love deceives,
And wrings with wrong, have shaped to me
Your face, and the God-curst sun, and a tree, 15
    And a pond edged with grayish leaves.

GERARD MANLEY HOPKINS *(1845–1889)*

Hopkins' rapid rhythm and flashing imagery might seem to preclude an elegiac mood. Certainly "Felix Randal" is witty, intellectual, and complex. But Hopkins does not lose sight of the personal feeling between priest and blacksmith. The last two stanzas are a compassionate celebration of Felix Randal's life (his afterlife having already been disposed of).

FELIX RANDAL*

Felix Randal the farrier, O he is dead then? my duty all ended
Who have watched his mould of man, big-boned and hardy-handsome
Pining, pining, till time when reason rambled in it and some
Fatal four disorders, fleshed there, all contended?

Sickness broke him. Impatient he cursed at first, but mended 5
Being anointed and all; though a heavenlier heart began some
Months earlier, since I had our sweet reprieve and ransom
Tendered to him. Ah well, God rest him all road ever he offended!

This seeing the sick endears them to us, us too it endears.
My tongue had taught thee comfort, touch had quenched thy tears, 10
Thy tears that touched my heart, child, Felix, poor Felix Randal;

How far from then forethought of, all thy more boisterous years,
When thou at the random grim forge, powerful amidst peers,
Didst fettle for the great grey drayhorse his bright and battering sandal!

WILLIAM BUTLER YEATS *(1865–1939)*

Yeats's own phrase "gaiety transfiguring all that dread" perhaps best characterizes the strategy of "Lapis Lazuli," which contemplates destruction without weeping, destruction transfigured by Yeats's vision of history as magnificent,

* From *Poems of Gerard Manley Hopkins*, Third Edition, edited by W. H. Gardner. Copyright 1948 by Oxford University Press, Inc. Reprinted by permission.

1 *farrier*: blacksmith.   8 *all road ever*: in whatever way.   13 *random*: irregularly built. 14 *fettle*: prepare.

inevitable, and violent. His vision precludes simple lamentation over change by incorporating immediate events into the vast making and unmaking of history. There are also the consolations of art, the ruin of the world being accompanied by mournful melodies, which "accomplished fingers" play.

LAPIS LAZULI*

I have heard that hysterical women say
They are sick of the palette and fiddle-bow,
Of poets that are always gay,
For everybody knows or else should know
That if nothing drastic is done   5
Aeroplane and Zeppelin will come out,
Pitch like King Billy bomb-balls in
Until the town lie beaten flat.

All perform their tragic play,
There struts Hamlet, there is Lear,   10
That's Ophelia, that Cordelia;
Yet they, should the last scene be there,
The great stage curtain about to drop,
If worthy their prominent part in the play,
Do not break up their lines to weep.   15
They know that Hamlet and Lear are gay;
Gaiety transfiguring all that dread.
All men have aimed at, found and lost;
Black out; Heaven blazing into the head:
Tragedy wrought to its uttermost.   20
Though Hamlet rambles and Lear rages,
And all the drop-scenes drop at once
Upon a hundred thousand stages,
It cannot grow by an inch or an ounce.

On their own feet they came, or on shipboard,   25
Camel-back, horse-back, ass-back, mule-back,
Old civilisations put to the sword.
Then they and their wisdom went to rack:
No handiwork of Callimachus,
Who handled marble as if it were bronze,   30
Made draperies that seemed to rise
When sea-wind swept the corner, stands;
His long lamp-chimney shaped like the stem
Of a slender palm, stood but a day;
All things fall and are built again,   35
And those that build them again are gay.

Two Chinamen, behind them a third,
Are carved in lapis lazuli,
Over them flies a long-legged bird,

A symbol of longevity;   40
The third, doubtless a serving-man,
Carries a musical instrument.

Every discoloration of the stone,
Every accidental crack or dent,
Seems a water-course or an avalanche,   45
Or lofty slope where it still snows
Though doubtless plum or cherry-branch
Sweetens the little half-way house
Those Chinamen climb towards, and I
Delight to imagine them seated there;   50
There, on the mountain and the sky,
On all the tragic scene they stare.
One asks for mournful melodies;
Accomplished fingers begin to play.
Their eyes mid many wrinkles, their eyes,
Their ancient, glittering eyes, are gay.

HART CRANE *(1899–1932)*

As the author of *Moby Dick*, Melville may leave his body entombed on land,
but his "fabulous shadow only the sea keeps." Crane's separation of the man
and the artist ("fabulous shadow" being a kind of prose-fiction equivalent of
"poetic spirit") allows him to relocate the novelist's grave in the eternal "azure
steeps" of his own works.

AT MELVILLE'S TOMB*

Often beneath the wave, wide from this ledge
The dice of drowned men's bones he saw bequeath
An embassy. Their numbers as he watched,
Beat on the dusty shore and were obscured.

And wrecks passed without sound of bells,   5
The calyx of death's bounty giving back
A scattered chapter, livid hieroglyph,
The portent wound in corridors of shells.

Then in the circuit calm of one vast coil,
Its lashings charmed and malice reconciled,   10
Frosted eyes there were that lifted altars;
And silent answers crept across the stars.

Compass, quadrant and sextant contrive
No farther tides...High in the azure steeps
Monody shall not wake the mariner.   15
This fabulous shadow only the sea keeps.

* From *The Collected Poems of Hart Crane.* By permission of Liveright, Publishers, N.Y.
Copyright © R, 1961 by Liveright Publishing Corp.

W. H. AUDEN *(1907–   )*

In commemorating Yeats's death, Auden at first bypasses most of the obvious poetic graces, beginning with a reasoned, honest, almost unmetrical voice that mocks elegiac conventions. But after a biting satire of those left behind, the third section becomes part incantation, part hymn, part exalted celebration of a great poet's powers, for it is the elegist who, confronted with "the nightmare of the dark," sings "of human unsuccess / In a rapture of distress" and by doing so makes "the healing fountains start."

IN MEMORY OF W. B. YEATS*

(d. Jan. 1939)

1

He disappeared in the dead of winter:
The brooks were frozen, the air-ports almost deserted,
And snow disfigured the public statues;
The mercury sank in the mouth of the dying day.
O all the instruments agree   5
The day of his death was a dark cold day.

Far from his illness
The wolves ran on through the evergreen forests,
The peasant river was untempted by the fashionable quays;
By mourning tongues   10
The death of the poet was kept from his poems.

But for him it was his last afternoon as himself,
An afternoon of nurses and rumours;
The provinces of his body revolted,
The squares of his mind were empty,   15
Silence invaded the suburbs,
The current of his feeling failed: he became his admirers.

Now he is scattered among a hundred cities
And wholly given over to unfamiliar affections;
To find his happiness in another kind of wood   20
And be punished under a foreign code of conscience.
The words of a dead man
Are modified in the guts of the living.

But in the importance and noise of to-morrow
When the brokers are roaring like beasts on the floor of the Bourse,   25
And the poor have the sufferings to which they are fairly accustomed,
And each in the cell of himself is almost convinced of his freedom;
A few thousand will think of this day
As one thinks of a day when one did something slightly unusual.

O all the instruments agree   30
The day of his death was a dark cold day.

2

You were silly like us: your gift survived it all;
The parish of rich women, physical decay,
Yourself; mad Ireland hurt you into poetry.
Now Ireland has her madness and her weather still,
For poetry makes nothing happen: it survives,   5
In the valley of its saying where executives
Would never want to tamper; it flows south
From ranches of isolation and the busy griefs,
Raw towns that we believe and die in; it survives,
A way of happening, a mouth.   10

3

Earth, receive an honoured guest;
William Yeats is laid to rest:
Let the Irish vessel lie
Emptied of its poetry.

Time that is intolerant   5
Of the brave and innocent,
And indifferent in a week
To a beautiful physique,

Worships language and forgives
Everyone by whom it lives;   10
Pardons cowardice, conceit,
Lays its honours at their feet.

Time that with this strange excuse
Pardoned Kipling and his views,
And will pardon Paul Claudel,   15
Pardons him for writing well.

In the nightmare of the dark
All the dogs of Europe bark,
And the living nations wait,
Each sequestered in its hate;   20

Intellectual disgrace
Stares from every human face,
And the seas of pity lie
Locked and frozen in each eye.

Follow, poet, follow right   25
To the bottom of the night,
With your unconstraining voice
Still persuade us to rejoice;

With the farming of a verse
Make a vineyard of the curse,   30

Sing of human unsuccess
In a rapture of distress;

In the deserts of the heart
Let the healing fountain start,
In the prison of his days   35
Teach the free man how to praise.

DYLAN THOMAS *(1914–1953)*

Like Yeats in "Lapis Lazuli," Thomas refuses to mourn a disaster, but for quite different reasons. Yeats's tragic vision is compounded of regret and joy together so that something like an oxymoronic fusion of the two emerges; Thomas' consolation is based on the "majesty of burning" of the child's death. Considering her return to the womb-like community of dead beside the un-mourning Thames, grave-side oratory ("grave truth") is hypocritical or at best irrelevant.

A REFUSAL TO MOURN THE DEATH, BY FIRE,
OF A CHILD IN LONDON*

Never until the mankind making
Bird beast and flower
Fathering and all humbling darkness
Tells with silence the last light breaking
And the still hour   5
Is come of the sea tumbling in harness

And I must enter again the round
Zion of the water bead
And the synagogue of the ear of corn
Shall I let pray the shadow of a sound   10
Or sow my salt seed
In the least valley of sackcloth to mourn

The majesty and burning of the child's death.
I shall not murder
The mankind of her going with a grave truth   15
Nor blaspheme down the stations of the breath
With any further
Elegy of innocence and youth.

Deep with the first dead lies London's daughter,
Robed in the long friends,   20
The grains beyond age, the dark veins of her mother,
Secret by the unmourning water
Of the riding Thames.
After the first death, there is no other.

Reflective, Religious, and Metaphysical Lyrics

In meditative lyrics, personal emotion is expressed in or filtered primarily through rational processes; the intellect shapes, qualifies, and defines emotion with the aid of the formal elements of verse. The reflective lyric, at least to a greater degree than songs, sonnets, odes, or elegies, is therefore a rationalized organization of experience, and to the extent that the poet subjects his experience to the processes of reason, he makes it available to the public—perhaps even to himself. In fact, one of the reasons that modern critics have devoted so much of their energies to the analysis of reflective lyrics is probably that analysis and paraphrase can account for more of the total poem than in genres stressing intangible formal devices.

But even in this apparently less formalized mode, the poet's art is never entirely paraphrasable. Reason is combined with elements of song and ceremony in meditational poems in much the same way that it is in other forms, the difference being that a reflective lyric, having practically no inherent limits on subject matter or mood, imitates more directly the movement of thought itself. In this respect, it is the most thematic of lyric forms (although poets like Herrick and Herbert are as musical as they are reflective). Consider the combination of theme, tone, and musical form in Donne's "Lovers' Infiniteness," for instance:

> If yet I have not all thy love,
> Dear, I shall never have it all,
> I cannot breathe one other sigh, to move;
> Nor can intreat one other tear to fall.
> And all my treasure, which should purchase thee,
> Sighs, tears, and oaths, and letters I have spent,
> Yet no more can be due to me,
> Than at the bargain made was meant,
> If then thy gift of love were partial,
> That some to me, some should to others fall,
>   Dear, I shall never have thee all.
>
> Or if then thou gavest me all,
> All was but all, which thou hadst then,
> But if in thy heart, since, there be or shall,
> New love created be, by other men,
> Which have their stocks intire, and can in tears,
> In sighs, in oaths, and letters outbid me,
> This new love may beget new fears,
> For, this love was not vowed by thee.
> And yet it was, thy gift being general,
> The ground, thy heart is mine, what ever shall
>   Grow there, dear, I should have it all.
>
> Yet I would not have all yet,
> He that hath all can have no more,

And since my love doth every day admit
New growth, thou shouldst have new rewards in store;
Thou canst not every day give me thy heart,
If thou canst give it, then thou never gavest it:
Love's riddles are, that though thy heart depart,
It stays at home, and thou with losing savest it:
But we will have a way more liberal,
Than changing hearts, to join them, so we shall
       Be one, and one another's all.

The poem is difficult to follow unless we catch the subtle, reflective, and modulated tone of the address. The "theme" of love's infiniteness is not for Donne
something to be considered separately and expounded as a proposition but
something to be experienced and worked out in the course of the meditation.
The frequency of the reversals in the first two stanzas is a sign that he is not
yet possessed of "infiniteness," by definition a static condition beyond change;
he must free himself first of legalistic and economic frames of thought and then
begin to think in terms of love's paradoxical riddles, of a total, "liberal" exchange
of identities. The last stanza is a series of leaps to new perspectives, not merely
intellectual but involving the speaker's whole sensibility. That the sepaker is
engaged in thinking through the nature of love while he writes (or speaks) we
understand from the careful spacing of pauses, especially the address "dear"
in the first stanza, and from the signals of logic, "yet," "if," "since." Tone,
image, and theme combine to give the impression of immediately experienced
thought and emotion seeking proper articulation, first in an inadequate stock
of metaphors and then in the joining of hearts.

The movement of rational thought and the style of the spoken voice are not
adequate in themselves, however, to account for the range of modes that reflective poetry may illustrate. A poem may be philosophic in implication, for
instance, rather than in statement, and the voice may seem less deliberative
than merely descriptive.

Consider Theodore Roethke's "The Heron"*:

The heron stands in water where the swamp
Has deepened to the blackness of a pool,
Or balances with one leg on a hump
Of marsh grass heaped above a musk-rat hole.

He walks the shallow with an antic grace.
The great feet break the ridges of the sand,
The long eye notes the minnow's hiding place.
His beak is quicker than a human hand.

He jerks a frog across his bony lip,
Then points his heavy bill above the wood.
The wide wings flap but once to lift him up.
A single ripple starts from where he stood.

It is clearly not the flow of thought or the cadence of speech that makes the poem seem reflective, but implication of another kind. Like some pastoral verse, it balances an implicit sense of rightness against something harsher that cuts into softer attitudes toward nature as the hard "k" sounds ("beak," "quicker," and "jerks") cut into the mellow sounds around them. The carefully modulated sound effects are, in fact, a clue to the poem's special kind of order. Seemingly, its sense of peace absorbs and transmutes the act of violence without stirring mud: the swamp and the hero are too anciently beautiful to raise, say, the spectre of Tennyson warning that nature is red in tooth and claw and that morality cries out against it.

Technically, the poem's meditative pace and phrasing urge us to look more closely. In the first stanza disorder subtly plays against the metrical norm in the off-rhymes and in some metrical irregularity. The phrasing carries past normal pauses at mid-line and end-line, the first line pausing at "water" and the next phrase unit carrying to the end of line two. The entire stanza, though divided firmly at the end of the second line, is much more a single unit than a strongly rhymed, end-stopped stanza of music would be. The mood, too, is modulated and ambivalent: our instinctive distrust of swamps is qualified by the wry humor of the one-legged stander. "Hump," "heaped," and "musk-rat hole" are the stuff of ironic children's verse.

Again in the last stanza, we are made to go slowly. After the short, lumbering strain of "wide wings flap," we coast out on gentle music, in a line whose regular meter is heightened by three softly alliterated words. But imagistically the focus remains on the pool as the heron escapes; we notice, in the past tense, the vacancy where he (and the frog) just were, and as we do so, we are led to ponder what's in a ripple: perhaps grace; nature's indifference; a symbol for afterthought itself, widening into insight; or calm—after a supper taken so quickly and with such precision that we haven't as yet had time to register what has happened. The deliberation, in other words, comes in part *after* the poem, in the silence of Roethke's nonstatement, in the reader's meditation on the spreading ring.

Besides questioning the relationship of herons and frogs, we are perhaps also led to raise a question that arises frequently in poetry written after older books of nature had ceased to offer ready-made concepts of animal, vegetable, and mineral phenomena—as they do in Milton's and Wordsworth's, for instance— namely, the kinds of parallel that exist between the human observer and the scene. What is Roethke's primeval swamp to us? What order rules there? Is there a "design" (to use the word Frost thinks of applying to a white spider in a white flower feasting on a white moth)? The poet's silence forces the imagery to make its statement indirectly, but one has only to think of Milton's Garden of Eden, and the emblematic world of Adam and Eve when they leave it, or of Wordsworth's pantheistic nature with its types and symbols of a divine mind, to see that there is in fact a "view of nature" implicit in the poem. The heron is scarcely graceful in terms comfortable to the human love of art and symmetry, and he is not fun for frogs either. Yet he is nonetheless graceful in his odd way. Hence the poet carefully distinguishes the bird kingdom from human orders by treating the heron with irony. As "antic" suggests, the great fellow and his swamp have an element of the absurd. The desire to domesticate him, to encompass him in some human calculus, is thus acknowledged but at the same time kept at arm's length. Graceful as he may be, he escapes. Does his efficiency—one motion of the beak, one gulp, one flap of the wings, a single ripple left behind—raise horror or delight? or amused irony and admiration? Is he droll, grotesque, quaint? If he is in any way typical of nature (one supposes that he is even though Roethke is careful not so say so), are we justified in inferring anything about man's own habitat?

The style of the saying is much like the style of the heron's enigmatic doing: economical and precise in its antic grace but difficult to plumb to the bottom. The poet's eye, like the heron's, is on the minnow's hiding place, where the meeting of deep and shallow water makes seeing into the swamp both possible and impossible. To one who reads this book of nature carefully, then, the understatement has an efficient eloquence as distinct as the heron's footprint on the sand—and as different from explicit, decipherable word-print.

In analyzing deliberative lyrics at either Donne's or Roethke's end of the spectrum—one intellectual and dramatic, the other descriptive and suggestive— the student obviously needs to draw upon resources different from those required by songs. At one extreme, reflective lyrics approach song and require careful attention to musical qualities, but they "roughen" them with counter forces, tension, irony, ambivalence, and the like; and at the other extreme they approach spoken drama in a dialectical crossing of points of view, the speaker's perspective being different from that of the poem's generally. In that direction lies the dramatic monologue, which we reserve for a separate section.

THE STORM RIDDLES

The "Storm Riddles" appear in an Anglo-Saxon manuscript known as the Exeter Book, which contains about ninety riddles altogether. As that would suggest, far from being the rather humorous and peripheral form it is today, the riddle was once a respectable and much-practiced genre. The speaker of a riddle is some sensory object—the moon or sun, an iceberg, a battle-ax, sword, falcon—and the poem itself moves from the object's descriptions of its physical details and functions to a concluding question, "What am I called?" The riddle thus enlists concrete images and sense impressions in the service of intellectual obliqueness, anticipating in some respects the metaphysical lyric of the seventeenth century. In the simplest riddles, the answer is more or less obvious and the element of transient intellectual "play" dominant. As the "Storm Riddles" indicate, however, the form can transcend playfulness and address itself to issues of enduring complexity. Whereas most Anglo-Saxon poetry deals in conventionally Christian sentiments, usually finding consolation for a life of hardship in the idea of divine providence, the "Storm Riddles" directly confront the terrifying in nature and God without the protection of theological orthodoxies.

Although some scholars regard the "Storm Riddles" as three separate poems brought together only because of shared subject matter, their structure—to which the translator has been entirely faithful—suggests that they are actually one extended poem probing the nature of God and the mystery of evil.

Translated by William H. Matchett*

1

What man is so wise as to explain
What it is that drives me on
When I rise in my strength, rage for a time,
Wondrously thunder, and throw my flames,
Blasting the earth, burning houses   5
And ravaging halls, till the ash-laden smoke
Pours from their roofs? Panic follows
And violent death, when I strike at the woods,
Shake the flourishing groves, fell the trees,
My unspeakable power, under rain-heavy clouds,   10
Propelled on its pathless way.
I hoist on my back what once clothed men—
Their broken, spiritless bodies.
Tell me who could escape—or just tell me my name:
Who am I that can bear such a burden?   15

2

I sometimes dive deeper than men can imagine
Beneath the waves' violence to seek the bottom,
The very floor of the ocean. The sea is churned,
Roiled in foam; the roaring breakers
Pummel the shores, pounding hour by hour   5
Against the steep headlands, with stones and sand,
Sea wrack and water, while I, raging,
Concealed in the force of the waves, shake the earth
From the briny depths. Nor from this dungeon
May I fly before he frees me, he, my master   10
On every occasion. Thoughtful man, tell me
Who is it wrests me from the sea's fathoms
When the waters again grow calm
And the waves that once hid me are gentle?

3

Sometimes my lord imprisons me firmly,
Buries me under the broad expanse
Of the flowering downs and, calling a halt,
Detains me in darkness by his might,
In confinement by his fury, with the heavy earth   5
Resting harshly on my back. Nor can I escape
That hardship; however, I still can shake
Men's citadels—their gabled mansions tremble,
The walls of their houses totter
Above the householders' heads. The air   10

Seems breathless over the land and the ocean is silent
Till I burst from restraint at a sign
From the one who, at the creation, first chained me
With bonds and shackles as guarantee
That I not defy his dominion, the one   15
Who marks out the tracks I must travel.

4

At times I must quicken the waves from above,
Weave counter-currents and hurl at the shores
The flint-grey flood. The foamy waves batter
Against the embankments; dark mountains multiply
Over the deep; one after another   5
The sombre combers follow relentlessly,
Hasting to meet, at the edge of the mainland,
The lofty bluffs. Then loud from shipboard
Come sailors' cries, while the silent rock-face
Lies in wait for the tumult,   10
For the impact of the waves when, mounting higher,
They drive against the cliffs. The seamen anticipate
Crueller torments if the current should bear
That shipload of souls to the bitter hour
When, out of control, it shall also be stripped   15
Of its human cargo, to roll on the crests
Of the boiling waves. There is a certain dread
Shown by men for him I must obey,
Invincible in his violence. Who alleviates that?

5

Sometimes I rush headlong through the lurid rain-clouds
That rode on my back, strewing them widely
Across the sea basin; then again I allow them
To slip together. There comes the vastest turmoil
Of noise over the cities, the loudest resonance,   5
When one cloud crashes against another,
Edge against edge. The black bodies,
Plunging overhead, ejaculate fire,
Bolts of vivid lightning, and generate,
Looming above humanity, a horrid clamor;   10
The attacking forces let fall to the earth
A certain dark gift: the sweat from their bosoms,
The rain from their wombs. As these dreadful troops
Continue the onslaught, terror mounts,
A desperate anguish within mankind;   15
There is panic in their dwellings when the ghastly assaulters
Flash by in brilliance with their sharp weapons.
Only a fool would not fear their fatal lances;
He dies notwithstanding, if the just God,
Unerringly, through the pelting rain,   20
Lets fly from the whirlwind

An urgent missile. Few of those survive
Who have met the spear of his lightning.

6

I bring about this orgy of destruction
When, through a turbulence of cloud-collisions,
I set out to rush with incredible force
Over the face of the waters; loudly resound
The thundering hordes. Then once again,   5
Under the dome of the sky, I dip near land
And load on my back whatever I must carry,
Strengthened by the authority of my lord.
Thus, a peerless servant, I sometimes labor
Under the earth; at times I must dive   10
Below the tallest waves; at times, above them,
I churn the surface; at times I mount up
To hasten the cloud-flow: I travel widely,
Swift and savage. Now tell me my name
And say who incites me when I may not rest,   15
And who keeps me in reserve when at last I am silent?

ADAM LAY I-BOWNDYN

The development in medieval lyrics of a theme, often paradoxical, through the
expansion of the range of a symbol is probably due in part to the iconological
or pictorial habit of religious meditation. In any case, the apple here (like "the
falcon" in the medieval elegy of that title) suggests a religious icon. In the
course of its development, the poem discovers consolation in the idea of the
"fortunate fall": the sin of Adam issues ultimately in the grace of "our lady"
and as proof of God's love in her "Son."

ANONYMOUS

Adam lay i-bowndyn,
        bowndyn in a bond,
Fowre thowsand wynter
        thowt he not to long;
And al was for an appil,   5
        an appil that he tok,
As clerkes fyndyn wretyn
        in here book.
Ne hadde the appil take ben,
        the appil taken ben,   10
Ne hadde never our lady
        a ben hevene quen.
Blyssid be the tyme
        that appil take was!
Therfore we momn syngyn   15
        Deo gracias.

---

1 *i-bowndyn*: bound.   8 *here*: their.   15 *mown*: must.

WESTERN WIND, WHEN WILL THOU BLOW

The difficulty of "Western Wind" lies essentially in its concern with the speaker's frame of mind rather than the narrative incidents that have brought it about. Without knowing where the lover has gone or why, we are forced to concentrate on the associations that that absence arouses in the speaker, namely, associations with the western wind, rain, and bed. Although the first two belong to the foreign world outside, which has the lover in its control, they are expected to offer relief. The bed is a protected, private place to which the speaker would retreat. Impatience is conditioned by anxiety, frank sensuousness by an unspoken fear.

ANONYMOUS

Western wind, when will thou blow,
    The small rain down can rain?
Christ, if my love were in my arms
    And I in my bed again!

SIR THOMAS WYATT *(1503?–1542)*

In the most personal and complex lyrics of his day, Wyatt characteristically finds himself in puzzling situations that provoke questions but suggest no definite course of action—except perhaps requital of those who have deserted him. The uncertainties of the love game and a sense that he alone is responsible to himself produce doubt in "It May Be Good"; the memory of better times causes him to ponder the ethics of "ranging" in continual change in "They Flee from Me"; and the failure of actual love to match a preconceived "eternal" idea of it results in his dismissal of the pseudo-Platonism of certain love conventions in "In Eternum."

IT MAY BE GOOD, LIKE IT WHO LIST

It may be good, like it who list,
    But I do doubt: who can me blame?
For oft assured yet have I missed,
    And now again I fear the same.
    The windy words, the eyes quaint game,   5
Of sudden change maketh me aghast:
For dread to fall I stand not fast.

Alas! I tread an endless maze
    That seeketh to accord two contraries;
And hope still and nothing have,   10
    Imprisoned in liberties;
    As one unheard, and still that cries;
Always thirsty, and yet nothing I taste;
For dread to fall I stand not fast.

Assured, I doubt I be not sure;   15
    And should I trust to such surety
That oft hath put the proof in ure

---

17 *ure*: use.

And never hath found it trusty?
Nay, sir, in faith it were great folly.
And yet my life thus I do waste;   20
For dread to fall I stand not fast.

THEY FLEE FROM ME

They flee from me that sometime did me seek,
With naked foot stalking in my chamber,
I have seen them gentle, tame, and meek,
That now are wild, and do not remember
That some time they put themselves in danger   5
To take bread at my hand; and now they range,
Busily seeking with a continual change.

Thanked be fortune, it hath been otherwise
Twenty times better; but once, in special,
In thin array, after a pleasant guise,   10
When her loose gown from her shoulders did fall,
And she me caught in her arms long and small,
Therewith all sweetly did me kiss,
And softly said, *Dear heart, how like you this?*

It was no dream; I lay broad awaking.   15
But all is turned now through my gentleness
Into a strange fashion of forsaking;
And I have leave to go of her goodness,
And she also to use newfangleness.
But since that I so kindly am served,   20
I fain would know what she hath deserved.

IN ETERNUM

In eternum I was once determined
For to have lovéd and my mind affirméd
That with my heart it should be confirméd
        In eternum.

Forthwith I found the thing that I might like,   5
And sought with love to warm her heart alike,
For, as me thought, I should not see the like
        In eternum.

To trace this dance I put my self in press;
Vain hope did lead and bade I should not cease   10
To serve, to suffer, and still to hold my peace
        In eternum.

14 *heart*: possibly "deer."
9 *press*: i.e., crowd, throng. To "put in press" means to push oneself, to compete, or to take a risk. "Press" also means an instrument for pressing, as a wine-press. All these meanings are possible here: the speaker joins the throng of suitors, thereby entering the competition for the lady, taking risks with his feelings, and subjecting himself to the pressures of love.

With this first rule I furthered me apace,
That, as me thought, my truth had taken place
With full assurance to stand in her grace   15
    In eternum.

It was not long or I by proof had found
That feeble building is on feeble ground;
For in her heart this word did never sound,
    In eternum.   20

In eternum then from my heart I cast
That I had first determined for the best;
Now in the place another thought doth rest,
    In eternum.

SIR WALTER RALEGH *(1552?–1618)*

The discrepancy between the appearance of the angelic lady, whom even a
traveler from the holy land remembers distinctly, and the looseness of her
conduct leads to two radically opposed conclusions in Ralegh's "Walsinghame."
The rejected lover assumes that because lovers are fickle, the word "love"
itself is without content, a mere illusion; the pilgrim holds that women and
particular incidents, not the concept of love itself, are false. Between embodied
and disembodied "love" (or the ideal of love in "the mind ever during"),
Ralegh leaves an indefinable gap. Thus "love" may be taken as representative
of the problem of uniting unchanging verities to the chaotic flux of the world, a
problem that has plagued philosophers since at least the pre-Socratics. It is
nearly always prominent in the love poetry of Wyatt, Sidney, Shakespeare,
Donne, and Marvell as well as that of Ralegh.

WALSINGHAME

"As you came from the holy land
    Of Walsinghame,
Met you not with my true love
    By the way as you came?"

"How shall I know your true love,   5
    That have met many a one
As I went to the holy land,
    That have come, that have gone?"

"She is neither white nor brown,
    But as the heavens fair,   10
There is none hath a form so divine
    In the earth or the air."

"Such an one did I meet, good Sir,
    Such an angelic face,
Who like a queen, like a nymph did appear   15
    By her gait, by her grace."

---

14 *truth* (trowghthe): sincerity, steadfastness. 17 *proof*: test, experiment.

"She hath left me here alone,
 All alone as unknown,
Who sometime did me lead with herself,
 And me loved as her own."   20

"What's the cause that she leaves you alone
 And a new way doth take,
Who loved you once as her own
 And her joy did you make?"

"I have loved her all my youth,   25
 But now old as you see,
Love likes not the falling fruit
 From the withered tree.

"Know that Love is a careless child,
 And forgets promise past;   30
He is blind, he is deaf when he list
 And in faith never fast.

"His desire is a dureless content
 And a trustless joy;
He is won with a world of despair   35
 And is lost with a toy."

"Of womenkind such indeed is the love
 Or the word love abused,
Under which many childish desires
 And conceits are excused.   40

"But love is a durable fire
 In the mind ever burning;
Never sick, never old, never dead,
 From itself never turning."

SIR PHILIP SIDNEY *(1554–1586)*

Sidney makes the Petrarchan game of pursuit and coy retreat appear almost its own reward. It goes on long enough that we nearly forget the lover's seriousness. But the ceremony is shattered in the final stanza, thanks to the lady's indifference to the suitor and her fear of discovery. The lover's disappointed outburst against the "lowts" (he has to take it out on someone) lifts the corner of the standard masks worn by cold ladies and their tortured worshipers.

WHO IS IT THAT THIS DARK NIGHT

'Who is it that this dark night
Underneath my window plaineth?'
 It is one who from thy sight
Being, ah, exiled, disdaineth
 Every other vulgar light.   5

 'Why, alas, and are you he?
Be not yet those fancies changëd?'
 Dear, when you find change in me,

Though from me you be estrangëd,
  Let my change to ruin be.   10

'Well, in absence this will die;
Leave to see, and leave to wonder.'
  Absence, sure, will help, if I
Can learn how much myself to sunder
  From what in my heart doth lie.   15

'But time will these thoughts remove;
Time doth work what no man knoweth.'
  Time doth as the subject prove;
With time still the affection groweth
  In the faithful turtle-dove.   20

'What if you new beauties see,
Will not they stir new affection?'
  I will think they pictures be,
(Image-like, of saints' perfection)
  Poorly counterfeiting thee.   25

'But your reason's purest light
Bids you leave such minds to nourish.'
  Dear, do reason no such spite:
Never doth thy beauty flourish
  More than in my reason's sight.   30

'But the wrongs Love bears will make
Love at length leave undertaking.'
  No, the more fools it do shake,
In a ground of so firm making
  Deeper still they drive the stake.   35

'Peace! I think that some give ear,
Come, no more, lest I get anger.'
  Bliss! I will my bliss forbear,
Fearing, sweet, you to endanger;
  But my soul shall harbour there.   40

'Well, be gone; be gone, I say!
Lest that Argus' eyes perceive you.'
  Oh, unjust is Fortune's sway,
Which can make me thus to leave you;
  And from lowts to run away.   45

JOHN HOSKINS *(1566–1638)*

Hoskins is Platonist enough to realize (with the Donne of "A Valediction
Forbidding Mourning") that parting is merely physical. But he also realizes the
limits of the consolations of philosophy.

ABSENCE

Absence hear my protestation
  Against thy strength
  Distance and length,

Do what thou canst for alteration:
   For hearts of truest metal   5
   Absence doth join, and time doth settle.

Who loves a mistress of right quality,
   His mind hath found
   Affections ground
Beyond time, place, and all mortality: 10
   To hearts that cannot vary
   Absence is present, time doth tarry:

My senses want their outward motion
   Which now within
   Reason doth win,   15
Redoubled by her secret notion:
   Like rich men that take pleasure
   In hiding more than handling treasure.

By absence this good means I gain
   That I can catch her   20
   Where none can watch her,
In some close corner of my brain:
   There I embrace and kiss her,
   And so enjoy her, and so miss her.

BEN JONSON *(1572?–1637)*

Jonson's realistic view of love is not a cynical inversion of unreflective love conventions, but it is a reconsideration of those conventions from the standpoint of one whom age and experience have educated.

WHY I WRITE NOT OF LOVE

Some act of Love's bound to rehearse,
I thought to bind him, in my verse:
Which when he felt, Away (quoth he)
Can poets hope to fetter me?
It is enough, they once did get   5
Mars, and my mother, in their net:
I wear not these my wings in vain.
With which he fled me: and again,
Into my rimes could ne're be got
By any art. Then wonder not,   10
That since, my numbers are so cold,
When Love is fled, and I grow old.

JOHN DONNE *(1573–1631)*

Although the form and many of the themes of Donne's lyrics derive from the tradition of love songs reflected in the title of his main collections, *Songs and Sonets,* formal regularity is made to encompass new subtleties of mood, imagery, and voice. (In the period of the "Donne revival" after the First World War, these qualities were considered the essential elements of a fully serious poetry that imitates the processes of thought and feeling rather than presenting the reasoned conclusions that emerge after the turmoil subsides.) "The Good Morrow," for instance, rather than treating love as an inescapable, given force, tests it from all sides by counter attitudes, staged as dialogues in progress. Ironic awareness, intricacy of movement, and explosiveness and frankness of language characterize Donne's religious lyrics as well as the *Songs and Sonets*.

THE GOOD MORROW

I wonder, by my troth, what thou and I
Did till we loved? were we not weaned till then,
But sucked on country pleasures, childishly?
Or snorted we in the Seven Sleepers' den?
'Twas so; but this, all pleasures fancies be.   5
If ever any beauty I did see
Which I desired, and got, 'twas but a dream of thee.

And now good morrow to our waking souls,
Which watch not one another out of fear;
For love all love of other sights controls,   10
And makes one little room an everywhere.
Let sea-discoverers to new worlds have gone;
Let maps to other, worlds on worlds have shown;
Let us possess one world; each hath one, and is one.

My face in thine eye, thine in mine appears,   15
And true, plain hearts do in the faces rest;
Where can we find two better hemispheres
Without sharp north, without declining west?
Whatever dies, was not mixed equally;
If our loves be one, or thou and I   20
Love so alike that none do slacken, none can die.

LOVE'S GROWTH

I scarce believe my love to be so pure
    As I had thought it was,
    Because it doth endure
Vicissitude, and season, as the grass;
Methinks I lied all winter, when I swore   5
My love was infinite, if spring make it more.

But if this medicine, love, which cures all sorrow
    With more, not only be no quintessence,
    But mix'd of all stuffs, vexing soul, or sense,
And of the sun his active vigour borrow,   10
Love's not so pure, and abstract, as they use
To say, which have no mistress but their Muse;
But as all else, being elemented too,
Love sometimes would contemplate, sometimes do.

And yet no greater, but more eminent,   15
    Love by the spring is grown;
    As in the firmament
Stars by the sun are not enlarged, but shown
Gentle love deeds, as blossoms on a bough,
From love's awaken'd root do bud out now.   20

If, as in water stirr'd more circles be
    Produced by one, love such additions take,
    Those like so many spheres but one heaven make,
For they are all concentric unto thee:
And though each spring do add to love new heat,   25
As princes do in times of action get
New taxes, and remit them not in peace,
No winter shall abate this spring's increase.

GEORGE HERBERT *(1593–1633)*

Although he frequently uses many images and themes of the Christian tradition, Herbert at his best re-examines and assimilates them. His dialogues with Hope, Love, and the God of "Temper" and "The Collar" are witty yet serious. More obviously graceful in technique than Donne, he shares Donne's sense of the incongruities of stretching a "crum of dust" to the most high—hence his reluctance as a sinner to accept Love's bidding and the impatience of the speaker of "Temper" and "The Collar" to end his trying colloquy with God. It is typical of Herbert, however, to submit after revolt to the divine injunction that sets grace above reason or justice.

HOPE

I gave to Hope a watch of mine: but he
    An anchor gave to me.
Then an old prayer-book I did present:
    And he an optic sent.
With that I gave a vial full of tears: 5
    But he a few green ears.
Ah loiterer! I'll no more, no more I'll bring:
    I did expect a ring.

LOVE

Love bade me welcome; yet my soul drew back,
    Guilty of dust and sin.
But quick-eyed Love, observing me grow slack
    From my first entrance in,
Drew nearer to me, sweetly questioning   5
    If I lacked anything.

"A guest," I answered, "worthy to be here":
    Love said, "You shall be he."
"I, the unkind, ungrateful? Ah, my dear,
    I cannot look on Thee."   10
Love took my hand, and smiling did reply,
    "Who made the eyes but I?"

"Truth, Lord; but I have marred them; let my shame
    Go where it doth deserve."
"And know you not," says Lord, "who bore the blame?"   15
    "My dear, then I will serve."
"You must sit down," says Love, "and taste my meat."
    So I did sit and eat.

TEMPER

How should I praise thee, Lord! how should my rimes
    Gladly engrave thy love in steel,
If what my soul doth feel sometimes,
    My soul might ever feel!

Although there were some forty heav'ns, or more,   5
    Sometimes I peer above them all;
Sometimes I hardly reach a score,
    Sometimes to hell I fall.

O rack me not to such a vast extent;
    Those distances belong to thee: 10
The world's too little for thy tent,
    A grave too big for me.

Wilt thou meet arms with man, that thou dost stretch
    A crum of dust from heav'n to hell?
Will great God measure with a wretch?   15
    Shall he thy stature spell?

O let me, when thy roof my soul hath hid,
    O let me roost and nestle there:
Then of a sinner thou art rid,
    And I of hope and fear.   20

Yet take thy way; for sure thy way is best:
    Stretch or contract me, thy poor debter:
This is but tuning of my breast,
    To make the music better.

Whether I fly with angels, fall with dust,   25
    Thy hands made both, and I am there:
Thy power and love, my love and trust
    Make one place ev'ry where.

VIRTUE

Sweet day, so cool, so calm, so bright,
    The bridal of the earth and sky!
The dew shall weep thy fall to-night;
    For thou must die.

Sweet rose, whose hue, angry and brave,   5
    Bids the rash gazer wipe his eye,
Thy root is ever in its grave,
    And thou must die.

Sweet spring, full of sweet days and roses,
    A box where sweets compacted lie,   10
My music shows ye have your closes,
    And all must die.

Only a sweet and virtuous soul,
    Like seasoned timber, never gives;

But though the whole world turn to coal,
    Then chiefly lives.   15

THE COLLAR*

I struck the board, and cry'd, No more.
    I will abroad.
What? shall I ever sigh and pine?
My lines and life are free; free as the road,
    Loose as the wind, as large as store.   5
      Shall I be still in suit?
Have I no harvest but a thorn
To let me blood, and not restore
What I have lost with cordial fruit?
      Sure there was wine   10
Before my sighs did dry it: there was corn
    Before my tears did drown it.
    Is the year only lost to me?
    Have I no bays to crown it?
No flowers, no garlands gay? all blasted?   15
    All wasted?
    Not so, my heart: but there is fruit,
      And thou has hands.
    Recover all thy sigh-blown age
On double pleasures: leave thy cold dispute   20
Of what is fit, and not. Forsake thy cage,
      Thy rope of sands,
Which petty thoughts have made, and made to thee
    Good cable, to enforce and draw,
      And be thy law,   25
While thou didst wink and wouldst not see.
      Away; take heed:
      I will abroad.
Call in thy deaths head there: tie up thy fears.
      He that forbears   30
    To suit and serve his need,
      Deserves his load.
But as I raved and grew more fierce and wild
      At every word,
Me thought I heard one calling, *Child!*   35
    And I replied, *My Lord.*

HERRICK, SHIRLEY, SUCKLING, LOVELACE

The statement of the lighter lyrics of Herrick, Shirley, Suckling, and Lovelace is normally too inconsiderable to be thought reflective; but the following seventeenth-century lyrics stress theme or unusual metaphor or planned irregularity

---

* "The Collar": the collar in Herbert's case is a special as well as a general restraint. It is a symbol for church discipline and the restraints of conscience.

---

6 *still*: ever.

of some kind, as well as musical grace. Deliberation is enhanced by the poets' skill in varying line lengths and exploiting the sound associations of individual words and phrases. Like Herbert, these lyricists combine the sounds of song with the sense of meditation.

TO DAFFODILS

ROBERT HERRICK *(1591–1674)*

Fair Daffodils, we weep to see
    You haste away so soon:
As yet the early-rising Sun
    Has not attain'd his noon.
      Stay, stay,   5
    Until the hasting day
      Has run
    But to the even-song;
And, having pray'd together, we
    Will go with you along.   10

We have short time to stay, as you,
    We have as short a pring;
As quick a growth to meet decay
    As you, or any thing.
      We die,   15
    As your hours do, and dry
      Away
    Like to the Summer's rain;
Or as the pearls of morning's dew,
    Ne'er to be found again.   20

DEATH THE LEVELLER

JAMES SHIRLEY *(1596–1666)*

The glories of our blood and state
    Are shadows, not substantial things;
There is no armour against Fate;
    Death lays his icy hand on kings:
      Sceptre and crown   5
      Must tumble down,
And in the dust be equal made
With the poor crooked scythe and spade.

Some men with swords may reap the field,
    And plant fresh laurels where they kill;   10
But their strong nerves at last must yield;
    They tame but one another still:
      Early or late
      They stoop to fate,
And must give up their murmuring breath   15
When they, pale captives, creep to death.

The garlands wither on your brow;
  Then boast no more your mighty deeds!
Upon Death's purple altar now
    See where the victor-victim bleeds.   20
        Your heads must come
          To the cold tomb:
Only the actions of the just
Smell sweet and blossom in their dust.

O FOR SOME HONEST LOVER'S GHOST

SIR JOHN SUCKLING *(1609–1642)*

O for some honest lover's ghost,
  Some kind unbodied post
    Sent from the shades below!
    I strangely long to know
Whether the noble chaplets wear,   5
Those that their mistress' scorn did bear
    Or those that were used kindly.

For whatsoe'er they tell us here
  To make those sufferings dear,
    'Twill there, I fear, be found   10
    That to the being crowned
T' have loved alone will not suffice,
Unless we also have been wise
    And have our loves enjoyed.

What posture can we think him in   15
  That, here unloved, again
    Departs, and 's thither gone
    Where each sits by his own?
Or how can that Elysium be
Where I my mistress still must see   20
    Circled in other's arms?

For there the judges all are just,
  And Sophonisba must
    Be his whom she held dear,
    Not his who loved her here.   25
The sweet Philoclea, since she died,
Lies by her Pirocles his side,
    Not by Amphialus.

Some bays, perchance, or myrtle bough
  For difference crowns the brow   30
    Of those kind souls that were
    The noble martyrs here;
And if that be the only odds
(As who can tell?), ye kinder gods,
    Give me the woman here!

---

23 *Sophonisba*: wife of Syphax, loved by Masinissa after the Romans took her captive.
26–28 *Philoclea, Pirocles, Amphialus*: from Sidney's *Arcadia*.

LA BELLA BONA ROBA

RICHARD LOVELACE *(1618–1658)*

I cannot tell who loves the skeleton
Of a poor marmoset, naught but bone, bone.
Give me a nakedness with her clothes on.

Such whose white satin upper coat of skin,
Cut upon velvet rich incarnadin,   5
Has yet a body (and of flesh) within.

Sure it is meant good husbandry in men,
Who do incorporate with aery lean,
T' repair their sides, and get their rib again.

Hard hap unto that huntsman that decrees   10
Fat joys for all his sweat, when as he sees,
After his 'say, naught but his keeper's fees.

Then Love I beg, when next thou tak'st thy bow,
Thy angry shafts, and dost heart-chasing go,
Pass rascal deer, strike me the largest doe.   15

HENRY VAUGHAN *(1621–1695)*

Unlike Herbert, Vaughan was not seriously concerned with stanzaic form and the grace notes of pronounced meter and rhyme. He does, however, "domesticate the infinite" with something of Herbert's colloquial turn of phrase. "I saw Eternity the other night" does just that before Vaughan turns to a satirical account of how the world looks from the perspective of eternity. Vaughan's vision is sometimes that of the mystic, sometimes that of the sharp-eyed lover of nature that has reminded some critics of Wordsworth. He sees traces of divinity in flowers, his method of pointing them out being often as narrative and allegorical as strictly rational or symbolic.

THE WORLD

I saw Eternity the other night,
Like a great ring of pure and endless light,
    All calm, as it was bright;
And round beneath it, Time in hours, days, years,
    Driven by the spheres   5
Like a vast shadow moved; in which the world
    And all her train were hurled.
The doting lover in his quaintest strain
    Did there complain;
Near him, his lute, his fancy, and his flights,   10
    Wit's sour delights;

---

3 *clothes*: skin. 12 *'say, naught but his keeper's fees*: It was customary in presenting a deer to the king or a noble to "assay" (or "essay") the quality of the meat by slitting the underside. The keeper's fee was generally the shoulder. 15 *rascal deer*: lean deer, but probably also a pun on "rascal dear" because the title, "La Bella Bona Roba," and "marmoset" are common expressions for a "harlot."

With gloves, and knots, the silly snares of pleasure,
    Yet his dear treasure,
All scattered lay, while he his eyes did pour
    Upon a flower.   15

The darksome statesman, hung with weights and woe
Like a thick midnight-fog, moved there so slow,
    He did not stay, nor go;
Condemning thoughts—like sad eclipses—scowl
    Upon his soul,   20
And clouds of crying witnesses without
    Pursued him with one shout.
Yet digged the mole, and lest his ways be found,
    Worked underground,
Where he did clutch his prey; but one did see   25
    That policy.
Churches and altars fed him; perjuries
    Were gnats and flies;
It rained about him blood and tears, but he
    Drank them as free.   30

The fearful miser on a heap of rust
Sat pining all his life there, did scarce trust
    His own hands with the dust,
Yet would not place one piece above, but lives
    In fear of thieves.   35
Thousands there were as frantic as himself,
    And hugged each one his pelf;
The downright epicure placed heav'n in sense,
    And scorned pretence;
While others, slipped into a wide excess,   40
    Said little less;
The weaker sort slight, trivial wares enslave,
    Who think them brave;
And poor, despisèd Truth sat counting by
    Their victory.   45

Yet some, who all this while did weep and sing,
And sing and weep, soared up into the ring;
    But most would use no wing.
Oh, fools—said I—thus to prefer dark night
    Before true light!   50
To live in grots and caves, and hate the day
    Because it shows the way;
The way, which from this dead and dark abode
    Leads up to God;
A way where you might tread the sun, and be   55
    More bright than he!
But as I did their madness so discuss,
    One whispered thus,
'This ring the Bridegroom did for none provide,
    But for His bride.'   60

ANDREW MARVELL *(1621–1678)*

In the tradition of both seventeenth-century metaphysical poets and the classicists, Marvell combines deceptive grace with sophistication. "On a Drop of Dew" and "A Dialogue" illustrate his alliance with the otherworldly leanings of Vaughan and Herbert and yet, too, his detached and sensuous manner of handling them. The "Definition of Love" is both a personal and a philosophical statement on a common theme uniquely handled. "To his Coy Mistress" counters the speaker's proposal with a deepening philosophical sense of the world lost to time and hasty love. In these poems, as in "The Garden," Marvell's learned and contemplative side gives full resonance to a well-regulated lyric medium.

DEFINITION OF LOVE

My love is of a birth as rare
As 'tis for object strange and high:
It was begotten by despair
Upon impossibility.

Magnanimous despair alone   5
Could show me so divine a thing,
Where feeble hope could ne'er have flown
But vainly flapt its tinsel wing.

And yet I quickly might arrive
Where my extended soul is fixt,   10
But fate does iron wedges drive,
And always crowds itself betwixt.

For fate with jealous eye does see
Two perfect loves, nor lets them close:
Their union would her ruin be,   15
And her tyrannic pow'r depose.

And therefore her decrees of steel
Us as the distant poles have plac'd,
(Though love's whole world on us does wheel)
Not by themselves to be embrac'd   20

Unless the giddy heaven fall
And earth some new convulsion tear,
And, us to join, the world should all
Be cramp'd into a planisphere.

As lines so loves oblique may well   25
Themselves in every angle greet;
But ours so truly parallel,
Though infinite can never meet.

Therefore the love which doth us bind,
But fate so enviously debars,   30
Is the conjunction of the mind,
And opposition of the stars.

TO HIS COY MISTRESS

Had we but world enough, and time,
This coyness, Lady, were no crime.
We would sit down and think which way
To walk and pass our long love's day.
Thou by the Indian Ganges' side   5
Shouldst rubies find: I by the tide
Of Humber would complain. I would
Love you ten years before the Flood,
And you should, if you please, refuse
Till the conversion of the Jews.   10

My vegetable love should grow
Vaster than empires, and more slow;
An hundred years should go to praise
Thine eyes and on thy forehead gaze;
Two hundred to adore each breast,   15
But thirty thousand to the rest;
An age at least to every part,
And the last age should show your heart.
For, Lady, you deserve this state,
Nor would I love at lower rate.   20

But at my back I always hear
Time's wingèd chariot hurrying near;
And yonder all before us lie
Deserts of vast eternity.
Thy beauty shall no more be found,   25
Nor, in thy marble vault, shall sound
My echoing song; then worms shall try
That long preserved virginity;
And your quaint honor turn to dust,
And into ashes all my lust: 30
The grave's a fine and private place,
But none, I think, do there embrace.

  Now therefore, while the youthful hue
Sits on thy skin like morning dew,
And while thy willing soul transpires   35
At every pore with instant fires,
Now let us sport us while we may,
And now, like amorous birds of prey,
Rather at once our time devour
Than languish in his slow-chapped power.   40
Let us roll all our strength and all
Our sweetness up into one ball,
And tear our pleasures with rough strife
Thorough the iron gates of life:
Thus, though we cannot make our sun   45
Stand still, yet we will make him run.

ON A DROP OF DEW

See how the orient dew,
  Shed from the bosom of the morn
  Into the blowing roses,
Yet careless of its mansion new;
For the clear region where 'twas born   5
  Round in itself encloses:
  And in its little globe's extent,
Frames as it can its native element.
  How it the purple flower does slight,
    Scarce touching where it lies,   10
  But gazing back upon the skies,
    Shines with a mournful light;
      Like its own tear,
Because so long divided from the sphere.
  Restless it rolls and unsecure,   15
    Trembling lest it grow impure:
  Till the warm sun pity its pain,
And to the skies exhale it back again.
    So the soul, that drop, that ray
Of the clear fountain of eternal day,   20
Could it within the human flower be seen,
  Rememb'ring still its former height,
  Shuns the sweet leaves and blossoms green;
  And, recollecting its own light,
Does, in its pure and circling thoughts, express   25
The greater heaven in a heaven less.
  In how coy a figure wound,
  Every way it turns away:
  So the world excluding round,
  Yet receiving in the day.   30
  Dark beneath, but bright above:
  Here disdaining, there in love.
  How loose and easy hence to go:
  How girt and ready to ascend.
  Moving but on a point below,   35
  It all about does upwards bend.
Such did the manna's sacred dew distill;
White, and entire, though congealed and chill.
Congealed on earth: but does, dissolving, run
Into the glories of the almighty sun.   40

A DIALOGUE BETWEEN THE RESOLVED SOUL
AND CREATED PLEASURE

Courage my Soul, now learn to wield
The weight of thine immortal shield.
Close on thy head thy helmet bright.
Balance thy sword against the fight.

See where an army, strong as fair,   5
With silken banners spreads the air.
Now, if thou bee'st that thing divine,
In this day's combat let it shine:
And show that Nature wants an art
To conquer one resolved heart.   10

PLEASURE

Welcome the creation's guest,
Lord of earth, and heaven's heir.
Lay aside that warlike crest,
And of Nature's banquet share:
Where the souls of fruits and flow'rs   15
Stand prepar'd to heighten yours.

SOUL

I sup above, and cannot stay
To bait so long upon the way.

PLEASURE

On these downy pillows lie,
Whose soft plumes will thither fly: 20
On these roses strow'd so plain
Lest one leaf thy side should strain.

SOUL

My gentler rest is on a thought,
Conscious of doing what I ought.

PLEASURE

If thou bee'st with perfumes pleas'd,   25
Such as oft the Gods appeas'd,
Thou in fragrant clouds shalt show
Like another God below.

SOUL

A soul that knows not to presume
Is heaven's and its own perfume.   30

PLEASURE

Every thing does seem to vie
Which should first attract thine eye:
But since none deserves that grace,
In this crystal view *thy* face.

SOUL

When the Creator's skill is priz'd,   35
The rest is all but earth disguis'd.

PLEASURE

Hark how music then prepares
For thy stay these charming airs;
Which the posting winds recall,
And suspend the river's fall.   40

SOUL

Had I but any time to lose,
On this I would it all dispose.
Cease tempter. None can chain a mind
Whom this sweet chordage cannot bind.

CHORUS

Earth cannot show so brave a sight   45
As when a single soul does fence
The batteries of alluring sense
And heaven views it with delight.
Then persevere: for still new charges sound:
And if thou overcom'st thou shalt be crown'd.   50

PLEASURE

All this fair, and soft, and sweet,
  Which scatteringly doth shine,
Shall within one beauty meet,
  And she be only thine.

SOUL

If things of sight such heavens be,   55
What heavens are those we cannot see?

PLEASURE

Where so e're thy foot shall go
  The minted gold shall lie;
Till thou purchase all below,
  And want new worlds to buy.   60

SOUL

Wer't not a price who'ld value gold?
And that's worth nought that can be sold.

PLEASURE

Wilt thou all the glory have
  That war or peace commend?
Half the world shall be thy slave   65
  The other half thy friend.

SOUL

What friends, if to myself untrue?
What slaves, unless I captive you?

PLEASURE

Thou shalt know each hidden cause;
    And see the future time: 70
Try what depth the center draws;
    And then to heaven climb.

SOUL

None thither mounts by the degree
Of knowledge, but humility.

CHORUS

Triumph, triumph, victorious Soul;   75
The world has not one pleasure more:
The rest does lie beyond the pole,
And is thine everlasting store.

EDWARD TAYLOR *(c. 1645–1729)*

In the manner of the English metaphysical poets, especially Herbert, Taylor
writes of exalted things in homespun language. The contrast between metaphor
and subject is a device of wit and an evidence that whereas the spirit of religious poems may be pure, the mind continues to be aware of the ironies of communication between disparate beings.

HUSWIFERY*

Make me, O Lord, Thy spinning-wheel complete
    Thy holy word my distaff make for me.
Make mine affections thy swift flyers neat,
    And make my soul Thy holy spool to be.
    My conversation make to be Thy reel,   5
    And reel the yarn thereon spun of Thy wheel.

Make me Thy loom then; knit therein this twine;
    And make Thy Holy Spirit, Lord, wind quills.
Then weave the web Thyself. The yarn is fine.
    Thine ordinances make my fulling mills.   10
    Then dye the same in heavenly colors choice,
    All pinked with varnished flowers of paradise.

Then clothe therewith mine understanding, will,
    Affections, judgment, conscience, memory,

---

2 *distaff*: a staff on which flax, wool, etc. is wound for use in spinning. 3 *flyers*: projecting
arms around which the "twine" is threaded to prevent its becoming entangled. 5 *reel*: on
which the finished thread is wound. 8 *quills*: hollow reeds on which thread is wound.
10 *ordinances*: church sacraments or rites ordered by authoritative decree. *fulling mills*:
simple machines for "fulling" (processing, refining, purifying) the cloth. 12 *pinked*: ornamented, perhaps by artful perforations.

My words and actions, that their shine may fill   15
My ways with glory and Thee glorify.
Then mine apparel shall display before Ye
That I am clothed in holy robes for glory.

WILLIAM BLAKE *(1757–1827)*

Although Blake's songs tend to follow pronounced metrical schemes and stanzaic forms, it is doubtful that anyone will set them to music for a Broadway production—or would catch all they have to offer in the musical net if he tried. They are disciplined probings of serious problems like the origin of the tiger's fearful symmetry and the copresence in creation of both the tiger and the Christlike lamb. Blake was a symbolic system-maker, if not a systematic thinker, and a given passage often connects with other lyrics on the basis of likenesses and contrasts in symbolism.

THE TYGER

Tyger! Tyger! burning bright
In the forests of the night,
What immortal hand or eye
Could frame thy fearful symmetry?

In what distant deeps or skies   5
Burnt the fire of thine eyes?
On what wings dare he aspire?
What the hand dare seize the fire?

And what shoulder, & what art,
Could twist the sinews of thy heart?   10
And when thy heart began to beat,
What dread hand? & what dread feet?

What the hammer? what the chain?
In what furnace was thy brain?
What the anvil? what dread grasp   15
Dare its deadly terrors clasp?

When the stars threw down their spears,
And water'd heaven with their tears,
Did he smile his work to see?
Did he who made the Lamb make thee?   20

Tyger! Tyger! burning bright
In the forests of the night,
What immortal hand or eye,
Dare frame thy fearful symmetry?

ROBERT BURNS *(1759–1796)*

Whereas the encyclopedic allegory of the medieval Book of Creatures offered a ready system of correspondence between the human, the natural, and the supernatural, Burns's lessons read in the book of the mouse are casual, personal, and dramatic, unfolding the particular details of the incident. As often in the "beast fable," the poet exploits the irony of taking seriously the fate of a beast, especially one "wee, sleekit, and cowrin," by making the differences between man and beast yield as much as their similarities.

TO A MOUSE

On Turning Her Up in Her Nest with the Plow, November, 1785

Wee, sleekit, cowrin, tim'rous beastie,
O, what a panic's in thy breastie!
Thou need na start awa sae hasty,
  Wi' bickering brattle!
I wad be laith to rin an' chase thee,   5
  Wi' murdering pattle!

I'm truly sorry man's dominion,
Has broken Nature's social union,
An' justifies that ill opinion
  Which makes thee startle   10
At me, thy poor, earth-born companion,
  An' fellow-mortal!

I doubt na, whyles, but thou may thieve;
What then? poor beastie, thou maun live!
A daimen icker in a thrave   15
  'S a sma' request:
I'll get a blessin wi' the lave,
  And never miss't!

Thy wee-bit housie, too, in ruin!
Its silly wa's the win's are strewin!   20
An' naething, now, to big a new ane,
  O' foggage green!
An' bleak December's win's ensuin,
  Baith snell an' keen!

Thou saw the fields laid bare and waste   25
An' weary winter comin' fast,
An' cozie here, beneath the blast,
  Thou thought to dwell,
Till, crash! the cruel coulter past
  Out thro' thy cell.   30

That wee bit heap o' leaves an' stibble
Has cost thee mony a weary nibble!
Now thou's turn'd out, for a' thy trouble,
  But house or hald,
To thole the winters' sleety dribble   35
  An' cranreuch cauld!

But, Mousie, thou art no thy lane
In proving foresight may be vain:

The best laid schemes o' mice an' men
Gang aft a-gley,   40
An' lea'e us nought but grief an' pain,
For promised joy.

Still thou art blest, compared wi' me!
The present only toucheth thee:
But, och! I backward cast my e'e   45
On prospects drear!
An' forward, tho' I canna see,
I guess an' fear!

GEORGE GORDON, LORD BYRON *(1788–1824)*

The ruminations on the decay of feeling in "There's Not a Joy" reveal why
Byron usually bypassed this species of lyric in favor of satire and romance.
The opening line, for instance, suggests that the world takes away more than
it gives without revealing the source of joy that exceeds the world's allowance—
a rather crucial omission if not a logical blunder. The second does not stipulate
why "thought" should decline in "feeling's decay," as though the two were
identical. In the images and proliferation of metaphors thereafter, Byron never
succeeds in articulating quite what it is he has lost or why we should care. We
have the uneasy feeling that he has wheeled into position an impressive artillery
of images and philosophy merely to squirt rosewater on a small stockpile of
self-pity.

THERE'S NOT A JOY THE WORLD CAN GIVE

There's not a joy the world can give like that it takes away,
When the glow of early thought declines in Feeling's dull decay;
'Tis not on Youth's smooth cheek the blush alone, which fades so fast,
But the tender bloom of heart is gone, ere Youth itself be past.

Then the few whose spirits float above the wreck of happiness   5
Are driven o'er the shoals of guilt or ocean of excess:
The magnet of their course is gone, or only points in vain
The shore to which their shivered sail shall never stretch again.

Then the mortal coldness of the soul like Death itself comes down;
It cannot feel for others' woes, it dare not dream its own;   10
That heavy chill has frozen o'er the fountain of our tears,
And though the eye may sparkle still, 'tis where the ice appears.

Though wit may flash from fluent lips, and mirth distract the breast,
Through midnight hours that yield no more their former hope of rest;
'Tis but as ivy-leaves around the ruined turret wreath,   15
All green and wildly fresh without, but worn and grey beneath.

Oh could I feel as I have felt,—or be what I have been,
Or weep as I could once have wept, o'er many a vanished scene;
As springs, in deserts found, seem sweet, all brackish though they be,
So, midst the withered waste of life, those tears would flow to me.   20

EDWARD FITZGERALD *(1809–1883)*

The universal themes of transience and the pleasures of wine and love gave FitzGerald's *Rubáiyát* a gentle nostalgia and a sense of doom attractive to a time that turned frequently toward Epicurean thought and the romance of far-off places.

THE RUBÁIYÁT OF OMAR KHAYYÁM

1

A Book of Verses underneath the Bough,
A Jug of Wine, a Loaf of Bread, and Thou
    Beside me singing in the Wilderness—
Oh, Wilderness were Paradise enow!

Some for the Glories of This World, and some   5
Sigh for the Prophet's Paradise to come—
    Ah, take the Cash and let the Credit go,
Nor heed the rumble of a distant Drum!

Look to the blowing Rose about us. 'Lo,
Laughing,' she says, 'into the world I blow,   10
    At once the silken tassel of my Purse
Tear, and its Treasure on the Garden throw.'

The Worldly Hope men set their Hearts upon
Turns Ashes, or it prospers; and anon,
    Like Snow upon the Desert's dusty Face   15
Lighting a little hour or two, is gone.

Think, in this batter'd Caravanserai
Whose Portals are alternate Night and Day,
    How Sultan after Sultan with his Pomp
Abode his destined Hour, and went his way.   20

They say the Lion and the Lizard keep
The Courts where Jamshyd gloried and drank deep:
    And Bahram, that great Hunter—the Wild Ass
Stamps o'er his Head, but cannot break his Sleep.

2

The Moving Fingers writes, and, having writ,
Moves on: nor all your Piety nor Wit
    Shall lure it back to cancel half a Line,
Nor all your Tears wash out a Word of it.

And that inverted Bowl we call the Sky,   5
Whereunder crawling coop'd we live and die,
    Lift not your hands to *It* for help—for It
As impotently moves as You or I.

With Earth's first Clay They did the Last Man knead,
And then of the Last Harvest sow'd the Seed: 10
    And the first Morning of Creation wrote
What the Last Dawn of Reckoning shall read. . . .

And this I know; whether the one True Light
Kindle to Love, or Wrath-consume me quite,
    One Flash of It within the Tavern caught   15
Better than in the Temple lost outright.

O Thou who didst with Pitfall and with Gin
Beset the Road I was to wander in,
    Thou wilt not with Predestination round
Enmesh me, and impute my Fall to Sin?...   20

Nay, but, for terror of his wrathful Face,
I swear I will not call Injustice Grace.
    Not one Good Fellow of the Tavern but
Would kick so poor a Coward from the place.

ALFRED, LORD TENNYSON *(1809–1892)*

The speaker's appeal to the maid to come down from the mountain is based
not so much on convincing reasons as on the indirect persuasions of image
and rhetoric. The reasons offered are important, however, and are reinforced
by Tennyson's rhythmical skills—the imitation of the journey down the mountain, for instance, and the sounds that make life pleasant down below. The
impressive display of imagery and imitative sounds of the broken waste of
water are followed by the logical injunction, "So waste not thou," which transforms—whether strictly according to logic or not—the impact of image to
rhetorical appeal. As in the best reflective poetry, thought, feeling, and the
techniques of verse are here inseparable.

COME DOWN, O MAID

Come down, O maid, from yonder mountain height:
What pleasure lives in height (the shepherd sang)
In height and cold, the splendour of the hills?
But cease to move so near the heavens, and cease
To glide a sunbeam by the blasted Pine,   5
To sit a star upon the sparkling spire;
And come, for Love is of the valley, come,
For Love is of the valley, come thou down
And find him; by the happy threshold, he,
Or hand in hand with Plenty in the maize,   10
Or red with spirted purple of the vats,
Or foxlike in the vine; nor cares to walk
With Death and Morning on the silver horns,
Nor wilt thou snare him in the white ravine,
Nor find him dropt upon the firths of ice   15
That huddling slant in furrow-cloven falls
To roll the torrent out of dusky doors:
But follow; let the torrent dance thee down
To find him in the valley; let the wild
Lean-headed Eagles yelp alone, and leave   20
The monstrous ledges there to slope, and spill
Their thousand wreaths of dangling water-smoke

That like a broken purpose waste in air:
So waste not thou; but come; for all the vales
Await thee; azure pillars of the hearth   25
Arise to thee; the children call, and I
Thy shepherd pipe, and sweet is every sound,
Sweeter thy voice, but every sound is sweet;
Myriads of rivulets hurrying thro' the lawn,
The moan of doves in immemorial elms,   30
And murmuring of innumerable bees.

EMILY DICKINSON *(1830–1886)*

Like her Puritan ancestors, the American transcendentalists, and the English metaphysical poets, Emily Dickinson puts the paradoxes of man's relation to the infinite and the intangible in compressed language. The following selections concern the discovery of the unknown in daily light. In what appears to be a common scene, simply described, something puzzling and scarcely nameable (though sometimes given an abstract title such as the "Beautiful") is suddenly manifest. Its appearance converts narrative movement to intellectual and spiritual journey.

A LIGHT EXISTS IN SPRING

A light exists in spring
Not present in the year
At any other period.
When March is scarcely here

A color stands abroad   5
On solitary hills
That science cannot overtake,
But human nature feels.

It waits upon the lawn;
It shows the furthest·tree   10
Upon the furthest slope we know;
It almost speaks to me.

Then, as horizons step,
Or noons report away,
Without the formula of sound,   15
It passes, and we stay:

A quality of loss
Affecting our content,
As trade had suddenly encroached
Upon a sacrament.   20

AS IMPERCEPTIBLY AS GRIEF

As imperceptibly as grief
The Summer lapsed away,—
Too imperceptible, at last,
To seem like perfidy.

A quietness distilled,   5
As twilight long begun,
Or Nature, spending with herself
Sequestered Afternoon.

The dusk drew earlier in,
The morning foreign shone,—   10
A courteous, yet harrowing grace,
As guest who would be gone.

And thus, without a wing,
Or service of a keel,
Our summer made her light escape   15
Into the beautiful.

THERE'S A CERTAIN SLANT OF LIGHT

There's a certain slant of light,
On winter afternoons,
That oppresses, like the weight
Of cathedral tunes.

Heavenly hurt it gives us;   5
We can find no scar,
But internal difference
Where the meanings are.

None may teach it anything,
'Tis the seal, despair,—   10
An imperial affliction
Sent us of the air.

When it comes, the landscape listens,
Shadows hold their breath;
When it goes, 'tis like the distance   15
On the look of death.

THOMAS HARDY *(1840–1928)*

Childhood faith is only one of the speaker's losses in "The Oxen." A protected
world of firesides and gentle fathers, the warmth of the "meek mild creatures,"
and perhaps above all the imaginative pleasure of an animal world obedient
to human and divine ends are out of place in "these years," which prompt a
skepticism incompatible with the shepherd's naive simplicity.

THE OXEN*

Christmas Eve, and twelve of the clock,
  "Now they are all on their knees,"
An elder said as we sat in a flock
  By the embers in hearthside ease.

* Reprinted from *Collected Poems of Thomas Hardy* by permission of the Estate, Macmillan
& Co., Ltd., London, and The Macmillan Company of Canada Limited.

We pictured the meek mild creatures where   5
    They dwelt in their strawy pen,
Nor did it occur to one of us there
    To doubt they were kneeling then.

So fair a fancy few would weave
    In these years! Yet, I feel,   10
If someone said on Christmas Eve,
    "Come; see the oxen kneel

"In the lonely barton by yonder coomb
    Our childhood used to know,"
I should go with him in the gloom,   15
    Hoping it might be so.

GERARD MANLEY HOPKINS *(1845–1889)*

The title and the dedication of "The Windhover" suggest the basic opposites of the poem, which the priest, his "heart in hiding" from nature (at least until he discoveres the windhover in flight), seeks to bring together: the windhover and Christ, the former being in a sense offered up to Christ, the spiritual "retriever." The key word in the speaker's transfer of admiration is "buckle" (line 10), which means "engage, unite, join together" and also "collapse, fall apart." A sacrificial object is annihilated in its use; similarly, the brute beauty, pride, and plume of the kestrel are "taken over" by Christ, who transcends them. They are engaged by him and they buckle before him. Although the speaker is not required to take back his admiration for the princely windhover, then, he acknowledges another prince "a billion times" lovelier in ways both like and unlike the beauty of nature.

THE WINDHOVER:*

To Christ Our Lord

I caught this morning morning's minion, king-
    dom of daylight's dauphin, dapple-dawn-drawn Falcon, in his riding
    Of the rolling level underneath him steady air, and striding
High there, how he rung upon the rein of a wimpling wing
In his ectasy! then off, off forth on swing,   5
    As a skate's heel sweeps smooth on a bow-bend: the hurl and gliding
    Rebuffed the big wind. My heart in hiding
Stirred for a bird,—the achieve of, the mastery of the thing!

Brute beauty and valor and act, oh, air, pride, plume, here
    Buckle! AND the fire that breaks from thee then, a billion   10
Times told lovelier, more dangerous, O my chevalier!
    No wonder of it: sheèr plòd makes plow down sillion
Shine, and blue-bleak embers, ah my dear,
    Fall, gall themselves, and gash gold-vermilion.

* From *Poems of Gerard Manley Hopkins*, Third Edition, edited by W. H. Gardner. Copyright 1948 by Oxford University Press, Inc. Reprinted by permission.

1 *minion*: favorite. 2 *dauphin*: prince. 4 *rung upon the rein*: as a horse performing at the end of a training line; *wimpling*: rippling. 10 *fire*: partly, sacrificial blood, as again in the "gold-vermilion" of the falling embers in line 14.

A. E. HOUSMAN *(1859–1936)*

The implicit tension of "Bredon Hill" is between a personal and momentarily outcast love (on the hill) and conventional society (in the valley). The capitulation of the speaker to the call of the noisy bells signals a collapse of independence, the beloved having "gone to church" without him. Nature's hostility to beauty and to private love (the girl dies in the season of snow) reinforces society's pressure on those who would not ordinarily come when called.

BREDON HILL*

In summertime on Bredon
  The bells they sound so clear;
Round both the shires they ring them
  In steeples far and near,
  A happy noise to hear.   5

Here of a Sunday morning
  My love and I would lie,
And see the colored counties,
  And hear the larks so high
  About us in the sky.   10

The bells would ring to call her
  In valleys miles away:
"Come all to church, good people;
  Good people, come and pray."
  But here my love would stay.   15

And I would turn and answer
  Among the springing thyme,
"Oh, peal upon our wedding,
  And we will hear the chime,
  And come to church in time."   20

But when the snows at Christmas
  On Bredon top were strown,
My love rose up so early
  And stole out unbeknown
  And went to church alone.   25

---

* From "A Shropshire Lad"—Authorised Edition—from *The Collected Poems of A. E. Housman*. Copyright 1939, 1940, © 1959 by Holt, Rinehart and Winston, Inc. Reprinted by permission of Holt, Rinehart and Winston, Inc. and The Society of Authors as the literary representative of the Estate of the late A. E. Housman, and Messrs, Jonathan Cape Ltd., publishers of A. E. Housman's *Collected Poems*.

---

12 *sillion*: overturned soil behind a plow, which shines when first turned up. The idea is that by putting himself under nature (by "buckling" himself), Christ has given nature a value not normally found in it, as an inner beauty is revealed when embers break open, "gall themselves." Perhaps also the priest indirectly suggests to himself that he should accept the burden of his calling (sheèr plòd) because, buckled in the harness, he discovers rewards greater than those symbolized by the free-flying bird.

They tolled the one bell only,
  Groom there was none to see,
The mourners followed after,
  And so to church went she,
  And would not wait for me.   30

The bells they sound on Bredon,
  And still the steeples hum.
"Come all to church, good people,—"
  Oh, noisy bells, be dumb;
  I hear you, I will come.   35

WILLIAM BUTLER YEATS *(1865–1939)*

As a philosophical and metaphysical poet, Yeats draws on a variety of sources, including Platonism, the esoteric tradition of Hermetic philosophy, and the more immediate aestheticism of the 1890's, which emerges even in the later Yeats in images like the golden form on the bough in "Sailing to Byzantium." Politically and socially, Yeats values the aristocratic poise and dignity of a former, prouder time of lords and ladies rather than the noisy market place of the contemporary scene. Hence in both "Sailing to Byzantium" and "Among School Children" he contrasts the present with the past or the distant. The difficulty for Yeats, as for Keats, is to have both life and the permanence of art at the same time, to make the dancer (the mortal) and the dance (the pattern) the same. It is more than a philosophical problem, of course, but Yeats considers it in its metaphysical dimensions as well as in terms of the speaker's own personal history.

SAILING TO BYZANTIUM*

That is no country for old men. The young
In one another's arms, birds in the trees,
—Those dying generations—at their song,
The salmon-falls, the mackerel-crowded seas,
Fish, flesh, or fowl, commend all summer long   5
Whatever is begotten, born, and dies.
Caught in that sensual music all neglect
Monuments of unaging intellect.

An aged man is but a paltry thing,
A tattered coat upon a stick, unless   10
Soul clap its hands and sing, and louder sing
For every tatter in its mortal dress,
Nor is there singing school but studying
Monuments of its own magnificence;
And therefore I have sailed the seas and come   15
To the holy city of Byzantium.

O sages standing in God's holy fire
As in the gold mosaic of a wall,
Come from the holy fire, perne in a gyre,
And be the singing-masters of my soul.   20
Consume my heart away; sick with desire
And fastened to a dying animal
It knows not what it is; and gather me
Into the artifice of eternity.

Once out of nature I shall never take   25
My bodily form from any natural thing,
But such a form as Grecian goldsmiths make
Of hammered gold and gold enameling
To keep a drowsy Emperor awake;
Or set upon a golden bough to sing   30
To lords and ladies of Byzantium
Of what is past, or passing, or to come.

AMONG SCHOOL CHILDREN

1

I walk through the long schoolroom questioning;
A kind old nun in a white hood replies;
The children learn to cipher and to sing,
To study reading-books and history,
To cut and sew, be neat in everything   5
In the best modern way—the children's eyes
In momentary wonder stare upon
A sixty year old smiling public man.

2

I dream of a Ledaean body, bent
Above a sinking fire, a tale that she   10
Told of a harsh reproof, or trivial event
That changed some childish day to tragedy—
Told, and it seemed that our two natures blent
Into a sphere from youthful sympathy,
Or else, to alter Plato's parable,   15
Into the yolk and white of the one shell.

3

And thinking of that fit of grief or rage
I look upon one child or t'other there
And wonder if she stood so at that age—
For even daughters of the swan can share   20
Something of every paddler's heritage—
And had that colour upon cheek or hair,
And thereupon my heart is driven wild:
She stands before me as a living child.

---

9 *Ledaean body*: Leda is a mythic Greek of great beauty. 15 *Plato's parable*: Aristophanes suggests that men and women are separate halves of what was once a single creature (*Symposium*).

4

Her present image floats into the mind—   25
Did Quattrocento finger fashion it
Hollow of cheek as though it drank the wind
And took a mess of shadows for its meat?
And I though never of Ledaean kind
Had pretty plumage once—enough of that,   30
Better to smile on all that smile, and show
There is a comfortable kind of scarecrow.

5

What youthful mother, a shape upon her lap
Honey of generation had betrayed,
And that must sleep, shriek, struggle to escape   35
As recollection or the drug decide,
Would think her son, did she but see that shape
With sixty or more winters on its head,
A compensation for the pang of his birth,
Or the uncertainty of his setting forth?   40

6

Plato thought nature but a spume that plays
Upon a ghostly paradigm of things;
Solider Aristotle played the taws
Upon the bottom of a king of kings;
World-famous golden-thighed Pythagoras   45
Fingered upon a fiddle-stick or strings
What a star sang and careless Muses heard:
Old clothes upon old sticks to scare a bird.

7

Both nuns and mothers worship images,
But those the candles light are not as those   50
That animate a mother's reveries,
But keep a marble or a bronze repose.
And yet they too break hearts—O Presences
That passion, piety or affection knows,
And that all heavenly glory symbolize—   55
O self-born mockers of man's enterprise;

8

Labour is blossoming or dancing where
The body is not bruised to pleasure soul,
Nor beauty born out of its own despair,
Nor blear-eyed wisdom out of midnight oil.   60
O chestnut tree, great rooted blossomer,
Are you the leaf, the blossom or the bole?
O body swayed to music, O brightening glance,
How can we know the dancer from the dance?

---

26 *Quattrocento finger*: fifteenth-century painter.   41–45 Plato, Aristotle, and Pythagoras
represent three different positions in Greek philosophy. (Yeats does not treat them
reverently.)

WALLACE STEVENS *(1879–1956)*

Perhaps no poet since Donne, Herbert, and Marvell, who were "metaphysical" in the primary sense of the word, is so distinctly a philosophical poet as Wallace Stevens. Taken as a whole, his poetry is a thorough exploration of what happens in the meeting of the mind and the external world, in both perception and conception. In "The Emperor of Ice-Cream," the command to let "be" be finale of "seem"—in other words, to imagine nothing different from what is— means accepting the reality of death untransfigured, though perhaps somewhat softened by the pleasures of eating ice cream. The rigid habits of bourgeois culture in "Disillusionment of Ten O'Clock" stifle the imagination, which when freed from restrictions runs riot among baboons and periwinkles. The order composed by the jar in Tennessee is like that of the mind imposing itself on chaos; but in disciplining the wilderness, the "jar" also deprives it of life and movement. These are three small but effective examples of Stevens' oblique way into basic negotiations between intellect, imagination, and what lies "out there."

ANECDOTE OF THE JAR*

I placed a jar in Tennessee,
And round it was, upon a hill.
It made the slovenly wilderness
Surround that hill.

The wilderness rose up to it,   5
And sprawled around, no longer wild.
The jar was round upon the ground
And tall and of a port in air.

It took dominion everywhere.
The jar was gray and bare.   10
It did not give of bird or bush,
Like nothing else in Tennessee.

DISILLUSIONMENT OF TEN O'CLOCK*

The houses are haunted
By white night-gowns.
None are green,
Or purple with green rings,
Or green with yellow rings,   5
Or yellow with blue rings.
None of them are strange,
With socks of lace
And beaded ceintures.
People are not going   10
To dream of baboons and periwinkles.

---

9 *Ceintures*: sashes.

Only, here and there, an old sailor,
Drunk and asleep in his boots,
Catches tigers
In red weather.

THE EMPEROR OF ICE-CREAM*

Call the roller of big cigars,
The muscular one, and bid him whip
In kitchen cups concupiscent curds.
Let the wenches dawdle in such dress
As they are used to wear, and let the boys   5
Bring flowers in last month's newspapers.
Let be be finale of seem.
The only emperor is the emperor of ice-cream.

Take from the dresser of deal,
Lacking the three glass knobs, that sheet   10
On which she embroidered fantails once
And spread it so as to cover her face.
If her horny feet protrude, they come
To show how cold she is, and dumb.
Let the lamp affix its beam.   15
The only emperor is the emperor of ice-cream.

WILLIAM CARLOS WILLIAMS *(1883–1964)*

Although the subject of his meditation is only a wheelbarrow, Williams poses a basic question about the meaning of meaning, the composition of a scene.

THE RED WHEELBARROW†

so much depends
upon

a red wheel
barrow

glazed with rain   5
water

beside the white
chickens.

JOHN CROWE RANSOM *(1888–   )*

"Philomela" illustrates the tendency of modern poetry to explore rather than to expound, but it also implies several statements concerning the kind of sensibility a democracy fosters and the relevance of myth to a culture too vehemently pragmatic to harbor stories of metamorphosed birds.

* Reprinted by permission of AAK, Inc. from *The Collected Poems of Wallace Stevens* by Wallace Stevens. Copyright 1923, 1951 by Wallace Stevens.
† From *Collected Earlier Pomes of William Carlos Williams* by William Carlos Williams. Copyright 1938 by New Directions. Reprinted by permission of New Directions.

PHILOMELA*

Procne, Philomela, and Itylus,
Your names are liquid, your improbable tale
Is recited in the classic numbers of the nightingale.
Ah, but our numbers are not felicitous,
It goes not liquidly for us.   5

Perched on a Roman ilex, and duly apostrophized,
The nightingale descanted unto Ovid;
She has even appeared to the Teutons, the swilled and gravid;
At Fontainebleau it may be the bird was gallicized;
Never was she baptized.   10

To England came Philomela with her pain,
Fleeing the hawk her husband; querulous ghost,
She wanders when he sits heavy on his roost,
Utters herself in the original again,
The untranslatable refrain.   15

Not to these shores she came! this other Thrace,
Environ barbarous to the royal Attic;
How could her delicate dirge run democratic,
Delivered in a cloudless boundless public place
To an inordinate race?   20

I pernoctated with the Oxford students once,
And in the quadrangles, in the cloisters, on the Cher,
Precociously knocked at antique doors ajar,
Fatuously touched the hems of the hierophants,
Sick of my dissonance.   25

I went out to Bagley Wood, I climbed the hill;
Even the moon had slanted off in a twinkling,
I heard the sepulchral owl and a few bells tinkling,
There was no more villainous day to unfulfil,
The diuturnity was still.   30

Up from the darkest wood where Philomela sat,
Her fairy numbers issued. What then ailed me?
My ears are called capacious but they failed me,
Her classics registered a little flat!
I rose, and venomously spat.   35

Philomela, Philomela, lover of song,
I am in despair if we may make us worthy,
A bantering breed sophistical and swarthy;
Unto more beautiful, persistently more young
Thy fabulous provinces belong.   40

* Reprinted by permission of AAK, Inc. from *Poems and Essays* by John Crowe Ransom. Copyright, 1924 by AAK, Inc. Renewed, 1952 by John Crowe Ransom.

1 *Procne, Philomela, and Itylus*: to avenge her husband Tereus' violence against her sister Philomela, Procne served her son Itylus to him for dinner. All four of the principal actors were transformed into birds.

ARCHIBALD MACLEISH *(1892–   )*

Like Amy Lowell, MacLeish felt that poetry should be largely a matter of visual particularity rather than abstract statement; but his imagery at its best, like hers, leads to and is based on an implicit, governing concept. The conceptual framework of "You, Andrew Marvell" is supplied by Marvell's famous lines, "At my back I always hear / Time's winged chariot hurrying near."

YOU, ANDREW MARVELL*

And here face down beneath the sun
And here upon earth's noonward height
To feel the always coming on
The always rising of the night

To feel creep up the curving east   5
The earthy chill of dusk and slow
Upon those under lands the vast
And ever climbing shadow grow

And strange at Ecbatan the trees
Take leaf by leaf the evening strange   10
The flooding dark about their knees
The mountains over Persia change

And now at Kermanshah the gate
Dark empty and the withered grass
And through the twilight now the late   15
Few travelers in the westward pass

And Baghdad darken and the bridge
Across the silent river gone
And through Arabia the edge
Of evening widen and steal on   20

And deepen on Palmyra's street
The wheel rut in the ruined stone
And Lebanon fade out and Crete
High through the clouds and overblown

And over Sicily the air   25
Still flashing with the landward gulls
And loom and slowly disappear
The sails above the shadowy hulls

And Spain go under and the shore
Of Africa the gilded sand   30
And evening vanish and no more
The low pale light across that land

Nor now the long light on the sea
And here face downward in the sun
To feel how swift how secretly   35
The shadow of the night comes on . . .

WILFRED OWEN *(1893–1918)*

An armed man such as Aeneas, to whom Owen's title refers, is much more easily made into an image of heroism than an armed boy. Reducing the age of the warrior, Owen reverses the epic process of heroic escalation by which the pursuit of war is made to seem noble. Here, the catalog of arms verges upon the satiric in its overturning of the propaganda value of flagwaving. But the tone is more sorrowful than bitter. The inversions are offered not as wit but as unadorned recognition of the brutalizing metamorphosis that war unmagically works.

ARMS AND THE BOY*

Let the boy try along this bayonet-blade
How cold steel is, and keen with hunger of blood;
Blue with all malice, like a madman's flash;
And thinly drawn with famishing for flesh.

Lend him to stroke these blind, blunt bullet-heads   5
Which long to nuzzle in the hearts of lads,
Or give him cartridges of fine zinc teeth,
Sharp with the sharpness of grief and death.

For his teeth seem for laughing round an apple.
There lurk no claws behind his fingers supple;   10
And god will grow no talons at his heels,
Nor antlers through the thickness of his curls.

E. E. CUMMINGS *(1894–1962)*

As the very shape of a printed Cummings poem suggests, Cummings was like Dylan Thomas in distrusting "categories": the normal movement of syntax and accepted logical structures for handling perception and thought. But the eccentric shape of his poems should not be mistaken for shapelessness. It is often a way of timing and emphasizing insights as well as getting maximum benefit from the sounds of words.

BUFFALO BILL 'S†

Buffalo Bill 's
defunct
    who used to
    ride a watersmooth-silver
               stallion   5
and break onetwothreefourfive pigeonsjustlikethat
                      Jesus

he was a handsome man
               and what i want to know is
how do you like your blueeyed boy   10
Mister Death

---

* From *Collected Poems of Wilfred Owen* by Wilfred Owen. Reprinted by permission of New Directions. Reprinted for Canadian circulation by permission of Chatto & Windus, Ltd. and Mr. Harold Owen.
† Copyright, 1923, 1951, by E. E. Cummings. Reprinted from *Poems 1923–1954*, by E. E. Cummings, by permission of Harcourt, Brace and World, Inc.

HART CRANE *(1899–1932)*

Crane's poetry could be characterized in Hopkins' terms as "things original, spare, and strange." It is a poetry of suggestion, "spare" in that all the suet of explicit statement has been worked off (along with some of its muscle, too, the reader may well feel) and what remains is an experience conveyed by implication. Although his poetry is reflective, it does not develop in terms of reason or logic; its "plot" is not an argument but a structure of tone and attitude controlled by imagistic associations. "Repose of Rivers" uses the topography of the delta country as a means of spatializing time, as a marshy geographical point to localize the meeting of the past and present and, "There, beyond the dykes," the future, while the process of temporal erosion goes on.

REPOSE OF RIVERS*

The willows carried a slow sound,
A sarabande the wind mowed on the mead.
I could never remember
That seething, steady leveling of the marshes
Till age had brought me to the sea.   5

Flags, weeds. And remembrance of steep alcoves
Where cypresses shared the noon's
Tyranny; they drew me into hades almost.
And mammoth turtles climbing sulphur dreams
Yielded, while sun-silt rippled them   10
Asunder...

How much I would have bartered! the black gorge
And all the singular nestings in the hills
Where beavers learn stitch and tooth.
The pond I entered once and quickly fled—   15
I remember now its singing willow rim.

And finally, in that memory all things nurse;
After the city that I finally passed
With scalding unguents spread and smoking darts
The monsoon cut across the delta   20
At gulf gates...There, beyond the dykes

I heard wind flaking sapphire, like this summer,
And willows could not hold more steady sound.

W. H. AUDEN *(1907–   )*

Auden's reflective poems are characteristically wry and flinty. In "Musée des Beaux Arts" he muses about human suffering in a leisurely and rambling monologue carefully staged for the benefit of casual listeners. In the delight we take in Auden's anecdotal riches, we should not lose sight of the logical and moral position that the illustrations gradually bring into focus.

MUSÉE DES BEAUX ARTS*

About suffering they were never wrong,
The Old Masters: how well they understood
Its human position; how it takes place
While someone else is eating or opening a window or just walking dully along;

How, when the aged are reverently, passionately waiting   5
For the miraculous birth, there always must be
Children who did not specially want it to happen, skating
On a pond at the edge of the wood:
They never forgot
That even the dreadful martyrdom must run its course   10
Anyhow in a corner, some untidy spot
Where the dogs go on with their doggy life and the torturer's horse
Scratches its innocent behind on a tree.

In Brueghel's *Icarus,* for instance: how everything turns away
Quite leisurely from the disaster; the ploughman may   15
Have heard the splash, the forsaken cry,
But for him it was not an important failure; the sun shone
As it had to on the white legs disappearing into the green
Water; and the expensive delicate ship that must have seen
Something amazing, a boy falling out of the sky,   20
Had somewhere to get to and sailed calmly on.

RICHARD WILBUR *(1921–   )*

Partly in the "imagist" tradition, Wilbur allows pattern and symbol to emerge
out of a finely articulated description, but they are given a decisive nudge in
"A Courtyard Thaw" by rational speculation.

A COURTYARD THAW†

The sun was strong enough today
To climb the well and loose the courtyard trees
(For two short hours, anyway)
From hardship of the January freeze.

Their icy cerements decayed   5
To silken moistures, which began to slip
In glints and spangles down, and made
On every twig a bauble at the tip.

No blossom, leaf or basking fruit
Showed ever such pure passion for the sun   10
As these cold drops that knew no root
Yet filled with light and swelled and one by one

(Or showered by a wingbeat, sown
From windbent branches in arpeggios)
Let go and took their shinings down   15
And brought their brittle season to a close.

O false gemmation! Flashy fall!
The eye is pleased when nature stoops to art,
Staging within a courtyard wall
Such twinkling scenes. But puzzling to the heart,   20

This spring was neither fierce nor gay;
This summary autumn fell without a tear:
No tinkling music-box can play
The slow, deep-grounded masses of the year.

Dramatic Monologue

We remarked earlier that art imposes form on personal feeling even when
the poet insists that he sings spontaneously (for even in making that claim
he is following a venerable convention). Another way of putting it is that the
speaker of a poem is never the poet himself but always in some sense a dramatic
invention. Even intensity of feeling is no guarantee that the emotion approxi-
mates the poet's. Thus all lyrics are in a sense dramatic monologues—*mono*
because one person speaks them and dramatic because the speaker is a projected
voice. But most lyrics do not make important use of the separation of speaker
and poet. Ordinarily, the term "dramatic monologue" is reserved for poems in
which the speaker is actually given a distinguishable character and perhaps a
separate name (such as "Andrea del Sarto") and placed in a situation that is
not likely to be confused with the poet's. This makes the poet relatively anonymous and allows character and dramatic encounter to dictate the style and
structural progress of the poem.

However, to emphasize the implications of dramatic technique, we have
included in this category some poems that might not normally be regarded as
dramatic monologues but that contain an address of a speaker to something
capable of drawing a response from him, hence of creating dialogue. The
crossfire of dialogue makes them *progressive negotiations,* or forms of dialectic,
and demands a certain kind of rhetoric. Insofar as the negotiating parties
disagree, there is an element of ordeal or agon: they "try" each other, ordeal
being dialogue intensified by conflict. From the standpoint of structure, the
parts of the poem are arranged not as in a past-tense narrative whose action
is completed before the beginning of the narration or as a rational argument
whose conclusions are implicit in the premises, but as present-tense statement
and answer.

Obviously the element foremost in a given poem, narrative, deliberation, or
drama is not always self-evident. For instance, we could consider Marvell's
"To his Coy Mistress" or Herrick's "Corinna Goes A-Maying" either as

dramatic monologues on the basis of their implicit dialectical progress or as reflective lyrics on the basis of their well-defined argumentative structures. Are they *set* speeches or *dramatic* speeches? Likewise, is the speaker of Amy Lowell's "Patterns" really negotiating with the garden—responding to it, letting it "speak" to her, in a progressive realization of the meaning of its patterns, or is she reciting to herself something she has already come to realize? (In placing these poems where we have, we are not implying final answers to these questions.)

The difficulty of determining what gives a poem its structural principle is complicated by considerations of tone, mood, and audience. We noticed that in many hymns and odes the poet approaches the thing addressed with veneration. He addresses it with the reverent "Thou," usually preceded by an "O" and followed by an exclamation point: "O wild West Wind, thou breath of Autumn's being...hear, oh, hear!" "O Attic shape! fair attitude!...Thou silent form...." Thus the odic or hymnal speaker may also be said to negotiate with the object; and certainly in most romantic odes his relationship with it is dramatic in the sense of progressive and present tense. But as we also suggested, an implicit *hierarchical* distance between the poet and the object results in a raising of the voice, as though to cross a *physical* distance. ("God," for instance, is often thought of as a long way "up.") Hence the negotiations are in the mode of imperative beseeching, like prayers. Much closer to the dramatic monologue's sense of spoken persuasion is the tone of *familiar* address in Donne's holy sonnets (p. 49) and Herbert's "The Collar" (p. 121). In these poems, as again in Herbert's dialogue poems "Hope" and "Love" and in most temptation poems (Marvell's "Dialogue between the Resolved Soul and Created Pleasure," for instance), the immediacy of the voice makes bargaining possible. The kind of "deal" one can strike at top voice across a chasm is limited.

Basic to dramatic monologues, therefore, is the notion of answerable dialogue, with one responder unheard so that we concentrate on the character of a single speaker—as though listening to one end of a telephone conversation or the address of someone to a low-voiced second party. We must guess from the speaker's changes of direction what his opponent says. The structure is that both of negotiation and of riddle. Lucrezia's silence must speak her mind for her in "Andrea del Sarto." And though Donne's speaker in "The Canonization" begins by shutting off debate, "For God's sake hold your tongue and let me love," he shapes his argument against what he supposes to be his listener's attitude. In "Patterns," the garden naturally does not speak, but it, too, plays a part in extracting certain statements from the speaker as she talks to herself.

By paying some attention to these matters—responsive address and the progressive unfolding of responses—the student can readily see that "drama" is one dimension of many lyrics he may have read with other things foremost in mind. Consider, for instance, the negotiations carried on (usually from a distance) between lover and mistress in Renaissance sonnets, or writer and addressee in epistles, interrogation and response in the ballad (notice also the outer framework of Keats's "La Belle Dame sans Merci" and Coleridge's "The Rime of the Ancient Mariner"), the speech of the bereaved to the dead or to other mourners in the elegy, the rhetorical figure of address (the "apostrophe") to an absent listener, which may crop up anywhere, and even dialogues held with the self, such as "The Love Song of J. Alfred Prufrock." The influence of the spoken voice on tone and rhythm in these poems is as important as the influence of music on songlike lyrics.

Perhaps equally important, the audience is situated differently: it is "entertained" by a song or listens in while the singer performs, but it is assumed to be officially absent in dramatic monologues. (Nor is it invited to share the poet's values as in satire, in which the second party is an object of attack rather than a negotiator.) Hence in songs we look less critically at the perspective of the performer than at his technique in performing; in dramatic monologues we look less critically at the speaker's technique than at what he sees and does not see: *point of view* becomes a critical consideration.

Consider, for instance, the opening lines of Browning's "Andrea del Sarto":

> But do not let us quarrel any more,
> No, my Lucrezia; bear with me for once:
> Sit down and all shall happen as you wish.
> You turn your face, but does it bring your heart?
> I'll work then for your friend's friend, never fear,
> Treat his own subject after his own way,
> Fix his own time, accept too his own price,
> And shut the money into this small hand
> When next it takes mine.

Though Andrea seeks quiet after a quarrel, the strain of anxiety remains; his mistress Lucrezia is not yet calm, and Andrea negotiates with her anger (over his refusal to pay her other lover's debts), buying it off too quickly, at too great a price ("all shall happen as you wish"). What he gets in return for his remarkable talent is the touch of a hand and a little sympathy. Hence the main negotiations are finished early and there remains only Lucrezia's upholding of her part of the bargain. She listens awhile in silence. Even as we find him largely sympathetic, Andrea forces us to judge him critically because her silence is stronger than his persuasion. He does not see himself or Lucrezia as we do or, presumably, as Browning does. The perspective of the reader and poet is therefore simultaneously inside and above that of the speaker, as again in "My Last Duchess," in which our detachment from the Duke, who is negotiating for a second wife soon after disposing of the first, is like that of a clinical psychologist. If the localizing of perspective and emotion in a personal speaker has much to do with the *lyric* quality of some poems, the crossing of the speaker's emotional curve with some outside perspective is partly what makes a monologue *dramatic*. It forces us to keep our distance and to counteract sympathy with judgment.

"Tithonus" is near the lyric end of the spectrum, "My Last Duchess" near the dramatic end, sympathy predominating in one and judgment in the other. The two elements seem to be nearly balanced in Eliot's "Gerontion," the speaker of which talks partly to himself, partly to something outside himself. The particular one to whom Gerontion would speak has long since departed, thus prompting Gerontion's freezing retreat into indecision in a world of warmed-over squalor and unrelenting self-appraisal.

JOHN DONNE *(1573–1631)*

THE CANONIZATION

For God's sake hold your tongue, and let me love;
    Or chide my palsy, or my gout;
My five gray hairs, or ruined fortune flout;
    With wealth your state, your mind with arts improve;
        Take you a course, get you a place,   5
        Observe his honour, or his grace;
Or the king's real, or his stamped face
    Contemplate; what you will, approve,
    So you will let me love.

Alas! alas! who's injured by my love?   10
    What merchants' ships have my sighs drowned?
Who says my tears have overflowed his ground?
    When did my colds a forward spring remove?
        When did the heats which my veins fill
        Add one more to the plaguy bill?   15
Soldiers find wars, and lawyers find out still
    Litigious men, which quarrels move,
    Though she and I do love.

Call us what you will, we are made such by love;
    Call her one, me another fly,   20
We'are tapers too, and at our own cost die,
    And we in us find th'eagle and the dove.
        The phoenix riddle hath more wit
        By us; we two being one, are it;
So, to one neutral thing both sexes fit.   25
    We die and rise the same, and prove
    Mysterious by this love.

We can die by it, if not live by love,
    And if unfit for tombs and hearse
Our legend be, it will be fit for verse;   30
    And if no piece of chronicle we prove,
        We'll build in sonnets pretty rooms;
        As well a well-wrought urn becomes
The greatest ashes, as half-acre tombs,
    And by these hymns all shall approve   35
    Us canonized for love;

And thus invoke us, "You, whom reverend love
    Made one another's hermitage;
You, to whom love was peace, that now is rage;
    Who did the whole world's soul contract, and drove   40
        Into the glasses of your eyes—
        So made such mirrors, and such spies,
That they did all to you epitomize—
    Countries, towns, courts beg from above
    A pattern of your love!"   45

ALFRED, LORD TENNYSON *(1809–1892)*

TITHONUS

The woods decay, the woods decay and fall,
The vapors weep their burthen to the ground,
Man comes and tills the field and lies beneath,
And after many a summer dies the swan.
Me only cruel immortality   5
Consumes; I wither slowly in thine arms,
Here at the quiet limit of the world,
A white-hair'd shadow roaming like a dream
The ever-silent spaces of the East,
Far-folded mists, and gleaming halls of morn.   10
   Alas! for this gray shadow, once a man—
So glorious in his beauty and thy choice,
Who madest him thy chosen, that he seem'd
To his great heart none other than a God!
I ask'd thee, 'Give me immortality.'   15
Then didst thou grant mine asking with a smile,
Like wealthy men who care not how they give.
But thy strong Hours indignant work'd their wills,
And beat me down and marr'd and wasted me,
And tho' they could not end me, left me maim'd   20
To dwell in presence of immortal youth,
Immortal age beside immortal youth,
And all I was in ashes. Can thy love,
Thy beauty, make amends, tho' even now,
Close over us, the silver star, thy guide,   25
Shines in those tremulous eyes that fill with tears
To hear me? Let me go; take back thy gift.
Why should a man desire in any way
To vary from the kindly race of men,
Or pass beyond the goal of ordinance   30
Where all should pause, as is most meet for all?
   A soft air fans the cloud apart; there comes
A glimpse of that dark world where I was born.
Once more the old mysterious glimmer steals
From thy pure brows, and from thy shoulders pure.   35
And bosom beating with a heart renew'd.
Thy cheek begins to redden thro' the gloom,
Thy sweet eyes brighten slowly close to mine,
Ere yet they blind the stars, and the wild team
Which love thee, yearning for thy yoke, arise   40
And shake the darkness from their loosen'd manes,
And beat the twilight into flakes of fire.
   Lo! ever thus thou growest beautiful
In silence, then before thine answer given
Departest, and thy tears are on my cheek.   45
   Why wilt thou ever scare me with thy tears,
And make me tremble lest a saying learnt,

In days far-off, on that dark earth, be true?
'The Gods themselves cannot recall their gifts.'
    Ay me! ay me! with what another heart   50
In days far-off, and with what other eyes
I used to watch—if I be he that watch'd—
The lucid outline forming round thee; saw
The dim curls kindle into sunny rings;
Changed with thy mystic change, and felt my blood   55
Glow with the glow that slowly crimson'd all
Thy presence and thy portals, while I lay,
Mouth, forehead, eyelids, growing dewy-warm
With kisses balmier than half-opening buds
Of April, and could hear the lips that kiss'd   60
Whispering I knew not what of wild and sweet,
Like that strange song I heard Apollo sing,
While Ilion like a mist rose into towers.
    Yet hold me not for ever in thine East;
How can my nature longer mix with thine?   65
Coldly thy rosy shadows bathe me, cold
Are all thy lights, and cold my wrinkled feet
Upon thy glimmering thresholds, when the steam
Floats up from those dim fields about the homes
Of happy men that have the power to die,   70
And grassy barrows of the happier dead.
Release me, and restore me to the ground.
Thou seest all things, thou wilt see my grave;
Thou wilt renew thy beauty morn by morn,
I earth in earth forget these empty courts,   75
And thee returning on thy silver wheels.

ROBERT BROWNING *(1812–1890)*

MY LAST DUCHESS

Ferrara

That's my last Duchess painted on the wall,
Looking as if she were alive. I call
That piece a wonder, now: Frà Pandolf's hands
Worked busily a day, and there she stands.
Will't please you sit and look at her? I said   5
"Frà Pandolf" by design, for never read
Strangers like you that pictured countenance,
The depth and passion of its earnest glance,
But to myself they turned (since none puts by
The curtain I have drawn for you, but I)   10
And seemed as they would ask me, if they durst,
How such a glance came there; so, not the first
Are you to turn and ask thus. Sir 'twas not
Her husband's presence only, called that spot
Of joy into the Duchess' cheek: perhaps   15

Frà Pandolf chanced to say, "Her mantle laps
Over my lady's wrist too much," or "Paint
Must never hope to reproduce the faint
Half-flush that dies along her throat." Such stuff
Was courtesy, she thought, and cause enough   20
For calling up that spot of joy. She had
A heart—how shall I say?—too soon made glad,
Too easily impressed; she liked whate'er
She looked on, and her looks went everywhere.
Sir, 'twas all one! My favor at her breast,   25
The drooping of the daylight in the West,
The bough of cherries some officious fool
Broke in the orchard for her, the white mule
She rode with round the terrace—all and each
Would draw from her alike the approving speech,   30
Or blush, at least. She thanked men,—good! but thanked
Somehow—I know not how—as if she ranked
My gift of a nine-hundred-years-old name
With anybody's gift. Who'd stoop to blame
This sort of trifling? Even had you skill   35
In speech—which I have not—to make your will
Quite clear to such an one, and say, "Just this
Or that in you disgusts me; here you miss,
Or there exceed the mark"—and if she let
Herself be lessoned so, nor plainly set   40
Her wits to yours, forsooth, and made excuse—
E'en then would be some stooping; and I choose
Never to stoop. Oh, sir, she smiled, no doubt,
Whene'er I passed her; but who passed without
Much the same smile? This grew; I gave commands;   45
Then all smiles stopped together. There she stands
As if alive. Will't please you rise? We'll meet
The company below, then. I repeat,
The Count your master's known munificence
Is ample warrant that no just pretense   50
Of mine for dowry will be disallowed;
Though his fair daughter's self, as I avowed
At starting, is my object. Nay, we'll go
Together down, sir. Notice Neptune, though,
Taming a sea-horse, thought a rarity,   60
Which Claus of Innsbruck cast in bronze for me!

ANDREA DEL SARTO*

Called "The Faultless Painter"

But do not let us quarrel any more,
No, my Lucrezia; bear with me for once:
Sit down and all shall happen as you wish.

---

* Andrea del Sarto (1486–1531) was a Florentine painter whom his student and biographer Giorgio Vasari thought had never fulfilled his promise as a painter. Lucrezia was in his wife.

You turn your face, but does it bring your heart?
I'll work then for your friend's friend, never fear,   5
Treat his own subject after his own way,
Fix his own time, accept too his own price,
And shut the money into this small hand
When next it takes mine. Will it? tenderly?
Oh, I'll content him,—but to-morrow, Love!   10
I often am much wearier than you think,
This evening more than usual, and it seems
As if—forgive now—should you let me sit
Here by the window with your hand in mine
And look a half-hour forth on Fiesole,   15
Both of one mind, as married people use,
Quietly, quietly the evening through,
I might get up to-morrow to my work
Cheerful and fresh as ever. Let us try.
To-morrow, how you shall be glad for this!   20
Your soft hand is a woman of itself,
And mine the man's bared breast she curls inside.
Don't count the time lost, neither; you must serve
For each of the five pictures we require:
It saves a model. So! keep looking so—   25
My serpentining beauty, rounds on rounds!
—How could you ever prick those perfect ears,
Even to put the pearl there! oh, so sweet—
My face, my moon, my everybody's moon,
Which everybody looks on and calls his,   30
And, I suppose, is looked on by in turn,
While she looks—no one's: very dear, no less.
You smile? why, there's my picture ready made,
There's what we painters call our harmony!
A common grayness silvers everything,—   35
All in a twilight, you and I alike
—You, at the point of your first pride in me
(That's gone you know),—but I, at every point;
My youth, my hope, my art, being all toned down
To yonder sober pleasant Fiesole.   40
There's the bell clinking from the chapel-top;
That length of convent-wall across the way
Holds the trees safer, huddled more inside;
The last monk leaves the garden; days decrease,
And autumn grows, autumn in everything.   45
Eh? the whole seems to fall into a shape
As if I saw alike my work and self
And all that I was born to be and do,
A twilight-piece. Love, we are in God's hand.
How strange now looks the life he makes us lead;   50
So free we seem, so fettered fast we are!

---

15 *Fiesole*: a suburb of Florence.

I feel he laid the fetter: let it lie!
This chamber for example—turn your head—
All that's behind us! You don't understand
Nor care to understand about my art,   55
But you can hear at least when people speak:
And that cartoon, the second from the door
—It is the thing, Love! so such things should be—
Behold Madonna!—I am bold to say.
I can do with my pencil what I know,   60
What I see, what at bottom of my heart
I wish for, if I ever wish so deep—
Do easily, too—when I say, perfectly,
I do not boast, perhaps: yourself are judge,
Who listened to the Legate's talk last week,   65
And just as much they used to say in France.
At any rate 'tis easy, all of it!
No sketches first, no studies, that's long past:
I do what many dream of all their lives,
—Dream? strive to do, and agonize to do,   70
And fail in doing. I could count twenty such
On twice your fingers, and not leave this town,
Who strive—you don't know how the others strive
To paint a little thing like that you smeared
Carelessly passing with your robes afloat,—   75
Yet do much less, so much less, Someone says,
(I know his name, no matter)—so much less!
Well, less is more, Lucrezia: I am judged.
There burns a truer light of God in them,
In their vexed beating stuffed and stopped-up brain,   80
Heart, or whate'er else, than goes on to prompt
This low-pulsed forthright craftsman's hand of mine.
Their works drop groundward, but themselves, I know,
Reach many a time a heaven that's shut to me,
Enter and take their place there sure enough,   85
Though they come back and cannot tell the world.
My works are nearer heaven, but I sit here.
The sudden blood of these men! at a word—
Praise them, it boils, or blame them, it boils too.
I, painting from myself and to myself,   90
Know what I do, am unmoved by men's blame
Or their praise either. Somebody remarks
Morello's outline there is wrongly traced,
His hue mistaken; what of that? or else,
Right traced and well ordered; what of that?   95
Speak as they please, what does the mountain care?
Ah, but a man's reach should exceed his grasp,
Or what's a heaven for? All is silver-gray
Placid and perfect with my art: the worse!

---

65 *Legate's*: a delegate of the Pope. 93 *Morello's*: a mountain near Florence.

I know both what I want and what might gain,   100
And yet how profitless to know, to sigh
"Had I been two, another and myself,
Our head would have o'erlooked the world!" No doubt.
Yonder's a work now, of that famous youth
The Urbinate who died five years ago.   105
('Tis copied, George Vasari sent it me.)
Well, I can fancy how he did it all,
Pouring his soul, with kings and popes to see,
Reaching, that heaven might so replenish him,
Above and through his art—for it gives way;   110
That arm is wrongly put—and there again—
A fault to pardon in the drawing's lines,
Its body, so to speak: its soul is right,
He means right—that, a child may understand.
Still, what an arm! and I could alter it: 115
But all the play, the insight, and the stretch—
Out of me! out of me! And wherefore out?
Had you enjoined them on me, given me soul,
We might have risen to Rafael, I and you!
Nay, Love, you did give all I asked, I think—   120
More than I merit, yes, by many times.
But had you—oh, with the same perfect brow,
And perfect eyes, and more than perfect mouth,
And the low voice my soul hears, as a bird
The fowler's pipe, and follows to the snare—   125
Had you, with these the same, but brought a mind!
Some women do so. Had the mouth there urged,
"God and the glory! never care for gain.
The present by the future, what is that?
Live for fame, side by side with Agnolo!   130
Rafael is waiting: up to God all three!"
I might have done it for you. So it seems—
Perhaps not. All is as God overrules.
Beside, incentives come from the soul's self;
The rest avail not. Why do I need you?   135
What wife had Rafael, or has Agnolo?
In this world, who can do a thing, will not;
And who would do it, cannot, I perceive:
Yet the will's somewhat—somewhat, too, the power—
And thus we half-men struggle. At the end,   140
God, I conclude, compensates, punishes.
'Tis safer for me, if the award be strict,
That I am something underrated here,
Poor this long while, despised, to speak the truth.
I dared not, do you know, leave home all day,   145

---

105 *The Urbinate*: Raphael Sanzio (1483–1520). 106 *George Vasari*: a student of Andrea del Sarto. 130 *Agnolo*: Michelangelo (1475–1564).

For fear of chancing on the Paris lords.
The best is when they pass and look aside;
But they speak sometimes; I must bear it all.
Well may they speak! That Francis, that first time,
And that long festal year at Fontainebleau!   150
I surely then could sometimes leave the ground,
Put on the glory, Rafael's daily wear,
In that humane great monarch's golden look,—
One finger in his beard or twisted curl
Over his mouth's good mark that made the smile,   155
One arm about my shoulder, round my neck,
The jingle of his gold chain in my ear,
I painting proudly with his breath on me,
All his court round him, seeing with his eyes,
Such frank French eyes, and such a fire of souls   160
Profuse, my hand kept plying by those hearts,—
And, best of all, this, this, this face beyond,
This in the background, waiting on my work,
To crown the issue with a last reward!
A good time, was it not, my kingly days?   165
And had you not grown restless...but I know—
'Tis done and past; 'twas right, my instinct said;
Too live the life grew, golden and not grey,
And I'm the weak-eyed bat no sun should tempt
Out of the grange whose four walls make his world.   170
How could it end in any other way?
You called me, and I came home to your heart.
The triumph was—to reach and stay there; since
I reached it ere the triumph, what is lost?
Let my hands frame your face in your hair's gold,   175
You beautiful Lucrezia that are mine!
"Rafael did this, Andrea painted that;
The Roman's is the better when you pray,
But still the other's Virgin was his wife"—
Men will excuse me. I am glad to judge   180
Both pictures in your presence; clearer grows
My better fortune, I resolve to think.
For, do you know, Lucrezia, as God lives,
Said one day Agnolo, his very self,
To Rafael...I have known it all these years...   185
(When the young man was flaming out his thoughts
Upon a palace-wall for Rome to see,
Too lifted up in heart because of it)
"Friend, there's a certain sorry little scrub
Goes up and down our Florence, none cares how,   190
Who, were he set to plan and execute
As you are, pricked on by your popes and kings,

---

149 *Francis*: King Francis I of France.

Would bring the sweat into that brow of yours!"
To Rafael's!—And indeed the arm is wrong.
I hardly dare...yet, only you to see,   195
Give the chalk here—quick, thus the line should go!
Ay, but the soul! he's Rafael! rub it out!
Still, all I care for, if he spoke the truth,
(What he? why, who but Michel Agnolo?
Do you forget already words like those?)   200
If really there was such a chance, so lost,—
Is, whether you're—not grateful—but more pleased.
Well, let me think so. And you smile indeed!
This hour has been an hour! Another smile?
If you would sit thus by me every night   205
I should work better, do you comprehend?
I mean that I should earn more, give you more.
See, it is settled dusk now; there's a star;
Morello's gone, the watch-lights show the wall,
The cue-owls speak the name we call them by.   210
Come from the window, love,—come in, at last,
Inside the melancholy little house
We built to be so gay with. God is just.
King Francis may forgive me: oft at nights
When I look up from painting, eyes tired out,   215
The walls become illumined, brick from brick
Distinct, instead of mortar, fierce bright gold,
That gold of his I did cement them with!
Let us but love each other. Must you go?
That Cousin here again? he waits outside?   220
Must see you—you, and not with me? Those loans?
More gaming debts to pay? you smiled for that?
Well, let smiles buy me! have you more to spend?
While hand and eye and something of a heart
Are left me, work's my ware, and what's it worth?   225
I'll pay my fancy. Only let me sit
The gray remainder of the evening out,
Idle, you call it, and muse perfectly
How I could paint, were I but back in France,
One picture, just one more—the Virgin's face,   230
Not yours this time! I want you at my side
To hear them—that is, Michel Agnolo—
Judge all I do and tell you of its worth.
Will you? To-morrow, satisfy your friend.
I take the subjects for his corridor,   235
Finish the portrait out of hand—there, there,
And throw him in another thing or two
If he demurs; the whole should prove enough
To pay for this same Cousin's freak. Beside,
What's better and what's all I care about,   240

Get you the thirteen scudi for the ruff!
Love, does that please you? Ah, but what does he,
The Cousin! what does he to please you more?
   I am grown peaceful as old age to-night.
I regret little, I would change still less.   245
Since there my past life lies, why alter it?
The very wrong to Francis!—it is true
I took his coin, was tempted and complied,
And built this house and sinned, and all is said.
My father and my mother died of want.   250
Well, had I riches of my own? you see
How one gets rich! Let each one bear his lot.
They were born poor, lived poor, and poor they died:
And I have labored somewhat in my time
And not been paid profusely. Some good son   255
Paint my two hundred pictures—let him try!
No doubt, there's something strikes a balance. Yes,
You loved me quite enough, it seems tonight.
This must suffice me here. What would one have?
In heaven, perhaps, new chances, one more chance—   260
Four great walls in the New Jerusalem,
Meted on each side by the angel's reed,
For Leonard, Rafael, Agnolo and me
To cover—the three first without a wife,
While I have mine! So—still they overcome   265
Because there's still Lucrezia—as I choose.
Again the Cousin's whistle! Go my Love.

AMY LOWELL *(1874–1925)*

PATTERNS*

I walk down the garden-paths,
And all the daffodils
Are blowing, and the bright blue squills.
I walk down the patterned garden-paths
In my stiff, brocaded gown.   5
With my powdered hair and jewelled fan,
I too am a rare
Pattern. As I wander down
The garden-paths.
My dress is richly figured,   10

* From *The Complete Poetical Works of Amy Lowell*. Copyright 1955 by Houghton Mifflin Company. Reprinted by permission of the publisher, Houghton Mifflin Company.

241 *scudi*: gold coins; *ruff*: perch.   262 *angel's reed*: measuring rod.   263 *Leonard*: Leonardo da Vinci (1452–1519).

And the train
Makes a pink and silver stain
On the gravel, and the thrift
Of the borders.
Just a plate of current fashion,   15
Tripping by in high-heeled, ribboned shoes.
Not a softness anywhere about me,
Only whalebone and brocade.
And I sink on a seat in the shade
Of a lime-tree. For my passion   20
Wars against the stiff brocade.
The daffodils and squills
Flutter in the breeze
As they please.
And I weep;   25
For the lime-tree is in blossom
And one small flower has dropped upon my bosom.

And the plashing of waterdrops
In the marble fountain
Comes down the garden-paths.   30
The dripping never stops.
Underneath my stiffened gown
Is the softness of a woman bathing in a marble basin,
A basin in the midst of hedges grown
So thick, she cannot see her lover hiding,   35
But she guesses he is near,
And the sliding of the water
Seems the stroking of a dear
Hand upon her.
What is Summer in a fine brocaded gown!   40
I should like to see it lying in a heap upon the ground.
All the pink and silver crumpled up on the ground.

I would be the pink and silver as I ran along the paths,
And he would stumble after,
Bewildered by my laughter.   45
I should see the sun flashing from his swordhilt and the buckles on his shoes.
I would choose
To lead him in a maze along the patterned paths,
A bright and laughing maze for my heavybooted lover.
Till he caught me in the shade,   50
And the buttons of his waistcoat bruised my body as he clasped me,
Aching, melting, unafraid.
With the shadows of the leaves and the sundrops,
And the plopping of the waterdrops,
All about us in the open afternoon—   55
I am very like to swoon
With the weight of this brocade,
For the sun sifts through the shade.

Underneath the fallen blossom
In my bosom   60
Is a letter I have hid.
It was brought to me this morning by a rider from the Duke.
"Madam, we regret to inform you that Lord Hartwell
Died in action Thursday se'nnight."
As I read it in the white, morning sunlight,   65
The letters squirmed like snakes.
"Any answer, Madam," said my footman.
"No," I told him.
"See that the messenger takes some refreshment.
No, no answer."   70
And I walked into the garden,
Up and down the patterned paths,
In my stiff, correct brocade.
The blue and yellow flowers stood up proudly in the sun,
Each one.   75
I stood upright too,
Held rigid to the pattern
By the stiffness of my gown;
Up and down I walked,
Up and down.   80

In a month he would have been my husband.
In a month, here, underneath this lime,
We would have broke the pattern;
He for me, and I for him,
He as Colonel, I as Lady,   85
On this shady seat.
He had a whim
That sunlight carried blessing.
And I answered, "It shall be as you have said."
Now he is dead.   90
In Summer and in Winter I shall walk
Up and down
The patterned garden paths
In my stiff, brocaded gown.
The squills and daffodils   95
Will give place to pillared roses, and to asters, and to snow.
I shall go
Up and down
In my gown.
Gorgeously arrayed,   100
Boned and stayed.
And the softness of my body will be guarded from embrace
By each button, hook, and lace.
For the man who should loose me is dead,
Fighting with the Duke in Flanders,   105
In a pattern called a war.
Christ! What are patterns for?

T. S. ELIOT *(1888–1964)*

GERONTION*

Thou hast nor youth nor age
But as it were an after dinner sleep
Dreaming of both.

Here I am, an old man in a dry month,
Being read to by a boy, waiting for rain.
I was neither at the hot gates
Nor fought in the warm rain
Nor knee deep in the salt marsh, heaving a cutlass,   5
Bitten by flies, fought.
My house is a decayed house,
And the Jew squats on the window sill, the owner,
Spawned in some estaminet of Antwerp,
Blistered in Brussels, patched and peeled in London.   10
The goat coughs at night in the field overhead;
Rocks, moss, stonecrop, iron, merds.
The woman keeps the kitchen, makes tea,
Sneezes at evening, poking the peevish gutter.
                                        I an old man,   15
A dull head among windy spaces.

Signs are taken for wonders. 'We would see a sign!'
The word within a word, unable to speak a word,
Swaddled with darkness. In the juvescence of the year
Came Christ the tiger   20

In depraved May, dogwood and chestnut, flowering judas,
To be eaten, to be divided, to be drunk
Among whispers; by Mr. Silvero
With caressing hands, at Limoges
Who walked all night in the next room;   25
By Hakagawa, bowing among the Titians;
By Madame de Tornquist, in the dark room
Shifting the candles; Fraülein von Kulp
Who turned in the hall, one hand on the door. Vacant shuttles
Weave the wind. I have no ghosts,   30
An old man in a draughty house
Under a windy knob.

After such knowledge, what forgiveness? Think now
History has many cunning passages, contrived corridors
And issues, deceives with whispering ambitions,   35

Guides us by vanities. Think now.
She gives when our attention is distracted
And what she gives, gives with such supple confusions
That the giving famishes the craving. Gives too late
What's not believed in, or if still believed,   40
In memory only, reconsidered passion. Gives too soon
Into weak hands, what's thought can be dispensed with
Till the refusal propagates a fear. Think
Neither fear nor courage saves us. Unnatural vices
Are fathered by our heroism. Virtues   45
Are forced upon us by our impudent crimes.
These tears are shaken from the wrath-bearing tree.
The tiger springs in the new year. Us he devours. Think at last
We have not reached conclusion, when I
Stiffen in a rented house. Think at last   50
I have not made this show purposelessly
And it is not by any concitation
Of the backward devils.
I would meet you upon this honestly.
I that was near your heart was removed therefrom   55
To lose beauty in terror, terror in inquisition.
I have lost my passion: why should I need to keep it
Since what is kept must be adulterated?
I have lost my sight, smell, hearing, taste and touch:
How should I use them for your closer contact?   60
These with a thousand small deliberations
Protract the profit of their chilled delirium,
Excite the membrane, when the sense has cooled,
With pungent sauces, multiply variety
In a wilderness of mirrors. What will the spider do,   65
Suspend its operations, will the weevil
Delay? De Bailhache, Fresca, Mrs. Cammel, whirled
Beyond the circuit of the shuddering Bear
In fractured atoms. Gull against the wind, in the windy straits
Of Belle Isle, or running on the Horn,   70
White feathers in the snow, the Gulf claims,
And an old man driven by the Trades
To a sleepy corner.

                         Tenants of the house,
Thoughts of a dry brain in a dry season.   75

Pastoral

Introduction

The view that pastorals are short poems constructed as dialogue or "eclogue" encounters among shepherds and are therefore pleasantly artificial and escapist is common but partly misleading. Pastorals *do* sometimes permit the reader to cavort (vicariously) on the greensward or mourn tunefully some sweet loss; but even in the *Idylls* (or "little pictures") of Theocritus, usually regarded as the originator of the form, the pleasantness of the scene is often undermined with irony and a certain amount of rural, colloquial realism. Nor are Theocritus' figures always rustics: they include not only shepherds and nymphs but fishermen and urban housewives. Even in the eighteenth century, when classical rules were more strictly observed than either before or since in English literature, pastoral types tended to proliferate, at a rate embarrassing to the purist, in burlesque eclogues, town eclogues, elegiac, satiric, and piscatory (fisherman) eclogues, and also in "topographical" poetry (which concerns a prominent geographical landmark such as a forest or hill and is written in a mood and style more exalted than normal shepherd poems). If these types—not to mention pastoral drama, pastoral opera, pastoral romance, pastoral-heroic combinations such as *Paradise Lost* and Sidney's *The Arcadia,* and the works of such poets as Blake, Keats, Wordsworth, and Frost—are allowed on the periphery of pastoral, we must revise the common view of it.

But if we claim a foothold for these variants and no longer derive the distinguishing feature of pastorals from pastors and pastures, what becomes of the concept of pastoral as a literary genre? Having taken away the sheep, what can we put in their place? Whatever beast offers itself, we must insist that it be two-sided, like Pan himself, the revered and reviled god of nature, half man and half goat—for pastoral is pre-eminently concerned with contrasts, the chief of which is the contrast of the simple life with some form of complexity. Simplicity usually finds a rural expression, whether it be the Arcadia of the old shepherd poem, the English countryside, or Keats's "untrodden region of [the] mind"; complexity is normally represented by life at court or in town or in a technological culture. Thus Blake's two collections of lyrics, *Songs of Innocence* and *Songs of Experience* present a series of contrasts between rural scenes and industrial life and between the uncomplicated play of children and psychological disturbances on the underside of experience. In a variation of the same principle of contrasts, Wordsworth's *Intimations Ode* sets childhood and the visionary experience of nature against an adult world of pain and mortality.

Pastoral, then, offers a working contrast, an outside view of a world in which lambs do not come home wagging tails behind them *from the perspective* of a world in which they do. A number of things may happen when two such radically different worlds are juxtaposed. They may *remain* poles apart, thus forcing us to adjust to their differences with some form of mental gymnastics (such as irony). Or one may be *transformed into* the other, perhaps by some magic or godlike power such as that which changes death to life in Milton's *Lycidas* or the idealist philosophy of Shelley's *Adonais*. Whatever the possibility of exchanging the real world for paradise, if the idyllic life is represented by rustics, the sophisticated poet and reader are likely to look down on it as well as yearn for it. This double attitude is a means of having it both ways—a little like urban dwellers, fleeing the city for the forest, who immediately set about "improving" the wilderness with canned food and refrigerators. In fact, the ambivalence that sophisticated people feel toward the simple life is no less prominent today than in the time of Theocritus. We associate rusticity with hillbillies and yokels at one moment and with folk songs and fishing poles at the next.

Most pastoral poems preserve something of this ambivalence of disdain and yearning. Anti-pastorals emphasize disdain alone, and escapist or purely idyllic poems offer a straightforward, sensuous absorption in nature—a flight from reality into a world of primrose paths and sylvan pleasure. The norm of pastoral, however, is something else.

Let us look at a typical case, Robert Frost's poem "Directive," which while appearing to take us on a pleasant journey into nature offers something quite different from escape:*

> Back out of all this now too much for us,
> Back in a time made simple by the loss
> Of detail, burned, dissolved, and broken off
> Like graveyard marble sculpture in the weather,
> There is a house that is no more a house   5
> Upon a farm that is no more a farm
> And in a town that is no more a town.
> The road there, if you'll let a guide direct you
> Who only has at heart your getting lost,
> May seem as if it should have been a quarry—   10
> Great monolithic knees the former town

Long since gave up pretence of keeping covered.
And there's a story in a book about it:
Besides the wear of iron wagon wheels
The ledges show lines ruled southeast northwest,   15
The chisel work of an enormous Glacier
That braced his feet against the Arctic Pole.
You must not mind a certain coolness from him
Still said to haunt this side of Panther Mountain.
Nor need you mind the serial ordeal   20
Of being watched from forty cellar holes
As if by eye pairs out of forty firkins.
As for the woods' excitement over you
That sends light rustle rushes to their leaves,
Charge that to upstart inexperience.   25
They think too much of having shaded out
A few old pecker-fretted apple trees.
Make yourself up a cheering song of how
Someone's road home from work this once was,
Who may be just ahead of you on foot   30
Or creaking with a buggy load of grain.
The height of the adventure is the height
Of country where two village cultures faded
Into each other. Both of them are lost.
And if you're lost enough to find yourself   35
By now, pull in your ladder road behind you
And put a sign up CLOSED for all but me.
Then make yourself at home. The only field
Now left's no bigger than a harness gall.
First there's the children's house of make believe,   40
Some shattered dishes underneath a pine,
The playthings in the playhouse of the children.
Weep for what little things could make them glad.
Then for the house that is no more a house,
But only a belilaced cellar hole,   45
Now slowly closing like a dent in dough.
This was no playhouse but a house in earnest.
Your destination and your destiny's
A brook that was the water of the house,
Cold as a spring as yet so near its source,   50
Too lofty and original to rage.
(We know the valley streams that when aroused
Will leave their tatters hung on barb and thorn.)
I have kept hidden in the instep arch
Of an old cedar at the waterside   55
A broken drinking goblet like the Grail
Under a spell so the wrong ones can't find it,
So can't get saved, as Saint Mark says they mustn't.
(I stole the goblet from the children's playhouse.)
Here are your waters and your watering place.   60
Drink and be whole again beyond confusion.

Whereas he maintains the traditional pastoralist's view of "all this now too much for us"—that is, the complexities of modern urban life—Frost beckons the reader into something other than a bower of bliss. We return to nature only to lose ourselves—in change, decay, and the disturbingly close presence of an indifferent world. We become aware only gradually of the irony of the first sentence, which suggests that nature's processes of burning and breaking off are simplifications on our behalf. Our full realization of what the "simple" life involves is delayed and cushioned by our guide, who stays at our elbow, reassuring us—apparently with good intentions and the best of manners— that he has our interests at heart. Finally, when we are indeed "lost" in nature, having grown downward and backward into a childhood where nature is too large and frighteningly anthropomorphic for us, we are told to "weep for what little things could make [the children] glad" and for the house that was a "house in earnest."

At this point many *anti*-pastoralists would have stopped: running from problems of civilization, we have encountered uncivilized problems of even greater magnitude. But Frost takes us one step further: our "destination" is the cold spring from which the poet drinks, "near its source" in primal nature. Unlike the stream of other poets (Frost elsewhere names Matthew Arnold in particular), this one is "too lofty and original to rage," and it is this loftiness that we are to share with him in order to be "whole again beyond confusion." This may be a diminished salvation compared with that of the Holy Grail legends, but it preserves something of the saving simplicity of the child's world. Hence we are not only consoled for the death that nature designs for us but are given a new perspective on the fate of houses, farms, and towns; we share in nature's inevitable reassertion of sovereignty.

II. Despite the frequent ambivalence of nature in pastoral, the contrast between simplicity and complexity, rustic and urban life often implies a contrast between *what is* (the real) and *what ought to be* (the ideal imaged as natural beauty). Because the idyllic world is characterized by innocence, freedom, and harmony between man and nature and reflects on the fragmentation and uprootedness of urban man, it is translatable "upward" as an image of perfection on a mythic level (the Golden Age, the Garden of Eden). Thus Pan and Venus appear frequently in pastoral landscapes, and rustics who have dealings with them clearly move in higher circles than asphalt men. Those gods exercise control over basic human experiences like love, work, and death, whereas the gods of the city-dweller are the time-clock, the actuarial tables of life insurance companies, and the local newspaper's Miss Lonelyhearts.

In this idealized form, pastoral, like one kind of romance (see the introduction to "Romance"), has an affinity to the wish-fulfillment dream, in which the imagination, well fueled with desire, soars beyond the leaden realities of fact and reason. Although myths are not always consoling and Venus, we may note, usually brings pain and suffering into the rustic world, love pangs in Arcadia are never quite what they are in Brooklyn or Chattanooga. Existence in Arcadia is transfigured by the imagination; its sharper edges are blunted, its suffering is diffused, and some of its ugliness purged.

We are well advised in saying "some" of its ugliness. In the hands of Theocritus, Virgil, Spenser, Milton, Marvell, Wordsworth, Hardy, Frost, and Stevens, the pastoral retreat is almost always both desirable *and* undesirable.

The idea of Arcadia is sometimes conceived simply to make the ravages of love and death, its two most formidable intruders, seem the more shocking. The intrusion of death, in fact, is more ominous and startling, less subject to idealization, than that of love, for one might suppose that death would seem to have no claim on Arcadia. In one recurrent pastoral motif, for instance, shepherds are shocked to discover in the midst of their idyllic landscape a tomb on which are inscribed the words of Death, *et in Arcadia ego* ("even in Arcadia, I am"). So the death of Lycidas forces Milton to "shatter leaves" with "forced fingers rude" before the mellowing year; the intrusion of Juliana causes Marvell's Mower to "mow" himself and prepare for his grave; and death itself becomes in Stevens' "Sunday Morning" the "mother of beauty."

Nevertheless, as the example from Stevens suggests, the poet frequently reasserts control over death, too, after it has gained entrance to Arcadia. Adonis may lie dead and bleeding in Bion's "Lament for Adonis," but he does not, as Claudio in *Measure for Measure* fears he himself will, "lie in cold obstruction and...rot"; rather, the "blood and tears become flowers upon the ground": "of the blood comes the rose, and of the tears the wild-flower." The mythic pastoralist, when he has reduced life to its rudiments, translates it upward as well, like Marvell's wanderer in "The Garden," who annihilates "all that's made / To a green thought in a green shade" and then creates "far other worlds and other seas" in the workshop of the imagination.

The success of his poem will depend on the degree to which pastoral innocence and painful experience reciprocally illuminate each other: innocence viewed from the perspective of experience is seen as frail and unrealistic; experience viewed from the perspective of innocence is seen as corrupt and artificial. The nostalgia for innocence—whether innocence is a lost phase of imaginative existence (as in Blake), an earlier historical time and place (the Biblical Eden or the Golden Age), or childhood seen in the soft focus of adult recollection (Hopkins' "Spring and Fall: To a Young Child")—presupposes in any case a diminished present, an "iron age" or fallen world.

In Marlowe's "The Passionate Shepherd to His Love" (p. 187), for instance, we seem at first glance to have only an unqualified idealization of the rustic world—a hopelessly unreal Arcadia where the rivers are too "shallow" to restrict human freedom of movement (too shallow also to require stand-by resuscitators for shepherd swimmers), where man has no need to conquer nature because she graciously yields up her treasures for his use, and where the rhythms of human experience are synchronized with those of nature. Moreover, the society that the passionate shepherd would have the nymph join is unlike any outside those populated by the imagination. There are no negotiations between shepherds and their employers, no wars, no frowning moralists to say they ought not: only a ring of merry dancers wearing gowns of finest wool and buckles of gold. The "contract" on which he would have her signature is based, then, on both an ideal nature and an ideal society. Naturally if one changes the scene, as Ralegh does in his answer to the poem (p. 188), or the society, as C. Day Lewis does in his modern answer (the speaker can offer only the peace and plenty that "chance employment may afford"), the terms of the bargain also change.

But if we regard Marlowe's poem as an example merely of escapist pastoral we are failing to observe that the shepherd, situated just within the borders of Arcadia, is speaking "out" to the nymph, who comes from the real world and stands indecisive, weighing the merits of Arcadia against those of an undefined reality. The nymph's hesitation, the conditional quality of Arcadia for her—"*If* these delights thy mind may move"—and our realization, therefore, that the shepherd is on his best rhetorical behavior, compel us to supply the contrast of ideal and real that the poem itself does not explicitly make.

III.   In a poem like "The Passionate Shepherd to His Love," then, the pastoral world includes the best of society and the best of nature, both delivered from the explicit anxieties of normal reality. We note simultaneously that shepherds, like others, use the tactics of salesmanship and yet that the world in which they live is more desirable than our own. But as the nymph's answer in Ralegh's poem illustrates, it is not impossible for pastoral to move in the opposite direction. Whereas in pastorals of the "Passionate Shepherd" type death and love are purged of their destructive potentials and take on the character of pastoral ideality or become somewhat isolated intruders, incongruous and rather puzzlingly foreign, in another kind of pastoral we find the tendency of the real world to encroach on the ideal given such prominence that the real world destroys either the ideal or man's relationship to it. Crabbe, for instance, reacting against an eighteenth-century pastoral that threatened to petrify in artificiality, rejects the notion of romantic rusticity and depicts the "real" life of the rural village with an eye to its poverty, shabbiness, and immorality. The light cast by the real on the ideal has greater candlepower than that cast in the reverse direction; in fact, the ideal tends to become indistinguishable from the real. Keats's "Ode to a Nightingale" varies that pattern by emphasizing not so much a diminution of the ideal as an attenuation of man's relations to it. At the close of the poem the nightingale, which stands for a permanence and beauty ardently desired by the poet, is "buried deep / In the next valley-glade," leaving the poet in bewilderment. In this poem the ideal remains ideal, but enduring communion with it is unavailable to man. Still another version of diminished pastoral can be seen in Marvell's "The Mower to the Glow-worms," where Juliana causes the Mower to go astray in the forest, never to find his "home." If man's basic links with nature are thus broken, the hope of reconciling dream and reality inevitably fails; in the jargon of the pastoral, the "greenness of the grass" is destroyed, just as Juliana destroys the Mower who cuts the grass: "She / What I do to the grass, does to my Thoughts and me." Instead of achieving a lasting rapport with nature, the shepherd must contemplate the descent of chaos: "And Flowers, and Grass, and I and all / Will in one common Ruin fall."

One basic pattern of pastoral, then, brings the ideal and the real into a contrast in which both are illuminated but in which the tendency is for the ideal to predominate. The other basic pattern diminishes the ideal so that it becomes merely another version of the real (Crabbe's *The Village*), or pictures the ideal as such, but then destroys it (the Mower poems), or stresses the impossibility of the ideal for man (Keats's "Ode to a Nightingale").

As twentieth-century readers we are more familiar with the latter kind of pastoral, or at least with the experience it describes. When Yeats places the modern world beside the old, comfortable myths, for example, it invariably fails to measure up to them—to provide the emotional, aesthetic, and imaginative satisfaction that they offer—yet it wins anyway:

> Locke sank into a swoon:
> The Garden died;
> God took the spinning-Jenny
> Out of his side.*

The companion of the modern Adam, his helpmate "Jenny," is not the nymph of the paradisal "Garden" but one of the primal machines of the Industrial Revolution, and Eden has been reduced to a deistic factory. Modern pastoral on the whole has only "one foot in Eden" and sometimes none at all. Thus in Frost's *New Hampshire*† we encounter the man with the double axe, who

> went alone against a grove of trees;
> But his heart failing him, he dropped the axe
> And ran for shelter quoting Matthew Arnold:
> "Nature is cruel, man is sick of blood;"...
> He had a special terror of the flux
> That showed itself in dendrophobia.

Many twentieth-century poets and their readers, although not exactly victims of dendrophobia (fear of trees), feel alienated from nature and highly dubious about idyllic landscapes. Since Darwin and Spencer, nature has been regarded more often as something brutal and mindless than as a verdurous Arcadia bequeathed to man by the gods and endowed with a sympathetic responsiveness to human feelings. Perhaps only in the nineteenth century could the established poetic practice of attributing human emotions to nature be suddenly (and disapprovingly) labeled a "pathetic fallacy." And perhaps only in the twentieth century could the following view of nature emerge with such starkness:‡

> When mountain rocks and leafy trees
> And clouds and things like these,
> With edges,
>
> Caricature the human face,
> Such scribblings have no grace
> Nor peace—
>
> The bulbous nose, the sunken chin,
> The ragged mouth in grin
> Of cretin.
>
> Nature is always so: you find
> That all she has of mind
> Is wind,
>
> Retching among the empty spaces,
> Ruffling the idiot grasses,
> The sheeps' fleeces.

> Whose pleasures are excreting, poking,
> Havocking and sucking,
> Sleepy licking.
>
> Whose griefs are melancholy,
> Whose flowers are oafish,
> Whose waters, silly,
> Whose birds, raffish,
> Whose fish, fish.

Here we begin to move outside the borders of pastoral toward invective and satire. The "greenness of the grass" is not destroyed; it never existed—it was all merely a quirk of the eye. In "The Passionate Shepherd to His Love," desire and imagination dominate fact and reason; but in "Nature's Lineaments," as in "The Nymph's Reply [to the Passionate Shepherd]," just the reverse is true. Yet the scathing tone of the speaker in "Nature's Lineaments" reflects an animus that looks suspiciously like disenchantment turned vicious, as though reason can be kept immune to desire only if given continuous injections of contempt; and in Ralegh's "The Nymph's Reply," although time destroys flowers, fields, and youth, and although the artifacts of the pastoral world are "in folly ripe, in reason rotten," still the imaginative appeal of the idyllic seeps back into the final stanza:

> But could youth last and love still breed,
> Had joys no date nor age no need,
> Then these delights my mind might move
> To live with thee and be thy love.

Thus even in poems of a radically "diminished" type we find an implicit suggestion of the contrast between simplicity and complexity characteristic of most pastoral.

IV.   Because an ideal is what-is-not, it is normally given some distance from sharp-edged, contemporary reality. The grammatical equivalent of that distance is the past or future tense and the contrary-to-fact subjunctive mood (the poet's "once long ago it was so" being another way of saying "would it were so now" or perhaps "it may be so sometime"). Partly because of this distance, the ideal landscape is useful as a framing device in other forms than the pastoral. The poet may combine pastoral with heroic modes, for instance. Since heroic modes emphasize the active life and pastoral modes the contemplative or even indolent life, the combination may seem strange, if not an outright contradiction. But heroic accomplishment is one way of *changing* the world to match one's idea of what it ought to be. Hence if the founding of empires is set in the context of some image of the Golden Age or paradise, the relation of action to contemplation or dream may become that of *accomplishment* to *program*. The function of the heroic element is to provide a means of transformation and of the pastoral element to envision a desired ideal.

Pastoral romances such as Sidney's *The Arcadia* and Shakespeare's *As You Like It* illustrate variations of that combination. They bring together shepherds and "high" society (knights, kings, noble lovers) in order to assess the relative merits of the quiet life and the life of heroic name-making and status codes. But any number of combinations is possible. For instance, Pope in *The Dunciad* combines both epic and pastoral elements with satire. An initial perfect creation, the product of the Word, or Logos, that said "let there be" and pronounced its cosmos good, contrasts with the uncreative words of Dulness, who instead of breathing life into clay sinks the spirit in a confusion of books; and the epic march of civilization westward, as in *The Aeneid*, contrasts with the encroaching reign of Dulness' herd of scribblers. Thus Queen Dulness *cancels out* both England's Eden (God's pastoral) and civilization (the accomplishment of heroes).

In these combinations, the means of *transforming* What Is into What Ought To Be is often critical, because given the contrasts in which pastoral functions, the inevitable question is what to do about them. How are we to "return to Eden" or move forward to Utopia or merely get rid of the dunces? Heroic modes such as Milton's *Paradise Lost* and Sidney's *The Arcadia* propose certain values and actions that represent real achievements against real obstacles. The most noticeable forces of transformation in pastoral proper are the generative powers of nature (manifest in cyclical rebirths of spring, for instance), the power of the gods to reinstate paradise, and the imagination, which reaches its destination with jet-like speed and without the high cost of fuel. (Each of these restorative and creative powers may be thought in some way analogous to the original power that made Arcadia or paradise "long ago," thus bringing the distant "myth" into the present.)

Consider the pastoral elegy, for instance. The poet begins with the given fact of someone's death: there has been a "heavy change" from better days, not so long ago in this case. The desired end is some kind of personal rebirth, and the question again is how to bring it about. The key to the poet's values is precisely the force he imagines to be capable of doing so. The Greek pastoralist is likely to return the dead one to nature, where he is reborn yearly as some vegetation figure. Milton answers in "Lycidas" that he "who walked the waves" will resurrect him. Shelley finds that Adonais, liberated from his body and from matter generally through death, has entered the realm of pure Ideas, which the imagination of the poet also penetrates. The goal in each of these elegies is to define "death" in a consoling fashion and thus to redefine nature as well.

It may be, however, that the poet, like Frost, finds no such transformative "machine" as Shelley's or Milton's (the Platonists' and Christians'), in which case he must find another alternative. Most likely he adopts an *attitude* that will make the discrepancy between the ideal and the real palatable. Pastoral transformations alter reality, and pastoral attitudes adjust to it as it is. Irony, for instance, because it allows two contrary statements to live side by side, is suited to such a purpose. If in the midst of a boiling heat-wave one says "marvelous weather we're having," he has done something linguistically (or "symbolically") where he could do nothing "industrially": because no amount of constructive exertion or magic will change the weather, he talks it away. The wry common-sensical humor of the rustic, the ceremonial sorrow of the elegist, the shrewd irony of a Frostian speaker, the nostalgic dream-state of the romantic are all means of nontransformational adjustment. (Notice in Edwin Muir's "One Foot in Eden," [p. 241], for example, the "fortunate fall" adjustment in which the speaker decides, philosophically, that the world outside Eden is better in its way than paradise because its trials extract higher virtues from us.)

Reducing these patterns to a set of formulas does some violence to the works in which they occur, but perhaps we can summarize them in this way: given the basic pastoral contrast of the ideal and the real, the poet can bring them together (1) for a satiric exposure of either, (2) as a framing device for defining heroic transformation, (3) as a measure of some other transformational power such as Shelley's "death" and Milton's Christ, and (4) as preparation for some attitudinal adjustment. In each case the "grammar" of pastoral alters accordingly. We may be implicitly urged to action in the imperative mood, led to yearn for What Is Not in the subjunctive, or made to ridicule those who do not measure up to the idyllic standard. In any case since pastoral elements may turn up as a dimension of forms as different as the epic (*Paradise Lost*), romantic narratives ("Lamia"), collections of lyrics (Blake's *Songs of Innocence* and *Songs of Experience*), and the novel (Hardy's *Tess*, Golding's *Lord of the Flies*), the student should be alert to the assistance that the concept gives him in approaching a diversity of works.

THEOCRITUS (*third century*, B.C.)

This justly famous dialogue between two fishermen, although very possibly not the work of Theocritus himself, illustrates the careful balance of attitudes toward rustic life that Theocritus frequently maintains in his *Idylls*. Hungry and poverty-stricken, the two fishermen scarcely lead ideal lives. But they are closer to the mythic sea than affluent urban dwellers are, and the dreamer of the two obviously enjoys fishing too much and knows his craft too well to be deflated by the realistic advice of his friend. From the clash of the idyllic, rustic element and the hard economic facts of the fishermen's lives, the poet fashions a humorous compromise.

TWENTY-FIRST IDYLL

Translated by J. M. Edmonds*

There's but one stirrer-up of the crafts, Diophantus, and her name is Poverty. She is the true teacher of labour; for a man of toil may not so much as sleep for the disquietude of his heart. Nay, if he nod ever so little o' nights, then is his slumber broke suddenly short by the cares that beset him.

One night against the leafy wall of a wattled cabin there lay together upon a bed of dry tangle two old catchers of fish. Beside them were laid the instruments of their calling: their creels, their rods, their hooks, their weedy nets and lines, their weels and rush-woven lobster-pots, some net-ropes, a pair of oars, and upon its props an aged coble. Beneath their heads lay a little mat, and for coverlets they had their jackets of frieze. This was all the means and all the riches of these poor fishermen. Key, door, watchdog, had they none; all such things were ill-store to the likes of them, seeing in that house kept Poverty watch and ward; neither dwelt there any neighbour at their gates, but the very cabin-walls were hemmed by the soft and delicate upflowing of the sea.

Now or ever the chariot of the Moon was halfway of its course, the fishermen's labour and trouble did rouse them, and thrusting slumber from their eyelids stirred up speech in their hearts.

Reprinted by permission of the publishers from *The Greek Bucolic Poets,* Trans. J. M. Edmonds, Harvard University Press.

ASPHALION

It seems they speak not true, friend, that say the summer nights grow less when they bring us the long days. Already I have had a thousand dreams, and the dawn is not yet. Or am I wrong when I say how long the watches of these nights are?

FRIEND

Asphalion, the pretty summer deserves not thy fault-finding. 'Tis not that Time hath truly and in himself over-run his course, but Care makes thy night long by curtailing thy slumber.

ASPHALION

Hast ever learnt to interpret a dream? I've had a good one this night, and am fain thou go shares in't.

FRIEND

Aye, we share our catch, and e'en let's share all our dreams. For shall I not be making conjecture of thee according to the saying, the best interpreter of dreams is he that learns of understanding? And what's more, we have time and to spare, for there's little enough for a man to do lying sleepless in a greenbed beside the sea. 'Faith, 'tis the ass in the thorns and the lamp in the town-hall, and they are the morals for waking. Come, thy dream; for a friend, look you, is always told a man's dreams.

ASPHALION

When I fell asleep last night after my labours o' the sea—and faith, 'twas not for fulness, if you mind, seeing we supped early to give our bellies short commons—I dreamt I was hard at my work upon a rock, seated watching for the fish and dangling my piece of deception from my rod's end, when there rose me a right gallant fellow—for mark you, I surmise a fish as a sleeping dog will a bear—, well hooked · too, for 'a showed blood, and my rod all bended wi' the pull of him, bended straining and bowing in my hand, insomuch that I questioned me sore how I was to deal with so great a fish with so weak tools to my hand. Howbeit I gently let him have line, and when he ran not away showed him the butt. Now was the prize mine. I drew up a golden fish, a fish smothered in gold, such indeed that I feared me lest he were a fish favoured of Poseidon, or mayhap a treasured possession of sea-green Amphitritè; aye, and unhooked him very carefully and slow lest ever the tackle should come away with gold from his mouth. Then, standing over, I sang the praises of that my glorious catch, my seaman made landsman, and sware I'ld nevermore set foot o' the sea, but I would rest ashore rather and king it there with my gold. And with that I awoke. And now, good friend, it remains for you to lend me your understanding; for troth, that oath I sware—

FRIEND

Be of good cheer; never you fear that. 'Twas no swearing when you sware that oath any more than 'twas seeing when you saw the golden fish. Howbeit there's wisdom to be had of empty shows; for if you will make real and waking search in these places there's hope of your sleep and your dreams. Go seek the fish of flesh and blood, or you'll die of hunger and golden visions.

VIRGIL *(70–19* B.C.*)*

Virgil's ninth eclogue can be read as a parable of the interaction of peace and strife, past and present, art and labor. Civilization is threatened by rapaciousness and violence. The shepherd Moeris is on his way to town taking what is now someone else's property to market, the harmony that he yearns for apparently a thing of the past. The eclogue is thus pervaded by a sense of melancholy and nostalgia: "time bears all away." The songs, especially Moeris' concerning the grotto laced with shadows, are fragmentary reminders of a better life, which shepherds are now powerless to preserve. Yet something of the golden quality of Arcadia is still available to them in the quiet place they come upon at the end of the poem, where they might escape their labors momentarily if they choose. Moeris feels compelled to go on, but the pain of his dispossession is partly dissolved in the pleasantness of memory and in the *locus amoenus* (pleasant place). Although such aspects of the contemplative, idyllic life cannot make the symbolic "long road" easier, they render it mellow and elegiac.

But it is a delicate question finally whether this mellowness serves to ameliorate the present by screening it through a hazy distance or renders it more poignant by contrast. In either case, the contrast is primarily between what is and what once was, with a slight hint of a further contrast between what *is* and what *might again be* if the right people become aware of the plight of shepherd-poets, for the parabolic dimension of the eclogue is supplemented by oblique reference to the politics of Virgil's own times.

NINTH ECLOGUE
Translated by John Dryden

When Virgil by the favour of Augustus had recover'd his patrimony near Mantua, and went in hope to take possession, he was in danger to be slain by Arius the Centurion, to whom those lands were assign'd by the Emperour in reward of his service against Brutus and Cassius. This pastoral therefore is fill'd with complaints of his hard usage; and the persons introduc'd, are the bayliff of Virgil, Moeris, and his friend Lycidas. (Dryden's note)

LYCIDAS

Ho Moeris! wither on thy way so fast?
This leads to Town.

MOERIS

O Lycidas at last
The time is come, I never thought to see,
(Strange revolution for my farm and me)   5
When the grim Captain in a surly tone

Cries out, pack up ye rascals and be gone.
Kick'd out, we set the best face on't we cou'd,
And these two kids, t' appease his angry mood
I bear, of which the Furies give him good.   10

LYCIDAS

Your country friends were told another tale;
That from the sloping mountain to the vale,
And dodder'd oak, and all the banks along,
Menalcas sav'd his fortune with a song.

MOERIS

Such was the news, indeed, but songs and rhimes   15
Prevail, as much in these hard iron times,
As would a plump of trembling fowl, that rise
Against an eagle sousing from the skies.
And had not Phoebus warn'd me by the croak
Of an old raven from a hollow oak,   20
To shun debate, Menalcas had been slain,
And Moeris not surviv'd him to complain.

LYCIDAS

Now heaven defend! could barbarous rage induce
The brutal son of Mars, t' insult the sacred muse!
Who then shou'd sing the nymphs, or who rehearse   25
The waters gliding in a smoother verse!
Or Amaryllis praise, that heavenly lay,
That shorten'd as we went, our tedious way;
O Tityrus, tend my herd and see them fed;
To morning pastures, evening waters led: 30
And 'ware the Lybian ridgils butting head.

MOERIS

Or what unfinish'd he to Varus read;
"Thy name, O Varus (if the kinder pow'rs
Preserve our plains, and shield the Mantuan tow'rs
Obnoxious by Cremonas neighb'ring crime,)   35
The wings of swans, and stronger pinion'd rhime,
Shall raise aloft, and soaring bear above
Th' immortal gift of gratitude to Jove."

LYCIDAS

Sing on, sing on, for I can ne're be cloy'd,
So may thy swarms the baleful eugh avoid: 40
So may thy cows their burden'd bags distend
And trees to goats their willing branches bend.
Mean as I am, yet have the muses made

---

13 *dodder'd*: aged, decayed. 14 *Menalcas*: Virgil. 17 *plump*: flock. 18 *sousing*: plunging.
31 *Lybian ridgils*: ram with one testicle. 32 *Varus*: Virgil's patron Alfenus Varus, or the
contemporary poet Lucius Varius. 40 *eugh*: yew-tree.

Me free, a member of the tuneful trade:
At least the shepherds seem to like my lays,   45
But I discern their flattery from their praise:
I nor to Cinna's ears, nor Varus dare aspire;
But gabble like a goose, amidst the swan-like quire.

MOERIS

'Tis what I have been conning in my mind:
Nor are they verses of a vulgar kind.   50
"Come Galatea, come, the seas forsake,
What pleasures can the tides with their hoarse murmurs make?
See on the shore inhabits purple spring;
Where nightingales their love-sick ditty sing;
See meads with purling streams, with flow'rs the ground,   55
The grottoes cool, with shady poplars crown'd,
And creeping vines on arbours weav'd around.
Come then and leave the waves tumultuous roar,
Let the wild surges vainly beat the shore."

LYCIDAS

Or that sweet song I heard with such delight;   60
The same you sung alone one starry night;
The tune I still retain, but not the words.

MOERIS

"Why, Daphnis, dost thou search in old records,
To know the seasons when the stars arise?
See Caesars lamp is lighted in the skies: 65
The star, whose rays the blushing grapes adorn,
And swell the kindly ripening ears of corn.
Under this influence, graft the tender shoot;
Thy childrens children shall enjoy the fruit."
The rest I have forgot, for cares and time   70
Change all things, and untune my soul to rhime:
I cou'd have once sung down a summers sun,
But now the chime of poetry is done.
My voice grows hoarse; I feel the notes decay,
As if the wolves had seen me first today.   75
But these, and more than I to mind can bring,
Menalcas has not yet forgot to sing.

Lycidas

Thy faint excuses but inflame me more;
And now the waves roll silent to the shore.
Husht winds the topmost branches scarcely bend   80
As if thy tuneful song they did attend:
Already we have half our way o'ercome;

---

49 *conning*: studying.

Far off I can discern Bianors tomb;
Here, where the labourers hands have form'd a bow'r
Of wreathing trees, in singing waste an hour.   85
Rest here thy weary limbs, thy kids lay down,
We've day before us yet, to reach the town:
Or if e're night the gathering clouds we fear,
A song will help the beating storm to bear.
And that thou maist not be too late abroad,   90
Sing, and I'le ease thy shoulders of thy load.

MOERIS

Cease to request me, let us mind our way;
Another song requires another day.
When good Menalcas comes, if he rejoice,
And find a friend at court, I'le find a voice   95

TORQUATO TASSO *(1544–1595)*

Tasso's lyric on the golden age, from the pastoral play *Aminta,* was well known
during the seventeenth and eighteenth centuries in England, partly because
the phrase "What you desire to do, you may" (*S'ei piace, ei lice*) expressed
a moral license tantalizingly appropriate to paradise. The play itself, however,
deals with the tension between unrestrained love and social constrictions without
necessarily arguing for one or the other.

FIRST CHORUS FROM *AMINTA,* O BELLA ETÀ DE L'ORO

Translated by Henry Reynolds (1628)

O happy Age of Gold; happy hours;
Not for with milk the rivers ran,
And honey dropped from every tree;
Nor that the Earth bore fruits, and flowers,
Without the toil or care of man,   5
And serpents were from poison free;
Nor for the air (ever calm to see)
Had quite exiled the lowring night;
Whilst clad in an eternal spring
(Nor fiery hot, or else freezing)   10
The cheeks of heaven smil'd with clear light;
Nor that the wandring pine of yore
Brought neither wars, nor wares from foreign shore;
    But therefore only happy days,
Because that vain and idle name,   15
That cozening idol of unrest
Whom the mad vulgar first did raise,
And called it Honor, whence it came
To tyrannize or'e every breast,

---

83 *Bianors tomb*: Bianor reportedly founded Mantua, a town near Virgil's village birthplace,
Andes.

Was not then suffered to molest   20
Poor lovers' hearts with new debate;
More happy they, by these his hard
And cruel laws, were not debarred
Their innate freedom; happy state;
The golden laws of Nature, they   25
Found in their breasts; and them they did obey.
Amid the silver streams and flowers,
The winged Genii then would dance,
Without their bow, without their brand;
The nymphs sat by their paramours,   30
Whisp'ring love-sports, and dalliance,
And joining lips, and hand to hand;
The fairest virgin in the land
Nor scorned, nor gloried to display
Her cheeks fresh roses to the eye,   35
Or ope her fair breasts to the day,
(Which now adays so veiléd lie),
But men and maidens spent free hours
In running rivers, lakes, or shady bowers.
   Then Honor, thou didst first devise   40
To mask the face of pleasure thus;
Bar water to the thirst of love,
And lewdly didst instruct fair eyes
They should be nice, and scrupulous,
And from the gazing world remove   45
Their beauties; thy hands new nets wove
T' intrap the wild curls, fair dispread
To th' open air; thou mad'st the sweet
Delight of love seem thus unmeet;
And (teaching how to look, speak, tread)   50
By thy ill laws this ill has left,
That what was first love's gift, is now our theft.
Nor ought thy mighty working brings,
But more annoyes, and woe to us;
But thou (of Nature and of love   55
The lord, and scourge of mighty kings)
Why do'st thou shroud thy greatness thus
In our poor cells? hence, and remove
Thy power; and it display above,
Disturbing great ones in their sleep;   60
And let us meaner men alone
T' enjoin again (when thou are gone)
And laws of our forefathers keep.
Live we in love, for our lives' hours
Haste on to death, that all at length devours.   65
   Love we while we may; the wain
Of heav'n can set, and rise again;
But we (when once we lose this light)
Must yield us to a never ending night.

EDMUND SPENSER *(1552?–1599)*

Initiations into love are traditional in pastoral from the Greeks to the present, from Longus' romance *Daphnis and Chloe* to film director Ingmar Bergman's *Virgin Spring*. Spenser's version of lost innocence, in the context of its tradition, is both charming and resonant.

MARCH ECLOGUE

ARGUMENT

In this Æglogue two shepheards boyes, taking occasion of the season, beginne to make purpose of love, and other pleasaunce which to spring-time is most agreeable. The speciall meaning hereof is to give certain markes and tokens to know Cupide, the poets god of love. But parti-cularlye, I thinke, in the person of Thomalin is meant some secrete freend, who scorned Love and his knights so long, till at length him selfe was entangled, and unwares wounded with the dart of some beautifull regard, which is Cupides arrow.

(E. K.)

WILLYE. THOMALIN.

WIL. Thomalin, why sytten we soe,
As weren overwent with woe,
 Upon so fayre a morow?
The joyous time now nigheth fast,
That shall alegge this bitter blast,   5
 And slake the winters sorowe.
THO. Sicker, Willye, thou warnest well:
For winters wrath beginnes to quell,
 And pleasant spring appeareth.
The grasse nowe ginnes to be refresht,   10
The swallow peepes out of her nest,
 And clowdie welkin cleareth.
WIL. Seest not thilke same hawthorne studde,
How bragly it beginnes to budde,
 And utter his tender head?   15
Flora now calleth forth eche flower,
And bids make ready Maias bowre,
 That newe is upryst from bedde.
Tho shall we sporten in delight,
And lerne with Lettice to wexe light,   20
 That scornefully lookes askaunce;
Tho will we little Love awake,
That nowe sleepeth in Lethe lake,
 And pray him leaden our daunce.
THO. Willye, I wene thou bee assott: 25
For lustie Love still sleepeth not,
 But is abroad at his game.
WIL. How kenst thou that he is awoke?

---

5 *alegge*: assuage. 12 *welkin*: sky. 13 *studde*: shoot. 14 *bragly*: briskly. 25 *wene*: think; *assott*: doting. 28 *kenst*: know.

Or hast thy selfe his slomber broke?
 Or made previe to the same?   30
THO. No, but happely I hym spyde,
Where in a bush he did him hide,
 With winges of purple and blewe.
And were not that my sheepe would stray,
The previe marks I would bewray,   35
 Whereby by chaunce I him knewe.
WIL. Thomalin, have no care forthy;
My selfe will have a double eye,
 Ylike to my flocke and thine:
For als at home I have a syre,   40
A stepdame eke, as whott as fyre,
 That dewly adayes counts mine.
THO. Nay, but thy seeing will not serve,
My sheepe for that may chaunce to swerve,
 And fall into some mischiefe.   45
For sithens is but the third morowe
That I chaunst to fall a sleepe with sorowe,
 And waked againe with griefe:
The while thilke same unhappye ewe,
Whose clouted legge her hurt doth shewe,   50
 Fell headlong into a dell,
And there unjoynted both her bones:
Mought her necke bene joynted attones,
 She shoulde have neede no more spell.
Thelf was so wanton and so wood,   55
(But now I trowe can better good)
 She mought ne gang on the greene.
WIL. Let be, as may be, that is past:
That is to come, let be forecast.
 Now tell us what thou hast seene.   60
THO. It was upon a holiday,
When shepheardes groomes han leave to play,
 I cast to goe a shooting.
Long wandring up and downe the land,
With bowe and bolts in either hand,   65
 For birds in bushes tooting,
At length within an yvie todde
(There shrouded was the little god)
 I heard a busie bustling.
I bent my bolt against the bush,   70
Listening if any thing did rushe,
 But then heard no more rustling.
Tho peeping close into the thicke,

---

30 *previe*: privy. 37 *forthy*: therefore. 50 *clouted*: covered. 51 *dell*: hole. 53 *attones*: at once. 54 *spell*: verse or charm. 55 *Thelf*: the elf; *wood*: mad. 52–57 "If she had dislocated her neck at the same time, she would no longer need charms. The elf was so wanton and mad (though now I trust she will be better) that she might no longer walk on the green." 66 *tooting*: looking.

Might see the moving of some quicke,
    Whose shape appeared not: 75
But were it faerie, feend, or snake,
My courage earnd it to awake,
    And manfully thereat shotte.
With that sprong forth a naked swayne,
With spotted winges like peacocks trayne,   80
    And laughing lope to a tree,
His gylden quiver at his backe,
And silver bowe, which was but slacke,
    Which lightly he bent at me.
That seeing I, levelde againe,   85
And shott at him with might and maine,
    As thicke as it had hayled.
So long I shott that al was spent:
Tho pumie stones I hastly hent,
    And threwe; but nought availed: 90
He was so wimble and so wight,
From bough to bough he lepped light,
    And oft the pumies latched.
Therewith affrayd I ranne away:
But he, that earst seemd but to playe,   95
    A shaft in earnest snatched,
And hit me running in the heele:
For then, I little smart did feele;
    But soone it sore encreased.
And now it ranckleth more and more,   100
And inwardly it festreth sore,
    Ne wote I how to cease it.
wil. Thomalin, I pittie thy plight.
Perdie, with Love thou diddest fight:
    I know him by a token.   105
For once I heard my father say,
How he him caught upon a day,
    (Whereof he wilbe wroken)
Entangled in a fowling net,
Which he for carrion crowes had set,   110
    That in our peeretree haunted.
Tho sayd, he was a winged lad,
But bowe and shafts as then none had,
    Els had he sore be daunted.
But see, the welkin thicks apace,   115
And stouping Phebus steepes his face:
Its time to hast us homeward.

---

77 *earnd*: desired. 91 *wimble and so wight*: nimble and so lively. 93 *latched*: caught,
102 *wote*: know. 108 *wroken*: revenged. 113 *but*: without. 113–114 Cupid was "without
bow and shafts...or else he [i.e., my father] had been sorely vanquished" (as Thomalin is
when Cupid seizes "a shaft in earnest").

Willyes embleme.
To be wise and eke to love,
Is graunted scarce to god above.

Thomalins embleme.
Of hony and of gaule in love there is store:
The honye is much, but the gaule is more.

MARLOWE AND RALEGH

"The Passionate Shepherd to His Love" and "The Nymph's Reply" are discussed in the introduction to this section.

THE PASSIONATE SHEPHERD TO HIS LOVE

CHRISTOPHER MARLOWE *(1564–1593)*

Come live with me and be my love,
And we will all the pleasures prove
That hills and valleys, dales and fields,
And all the craggy mountains yields.

There will we sit upon the rocks   5
And see the shepherds feed their flocks,
By shallow rivers, to whose falls
Melodious birds sing madrigals.

There will I make thee beds of roses
And a thousand fragrant posies,   10
A cap of flowers, and a kirtle
Embroider'd all with leaves of myrtle.

A gown made of the finest wool,
Which from our pretty lambs we pull,
Fair linèd slippers for the cold,   15
With buckles of the purest gold.

A belt of straw and ivy buds
With coral clasps and amber studs:
And if these pleasures may thee move,
Come live with me and be my love.   20

The shepherd swains shall dance and sing
For thy delight each May-morning:
If these delights thy mind may move,
Then live with me and be my love.

THE NYMPH'S REPLY TO THE SHEPHERD

SIR WALTER RALEGH *(1552–1618)*

If all the world and love were young,
And truth in every shepherd's tongue,
These pretty pleasures might me move
To live with thee and be thy love.

But time drives flocks from field to fold,   5
When rivers rage and rocks grow cold;
And Philomel becometh dumb;
The rest complains of cares to come.

The flowers do fade, and wanton fields
To wayward winter reckoning yields: 10
A honey tongue, a heart of gall,
Is fancy's spring, but sorrow's fall.

Thy gowns, thy shoes, thy beds of roses,
Thy cap, thy kirtle, and thy posies
Soon break, soon wither, soon forgotten,   15
In folly ripe, in reason rotten.

Thy belt of straw and ivy buds,
Thy coral clasps and amber studs,
All these in me no means can move
To come to thee and be thy love.   20

But could youth last, and love still breed,
Had joys no date, nor age no need,
Then these delights my mind might move
To live with thee and be thy love.

ROBERT GREENE *(1560?–1592)*

Like Spenser, Greene is concerned with the forcible intrusion of love into
nature's flowering season. His medium, however, is a Blakean lyric that plays
on the contrasting states of innocence and experience. The shepherd in his
self-constructed maze is barely able to note the life that blossoms around him,
yet he chooses to burn with, rather than abandon, desire.

WHEN FLORA PROUD
(The Shepherd Eurymachus to his fair shepherdess Mirimida)

When Flora proud in pomp of all her flowers
      Sat bright and gay:
And gloried in the dew of Iris showers,
      And did display
Her mantle checkered all with gaudy green,   5
      Then I
      Alone
A mournful man in Ericine was seen.

With folded arms I trampled through the grass,
      Tracing as he   10
That held the throne of fortune brittle glass,
      And love to be
Like fortune fleeting, as the restless wind
      Mixed
      With mists   15
Whose damp doth make the clearest eyes grow blind.

---

10 *tracing*: traversing.

Thus in a maze, I spied a hideous flame,
      I cast my sight,
And saw where blithely bathing in the same
      With great delight   20
A worm did lie, wrapt in a smoky sweat:
      And yet
      Twas strange,
It careless lay, and shrunk not at the heat.

I stood amaz'd, and wondring at the sight,   25
      While that a dame,
That shone like to the heavens rich sparkling light,
      Discoursed the same,
And said, "My friend, this worm within the fire:
      Which lies   30
      Content,
Is Venus' worm, and represents desire.

A salamander is this princely beast,
      Decked with a crown,
Given him by Cupid as a gorgeous crest,   35
      Gainst fortune's frown.
Content he lies, and bathes him in the flame,
      And goes
      Not forth,
For why, he cannot live without the same.   40

As he, so lovers live within the fire
      Of fervent love:
And shrink not from the flame of hot desire,
      Nor will not move
From any heat that Venus force imparts: 45
      But lie
      Content,
Within a fire, and waste away their hearts."

Up flew the dame, and vanished in a cloud,
      But there stood I,   50
And many thoughts within my mind did shroud
      My love: for why
I felt within my heart a scorching fire,
      And yet
      As did   55
The salamander, twas my whole desire.

ROBERT HERRICK *(1591–1674)*

Herrick sets the enjoyment of spring in the context of the swift passage of
time so that death and joy intensify each other. The inherently contrastive
structure of pastoral is here accommodated to the general rhetorical appeal of
the *carpe diem* theme.

40, 52 *for why*: because.

CORINNA'S GOING A-MAYING

Get up, get up for shame, the blooming morn
Upon her wings presents the god unshorn.
  See how Aurora throws her fair
  Fresh-quilted colors through the air:
  Get up, sweet slug-a-bed, and see   5
  The dew bespangling herb and tree.
Each flower has wept and bowèd toward the east
Above an hour since: yet you not dressed;
  Nay! not so much as out of bed?
  When all the birds have matins said   10
  And sung their thankful hymns, 'tis sin,
  Nay, profanation to keep in,
Whenas a thousand virgins on this day
Spring, sooner than the lark, to fetch in May.

Rise and put on your foliage, and be seen   15
To come forth like the springtime, fresh and green,
  And sweet as Flora. Take no care
  For jewels for your gown or hair;
  Fear not, the leaves will strew
  Gems in abundance upon you;   20
Besides, the childhood of the day has kept,
Against you come, some orient pearls unwept;
  Come and receive them while the light
  Hangs on the dew-locks of the night,
  And Titan on the eastern hill   25
  Retires himself, or else stands still
Till you come forth. Wash, dress, be brief in praying:
Few beads are best when once we go a-Maying.

Come, my Corinna, come; and coming, mark
How each field turns a street, each street a park   30
  Made green and trimmed with trees; see how
  Devotion gives each house a bough
  Or branch; each porch, each door, ere this,
  An ark, a tabernacle is,
Made up of white-thorn neatly interwove,   35
As if here were those cooler shades of love.
  Can such delights be in the street
  And open fields, and we not see't?
  Come, we'll abroad, and let's obey
  The proclamation made for May,   40
And sin no more, as we have done, by staying;
But, my Corinna, come, let's go a-Maying.

There's not a budding boy or girl this day
But is got up, and gone to bring in May.
  A deal of youth, ere this, is come   45
  Back, and with white-thorn laden, home.

Some have dispatched their cakes and cream
Before that we have left to dream:
And some have wept, and wooed, and plighted troth,
And chose their priest, ere we can cast off sloth: 50
  Many a green-gown has been given;
  Many a kiss, both odd and even:
  Many a glance too has been sent
  From out the eye, love's firmament;
Many a jest told of the keys betraying   55
This night, and locks picked, yet we're not a-Maying.

Come, let us go while we are in our prime;
And take the harmless folly of the time.
  We shall grow old apace, and die
  Before we know our liberty.   60
  Our life is short, and our days run
  As fast away as does the sun;
And, as a vapor or a drop of rain,
Once lost, can ne'er be found again,
  So when or you or I are made   65
  A fable, song, or fleeting shade,
  All love, all liking, all delight
  Lies drowned with us in endless night.
Then while time serves, and we are but decaying,
Come, my Corinna, come let's go a-Maying.   70

JOHN MILTON *(1608–1674)*

One side of Milton's "uncouth swain," the speaker of "Lycidas," wants to celebrate the death of his friend ceremonially, with the participation of various elements of nature—nymphs, flowers, and the like. But a more realistic voice insists on breaking into the ceremony, as though Marlowe's shepherd were speaking one part and Ralegh's nymph the other. Both the movement and the imagery of the poem are initially dictated by the flux and reflux of these counter impulses, a good capsule example of which is the two paragraphs beginning "Together both..." (line 25) and "But O the heavy change..." (line 37). The image of flowers wearing frost with "their gay wardrobe" compresses this twofold awareness into a single symbol of natural beauty that changes, on second look, into a symbol of blight.

Hence "poetry" in the sense of a traditional "pagan" elegy proves inadequate; it is as helpless in offering Lycidas the "meed of some melodious tear" as "the muse herself" was in saving the archetype of nature poets, Orpheus, who like Lycidas was slain with anything but ceremony and sweet music. The supernatural rather than nature and the unexpressive nuptial song rather than the poet's loudly swept string must offer consolation—not the watery bier, shepherd songs, and flowers, but Him who walked the waves and the celestial choirs moving along "other streams." The contrast of the two natures—sweet and vicious—is thus dissolved by the transformational power of grace.

LYCIDAS

Yet once more, O ye laurels, and once more
Ye myrtles brown, with ivy never-sear,
I come to pluck your berries harsh and crude,
And with forc'd fingers rude,
Shatter your leaves before the mellowing year.   5
Bitter constraint and sad occasion dear
Compels me to disturb your season due:
For Lycidas is dead, dead ere his prime,
Young Lycidas, and hath not left his peer.
Who would not sing for Lycidas? he knew   10
Himself to sing, and build the lofty rhyme.
He must not float upon his watery bier
Unwept, and welter to the parching wind,
Without the meed of some melodious tear.
   Begin then, sisters of the sacred well   15
That from beneath the seat of Jove doth spring;
Begin, and somewhat loudly sweep the string;
Hence with denial vain and coy excuse:
So may some gentle muse
With lucky words favor my destined urn;   20
And as he passes, turn
And bid fair peace be to my sable shroud.
   For we were nursed upon the self-same hill,
Fed the same flock by fountain, shade, and rill.
Together both, ere the high lawns appeared   25
Under the opening eye-lids of the morn,
We drove a-field, and both together heard
What time the gray-fly winds her sultry horn,
Battening our flocks with the fresh dews of night;
Oft till the star, that rose at evening bright,   30
Toward heaven's descent had sloped his westering wheel.
Meanwhile the rural ditties were not mute;
Tempered to the oaten flute,
Rough satyrs danced, and fauns with cloven heel
From the glad sound would not be absent long;   35
And old Damoetas loved to hear our song.
   But, O! the heavy change, now thou art gone,
Now thou art gone, and never must return!
Thee, shepherd, thee the woods and desert caves,
With wild thyme and the gadding vine o'ergrown,   40
And all their echoes, mourn:
The willows and the hazel copses green
Shall now no more be seen
Fanning their joyous leaves to thy soft lays.
As killing as the canker to the rose,   45
Or taint-worm to the weanling herds that graze,

---

3 *crude*: not yet ripe. 28 *winds*: blows. 29 *battening*: feeding. 36 *Damoetas*: a tutor at Cambridge. 40 *gadding*: straying. 45 *the canker*: the cankerworm.

Or frost to flowers, that their gay wardrobe wear
When first the white-thorn blows;
Such, Lycidas, thy loss to shepherd's ear.
    Where were ye, nymphs, when the remorseless deep   50
Closed o'er the head of your loved Lycidas?
For neither were ye playing on the steep
Where your old bards, the famous Druids, lie,
Nor on the shaggy top of Mona high,
Nor yet where Deva spreads her wizard stream.   55
Ay me! I fondly dream
"Had ye been there,"—for what could that have done?
What could the muse herself that Orpheus bore,
The muse herself, for her enchanting son,
Whom universal nature did lament,   60
When by the rout that made the hideous roar
His gory visage down the stream was sent,
Down the swift Hebrus to the Lesbian shore?
    Alas! what boots it with uncessant care
To tend the homely, slighted, shepherd's trade   65
And strictly meditate the thankless muse?
Were it not better done, as others use,
To sport with Amaryllis in the shade,
Or with the tangles of Neaera's hair?
Fame is the spur that the clear spirit doth raise   70
(That last infirmity of noble mind)
To scorn delights, and live laborious days;
But the fair guerdon when we hope to find,
And think to burst out into sudden blaze,
Comes the blind fury with the abhorred shears   75
And slits the thin-spun life. "But not the praise,"
Phoebus replied, and touched my trembling ears:
"Fame is no plant that grows on mortal soil,
Nor in the glistering foil
Set off to the world, nor in broad rumor lies: 80
But lives and spreads aloft by those pure eyes
And perfect witness of all-judging Jove;
As he pronounces lastly on each deed,
Of so much fame in heaven expect thy meed."
    O fountain Arethuse, and thou honored flood,   85
Smooth-sliding Mincius, crowned with vocal reeds,
That strain I heard was of a higher mood.
But now my oat proceeds,
And listens to the herald of the sea
That came in Neptune's plea.   90
He asked the waves, and asked the felon winds,

---

53 *Druids*: members of an ancient religious order. 54 *Mona*: Anglesey, an island off the coast of Wales. 55 *Deva*: river Dee of Chester. 58 *muse*: Calliope, Orpheus' mother. 64 *boots*: avails. 75 *blind fury*: Atropos, one of the three fates, who cuts off life. 77 *Phoebus*: Apollo. 85 *Arethuse*: in Sicily, hence Greek pastoral. 86 *Mincius*: in Italy, hence Roman pastoral. 89 *herald*: Triton, Poseidon's son.

What hard mishap hath doomed this gentle swain?
And questioned every gust of rugged wings
That blows from off each beakèd promontory.
They knew not of his story;   95
And sage Hippotades their answer brings,
That not a blast was from his dungeon strayed:
The air was calm, and on the level brine
Sleek Panope with all her sisters played.
It was that fatal and perfidious bark,   100
Built in the eclipse, and rigged with curses dark,
That sunk so low that sacred head of thine.
   Next, Camus, reverend sire, went footing slow,
His mantle hairy, and his bonnet sedge,
Inwrought with figures dim, and on the edge   105
Like to that sanguine flower inscribed with woe.
"Ah! who hath reft," quoth he, "my dearest pledge?"
Last came, and last did go,
The Pilot of the Galilean Lake;
Two massy keys he bore of metals twain   110
(The golden opes, the iron shuts amain).
He shook his mitred locks, and stern bespake:—
"How well could I have spared for thee, young swain,
Enow of such as, for their bellies' sake,
Creep, and intrude, and climb into the fold!   115
Of other care they little reckoning make
Than how to scramble at the shearers' feast,
And shove away the worthy bidden guest.
Blind mouths! that scarce themselves know how to hold
A sheephook, or have learnt aught else the least   120
That to the faithful herdman's art belongs!
What recks it them? What need they? They are sped;
And, when they list, their lean and flashy songs
Grate on their scrannel pipes of wretched straw;
The hungry sheep look up, and are not fed,   125
But, swoln with wind and the rank mist they draw,
Rot inwardly, and foul contagion spread;
Besides what the grim wolf with privy paw
Daily devours apace, and nothing said.
But that two-handed engine at the door   130
Stands ready to smite once, and smite no more."
   Return, Alpheus; the dread voice is past
That shrunk thy streams; return, Sicilian muse,
And call the vales, and bid them hither cast
Their bells and flowerets of a thousand hues.   135
Ye valleys low, where the mild whispers use

---

96 *Hippotades*: Aeolus, god of the winds. 103 *Camus*: personification of the river Cam
and Cambridge University. 106 *that sanguine flower*: hyacinth. 109 *The Pilot*: probably
St. Peter. 122 *What recks it*: what do they care; *They are sped*: they are prosperous.
124 *scrannel*: feeble. 128 *grim Wolf*: Roman Catholic Church. 132 *Alpheus*: Arcadian
river.

Of shades, and wanton winds, and gushing brooks,
On whose fresh lap the swart star sparely looks,
Throw hither all your quaint enamelled eyes,
That on the green turf sucked the honeyed showers,　　　140
And purple all the ground with vernal flowers.
Bring the rathe primrose that forsaken dies,
The tufted crow-toe, and pale jessamine,
The white pink, and the pansy freaked with jet,
The glowing violet,　　　145
The musk-rose, and the well-attired woodbine,
With cowslips wan that hang the pensive head,
And every flower that sad embroidery wears;
Bid amaranthus all his beauty shed,
And daffodillies fill their cups with tears,　　　150
To strew the laureate hearse where Lycid lies.
For so, to interpose a little ease,
Let our frail thoughts dally with false surmise:
Ay me! whilst thee the shores and sounding seas
Wash far away, where'er thy bones are hurled;　　　155
Whether beyond the stormy Hebrides,
Where thou perhaps under the whelming tide
Visit'st the bottom of the monstrous world;
Or whether thou, to our moist vows denied,
Sleep'st by the fable of Bellerus old,　　　160
Where the great Vision of the guarded mount
Looks toward Namancos and Bayona's hold.
Look homeward, angel, now, and melt with ruth;
And, O ye dolphins, waft the hapless youth.
　Weep no more, woeful shepherds, weep no more,　　　165
For Lycidas, your sorrow, is not dead,
Sunk though he be beneath the watery floor;
So sinks the day-star in the ocean bed,
And yet anon repairs his drooping head,
And tricks his beams, and with new-spangled ore　　　170
Flames in the forehead of the morning sky:
So Lycidas sunk low, but mounted high
Through the dear might of Him that walked the waves;
Where, other groves and other streams along,
With nectar pure his oozy locks he laves,　　　175
And hears the unexpressive nuptial song
In the blest kingdoms meek of joy and love.
There entertain him all the saints above
In solemn troops, and sweet societies,
That sing, and singing in their glory move,　　　180
And wipe the tears for ever from his eyes.

---

138 *swart star sparely looks*: "the Dog Star (associated with withered vegetation) seldom looks." 149 *Amaranthus*: unfading flower. 156 *Hebrides*: islands west of Scotland. 160 *Bellerus*: mythical giant associated with "Land's End" at the southwest tip of Cornwall. 162 *Namacos and Bayona*: Spanish strongholds toward which Michael (the angel, of line 163) looks. 168 *day-star*: the sun.

Now, Lycidas, the shepherds weep no more;
Henceforth thou art the genius of the shore
In thy large recompense, and shalt be good
To all that wander in that perilous flood. 185
   Thus sang the uncouth swain to the oaks and rills,
While the still morn went out with sandals gray;
He touched the tender tops of various quills,
With eager thought warbling his Doric lay:
And now the sun had stretched out all the hills. 190
And now was dropt into the western bay.
At last he rose, and twitched his mantle blue:
Tomorrow to fresh woods, and pastures new.

HENRY VAUGHAN *(1621–1695)*

The Christian equivalent to the descent of the gods in Arcadia is the birth of
Christ among shepherds in the stable and perhaps also the subsequent contrast
in Christ's life between the humble and the money-changers in the temple:
The poor are blessed, and the rich find entrance into heaven difficult. Vaughan
is as aware of this pastoralism inherent in the tradition as he is of the presence
of divine emblems in nature.

THE SHEPHERDS

Sweet, harmless livers! (on whose holy leisure
   Waits innocence and pleasure)
Whose leaders to those pastures, and clear springs,
   Were patriarchs, saints, and kings,
How happened it that in the dead of night 5
   You only saw true light,
While Palestine was fast asleep, and lay
   Without one thought of day?
Was it because those first and blessèd swains
   Were pilgrims on those plains 10
When they receiv'd the promise, for which now
   'Twas there first shown to you?
'Tis true, he loves that dust whereon they go
   That serve him here below,
And therefore might for memory of those 15
   His love there first disclose;
But wretched Salem once his love, must now
   No voice, nor vision know,
Her stately piles with all their height and pride
   Now languishèd and died, 20
And Bethlem's humble cots above them step
   While all her seers slept;
Her cedar, fir, hew'd stones and gold were all
   Polluted through their fall,
And those once sacred mansions were now 25

---

183 *genius*: protective spirit.　189 *Doric*: Greek dialect often used in pastorals.

Mere emptiness and show,
This made the angel call at reeds and thatch,
    Yet where the shepherds watch,
And God's own lodging (though he could not lack)
    To be a common rack;   30
No costly pride, no soft-clothed luxury
    In those thin cells could lie,
Each stirring wind and storm blew through their cots
    Which never harbour'd plots,
Only content, and love, and humble joys   35
    Lived there without all noise,
Perhaps some harmless cares for the next day
    Did in their bosoms play,
As where to lead their sheep, what silent nook,
    What springs or shades to look,   40
But that was all; and now with gladsome care
    They for the town prepare,
They leave their flock, and in a busy talk
    All towards Bethlem walk
To see their souls' great shepherd, who was come   45
    To bring all stragglers home,
Where now they find him out, and taught before
    That Lamb of God adore,
That Lamb whose days great kings and prophets wish'd
    And long'd to see, but miss'd.   50
The first light they beheld was bright and gay
    And turn'd their night to day,
But to this later light they saw in him,
    Their day was dark, and dim.

ANDREW MARVELL *(1621–1678)*

In "The Coronet" Marvell reflects the concern of both Herbert and Milton for the gulf between nature and grace. The poet sacrifices his pastoral garland at Christ's feet with faint hope that Christ will disentangle Satan from it rather than crush it. "The Garden" has no such doubts about the wholesomeness of herbs and flowers, but the mind dwells partly elsewhere.

THE GARDEN

How vainly men themselves amaze
To win the palm, the oak, or bays,
And their incessant labors see
Crown'd from some single herb or tree,
Whose short and narrowed vergèd shade   5
Does prudently their toils upbraid;
While all flow'rs and all trees do close
To weave the garlands of repose.

Fair Quiet, have I found thee here,
And Innocence, thy sister dear!   10

Mistaken long, I sought you then
In busy companies of men.
Your sacred plants, if here below,
Only among the plants will grow.
Society is all but rude,   15
To this delicious solitude.

No white nor red was ever seen
So am'rous as this lovely green.
Fond lovers, cruel as their flame,
Cut in these trees their mistress' name;   20
Little, alas, they know, or heed,
How far these beauties hers exceed!
Fair trees, where s'eer your barks I wound
No name shall but your own be found.

When we have run our passion's heat,   25
Love hither makes his best retreat.
The gods that mortal beauty chase,
Still in a tree did end their race:
Apollo hunted Daphne so,
Only that she might laurel grow;   30
And Pan did after Syrinx speed,
Not as a nymph, but for a reed.

What wondrous life is this I lead!
Ripe apples drop about my head;
The luscious clusters of the vine   35
Upon my mouth do crush their wine;
The nectarine, and curious peach,
Into my hands themselves do reach;
Stumbling on melons, as I pass,
Ensnared with flowers, I fall on grass.   40

Meanwhile the mind, from pleasure less,
Withdraws into its happiness;
The mind, that ocean where each kind
Does straight its own resemblance find:
Yet it creates, transcending these,   45
Far other worlds and other seas,
Annihilating all that's made
To a green thought in a green shade.

Here at the fountain's sliding foot,
Or at some fruit tree's mossy root,   50
Casting the body's vest aside,
My soul into the boughs does glide;
There, like a bird, it sits and sings,
Then whets and combs its silver wings,
And till prepared for longer flight,   55
Waves in its plumes the various light.

Such was that happy garden-state,
While man there walked without a mate:

After a place so pure and sweet,
What other help could yet be meet!   60
But 'twas beyond a mortal's share
To wander solitary there:
Two paradises 'twere, in one,
To live in paradise alone.

How well the skilful gardener drew   65
Of flowers and herbs this dial new,
Where, from above, the milder sun
Does through a fragrant zodiac run;
And as it works, th' industrious bee
Computes its time as well as we.   70
How could such sweet and wholesome hours
Be reckoned but with herbs and flowers!

THE CORONET

When for the thorns with which I long, too long,
  With many a piercing wound,
  My saviour's head have crown'd,
I seek with garlands to redress that wrong:
  Through every garden, every mead,   5
I gather flow'rs (my fruits are only flow'rs)
  Dismantling all the fragrant towers
That once adorn'd my shepherdess's head.
And now when I have summ'd up all my store,
  Thinking (so I myself deceive)   10
  So rich a chaplet thence to weave
As never yet the king of glory wore:
  Alas I find the serpent old
  That, twining in his speckled breast,
  About the flow'rs disguis'd does fold,   15
  With wreaths of fame and interest. .
Ah, foolish man, that would'st debase with them,
And mortal glory, heaven's diadem!
But thou who only could'st the serpent tame,
Either his slipp'ry knots at once untie,   20
And disentangle all his winding snare:
Or shatter too with him my curious frame:
And let these wither, so that he may die,
Though set with skill and chosen out with care.
That they, while Thou on both their spoils dost tread,   25
May crown thy feet, that could not crown thy head.

THE MOWER TO THE GLOWWORMS

1

Ye living lamps, by whose dear light
The nightingale does sit so late,
And studying all the summer night,
Her matchless songs does mediate;

2

Ye country comets, that portend   5
No war, nor prince's funeral,
Shining unto no higher end
Than to presage the grass's fall;

3

Ye glowworms, whose officious flame
To wandring mowers shows the way,   10
That in the night have lost their aim,
And after foolish fires do stray;

4

Your courteous lights in vain you waste,
Since Juliana here is come,
For she my mind hath so displac'd   15
That I shall never find my home.

JONATHAN SWIFT *(1667–1745)*

Swift's parody of the nymph's creation of beauty in the boudoir is in part a
comment on the relations of art and nature. In comparison, note Pope's description of Belinda's rites of the mirror in the *Rape of the Lock,* in which the
family relation of satire and pastoral is also momentarily evident.

THE PROGRESS OF BEAUTY

When first Diana leaves her bed,
Vapors and steams her looks disgrace;
A frouzy dirty colour'd red
Sits on her cloudy wrinckled face.

But by degrees when mounted high   5
Her artificial face appears
Down from her window in the sky;
Her spots are gone, her visage clears.

'Twixt earthly femals and the moon
All parallells exactly run;   10
If Celia should appear too soon
Alas, the nymph would be undone.

To see her from her pillow rise
All reeking in a cloudy steam,
Crackt lips, foul teeth, and gummy eyes,   15
Poor Strephon, how would he blaspheme!

The soot or powder which was wont
To make her hair look black as jet,
Falls from her tresses on her front,
A mingled mass of dirt and sweat.   20

Three colours, black, and red, and white,
So graceful in their proper place,
Remove them to a diff'rent light
They form a frightful hideous Face;

For instance: when the lilly slipps   25
Into the precincts of the rose,
And takes possession of the lips,
Leaving the purple to the nose.

So Celia went entire to bed,
All her complexions safe and sound;   30
But when she rose, the black and red,
Though still in sight, had chang'd their ground.

The black, which would not be confin'd,
A more inferior station seeks,
Leaving the fiery red behind,   35
And mingles in her muddy cheeks.

The paint by perspiration cracks,
And falls in rivulets of sweat,
On either side you see the tracks,
While at her chin the confluents met.   40

A skillful housewife thus her thumb
With spittle while she spins, anoints,
And thus the brown meanders come
In trickling streams betwixt her joynts.

But Celia can with ease reduce   45
By help of pencil, paint and brush
Each colour to it's place and use,
And teach her cheeks again to blush.

She knows her early self no more,
But fill'd with admiration, stands,   50
As other painters oft adore
The workmanship of their own hands.

Thus after four important hours
Celia's the wonder of her sex;
Say, which among the heav'nly pow'rs   55
Could cause such wonderfull effects.

Venus, indulgent of her kind,
Gave women all their hearts could wish
When first she taught them where to find
White lead, and Lusitanian dish.   60

Love with white lead cements his wings,
White lead was sent us to repair
Two brightest, brittlest earthly things,
A Lady's face, and China ware.

She ventures now to lift the sash,   65
The window is her proper sphear;
Ah lovely nymph, be not too rash,
Nor let the beaux approach too near.

Take pattern by your sister star,
Delude at once and bless our sight;   70
When you are seen, be seen from far,
And chiefly chuse to shine by night.

In the pell-mell when passing by,
Keep up the glasses of your chair;
Then each transported fop will cry,   75
G—d d—m me, Jack, she's wondrous fair!

But art no longer can prevayl
When the materialls all are gone;
The best mechanick hand must fayl
Where nothing's left to work upon.   80

Matter, as wise logicians say,
Cannot without a form subsist;
And form, say I, as well as they,
Must fayl if matter brings no grist.

And this is fair Diana's Case: 85
For all astrologers maintain
Each night a bit drops off her face
When mortals say she's in her wain.

While Partridge wisely shews the cause
Efficient of the moon's decay,   90
That Cancer with his pois'nous claws
Attacks her in the milky Way;

But Gadbury in art profound
From her pale cheeks pretends to show
That swain Endymion is not sound,   95
Or else that Mercury's her foe.

But let the cause be what it will,
In half a month she looks so thin
That Flamstead can with all his skill
See but her forehead and her chin.   100

Yet as she wasts, she grows discreet,
Till midnight never shows her head;
So rotting Celia stroles the street
When sober folks are all a-bed.

For sure if this be Luna's fate,   105
Poor Celia, but of mortall race,
In vain expects a longer date
To the materialls of her face.

---

89 *Partridge*: contemporary almanac writer satirized in Swift's "The Bickerstaff Papers."
Swift recites theories of the moon's "spots" in "Gadbury" and the "Observations of
Flamstead."   95 *Endymion*: mythical shepherd-lover of Cynthia, the moon.

When Mercury her tresses mows,
To think of oyl and soot is vain,   110
No painting can restore a nose,
Nor will her teeth return again.

Two balls of glass may serve for eyes,
White lead can plaister up a cleft;
But these, alas, are poor supplyes   115
If neither cheeks, nor lips, be left.

Ye pow'rs who over love preside,
Since mortal beautys drop so soon,
If you would have us well supply'd,
Send us new nymphs with each new moon.   120

JOHN GAY *(1685–1732)*

Lines were drawn in Gay's time between "elegant" pastoral after the manner
of Virgil and Pope, and rustic, or crude, pastoral. Gay, like Pope, disliked the
kind of rustic realism that certain eighteenth-century pastoralists wrote, imitating the manner of Spenser. What Pope argues in prose against it, Gay demonstrates through a parody of country bumpkins whose manners, he suggests,
are some kind of ultimate in naturalism.

THE SHEPHERD'S WEEK

from Wednesday; or, the Dumps

The wailings of a maiden I recite,
A maiden fair, that Sparabella hight.
Such strains ne'er warble in the linnets throat,
Nor the gay goldfinch chaunts so sweet a note,
No mag-pye chatter'd, nor the painted jay,   5
Nor ox was heard to low, nor ass to bray.
No rustling breezes play'd the leaves among,
While thus her madrigal the damsel sung.
  A while, O D——y, lend an ear or twain,
Nor, though in homely guise, my verse disdain;   10
Whether thou seek'st new kingdoms in the sun,
Whether thy muse does at New-market run,
Or does with gossips at a feast regale,
And heighten her conceits with sack and ale,
Or else at wakes with Joan and Hodge rejoice,   15
Where D——y's lyricks swell in every voice;
Yet suffer me, thou bard of wond'rous meed,
Amid thy bays to weave this rural weed.
  Now the sun drove adown the western road,
And oxen laid at rest forget the goad,   20
The clown fatigu'd trudg'd homeward with his spade,
Across the meadows stretch'd the lengthen'd shade;

---

9 *D——y's:* D'Urfey (Thomas), an English songwriter and dramatist.

When Sparabella pensive and forlorn,
Lean'd on her rake, and straight with doleful guise
Did this sad plaint in moanful notes devise: 25
    Come night as dark as pitch, surround my head,
From Sparabella Bumkinet is fled;
The ribbon that his val'rous cudgel won,
Last Sunday happier Clumsilis put on.   30
Sure, if he'd eyes (but love, they say, has none)
I whilome by that ribbon had been known.
Ah, well-a-day! I'm shent with baneful smart,
For with the ribbon he bestow'd his heart.
    My plaint, ye lasses, with this burthen aid,   35
'Tis hard so true a damsel dies a maid.
    Shall heavy Clumsilis with me compare?
View this, ye lovers, and like me despair.
Her blubber'd lip by smutty pipes is worn,
And in her breath tobacco whiffs are born;   40
The cleanly cheese-press she could never turn,
Her awkward fist did ne'er employ the churn;
If e'er she brew'd, the drink wou'd straight grow sour,
Before it ever felt the thunder's pow'r:
No huswifry the dowdy creature knew;   45
To sum up all, her tongue confess'd the shrew.
    My plaint, ye lasses, with this burthen aid,
'Tis hard so true a damsel dies a maid.

. . . .

    Ah! didst thou know what proffers I withstood,   75
When late I met the squire in yonder wood!
To me he sped, regardless of his game,
Whilst all my cheek was glowing red with shame;
My lips he kiss'd, and prais'd my healthful look,
Then from his purse of silk a guinea took,   80
Into my hand he forc'd the tempting gold,
While I with modest struggling broke his hold.
He swore that Dick in liv'ry strip'd with lace,
Should wed me soon to keep me from disgrace;
But I nor footman priz'd nor golden fee,   85
For what is lace or gold compar'd to thee?
    My plaint, ye lasses, with this burthen aid,
'Tis hard so true a damsel dies a maid.

. . . .

    Farewel, ye woods, yet meads, ye streams that flow;
A sudden death shall rid me of my woe,   100
This penknife keen my windpipe shall divide—
What, shall I fall as squeaking pigs have dy'd!
No—to some tree this carcass I'll suspend—

---

33 *shent*: hurt.

But worrying curs find such untimely end!
I'll speed me to the pond, where the high stool   105
On the long plank hangs o'er the muddy pool,
That stool, the dread of ev'ry scolding Quean—
Yet, sure a lover should not dye so mean!
There plac'd aloft, I'll rave and rail by fits,
Though all the parish say I've lost my wits;   110
And thence, if courage holds, my self I'll throw,
And quench my passion in the lake below.
 Yet lasses, cease your burthen, cease to moan,
And, by my case forewarn'd, go mind your own.
 The sun was set; the night came on a-pace,   115
And falling dews bewet around the place,
The bat takes airy rounds on leathern wings,
And the hoarse owl his woeful dirges sings;
The prudent maiden deems it now too late,
And 'till to morrow comes, defers her fate.   120

ALEXANDER POPE *(1688–1744)*

Most topographical poems mix description of a given scene with reflections on moral, literary, and political topics. They belong loosely in what has been described as the "happy wanderer" tradition, in which a leisurely stroll evokes certain reactions in the poet to the natural and human orders. The poet's detached perspective is often symbolized by the hillside location of his wanderings. Although the paradisal aspects of the scene may be contested by less pleasant features, they ordinarily prevail because they are "higher," even the public order agreeing basically with the law of nature—as the government of Queen Anne in *Windsor Forest* reflects and preserves the harmony of sacred groves. Whether a Neoplatonist whose commerce is with Ideas or an Isaac Walton angling in the local fish pond, then, the poet does not let the troubles of the outside world ruin his private hour. He may hold with Abraham Cowley that "To be a husbandman is but a retreat from the city; to be a philosopher, from the world, or rather, a retreat from the world as it is man's, into the world as it is God's," but looking back toward society, he is likely to find some possibility of molding it, too, after the divine will.

 Properly understood, Pope indicates, nature is the model for all orders including art and society—not nature untamed and undisciplined such as that which Norman tyrants unleased in their savagery, but nature "methodized." As the *Essay on Criticism* explains,

  First follow Nature, and your judgment frame
  By her just standard, which is still the same:
  Unerring Nature, still divinely bright,
  One clear, unchang'd, and universal light,
  Life, force, and beauty, must to all impart,
  At once the source, and end, and test of art.

Between the extremes of democracy and despotism, both "unnatural," Queen Anne has carved a peace suitable to her subjects and in keeping with nature;

and the poet, far from rejecting that public order, models his own sense of form to fit it.

As the epic-sounding beginning of the poem reveals, Pope thought of the topographical poem as slightly more elevated than pastoral proper because it has to do with the accomplishments of a nation as well as with the quiet life. *Windsor Forest* is therefore pastoral on one level only. Cast in a middle style, it is capable of rising to patriotic fervor and high eulogy or of descending to praise of unambitious solitude. Both the haunts of muses and the seat of monarchy come within its scope, and the happy wanderer is both a courtier and a quiet scholar.

WINDSOR FOREST

Thy forests, Windsor! and thy green retreats,
At once the monarch's and the muse's seats,
Invite my lays. Be present, sylvan maids!
Unlock your springs, and open all your shades.
Granville commands: your aid O muses bring!   5
What muse for Granville can refuse to sing?
  The groves of Eden, vanish'd now so long,
Live in description, and look green in song:
These were my breast inspir'd with equal flame,
Like them in beauty, should be like in fame.   10
Here hills and vales, the woodland and the plain,
Here earth and water seem to strive again,
Not chaos-like together crush'd and bruis'd,
But as the world, harmoniously confus'd:
Where order in variety we see,   15
And where, tho' all things differ, all agree.
Here waving groves a checquer'd scene display,
And part admit and part exclude the day;
As some coy nymph her lover's warm address
Nor quite indulges, nor can quite repress.   20
There, interspers'd in lawns and opening glades,
Thin trees arise that shun each other's shades.
Here in full light the russet plains extend;
There wrapt in clouds the blueish hills ascend:
Ev'n the wild heath displays her purple dyes,   25
And 'midst the desert fruitful fields arise,
That crown'd with tufted trees and springing corn,
Like verdant isles the sable waste adorn.
Let India boast her plants, nor envy we
The weeping amber or the balmy tree,   30
While by our oaks the precious loads are born,
And realms commanded which those trees adorn.
Not proud Olympus yields a nobler sight,
Tho' gods assembled grace his tow'ring height,
Than what more humble mountains offer here,   35

---

5 *Granville*: George Granville, Lord Lansdown (1666–1735), to whom the poem is addressed. He wrote poems enthusiastic about nature and disliked the reign of William III, which Pope obliquely likens to that of William I (lines (43ff.). 31 *Oaks*: ships.

Where, in their blessings, all those gods appear.
See Pan with flocks, with fruits Pomona crown'd,
Here blushing Flora paints th'enamel'd ground,
Here Ceres' gifts in waving prospect stand,
And nodding tempt the joyful reaper's hand,   40
Rich industry sits smiling on the plains,
And peace and plenty tell, a Stuart reigns.
   Not thus the land appear'd in ages past,
A dreary desert and a gloomy waste,
To savage beasts and savage laws a prey,   45
And kings more furious and severe than they:
Who claim'd the skies, dispeopled air and floods,
The lonely lords of empty wilds and woods.
Cities laid waste, they storm'd the dens and caves,
(For wiser brutes were backward to be slaves).   50
What could be free, when lawless beasts obey'd,
And ev'n the elements a tyrant sway'd?
In vain kind seasons swell'd the teeming grain,
Soft show'rs distill'd, and suns grew warm in vain;
The swain with tears his frustrate labour yields,   55
And famish'd dies amidst his ripen'd fields.
What wonder then, a beast or subject slain
Were equal crimes in a despotic reign;
Both doom'd alike for sportive tyrants bled,
But while the subject starv'd, the beast was fed.   60
Proud Nimrod first the bloody chase began,
A mighty hunter, and his prey was man.
Our haughty Norman boasts that barb'rous name,
And makes his trembling slaves the royal game.
The fields are ravish'd from th'industrious swains,   65
From men their cities, and from gods their fanes:
The levell'd towns with weeds lie cover'd o'er,
The hollow winds thro' naked temples roar;
Round broken columns clasping ivy twin'd;
O'er heaps of ruin stalk'd the stately hind;   70
The fox obscene to gaping tombs retires,
And savage howlings fill the sacred quires.
Aw'd by his nobles, by his commons curst,
Th'oppressor rul'd tyrannic where he durst,
Stretch'd o'er the poor, and church, his iron rod,   75
And serv'd alike his vassals and his God.
Whom ev'n the Saxon spar'd, and bloody Dane,
The wanton victims of his sport remain.
But see the man who spacious regions gave
A waste for beasts, himself denied a grave!   80

---

37 *Pomona*: goddess of the fruit of trees. 38 *enamel'd*: certain metals were covered with enamel before being painted. 61 *Nimrod*: on the basis of the text in Genesis, Nimrod the hunter was commonly taken to be a type of the tyrant. 63 *Norman*: William I. 80 *denied a grave*: Pope finds ironic justice in the fact that Norman royalty was the victim of its own savagery because it had introduced the "forest law," which set land outside (*foris*) the common law, making it the king's hunting ground.

Stretch'd on the lawn his second hope survey,
At once the chaser and at once the prey.
Lo Rufus, tugging at the deadly dart,
Bleeds in the forest, like a wounded hart.
Succeeding monarchs heard the subjects cries,   85
Nor saw displeas'd the peaceful cottage rise.
Then gath'ring flocks on unknown mountains fed,
O'er sandy wilds were yellow harvests spread,
The forests wonder'd at th'unusual grain,
And secret transport touch'd the conscious swain.   90
Fair Liberty, Britannia's goddess, rears
Her cheerful head, and leads the golden years.
    Ye vig'rous swains! while youth ferments your blood,
And purer spirits swell the sprightly flood,
Now range the hills, the gameful woods beset,   95
Wind the shrill horn, or spread the waving net.
When milder autumn summer's heat succeeds,
And in the new-shorn field the partridge feeds,
Before his lord the ready spaniel bounds,
Panting with hope, he tries the furrow'd grounds,   100
But when the tainted gales the game betray,
Couch'd close he lies, and meditates the prey;
Secure they trust th'unfaithful field, beset,
Till hov'ring o'er 'em sweeps the swelling net.
Thus (if small things we may with great compare)   105
When Albion sends her eager sons to war,
Some thoughtless town, with ease and plenty blest,
Near, and the more near, the closing lines invest;
Sudden they seize th'amaz'd, defenceless prize
And high in air Britannia's standard flies.   110
    See! from the brake the whirring pheasant springs,
And mounts exulting on triumphant wings;
Short is his joy! he feels the fiery wound,
Flutters in blood, and panting beats the ground.
Ah! what avail his glossie, varying dyes,   115
His purple crest, and scarlet-circled eyes,
The vivid green his shining plumes unfold;
His painted wings, and breast that flames with gold?

. . . .

    Happy the man whom this bright court approves,   235
His sov'reign favours, and his country loves;
Happy next him who to these shades retires,
Whom nature charms, and whom the muse inspires,
Whom humbler joys of home-felt quiet please,

---

81 *second hope*: Richard, second son of William the Conqueror. (P) 83 *Rufus*: William Rufus. 94 *purer spirits*: animal spirits were believed to enter the bloodstream and make it more vigorous. 101 *tainted*: scented with game. 102 *meditates*: observes intently 118–234 In the lines omitted, Pope describes further hunting and fishing scenes and the transformation of the nymph Lodona into the river Lodona.

Successive study, exercise and ease.   240
He gathers health from herbs the forest yields,
And of their fragrant physic spoils the fields:
With chymic art exalts the min'ral pow'rs,
And draws the aromatic souls of flow'rs.
Now marks the course of rolling orbs on high;   245
O'er figur'd worlds now travels with his eye.
Of ancient writ unlocks the learned store,
Consults the dead, and lives past ages o'er.
Or wandring thoughtful in the silent wood,
Attends the duties of the wise and good,   250
T'observe a mean, be to himself a friend,
To follow nature, and regard his end.
Or looks on heav'n with more than mortal eyes,
Bids his free soul expatiate in the skies,
Amid her kindred stars familiar roam,   255
Survey the region, and confess her home!
Such was the life great Scipio once admir'd,
Thus Atticus, and Trumbal thus retir'd.
     Ye sacred nine! that all my soul possess,
Whose raptures fire me, and whose visions bless,   260
Bear me, oh bear me to sequester'd scenes,
The bow'ry mazes and surrounding greens;
To Thames's banks which fragrant breezes fill,
Or where ye muses sport on Cooper's Hill.
(On Cooper's Hill eternal wreaths shall grow,   265
While lasts the mountain, or while Thames shall flow)
I seem thro' consecrated walks to rove,
I hear soft music die along the grove;
Led by the sound I roam from shade to shade,
By god-like poets venerable made: 270
Here his first lays majestic Denham sung;
There the last numbers flow'd from Cowley's tongue.
O early lost! what tears the river shed
When the sad pomp along his banks was led?
His drooping swans on ev'ry note expire,   275
And on his willows hung each muse's lyre.
     Since fate relentless stop'd their heav'nly voice,
No more the forests ring, or groves rejoice;
Who now shall charm the shades where Cowley strung
His living harp, and lofty Denham sung?   280
But hark! the groves rejoice, the forest rings!
Are these reviv'd? or is it Granville sings?

---

242 *spoils*: gathers. The "happy man," unlike the tyrant who "spoils" the fields in a different
way or even the swains who pursue their gentler sports at the expense of birds and fish,
makes nature yield its innermost secrets. His is an intellectual and healing spoilage. 243
exalts: raises to a higher degree. 254 *expatiate*: literally, to walk about. 258 *Atticus*: Titus
Pomponius, a friend of Cicero's who retired from public life in Rome to pursue studies in
Athens; *Trumbal*: Sir William Trumbull (1639–1716), to whom Pope dedicated the "Spring"
pastoral. He retired to Windsor Forest after resigning as Secretary of State in the reign of
William III. 265 *Cooper's Hill*: subject of Denham's poem, which Pope used for a model.
273 *early lost*: Cowley died at age forty-nine in 1667.

'Tis yours, my lord, to bless our soft retreats,
And call the muses to their ancient seats,
To paint anew the flow'ry sylvan scenes,   285
To crown the forest with immortal greens,
Make Windsor hills in lofty numbers rise,
And lift her turrets nearer to the skies;
To sing those honours you deserve to wear,
And add new lustre to her silver star.   290

....

Behold! Augusta's glitt'ring spires increase,
And temples rise, the beauteous works of peace.
I see, I see where two fair cities bend
Their ample bow, a new White-Hall ascend!   380
There mighty nations shall inquire their doom,
The world's great oracle in times to come;
There kings shall sue, and suppliant states be seen
Once more to bend before a British queen.
   Thy trees, fair Windsor! now shall leave their woods,   385
And half thy forests rush into my floods,
Bear Britain's thunder, and her cross display,
To the bright regions of the rising day;
Tempt icy seas, where scarce the waters roll,
Where clearer flames glow round the frozen pole;   390
Or under southern skies exalt their sails,
Led by new stars, and born by spicy gales!
For me the balm shall bleed, and amber flow,
The coral redden, and the ruby glow,
The pearly shell its lucid globe infold,   395
And Phoebus warm the ripening ore to gold.
The time shall come, when free as seas or wind
Unbounded Thames shall flow for all mankind,
Whole nations enter with each swelling tide,
And seas but join the regions they divide;   400
Earth's distant ends our glory shall behold,
And the new world launch forth to seek the old.
Then ships of uncouth form shall stem the tide,
And feather'd people crowd my wealthy side,
And naked youths and painted chiefs admire   405
Our speech, our colour, and our strange attire!
Oh stretch thy reign, fair Peace! from shore to shore,
Till conquest cease, and slav'ry be no more:

---

290 *silver star*: Star of the Order of the Garter. Edward III rebuilt Windsor Castle as a
meeting place for the Order. 291–376 At the beginning of the section added in the 1713
edition of the poem, Pope catalogues the poets of England and the trials they have confronted. The God of the river Thames then rises up and foretells the future, Queen Anna
having pronounced, "Let discord cease!" In the patriotic fervor of the conclusion, Pope
thinks of "peace" in terms of vigorous commercial pursuits. 380 *new White-Hall*: the old
Whitehall Palace, often the king's residence, was burned in 1698. 384 *once more*: as in
the days of Queen Elizabeth. 386 *half thy forests rush...*: as ships. 393 *balm shall bleed*:
sap shall be drawn off. 398 *Unbounded Thames*: a wish that London may be made a free
port. (P)

Till the freed Indians in their native groves
Reap their own fruits, and woo their sable loves,   410
Peru once more a race of kings behold,
And other Mexico's be roof'd with gold.
Exil'd by thee from earth to deepest hell,
In brazen bonds shall barb'rous Discord dwell:
Gigantic Pride, pale Terror, gloomy Care,   415
And mad ambition, shall attend her there.
There purple vengeance bath'd in gore retires,
Her weapons blunted, and extinct her fires:
There hateful Envy her own snakes shall feel,
And Persecution mourn her broken wheel: 420
There Faction roar, Rebellion bite her chain,
And gasping furies thirst for blood in vain.
   Here cease thy flight, nor with unhallow'd lays
Touch the fair fame of Albion's golden days.
The thoughts of gods let Granville's verse recite,   425
And bring the scenes of opening fate to light.
My humble muse, in unambitious strains,
Paints the green forests and the flow'ry plains,
Where peace descending bids her olives spring,
And scatters blessings from her dove-like wing.   430
Ev'n I more sweetly pass my careless days,
Pleas'd in the silent shade with empty praise;
Enough for me, that to the listning swains
First in these fields I sung the sylvan strains.

GEORGE CRABBE *(1754–1832)*

With Dr. Johnson's approval, Crabbe revolted against the notion of making
shepherds noblemen in disguise. He found such literary figures as alien to
genuine peasant life as are picture-postcard versions of small-town life to
England's poverty-stricken villagers. In *The Village* he therefore infuses realism
into what he considered a moribund tradition.

from THE VILLAGE

The village life, and every care that reigns
O'er youthful peasants and declining swains;
What labour yields, and what, that labour past,
Age, in its hour of languor, finds at last;
What form the real picture of the poor,   5
Demand a song—the muse can give no more.
   Fled are those times, when, in harmonious strains,
The rustic poet praised his native plains:
No shepherds now, in smooth alternate verse,
Their country's beauty or their nymphs' rehearse;   10
Yet still for these we frame the tender strain,

---

409 *freed Indians*: Pope (or the river god) foresees the liberating of those now under
Spanish yoke.

Still in our lays fond Corydons complain,
And shepherds' boys their amorous pains reveal,
The only pains, alas! they never feel.
　　On Mincio's banks, in Caesar's bounteous reign,　　15
If Tityrus found the Golden Age again,
Must sleepy bards the flattering dream prolong,
Mechanic echoes of the Mantuan song?
From Truth and Nature shall we widely stray,
Where Virgil, not where fancy, leads the way?　　20
　　Yes, thus the muses sing of happy swains,
Because the muses never knew their pains:
They boast their peasants' pipes; but peasants now
Resign their pipes and plod behind the plough;
And few, amid the rural-tribe, have time　　25
To number syllables, and play with rhyme;
Save honest Duck, what son of verse could share
The poet's rapture, and the peasant's care?
Or the great labours of the field degrade,
With the new peril of a poorer trade?　　30
　　From this chief cause these idle praises spring,
That themes so easy few forbear to sing;
For no deep thought the trifling subjects ask;
To sing of shepherds is an easy task:
The happy youth assumes the common strain,　　35
A nymph his mistress, and himself a swain;
With no sad scenes he clouds his tuneful prayer,
But all, to look like her, is painted fair.
　　I grant indeed that fields and flocks have charms
For him that grazes or for him that farms;　　40
But when amid such pleasing scenes I trace
The poor laborious natives of the place,
And see the mid-day sun, with fervid ray,
On their bare heads and dewy temples play;
While some, with feebler heads and fainter hearts,　　45
Deplore their fortune, yet sustain their parts:
Then shall I dare these real ills to hide
In tinsel trappings of poetic pride?
　　No; cast by Fortune on a frowning coast,
Which neither groves nor happy valleys boast;　　50
Where other cares than those the muse relates,
And other shepherds dwell with other mates;
By such examples taught, I paint the cot,
As truth will paint it, and as bards will not:
Nor you, ye poor, of letter'd scorn complain,　　55
To you the smoothest song is smooth in vain;
O'ercome by labour, and bow'd down by time,
Feel you the barren flattery of a rhyme?

---

15 *Mincio*: scene of Roman pastoral.　16 *Tityrus*: Virgil, poet of Mantua.　27 *Duck*: rural
poet of some fame in the eighteenth century.

Can poets soothe you, when you pine for bread,
By winding myrtles round your ruin'd shed?   60
Can their light tales your weighty griefs o'erpower,
Or glad with airy mirth the toilsome hour?...

WILLIAM BLAKE *(1757–1827)*

Blake's *Songs of Innocence* and *Songs of Experience* place experience and
innocence in a double perspective, implying that neither exists separately,
either in childhood or in adult life. Like other pastoralists, Blake is also concerned with the relationship between art and nature and hence with the kind
of *song* that issues from each state, with results that a comparison of the
"Introduction" (from the *Songs of Innocence*) and "Mad Song" will suggest—
or, "The Blossom" and "The Sick Rose" (see the section on Songs).

THE GARDEN OF LOVE
from Songs of Experience

I went to the Garden of Love
And saw what I never had seen:
A chapel was built in the midst,
Where I used to play on the green.

And the gates of this chapel were shut,   5
And "Thou shalt not" writ over the door;
So I turn'd to the Garden of Love
That so many sweet flowers bore;

And I saw it was filled with graves,
And tomb-stones where flowers should be;   10
And priests in black gowns were walking their rounds,
And binding with briars my joys and desires.

HOW SWEET I ROAM'D

How sweet I roam'd from field to field
And tasted all the summer's pride,
Till I the Prince of Love beheld,
Who in the sunny beams did glide!

He shew'd me lilies for my hair,   5
And blushing roses for my brow;
He led me through his gardens fair,
Where all his golden pleasures grow.

With sweet May dews my wings were wet,
And Phoebus fired my vocal rage;   10
He caught me in his silken net,
And shut me in his golden cage.

He loves to sit and hear me sing;
Then, laughing, sports and plays with me;
Then stretches out my golden wing,   15
And mocks my loss of liberty.

THE CHIMNEY SWEEPER

When my mother died I was very young,
And my father sold me while yet my tongue
Could scarcely cry " 'weep! 'weep! 'weep! 'weep!"
So your chimneys I sweep, & in soot I sleep.

There's little Tom Dacre, who cried when his head,   5
That curl'd like a lamb's back, was shav'd: so I said
"Hush, Tom! never mind it, for when your head's bare
You know that the soot cannot spoil your white hair."

And so he was quiet, & that very night,
As Tom was a-sleeping, he had such a sight!   10
That thousands of sweepers, Dick, Joe, Ned, & Jack,
Were all of them lock'd up in coffins of black.

And by came an Angel who had a bright key,
And he open'd the coffins & set them all free;
Then down a green plain leaping, laughing, they run,   15
And wash in a river, and shine in the Sun.

Then naked & white, all their bags left behind,
They rise upon clouds and sport in the wind;
And the Angel told Tom, if he'd be a good boy,
He'd have God for his father, & never want joy.   20

And so Tom awoke; and we rose in the dark,
And got with our bags & our brushes to work.
Tho' the morning was cold, Tom was happy & warm;
So if all do their duty they need not fear harm.

THE SICK ROSE

from Songs of Experience

O Rose, thou art sick!
The invisible worm
That flies in the night,
In the howling storm,

Has found out thy bed   5
Of crimson joy,
And his dark secret love
Does thy life destroy.

WILLIAM WORDSWORTH *(1770–1850)*

Like other poems in Wordsworth's and Coleridge's joint collection of lyrical
ballads, these "Matthew" and "Lucy" poems bring together a pastoral concern
with idyllic nature, the narrative-dialogue technique of the ballad, and lyric
screening of the narrative events through a speaker's personal response. In
"kindling" and "restraining" those whom it chooses for its own, nature has

two quite different effects on them: "kindling" ranges upward from the arousing of sportive delight to the generating of a feeling of communion with the universe, and "restraining" ranges downward from mere calm and self-discipline to "death," for nature kills someone in each poem. (In "A Slumber Did My Spirit Seal," for instance, it imprisons its victim in a mechanical generality of rocks, stones, and trees.) Thus descriptive phrases that on first glance seem to present a pleasantly idyllic scene disclose something on second glance that is sinister in nature's deathly quiet. "Looking twice" at the natural order is the source of irony in all these poems but is especially so in "The Two April Mornings," in which the recalling of the past (the death of Matthew's daughter) imposes a new dimension on the present (a pleasant fishing excursion). The old man *has* looked twice, and the young one *learns to do so* in the course of the poem, thus the mixture of "eclogue" discussion between them and the lyric dimension of the speaker's enclosing narrative.

Yet despite nature's ambiguity as the source of life and death, the first look is merely qualified by the second, not *dis*qualified. With the aid of irony, the poems encompass the two views without disturbing the poet's basic equilibrium.

THREE YEARS SHE GREW

Three years she grew in sun and shower,
Then Nature said, "A lovelier flower
On earth was never sown;
This Child I to myself will take;
She shall be mine, and I will make   5
A Lady of my own.

"Myself will to my darling be
Both law and impulse: and with me
The Girl, in rock and plain,
In earth and heaven, in glade and bower,   10
Shall feel an overseeing power
To kindle or restrain.

"She shall be sportive as the fawn
That wild with glee across the lawn
Or up the mountain springs;   15
And hers shall be the breathing balm,
And hers the silence and the calm
Of mute insensate things.

"The floating clouds their state shall lend
To her; for her the willow bend;   20
Nor shall she fail to see
Even in the motions of the Storm
Grace that shall mould the Maiden's form
By silent sympathy.

"The stars of midnight shall be dear   25
To her; and she shall lean her ear
In many a secret place

Where rivulets dance their wayward round,
And beauty born of murmuring sound
Shall pass into her face.   30

   And vital feelings of delight
Shall rear her form to stately height,
Her virgin bosom swell;
Such thoughts to Lucy I will give
While she and I together live   35
Here in this happy dell."

Thus Nature spake — The work was done —
How soon my Lucy's race was run!
She died, and left to me
This heath, this calm, and quiet scene;   40
The memory of what has been,
And never more will be.

A SLUMBER DID MY SPIRIT SEAL

A slumber did my spirit seal;
   I had no human fears:
She seemed a thing that could not feel
   The touch of earthly years.

No motion has she now, no force;   5
   She neither hears nor sees;
Rolled round in earth's diurnal course,
   With rocks, and stones, and trees.

THE FOUNTAIN

A Conversation

We talked with open heart, and tongue
Affectionate and true,
A pair of friends, though I was young,
And Matthew seventy-two.

We lay beneath a spreading oak,   5
Beside a mossy seat;
And from the turf a fountain broke,
And gurgled at our feet.

"Now, Matthew!" said I, "let us match
This water's pleasant tune   10
With some old border-song, or catch
That suits a summer's noon;

"Or of the church-clock and the chimes
Sing here beneath the shade,
That half-mad thing of witty rhymes   15
Which you last April made!"

In silence Matthew lay, and eyed
The spring beneath the tree;

And thus the dear old Man replied,
The grey-haired man of glee: 20

"No check, no stay, this Streamlet fears;
How merrily it goes!
'Twill murmur on a thousand years,
And flow as now it flows.

"And here, on this delightful day,   25
I cannot choose but think
How oft, a vigorous man, I lay
Beside this fountain's brink.

"My eyes are dim with childish tears,
My heart is idly stirred,   30
For the same sound is in my ears
Which in those days I heard.

"Thus fares it still in our decay:
And yet the wiser mind
Mourns less for what age takes away   35
Than what it leaves behind.

"The blackbird amid leafy trees,
The lark above the hill,
Let loose their carols when they please,
Are quiet when they will.   40

"With Nature never do *they* wage
A foolish strife; they see
A happy youth, and their old age
Is beautiful and free:

"But we are pressed by heavy laws;   45
And often, glad no more,
We wear a face of joy, because
We have been glad of yore.

"If there be one who need bemoan
His kindred laid in earth,   50
The household hearts that were his own;
It is the man of mirth.

"My days, my Friend, are almost gone,
My life has been approved,
And many love me! but by none   55
Am I enough beloved."

"Now both himself and me he wrongs,
The man who thus complains!
I live and sing my idle songs
Upon these happy plains;   60

"And, Matthew, for thy children dead
I'll be a son to thee!"
At this he grasped my hand, and said,
"Alas! that cannot be."

We rose up from the fountain-side;   65
And down the smooth descent
Of the green sheep-track did we glide;
And through the wood we went;

And, ere we came to Leonard's rock,
He sang those witty rhymes   70
About the crazy old church-clock,
And the bewildered chimes.

THE TWO APRIL MORNINGS

We walked along, while bright and red
Uprose the morning sun;
And Matthew stopped, he looked, and said,
"The will of God be done!"

A village schoolmaster was he,   5
With hair of glittering grey;
As blithe a man as you could see
On a spring holiday.

And on that morning, through the grass,
And by the steaming rills,   10
We travelled merrily, to pass
A day among the hills.

"Our work," said I, "was well begun,
Then from thy breast what thought,
Beneath so beautiful a sun,   15
So sad a sigh has brought?"

A second time did Matthew step;
And fixing still his eye
Upon the eastern mountain-top,
To me he made reply: 20

"Yon cloud with that long purple cleft
Brings fresh into my mind
A day like this which I have left
Full thirty years behind.

"And just above yon slope of corn   25
Such colours, and no other,
Were in the sky, that April morn,
Of this the very brother.

"With rod and line I sued the sport
Which that sweet season gave,   30
And, to the churchyard come, stopped short
Beside my daughter's grave.

"Nine summers had she scarcely seen,
The pride of all the vale;
And then she sang;—she would have been   35
A very nightingale.

"Six feet in earth my Emma lay;
And yet I loved her more,
For so it seemed, than till that day
I e'er had loved before.   40

"And, turning from her grave, I met,
Beside the churchyard yew,
A blooming Girl, whose hair was wet
With points of morning dew.

"A basket on her head she bare;   45
Her brow was smooth and white:
To see a child so very fair,
It was a pure delight!

"No fountain from its rocky cave
E'er tripped with foot so free;   50
She seemed as happy as a wave
That dances on the sea.

"There came from me a sigh of pain
Which I could ill confine;
I looked at her, and looked again: 55
And did not wish her mine!"

Matthew is in his grave, yet now,
Methinks, I see him stand,
As at that moment, with a bough
Of wilding in his hand.   60

SAMUEL TAYLOR COLERIDGE *(1772–1834)*

The range of contrasts in "Frost at Midnight" extends beyond the pastoral
contrast of city and country but is directly related to it; it includes contrasts
of the sophisticated speaker and his innocent child, of "abstruse" wisdom and
the spontaneous lore learned from dreams and from the "eternal language"
of nature. The poem is a "romantic" version of pastoral, then, its thematic
concern being how nature "means" and its method an extension of nature
imagery into the kind of symbolism typical of the romantics (the frost's "secret"
ministry suggests a dreamlike reality beyond the boundaries of reason). The
central paradox, too, is both romantic and pastoral: quiet peacefulness and
silence speak the unhearable; moonlight encourages the perception of the
invisible. These instruments of "the great universal Teacher" transcend the
"stern perceptor" who once interrupted the poet's prefiguring dreams, in
which, though pent up in the city, he intuited the "dim sympathies" that
nature now urges upon him more forcefully.

FROST AT MIDNIGHT

The Frost performs its secret ministry,
Unhelped by any wind. The owlet's cry
Came loud—and hark, again! loud as before.
The inmates of my cottage, all at rest,

Have left me to that solitude, which suits 5
Abstruser musings: save that at my side
My cradled infant slumbers peacefully.
'Tis calm indeed! so calm, that it disturbs
And vexes meditation with its strange
And extreme silentness. Sea, hill, and wood, 10
This populous village! Sea, and hill, and wood,
With all the numberless goings-on of life,
Inaudible as dreams! the thin blue flame
Lies on my low-burnt fire, and quivers not;
Only that film, which fluttered on the grate, 15
Still flutters there, the sole unquiet thing.
Methinks, its motion in this hush of nature
Gives it dim sympathies with me who live,
Making it a companionable form,
Whose puny flaps and freaks the idling Spirit 20
By its own moods interprets, every where
Echo or mirror seeking of itself,
And makes a toy of Thought.

                    But O! how oft,
How oft, at school, with most believing mind, 25
Presageful, have I gazed upon the bars,
To watch that fluttering *stranger!* and as oft
With unclosed lids, already had I dreamt
Of my sweet birth-place, and the old church-tower,
Whose bells, the poor man's only music, rang 30
From morn to evening, all the hot Fair-day,
So sweetly, that they stirred and haunted me
With a wild pleasure, falling on mine ear
Most like articulate sounds of things to come!
So gazed I, till the soothing things, I dreamt, 35
Lulled me to sleep, and sleep prolonged my dreams!
And so I brooded all the following morn,
Awed by the stern preceptor's face, mine eye
Fixed with mock study on my swimming book:
Save if the door half opened, and I snatched 40
A hasty glance, and still my heart leaped up,
For still I hoped to see the *stranger's* face,
Townsman, or aunt, or sister more beloved,
My play-mate when we both were clothed alike!

  Dear Babe, that sleepest cradled by my side, 45
Whose gentle breathings, heard in this deep calm,
Fill up the interspersèd vacancies
And momentary pauses of the thought!
My babe so beautiful! it thrills my heart
With tender gladness, thus to look at thee, 50
And think that thou shalt learn far other lore,
And in far other scenes! For I was reared
In the great city, pent 'mid cloisters dim,

And saw nought lovely but the sky and stars.
But *thou,* my babe! shalt wander like a breeze   55
By lakes and sandy shores, beneath the crags
Of ancient mountain, and beneath the clouds,
Which image in their bulk both lakes and shores
And mountain crags: so shalt thou see and hear
The lovely shapes and sounds intelligible   60
Of that eternal language, which thy God
Utters, who from eternity doth teach
Himself in all, and all things in himself.
Great universal Teacher! he shall mould
Thy spirit, and by giving make it ask.   65

   Therefore all seasons shall be sweet to thee,
Whether the summer clothe the general earth
With greenness, or the redbreast sit and sing
Betwixt the tufts of snow on the bare branch
Of mossy apple-tree, while the nigh thatch   70
Smokes in the sun-thaw; whether the eave-drops fall
Heard only in the trances of the blast,
Or if the secret ministry of frost
Shall hang them up in silent icicles,
Quietly shining to the quiet Moon.   75

JOHN KEATS *(1795–1821)*

Implicit in Keats's odes is a basic tension between truth and beauty, which can be equated roughly with the real and the ideal, for Keats associates truth (on one level) with change, fever, and mortality and beauty with art, permanence, and "happiness." Keats's definition of the last of these terms suggests that his mode of *transforming* one state into the other depends on the poet's communion with "essence":

> Wherein lies happiness? In that which becks
> Our ready mind to fellowship divine,
> A fellowship with essence; till we shine,
> Full alchemized, and free of space.

In a letter to Benjamin Bailey (November 22, 1817), Keats finds imagination the human faculty by which "essential Beauty" is seized. Imagination prefigures as in a *dream* what is to come in *reality*; that is, beauty seized by the imagination adumbrates the truth-to-come and this beauty-truth is the "essence" of the happy life, the basis of "fellowship divine" between the subject and the object:

I am certain of nothing but of the holiness of the Heart's affections and the truth of Imagination—What the imagination seizes as Beauty must be truth—whether it existed before or not. . . . The Imagination may be compared to Adam's dream [Milton's Adam dreams of Eve and awakens to find that God has created her]—he awoke and found it truth. . . . We shall enjoy ourselves hereafter by having what we called happiness on Earth repeated in a finer tone and so repeated—And yet such a fate can only befall those who delight in sensation rather than hunger as you do after Truth—Adam's dream will do here and seems to be a conviction that Imagination and its empyreal reflection is the same as human life and its spiritual repetition.

(By "spiritual repetition" Keats does not mean disembodied repetition but "essentialized" communion with sense objects in nature.)

At the same time, Keats rejected the Christian *means* of such transformation (divine creative power) and so was left with "magic" and the power of poetry itself as its instrument. The weakness of the imagination as the means of transformation is the subject of much of his later poetry. In "Ode to a Nightingale," the speaker has already experienced such an alchemized state in communion with the nightingale but has returned to a painful state of drowsy numbness. The poem concerns various ways to escape from that uncomfortable reminder of "leaden-eyed despairs" and to return to the nightingale. All of them fail: Keats finds that "fancy"—the alchemical power that prefigures and brings about the beautiful life—cannot "cheat" as well as he had thought.

The difficulty in "Ode on a Grecian Urn" lies in the speaker's sharing in the joy of the figures depicted in art, frozen beyond change in attitudes of near-paradisal completion. The urn's equation of truth and beauty has relevance for *them*. But by having the urn state that equation, Keats leaves open the possibility that those *not* made of marble are subject still to sorrowful and cloyed hearts.

In both the nightingale and Grecian-urn poems, then, the "pastoralism" consists in part of a confrontation between ideal beauty (green boughs, music, and love) and the painful condition of the speaker, whose desire is implicitly to transform himself, to approach the permanent ideality of art, and thus to achieve "fellowship divine" with nature. In "To Autumn," Keats settles for the ambivalent quality of autumn's tuneful things at the point of fruition (therefore near harvest). Rather than asking for a transformation of nature or a freezing of process at some moment of beauty, he is resigned to autumn's joyful-elegiac processes of change. The poem is thus concerned not with the permanence of art but with a seasonal music quite unlike "ditties of no tone" that play permanently to the spirit.

ODE ON A GRECIAN URN

1

Thou still unravish'd bride of quietness,
   Thou foster-child of silence and slow time,
Sylvan historian, who canst thus express
   A flowery tale more sweetly than our rhyme:
What leaf-fring'd legend haunts about thy shape   5
   Of deities or mortals, or of both,
     In Tempe or the dales of Arcady?
What men or gods are these? What maidens loth?
What mad pursuit? What struggle to escape?
     What pipes and timbrels? What wild ecstasy?   10

2

Heard melodies are sweet, but those unheard
   Are sweeter; therefore, ye soft pipes, play on;

Not to the sensual ear, but, more endear'd,
    Pipe to the spirit ditties of no tome:
Fair youth, beneath the trees, thou canst not leave   15
    Thy song, nor ever can those trees be bare;
        Bold Lover, never, never canst thou kiss,
Though winning near the goal—yet, do not grieve;
    She cannot fade, though thou hast not thy bliss,
        For ever wilt thou love, and she be fair!   20

3

Ah, happy, happy boughs! that cannot shed
    Your leaves, nor ever bid the Spring adieu;
And, happy melodist, unwearièd,
    For ever warm and still to be enjoy'd,
More happy love! more happy, happy love!   25
    For ever warm and still to be enjoy'd,
        For ever panting, and for ever young;
All breathing human passion far above,
    That leaves a heart high-sorrowful and cloy'd,
        A burning forehead, and a parching tongue.   30

4

Who are these coming to the sacrifice?
    To what green altar, O mysterious priest,
Lead'st thou that heifer lowing at the skies,
    And all her silken flanks with garlands drest?
What little town by river or sea shore,   35
    Or mountain-built with peaceful citadel,
        Is emptied of this folk, this pious morn?
And, little town, thy streets for evermore
    Will silent be; and not a soul to tell
        Why thou art desolate, can e'er return.   40

5

O Attic shape! Fair attitude! with brede
    Of marble men and maidens overwrought,
With forest branches and the trodden weed;
    Thou, silent form, dost tease us out of thought
As doth eternity: Cold Pastoral!   45
    When old age shall this generation waste,
        Thou shalt remain, in midst of other woe
Than ours, a friend to man, to whom thou say'st,
"Beauty is truth, truth beauty,"—that is all
    Ye know on earth, and all ye need to know.   50

ODE TO A NIGHTINGALE

1

My heart aches, and a drowsy numbness pains
    My sense, as though of hemlock I had drunk,
Or emptied some dull opiate to the drains
    One minute past, and Lethe-wards had sunk:

'Tis not through envy of thy happy lot,   5
   But being too happy in thine happiness,—
      That thou, light-wingèd Dryad of the trees,
         In some melodious plot
   Of beechen green, and shadows numberless,
      Singest of summer in full-throated ease.   10

2

O, far a draught of vintage! that hath been
   Cool'd a long age in the deep-delved earth,
Tasting of Flora and the country green,
   Dance, and Provençal song, and sunburnt mirth!
O for a beaker full of the warm South,   15
   Full of the true, the blushful Hippocrene,
      With beaded bubbles winking at the brim,
         And purple-stained mouth;
   That I might drink, and leave the world unseen,
      And with thee fade away into the forest dim: 20

3

Fade far away, dissolve, and quite forget
   What thou among the leaves hast never known.
The weariness, the fever, and the fret
   Here, where men sit and hear each other groan;
Where palsy shakes a few, sad, last gray hairs,   25
      Where youth grows pale, and spectre-thin, and dies;
       Where but to think is to be full of sorrow
      And leaden-eyed despairs.
   Where Beauty cannot keep her lustrous eyes,
      Or new Love pine at them beyond tomorrow.   30

4

Away! away! for I will fly to thee,
   Not charioted by Bacchus and his pards,
But on the viewless wings of Poesy,
   Though the dull brain perplexes and retards:
Already with thee! tender is the night,   35
   And haply the Queen-Moon is on her throne,
      Cluster'd around by all her starry fays;
         But here there is no light,
   Save what from heaven is with the breezes blown
      Through verdurous glooms and winding mossy ways.   40

5

I cannot see what flowers are at my feet,
   Nor what soft incense hangs upon the boughs,
But, in embalmèd darkness, guess each sweet
   Wherewith the seasonable month endows
The grass, the thicket, and the fruit-tree wild;   45
      White hawthorn, and the pastoral eglantine;
       Fast fading violets cover'd up in leaves;

And mid-May's eldest child,
  The coming musk-rose, full of dewy wine,
    The murmurous haunt of flies on summer eves.   50

6

Darkling I listen; and, for many a time
  I have been half in love with easeful death.
Call'd him soft names in many a musèd rhyme,
  To take into the air my quiet breath;
Now more than ever seems it rich to die,   55
  To cease upon the midnight with no pain,
    While thou art pouring forth thy soul abroad
      In such an ecstasy!
Still wouldst thou sing, and I have ears in vain—
To thy high requiem become a sod.   60

7

Thou wast not born for death, immortal Bird!
  No hungry generations tread thee down;
The voice I hear this passing night was heard
  In ancient days by emperor and clown:
Perhaps the self-same song that found a path   65
  Through the sad heart of Ruth, when, sick for home,
    She stood in tears amid the alien corn;
      The same that oft-times hath
Charm'd magic casements, opening on the foam
Of perilous seas, in faery lands forlorn.   70

8

Forlorn! the very word is like a bell
  To toll me back from thee to my sole self!
Adieu! the fancy cannot cheat so well
  As she is fam'd to do, deceiving elf.
Adieu! adieu! thy plaintive anthem fades   75
  Past the near meadows, over the still stream,
    Up the hill-side; and now 'tis buried deep
      In the next valley-glades:
Was it a vision, or a waking dream?
  Fled is that music:—Do I wake or sleep?   80

TO AUTUMN

Season of mists and mellow fruitfulness,
  Close bosom-friend of the maturing sun;
Conspiring with him how to load and bless
  With fruit the vines that round the thatch-eaves run;
To bend with apples the moss'd cottage-trees,   5
  And fill all fruit with ripeness to the core;
    To swell the gourd, and plump the hazel shells
  With a sweet kernel; to set budding more,
And still more, later flowers for the bees,

Until they think warm days will never cease;　　　　　　　10
　　For Summer has o'erbrimm'd their clammy cells.

Who hath not seen thee oft amid thy store?
　　Sometimes whoever seeks abroad may find
Thee sitting careless on a granary floor,
　　Thy hair soft-lifted by the winnowing wind;　　　　　15
Or on a half-reap'd furrow sound asleep,
　　Drows'd with the fume of poppies, while thy hook
　　　Spares the next swath and all its twinéd flowers;
And sometimes like a gleaner thou dost keep
　　Steady thy laden head across a brook;　　　　　　　20
Or by a cider-press, with patient look,
　　Thou watchest the last oozings, hours by hours.

Where are the songs of Spring? Aye, where are they?
　　Think not of them,—thou hast thy music too,
While barred clouds bloom the soft-dying day　　　　　25
　　And touch the stubble-plains with rosy hue;
Then in a wailful choir the small gnats mourn
　　Among the river sallows, borne aloft
　　　Or sinking as the light wind lives or dies;
And full-grown lambs loud bleat from hilly bourn;　　30
　　Hedge-crickets sing, and now with treble soft
　　The redbreast whistles from a garden-croft,
　　　And gathering swallows twitter in the skies.

PERCY BYSSHE SHELLEY *(1792–1822)*

Unlike *Lycidas,* Shelley's pastoral elegy finds no use for nature, even as a subordinate force prefiguring the saving of the dead shepherd. Adonais has gone not to a land of higher pastoralism, as Lycidas does, but to a place devoid of images altogether. Nature is a many colored dome that the poet would trample to fragments in order to discover the white radiance of eternity. For this reason, it would not be unreasonable to consider Shelley's elegy an antipastoral poem using motives and images of the tradition as erroneous conjectures to be transcended.

FROM ADONAIS

An Elegy on the Death of John Keats*

1

I weep for Adonais—he is dead!
Oh, weep for Adonais! though our tears

---

* In a prefatory note to the poem, Shelley remarks that Keats "was buried in the romantic and lonely cemetery of the Protestants" in Rome, "under the pyramid which is the tomb of Cestius, and the massy walls and towers, now mouldering and desolate, which formed the circuit of ancient Rome. The cemetery is an open space among the ruins....It might make one in love with death, to think that one should be buried in so sweet a place." He then (erroneously) holds the critics of Keats's *Endymion* responsible for Keats's death:

The genius of the lamented person to whose memory I have dedicated these unworthy

Thaw not the frost which binds so dear a head!
And thou, sad Hour, selected from all years
To mourn our loss, rouse thy obscure compeers,   5
And teach them thine own sorrow, say: "With me
Died Adonais; till the Future dares
Forget the Past, his fate and fame shall be
An echo and a light unto eternity!"

2

Where wert thou, mighty Mother, when he lay,   10
When thy Son lay, pierced by the shaft which flies
In darkness? where was lorn Urania
When Adonais died? With veilèd eyes,
'Mid listening Echoes, in her Paradise
She sat, while one, with soft enamored breath,   15
Rekindled all the fading melodies,
With which, like flowers that mock the corse beneath,
He had adorned and hid the coming bulk of Death.

3

Oh, weep for Adonais—he is dead!
Wake, melancholy Mother, wake and weep!   20
Yet wherefore? Quench within their burning bed
Thy fiery tears, and let thy loud heart keep
Like his, a mute and uncomplaining sleep;
For he is gone where all things wise and fair
Descend.—Oh, dream not that the amorous Deep   25
Will yet restore him to the vital air;
Death feeds on his mute voice, and laughs at our despair.

. . . .

[Urania is asked to weep "anew."]

7

To that high Capital, where kingly Death   55
Keeps his pale court in beauty and decay,
He came; and bought, with price of purest breath,
A grave among the eternal.—Come away!
Haste, while the vault of blue Italian day

---

verses was not less delicate and fragile than it was beautiful; and where cankerworms abound, what wonder if its young flower was blighted in the bud? The savage criticism on his *Endymion*, which appeared in the *Quarterly Review*, produced the most violent effect on his susceptible mind; the agitation thus originated ended in the rupture of a blood-vessel in the lungs; a rapid consumption ensued.

These biographical facts are translated in the poem into a polar tension between nature and the "white radiance" of eternity and between death-dealing critics and the (eventually) liberated spirit of the poet. Keats himself becomes "Adonais," which name, as Earl Wasserman points out, combines "Adonai," the Hebrew word for Lord, and "Adonis," a Greek hunter loved by Venus and slain by a boar. Adonis had been associated with the death of vegetation in Bion and in later pastoral poems with flowers and vernal rebirth.

---

12 *Urania*: muse of astronomy, daughter of Jupiter and Mnemosyne.

Is yet his fitting charnel-roof! while still 60
He lies, as if in dewy sleep he lay;
Awake him not! surely he takes his fill
Of deep and liquid rest, forgetful of all ill.

8

He will awake no more, oh, never more!—
Within the twilight chamber spreads apace 65
The shadow of white Death, and at the door
Invisible Corruption waits to trace
His extreme way to her dim dwelling-place;
The eternal Hunger sits, but pity and awe
Soothe her pale rage, nor dares she to deface 70
So fair a prey, till darkness and the law
Of change shall o'er his sleep the mortal curtain draw.

. . . .

[Various allegorical force—winged Persuasions, veiled Des-
tines, Splendors—and then Echo and Albion mourn their loss.]

18

Ah, woe is me! Winter is come and gone,
But grief returns with the revolving year; 155
The airs and streams renew their joyous tone;
The ants, the bees, the swallows reappear;
Fresh leaves and flowers deck the dead Seasons' bier;
The amorous birds now pair in every brake,
And build their mossy homes in field and brere; 160
And the green lizard and the golden snake,
Like unimprisoned flames, out of their trance awake.

19

Through wood and stream and field and hill and Ocean
A quickening life from the Earth's heart has burst,
As it has ever done, with change and motion, 165
From the great morning of the world when first
God dawned on Chaos; in its stream immersed,
The lamps of Heaven flash with a softer light;
All baser things pant with life's sacred thirst;
Diffuse themselves; and spend in love's delight 170
The beauty and the joy of their renewèd might.

20

The leprous corpse, touched by this spirit tender,
Exhales itself in flowers of gentle breath;
Like incarnations of the stars, when splendor
Is changed to fragrance, they illumine death 175
And mock the merry worm that wakes beneath.
Nought we know, dies. Shall that alone which knows
Be as a sword consumed before the sheath
By sightless lightning?—the intense atom glows
A moment, then is quenched in a most cold repose. 180

21

Alas! that all we loved of him should be,
But for our grief, as if it had not been,
And grief itself be mortal! Woe is me!
Whence are we, and why are we? of what scene
The actors or spectators? Great and mean   185
Meet massed in death, who lends what life must borrow.
As long as skies are blue and fields are green,
Evening must usher night, night urge the morrow,
Month follow month with woe, and year wake year to sorrow.

22

He will awake no more, oh, never more!   190
"Wake thou," cried Misery, "childless Mother, rise
Out of thy sleep, and slake, in thy heart's core,
A wound more fierce than his with tears and sighs."
And all the Dreams that watched Urania's eyes,
And all the Echoes whom their sister's song   195
Had held in holy silence, cried, "Arise!"
Swift as a Thought by the snake Memory stung,
From her ambrosial rest the fading Splendor sprung.

23

She rose like an autumnal Night, that springs
Out of the East, and follows wild and drear   200
The golden Day, which, on eternal wings,
Even as a ghost abandoning a bier,
Had left the Earth a corpse. Sorrow and fear
So struck, so roused, so rapt Urania:
So saddened round her like an atmosphere   205
Of stormy mist; so swept her on her way
Even to the mournful place where Adonais lay.

. . . .

[Urania visits the death chamber and laments. Afterwards various poet-shepherds, Shelley among them, pay tribute to Adonais.

In reaction to the "viper critics" blamed for the death of Adonais, the poet reverses the previous definitions of life and death: Adonais is now more fully alive.]

38

Nor let us weep that our delight is fled
Far from these carrion kites that scream below;   335
He wakes or sleeps with the enduring dead;
Thou canst not soar where he is sitting now.—
Dust to the dust! but the pure spirit shall flow
Back to the burning fountain whence it came,
A portion of the Eternal, which must glow   340
Through time and change, unquenchably the same,
Whilst thy cold embers choke the sordid hearth of shame.

---

191 *childless mother*: Urania.

39

Peace, peace! he is not dead; he doth not sleep—
He hath awakened from the dream of life—
'Tis we who, lost in stormy visions, keep   345
With phantoms an unprofitable strife,
And in mad trance strike with our spirit's knife
Invulnerable nothings.—*We* decay
Like corpses in a charnel; fear and grief
Convulse us and consume us day by day,   350
And cold hopes swarm like worms within our living clay.

40

He has outsoared the shadow of our night;
Envy and calumny and hate and pain,
And that unrest which men miscall delight,
Can touch him not and torture not again;   355
From the contagion of the world's slow stain
He is secure, and now can never mourn
A heart grown cold, a head grown gray in vain;
Nor, when the spirit's self has ceased to burn,
With sparkless ashes load an unlamented urn.   360

41

He lives, he wakes—'tis Death is dead, not he;
Mourn not for Adonais.—Thou young Dawn,
Turn all thy dew to splendor, for from thee
The spirit thou lamentest is not gone;
Ye caverns and ye forests, cease to moan!   365
Cease, ye faint flowers and fountains, and thou Air,
Which like a mourning veil thy scarf hadst thrown
O'er the abandoned Earth, now leave it bare
Even to the joyous stars which smile on its despair!

42

He is made one with Nature: there is heard   370
His voice in all her music, from the moan
Of thunder, to the song of night's sweet bird;
He is a presence to be felt and known
In darkness and in light, from herb and stone,
Spreading itself where'er that Power may move   375
Which has withdrawn his being to its own;
Which wields the world with never-wearied love,
Sustains it from beneath, and kindles it above.

43

He is a portion of the loveliness
Which once he made more lovely: he doth bear   380
His part, while the one Spirit's plastic stress
Sweeps through the dull dense world, compelling there
All new successions to the forms they wear;

Torturing the unwilling dross that checks its fight
To its own likeness, as each mass may bear;   385
And bursting in its beauty and its might
From trees and beasts and men into the Heaven's light.

44

The splendors of the firmament of time
May be eclipsed, but are extinguished not;
Like stars to their appointed height they climb,   390
And death is a low mist which cannot blot
The brightness it may veil. When lofty thought
Lifts a young heart above its mortal lair,
And love and life contend in it, for what
Shall be its earthly doom, the dead live there   395
And move like winds of light on dark and stormy air.

45

The inheritors of unfulfilled renown
Rose from their thrones, built beyond mortal thought,
Far in the Unapparent. Chatterton
Rose pale,—his solemn agony had not   400
Yet faded from him; Sidney, as he fought
And as he fell and as he lived and loved
Sublimely mild, a Spirit without spot,
Arose; and Lucan, by his death approved;
Oblivion as they rose shrank like a thing reproved.   405

46

And many more, whose names on Earth are dark,
But whose transmitted effluence cannot die
So long as fire outlives the parent spark,
Rose, robed in dazzling immortality.
"Thou art become as one of us," they cry;   410
"It was for thee yon kingless sphere has long
Swung blind in unascended majesty,
Silent alone amid an Heaven of song.
Assume thy wingèd throne, thou Vesper of our throng!"

47

Who mourns for Adonais? Oh, come forth,   415
Fond wretch! and know thyself and him aright.
Clasp with thy panting soul the pendulous Earth;
As from a center, dart thy spirit's light
Beyond all worlds, until its spacious might
Satiate the void circumference; then shrink   420
Even to a point within our day and night;
And keep thy heart light lest it make thee sink
When hope has kindled hope, and lured thee to the brink.

---

399 *Chatterton*: poet who committed suicide at eighteen (1752–1770). 401 *Sidney*: died at
thirty-two from a battle wound. 404 *Lucan*: Roman poet who committed suicide at
twenty-six.

48

Or go to Rome, which is the sepulchre,
Oh, not of him, but of our joy: 'tis nought   425
That ages, empires, and religions there
Lie buried in the ravage they have wrought;
For such as he can lend,—they borrow not
Glory from those who made the world their prey;
And he is gathered to the kings of thought   430
Who waged contention with their time's decay,
And of the past are all that cannot pass away.

49

Go thou to Rome,—at once the Paradise,
The grave, the city, and the wilderness;
And where its wrecks like shattered mountains rise,   435
And flowering weeds and fragrant copses dress
The bones of Desolation's nakedness
Pass, till the Spirit of the spot shall lead
Thy footsteps to a slope of green access
Where, like an infant's smile, over the dead   440
A light of laughing flowers along the grass is spread.

50

And gray walls molder round, on which dull Time
Feeds, like slow fire upon a hoary brand;
And one keen pyramid with wedge sublime,
Pavilioning the dust of him who planned   445
This refuge for his memory, doth stand
Like flame transformed to marble; and beneath,
A field is spread, on which a newer band
Have pitched in Heaven's smile their camp of death,
Welcoming him we lose with scarce extinguished breath.   450

51

Here pause: these graves are all too young as yet
To have outgrown the sorrow which consigned
Its charge to each; and if the seal is set,
Here, on one fountain of a mourning mind,
Break it not thou! too surely shalt thou find   455
Thine own well full, if thou returnest home,
Of tears and gall. From the world's bitter wind
Seek shelter in the shadow of the tomb.
What Adonais is, why fear we to become?

52

The One remains, the many change and pass;   460
Heaven's light forever shines, Earth's shadows fly;
Life, like a dome of many-colored glass,
Stains the white radiance of Eternity,

---

444 *one keen pyramid*: tomb of Caius Cestius. 451 *these graves*: graves of Keats and Shelley's son William.

Until Death tramples it to fragments.—Die,
If thou wouldst be with that which thou dost seek! 465
Follow where all is fled!—Rome's azure sky,
Flowers, ruins, statues, music, words, are weak
The glory they transfuse with fitting truth to speak.

53
Why linger, why turn back, why shrink, my Heart?
Thy hopes are gone before; from all things here 470
They have departed; thou shouldst now depart!
A light is passed from the revolving year,
And man, and woman; and what still is dear
Attracts to crush, repels to make thee wither.
The soft sky smiles,—the low wind whispers near; 475
'Tis Adonais calls! oh, hasten thither,
No more let Life divide what Death can join together.

54
That Light whose smile kindles the Universe,
That Beauty in which all things work and move,
That Benediction which the eclipsing Curse 480
Of birth can quench not, that sustaining Love
Which, through the web of being blindly wove
By man and beast and earth and air and sea,
Burns bright or dim, as each are mirrors of
The fire for which all thirst, now beams on me, 485
Consuming the last clouds of cold mortality.

55
The breath whose might I have invoked in song
Descends on me; my spirit's bark is driven
Far from the shore, far from the trembling throng
Whose sails were never to the tempest given; 490
The massy earth and sphered skies are riven!
I am borne darkly, fearfully, afar;
Whilst, burning through the inmost veil of Heaven,
The soul of Adonais, like a star,
Beacons from the abode where the Eternal are. 495

ELIZABETH BARRETT BROWNING *(1806–1861)*

Like Blake's piper in the introduction to the *Songs of Innocence*, Elizabeth Barrett Browning's speaker assesses the cost of a "musical instrument" in pastoral terms, the transformation of nature into art both killing and immortalizing its particular objects.

A MUSICAL INSTRUMENT

What was he doing, the great god Pan,
    Down in the reeds by the river?
Spreading ruin and scattering ban,
Splashing and paddling with hoofs of a goat,

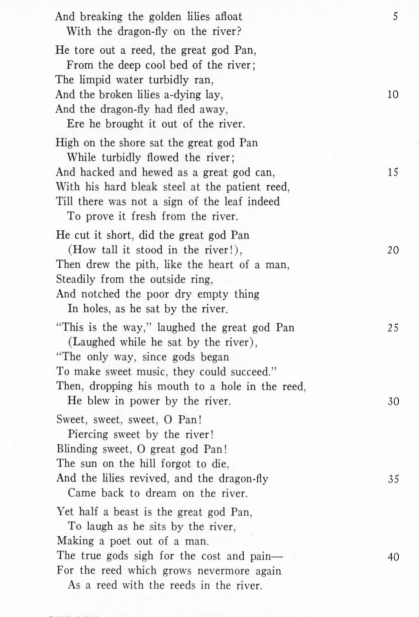

And breaking the golden lilies afloat   5
    With the dragon-fly on the river?

He tore out a reed, the great god Pan,
    From the deep cool bed of the river;
The limpid water turbidly ran,
And the broken lilies a-dying lay,   10
And the dragon-fly had fled away,
    Ere he brought it out of the river.

High on the shore sat the great god Pan
    While turbidly flowed the river;
And hacked and hewed as a great god can,   15
With his hard bleak steel at the patient reed,
Till there was not a sign of the leaf indeed
    To prove it fresh from the river.

He cut it short, did the great god Pan
    (How tall it stood in the river!),   20
Then drew the pith, like the heart of a man,
Steadily from the outside ring,
And notched the poor dry empty thing
    In holes, as he sat by the river.

"This is the way," laughed the great god Pan   25
    (Laughed while he sat by the river),
"The only way, since gods began
To make sweet music, they could succeed."
Then, dropping his mouth to a hole in the reed,
    He blew in power by the river.   30

Sweet, sweet, sweet, O Pan!
    Piercing sweet by the river!
Blinding sweet, O great god Pan!
The sun on the hill forgot to die,
And the lilies revived, and the dragon-fly   35
    Came back to dream on the river.

Yet half a beast is the great god Pan,
    To laugh as he sits by the river,
Making a poet out of a man.
The true gods sigh for the cost and pain—   40
For the reed which grows nevermore again
    As a reed with the reeds in the river.

GERARD MANLEY HOPKINS *(1845–1889)*

As the double titles of the following selections suggest, Hopkins frequently
sets opposites against each other—spring and fall, spring and death—and out
of their clash fashions a question: not which shall it be, but why is it both
and how shall it be both at once. The method and some of the themes here
as in "God's Grandeur" and "The Windhover" are familiar in pastoral literature; much is uniquely Hopkinsian. (For remarks about "Spring and Fall,"
see the appendix on Literature and Literary Genres, pp. 591.)

SPRING AND FALL: TO A YOUNG CHILD*

Márgarét, are you grieving
Over Goldengrove unleaving?
Leáves, líke the things of man, you
With your fresh thoughts care for, can you?
Áh! ás the heart grows older   5
It will come to such sights colder
By and by, nor spare a sigh
Though worlds of wanwood leafmeal lie;
And yet you wíll weep and know why.
Now no matter, child, the name: 10
Sórrow's spríngs áre the same.
Nor mouth had, no nor mind, expressed
What heart heard of, ghost guessed:
It ís the blight man was born for,
It is Margaret you mourn for.   15

SPRING AND DEATH*

I had a dream. A wondrous thing:
It seem'd an evening in the Spring:
—A little sickness in the air
From too much fragrance everywhere:—
As I walk'd a stilly wood,   5
Sudden, Death before me stood:
In a hollow lush and damp,
He seem'd a dismal mirky stamp
On the flowers that were seen
His charnelhouse-grate ribs between,   10
And with coffin-black he barr'd the green.
"Death," said I, "what do you here
At this Spring season of the year?"
"I mark the flowers ere the prime
Which I may tell at Autumn-time."   15
Ere I had further question made
Death was vanish'd from the glade.
Then I saw that he had bound
Many trees and flowers round
With a subtle web of black,   20
And that such a sable track
Lay along the grasses green
From the spot where he had been.
  But the Spring-tide pass'd the same;
Summer was as full of flame;   25
Autumn-time no earlier came.
And the flowers that he had tied,
As I mark'd not always died

Sooner than their mates; and yet
Their fall was fuller of regret: 30
  It seem'd so hard and dismal thing,
Death, to mark them in the Spring.

ROBERT FROST *(1875–1963)*

In "The Most of It," communication between man and nature is both something more and something less than the speaker originally wants it to be.
Calling for nature to acknowledge him in some sort of reciprocal dialogue, he
discovers instead a magnificent buck, indifferent to him, which takes its own
course, crashes through the brush, and leaves him in his original solitude. "The
Oven Bird" is much like the poet himself in singing of diminished things—
diminished twofold if one has been led by the American transcendentalists
or English romantics to look for boundless moments in nature. The woodpile,
too, is another of Frost's diminished things, slowly deteriorating in nature's all-
consuming swamp. In a sense it is a work of art and a fitting end of the speaker's
aimless search, and even the frozen wasteland has its grace, its "tall slim trees";
but the trees "add up" to chaos, and the four by four by eight pile of wood,
so exactly measured and stacked, is no more a permanent monument than other
works of art in Frost: it is merely a "momentary stay against confusion." In
each of these poems, "making the most of it" requires a tactical readjustment
of the speaker's expectations.

THE WOODPILE*

Out walking in the frozen swamp one grey day
I paused and said, "I will turn back from here.
No, I will go on farther—and we shall see."
The hard snow held me, save where now and then
One foot went down. The view was all in lines   5
Straight up and down of tall slim trees
Too much alike to mark or name a place by
So as to say for certain I was here
Or somewhere else: I was just far from home.
A small bird flew before me. He was careful   10
To put a tree between us when he lighted,
And say no word to tell me who he was
Who was so foolish as to think what *he* thought.
He thought that I was after him for a feather—
The white one in his tail; like one who takes   15
Everything said as personal to himself.
One flight out sideways would have undeceived him.
And then there was a pile of wood for which
I forgot him and let his little fear
Carry him off the way I might have gone,   20

Without so much as wishing him good-night.
He went behind it to make his last stand.
It was a cord of maple, cut and split
And piled—and measured, four by four by eight.
And not another like it I could see.   25
No runner tracks in this year's snow looped near it.
And it was older sure than this year's cutting,
Or even last year's or the year's before.
The wood was grey and the bark warping off it
And the pile somewhat sunken. Clematis   30
Had wound strings round and round it like a bundle.
What held it though on one side was a tree
Still growing, and on one a stake and prop,
These latter about to fall. I thought that only
Someone who lived in turning to fresh tasks   35
Could so forget his handiwork on which
He spent himself, the labor of his axe,
And leave it there far from a useful fireplace
To warm the frozen swamp as best it could
With the slow smokeless burning of decay.   40

THE OVEN BIRD*

There is a singer everyone has heard,
Loud, a mid-summer and mid-wood bird,
Who makes the solid tree trunks sound again.
He says that leaves are old and that for flowers
Mid-summer is to spring as one to ten.   5
He says the early petal-fall is past
When pear and cherry bloom went down in showers
On sunny days a moment overcast;
And comes that other fall we name to fall.
He says the highway dust is over all.   10
The bird would cease and be as other birds
But that he knows in singing not to sing.
The question that he frames in all but words
Is what to make of a diminished thing.

THE MOST OF IT*

He thought he kept the universe alone;
For all the voice in answer he could wake
Was but the mocking echo of his own
From some tree-hidden cliff across the lake.
Some morning from the boulder-broken beach   5
He would cry out on life, that what it wants

Is not its own love back in copy speech,
But counter-love, original response.
And nothing ever came of what he cried
Unless it was the embodiment that crashed   10
In the cliff's talus on the other side,
And then in the far distant water splashed,
But after a time allowed for it to swim,
Instead of proving human when it neared
And someone else additional to him,   15
As a great buck it powerfully appeared,
Pushing the crumpled water up ahead,
And landed pouring like a waterfall,
And stumbled through the rocks with horny tread,
And forced the underbrush—and that was all.   20

WALLACE STEVENS *(1879–1956)*

Unlike traditional pastoral elegies, "Sunday Morning" is not concerned with
a particular death but with the effect of death in general on the concept of
"paradise." Stevens' musing lady finds it the "mother of beauty" and so wel-
comes the chaos of the sun, which neither weeps nor rejoices with man but
with which one nonetheless identifies in an "old dependency of day and night."
Christ remains dead in the tomb, but deer and quail live now in the wilderness.

SUNDAY MORNING*

1

Complacencies of the peignoir, and late
Coffee and oranges in a sunny chair,
And the green freedom of a cockatoo
Upon a rug mingle to dissipate
The holy hush of ancient sacrifice.   5
She dreams a little, and she feels the dark
Encroachment of that old catastrophe,
As a calm darkens among water-lights.
The pungent oranges and bright, green wings
Seem things in some procession of the dead,   10
Winding across wide water, without sound.
The day is like wide water, without sound,
Stilled for the passing of her dreaming feet
Over the seas, to silent Palestine,
Dominion of the blood and sepulchre.   15

2

Why should she give her bounty to the dead?
What is divinity if it can come
Only in silent shadows and in dreams?
Shall she not find in comforts of the sun,

---

* Reprinted by permission of AAK, Inc. from *The Collected Poems of Wallace Stevens*
by Wallace Stevens. Copyright 1923, 1951 by Wallace Stevens.

In pungent fruit and bright, green wings, or else   20
In any balm or beauty of the earth,
Things to be cherished like the thought of heaven?
Divinity must live within herself:
Passions of rain, or moods in falling snow;
Grievings in loneliness, or unsubdued   25
Elations when the forest blooms; gusty
Emotions on wet roads on autumn nights;
All pleasures and all pains, remembering
The bough of summer and the winter branch.
These are the measures destined for her soul.   30

3

Jove in the clouds had his inhuman birth.
No mother suckled him, no sweet land gave
Large-mannered motions to his mythy mind.
He moved among us, as a muttering king,
Magnificent, would move among his hinds,   35
Until our blood, commingling, virginal,
With heaven, brought such requital to desire
The very hinds discerned it, in a star.
Shall our blood fail? Or shall it come to be
The blood of paradise? And shall the earth   40
Seem all of paradise that we shall know?
The sky will be much friendlier then than now,
A part of labor and a part of pain,
And next in glory to enduring love,
Not this dividing and indifferent blue.   45

4

She says, "I am content when wakened birds,
Before they fly, test the reality
Of misty fields, by their sweet questionings;
But when the birds are gone, and their warm fields
Return no more, where, then, is paradise?"   50
There is not any haunt of prophecy,
Nor any old chimera of the grave,
Neither the golden underground, nor isle
Melodious, where spirits gat them home,
Nor visionary south, nor cloudy palm   55
Remote on heaven's hill, that has endured
As April's green endures; or will endure
Like her remembrance of awakened birds,
Or her desire for June and evening, tipped
By the consummation of the swallow's wings.   60

5

She says, "But in contentment I still feel
The need of some imperishable bliss."
Death is the mother of beauty; hence from her,
Alone, shall come fulfilment to our dreams

And our desires. Although she strews the leaves   65
Of sure obliteration on our paths,
The path sick sorrow took, the many paths
Where triumph rang its brassy phrase, or love
Whispered a little out of tenderness,
She makes the willow shiver in the sun   70
For maidens who were wont to sit and gaze
Upon the grass, relinquished to their feet.
She causes boys to pile new plums and pears
On disregarded plate. The maidens taste
And stray impassioned in the littering leaves.   75

6

Is there no change of death in paradise?
Does ripe fruit never fall? Or do the boughs
Hang always heavy in that perfect sky,
Unchanging, yet so like our perishing earth,
With rivers like our own that seek for seas   80
They never find, the same receding shores
That never touch with inarticulate pang?
Why set the pear upon those river-banks
Or spice the shores with odors of the plum?
Alas, that they should wear our colors there,   85
The silken weavings of our afternoons,
And pick the strings of our insipid lutes!
Death is the mother of beauty, mystical,
Within whose burning bosom we devise
Our earthly mothers waiting, sleeplessly.   90

7

Supple and turbulent, a ring of men
Shall chant in orgy on a summer morn
Their boisterous devotion to the sun,
Not as a god, but as a god might be,
Naked among them, like a savage source.   95
Their chant shall be a chant of paradise,
Out of their blood, returning to the sky;
And in their chant shall enter, voice by voice,
The windy lake wherein their lord delights,
The trees, like serafin, and echoing hills,   100
That choir among themselves long afterward.
They shall know well the heavenly fellowship
Of men that perish and of summer morn.
And whence they came and whither they shall go
The dew upon their feet shall manifest.   105

8

She hears, upon that water without sound,
A voice that cries, "The tomb in Palestine
Is not the porch of spirits lingering.
It is the grave of Jesus, where he lay."

We live in an old chaos of the sun,   110
Or old dependency of day and night,
Or island solitude, unsponsored, free,
Of that wide water, inescapable.
Deer walk upon our mountains, and the quail
Whistle about us their spontaneous cries;   115
Sweet berries ripen in the wilderness;
And, in the isolation of the sky,
At evening, casual flocks of pigeons make
Ambiguous undulations as they sink,
Downward to darkness, on extended wings.   120

EDWIN MUIR *(1887–1958)*

Like Blake's contrasting states of innocence and experience, Muir's Eden and
the world outside it do not cancel each other but serve as necessary opposites
in a comprehensive set of terms and in the emergence of a third condition,
neither one nor the other. Each demands its opposite as "yes" demands "no"
and "morality" "immorality." The third term is (metaphorically) the new
"blossom" that grows in famished fields, or virtue's "strange blessing," which
can be known only outside Eden by those who remember Eden.

ONE FOOT IN EDEN*

One foot in Eden still, I stand
And look across the other land.
The world's great day is growing late,
Yet strange these fields that we have planted
So long with crops of love and hate.   5
Time's handiworks by time are haunted,
And nothing now can separate
The corn and tares compactly grown.
The armorial weed in stillness bound
About the stalk; these are our own.   10
Evil and good stand thick around
In the fields of charity and sin
Where we shall lead our harvest in.

Yet still from Eden springs the root
As clean as on the starting day.   15
Time takes the foliage and the fruit
And burns the archetypal leaf
To shapes of terror and of grief
Scattered along the winter way.
But famished field and blackened tree   20
Bear flowers in Eden never known.
Blossoms of grief and charity
Bloom in these darkened fields alone.

* Reprinted from *Collected Poems 1921–1951* by Edwin Muir. Copyright © 1957 by Edwin
Muir, published by Grove Press, Inc.

What had Eden ever to say
Of hope and faith and pity and love   25
Until was buried all its day
And memory found its treasure trove?
Strange blessings never in Paradise
Fall from these beclouded skies.

JOHN CROWE RANSOM *(1888–   )*

Ransom's elegy for John Whiteside's daughter could obviously be considered under other headings. But the contrast of the girl's innocent games to her final condition, primly propped in death, is essentially a pastoral strategy. And like many of the best pastoralists, Ransom does not settle for one or the other view of the girl but suggests that she is something of both, dead in fact but still alive in the poet's precise and unsentimental memory of her.

BELLS FOR JOHN WHITESIDE'S DAUGHTER*

There was such speed in her little body,
And such lightness in her footfall,
It is no wonder that her brown study
Astonishes us all.

Her wars were bruited in our high window.   5
We looked among orchard trees and beyond,
Where she took arms against her shadow,
Or harried unto the pond

The lazy geese, like a snow cloud
Dripping their snow on the green grass,   10
Tricking and stopping, sleepy and proud,
Who cried in goose, Alas,

For the tireless heart within the little
Lady with rod that made them rise
From their noon apple dreams, and scuttle   15
Goose-fashion under the skies!

But now go the bells, and we are ready;
In one house we are sternly stopped
To say we are vexed at her brown study,
Lying so primly propped.   20

STEPHEN SPENDER *(1909–   )*

Spender suggests that for children in a slum, images of unattainable flowers and valleys are a needless cruelty, the contrast with their condition merely heightening their discomfort. But there is an "unless clause: if the slum can be broken open and the children restored to nature and to the world of books (to "leaves" white and green), they may yet have the best of both worlds.

---

* Reprinted by permission of AAK, Inc. from *Poems and Essays* by John Crowe Ransom. Copyright, 1924 by AAK, Inc. Renewed, 1952 by John Crowe Ransom.

AN ELEMENTARY SCHOOL CLASSROOM IN A SLUM*

Far far from gusty waves, these children's faces.
Like rootless weeds the torn hair round their paleness.
The tall girl with her weighed-down head. The paper-
seeming boy with rat's eyes. The stunted unlucky heir
Of twisted bones, reciting a father's gnarled disease,   5
His lesson from his desk. At back of the dim class
One unnoted, mild and young: his eyes live in a dream
Of squirrels' game, in tree room, other than this.

On sour cream walls, donations. Shakespeare's head
Cloudless at dawn, civilized dome riding all cities.   10
Belled, flowery, Tyrolese valley. Open-handed map
Awarding the world its world. And yet, for these
Children, these windows, not this world, are world,
Where all their future's painted with a fog,
A narrow street sealed in with a lead sky,   15
Far far from rivers, capes, and stars of words.

Surely Shakespeare is wicked, the map a bad example
With ships and sun and love tempting them to steal—
For lives that slyly turn in their cramped holes
From fog to endless night? On their slag heap, these children   20
Wear skins peeped through by bones, and spectacles of steel
With mended glass, like bottle bits in slag.
Tyrol is wicked; map's promising a fable:
All of their time and space are foggy slum,
So blot their maps with slums as big as doom.   25

Unless, governor, teacher, inspector, visitor,
This map becomes their window and these windows
That open on their lives like crouching tombs
Break, O break open, till they break the town
And show the children to the fields and all their world   30
Azure on their sands, to let their tongues
Run naked into books, the white and green leaves open
The history theirs whose language is the sun.

DYLAN THOMAS *(1914–1953)*

Retrospection, which superimposes adulthood on youth, is the main source of
tension in "Fern Hill," for memory is automatically dialectical in its crossing
of present and past and may be the source of "pastoral dialectic" if the
two periods are contraries of a certain kind. For Thomas, youth is a time
of joy "under apple boughs." It lasts only while time, "in the mercy of
his means," permits. The childhood of the race in Eden, "in the first spinning place" after the birth of simple light, must have been similar, Thomas
suggests. But the past tense and the concept of time as the guardian of

---

paradise imply throughout that time is also a prison-keeper. In the present, the farm has fled the childless land, and the speaker is "green and dying." Both the sea and the poet "sing," however, because time (and tide) moves them. The "force" of "The Force that through the Green Fuse..." has much the same goading function: it simultaneously makes things grow green and destroys them in the processes of time, making the stem of the flower both its supply line and its fuse.

THE FORCE THAT THROUGH THE GREEN FUSE DRIVES THE FLOWER*

The force that through the green fuse drives the flower
Drives my green age; that blasts the roots of trees
Is my destroyer.
And I am dumb to tell the crooked rose
My youth is bent by the same wintry fever.   5

The force that drives the water through the rocks
Drives my red blood; that dries the mouthing streams
Turns mine to wax.
And I am dumb to mouth unto my veins
How at the mountain spring the same mouth sucks.   10

The hand that whirls the water in the pool
Stirs the quicksand; that ropes the blowing wind
Hauls my shroud sail.
And I am dumb to tell the hanging man
How of my clay is made the hangman's lime.   15

The lips of time leech to the fountain head;
Love drips and gathers, but the fallen blood
Shall calm her sores.
And I am dumb to tell a weather's wind
How time has ticked a heaven round the stars.   20

And I am dumb to tell the lover's tomb
How at my sheet goes the same crooked worm.

FERN HILL*

Now as I was young and easy under the apple boughs
About the lilting house and happy as the grass was green,
    The night above the dingle starry,
        Time let me hail and climb
        Golden in the heydays of his eyes,   5
And honoured among wagons I was prince of the apple towns
And once below a time I lordly had the trees and leaves

Trail with daisies and barley
Down the rivers of the windfall light.

And as I was green and carefree, famous among the barns   10
About the happy yard and singing as the farm was home,
     In the sun that is young once only,
       Time let me play and be
     Golden in the mercy of his means,
And green and golden I was huntsman and herdsman, the calves   15
Sang to my horn, the foxes on the hills barked clear and cold,
       And the sabbath rang slowly
     In the pebbles of the holy streams.

All the sun long it was running, it was lovely, the hay
Fields high as the house, the tunes from the chimneys, it was air   20
     And playing, lovely and watery
      And fire green as grass.
     And nightly under the simple stars
As I rode to sleep the owls were bearing the farm away,
All the moon long I heard, blessed among stables, the nightjars   25
     Flying with the ricks, and the horses
     Flashing into the dark.

And then to awake, and the farm, like a wanderer white
With the dew, come back, the cock on his shoulder: it was all
     Shining, it was Adam and maiden,   30
      The sky gathered again
     And the sun grew round that very day.
So it must have been after the birth of the simple light
In the first, spinning place, the spellbound horses walking warm
     Out of the whinnying green stable ·   35
      On to the fields of praise.

And honoured among foxes and pheasants by the gay house
Under the new made clouds and happy as the heart was long,
     In the sun born over and over,
      I ran my heedless ways,   40
     My wishes raced through the house-high hay
And nothing I cared, at my sky blue trades, that time allows
In all his tuneful turning so few and such morning songs
     Before the Children green and golden
      Follow him out of grace,   45

Nothing I cared, in the lamb white days, that time would take me
Up to the swallow thronged loft by the shadow of my hand,
     In the moon that is always rising,
      Nor that riding to sleep
     I should hear him fly with the high fields   50
And wake to the farm forever fled from the childless land.
Oh as I was young and easy in the mercy of his means,
      Time held me green and dying
     Though I sang in my chains like the sea.

ALVIN FEINMAN *(1929–   )*

The response of the mind to the scene in Feinman's urban setting is based not on some underlying intelligible order or specific meaning but on the momentary overlapping of poetry and nature. Both are tuned and emblaze a radiance in a style of precise austerity, stripped bare, corrected to a "severe essential elegance"; both reflect images as in "rigid water," composing what they mirror; both have a light that "exacts" all good as it cleanses what it shines on. These parallels suggest that nature at its best *is* poetry and that this is as it should be—a "proper" pastoral. Even so, the poet's reading of the scene is implicitly rare and shortlived. The intrusion of other elements (heavier traffic, for instance), and hence the decomposing of the scene, awaits an imminent cue.

NOVEMBER SUNDAY MORNING*

And the light, a wakened heyday of air
Tuned low and clear and wide,
A radiance now that would emblaze
And veil the most golden horn
Or any entering of a sudden clearing   5
To a standing, astonished, revealed...

That the actual streets I loitered in
Lay lit like fields, or narrow channels
About to open to a burning river;
All brick and window vivid and calm   10
As though composed in a rigid water
No random traffic would dispel...

As now through the park, and across
The chill nailed colors of the roofs,
And on near trees stripped bare,   15
Corrected in the scant remaining leaf
To their severe essential elegance,
Light is the all-exacting good,
That dry, forever virile stream
That wipes each thing to what it is,   20
The whole, collage and stone, cleansed
To its proper pastoral...
                                          I sit
And smoke, and linger out desire.

* From *Preambles and Other Poems* by Alvin Feinman. Copyright © 1964 by Alvin Feinman. Reprinted by permission of Oxford University Press, Inc.

Heroic Modes

Introduction

I. The Hero As the words *epikos* and *epos* ("oral recitation" or "song") indicate, the Greek concept of heroic poetry derived in part from its public mode of presentation; but it also described a certain attitude, subject, and style. In Homer the epic was magnificent, dignified in movement, and elevated in style, and it contained long speeches, sweeping periods, and formal introductions. By Virgil's time an invocation to the muses, extended similes, the descent of messengers from Mount Olympus, and elaborate descriptions of funeral games and military encounters had become conventional. To both Greeks and Romans, "epic" thus meant primarily a formal account of heroic trials narrated in a heightened style.

Although in some ways the boundaries of epic widened with later Roman and European writers, the conventions themselves changed very little. Because they were based on a particular concept of the narrative voice and the presence of the narrator before an audience, these conventions proved ill-adapted to the rise of the printing press, middle-class realism, the inner probings of private consciousness, and the domestic experience of the modern nonhero—the domains of documentary fiction, lyric, romance, drama, and cinema. It is not surprising, therefore, that many literary historians consider the epic form after Milton moribund, tracing its decline in the seventeenth and eighteenth centuries in the rise of mock-heroic forms. Although such satiric and novelistic works as *The Rape of the Lock* and *Tom Jones,* for example, retain residual elements of epic technique, they are put largely to comic employment, turning the hero wrong side out. Picaresque heroes like Tom Jones and Humphrey Clinker come from the middle class; their exploits are played *against* heroic conventions but are not presented straightforwardly *as* heroic. Although the novelist may give such protagonists a modified heroic stature, it is screened through the qualifying medium of satire. In some mock-epic forms, the contrast between the expectations of convention and the trivialities of society may either deflate epic pretensions (as in Pope's incongruous image of the "stern Achilles" stalking "through a mead of daffodillies") or suggest obliquely that by comparison with ancient heroes the modern "hero" should stick to sweeping out tents. By contrasting Belinda's tinsel world of flirtation, lap dogs, and rites of the mirror with the action of several epics, Pope's *The Rape of the Lock* both dignifies and mocks the heroine's "name." The muse "consecrates to fame" the exploits of the hero and heroine, but at the same time the poet suggests that only the beau monde of the London social set will discern them. Other eighteenth-century heroes and heroines, such as Robinson Crusoe and Moll Flanders, although their exploits may be adventurous and extraordinary, have little to do with the virtues of nobility, even by contrast. Crusoe travels to his deserted island to establish a burgher economy of goats, farm crops, and eventually an owner-worker society. Moll Flanders' feats of thievery, plotting, and sexual bargaining are eventually rewarded with a well-stocked Virginia plantation. The chief concerns of both are the daily mechanics of economic survival.

To the romantics, the heroic was likewise not a matter of public service or inherited nobility, and to post-romantic writers, exemplary religious and martial heroes proved even less appealing. The hero of the modern novel has little influence on his environment; he is circumscribed by the manners, scene, and economic class into which he is born. Stream-of-consciousness techniques, first-person narrative—"inside" perspectives capable of embracing confession and dream fantasy, comedy, irony, and the realism of world wars—have replaced the conventions of oral recitation in nearly all long narrative works. The modern wanderer, like Joyce's Ulysses, is half in and half out of society—a Huck Finn, Humbert Humbert, or Augie March, an expatriate of the lost generation, a dope addict, a homosexual, or a rebel against the household gods. Whatever nobility he may have—and an Augie March or a Huck Finn may salvage some—must take shape out of a controlling, generally urban scene and be defined partly in terms of the hero's capacity to *resist* society. Far from belonging to a messenger from Olympus, the voice that delivers oracles to the modern hero comes from social consciousness, within or without, and its messages concern the mandates of money, sex, and power. Like that of Milton's Satan (perhaps the first epic figure to realize the tempting power of self-aggrandizement and free enterprise), it entices the hero with forms of conspicuous consumption. It is in reaction to such voices from officialdom that the heroes of many picaresque narratives—myths of the West, the outcast-romances of Steinbeck, the return-to-childhood adventures of Twain—refuse to adopt public roles at all. Huck Finn perhaps speaks for all of them when he says, "I reckon I got to light out for the territory ahead...because Aunt Sally she's goin' to adopt me and sivilize me, and I can't stand it. I been there before." The partly comic picaresque hero of the eighteenth century at least returns to society at the end of his travels, but the modern wanderer is likely to remain homeless.

Hence as a social paradigm, the epic hero is a creature of the past. A representative of the best elements of a bygone culture, he could not survive the fragmentation of social values, the discovery of antiheroic motives in Freudian depth-psychology, and the realism of an industrial age.

Yet the word "epic" is still spendable currency—albeit sometimes as a publicity term for historical movies featuring chariot races and barbarian hordes—and the epic spirit is no more bound to strict conventions than tragedy to the fall of kings. Even historically, literary theorists have applied the word liberally to all variations of the heroic mode that have sufficient magnitude. The line between epic and heroic and between epic and romance has never been easy to draw. Several Renaissance critics, for instance, consider the epic hero both a public "mold of form" and a romantic lover. Believing that "hero" and "eros" had a common etymology, Tasso ranked the several heroes of *Jerusalem Delivered* according to their place in a hierarchy of neoplatonic loves. Even some primitive epics (or "folk" as distinguished from "literary" modes) resemble romance more than they do epics like *The Iliad* or *The Aeneid*.

Consider, for instance, the kinds of journeys undertaken by the heroes in each. Nearly all heroic modes have in common a quest motif. Ulysses journeys from the Trojan wars toward Ithaca and Penelope, Aeneas from an empire in flames toward a new empire that he is to found, and Milton's Satan from Hell toward Eden to seduce man. But in epic quests proper, the journey is normally toward a social institution like the family in *The Odyssey* or the Roman empire in *The Aeneid*. The journeys of romance heroes, on the other hand, reflect primarily the hero's own internal state. If the epic hero struggles against known and recognized combatants on the open plain—more likely than not in full view of his people, who are depending on him—the romance hero travels through obscure forests, alone or with a symbolic psychic guide of some kind (a dwarf, for instance), perhaps in behalf of a lady. He struggles against mysterious, unknowable forces, in a world of erotic, religious, or psychic cross-currents. His encounters may well have social relevance, but at one remove (as social behavior is eventually changed by psychological experience).

There are also differences in the *presentation* of the quest. Whereas the epic journey is ordinarily a central, dominant action around which the main elements of the poem are organized, in romances the journeys are multiple, asocial, and unhistorical—located in a past that never was. Several heroes are likely to undertake them, and their occurrence outside historical space and time, combined with a large admixture of the marvelous, gives them the qualities of distortion and displacement characteristic of dream fantasy. Although Tasso argued that a heroic poem may concern inner passions, opinions, and character (made manifest through allegory) and at the same time external social and heroic action (presented by direct imitation), it is obviously difficult to combine the two interests and modes in a single work: one tends to fall to the epic, the other to the romance. The principles of organization, the surface texture, and the concept of character in dream technique differ from those in epic proper much as Spenser's Redcross Knight differs from Homer's Achilles: one is a single character engaged in a continuous action, the other an allegorical or programmatic figure representing one of several virtues that make up the perfect Christian gentleman.

Romance and epic heroes thus pass through different landscapes and obey different laws. The episodic construction of allegory and romance results from the free use of action and scene to embody spiritual and psychological forces, which provide the inner logic of the work. *The Faerie Queene* is no less organized than *The Aeneid*, but its principle of order does not lie in the history or geography of its scene or in the external action of its hero. Malory's account of the grail quests, although articulately organized in terms of theme, deals with several major knights, each illustrating a different relationship with holiness and arriving at a different goal. The structural principle in such works depends on balance, contrast, dream-association, and a distinction between surface "fable" and underlying meaning. The laws of epic, on the other hand, are closer to the normal laws of cause and effect governing the external world of politics and manners. Whereas Cuchulain may have seven pupils in each eye and spout flames from his mouth, Aeneas must see and speak normally.

The distinction between romance and epic, however, is often less decisive in practice than we have suggested because many works combine something of both forms. In the old Babylonian and Sumerian *Epic of Gilgamesh* (seventeenth or eighteenth century B.C.) the adventures of the hero are neither "probable" nor unified in a single journey, although on the whole the work seems more epic than allegorical or romantic. The distinction between hero and god, mortal and divine, dissolves in their continual interplay (Gilgamesh is himself two-thirds god) and in the emphasis on the marvelous. But eventually an epic hero's debt to society and to his own mortality must be made apparent. Beowulf, although possessed of divine favor and quasi-magical power, dies while attempting to protect his people from disaster. His readiness to make that attempt and his inability to survive it indicate the necessary interaction of politics and mortal limitation. Even the divine Gilgamesh learns to fear death like other men. Although in his romantic quest for eternal youth he is given a magic plant-of-promise, he loses it to a serpent. His friend Engidu miraculously returns from the dead, but only to tell Gilgamesh of the sorrows of the afterlife:

> See, the body which thou hast clasped
> So that thy heart was glad—
> The worms eat it like an old garment.
> My body...
> Is vanished away, full of dust,
> In dust is it sunken away.

And so Gilgamesh realizes that he has worked no good for himself: "For the worm of the earth have I wrought good."

In contrast, the romantic hero has the privilege of springing back to life again, either literally or behind another face (as in the transfers of identity in dreams). The tendency in romance to scatter the heroic image among several protagonists makes it difficult for a particular hero to illustrate both the triumph and the limitations of human heroism, as the epic hero on his single journey usually does. Whereas Tristram, Sir Bors, Lancelot, and Galahad in Malory and the Redcross Knight, Sir Guyon, Sir Artegall, and Sir Calidore in Spenser represent different heroic potentials, Milton's Adam falls *and* rises, Aeneas founds his empire in sorrow as well as in triumph, and Beowulf becomes even more impressive in death, as a mortal, than in triumph over Grendel, as a supernaturally gifted figure. The epic hero thus tends to represent both the highest achievements of his culture and the limitations of the human condition that make those achievements difficult and meaningful.

Since the epic hero has no magic potions ot cure wounds or marvelous steeds with which to escape danger and hence confronts ultimate defeat or the threat of it, he is also distinguishable from journeying heroes who have stronger divine sanctions. A pilgrim like Bunyan's Christian, for instance, is less epic than allegorical, although in a way different from the hero of romance; he represents something like Bunyan's notion of the potential Christian. (Although he might indeed have failed to reach the eternal city, he would have failed not as a Christian but as a sinner.) Insofar as he is representative rather than singular or historical, he is the allegorical equivalent to a mythic hero, a fictional convenience whose goal in this case is not to reform or protect society but to leave it. Much closer to the traditional epic hero is the character "Dante" in *The Divine Comedy,* another variation of the pilgrim figure. It is true that the actual location of his travels is a land never seen by earth-dwellers and the subject of the poem is the timeless scheme of man's salvation as well as certain topical events. But the pilgrim thinks frequently of his contemporary Italy, and his eventual return there is not a sign of his failure to attain paradise: It is a precondition of his journey into myth and of the mortal condition that he never abandons. The shadow of his mortal body accompanies him everywhere. Dante thus combines epic and allegory by giving the quest the appearance of literal, historical truth while making it also "the journey of our life."

In contrast to the pilgrim figure who travels into the unknown, Milton's Adam and Eve are mythic figures who descend into history through the Fall, becoming human—and in becoming human, becoming heroic. Likewise, Christ in *Paradise Regained,* Milton's "brief epic," after triumphing over Satan, is celebrated not as the accomplished savior but as a heroic model about to begin the work of salvation:

> Hail Son of the most High, heir of both worlds,
> Queller of Satan, on thy glorious work
> Now enter, and begin to save mankind.

And the place to enter and begin is "his Mother's house private," among unmythic and humble people of a household, in a fixed geographical location. The Christian or allegorical hero is "epic," then, only when he remains involved in the social and political affairs of a historical scene.

We may also distinguish the epic hero from the Utopian wanderer who journeys through another kind of fantasy landscape, a place of pigmies or giants, for instance, or of model governments and social systems. The scene of this kind of heroic adventure is distorted for satiric and didactic purposes. The hero serves not so much to establish a pattern of heroic achievement-within-limitations as to bring into contrast the values of a given society and those of a foreign order. Among the horses and the Brobdingnagians, Gulliver is a walking series of contrasts, an extended "conceit" that brings together dissimilar societies. To see the human body magnified, as Gulliver does in the land of the giants, for instance, is implicitly to contrast the ordinary assumption that it is comely and well proportioned with an ant's view of its grossness. Swift makes it difficult for those who would define man as a rational and spiritual being to ignore the mechanics of living physically in a physical world. Such "perspective-by-incongruity" does not require a "hero" in the usual sense of the term: It demands a representative of common experience and undermines any concept of heroism that disregards commonness.

II.   The Fable and Style   Apart from the hero's involvement in a geographical, historical, social world, the major epics have little in common with respect to fable and subject matter. It is not true, for instance, that all epics are nationalistic or concerned primarily with great battles. Some do not concern traveling heroes at all, although *most* do—if only because epic trials are not easily come by in the living room or the shopping center. The quests themselves may carry the hero toward nearly any kind of fulfilment (the founding of an empire or a return home from war), destruction, or some mixed condition. Dante's poem is a "comedy" because the pilgrim may eventually achieve permanently the vision he is granted temporarily and because, whether or not a particular pilgrim is saved, the cosmos is clearly in good hands. Ulysses' quest in *The Odyssey* is also "comic" in its satisfactory ending, but in a domestic rather than a social or divine way. *The Iliad* and *Beowulf* lean toward tragedy; *Paradise Lost* and *The Aeneid* are mixed in tone and mood. Moreover, the basic comic, tragic, and mixed patterns of epic journeys are complicated by other considerations, especially those of symbolic level and direction. Ulysses' journey is largely without symbolic dimensions. Despite the magic of Circe and the monstrosity of certain creatures he encounters, things are by and large just what they seem to be. If Ulysses grows wiser, it is only in terms of his accumulated experience. Dante's pilgrim, on the other hand, travels vertically, as we have seen, both in the literal geography of the inferno and purgatory and in spiritual and intellectual ways as well. His journey results ultimately in the equation of vision and ecstasy: to *see* is to be blessed. And although Dante is unique in making the vertical quest so predominantly the structural principle of his poem, the vertical framework can be important in other epics as well, especially in those bordering on allegory or approaching fables of self-discovery.

As a general rule, the more personal or inward the hero's experience becomes, the more allegorical the epic method will be and the more important the vertical dimension of the quest. Under these circumstances epic trials become spiritual and intellectual rather than muscular. Forms of autobiography like Wordsworth's *The Prelude* (which has a key mountain-illumination scene) and Whitman's *Leaves of Grass* may thus be viewed as extensions of traditional vertical quests. They replace the "fable" of the older epic with the processes of defining identity, and they alter the concept of the hero correspondingly; he tends to become a mask for the poet or even the poet without a mask. Some of the machinery and conventions of traditional oral recitation are converted to lyric equivalents, and some are dropped altogether.

Yet despite the variety of quests, we can still discover much that is common in the *manner* of poems we instinctively call epic. Aristotle distinguishes not only three methods of literary presentation (epic, lyric, and dramatic) but also three *attitudes*—meliorative, normative, and pejorative—which in turn involve high, middle, and humble styles. Whereas comedy deals with worse-than-average men in a generally pejorative or low style, epic is meliorative: it imitates men who are better than ourselves, whether idealizations of the best qualities abstracted from normal men and synthesized in one figure or simply historical figures seen at their best. Although the stylistic range may include some documentary realism, as in Homer, the normal manner of epic is that of a dignified, exalted voice.

Paradise Lost, for instance, is unlike other epics in the virtues it gives its heroes and in its use of the journey motif but is typical in granting those virtues a certain stature, a "style." Even Satan's pseudo-heroics have a qualified magnitude; they are absurd, but from the standpoint of human history filled with pain and guilt, they are also impressively powerful. The style of the poem as a whole maintains a dignity answerable to the cosmic importance of the fable. Satan's "comedy" is in part a parody of epic dignity, a perversion of a higher order; his manner is Heaven's style in decay. The effectiveness of his epic-size propaganda is founded on the genuine dignity of God, as his throne imitates but also vulgarizes God's throne:

> High on a Throne of Royal State, which far
> Outshone the wealth of Ormus and of Ind,
> Or where the gorgeous East with richest hand
> Show'rs on her Kings Barbaric Pearl and Gold,
> Satan exalted sat, by merit rais'd
> To that bad eminence; and from despair
> Thus high uplifted beyond hope, aspires
> Beyond thus high, insatiate to pursue
> Vain war with Heav'n, and by success untaught
> His proud imaginations thus display'd.   (II. 1–10)

As with his throne, so with his language generally. He benefits from many of the stylistic gifts that Milton gives genuine heroes—the slow, elaborate movement of the syntax and the postponed, inverted adjective and verb ("Satan exalted sat," for instance).

Perhaps no other epic in English encompasses the stylistic range of *Paradise Lost* from epic parody to exalted hymn and warlike speech; but all works of epic pretension establish a dignified norm. The difficulty in epics after Milton, especially in those dealing with inherently less exalted subjects, is that once a heightened norm has been established—usually with a rather impressive opening paragraph—the poet must manage his descents from that norm with the utmost care or risk falling into unintentional parody. In putting his own growth as a philosophical poet in partly epic terms, for instance, Wordsworth risks dressing his poem in armor too big for it. If he does not "tailor" his style adroitly, the descent from high Miltonic altitudes into personal reminiscence and anecdote will be as sudden as Satan's descent into egoism and mere display. Wordsworth can afford the familiar but not the comic:

> When summer came,
> Our pastime was, on bright half-holidays,
> To sweep along the plain of Windermere
> With rival oars; and the selected bourne
> Was now an Island musical with birds
> That sang and ceased not; now a Sister Isle
> Beneath the oaks' umbrageous covert, sown
> With lilies of the valley like a field;
> And now a third small Island, where survived
> In solitude the ruins of a shrine
> Once to Our Lady dedicate, and served
> Daily with chaunted rites.   (II. 54–64)

The Latinate quality of "umbrageous covert" (probably from Virgil by way of Milton), the Biblical echo in "lilies of the valley like a field," the syntactical inversion of "sang and ceased not" and "where survived / In solitude," the run-on lines that accumulate into a sweeping paragraph, the slow dignity of rhythm and vowel manipulation, and the Virgilian technique of the "now" signals that set up different aspects of a panoramic view: these stylistic features convert an ordinary childhood scene into something of special importance. At the same time, the basic "grammar" of the passage is simply that of a personal, rather miscellaneous remembrance, beginning quite naturally with "when summer came / Our pastime was...." Unlike Milton's Eden, this paradise does not directly manifest a divine order, nor does the future of mankind hinge on Wordsworth's boat races. The voice of the narrator is not that of a reciter before a large audience but of a poet in conversation, partly with himself and partly with a circle of interested friends (such as Coleridge, addressed several times in the poem). The stylistic norms are still recognizably epic, but epic as a search for private and personal dignity, not as public record. Milton's religious exaltation becomes "emotion recollected in tranquillity," and traditional heroic games become friendly rowing contests, although the idiom ("sweep...with rival oars") recalls greater engagements. Here the crucial trials of the hero are neither moral nor muscular but crises of the imagination in the act of grasping and rendering reality. The creative processes rather than the fall of mankind are at stake and form the basis of the "plot."

The interjection of irony in this imposing edifice of epic attitudinizing would be disastrous. The encyclopedic lists of diseases and vices in Swift's *Guilliver*, for instance, could not be assimilated by Wordsworth's scheme or by any imaginable epic world:

But, in order to feed the luxury and intemperance of the males, and the vanity of the females, we sent away the greatest part of our necessary things to other countries, from whence in return we brought the materials of disease, folly, and vice, to spend among ourselves. Hence it follows of necessity that vast numbers of our people are compelled to seek their livelihood by begging, robbing, stealing, cheating, pimping, forswearing, flattering, suborning, forging, gaming, lying, fawning, hectoring, voting, scribbling, star-gazing, poisoning, whoring, canting, libelling, freethinking, and the like occupations: every one of which terms, I was at much pains to make him understand.

Like the king of the Houynhnms to whom Gulliver is speaking, epic has only a limited range of words. It would be as out of place to introduce Guilliver's terms into Wordsworthian decorum as to allow Gulliver to talk in the meditative manner of John Donne or in the blank verse of Milton.

On the other hand, we should recognize that epic style is no more limiting than that of other modes, all of which have their own principle of selectivity. Epic style screens certain kinds of experience *through* its decorum and others *out*. Defining the epic manner is thus largely an attempt to identify the mesh of the "screen" itself, as distinct from others. Compared with a romance or Utopian vocabulary, for instance, the diction of the epic is in some ways "realistic." Wordsworth's reminiscences concern a number of literal geographical places and events; Whitman's *Leaves of Grass*—which might be thought of as another variation of the poem of the self in "high" rather than strictly lyric style—is flooded with topographical details, urban description, and the sense data of particular times and places. Even the most documentary of passages in *Gulliver's Travels*, on the other hand, is distanced by the fantasy of the entire venture. The list of human vices quoted above, though realistic, has something of a *theoretical* quality; a Utopian work, whether satiric or exemplary in aim, is situated in an imaginary realm, like Alice's land behind the looking glass. It may be both grotesquely realistic and yet "unreal."

Moreover, whereas Swift's specificity of detail serves for *derision,* that of Wordsworth and Whitman is devoted to *celebration.* Epic is a heroic mode in which stylization is limited not only by the assumed reality of its geographical and historical situation but also by the assumed magnitude of its action. Whether or not the action would actually be of magnitude to most observers outside the poem, the epic poet assumes it to be so in the poem. Without sacrificing the sense of place, he filters it through a certain kind of lens as though seeing a distant action up close through high-power binoculars. Although Adam and Eve's quarrels, for instance, might be grist for another poet's satiric mill, in Milton's handling they are epic. Quests, too, may differ radically according to the decorum within which they are treated, although they normally involve the key issues of an age—the founding of empire in Virgil, the merger of Christianity and tribal culture in *Beowulf,* the justification of God's ways to man in *Paradise Lost,* the interaction of "self" and "other" in Wordsworth. Quests are epic only if the poem lends them dignity—dignity that hearkens back to the voice of the poet offering an immediate audience an image of their noble past and their high and compelling destiny.

JOHN MILTON

The concept of nobility and heroic virtue in *Paradise Lost* requires a flexible and mixed mode, a style of contrasts capable of setting off genuine dignity against absurdity, good against evil, the humble against the exalted and pseudo-exalted. Because of this flexibility, Milton's is perhaps the most difficult of the major epics to describe stylistically. It combines elements of romance, autobiographical (lyric) passages, and eventually a paradoxical mixture of tragic and comic modes as the post-fall Adam and Eve are made aware of both their mortal limitations and the "fortune" of their sin. Moreover, in Satan, the poem anticipates the modern hero as outsider and rebel. Hence virtually all modes of the heroic from romance to religious allegory and parody meet in *Paradise Lost.*

From the viewpoint of classical precedents, one of the basic innovations of the poem is a redefinition of "heroism," which Milton dissociated not only from the battle-heroics of the military hero but also from the concept of nobility inherent in the class structure of most earlier heroic modes. The Protestant concept of heroism in the seventeenth century favored lower- and middle-class virtues: *Pilgrim's Progress* is the product of an uneducated shoemaker who spent much of his life in prison; before Bunyan, Arthur Dent revealed a similar Puritan bias in the *Plain Man's Pathway to Heaven.* As a Puritan who had recently taken part in the Civil War and served in Cromwell's cabinet, Milton believed that the humble Christian is potentially heroic. The only legitimate hierarchy for him was a hierarchy of the spiritually fit, which obviously was not suited to Arthurian romance of the kind he originally planned to write. Hence he substitutes marital love for romantic extramarital love and the invisible church for the kingship and the Round Table. He associates the trappings of kingship with Satan and Nimrod, the builder of the Tower of Babel (both rebels against the only true "king") and has Eve fall because she aspires to queenliness above her domestic situation. Only in learning to be Adam's humble and repentant helpmate after the Fall does she model the kind of consort that Milton finds suitable for a religious household (as his divorce tracts make clear). Certainly Adam and Eve, even before the Fall, need no status symbols or codes of chivalric dignity: because they have inner light and spiritual discipline (and later, the scriptural vision that will be available to everyone through the Bible), they need no vestments, seek no Holy Grail, and possess no sacramental magic. Despite their unique situation as the parents of mankind, then, they are in a sense the first "democratic" epic heroes, whereas Satan, as a *tyrannos*, or despotic ruler—a blustering military chief proud of physical strength and courage and a magician more potent than Merlin—parodies the old epic and romance heroes and the values they represent. Other epic and romance elements Milton finds useful without parody or inversion: invocations to the muses become modes of prayer and meditation; messengers from Heaven become modes of revelation in the system of communications between man and God.

The democratic implications of the story of Adam and Eve ("When Adam delved and Eve span / Who was then the gentleman?"), however, are secondary to the moral and religious implications. The drama that Adam and Eve enact stands outside time as the pattern of Everyman, tempted, incapable of resisting, in need of repentance and Christ's mercy. Even so, Milton does not allow the all-inclusiveness of the Christian perspective to reduce the central figures to mere specks on the allegorical landscape. The technique of *Paradise Lost* consists in part of shifting perspectives: in some passages the narrator traverses the cosmos but in others moves nearer Adam and Eve or Satan and sees them as particular historical creatures, more human than mythical. Likewise, the style of the poem ranges from vast descriptive amplitude to intimate conversation. It encompasses the spaciousness of the creation, the imperative urgency of God's decrees, and the exaltation of the angels' songs; yet it also adjusts to the homeliness of Adam and Eve's domestic scene. Except for the war in heaven, the style of most of the scenes after the opening books is set by the range of Adam's experience, from conversation with Eve and the angle Raphael to Adam's own hymns to the creation. The pseudo-heroic action of Satan is reduced to the infighting of man's spiritual warfare. This reduction has seemed to some critics to leave little epic dimension in the poem. Moreover, Milton has a still more difficult stylistic problem in handling voices that might naturally command power. God's language, for instance, must manifest dignity, all-seeing vision, and moral indignation without becoming merely tyrannical or petulant.

Milton's solution to these problems is unpredictable if we come to the poem expecting merely traditional epic style. He casts the speeches of Satan and the fallen angels in Books I and II in a high mode but undercuts them with irony and editorial indications of their pretentiousness. Satan's rhetorical force is a compensation for rational shortcomings and a multitude of contradictions, which expose the host's need to find a principle of unity once they have abandoned the true center of their being. In contrast to Satan's linguistic inflation, the speeches of Adam and Eve before the Fall have a natural simplicity and innocence that suggest inherent grace, even modest grandeur. (In books not included here, the unfallen host is also given an impressive rhetoric of hymns and celebrations, which lends itself to such subjects as Christ's exaltation,

God's manifestation of mercy, the creation, and the victories over the fallen.) The range and contrasts of heavenly and infernal styles thus provide a defining context for human speech in Eden. Although not of high magnitude in itself, then, this speech lies at the center of a grand cosmos and a critical contest between extremes of good and evil. Moreover, Milton has the narrator react to the subject, speaking as though in his own voice in a generally elevated style and making clear that no other epic has had so much riding on the moral choice of its heroes—nor has any other epic poet had Holy Light for his muse. Prepared for in this way, the domestic conversations of the simple swain and his newly-made consort in Eden take on such proportions that Milton can afford *not* to elevate them too much stylistically.

After the Fall, Milton's stylistic task is quite different. He must allow the "mythic" native dignity and grace of Adam and Eve to shrink into the merely human without becoming pathetic or comic. We see the first signs of his technique in their dispute, on the morning of the Fall, over a domestic problem of the sort not likely to trouble Aeneas or Achilles. Because of the pressure of the event, it does not become an ordinary domestic comedy. (Had Milton pitched the quarrel too low, there would have been nothing of Paradise left to lose.) Since their horticultural quibble not only lies at the center of the larger contest between God and Satan but also reveals the difficulty that unequals in God's Chain of Being have in communicating with one another, their dialogue suggests certain metaphysical problems worked out in dramatic, human terms. The "flaw" of the epic hero and heroine is linked thematically to the question of free will and the independence of creatures in a universe governed by an omnipotent force. In the course of their conversation Adam is searching for the right *mode* to influence Eve, an inferior in God's scheme: he cannot order her to stay with him because that would be equivalent to God's forcing his will on creatures; yet he cannot let her go unwarned without failing as her natural superior in the hierarchy. Eve's decision to go out on her own is essentially a decision to put herself in another order in which she will no longer be merely Adam's helpmate but an independent creature capable of probing on her own anything in creation—with the help of the "Mother of Science," the apple. At Satan's urging, she replaces her assigned identity with one of *her* making.

Milton thus makes the family quarrel a contest of identity within the given hierarchical order. Yet he cannot afford to have Adam and Eve become the tragic *victims* of that system, over which they may seem to have little control, the universe being so large and they so small. The Fall must not explode our sympathy for the stumbling hero and heroine, and yet, unlike Prometheus, Adam cannot be given dignity at God's expense. He must fall for reasonable and elevated motives and yet make a distinctly bad choice. Milton thus makes his decision essentially a choice of the domestic over the religious; Adam takes himself out of the cosmic drama in the interests of earthly and especially marital happiness. This does in fact lead to his becoming a "human" hero struggling with the pain and ambiguities of the fallen world, but God does not let him forget the rest of the universe. Both Adam and Eve are made to recognize the implications of their mistake before they repent and begin the long journey back to Paradise through history. Milton handles the situation immediately after the Fall by imitating to a degree the confusion and moral uncertainty that results from the loss of innocence and yet keeping in view both the potential in Adam and Eve for a new mode of human dignity and the view heaven takes of them. He maintains heightened stylistic norms but makes them encompass some of the wrangling of love-gone-sour. In fact, their style of dignified, repentant prayer and moral enlightenment becomes the norm of Christian heroism. The lyric intensity and grandeur of the invocations, the "epic" force of Satanic speech-making, and the hymns of angels give way to a less magnificent decorum suitable to·the unmythic experience of fallen mankind, which is too chastened to allow soaring exaltation but too dignified to drop entirely out of the epic range.

Satan meanwhile has been diminished and set aside (although the cosmic dimensions of the struggle between God and Satan are residual in the daily battles of mankind). It is Satan who makes the discipline of Adam and Eve meaningful and urgent despite its rather unheroic appearance in Michael's Protestant rhetoric:

> thou hast attained the summe
> Of wisdom; hope no higher, though all the stars
> Thou knewest by name, and all th' ethereal powers,
> All secrets of the deep, all nature's works,
> Of works of God in heav'n, air, earth, or sea,
> And all the riches of this world enjoydst,
> And all the rule, one empire; only add
> Deeds to thy knowledge answerable, add faith,
> Add vertue, patience, temperance, add love,
> By name to come call'd charity, the soul
> Of all the rest: then wilt thou not be loath
> To leave this paradise, but shalt possess
> A paradise within thee, happier far.   (XII. 574ff.)

Adam has had knowledge before, but he has not needed deeds; he has had no opportunity to exercise most of the virtues on Michael's list. Thanks to Satan, he has increased his heroic vocabulary, and although Achilles might scoff at the terms, to Milton they are the terms of all Christian warfare.

PARADISE LOST

BOOK I
THE ARGUMENT

This first Book proposes, first in brief, the whole Subject, *Man's disobedience, and the loss thereupon of Paradise wherein he was plac't:* Then touches *the prime cause of his fall, the Serpent, or rather* Satan *in the Serpent; who revolting from God, and drawing to his side many Legions of Angels, was by the command of God driven out of Heaven with all his Crew into the great Deep.* Which action past over, the Poem hastes into the midst of things, presenting *Satan with his Angels now fallen into Hell,* describ'd here, *not in the Centre* (for Heaven and Earth may be suppos'd as yet not made, certainly not yet accurst) *but in a place of utter darkness, fitliest call'd* Chaos: *Here* Satan *with his Angels lying on the burning Lake, thunderstruck and astonisht, after a certain space recovers, as from confusion, calls up him who next in Order and Dignity lay by him; they confer of their miserable fall.* Satan *awakens all his Legions, who lay till then in the same manner confounded; They rise, thir Numbers, array of Battle, thir chief Leaders nam'd, according to the Idols known afterwards in* Canaan *and the Countries adjoining. To these* Satan *directs his Speech, comforts them with hope yet of regaining Heaven, but tells them lastly of a new World and new kind of Creature to be created, according to an ancient Prophecy or report in Heaven;* for that Angels were long before this visible Creation, was the opinion of many ancient Fathers. *To find out the truth of this Prophecy, and what to determine thereon he refers to a full Council. What his Associates thence attempt.* Pandemonium *the Palace of* Satan *rises, suddenly built out of the Deep: The infernal Peers there sit in Council.*

Of Man's First Disobedience, and the Fruit	
Of that Forbidden Tree, whose mortal taste	
Brought Death into the World, and all our woe,	
With loss of *Eden,* till one greater Man	
Restore us, and regain in blissful Seat,	5
Sing Heav'nly Muse, that on the secret top	
Of *Oreb,* or of *Sinai,* didst inspire	
That Shepherd, who first taught the chosen Seed,	
In the Beginning how the Heav'ns and Earth	
Rose out of *Chaos:* Or if *Sion* Hill	10
Delight thee more, and *Siloa's* Brook that flow'd	
Fast by the Oracle of God; I thence	
Invoke thy aid to my advent'rous Song,	
That with no middle flight intends to soar	
Above th' *Aonian* Mount, while it pursues	15
Things unattempted yet in Prose or Rhyme.	
And chiefly Thou O Spirit, that dost prefer	
Before all Temples th' upright heart and pure,	
Instruct me, for Thou know'st; Thou from the first	
Wast present, and with mighty wings outspread	20
Dove-like satst brooding on the vast Abyss	
And mad'st it pregnant: What in me is dark	
Illumine, what is low raise and support;	
That to the highth of this great Argument	
I may assert Eternal Providence,	25
And justify the ways of God to men.	
Say first, for Heav'n hides nothing from thy view	
Nor the deep Tract of Hell, say first what cause	
Mov'd our Grand Parents in that happy State,	
Favour'd of Heav'n so highly, to fall off	30

---

8 *That Shepherd*: Moses, transmitting the law to the chosen people from Mount Oreb and Mount Sinai. 10–12 *Sion Hill, Siloa's Brook*: God's voice spoke to Hebrew prophets at Mount Zion near the brook Siloam. 15 *Aonian Mount*: home of Greek muses. 17 *Thou O Spirit*: the creative force through which God turns chaos to order, darkness to light, Milton invokes it in the name of Light at the beginning of Book III. In *Christian Doctrine,* Milton discusses it under the heading of God's "external efficiency," suggesting that whatever specific form it takes, it is an instrument of divine epiphany.

From thir Creator, and transgress his Will
For one restraint, Lords of the World besides?
Who first seduc'd them to that foul revolt?
Th' infernal Serpent; he it was, whose guile
Stirr'd up with Envy and Revenge, deceiv'd   35
The Mother of Mankind, what time his Pride
Had cast him out from Heav'n, with all his Host
Of Rebel Angels, by whose aid aspiring
To set himself in Glory above his Peers,
He trusted to have equall'd the most High,   40
If he oppos'd; and with ambitious aim
Against the Throne and Monarchy of God
Rais'd impious War in Heav'n and Battle proud
With vain attempt. Him the Almighty Power
Hurl'd headlong flaming from th' Ethereal Sky   45
With hideous ruin and combustion down
To bottomless perdition, there to dwell
In Adamantine Chains and penal Fire,
Who durst defy th' Omnipotent to Arms.
Nine times the Space that measures Day and Night   50
To mortal men, hee with his horrid crew
Lay vanquisht, rolling in the fiery Gulf
Confounded though immortal; But his doom
Reserv'd him to more wrath; for now the thought
Both of lost happiness and lasting pain   55
Torments him; round he throws his baleful eyes
That witness'd huge affliction and dismay
Mixt with obdurate pride and steadfast hate:
At once as far as Angels ken he views
The dismal Situation waste and wild,   60
A Dungeon horrible, on all sides round
As one great Furnace flam'd, yet from those flames
No light, but rather darkness visible
Serv'd only to discover sights of woe,
Regions of sorrow, doleful shades, where peace   65
And rest can never dwell, hope never comes
That comes to all; but torture without end .
Still urges, and a fiery Deluge, fed
With ever-burning Sulphur unconsum'd:
Such place Eternal Justice had prepar'd   70
For those rebellious, here thir Prison ordained
In utter darkness, and thir portion set
As far remov'd from God and light of Heav'n
As from the Center thrice to th' utmost Pole.
O how unlike the place from whence they fell!   75
There the companions of his fall, o'erwhelm'd
With Floods and Whirlwinds of tempestuous fire,
He soon discerns, and welt'ring by his side
One next himself in power, and next in crime,
Long after known in *Palestine,* and nam'd   80

Beëlzebub. To whom th' Arch-Enemy,
And thence in Heav'n call'd Satan, with bold words
Breaking the horrid silence thus began.
    If thou beest he; But O how fall'n! how chang'd
From him, who in the happy Realms of Light   85
Cloth'd with transcendent brightness didst outshine
Myriads though bright: If he whom mutual league,
United thoughts and counsels, equal hope,
And hazard in the Glorious Enterprise,
Join'd with me once, now misery hath join'd   90
In equal ruin: into what Pit thou seest
From what highth fall'n, so much the stronger prov'd
He with his Thunder: and till then who knew
The force of those dire Arms? yet not for those,
Nor what the Potent Victor in his rage   95
Can else inflict, do I repent or change,
Though chang'd in outward lustre; that fixt mind
And high disdain, from sense of injur'd merit,
That with the mightiest rais'd me to contend,
And to the fierce contention brought along   100
Innumerable force of Spirits arm'd
That durst dislike his reign, and me preferring,
His utmost power with adverse power oppos'd
In dubious Battle on the Plains of Heav'n,
And shook his throne. What though the field be lost?   105
All is not lost; the unconquerable will,
And study of revenge, immortal hate,
And courage never to submit or yield:
And what is else not to be overcome?
That Glory never shall his wrath or might   110
Extort from me. To bow and sue for grace
With suppliant knee, and deify his power
Who from the terror of this Arm so late
Doubted his Empire, that were low indeed,
That were an ignominy and shame beneath   115
This downfall; since by Fate the strength of Gods
And this Empyreal substance cannot fail,
Since through experience of this great event
In Arms not worse, in foresight much advanc't,
We may with more successful hope resolve   120
To wage by force or guile eternal War
Irreconcilable to our grand Foe,
Who now triumphs, and in th' excess of joy
Sole reigning holds the Tyranny of Heav'n.
    So spake th' Apostate Angel, though in pain,   125
Vaunting aloud, but rackt with deep despair:
And him thus answer'd soon his bold Compeer.
    O Prince, O Chief of many Throned Powers,
That led th' imbattl'd Seraphim to War
Under thy conduct, and in dreadful deeds   130

Fearless, endanger'd Heav'n's perpetual King;
And put to proof his high Supremacy,
Whether upheld by strength, or Chance, or Fate;
Too well I see and rue the dire event,
That with sad overthrow and foul defeat   135
Hath lost us Heav'n, and all this mighty Host
In horrible destruction laid thus low,
As far as Gods and Heav'nly Essences
Can perish: for the mind and spirit remains
Invincible, and vigor soon returns,   140
Though all our Glory extinct, and happy state
Here swallow'd up in endless misery.
But what if he our Conqueror, (whom I now
Of force believe Almighty, since no less
Than such could have o'erpow'rd such force as ours)   145
Have left us this our spirit and strength entire
Strongly to suffer and support our pains,
That we may so suffice his vengeful ire,
Or do him mightier service as his thralls
By right of War, whate'er his business be   150
Here in the heart of Hell to work in Fire,
Or do his Errands in the gloomy Deep;
What can it then avail though yet we feel
Strength undiminisht, or eternal being
To undergo eternal punishment?   155
Whereto with speedy words th' Arch-fiend repli'd.
  Fall'n Cherub, to be weak is miserable
Doing or Suffering: but of this be sure,
To do aught good never will be our task,
But ever to do ill our sole delight,   160
As being the contrary to his high will
Whom we resist. If then his Providence
Out of our evil seek to bring forth good,
Our labour must be to pervert that end,
And out of good still to find means of evil;   165
Which oft-times may succeed, so as perhaps
Shall grieve him, if I fail not, and disturb
His inmost counsels from thir destin'd aim.
But see the angry Victor hath recall'd
His Ministers of vengeance and pursuit   170
Back to the Gates of Heav'n: the Sulphurous Hail
Shot after us in storm, o'erblown hath laid
The fiery Surge, that from the Precipice
Of Heav'n receiv'd us falling, and the Thunder,
Wing'd with red Lightning and impetuous rage,   175
Perhaps hath spent his shafts, and ceases now
To bellow through the vast and boundless Deep.
Let us not slip th' occasion, whether scorn,
Or satiate fury yield it from our Foe.
Seest thou yon dreary Plain, forlorn and wild,   180

The seat of desolation, void of light,
Save what the glimmering of these livid flames
Casts pale and dreadful? Thither let us tend
From off the tossing of these fiery waves,
There rest, if any rest can harbour there,   185
And reassembling our afflicted Powers,
Consult how we may henceforth most offend
Our Enemy, our own loss how repair,
How overcome this dire Calamity,
What reinforcement we may gain from Hope,   190
If not what resolution from despair.
   Thus Satan talking to his nearest Mate
With Head up-lift above the wave, and Eyes
That sparkling blaz'd, his other Parts besides
Prone on the Flood, extended long and large   195
Lay floating many a rood, in bulk as huge
As whom the Fables name of monstrous size,
Titanian, or *Earth-born*, that warr'd on *Jove*,
Briareos or *Typhon*, whom the Den
By ancient *Tarsus* held, or that Sea-beast   200
Leviathan, which God of all his works
Created hugest that swim th' Ocean stream:
Him haply slumb'ring on the *Norway* foam
The Pilot of some small night-founder'd Skiff,
Deeming some Island, oft, as Seamen tell,   205
With fixed Anchor in his scaly rind
Moors by his side under the Lee, while Night
Invests the Sea, and wished Morn delays:
So stretcht out huge in length the Arch-fiend lay
Chain'd on the burning Lake, nor ever thence   210
Had ris'n or heav'd his head, but that the will
And high permission of all-ruling Heaven
Left him at large to his own dark designs,
That with reiterated crimes he might
Heap on himself damnation, while he sought   215
Evil to others, and enrag'd might see
How all his malice serv'd but to bring forth
Infinite goodness, grace and mercy shown
On Man by him seduc't, but on himself
Treble confusion, wrath and vengeance pour'd.   220
Forthwith upright he rears from off the Pool
His mighty Stature; on each hand the flames
Driv'n backward slope their pointing spires, and roll'd
In billows, leave i' th' midst a horrid Vale.
Then with expanded wings he steers his flight   225
Aloft, incumbent on the dusky Air

198–201 *Titanian* (Titan), son of Coelus and Terra. He gave his brother Saturn the kingdom of the world provided that Saturn would raise no male children. He then made war against Saturn when the latter concealed the birth of Jupiter; *Briareus*: Jupiter's strong man; *Typhon*: one of those who attacked Jupiter; *Leviathan*: treacherous whale.

That felt unusual weight, till on dry Land
He lights, if it were Land that ever burn'd
With solid, as the Lake with liquid fire;
And such appear'd in hue, as when the force   230
Of subterranean wind transports a Hill
Torn from *Pelorus,* or the shatter'd side
Of thund'ring *Ætna,* whose combustible
And fuell'd entrails thence conceiving Fire,
Sublim'd with Mineral fury, aid the Winds,   235
And leave a singed bottom all involv'd
With stench and smoke: Such resting found the sole
Of unblest feet. Him follow'd his next Mate,
Both glorying to have scap't *Stygian* flood
As Gods, and by thir own recover'd strength,   240
Not by the sufferance of supernal Power.
   Is this the Region, this the Soil, the Clime,
Said then the lost Arch-Angel, this the seat
That we must change for Heav'n, this mournful gloom
For that celestial light? Be it so, since hee   245
Who now is Sovran can dispose and bid
What shall be right: fardest from him is best
Whom reason hath equall'd, force hath made supreme
Above his equals. Farewell happy Fields
Where Joy for ever dwells: Hail horrors, hail   250
Infernal world, and thou profoundest Hell
Receive thy new Possessor: One who brings
A mind not to be chang'd by Place or Time.
The mind is its own place, and in itself
Can make a Heav'n of Hell, a Hell of Heav'n.   255
What matter where, if I be still the same,
And what I should be, all but less than hee
Whom Thunder hath made greater? Here at least
We shall be free; th' Almighty hath not built
Here for his envy, will not drive us hence: 260
Here we may reign secure, and in my choice
To reign is worth ambition though in Hell:
Better to reign in Hell, than serve in Heav'n.
But wherefore let we then our faithful friends,
Th' associates and copartners of our loss   265
Lie thus astonisht on th' oblivious Pool,
And call them not to share with us their part
In this unhappy Mansion, or once more
With rallied Arms to try what may be yet
Regain'd in Heav'n, or what more lost in Hell?   270
   So *Satan* spake, and him *Beëlzebub*
Thus answer'd. Leader of those Armies bright,
Which but th' Omnipotent none could have foiled,

232–33 *Pelorus* and *Ætna*: mountains in Sicily. 235 *Sublim'd*: purified with mineral energy (alchemical term). 266 *oblivious Pool*: renders the angels oblivious.

If once they hear that voice, thir liveliest pledge
Of hope in fears and dangers, heard so oft   275
In worst extremes, and on the perilous edge
Of battle when it rag'd, in all assaults
Thir surest signal, they will soon resume
New courage and revive, though now they lie
Groveling and prostrate on yon Lake of Fire,   280
As we erewhile, astounded and amaz'd,
No wonder, fall'n such a pernicious highth.
   He scarce had ceas't when the superior Fiend
Was moving toward the shore; his ponderous shield
Ethereal temper, massy, large and round,   285
Behind him cast; the broad circumference
Hung on his shoulders like the Moon, whose Orb
Through Optic Glass the *Tuscan* Artist views
At Ev'ning from the top of *Fesole,*
Or in *Valdarno,* to descry new Lands,   290
Rivers or Mountains in her spotty Globe.
His Spear, to equal which the tallest Pine
Hewn on *Norwegian* hills, to be the Mast
Of some great Ammiral, were but a wand,
He walkt with to support uneasy steps   295
Over the burning Marl, not like those steps
On Heaven's Azure, and the torrid Clime
Smote on him sore besides, vaulted with Fire;
Nathless he so endur'd, till on the Beach
Of that inflamed Sea, he stood and call'd   300
His Legions, Angel Forms, who lay intrans't
Thick as Autumnal Leaves that strow the Brooks
In *Vallombrosa,* where th' *Etrurian* shades
High overarch't imbow'r; or scatter'd sedge
Afloat, when with fierce Winds *Orion* arm'd   305
Hath vext the Red-Sea Coast, whose waves o'erthrew
Busiris and his *Memphian* Chivalry,
While with perfidious hatred they pursu'd
The Sojourners of *Goshen,* who beheld
From the safe shore thir floating Carcasses   310
And broken Chariot Wheels, so thick bestrown
Abject and lost lay these, covering the Flood,
Under amazement of thir hideous change.
He call'd so loud, that all the hollow Deep
Of Hell resounded. Princes, Potentates,   315
Warriors, the Flow'r of Heav'n, once yours, now lost,
If such astonishment as this can seize
Eternal spirits; or have ye chos'n this place

288–290 *Tuscan Artist*: Galileo, in Florence at the heights of Fiesole above the Arno (Valdarno). 303–309 *Etruria*: a country northwest of the Tiber; the winds of Orion were supposed to blow as the constellation of Orion rises on about March 9th; *Busiris*: a king of Egypt, son of Neptune; *Memphis*: a town of Egypt on the Nile above the Delta; *Sojourners of Goshen*: persecuted by a Pharoah (not Busiris—Milton has mixed two legends together).

After the toil of Battle to repose
Your wearied virtue, for the ease you find   320
To slumber here, as in the Vales of Heav'n?
Or in this abject posture have ye sworn
To adore the Conqueror? who now beholds
Cherub and Seraph rolling in the Flood
With scatter'd Arms and Ensigns, till anon   325
His swift pursuers from Heav'n Gates discern
Th' advantage, and descending tread us down
Thus drooping, or with linked Thunderbolts
Transfix us to the bottom of this Gulf.
Awake, arise, or be for ever fall'n.   330
    They heard, and were abasht, and up they sprung
Upon the wing, as when men wont to watch
On duty, sleeping found by whom they dread,
Rouse and bestir themselves ere well awake.
Nor did they not perceive the evil plight   335
In which they were, or the fierce pains not feel;
Yet to thir General's Voice they soon obey'd
Innumerable. As when the potent Rod
Of *Amram's* Son in *Egypt's* evil day
Wav'd round the Coast, up call'd a pitchy cloud   340
Of *Locusts,* warping on the Eastern Wind,
That o'er the Realm of impious *Pharaoh* hung
Like Night, and darken'd all the Land of *Nile:*
So numberless were those bad Angels seen
Hovering on wing under the Cope of Hell   345
'Twixt upper, nether, and surrounding Fires;
Till, as a signal giv'n, th' uplifted Spear
Of thir great Sultan waving to direct
Thir course, in even balance down they light
On the firm brimstone, and fill all the Plain;   350
A multitude, like which the populous North
Pour'd never from her frozen loins, to pass
Rhene or the *Danaw,* when her barbarous Sons
Came like a Deluge on the South, and spread
Beneath *Gibraltar* to the *Lybian* sands.   355
Forthwith from every Squadron and each Band
The Heads and Leaders thither haste where stood
Thir great Commander; Godlike shapes and forms
Excelling human, Princely Dignities,
And Powers that erst in Heaven sat on Thrones;   360
Though of thir Names in heav'nly Records now
Be no memorial, blotted out and ras'd
By thir Rebellion, from the Books of Life.
Nor had they yet among the Sons of *Eve*
Got them new Names, till wand'ring o'er the Earth,   365

---

339 *Amram's Son:* Moses, who cursed the Egyptians with a cloud of locusts.   353 *Rhene* or
Danaw: Rhine or Danube.

Through God's high sufferance for the trial of man,
By falsities and lies the greatest part
Of Mankind they corrupted to forsake
God thir Creator, and th' invisible
Glory of him, that made them, to transform   370
Oft to the Image of a Brute, adorn'd
With gay Religions full of Pomp and Gold,
And Devils to adore for Deities:
Then were they known to men by various Names,
And various Idols through the Heathen World.   375

[Milton lists the devils.]

All these and more came flocking; but with looks
Downcast and damp, yet such wherein appear'd
Obscure some glimpse of joy, to have found thir chief
Not in despair, to have found themselves not lost   525
In loss itself; which on his count'nance cast
Like doubtful hue: but he his wonted pride
Soon recollecting, with high words, that bore
Semblance of worth, not substance, gently rais'd
Thir fainting courage, and dispell'd thir fears.   530
Then straight commands that at the warlike sound
Of Trumpets loud and Clarions be uprear'd
His mighty Standard; that proud honour claim'd
Azazel as his right, a Cherub tall:
Who forthwith from the glittering Staff unfurl'd   535
Th' Imperial Ensign, which full high advanc't
Shone like a Meteor streaming to the Wind
With Gems and Golden lustre rich imblaz'd,
Seraphic arms and Trophies: all the while
Sonorous metal blowing Martial sounds: 540
At which the universal Host upsent
A shout that tore Hell's Concave, and beyond
Frighted the Reign of *Chaos* and old Night.
All in a moment through the gloom were seen
Ten thousand Banners rise into the Air   545
With Orient Colours waving: with them rose
A Forest huge of Spears: and thronging Helms
Appear'd, and serried Shields in thick array
Of depth immeasurable: Anon they move
In perfect *Phalanx* to the *Dorian* mood   550
Of Flutes and soft Recorders; such as rais'd
To highth of noblest temper Heroes old
Arming to Battle, and instead of rage
Deliberate valour breath'd, firm and unmov'd
With dread of death to flight or foul retreat,   555
Nor wanting power to mitigate and swage
With solemn touches, troubl'd thoughts and chase
Anguish and doubt and fear and sorrow and pain
From mortal or immortal minds. Thus they

Breathing united force with fixed thought   560
Mov'd on in silence to soft Pipes that charm'd
Thir painful steps o'er the burnt soil; and now
Advanc't in view they stand, a horrid Front
Of dreadful length and dazzling Arms, in guise
Of Warriors old with order'd Spear and Shield,   565
Awaiting what command thir mighty Chief
Had to impose: He through the armed Files
Darts his experienc't eye, and soon traverse
The whole Battalion views, thir order due,
Thir visages and stature as of Gods,   570
Thir number last he sums. And now his heart
Distends with pride, and hard'ning in his strength
Glories: For never since created man,
Met such imbodied force, as nam'd with these
Could merit more than that small infantry   575
Warr'd on by Cranes: though all the Giant brood
Of *Phlegra* with th' Heroic Race were join'd
That fought at *Thebes* and *Ilium,* on each side
Mixt with auxiliar Gods; and what resounds
In Fable or *Romance* of *Uther's* Son   580
Begirt with *British* and *Armoric* Knights;
And all who since, Baptiz'd or Infidel
Jousted in *Aspramont* or *Montalban,*
Damasco, or *Marocco* or *Trebisond,*
Or whom *Biserta* sent from *Afric* shore   585
When *Charlemain* with all his Peerage fell
By *Fontarabbia.* Thus far these beyond
Compare of mortal prowess, yet observ'd
Thir dread commander: he above the rest
In shape and gesture proudly eminent   590
Stood like a Tow'r; his form had yet not lost
All her Original brightness, nor appear'd
Less then Arch Angel ruin'd, and th' excess
Of Glory obscur'd: As when the Sun new ris'n
Looks through the Horizontal misty Air   595
Shorn of his Beams, or from behind the Moon
In dim Eclipse disastrous twilight sheds
On half the Nations, and with fear of change
Perplexes Monarchs. Dark'n'd so, yet shone
Above them all th' Arch Angel: but his face   600
Deep scars of Thunder had intrencht, and care
Sat on his faded cheek, but under Brows
Of dauntless courage, and considerate Pride

---

575 *that small infantry*: cf. lines 780–81 following, "that Pigmean Race / Beyond the Indian Mount." Migrating cranes were thought to bring death to the Pygmies. 577 *Phlegra*: sometimes called Pallene, a place in Macedonia where the giants attacked the gods and were defeated by Hercules. 580 *Uther's son*: King Arthur. 583 *Asparamont or Montalban*: places in Italian romances. 585–88 *Damasco, Marocco, Trebisond, Biserta, Fontarabbia*: figures and places prominent in the battles of renaissance romance.

Waiting revenge: cruel his eye, but cast
Signs of remorse and passion to behold   605
The fellows of his crime, the followers rather
(Far other once beheld in bliss) condemn'd
For ever now to have thir lot in pain,
Millions of Spirits for his fault amerc't
Of Heav'n, and from Eternal Splendors flung   610
For his revolt, yet faithful how they stood,
Thir Glory wither'd. As when Heaven's Fire
Hath scath'd the Forest Oaks, or Mountain Pines,
With singed top thir stately growth though bare
Stands on the blasted Heath. He now prepar'd   615
To speak; whereat thir doubl'd Ranks they bend
From wing to wing, and half enclose him round
With all his Peers: attention held them mute.
Thrice he assay'd, and thrice in spite of scorn,
Tears such as Angels weep, burst forth: at last   620
Words interwove with sighs found out thir way.
   O Myriads of immortal Spirits, O Powers
Matchless, but with th' Almighty, and that strife
Was not inglorious, though th' event was dire,
As this place testifies, and this dire change   625
Hateful to utter: but what power of mind
Foreseeing or presaging, from the Depth
Of knowledge past or present, could have fear'd,
How such united force of Gods, how such
As stood like these, could ever know repulse?   630
For who can yet believe, though after loss,
That all these puissant Legions, whose exíle
Hath emptied Heav'n, shall fail to re-ascend
Self-rais'd, and repossess thir native seat?
For mee, be witness all the Host of Heav'n,   635
If counsels different, or danger shunn'd
By mee, have lost our hopes. But he who reigns
Monarch in Heav'n, till then as one secure
Sat on his Throne, upheld by old repute,
Consent or custom, and his Regal State   640
Put forth at full, but still his strength conceal'd,
Which tempted our attempt, and wrought our fall.
Henceforth his might we know, and know our own
So as not either to provoke, or dread
New war, provok't; our better part remains   645
To work in close design, by fraud or guile
What force effected not: that he no less
At length from us may find, who overcomes
By force, hath overcome but half his foe.
Space may produce new Worlds; whereof so rife   650
There went a fame in Heav'n that he ere long

---

609 *amerc't*: punished.

Intended to create, and therein plant
A generation, whom his choice regard
Should favour equal to the Sons of Heaven:
Thither, if but to pry, shall be perhaps   655
Our first eruption, thither or elsewhere:
For this Infernal Pit shall never hold
Celestial Spirits in Bondage, nor th' Abyss
Long under darkness cover. But these thoughts
Full Counsel must mature: Peace is despair'd,   660
For who can think Submission? War then, War
Open or understood, must be resolv'd.
   He spake: and to confirm his words, out-flew
Millions of flaming swords, drawn from the thighs
Of mighty Cherubim; the sudden blaze   665
Far round illumin'd hell: highly they rag'd
Against the Highest, and fierce with grasped Arms
Clash'd on thir sounding shields the din of war,
Hurling defiance toward the Vault of Heav'n.
   There stood a Hill not far whose grisly top   670
Belch'd fire and rolling smoke; the rest entire
Shone with a glossy scurf, undoubted sign
That in his womb was hid metallic Ore,
The work of Sulphur. Thither wing'd with speed
A numerous Brígad hasten'd. As when bands   675
Of Píoners with Spade and Pickax arm'd
Forerun the Royal Camp, to trench a Field,
Or cast a Rampart. *Mammon* led them on,
Mammon, the least erected Spirit that fell
From heav'n, for ev'n in heav'n his looks and thoughts   680
Were always downward bent, admiring more
The riches of Heav'n's pavement, trodd'n Gold,
Than aught divine or holy else enjoy'd
In vision beatific: by him first
Men also, and by his suggestion taught,   685
Ransack'd the Centre, and with impious hands
Rifl'd the bowels of thir mother Earth
For Treasures better hid. Soon had his crew
Op'n'd into the Hill a spacious wound
And digg'd out ribs of Gold. Let none admire   690
That riches grow in Hell; that soil may best
Deserve the precious bane. And here let those
Who boast in mortal things, and wond'ring tell
Of *Babel,* and the works of *Memphian* Kings,
Learn how thir greatest Monuments of Fame,   695
And Strength and Art are easily outdone
By Spirits reprobate, and in an hour
What in an age they with incessant toil

---

694 *Babel, Memphian*: Milton associates the tower of Babel with Egyptian (Memphian) "Monuments of Fame."

And hands innumerable scarce perform.
Nigh on the Plain in many cells prepar'd,   700
That underneath had veins of liquid fire
Sluic'd from the Lake, a second multitude
With wondrous Art founded the massy Ore,
Severing each kind, and scumm'd the Bullion dross:
A third as soon had form'd within the ground   705
A various mould, and from the boiling cells
By strange conveyance fill'd each hollow nook,
As in an Organ from one blast of wind
To many a row of Pipes the sound-board breathes.
Anon out of the earth a Fabric huge   710
Rose like an Exhalation, with the sound
Of Dulcet Symphonies and voices sweet,
Built like a Temple, where *Pilasters* round
Were set, and Doric pillars overlaid
With Golden Architrave; nor did there want   715
Cornice or Frieze, with bossy Sculptures grav'n,
The Roof was fretted Gold. Not *Babylon*,
Nor great *Alcairo* such magnificence
Equall'd in all thir glories, to inshrine
Belus or *Serapis* thir Gods, or seat   720
Thir Kings, when *Egypt* with *Assyria* strove
In wealth and luxury. Th' ascending pile
Stood fixt her stately highth, and straight the doors
Op'ning thir brazen folds discover wide
Within, her ample spaces, o'er the smooth   725
And level pavement: from the arched roof
Pendant by subtle Magic many a row
Of Starry Lamps and blazing Cressets fed
With *Naphtha* and *Asphaltus* yielded light
As from a sky. The hasty multitude   730
Admiring enter'd, and the work some praise
And some the Architect: his hand was known
In Heav'n by many a Tow'red structure high,
Where Scepter'd Angels held thir residence,
And sat as Princes, whom the supreme King   735
Exalted to such power, and gave to rule,
Each in his Hierarchy, the Orders bright.
Nor was his name unheard or unador'd
In ancient *Greece;* and in *Ausonian* land
Men call'd him *Mulciber;* and how he fell   740
From Heav'n, they fabl'd, thrown by angry *Jove*
Sheer o'er the Crystal Battlements: from Morn
To Noon he fell, from Noon to dewy Eve,
A Summer's day; and with the setting Sun
Dropt from the Zenith like a falling Star,   745

718 *Alcairo*: Cairo, Egypt. 720 *Belus, Serapis*: Baal (Babylonian god) and Osiris (Egyptian god). 728 *blazing Cressets*: burning pots filled with naphtha and asphalt (line 729). 739 *Ausonian land*: Italy.

On *Lemnos* th' *Ægæan* Isle: thus they relate,
Erring; for he with this rebellious rout
Fell long before; nor aught avail'd him now
To have built in Heav'n high Tow'rs; nor did he scape
By all his Engines, but was headlong sent   750
With his industrious crew to build in hell.
Meanwhile the winged Heralds by command
Of Sovran power, with awful Ceremony
And Trumpets' sound throughout the Host proclaim
A solemn Council forthwith to be held   755
At *Pandæmonium*, the high Capital
Of Satan and his Peers: thir summons call'd
From every Band and squared Regiment
By place or choice the worthiest; they anon
With hundreds and with thousands trooping came   760
Attended: all access was throng'd, the Gates
And Porches wide, but chief the spacious Hall
(Though like a cover'd field, where Champions bold
Wont ride in arm'd, and at the Soldan's chair
Defi'd the best of *Paynim* chivalry   765
To mortal combat or career with Lance)
Thick swarm'd, both on the ground and in the air,
Brusht with the hiss of rustling wings. As Bees
In spring time, when the Sun with *Taurus* rides,
Pour forth thir populous youth about the Hive   770
In clusters; they among fresh dews and flowers
Fly to and fro, or on the smoothed Plank,
The suburb of thir Straw-built Citadel,
New rubb'd with Balm, expatiate and confer
Thir State affairs. So thick the aery crowd   775
Swarm'd and were strait'n'd; till the Signal giv'n,
Behold a wonder! they but now who seem'd
In bigness to surpass Earth's Giant Sons
Now less than smallest Dwarfs, in narrow room
Throng numberless, like that Pigmean Race   780
Beyond the *Indian* Mount, or Faery Elves,
Whose midnight Revels, by a Forest side
Or Fountain some belated Peasant sees,
Or dreams he sees, while over-head the Moon
Sits Arbitress, and nearer to the Earth   785
Wheels her pale course, they on thir mirth and dance
Intent, with jocund Music charm his ear;
At once with joy and fear his heart rebounds.
Thus incorporeal Spirits to smallest forms
Reduc'd thir shapes immense, and were at large,   790
Though without number still amidst the Hall

---

746 *Lemnos*: an island in the Aegean sea sacred to Vulcan, the Roman equivalent to Hephaetus, the Greek god of fire. Milton makes Mulciber the archetype of the Greek and Roman gods ejected from heaven. 765 *Paynim*: pagan, Saracen. 769 *Taurus*: sign of the Bull (in April). 780 Cf. line 575.

Of that infernal Court. But far within
And in thir own dimensions like themselves
The great Seraphic Lords and Cherubim
In close recess and secret conclave sat 795
A thousand Demi-Gods on golden seats,
Frequent and full. After short silence then
And summons read, the great consult began.

The End of the First Book.

BOOK II

THE ARGUMENT

The Consultation begun, Satan *debate whether another Battle be to be
hazarded for the recovery of Heaven: some advise it, others dissuade:
A third proposal is preferr'd, mention'd before by* Satan, *to search the
truth of that Prophecy or Tradition in Heaven concerning another world,
and another kind of creature equal or not much inferior to themselves,
about this time to be created: Thir doubt who shall be sent on this difficult search:* Satan *thir chief undertakes alone the voyage, is honour'd and
applauded. The Council thus ended, the rest betake them several ways
and to several employments, as thir inclinations lead them, to entertain
the time till* Satan *return. He passes on his Journey to Hell Gates, finds
them shut, and who sat there to guard them, by whom at length they are
op'n'd, and discover to him the great Gulf between Hell and Heaven;
with what difficulty he passes through, directed by* Chaos, *the Power of
that place, to the sight of this new World which he sought.*

High on a Throne of Royal State, which far
Outshone the wealth of *Ormus* and of *Ind,*
Or where the gorgeous East with richest hand
Show'rs on her Kings *Barbaric* Pearl and Gold,
Satan exalted sat, by merit rais'd 5
To that bad eminence; and from despair
Thus high uplifted beyond hope, aspires
Beyond thus high, insatiate to pursue
Vain War with Heav'n, and by success untaught
His proud imaginations thus display'd. 10
Powers and Dominions, Deities of Heav'n,
For since no deep within her gulf can hold
Immortal vigor, though opprest and fall'n,
I give not Heav'n for lost. From this descent
Celestial virtues rising, will appear 15
More glorious and more dread than from no fall,
And trust themselves to fear no second fate:
Mee though just right, and the fixt Laws of Heav'n
Did first create your Leader, next, free choice,
With what besides, in Counsel or in Fight, 20
Hath been achiev'd of merit, yet this loss
Thus far at least recover'd, hath much more

---

2 *Ormus, Ind:* a rich city in the Persian Gulf, and India. Ormus was famous as a center
of despotism, greed, and exotic depravity.

Establisht in a safe unenvied Throne
Yielded with full consent. The happier state
In Heav'n, which follows dignity, might draw   25
Envy from each inferior; but who here
Will envy whom the highest place exposes
Foremost to stand against the Thunderer's aim
Your bulwark, and condemns to greatest share
Of endless pain? where there is then no good   30
For which to strive, no strife can grow up there
From Faction; for none sure will claim in Hell
Precedence, none, whose portion is so small
Of present pain, that with ambitious mind
Will covet more. With this advantage then   35
To union, and firm Faith, and firm accord,
More than can be in Heav'n, we now return
To claim our just inheritance of old,
Surer to prosper than prosperity
Could have assur'd us; and by what best way,   40
Whether of open War or covert guile,
We now debate; who can advise, may speak.
     He ceas'd, and next him *Moloch,* Scepter'd King
Stood up, the strongest and the fiercest Spirit
That fought in Heav'n; now fiercer by despair: 45
His trust was with th' Eternal to be deem'd
Equal in strength, and rather than be less
Car'd not to be at all; with that care lost
Went all his fear: of God, or Hell, or worst
He reck'd not, and these words thereafter spake.   50
     My sentence is for open War: Of Wiles,
More unexpert, I boast not: them let those
Contrive who need, or when they need, not now.
For while they sit contriving, shall the rest,
Millions that stand in Arms, and longing wait   55
The Signal to ascend, sit ling'ring here
Heav'n's fugitives, and for thir dwelling place
Accept this dark opprobrious Den of shame,
The Prison of his Tyranny who Reigns
By our delay? no, let us rather choose   60
Arm'd with Hell flames and fury all at once
O'er Heav'n's high Tow'rs to force resistless way,
Turning our Tortures into horrid Arms
Against the Torturer; when to meet the noise
Of his Almighty Engine he shall hear   65
Infernal Thunder, and for Lightning see
Black fire and horror shot with equal rage
Among his Angels; and his Throne itself
Mixt with *Tartarean* Sulphur, and strange fire,

---

25 Because greater worth ("dignity") in heaven brings greater happiness, inferiors in the hierarchy might envy those set above them.   69 *Tartarean*: Tartarus is the Greek equivalent to hell.

His own invented Torments. But perhaps   70
The way seems difficult and steep to scale
With upright wing against a higher foe.
Let such bethink them, if the sleepy drench
Of that forgetful Lake benumb not still,
That in our proper motion we ascend   75
Up to our native seat: descent and fall
To us is adverse. Who but felt of late
When the fierce Foe hung on our brok'n Rear
Insulting, and pursu'd us through the Deep,
With what compulsion and laborious flight   80
We sunk thus low? Th' ascent is easy then;
Th' event is fear'd; should we again provoke
Our stronger, some worse way his wrath may find
To our destruction: if there be in Hell
Fear to be worse destroy'd: what can be worse   85
Than to dwell here, driv'n out from bliss, condemn'd
In this abhorred deep to utter woe;
Where pain of unextinguishable fire
Must exercise us without hope of end
The Vassals of his anger, when the Scourge   90
Inexorably, and the torturing hour
Calls us to Penance? More destroy'd than thus
We should be quite abolisht and expire.
What fear we then? what doubt we to incense
His utmost ire? which to the highth enrag'd,   95
Will either quite consume us, and reduce
To nothing this essential, happier far
Than miserable to have eternal being:
Or if our substance be indeed Divine,
And cannot cease to be, we are at worst   100
On this side nothing; and by proof we feel
Our power sufficient to disturb his Heav'n,
And with perpetual inroads to Alarm,
Though inaccessible, his fatal Throne:
Which if not Victory is yet Revenge.   105
   He ended frowning, and his look denounc'd
Desperate revenge, and Battle dangerous
To less than Gods. On th' other side up rose
Belial, in act more graceful and humane;
A fairer person lost not Heav'n; he seem'd   110
For dignity compos'd and high exploit:
But all was false and hollow; though his Tongue
Dropt Manna, and could make the worse appear
The better reason, to perplex and dash
Maturest Counsels: for his thoughts were low;   115
To vice industrious, but to Nobler deeds

---

74 *that forgetful Lake*: equivalent to the river Lethe, drinking from which causes oblivion.
97 *essential*: essence.

Timorous and slothful: yet he pleas'd the ear,
And with persuasive accent thus began.
   I should be much for open War, O Peers,
As not behind in hate; if what was urg'd   120
Main reason to persuade immediate War,
Did not dissuade me most, and seem to cast
Ominous conjecture on the whole success:
When he who most excels in fact of Arms,
In what he counsels and in what excels   125
Mistrustful, grounds his courage on despair
And utter dissolution, as the scope
Of all his aim, after some dire revenge.
First, what Revenge? the Tow'rs of Heav'n are fill'd
With Armed watch, that render all access   130
Impregnable; oft on the bordering Deep
Encamp thir Legions, or with obscure wing
Scout far and wide into the Realm of night,
Scorning surprise. Or could we break our way
By force, and at our heels all Hell should rise   135
With blackest Insurrection, to confound
Heav'n's purest Light, yet our great Enemy
All incorruptible would on his Throne
Sit unpolluted, and the Ethereal mould
Incapable of stain would soon expel   140
Her mischief, and purge off the baser fire
Victorious. Thus repuls'd, our final hope
Is flat despair; we must exasperate
Th' Almighty Victor to spend all his rage,
And that must end us, that must be our cure,   145
To be no more; sad cure; for who would lose,
Though full of pain, this intellectual being,
Those thoughts that wander through Eternity,
To perish rather, swallow'd up and lost
In the wide womb of uncreated night,   150
Devoid of sense and motion? and who knows,
Let this be good, whether our angry Foe
Can give it, or will ever? how he can
Is doubtful; that he never will is sure.
Will he, so wise, let loose at once his ire,   155
Belike through impotence, or unaware,
To give his Enemies thir wish, and end
Them in his anger, whom his anger saves
To punish endless? wherefore cease we then?
Say they who counsel War, we are decreed,   160
Reserv'd and destin'd to Eternal woe;
Whatever doing, what can we suffer more,
What can we suffer worse? is this then worst,
Thus sitting, thus consulting, thus in Arms?
What when we fled amain, pursu'd and strook   165
With Heav'n's afflicting Thunder, and besought

The Deep to shelter us? this Hell then seem'd
A refuge from those wounds: or when we lay
Chain'd on the burning Lake? that sure was worse.
What if the breath that kindl'd those grim fires   170
Awak'd should blow them into sevenfold rage
And plunge us in the flames? or from above
Should intermitted vengeance arm again
His red right hand to plague us? what if all
Her stores were op'n'd, and this Firmament   175
Of Hell should spout her Cataracts of Fire,
Impendent horrors, threat'ning hideous fall
One day upon our heads; while we perhaps
Designing or exhorting glorious war,
Caught in a fiery Tempest shall be hurl'd   180
Each on his rock transfixt, the sport and prey
Of racking whirlwinds, or for ever sunk
Under yon boiling Ocean, wrapt in Chains;
There to converse with everlasting groans,
Unrespited, unpitied, unrepriev'd,   185
Ages of hopeless end; this would be worse.
War therefore, open or conceal'd, alike
My voice dissuades; for what can force or guile
With him, or who deceive his mind, whose eye
Views all things at one view? he from heav'n's highth   190
All these our motions vain, sees and derides;
Not more Almighty to resist our might
Than wise to frustrate all our plots and wiles.
Shall we then live thus vile, the race of Heav'n
Thus trampl'd, thus expell'd to suffer here   195
Chains and these Torments? better these than worse
By my advice; since fate inevitable
Subdues us, and Omnipotent Decree
The Victor's will. To suffer, as to do,
Our strength is equal, nor the Law unjust   200
That so ordains: this was at first resolv'd,
If we were wise, against so great a foe
Contending, and so doubtful what might fall.
I laugh, when those who at the Spear are bold
And vent'rous, if that fail them, shrink and fear   205
What yet they know must follow, to endure
Exile, or ignominy, or bonds or pain,
The sentence of thir Conqueror: This is now
Our doom; which if we can sustain and bear,
Our Supreme Foe in time may much remit   210
His anger, and perhaps thus far remov'd
Not mind us not offending, satisfi'd
With what is punish't; whence these raging fires
Will slack'n, if his breath stir not thir flames.
Our purer essence then will overcome   215
Thir noxious vapour, or enur'd not feel,

Or chang'd at length, and to the place conform'd
In temper and in nature, will receive
Familiar the fierce heat, and void of pain;
This horror will grow mild, this darkness light,   220
Besides what hope the never-ending flight
Of future days may bring, what chance, what change
Worth waiting, since our present lot appears
For happy though but ill, for ill not worst,
If we procure not to ourselves more woe.   225
  Thus *Belial* with words cloth'd in reason's garb
Counsell'd ignoble ease, and peaceful sloth,
Not peace: and after him thus *Mammon* spake.
  Either to disinthrone the King of Heav'n
We war, if war be best, or to regain   230
Our own right lost: him to unthrone we then
May hope, when everlasting Fate shall yield
To fickle Chance, and *Chaos* judge the strife:
The former vain to hope argues as vain
The latter: for what place can be for us   235
Within Heav'n's bound, unless Heav'n's Lord supreme
We overpower? Suppose he should relent
And publish Grace to all, on promise made
Of new Subjection; with what eyes could we
Stand in his presence humble, and receive   240
Strict Laws impos'd, to celebrate his Throne
With warbl'd Hymns, and to his Godhead sing
Forc't Halleluiahs; while he Lordly sits
Our envied Sovran, and his Altar breathes
Ambrosial Odours and Ambrosial Flowers,   245
Our servile offerings. This must be our task
In Heav'n, this our delight; how wearisome
Eternity so spent in worship paid
To whom we hate. Let us not then pursue
By force impossible, by leave obtain'd   250
Unácceptable, though in Heav'n, our state
Of splendid vassalage, but rather seek
Our own good from ourselves, and from our own
Live to ourselves, though in this vast recess,
Free, and to none accountable, preferring   255
Hard liberty before the easy yoke
Of servile Pomp. Our greatness will appear
Then most conspicuous, when great things of small,
Useful of hurtful, prosperous of adverse
We can create, and in what place soe'er   260
Thrive under evil, and work ease out of pain
Through labour and endurance. This deep world
Of darkness do we dread? How oft amidst
Thick clouds and dark doth Heav'n's all-ruling Sire
Choose to reside, his Glory unobscur'd,   265
And with the Majesty of darkness round

Covers his Throne; from whence deep thunders roar
Must'ring thir rage, and Heav'n resembles Hell?
As he our darkness, cannot we his Light
Imitate when we please? This Desert soil   270
Wants not her hidden lustre, Gems and Gold;
Nor want we skill or art, from whence to raise
Magnificence; and what can Heav'n show more?
Our torments also may in length of time
Become our Elements, these piercing Fires   275
As soft as now severe, our temper chang'd
Into their temper; which must needs remove
The sensible of pain. All things invite
To peaceful Counsels, and the settl'd State
Of order, how in safety best we may   280
Compose our present evils, with regard
Of what we are and where, dismissing quite
All thoughts of War; ye have what I advise.
    He scarce had finisht, when such murmur fill'd
Th' Assembly, as when hollow Rocks retain   285
The sound of blust'ring winds, which all night long
Had rous'd the Sea, now with hoarse cadence lull
Sea-faring men o'erwatcht, whose Bark by chance
Or Pinnance anchors in a craggy Bay
After the Tempest: Such applause was heard   290
As *Mammon* ended, and his Sentence pleas'd,
Advising peace: for such another Field
They dreaded worse than Hell: so much the fear
Of Thunder and the Sword of *Michaël*
Wrought still within them; and no less desire   295
To found this nether Empire, which might rise
By policy, and long process of time,
In emulation opposite to Heav'n.
Which when *Beëlzebub* perceiv'd, than whom,
Satan except, none higher sat, with grave   300
Aspect he rose, and in his rising seem'd
A Pillar of State; deep on his Front engraven
Deliberation sat and public care;
And Princely counsel in his face yet shone,
Majestic though in ruin: sage he stood   305
With *Atlantean* shoulders fit to bear
The weight of mightiest Monarchies; his look
Drew audience and attention still as Night
Or Summer's Noon-tide air, while thus he spake.
    Thrones and imperial Powers, off-spring of heav'n,   310
Ethereal Virtues; or these Titles now
Must we renounce, and changing style be call'd
Princes of Hell? for so the popular vote
Inclines, here to continue, and build up here

---

302 *Front*: forehead. 306 *Atlantean*: Atlas-like.

A growing Empire; doubtless; while we dream,   315
And know not that the King of Heav'n hath doom'd
This place our dungeon, not our safe retreat
Beyond his Potent arm, to live exempt
From Heav'n's high jurisdiction, in new League
Banded against his Throne, but to remain   320
In strictest bondage, though thus far remov'd,
Under th' inevitable curb, reserv'd
His captive multitude: For he, be sure,
In highth or depth, still first and last will Reign
Sole King, and of his Kingdom lose no part   325
By our revolt, but over Hell extend
His Empire, and with Iron Sceptre rule
Us here, as with his Golden those in Heav'n.
What sit we then projecting peace and War?
War hath determin'd us, and foil'd with loss   330
Irreparable; terms of peace yet none
Voutsaf't or sought; for what peace will be giv'n
To us enslav'd, but custody severe,
And stripes, and arbitrary punishment
Inflicted? and what peace can we return,   335
But to our power hostility and hate,
Untam'd reluctance, and revenge though slow,
Yet ever plotting how the Conqueror least
May reap his conquest, and may least rejoice
In doing what we most in suffering feel?   340
Nor will occasion want, nor shall we need
With dangerous expedition to invade
Heav'n, whose high walls fear no assault or Siege,
Or ambush from the Deep. What if we find
Some easier enterprise? There is a place   345
(If ancient and prophetic fame in Heav'n
Err not) another World, the happy seat
Of some new Race call'd *Man,* about this time
To be created like to us, though less
In power and excellence, but favour'd more   350
Of him who rules above; so was his will
Pronounc'd among the Gods, and by an Oath,
That shook Heav'n's whole circumference, confirm'd.
Thither let us bend all our thoughts, to learn
What creatures there inhabit, of what mould,   355
Or substance, how endu'd, and what thir Power,
And where thir weakness, how attempted best,
By force or subtlety: Though Heav'n be shut,
And Heav'n's high Arbitrator sit secure
In his own strength, this place may lie expos'd   360
The utmost border of his Kingdom, left

---

336 *But to our power hostility and hate*: "But endure to our limit hostility...."   356 *endu'd*: endowed.

To their defence who hold it: here perhaps
Some advantageous act may be achiev'd
By sudden onset, either with Hell fire
To waste his whole Creation, or possess   365
All as our own, and drive as we were driven,
The puny habitants, or if not drive,
Seduce them to our Party, that thir God
May prove thir foe, and with repenting hand
Abolish his own works. This would surpass   370
Common revenge, and interrupt his joy
In our Confusion, and our Joy upraise
In his disturbance; when his darling Sons
Hurl'd headlong to partake with us, shall curse
Thir frail Original, and faded bliss,   375
Faded so soon. Advise if this be worth
Attempting, or to sit in darkness here
Hatching vain Empires. Thus *Beëlzebub*
Pleaded his devilish Counsel, first devis'd
By *Satan,* and in part propos'd: for whence,   380
But from the Author of all ill could Spring
So deep a malice, to confound the race
Of mankind in one root, and Earth with Hell
To mingle and involve, done all to spite
The great Creator? But thir spite still serves   385
His glory to augment. The bold design
Pleas'd highly those infernal States, and joy
Sparkl'd in all thir eyes; with full assent
They vote: whereat his speech he thus renews.
    Well have ye judg'd, well ended long debate,   390
Synod of Gods, and like to what ye are,
Great things resolv'd, which from the lowest deep
Will once more lift us up, in spite of Fate,
Nearer our ancient Seat; perhaps in view
Of those bright confines, whence with neighbouring Arms   395
And opportune excursion we may chance
Re-enter Heav'n; or else in some mild Zone
Dwell not unvisited of Heav'n's fair Light
Secure, and at the bright'ning Orient beam
Purge off this gloom; the soft delicious Air,   400
To heal the scar of these corrosive Fires
Shall breathe her balm. But first whom shall we send
In search of this new world, whom shall we find
Sufficient? who shall tempt with wand'ring feet
The dark unbottom'd infinite Abyss   405
And through the palpable obscure find out
His uncouth way, or spread his aery flight
Upborne with indefatigable wings
Over the vast abrupt, ere he arrive

---

375 *frail Original*: Adam, the origin of men.

The happy Isle; what strength, what art can then   410
Suffice, or what evasion bear him safe
Through the strict Senteries and Stations thick
Of Angels watching round? Here he had need
All circumspection, and we now no less
Choice in our suffrage; for on whom we send,   415
The weight of all and our last hope relies.
   This said, he sat; and expectation held
His look suspense, awaiting who appear'd
To second, or oppose, or undertake
The perilous attempt; but all sat mute,   420
Pondering the danger with deep thoughts; and each
In other's count'nance read his own dismay
Astonisht: none among the choice and prime
Of those Heav'n-warring Champions could be found
So hardy as to proffer or accept   425
Alone the dreadful voyage; till at last
Satan, whom now transcendent glory rais'd
Above his fellows, with Monarchal pride
Conscious of highest worth, unmov'd thus spake.
   O Progeny of Heav'n, Empyreal Thrones,   430
With reason hath deep silence and demur
Seiz'd us, though undismay'd: long is the way
And hard, that out of Hell leads up to light;
Our prison strong, this huge convex of Fire,
Outrageous to devour, immures us round   435
Ninefold, and gates of burning Adamant
Barr'd over us prohibit all egress.
These past, if any pass, the void profound
Of unessential Night receives him next
Wide gaping, and with utter loss of being   440
Threatens him, plung'd in that abortive gulf.
If thence he scape into whatever world,
Or unknown Region, what remains him less
Than unknown dangers and as hard escape.
But I should ill become this Throne, O Peers,   445
And this Imperial Sov'ranty, adorn'd
With splendor, arm'd with power, if aught propos'd
And judg'd of public moment, in the shape
Of difficulty or danger could deter
Me from attempting. Wherefore do I assume   450
These Royalties, and not refuse to Reign,
Refusing to accept as great a share
Of hazard as of honour, due alike
To him who Reigns, and so much to him due
Of hazard more, as he above the rest   455
High honour'd sits? Go therefore mighty Powers.
Terror of Heav'n, though fall'n; intend at home,
While here shall be our home, what best may ease
The present misery, and render Hell

More tolerable; if there be cure or charm   460
To respite or deceive, or slack the pain
Of this ill Mansion: intermit no watch
Against a wakeful Foe, while I abroad
Through all the Coasts of dark destruction seek
Deliverance for us all: this enterprise   465
None shall partake with me. Thus saying rose
The Monarch, and prevented all reply,
Prudent, lest from his resolution rais'd
Others among the chief might offer now
(Certain to be refus'd) what erst they fear'd;   470
And so refus'd might in opinion stand
His Rivals, winning cheap the high repute
Which he through hazard huge must earn. But they
Dreaded not more th' adventure than his voice
Forbidding; and at once with him they rose;   475
Thir rising all at once was as the sound
Of Thunder heard remote. Towards him they bend
With awful reverence prone; and as a God
Extol him equal to the highest in Heav'n:
Nor fail'd they to express how much they prais'd,   480
That for the general safety he despis'd
His own: for neither do the Spirits damn'd
Lose all thir virtue; lest bad men should boast
Thir specious deeds on earth, which glory excites,
Or close ambition varnisht o'er with zeal.   485
Thus they thir doubtful consultations dark
Ended rejoicing in their matchless Chief:
As when from mountain tops the dusky clouds
Ascending, while the North wind sleeps, o'erspread
Heav'n's cheerful face, the low'ring Element   490
Scowls o'er the dark'n'd lantskip Snow, or show'r;
If chance the radiant Sun with farewell sweet
Extend his ev'ning beam, the fields revive,
The birds thir notes renew, and bleating herds
Attest thir joy, that hill and valley rings.   495
O shame to men! Devil with Devil damn'd
Firm concord holds, men only disagree
Of Creatures rational, though under hope
Of heavenly Grace; and God proclaiming peace,
Yet live in hatred, enmity, and strife   500
Among themselves, and levy cruel wars,
Wasting the Earth, each other to destroy:
As if (which might induce us to accord)
Man had not hellish foes anow besides,
That day and night for his destruction wait.   505
    The *Stygian* Council thus dissolv'd; and forth
In order came the grand infernal Peers,
Midst came thir mighty Paramount, and seem'd
Alone th' Antagonist of Heav'n, nor less

Than Hell's dread Emperor with pomp Supreme,   510
And God-like imitated State; him round
A Globe of fiery Seraphim inclos'd
With bright imblazonry, and horrent Arms.
Then of thir Session ended they bid cry
With Trumpet's regal sound the great result: 515
Toward the four winds four speedy Cherubim
Put to thir mouths the sounding Alchymy
By Herald's voice explain'd: the hollow Abyss
Heard far and wide, and all the host of Hell
With deaf'ning shout, return'd them loud acclaim.   520
Thence more at ease thir minds and somewhat rais'd
By false presumptuous hope, the ranged powers
Disband, and wand'ring, each his several way
Pursues, as inclination or sad choice
Leads him perplext, where he may likeliest find   525
Truce to his restless thoughts, and entertain
The irksome hours, till his great Chief return.
Part on the Plain, or in the Air sublime
Upon the wing, or in swift Race contend,
As at th' Olympian Games or *Pythian* fields;   530
Part curb thir fiery Steeds, or shun the Goal
With rapid wheels, or fronted Brígads form.
As when to warn proud Cities war appears
Wag'd in the troubl'd Sky, and Armies rush
To Battle in the Clouds, before each Van   535
Prick forth the Aery Knights, and couch thir spears
Till thickest Legions close; with feats of Arms
From either end of Heav'n the welkin burns.
Others with vast *Typhœan* rage more fell
Rend up both Rocks and Hills, and ride the Air   540
In whirlwind; Hell scarce holds the wild uproar.
As when *Alcides* from *Oechalia* Crown'd
With conquest, felt th' envenom'd robe, and tore
Through pain up by the roots *Thessalian* Pines,
And *Lichas* from the top of *Oeta* threw   545
Into th' *Euboic* Sea. Others more mild,
Retreated in a silent valley, sing
With notes Angelical to many a Harp
Thir own Heroic deeds and hapless fall
By doom of Battle; and complain that Fate   550
Free Virtue should enthrall to Force or Chance.
Thir song was partial, but the harmony
(What could it less when Spirits immortal sing?)

---

517 *Alchymy*: golden instruments. 530 *Olympian Games or Pythian fields*: games were
held every four years at Olympia. The Pythian games were held at Delphi. 539 *Typhoean*:
after the Titan Typhon. 542–46 *Alcides, Oechalia, Thessalian, Lichas, Oeta, Euboic*:
Hercules (Alcides), after marrying Deianira, fell in love with Iole. Deianira sent him, through
Lichas, a poisoned robe that caused Hercules to fall into a desperate distemper. Hercules
then threw Lichas from Mount Otea (in Thessaly) into the neighboring Euboean sea.

Suspended Hell, and took with ravishment
The thronging audience. In discourse more sweet   555
(For Eloquence the Soul, Song charms the Sense,)
Others apart sat on a Hill retir'd,
In thoughts more elevate, and reason'd high
Of Providence, Foreknowledge, Will, and Fate,
Fixt Fate, free will, foreknowledge absolute,   560
And found no end, in wand'ring mazes lost.
Of good and evil much they argu'd then,
Of happiness and final misery,
Passion and Apathy, and glory and shame,
Vain wisdom all, and false Philosophie: 565
Yet with a pleasing sorcery could charm
Pain for a while or anguish, and excite
Fallacious hope, or arm th' obdured breast
With stubborn patience as with triple steel.
Another part in Squadrons and gross Bands,   570
On bold adventure to discover wide
That dismal World, if any Clime perhaps
Might yield them easier habitation, bend
Four ways thir flying March, along the Banks
Of four infernal Rivers that disgorge   575
Into the burning Lake thir baleful streams;
Abhorred *Styx* the flood of deadly hate,
Sad *Acheron* of Sorrow, black and deep;
Cocytus, nam'd of lamentation loud
Heard on the rueful stream; fierce *Phlegeton*   580
Whose waves of torrent fire inflame with rage.
Far off from these a slow and silent stream,
Lethe the River of Oblivion rolls
Her wat'ry Labyrinth, whereof who drinks,
Forthwith his former state and being forgets,   585
Forgets both joy and grief, pleasure and pain.
Beyond this flood a frozen Continent
Lies dark and wild, beat with perpetual storms
Of Whirlwind and dire Hail, which on firm land
Thaws not, but gathers heap, and ruin seems   590
Of ancient pile; all else deep snow and ice,
A gulf profound as that *Serbonian* Bog
Betwixt *Damiata* and mount *Casius* old,
Where Armies whole have sunk: the parching Air
Burns frore, and cold performs th' effect of Fire.   595
Thither by harpy-footed Furies hal'd,
At certain revolutions all the damn'd
Are brought: and feel by turns the bitter change
Of fierce extremes, extremes by change more fierce,
From Beds of raging Fire to starve in Ice   600
Thir soft Ethereal warmth, and there to pine
Immovable, infixt, and frozen round,
Periods of time, thence hurried back to fire.

They ferry over this *Lethean* Sound
Both to and fro, thir sorrow to augment,   605
And wish and struggle, as they pass, to reach
The tempting stream, with one small drop to lose
In sweet forgetfulness all pain and woe,
All in one moment, and so near the brink;
But fate withstands, and to oppose th' attempt   610
Medusa with *Gorgonian* terror guards
The Ford, and of itself the water flies
All taste of living wight, as once it fled
The lip of *Tantalus*. Thus roving on
In confus'd march forlorn, th' advent'rous Bands   615
With shudd'ring horror pale, and eyes aghast
View'd first thir lamentable lot, and found
No rest: through many a dark and dreary Vale
They pass'd, and many a Region dolorous,
O'er many a Frozen, many a Fiery Alp,   620
Rocks, Caves, Lakes, Fens, Bogs, Dens, and shades of death,
A Universe of death, which God by curse
Created evil, for evil only good,
Where all life dies, death lives, and Nature breeds,
Perverse, all monstrous, all prodigious things,   625
Abominable, inutterable, and worse
Than Fables yet have feign'd, or fear conceiv'd,
Gorgons and *Hydras*, and *Chimeras* dire.
      Meanwhile the Adversary of God and Man,
Satan with thoughts inflam'd of highest design,   630
Puts on swift wings, and toward the Gates of Hell
Explores his solitary flight; sometimes
He scours the right hand coast, sometimes the left,
Now shaves with level wing the Deep, then soars
Up to the fiery concave tow'ring high.   635
As when far off at Sea a Fleet descri'd
Hangs in the Clouds, by *Equinoctial* Winds
Close sailing from *Bengala*, or the Isles
Of *Ternate* and *Tidore*, whence Merchants bring
Thir spicy Drugs: they on the Trading Flood   640
Through the wide *Ethiopian* to the Cape
Ply stemming nightly toward the Pole. So seem'd
Far off the flying Fiend: at last appear
Hell bounds high reaching to the horrid Roof
And thrice threefold the Gates; three folds were Brass,   645
Three Iron, three of Adamantine Rock,
Impenetrable, impal'd with circling fire,
Yet unconsum'd. Before the Gates there sat
On either side a formidable shape;

---

611 *Medusa*: one of the three Gorgons, with serpents for locks of hair. 614 *Tantalus*:
punished with insatiable thirst in the midst of a pool which he can never quite taste. 628
Gorgons, Hydras, Chimeras: all rather intangible monsters in classical infernos. 637–641
The reference is to the Spice Islands, which had been newly opened to trade in Milton's time.

The one seem'd Woman to the waist, and fair, 650
But ended foul in many a scaly fold
Voluminous and vast, a Serpent arm'd
With mortal sting: about her middle round
A cry of Hell Hounds never ceasing bark'd
With wide *Cerberean* mouths full loud, and rung 655
A hideous Peal: yet, when they list, would creep,
If aught disturb'd thir noise, into her womb,
And kennel there, yet there still bark'd and howl'd
Within unseen. Far less abhorr'd than these
Vex'd *Scylla* bathing in the Sea that parts 660
Calabria from the hoarse *Trinacrian* shore:
Nor uglier follow the Night-Hag, when call'd
In secret, riding through the Air she comes
Lur'd with the smell of infant blood, to dance
With *Lapland* Witches, while the labouring Moon 665
Eclipses at thir charms. The other shape,
If shape it might be call'd that shape had none
Distinguishable in member, joint, or limb,
Or substance might be call'd that shadow seem'd,
For each seem'd either; black it stood as Night, 670
Fierce as ten Furies, terrible as Hell,
And shook a dreadful Dart; what seem'd his head
The likeness of a Kingly Crown had on.
Satan was now at hand, and from his seat
The Monster moving onward came as fast, 675
With horrid strides Hell trembled as he strode.
Th' undaunted Fiend what this might be admir'd,
Admir'd, not fear'd; God and his Son except,
Created thing naught valu'd he nor shunn'd;
And with disdainful look thus first began. 680
    Whence and what art thou, execrable shape,
That dar'st, though grim and terrible, advance
Thy miscreated Front athwart my way
To yonder Gates? through them I mean to pass,
That be assured, without leave askt of thee: 685
Retire, or taste thy folly, and learn by proof,
Hell-born, not to contend with Spirits of Heav'n.
    To whom the Goblin full of wrath repli'd,
Art thou that Traitor Angel, art thou hee,
Who first broke peace in Heav'n and Faith, till then 690
Unbrok'n, and in proud rebellious Arms
Drew after him the third part of Heav'n's Sons
Conjur'd against the highest, for which both Thou
And they outcast from God, are here condemn'd
To waste Eternal days in woe and pain? 695
And reck'n'st thou thyself with Spirits of Heav'n,

---

661 *Calabria, Trinacrian shore*: the southern tip of Italy and Sicily. 662 *the Night-Hag*:
possibly Hecate, who helped Circe charm Scylla.

Hell-doom'd, and breath'st defiance here and scorn,
Where I reign King, and to enrage thee more,
Thy King and Lord? Back to thy punishment,
False fugitive, and to thy speed add wings,   700
Lest with a whip of Scorpions I pursue
Thy ling'ring, or with one stroke of this Dart
Strange horror seize thee, and pangs unfelt before.
   So spake the grisly terror, and in shape,
So speaking and so threat'ning, grew tenfold   705
More dreadful and deform: on th' other side
Incens't with indignation *Satan* stood
Unterrifi'd, and like a Comet burn'd,
That fires the length of *Ophiucus* huge
In th' Arctic Sky, and from his horrid hair   710
Shakes Pestilence and War. Each at the Head
Levell'd his deadly aim; thir fatal hands
No second stroke intend, and such a frown
Each cast at th' other, as when two black Clouds
With Heav'n's Artillery fraught, come rattling on   715
Over the *Caspian,* then stand front to front
Hov'ring a space, till Winds the signal blow
To join thir dark Encounter in mid air:
So frown'd the mighty Combatants, that Hell
Grew darker at thir frown, so matcht they stood;   720
For never but once more was either like
To meet so great a foe: and now great deeds
Had been achiev'd, whereof all Hell had rung,
Had not the Snaky Sorceress that sat
Fast by Hell Gate, and kept the fatal Key,   725
Ris'n, and with hideous outcry rush'd between.
   O Father, what intends thy hand, she cri'd,
Against thy only Son? What fury O Son,
Possesses thee to bend that mortal Dart
Against thy Father's head? and know'st for whom;   730
For him who sits above and laughs the while
At thee ordain'd his drudge, to execute
Whate'er his wrath, which he calls Justice, bids,
His wrath which one day will destroy ye both.
   She spake, and at her words the hellish Pest   735
Forbore, then these to her *Satan* return'd:
   So strange thy outcry, and thy words so strange
Thou interposest, that my sudden hand
Prevented spares to tell thee yet by deeds
What it intends; till first I know of thee,   740
What thing thou art, thus double-form'd, and why
In this infernal Vale first met thou call'st
Me Father, and that Phantasm call'st my Son?

709 *Ophiuchus:* a large constellation with comets and "horrid hair" suggestive of serpents.

I know thee not, nor ever saw till now
Sight more detestable than him and thee.   745
   T' whom thus the Portress of Hell Gate repli'd:
Hast thou forgot me then, and do I seem
Now in thine eye so foul, once deem'd so fair
In Heav'n, when at th' Assembly, and in sight
Of all the Seraphim with thee combin'd   750
In bold conspiracy against Heav'n's King,
All on a sudden miserable pain
Surpris'd thee, dim thine eyes, and dizzy swum
In darkness, while thy head flames thick and fast
Threw forth, till on the left side op'ning wide,   755
Likest to thee in shape and count'nance bright,
Then shining heav'nly fair, a Goddess arm'd
Out of thy head I sprung; amazement seiz'd
All th' Host of Heav'n; back they recoil'd afraid
At first, and call'd me *Sin,* and for a Sign   760
Portentous held me; but familiar grown,
I pleas'd, and with attractive graces won
The most averse, thee chiefly, who full oft
Thyself in me thy perfect image viewing
Becam'st enamor'd, and such joy thou took'st   765
With me in secret, that my womb conceiv'd
A growing burden. Meanwhile War arose,
And fields were fought in Heav'n; wherein remain'd
(For what could else) to our Almighty Foe
Clear Victory, to our part loss and rout   770
Through all the Empyrean: down they fell
Driv'n headlong from the Pitch of Heaven, down
Into this Deep, and in the general fall
I also; at which time this powerful Key
Into my hand was giv'n, with charge to keep   775
These Gates for ever shut, which none can pass
Without my op'ning. Pensive here I sat
Alone, but long I sat not, till my womb
Pregnant by thee, and now excessive grown
Prodigious motion felt and rueful throes.   780
At last this odious offspring whom thou seest
Thine own begotten, breaking violent way
Tore through my entrails, that with fear and pain
Distorted, all my nether shape thus grew
Transform'd: but he my inbred enemy   785
Forth issu'd, brandishing his fatal Dart
Made to destroy: I fled, and cri'd out *Death;*
Hell trembl'd at the hideous Name, and sigh'd
From all her Caves, and back resounded *Death.*
I fled, but he pursu'd (though more, it seems,   790
Inflam'd with lust than rage) and swifter far,
Mee overtook his mother all dismay'd,

And in embraces forcible and foul
Ingend'ring with me, of that rape begot
These yelling Monsters that with ceaseless cry   795
Surround me, as thou saw'st, hourly conceiv'd
And hourly born, with sorrow infinite
To me, for when they list into the womb
That bred them they return, and howl and gnaw
My Bowels, thir repast; then bursting forth   800
Afresh with conscious terrors vex me round,
That rest or intermission none I find.
Before mine eyes in opposition sits
Grim *Death* my Son and foe, who sets them on,
And me his Parent would full soon devour   805
For want of other prey, but that he knows
His end with mine involv'd; and knows that I
Should prove a bitter Morsel, and his bane,
Whenever that shall be; so Fate pronounc'd.
But thou O Father, I forewarn thee, shun   810
His deadly arrow; neither vainly hope
To be invulnerable in those bright Arms,
Though temper'd heav'nly, for that mortal dint,
Save he who reigns above, none can resist.
  She finish'd, and the subtle Fiend his lore   815
Soon learn'd, now milder, and thus answer'd smooth.
Dear Daughter, since thou claim'st me for thy Sire,
And my fair Son here show'st me, the dear pledge
Of dalliance had with thee in Heav'n, and joys
Then sweet, now sad to mention, through dire change   820
Befall'n us unforeseen, unthought of, know
I come no enemy, but to set free
From out this dark and dismal house of pain,
Both him and thee, and all the heav'nly Host
Of Spirits that in our just pretenses arm'd   825
Fell with us from on high: from them I go
This uncouth errand sole, and one for all
Myself expose, with lonely steps to tread
Th' unfounded deep, and through the void immense
To search with wand'ring quest a place foretold   830
Should be, and, by concurring signs, ere now
Created vast and round, a place of bliss
In the Purlieus of Heav'n, and therein plac't
A race of upstart Creatures, to supply
Perhaps our vacant room, though more remov'd,   835
Lest Heav'n surcharg'd with potent multitude
Might hap to move new broils: Be this or aught
Than this more secret now design'd, I haste
To know, and this once known, shall soon return,
And bring ye to the place where Thou and Death   840
Shall dwell at ease, and up and down unseen
Wing silently the buxom Air, imbalm'd

With odours; there ye shall be fed and fill'd
Immeasurably, all things shall be your prey.
He ceas'd, for both seem'd highly pleas'd, and Death   845
Grinn'd horrible a ghastly smile, to hear
His famine should be fill'd, and blest his maw
Destin'd to that good hour: no less rejoic'd
His mother bad, and thus bespake her Sire.
　　The key of this infernal Pit by due,   850
And by command of Heav'n's all-powerful King
I keep, by him forbidden to unlock
These Adamantine Gates; against all force
Death ready stands to interpose his dart,
Fearless to be o'ermatcht by living might.   855
But what owe I to his commands above
Who hates me, and hath hither thrust me down
Into this gloom of *Tartarus* profound,
To sit in hateful Office here confin'd,
Inhabitant of Heav'n, and heav'nly-born,   860
Here in perpetual agony and pain,
With terrors and with clamors compasst round
Of mine own brood, that on my bowels feed:
Thou art my Father, thou my Author, thou
My being gav'st me; whom should I obey   865
But thee, whom follow? thou wilt bring me soon
To that new world of light and bliss, among
The Gods who live at ease, where I shall Reign
At thy right hand voluptuous, as beseems
Thy daughter and thy darling, without end.   870
　　Thus saying, from her side the fatal Key,
Sad instrument of all our woe, she took;
And towards the Gate rolling her bestial train,
Forthwith the huge Portcullis high up drew,
Which but herself not all the *Stygian* powers   875
Could once have mov'd; then in the key-hole turns
Th' intricate wards, and every Bolt and Bar
Of massy Iron or solid Rock with ease
Unfast'ns: on a sudden op'n fly
With impetuous recoil and jarring sound   880
Th' infernal doors, and on thir hinges grate
Harsh Thunder, that the lowest bottom shook
Of *Erebus*. She op'n'd, but to shut
Excell'd her power; the Gates wide op'n stood,
That with extended wings a Banner'd Host   885
Under spread Ensigns marching might pass through
With Horse and Chariots rankt in loose array;
So wide they stood, and like a Furnace mouth
Cast forth redounding smoke and ruddy flame.
Before thir eyes in sudden view appear   890

---

883 *Erebus*: mythological child of chaos.

The secrets of the hoary deep, a dark
Illimitable Ocean without bound,
Without dimension, where length, breadth, and highth,
And time and place are lost; where eldest Night
And *Chaos,* Ancestors of Nature, hold   895
Eternal *Anarchy,* amidst the noise
Of endless wars, and by confusion stand.
For hot, cold, moist, and dry, four Champions fierce
Strive here for Maistry, and to Battle bring
Thir embryon Atoms; they around the flag   900
Of each his Faction, in thir several Clans,
Light-arm'd or heavy, sharp, smooth, swift or slow,
Swarm populous, unnumber'd as the Sands
Of *Barca* or *Cyrene*'s torrid soil,
Levied to side with warring Winds, and poise   905
Thir lighter wings. To whom these most adhere,
Hee rules a moment; *Chaos* Umpire sits,
And by decision more imbroils the fray
By which he Reigns: next him high Arbiter
Chance governs all. Into this wild Abyss,   910
The Womb of nature and perhaps her Grave,
Of neither Sea, nor Shore, nor Air, nor Fire,
But all these in thir pregnant causes mixt
Confus'dly, and which thus must ever fight,
Unless th' Almighty Maker them ordain   915
His dark materials to create more Worlds,
Into this wild Abyss the wary fiend
Stood on the brink of Hell and look'd a while,
Pondering his Voyage: for no narrow frith
He had to cross. Nor was his ear less peal'd   920
With noises loud and ruinous (to compare
Great things with small) than when *Bellona* storms,
With all her battering Engines bent to rase
Some Capital City, or less than if this frame
Of Heav'n were falling, and these Elements   925
In mutiny had from her Axle torn
The steadfast Earth. At last his Sail-broad Vans
He spreads for flight, and in the surging smoke
Uplifted spurns the ground, thence many a League
As in a cloudy Chair ascending rides   930
Audacious, but that seat soon failing, meets
A vast vacuity: all unawares
Flutt'ring his pennons vain plumb down he drops
Ten thousand fadom deep, and to this hour
Down had been falling, had not by ill chance   935
The strong rebuff of some tumultuous cloud
Instinct with Fire and Nitre hurried him
As many miles aloft: that fury stay'd,

---

904 *Barca, Cyrene*: a desert of northern Africa and a city near what is now Tripoli.   920
peal'd: struck.   922 *Bellona*: goddess of war, daughter of Phorcys and Ceto.

Quencht in a Boggy *Syrtis,* neither Sea,
Nor good dry Land: nigh founder'd on he fares,   940
Treading the crude consistence, half on foot,
Half flying; behoves him now both Oar and Sail.
As when a Gryfon through the Wilderness
With winged course o'er Hill or moory Dale,
Pursues the *Arimaspian,* who by stealth   945
Had from his wakeful custody purloin'd
The guarded Gold: So eagerly the fiend
O'er bog or steep, through strait, rough, dense, or rare,
With head, hands, wings, or feet pursues his way,
And swims or sinks, or wades, or creeps, or flies: 950
At length a universal hubbub wild
Of stunning sounds and voices all confus'd
Borne through the hollow dark assaults his ear
With loudest vehemence: thither he plies,
Undaunted to meet there whatever power   955
Or Spirit of the nethermost Abyss
Might in that noise reside, of whom to ask
Which way the nearest coast of darkness lies
Bordering on light; when straight behold the Throne
Of *Chaos,* and his dark Pavilian spread   960
Wide on the wasteful Deep; with him Enthron'd
Sat Sable-vested Night, eldest of things,
The Consort of his Reign; and by them stood
Orcus and *Ades,* and the dreaded name
Of *Demogorgon; Rumor* next and *Chance,*   965
And *Tumult* and *Confusion* all imbroil'd,
And *Discord* with a thousand various mouths.
     T' whom *Satan* turning boldly, thus. Ye Powers
And Spirits of this nethermost Abyss,
Chaos and *ancient Night,* I come no Spy,   970
With purpose to explore or to disturb
The secrets of your Realm, but by constraint
Wand'ring this darksome Desert, as my way
Lies through your spacious Empire up to light,
Alone, and without guide, half lost, I seek   975
What readiest path leads where your gloomy bounds
Confine with Heav'n; or if some other place
From your Dominion won, th' Ethereal King
Possesses lately, thither to arrive
I travel this profound, direct my course;   980
Directed, no mean recompence it brings
To your behoof, if I that Region lost,
All usurpation thence expell'd, reduce
To her original darkness and your sway

---

939 *Syrtis*: gulf near Tripoli, half land and half water.   945 *Arimaspian*: Arimaspias was
a river of Scythia. Its neighboring inhabitants were one-eyed and fought the griffins to
prevent them from taking the gold of the river.   964 *Orcus and Ades*: Hell and Hades.   965
Demogorgon: a relative newcomer among those who preside over Hell, stationed by Spenser
at the "bottome of the deepe Abysse."

(Which is my present journey) and once more   985
Erect the Standard there of *ancient Night;*
Yours be th' advantage all, mine the revenge.
  Thus *Satan;* and him thus the Anarch old
With falt'ring speech and visage incompos'd
Answer'd. I know thee, stranger, who thou art,   990
That mighty leading Angel, who of late
Made head against Heav'n's King, though overthrown.
I saw and heard, for such a numerous Host
Fled not in silence through the frighted deep
With ruin upon ruin, rout on rout,   995
Confusion worse confounded; and Heav'n Gates
Pour'd out by millions her victorious Bands
Pursuing. I upon my Frontiers here
Keep residence; if all I can will serve,
That little which is left so to defend   1000
Encroacht on still through our intestine broils
Weak'ning the Sceptre of old Night: first Hell
Your dungeon stretching far and wide beneath;
Now lately Heaven and Earth, another World
Hung o'er my Realm, link'd in a golden Chain   1005
To that side Heav'n from whence your Legions fell:
If that way be your walk, you have not far;
So much the nearer danger; go and speed;
Havoc and spoil and ruin are my gain.
  He ceas'd; and *Satan* stay'd not to reply,   1010
But glad that now his Sea should find a shore,
With fresh alacrity and force renew'd
Springs upward like a Pyramid of fire
Into the wild expanse, and through the shock
Of fighting Elements, on all sides round   1015
Environ'd wins his way; harder beset
And more endanger'd, than when *Argo* pass'd
Through *Bosporus* betwixt the justling Rocks:
Or when *Ulysses* on the Larboard shunn'd
Charybdis, and by th' other whirlpool steer'd.   1020
So he with difficulty and labour hard
Mov'd on, with difficulty and labour hee;
But hee once past, soon after when man fell,
Strange alteration! Sin and Death amain
Following his track, such was the will of Heav'n,   1025
Pav'd after him a broad and beat'n way
Over the dark Abyss, whose boiling Gulf
Tamely endur'd a Bridge of wondrous length
From Hell continu'd reaching th' utmost Orb
Of this frail World; by which the Spirits pervers,   1030
With easy intercourse pass to and fro

1017 *Argo:* the name of the ship Jason used in his quest for the golden fleece. 1018
Bosporus: Straits of Constantinople. 1020 *Charybdis:* the Sicilian whirlpool that proved
fatal to part of Ulysses' fleet.

To tempt or punish mortals, except whom
God and good Angels guard by special grace.
But now at last the sacred influence
Of light appears, and from the walls of Heav'n 1035
Shoots far into the bosom of dim Night
A glimmering dawn; here Nature first begins
Her fardest verge, and *Chaos* to retire
As from her outmost works a brok'n foe
With tumult less and with less hostile din, 1040
That *Satan* with less toil, and now with ease
Wafts on the calmer wave by dubious light
And like a weather-beaten Vessel holds
Gladly the Port, though Shrouds and Tackle torn;
Or in the emptier waste, resembling Air, 1045
Weighs his spread wings, at leisure to behold
Far off th' Empyreal Heav'n, extended wide
In circuit, undetermin'd square or round,
With Opal Tow'rs and Battlements adorn'd
Of living Sapphire, once his native Seat; 1050
And fast by hanging in a golden Chain
This pendant world, in bigness as a Star
Of smallest Magnitude close by the Moon.
Thither full fraught with mischievous revenge,
Accurst, and in a cursed hour he hies. 1055

The End of the Second Book.

BOOK III

THE ARGUMENT

God *sitting on his Throne sees* Satan *flying towards this world, then newly created; shows him to the Son who sat at his right hand; foretells the success of* Satan *in perverting mankind; clears his own Justice and Wisdom from all imputation, having created Man free and able enough to have withstood his Tempter; yet declares his purpose of grace towards him, in regard he fell not of his own malice, as did* Satan, *but by him seduc't. The Son of God renders praises to his Father for the manifestation of his gracious purpose towards Man; but God again declares, that Grace cannot be extended towards Man without the satisfaction of divine Justice; Man hath offended the majesty of God by aspiring to Godhead, and therefore with all his Progeny devoted to death must die, unless some one can be found sufficient to answer for his offence, and undergo his Punishment. The Son of God freely offers himself a Ransom for Man: the Father accepts him, ordains his incarnation, pronounces his exaltation above all Names in Heaven and Earth; commands all the Angels to adore him; they obey, and hymning to thir Harps in full Quire, celebrate the Father and the Son. Meanwhile* Satan *alights upon the bare convex of this World's outermost Orb; where wand'ring he first finds a place since call'd The Limbo of Vanity; what persons and things fly up thither; thence comes to the Gate of Heaven, describ'd ascending by stairs, and the waters above the Firmament that flow about it: His passage thence to the Orb of the Sun; he finds there* Uriel *the Regent of that Orb, but first changes himself into the shape of a meaner Angel; and pretending a zealous desire to behold the new Creation and Man whom God had plac't here, inquires of him the place of his habitation, and is directed; alights first on Mount* Niphates.

Hail holy Light, offspring of Heav'n first-born,
Or of th' Eternal Coeternal beam
May I express thee unblam'd? since God is light,
And never but in unapproached light
Dwelt from Eternity, dwelt then in thee,   5
Bright effluence of bright essence increate.
Or hear'st thou rather pure Ethereal stream,
Whose Fountain who shall tell? before the Sun,
Before the Heavens thou wert, and at the voice
Of God, as with a Mantle didst invest   10
The rising world of waters dark and deep,
Won from the void and formless infinite.
Thee I revisit now with bolder wing,
Escap't the *Stygian* Pool, though long detain'd
In that obscure sojourn, while in my flight   15
Through utter and through middle darkness borne
With other notes than to th' *Orphean* Lyre
I sung of *Chaos* and *Eternal Night*,
Taught by the heav'nly Muse to venture down
The dark descent, and up to reascend,   20
Though hard and rare: thee I revisit safe,
And feel thy sovran vital Lamp; but thou
Revisit'st not these eyes, that roll in vain
To find thy piercing ray, and find no dawn;
So thick a drop serene hath quencht thir Orbs,   25
Or dim suffusion veil'd. Yet not the more
Cease I to wander where the Muses haunt
Clear Spring, or shady Grove, or Sunny Hill,
Smit with the love of sacred song; but chief
Thee *Sion* and the flow'ry Brooks beneath   30
That wash thy hallow'd feet, and warbling flow,
Nightly I visit: nor sometimes forget
Those other two equall'd with me in Fate,
So were I equall'd with them in renown,
Blind *Thamyris* and blind *Mæonides*,   35
And *Tiresias* and *Phineus* Prophets old.
Then feed on thoughts, that voluntary move
Harmonious numbers; as the wakeful Bird
Sings darkling, and in shadiest Covert hid
Tunes her nocturnal Note. Thus with the Year   40
Seasons return, but not to me returns

---

35 *Thamyris, Maeonides*: Homer mentions Thamyris in the *Iliad*. Maeonides is Homer himself. 36 *Tiresias*: blind priest in *Oedipus Rex*; *Phineus*: a Thracian prophet blinded by the sun.

Day, or the sweet approach of Ev'n or Morn,
Or sight of vernal bloom, or Summer's Rose,
Or flocks, or herds, or human face divine;
But cloud instead, and ever-during dark   45
Surrounds me, from the cheerful ways of men
Cut off, and for the Book of knowledge fair
Presented with a Universal blanc
Of Nature's works to mee expung'd and ras'd,
And wisdom at one entrance quite shut out.   50
So much the rather thou Celestial light
Shine inward, and the mind through all her powers
Irradiate, there plant eyes, all mist from thence
Purge and disperse, that I may see and tell
Of things invisible to mortal sight.   55

[Milton proceeds to describe the counsel in
Heaven in which God foretells Adam's fall and
proclaims that either Adam or justice must die.
Christ offers to ransom man with his own death,
and in response God promises to raise those who are
redeemed higher than ever: they will become "All
in All." Meanwhile Satan approaches Eden, where
Adam and Eve are situated in "excellent form and
happy state." Raphael descends to them to warn
them of their danger from Satan and describes
both the creation and the war in Heaven. Having
instructed them in the laws of the universe and
their duty, he leaves a parting admonition with
Adam, "take heed lest Passion sway / Thy Judgment . . . beware."]

BOOK IX
THE ARGUMENT

Satan *having compast the Earth, with meditated guile returns as a mist
by Night into Paradise, enters into the Serpent sleeping.* Adam *and* Eve
in the Morning go forth to thir labours, which Eve *proposes to divide in
several places, each labouring apart:* Adam *consents not, alleging the
danger, lest that Enemy, of whom they were forewarn'd, should attempt
her found alone:* Eve *loath to be thought not circumspect or firm enough,
urges her going apart, the rather desirous to make trial of her strength;*
Adam *at last yields: The Serpent finds her alone; his subtle approach, first
gazing, then speaking, with much flattery extolling* Eve *above all other
Creatures.* Eve *wond'ring to hear the Serpent speak, asks how he attain'd
to human speech and such understanding not till now; the Serpent answers, that by tasting of a certain Tree in the Garden he attain'd both to
Speech and Reason, till then void of both:* Eve *requires him to bring her
to that Tree, and finds it to be the Tree of Knowledge forbidden: The Serpent now grown bolder, with many wiles and arguments induces her at
length to eat; she pleas'd with the taste deliberates awhile whether to
impart thereof to* Adam *or not, at last brings him of the Fruit, relates
what persuaded her to eat thereof:* Adam *at first amaz'd, but perceiving
her lost, resolves through vehemence of love to perish with her; and*

extenuating the trespass, eats also of the Fruit: The effects thereof in them
both; they seek to cover thir nakedness; then fall to variance and accusa-
tion of one another.

No more of talk where God or Angel Guest
With Man, as with his Friend, familiar us'd
To sit indulgent, and with him partake
Rural repast, permitting him the while
Venial discourse unblam'd: I now must change   5
Those Notes to Tragic; foul distrust, and breach
Disloyal on the part of Man, revolt,
And disobedience: On the part of Heav'n
Now alienated, distance and distaste,
Anger and just rebuke, and judgment giv'n,   10
That brought into this World a world of woe,
Sin and her shadow Death, and Misery
Death's Harbinger: Sad task, yet argument
Not less but more Heroic than the wrath
Of stern *Achilles* on his Foe pursu'd   15
Thrice Fugitive about *Troy* Wall; or rage
Of *Turnus* for *Lavinia* disespous'd,
Or *Neptune's* ire or *Juno's,* that so long
Perplex'd the *Greek* and *Cytherea's* Son;
If answerable style I can obtain   20
Of my Celestial Patroness, who deigns
Her nightly visitation unimplor'd,
And dictates to me slumb'ring, or inspires
Easy my unpremeditated Verse:
Since first this Subject for Heroic Song   25
Pleas'd me long choosing, and beginning late;
Not sedulous by Nature to indite
Wars, hitherto the only Argument
Heroic deem'd, chief maistry to dissect
With long and tedious havoc fabl'd Knights   30
In Battles feign'd; the better fortitude
Of Patience and Heroic Martyrdom
Unsung; or to describe Races and Games,
Or tilting Furniture, emblazon'd Shields,
Impreses quaint, Caparisons and Steeds;   35
Bases and tinsel Trappings, gorgeous Knights
At Joust and Tournament; then marshall'd Feast
Serv'd up in Hall with Sewers, and Seneschals;
The skill of Artifice or Office mean,
Not that which justly gives Heroic name   40
To Person or to Poem. Mee of these
Nor skill'd nor studious, higher Argument

---

15 *Achilles*: a reference to *Iliad*.   17 Aeneas contended against Turnus in winning Lavinia.
18 Neptune's anger was directed against Ulysses, Neptune's against Cytherea's son Aeneas.
34 *tilting Furniture*: trappings of knights in jousts.   35 *Impreses quaint*: emblems im-
printed on shields.   36 *Bases*: places from which the chargers issued.   38 *Sewers*: those
who arranged seating at banquets.

Remains, sufficient of itself to raise
That name, unless an age too late, or cold
Climate, or Years damp my intended wing   45
Deprest, and much they may, if all be mine,
Not Hers who brings it nightly to my Ear.
  The Sun was sunk, and after him the Star
Of *Hesperus,* whose Office is to bring
Twilight upon the Earth, short Arbiter   50
Twixt Day and Night, and now from end to end
Night's Hemisphere had veil'd the Horizon round:
When *Satan* who late fled before the threats
Of *Gabriel* out of *Eden,* now improv'd
In meditated fraud and malice, bent   55
On man's destruction, maugre what might hap
Of heavier on himself, fearless return'd.
By Night he fled, and Midnight return'd
From compassing the Earth, cautious of day,
Since *Uriel* Regent of the Sun descri'd   60
His entrance, and forewarn'd the Cherubim
That kept thir watch; thence full of anguish driv'n,
The space of seven continu'd Nights he rode
With darkness, thrice the Equinoctial Line
He circl'd, four times cross'd the Car of Night   65
From Pole to Pole, traversing each Colure;
On the eighth return'd, and on the Coast averse
From entrance or Cherubic Watch, by stealth
Found unsuspected way. There was a place,
Now not, though Sin, not Time, first wrought the change,   70
Where *Tigris* at the foot of Paradise
Into a Gulf shot under ground, till part
Rose up a Fountain by the Tree of Life;
In with the River sunk, and with it rose
Satan involv'd in rising Mist, then sought   75
Where to lie hid; Sea he had searcht and Land
From *Eden* over *Pontus,* and the Pool
Mæotis, up beyond the River *Ob;*
Downward as far Antarctic; and in length
West from *Orontes* to the Ocean barr'd   80
At *Darien,* thence to the Land where flows
Ganges and *Indus:* thus the Orb he roam'd
With narrow search; and with inspection deep
Consider'd every Creature, which of all
Most opportune might serve his Wiles, and found   85
The Serpent subtlest Beast of all the Field.

---

49 *Hesperus:* the evening star, Venus. 56 *maugre:* in spite of. 66 *Colure:* one of two circles
of the celestial sphere intersecting at the poles, one passing through the equinoctial points
and the other at right angles to it. Satan first flew around the world three times at the
equator and then flew along each colure twice, keeping always in the dark. 67 *averse:*
opposite. 77 *Pontus:* the Black Sea. 78 *Maeotis* and *the River Ob:* Sea of Azof north of
the river Obi in Siberia. 80 *Orontes:* river in Syria. 81 *Darien:* isthmus of Panama;
where flows: India.

Him after long debate, irresolute
Of thoughts revolv'd, his final sentence chose
Fit Vessel, fittest Imp of fraud, in whom
To enter, and his dark suggestions hide   90
From sharpest sight: for in the wily Snake,
Whatever sleights none would suspicious mark,
As from his wit and native subtlety
Proceeding, which in other Beasts observ'd
Doubt might beget of Diabolic pow'r   95
Active within beyond the sense of brute.
Thus he resolv'd, but first from inward grief
His bursting passion into plaints thus pour'd:
   O Earth, how like to Heav'n, if not preferr'd
More justly, Seat worthier of Gods, as built   100
With second thoughts, reforming what was old!
For what God after better worse would build?
Terrestrial Heav'n, danc't round by other Heav'ns
That shine, yet bear thir bright officious Lamps,
Light above Light, for thee alone, as seems,   105
In thee concentring all thir precious beams
Of sacred influence: As God in Heav'n
Is Centre, yet extends to all, so thou
Centring receiv'st from all those Orbs; in thee,
Not in themselves, all thir known virtue appears   110
Productive in Herb, Plant, and nobler birth
Of Creatures animate with gradual life
Of Growth, Sense, Reason, all summ'd up in Man.
With what delight could I have walkt thee round,
If I could joy in aught, sweet interchange   115
Of Hill and Valley, Rivers, Woods and Plains,
Now Land, now Sea, and Shores with Forest crown'd,
Rocks, Dens, and Caves; but I in none of these
Find place or refuge; and the more I see
Pleasures about me, so much more I feel   120
Torment within me, as from the hateful siege
Of contraries; all good to me becomes
Bane, and in Heav'n much worse would be my state.
But neither here seek I, no nor in Heav'n
To dwell, unless by maistring Heav'n's Supreme;   125
Nor hope to be myself less miserable
By what I seek, but others to make such
As I, though thereby worse to me redound:
For only in destroying I find ease
To my relentless thoughts; and him destroy'd,   130
Or won to what may work his utter loss,
For whom all this was made, all this will soon
Follow, as to him linkt in weal or woe,
In woe then; that destruction wide may range:
To me shall be the glory sole among   135
The infernal Powers, in one day to have marr'd

What he *Almighty* styl'd, six Nights and Days
Continu'd making, and who knows how long
Before had been contriving, though perhaps
Not longer than since I in one Night freed   140
From servitude inglorious well nigh half
Th' Angelic Name, and thinner left the throng
Of his adorers: hee to be aveng'd,
And to repair his numbers thus impair'd,
Whether such virtue spent of old now fail'd   145
More Angels to Create, if they at least
Are his Created, or to spite us more,
Determin'd to advance into our room
A Creature form'd of Earth, and him endow,
Exalted from so base original,   150
With Heav'nly spoils, our spoils; What he decreed
He effected; Man he made, and for him built
Magnificent this World, and Earth his seat,
Him Lord pronounc'd, and, O indignity!
Subjected to his service Angel wings,   155
And flaming Ministers to watch and tend
Thir earthy Charge: Of these the vigilance
I dread, and to elude, thus wrapt in mist
Of midnight vapour glide obscure, and pry
In every Bush and Brake, where hap may find   160
The Serpent sleeping, in whose mazy folds
To hide me, and the dark intent I bring.
O foul descent! that I who erst contended
With Gods to sit the highest, am now constrain'd
Into a Beast, and mixt with bestial slime,   165
This essence to incarnate and imbrute,
That to the highth of Deity aspir'd;
But what will not Ambition and Revenge
Descend to? who aspires must down as low
As high he soar'd, obnoxious first or last   170
To basest things. Revenge, at first though sweet,
Bitter ere long back on itself recoils;
Let it; I reck not, so it light well aim'd,
Since higher I fall short, on him who next
Provokes my envy, this new Favorite   175
Of Heav'n, this Man of Clay, Son of despite,
Whom us the more to spite his Maker rais'd
From dust: spite then with spite is best repaid.
    So saying, through each Thicket Dank or Dry,
Like a black mist low creeping, he held on   180
His midnight search, where soonest he might find
The Serpent: him fast sleeping soon he found
In Labyrinth of many a round self-roll'd,
His head the midst, well stor'd with subtle wiles:
Not yet in horrid Shade or dismal Den,   185
Nor nocent yet, but on the grassy Herb

Fearless unfear'd he slept: in at his Mouth
The Devil enter'd, and his brutal sense,
In heart or head, possessing soon inspir'd
With act intelligential; but his sleep   190
Disturb'd not, waiting close th' approach of Morn.
Now whenas sacred Light began to dawn
In *Eden* on the humid Flow'rs, that breath'd
Thir morning incense, when all things that breathe
From th' Earth's great Altar send up silent praise   195
To the Creator, and his Nostrils fill
With grateful Smell, forth came the human pair
And join'd thir vocal Worship to the Quire
Of Creatures wanting voice, that done, partake
The season, prime for sweetest Scents and Airs: 200
Then cómmune how that day they best may ply
Thir growing work: for much thir work outgrew
The hands' dispatch of two Gard'ning so wide.
And *Eve* first to her Husband thus began.
    Adam, well may we labour still to dress   205
This Garden, still to tend Plant, Herb and Flow'r.
Our pleasant task enjoin'd, but till more hands
Aid us, the work under our labour grows,
Luxurious by restraint; what we by day
Lop overgrown, or prune, or prop, or bind,   210
One night or two with wanton growth derides
Tending to wild. Thou therefore now advise
Or hear what to my mind first thoughts present,
Let us divide our labours, thou where choice
Leads thee, or where most needs, whether to wind   215
The Woodbine round this Arbour, or direct
The clasping Ivy where to climb, while I
In yonder Spring of Roses intermixt
With Myrtle, find what to redress till Noon:
For while so near each other thus all day   220
Our task we choose, what wonder if so near
Looks intervene and smiles, or object new
Casual discourse draw on, which intermits
Our day's work brought to little, though begun
Early, and th' hour of Supper comes unearn'd.   225
    To whom mild answer *Adam* thus return'd.
Sole *Eve,* Associate sole, to me beyond
Compare above all living Creatures dear,
Well hast thou motion'd, well thy thoughts imploy'd
How we might best fulfil the work which here   230
God hath assign'd us, nor of me shalt pass
Unprais'd: for nothing lovelier can be found
In Woman, than to study household good,
And good works in her Husband to promote.
Yet not so strictly hath our Lord impos'd   235
Labour, as to debar us when we need

Refreshment, whether food, or talk between,
Food of the mind, or this sweet intercourse
Of looks and smiles, for smiles from Reason flow,
To brute deni'd, and are of Love the food,   240
Love not the lowest end of human life.
For not to irksome toil, but to delight
He made us, and delight to Reason join'd.
These paths and Bowers doubt not but our joint hands
Will keep from Wilderness with ease, as wide   245
As we need walk, till younger hands ere long
Assist us: But if much converse perhaps
Thee satiate, to short absence I could yield.
For solitude sometimes is best society,
And short retirement urges sweet return.   250
But other doubt possesses me, lest harm
Befall thee sever'd from me; for thou know'st
What hath been warn'd us, what malicious Foe
Envying our happiness, and of his own
Despairing, seeks to work us woe and shame   255
By sly assault; and somewhere nigh at hand
Watches, no doubt, with greedy hope to find
His wish and best advantage, us asunder,
Hopeless to circumvent us join'd, where each
To other speedy aid might lend at need;   260
Whether his first design be to withdraw
Our fealty from God, or to disturb
Conjugal Love, than which perhaps no bliss
Enjoy'd by us excites his envy more;
Or this, or worse, leave not the faithful side   265
That gave thee being, still shades thee and protects.
The Wife, where danger or dishonour lurks,
Safest and seemliest by her Husband stays,
Who guards her, or with her the worst endures.
⠀⠀⠀To whom the Virgin Majesty of *Eve,*   270
As one who loves, and some unkindness meets,
With sweet austere composure thus repli'd.
⠀⠀⠀Offspring of Heav'n and Earth, and all Earth's Lord,
That such an Enemy we have, who seeks
Our ruin, both by thee inform'd I learn,   275
And from the parting Angel over-heard
As in a shady nook I stood behind,
Just then return'd at shut of Ev'ning Flow'rs.
But that thou shouldst my firmness therefore doubt
To God or thee, because we have a foe   280
May tempt it, I expected not to hear.
His violence thou fear'st not, being such,
As wee, not capable of death or pain,
Can either not receive, or can repel.
His fraud is then thy fear, which plain infers   285
Thy equal fear that my firm Faith and Love

Can by his fraud be shak'n or seduc't;
Thoughts, which how found they harbour in thy breast,
Adam, misthought of her to thee so dear?
   To whom with healing words *Adam* repli'd.   290
Daughter of God and Man, immortal *Eve,*
For such thou art, from sin and blame entire:
Not diffident of thee do I dissuade
Thy absence from my sight, but to avoid
Th' attempt itself, intended by our Foe.   295
For hee who tempts, though in vain, at least asperses
The tempted with dishonour foul, suppos'd
Not incorruptible of Faith, not proof
Against temptation: thou thyself with scorn
And anger wouldst resent the offer'd wrong,   300
Though ineffectual found: misdeem not then,
If such affront I labour to avert
From thee alone, which on us both at once
The Enemy, though bold, will hardly dare,
Or daring, first on mee th' assault shall light.   305
Nor thou his malice and false guile contemn;
Subtle he needs must be, who could seduce
Angels, nor think superfluous others' aid.
I from the influence of thy looks receive
Access in every Virtue, in thy sight   310
More wise, more watchful, stronger, if need were
Of outward strength; while shame, thou looking on,
Shame to be overcome or over-reacht
Would utmost vigor raise, and rais'd unite.
Why shouldst not thou like sense within thee feel   315
When I am present, and thy trial choose
With me, best witness of thy Virtue tri'd.
   So spake domestic *Adam* in his care
And Matrimonial Love, but *Eve,* who thought
Less attribúted to her Faith sincere,   320
Thus her reply with accent sweet renew'd.
   If this be our condition, thus to dwell
In narrow circuit strait'n'd by a Foe,
Subtle or violent, we not endu'd
Single with like defence, wherever met,   325
How are we happy, still in fear of harm?
But harm precedes not sin: only our Foe
Tempting affronts us with his foul esteem
Of our integrity: his foul esteem
Sticks no dishonour on our Front, but turns   330
Foul on himself; then wherefore shunn'd or fear'd
By us? who rather double honour gain
From his surmise prov'd false, find peace within,
Favour from Heav'n, our witness from th' event.
And what is Faith, Love, Virtue unassay'd   335
Alone, without exterior help sustain'd?

Let us not then suspect our happy State
Left so imperfet by the Maker wise,
As not secure to single or combin'd.
Frail is our happiness, if this be so,   340
And *Eden* were no *Eden* thus expos'd.
   To whom thus *Adam* fervently repli'd.
O Woman, best are all things as the will
Of God ordain'd them, his creating hand
Nothing imperfet or deficient left   345
Of all that he Created, much less Man,
Or aught that might his happy State secure,
Secure from outward force; within himself
The danger lies, yet lies within his power:
Against his will he can receive no harm   350
But God left free the Will, for what obeys
Reason, is free, and Reason he made right,
But bid her well beware, and still erect,
Lest by some fair appearing good surpris'd
She dictate false, and misinform the Will   355
To do what God expressly hath forbid.
Not then mistrust, but tender love enjoins,
That I should mind thee oft, and mind thou me.
Firm we subsist, yet possible to swerve,
Since Reason not impossibly may meet   360
Some specious object by the Foe suborn'd,
And fall into deception unaware,
Not keeping strictest watch, as she was warn'd.
Seek not temptation then, which to avoid
Were better, and most likely if from mee   365
Thou sever not: Trial will come unsought.
Wouldst thou approve thy constancy, approve
First thy obedience; th' other who can know,
Not seeing thee attempted, who attest?
But if thou think, trial unsought may find   370
Us both securer than thus warn'd thou seem'st,
Go; for thy stay, not free, absents thee more;
Go in thy native innocence, rely
On what thou hast of virtue, summon all.
For God towards thee hath done his part, do thine.   375
   So spake the Patriarch of Mankind, but *Eve*
Persisted, yet submiss, though last, repli'd.
   With thy permission then, and thus forewarn'd
Chiefly by what thy own last reasoning words
Touch'd only, that our trial, when least sought,   380
May find us both perhaps far less prepar'd,
The willinger I go, nor much expect
A Foe so proud will first the weaker seek;
So bent, the more shall shame him his repulse.
Thus saying, from her Husband's hand her hand   385
Soft she withdrew, and like a Wood-Nymph light,

Oread or *Dryad,* or of *Delia's* Train,
Betook her to the Groves, but *Delia's* self
In gait surpass'd and Goddess-like deport,
Though not as shee with Bow and Quiver arm'd,   390
But with such Gard'ning Tools as Art yet rude,
Guiltless of fire had form'd, or Angels brought.
To *Pales,* or *Pomona,* thus adorn'd,
Likest she seem'd, *Pomona* when she fled
Vertumnus, or to *Ceres* in her Prime,   395
Yet Virgin of *Proserpina* from *Jove.*
Her long with ardent look his Eye pursu'd
Delighted, but desiring more her stay.
Oft he to her his charge of quick return
Repeated, shee to him as oft engag'd   400
To be return'd by Noon amid the Bow'r,
And all things in best order to invite
Noontide repast, or Afternoon's repose.
O much deceiv'd, much failing, hapless *Eve,*
Of thy presum'd return! event perverse!   405
Thou never from that hour in Paradise
Found'st either sweet repast, or sound repose;
Such ambush hid among sweet Flow'rs and Shades
Waited with hellish rancour imminent
To intercept thy way, or send thee back   410
Despoil'd of Innocence, of Faith, of Bliss.
For now, and since first break of dawn the Fiend,
Mere Serpent in appearance, forth was come,
And on his Quest, where likeliest he might find
The only two of Mankind, but in them   415
The whole included Race, his purpos'd prey.
In Bow'r and Field he sought, where any tuft
Of Grove or Garden-Plot more pleasant lay,
Thir tendance or Plantation for delight,
By Fountain or by shady Rivulet.   420
He sought them both, but wish'd his hap might find
Eve separate, he wish'd but not with hope
Of what so seldom chanc'd, when to his wish,
Beyond his hope, *Eve* separate he spies,
Veil'd in a Cloud of Fragrance, where she stood,   425
Half spi'd, so thick the Roses bushing round
About her glow'd, oft stooping to support
Each Flow'r of slender stalk, whose head though gay
Carnation, Purple, Azure, or speckt with Gold,
Hung drooping unsustain'd, them she upstays   430

---

387 *Delia:* Diana, who was born in Delos. The *Oreades* were mountain nymphs, daughters of
Phoroneus and Hecate, who followed in Diana's train along with the Dryades.   393 *Pales:*
Roman goddess of sheepfolds; *Pomona:* a Roman nymph who presided over gardens and
fruit trees. Although she was sworn to chastity, Vertumnus, by assuming different shapes
and finally becoming an old woman, got near enough to her to convince her to marry him.
395 *Ceres:* the Greek goddess of corn and harvests, whom Milton thinks of here as she
was before bearing Proserpina and having to search for her throughout the world, the
heavens, and the underworld.

Gently with Myrtle band, mindless the while,
Herself, though fairest unsupported Flow'r,
From her best prop so far, and storm so nigh.
Nearer he drew, and many a walk travers'd
Of stateliest Covert, Cedar, Pine, or Palm,   435
Then voluble and bold, now hid, now seen
Among thick-wov'n Arborets and Flow'rs
Imborder'd on each Bank, the hand of *Eve:*
Spot more delicious than those Gardens feign'd
Or of reviv'd *Adonis,* or renown'd   440
Alcinoüs, host of old *Laertes'* Son,
Or that, not Mystic, where the Sapient King
Held dalliance with his fair *Egyptian* Spouse.
Much hee the Place admir'd, the Person more.
As one who long in populous City pent,   445
Where Houses thick and Sewers annoy the Air,
Forth issuing on a Summer's Morn to breathe
Among the pleasant Villages and Farms
Adjoin'd, from each thing met conceives delight,
The smell of Grain, or tedded Grass, or Kine,   450
Or Dairy, each rural sight, each rural sound;
If chance with Nymphlike step fair Virgin pass,
What pleasing seem'd, for her now pleases more,
She most, and in her look sums all Delight.
Such Pleasure took the Serpent to behold   455
This Flow'ry Plat, the sweet recess of *Eve*
Thus early, thus alone; her Heav'nly form
Angelic, but more soft, and Feminine,
Her graceful Innocence, her every Air
Of gesture or least action overaw'd   460
His Malice, and with rapine sweet bereav'd
His fierceness of the fierce intent it brought:
That space the Evil one abstracted 'stood
From his own evil, and for the time remain'd
Stupidly good, of enmity disarm'd,   465
Of guile, of hate, of envy, of revenge;
But the hot Hell that always in him burns,
Though in mid Heav'n, soon ended his delight,
And tortures him now more, the more he sees
Of pleasure not for him ordain'd: then soon   470
Fierce hate he recollects, and all his thoughts
Of mischief, gratulating, thus excites.
    Thoughts, whither have ye led me, with what sweet
Compulsion thus transported to forget
What hither brought us, hate, not love, nor hope   475
Of Paradise for Hell, hope here to taste
Of pleasure, but all pleasure to destroy,

---

440 Venus helped restore Adonis to health in the garden of Adonis. 441 *Alcinoüs:* King of Phaecia who entertained Ulysses, Laertes' son, after the latter had been shipwrecked on his coast.

Save what is in destroying, other joy
To me is lost. Then let me not let pass
Occasion which now smiles, behold alone   480
The Woman, opportune to all attempts,
Her Husband, for I view far round, not nigh,
Whose higher intellectual more I shun,
And strength, of courage haughty, and of limb
Heroic built, though of terrestrial mould,   485
Foe not informidable, exempt from wound,
I not; so much hath Hell debas'd, and pain
Infeebl'd me, to what I was in Heav'n.
Shee fair, divinely fair, fit Love for Gods,
Not terrible, though terror be in Love   490
And beauty, not approacht by stronger hate,
Hate stronger, under show of Love well feign'd,
The way which to her ruin now I tend.
   So spake the Enemy of Mankind, enclos'd
In Serpent, Inmate bad, and toward *Eve*   495
Address'd his way, not with indented wave,
Prone on the ground, as since, but on his rear,
Circular base of rising folds, that tow'r'd
Fold above fold a surging Maze, his Head
Crested aloft, and Carbuncle his Eyes;   500
With burnisht Neck of verdant Gold, erect
Amidst his circling Spires, that on the grass
Floated redundant: pleasing was his shape,
And lovely, never since of Serpent kind
Lovelier, not those that in *Illyria* chang'd   505
Hermione and *Cadmus,* or the God
In *Epidaurus;* nor to which transform'd
Ammonian Jove, or *Capitoline* was seen,
Hee with *Olympias,* this with her who bore
Scipio the highth of *Rome.* With tract oblique   510
At first, as one who sought access, but fear'd
To interrupt, side-long he works his way.
As when a Ship by skilful Steersman wrought
Nigh River's mouth or Foreland, where the Wind
Veers oft, as oft so steers, and shifts her Sail;   515
So varied hee, and of his tortuous Train
Curl'd many a wanton wreath in sight of *Eve,*
To lure her Eye; shee busied heard the sound
Of rustling Leaves, but minded not, as us'd
To such disport before her through the Field,   520

506–507 *Cadmus and Harmonia* (Milton's Hermione), growing old in Illyria, had the Gods change them into serpents to escape the misfortunes of living; the "god in Epidaurus" is Aesculapius, who had a temple there. Serpents, among other things, were sacred to him; he supposedly visited Rome in the form of a serpent. 508 *Ammonian Jove, or Capitoline*: Ammon or Hammon was a name for Jupiter in Libia, Capitolinus a surname deriving from Jupiter's temple on Mount Capitolinus. Olympias, Alexander's mother, claimed that Jupiter had fathered Alexander in the shape of a serpent. 510 *Scipio*: Scipio Africanus, whose mother was Sempronia and whose father was supposedly Jove.

From every Beast, more duteous at her call,
Than at *Circean* call the Herd disguis'd.
Hee bolder now, uncall'd before her stood;
But as in gaze admiring: Oft he bow'd
His turret Crest, and sleek enamell'd Neck,   525
Fawning, and lick'd the ground whereon she trod.
His gentle dumb expression turn'd at length
The Eye of *Eve* to mark his play; he glad
Of her attention gain'd, with Serpent Tongue
Organic, or impulse of vocal Air,   530
His fraudulent temptation thus began.
   Wonder not, sovran Mistress, if perhaps
Thou canst, who art sole Wonder, much less arm
Thy looks, the Heav'n of mildness, with disdain,
Displeas'd that I approach thee thus, and gaze   535
Insatiate, I thus single, nor have fear'd
Thy awful brow, more awful thus retir'd.
Fairest resemblance of thy Maker fair,
Thee all things living gaze on, all things thine
By gift, and thy Celestial Beauty adore   540
With ravishment beheld, there best beheld
Where universally admir'd: but here
In this enclosure wild, these Beasts among,
Beholders rude, and shallow to discern
Half what in thee is fair, one man except,   545
Who sees thee? (and what is one?) who shouldst be seen
A Goddess among Gods, ador'd and serv'd
By Angels numberless, thy daily Train.
   So gloz'd the Tempter, and his Proem tun'd;
Into the Heart of *Eve* his words made way,   550
Though at the voice much marvelling; at length
Not unamaz'd she thus in answer spake.
What may this mean? Language of Man pronounc't
By Tongue of Brute, and human sense exprest?
The first at least of these I thought deni'd   555
To Beasts, whom God on thir Creation-Day
Created mute to all articulate sound;
The latter I demur, for in thir looks
Much reason, and in thir actions oft appears.
Thee, Serpent, subtlest beast of all the field   560
I knew, but not with human voice endu'd;
Redouble then this miracle, and say,
How cam'st thou speakable of mute, and how
To me so friendly grown above the rest
Of brutal kind, that daily are in sight?   565
Say, for such wonder claims attention due.
   To whom the guileful Tempter thus repli'd.
Empress of this fair World, resplendent *Eve,*

---

532 Circe's herd of metamorphosed travellers was noted for devotion to her.

Easy to mee it is to tell thee all
What thou command'st and right thou shouldst be obey'd: 570
I was at first as other Beasts that graze
The trodden Herb, of abject thoughts and low,
As was my food, nor aught but food discern'd
Or Sex, and apprehended nothing high:
Till on a day roving the field, I chanc'd   575
A goodly Tree far distant to behold
Loaden with fruit of fairest colours mixt,
Ruddy and Gold: I nearer drew to gaze;
When from the boughs a savoury odour blown,
Grateful to appetite, more pleas'd my sense   580
Than smell of sweetest Fennel, or the Teats
Of Ewe or Goat dropping with Milk at Ev'n,
Unsuckt of Lamb or Kid, that tend thir play.
To satisfy the sharp desire I had
Of tasting those fair Apples, I resolv'd   585
Not to defer; hunger and thirst at once,
Powerful persuaders, quick'n'd at the scent
Of that alluring fruit, urg'd me so keen.
About the Mossy Trunk I wound me soon,
For high from ground the branches would require   590
Thy utmost reach or *Adam's:* Round the Tree
All other Beasts that saw, with like desire
Longing and envying stood, but could not reach.
Amid the Tree now got, where plenty hung
Tempting so nigh, to pluck and eat my fill   595
I spar'd not, for such pleasure till that hour
At Feed or Fountain never had I found.
Sated at length, ere long I might perceive
Strange alteration in me, to degree
Of Reason in my inward Powers, and Speech   600
Wanted not long, though to this shape retain'd.
Thenceforth to Speculations high or deep
I turn'd my thoughts, and with capacious mind
Consider'd all things visible in Heav'n,
Or Earth, or Middle, all things fair and good;   605
But all that fair and good in thy Divine
Semblance, and in thy Beauty's heav'nly Ray
United I beheld; no Fair to thine
Equivalent or second, which compell'd
Mee thus, though importune perhaps, to come   610
And gaze, and worship thee of right declar'd
Sovran of Creatures, universal Dame.
　　So talk'd the spirited sly Snake; and *Eve*
Yet more amaz'd unwary thus repli'd.
　　Serpent, thy overpraising leaves in doubt   615
The virtue of that Fruit, in thee first prov'd:

---

605 *Middle*: the sky.

But say, where grows the Tree, from hence how far?
For many are the Trees of God that grow
In Paradise, and various, yet unknown
To us, in such abundance lies our choice,   620
As leaves a greater store of Fruit untoucht,
Still hanging incorruptible, till men
Grow up to thir provision, and more hands
Help to disburden Nature of her Birth.
   To whom the wily Adder, blithe and glad.   625
Empress, the way is ready, and not long,
Beyond a row of Myrtles, on a Flat,
Fast by a Fountain, one small Thicket past
Of blowing Myrrh and Balm; if thou accept
My conduct, I can bring thee thither soon.   630
   Lead then, said *Eve*. Hee leading swiftly roll'd
In tangles, and made intricate seem straight,
To mischief swift. Hope elevates, and joy
Bright'ns his Crest, as when a wand'ring Fire,
Compact of unctuous vapour, which the Night   635
Condenses, and the cold invirons round,
Kindl'd through agitation to a Flame,
Which oft, they say, some evil Spirit attends,
Hovering and blazing with delusive Light,
Misleads th' amaz'd Night-wanderer from his way   640
To Bogs and Mires, and oft through Pond or Pool,
There swallow'd up and lost, from succour far.
So glister'd the dire Snake, and into fraud
Led *Eve* our credulous Mother, to the Tree
Of prohibition, root of all our woe;   645
Which when she saw, thus to her guide she spake.
   Serpent, we might have spar'd our coming hither,
Fruitless to mee, though Fruit be here to excess,
The credit of whose virtue rest with thee,
Wondrous indeed, if cause of such effects.   650
But of this Tree we may not taste nor touch;
God so commanded, and left that Command
Sole Daughter of his voice; the rest, we live
Law to ourselves, our Reason is our Law.
   To whom the Tempter guilefully repli'd.   655
Indeed? hath God then said that of the Fruit
Of all these Garden Trees ye shall not eat,
Yet Lords declar'd of all in Earth or Air?
   To whom thus *Eve* yet sinless. Of the Fruit
Of each Tree in the Garden we may eat,   660
But of the Fruit of this fair Tree amidst
The Garden, God hath said, Ye shall not eat
Thereof, nor shall ye touch it, lest ye die.
   She scarce had said, though brief, when now more bold
The Tempter, but with show of Zeal and Love   665
To Man, and indignation at his wrong,

New part puts on, and as to passion mov'd,
Fluctuates disturb'd, yet comely, and in act
Rais'd, as of some great matter to begin.
As when of old some Orator renown'd   670
In *Athens* or free *Rome,* where Eloquence
Flourish'd, since mute, to some great cause addrest,
Stood in himself collected, while each part,
Motion, each act won audience ere the tongue,
Sometimes in highth began, as no delay   675
Of Preface brooking through his Zeal of Right.
So standing, moving, or to highth upgrown
The Tempter all impassion'd thus began.
  O Sacred, Wise, and Wisdom-giving Plant,
Mother of Science, Now I feel thy Power   680
Within me clear, not only to discern
Things in thir Causes, but to trace the ways
Of highest Agents, deem'd however wise.
Queen of this Universe, do not believe
Those rigid threats of Death; ye shall not Die: 685
How should ye? by the Fruit? it gives you Life
To Knowledge: By the Threat'ner? look on mee,
Mee who have touch'd and tasted, yet both live,
And life more perfet have attain'd than Fate
Meant mee, by vent'ring higher than my Lot.   690
Shall that be shut to Man, which to the Beast
Is open? or will God incense his ire
For such a petty Trespass, and not praise
Rather your dauntless virtue, whom the pain
Of Death denounc't, whatever thing Death be,   695
Deterr'd not from achieving what might lead
To happier life, knowledge of Good and Evil;
Of good, how just? of evil, if what is evil
Be real, why not known, since easier shunn'd?
God therefore cannot hurt ye, and be just;   700
Not just, not God; not fear'd then, nor obey'd:
Your fear itself of Death removes the fear.
Why then was this forbid? Why but to awe,
Why but to keep ye low and ignorant,
His worshippers; he knows that in the day   705
Ye Eat thereof, your Eyes that seem so clear,
Yet are but dim, shall perfetly be then
Op'n'd and clear'd, and ye shall be as Gods,
Knowing both Good and Evil as they know.
That ye should be as Gods, since I as Man,   710
Internal Man, is but proportion meet,
I of brute human, yee of human Gods.
So ye shall die perhaps, by putting off
Human, to put on Gods, death to be wisht,
Though threat'n'd, which no worse than this can bring.   715
And what are Gods that Man may not become

As they, participating God-like food?
The Gods are first, and that advantage use
On our belief, that all from them proceeds;
I question it, for this fair Earth I see,   720
Warm'd by the Sun, producing every kind,
Them nothing: If they all things, who enclos'd
Knowledge of Good and Evil in this Tree,
That whoso eats thereof, forthwith attains
Wisdom without their leave? and wherein lies   725
Th' offence, that Man should thus attain to know?
What can your knowledge hurt him, or this Tree
Impart against his will if all be his?
Or is it envy, and can envy dwell
In heav'nly breasts? these, these and many more   730
Causes import your need of this fair Fruit.
Goddess humane, reach then, and freely taste.
   He ended, and his words replete with guile
Into her heart too easy entrance won:
Fixt on the Fruit she gaz'd, which to behold   735
Might tempt alone, and in her ears the sound
Yet rung of his persuasive words, impregn'd
With Reason, to her seeming, and with Truth;
Meanwhile the hour of Noon drew on, and wak'd
An eager appetite, rais'd by the smell   740
So savoury of that Fruit, which with desire,
Inclinable now grown to touch or taste,
Solicited her longing eye; yet first
Pausing a while, thus to herself she mus'd.
   Great are thy Virtues, doubtless, best of Fruits,   745
Though kept from Man, and worthy to be admir'd,
Whose taste, too long forborne, at first assay
Gave elocution to the mute, and taught
The Tongue not made for Speech to speak thy praise:
Thy praise hee also who forbids thy use,   750
Conceals not from us, naming thee the Tree
Of Knowledge, knowledge both of good and evil;
Forbids us then to taste, but his forbidding
Commends thee more, while it infers the good
By thee communicated, and our want: 755
For good unknown, sure is not had, or had
And yet unknown, is as not had at all.
In plain then, what forbids he but to know,
Forbids us good, forbids us to be wise?
Such prohibitions bind not. But if Death   760
Bind us with after-bands, what profits then
Our inward freedom? In the day we eat
Of this fair Fruit, our doom is, we shall die.
How dies the Serpent? hee hath eat'n and lives,
And knows, and speaks, and reasons, and discerns,   765
Irrational till then. For us alone

Was death invented? or to us deni'd
This intellectual food, for beasts reserv'd?
For Beasts it seems: yet that one Beast which first
Hath tasted, envies not, but brings with joy   770
The good befall'n him, Author unsuspect,
Friendly to man, far from deceit or guile.
What fear I then, rather what know to fear
Under this ignorance of Good and Evil,
Of God or Death, of Law or Penalty?   775
Here grows the Cure of all, this Fruit Divine,
Fair to the Eye, inviting to the Taste,
Of virtue to make wise: what hinders then
To reach, and feed at once both Body and Mind?
   So saying, her rash hand in evil hour   780
Forth reaching to the Fruit, she pluck'd, she eat:
Earth felt the wound, and Nature from her seat
Sighing through all her Works gave signs of woe,
That all was lost. Back to the Thicket slunk
The guilty Serpent, and well might, for *Eve*   785
Intent now wholly on her taste, naught else
Regarded, such delight till then, as seem'd,
In Fruit she never tasted, whether true
Or fancied so, through expectation high
Of knowledge, nor was God-head from her thought.   790
Greedily she ingorg'd without restraint,
And knew not eating Death: Satiate at length,
And hight'n'd as with Wine, jocund and boon,
Thus to herself she pleasingly began.
   O Sovran, virtuous, precious of all Trees   795
In Paradise, of operation blest
To Sapience, hitherto obscur'd, infam'd,
And thy fair Fruit let hang, as to no end
Created; but henceforth my early care,
Not without Song, each Morning, and due praise   800
Shall tend thee, and the fertile burden ease
Of thy full branches offer'd free to all;
Till dieted by thee I grow mature
In knowledge, as the Gods who all things know;
Though others envy what they cannot give;   805
For had the gift been theirs, it had not here
Thus grown. Experience, next to thee I owe,
Best guide; not following thee, I had remain'd
In ignorance, thou op'n'st Wisdom's way,
And giv'st access, though secret she retire.   810
And I perhaps am secret; Heav'n is high,
High and remote to see from thence distinct
Each thing on Earth; and other care perhaps
May have diverted from continual watch
Our great Forbidder, safe with all his Spies   815
About him. But to *Adam* in what sort

Shall I appear? shall I to him make known
As yet my change, and give him to partake
Full happiness with mee, or rather not,
But keep the odds of Knowledge in my power   820
Without Copartner? so to add what wants
In Female Sex, the more to draw his Love,
And render me more equal, and perhaps,
A thing not undesirable, sometime
Superior: for inferior who is free?   825
This may be well: but what if God have seen
And Death ensue? then I shall be no more,
And *Adam* wedded to another *Eve,*
Shall live with her enjoying, I extinct;
A death to think. Confirm'd then I resolve,   830
Adam shall share with me in bliss or woe:
So dear I love him, that with him all deaths
I could endure, without him live no life.
    So saying, from the Tree her step she turn'd.
But first low Reverence done, as to the power   835
That dwelt within, whose presence had infus'd
Into the plant sciential sap, deriv'd
From Nectar, drink of Gods. *Adam* the while
Waiting desirous her return, had wove
Of choicest Flow'rs a Garland to adorn   840
Her Tresses, and her rural labours crown,
As Reapers oft are wont thir Harvest Queen.
Great joy he promis'd to his thoughts, and new
Solace in her return, so long delay'd;
Yet oft his heart, divine of something ill,   845
Misgave him; hee the falt'ring measure felt;
And forth to meet her went, the way she took
That Morn when first they parted; by the Tree
Of Knowledge he must pass, there he her met,
Scarce from the Tree returning; in her hand   850
A bough of fairest fruit that downy smil'd,
New gather'd, and ambrosial smell diffus'd.
To him she hasted, in her face excuse
Came Prologue, and Apology to prompt,
Which with bland words at will she thus addrest.   855
    Hast though not wonder'd, *Adam,* at my stay?
Thee I have misst, and thought it long, depriv'd
Thy presence, agony of love till now
Not felt, nor shall be twice, for never more
Mean I to try, what rash untri'd I sought,   860
The pain of absence from thy sight. But strange
Hath been the cause, and wonderful to hear:
This Tree is not as we are told, a Tree
Of danger tasted, nor to evil unknown
Op'ning the way, but of Divine effect   865
To open Eyes, and make them Gods who taste;

And hath been tasted such: the Serpent wise,
Or not restrain'd as wee, or not obeying,
Hath eat'n of the fruit, and is become,
Not dead, as we are threat'n'd, but thenceforth   870
Endu'd with human voice and human sense,
Reasoning to admiration, and with mee
Persuasively hath so prevail'd, that I
Have also tasted, and have also found
Th' effects to correspond, opener mine Eyes,   875
Dim erst, dilated Spirits, ampler Heart,
And growing up to Godhead; which for thee
Chiefly I sought, without thee can despise.
For bliss, as thou hast part, to me is bliss,
Tedious, unshar'd with thee, and odious soon.   880
Though therefore also taste, that equal Lot
May join us, equal Joy, as equal Love;
Lest thou not tasting, different degree
Disjoin us, and I then too late renounce
Deity for thee, when Fate will not permit.   885
    Thus *Eve* with Count'nance blithe her story told;
But in her Cheek distemper flushing glow'd.
On th' other side, *Adam*, soon as he heard
The fatal Trespass done by *Eve*, amaz'd,
Astonied stood and Blank, while horror chill   890
Ran through his veins, and all his joints relax'd;
From his slack hand the Garland wreath'd for *Eve*
Down dropp'd, and all the faded Roses shed:
Speechless he stood and pale, till thus at length
First to himself he inward silence broke.   895
    O fairest of Creation, last and best
Of all God's Works, Creature in whom excell'd
Whatever can to sight or thought be form'd,
Holy, divine, good, amiable, or sweet!
How art thou lost, how on a sudden lost,   900
Defac't, deflowr'd, and now to Death devote?
Rather how hast thou yielded to transgress
The strict forbiddance, how to violate
The sacred Fruit forbidd'n! some cursed fraud
Of Enemy hath beguil'd thee, yet unknown,   905
And mee with thee hath ruin'd, for with thee
Certain my resolution is to Die;
How can I live without thee, how forgo
Thy sweet Converse and Love so dearly join'd,
To live again in these wild Woods forlorn?   910
Should God create another *Eve*, and I
Another Rib afford, yet loss of thee
Would never from my heart; no no, I feel
The Link of Nature draw me: Flesh of Flesh,
Bone of my Bone thou art, and from thy State   915
Mine never shall be parted, bliss or woe.

So having said, as one from sad dismay
Recomforted, and after thoughts disturb'd
Submitting to what seem'd remediless,
Thus in calm mood his Words to *Eve* he turn'd.   920
    Bold deed thou hast presum'd, advent'rous *Eve,*
And peril great provok't, who thus hast dar'd
Had it been only coveting to Eye
That sacred Fruit, sacred to abstinence,
Much more to taste it under ban to touch.   925
But past who can recall, or done undo?
Not God Omnipotent, nor Fate, yet so
Perhaps thou shalt not Die, perhaps the Fact
Is not so heinous now, foretasted Fruit,
Profan'd first by the Serpent, by him first   930
Made common and unhallow'd ere our taste;
Nor yet on him found deadly, he yet lives,
Lives, as thou said'st, and gains to live as Man
Higher degree of Life, inducement strong
To us, as likely tasting to attain   935
Proportional ascent, which cannot be
But to be Gods, or Angels Demi-gods.
Nor can I think that God, Creator wise,
Though threat'ning, will in earnest so destroy
Us his prime Creatures, dignifi'd so high,   940
Set over all his Works, which in our Fall,
For us created, needs with us must fail,
Dependent made; so God shall uncreate,
Be frustrate, do, undo, and labour lose,
Not well conceiv'd of God, who though his Power   945
Creation could repeat, yet would be loath
Us to abolish, lest the Adversary
Triumph and say; Fickle their State whom God
Most Favours, who can please him long? Mee first
He ruin'd, now Mankind; whom will be next?   950
Matter of scorn, not to be given the Foe.
However I with thee have fixt my Lot,
Certain to undergo like doom, if Death
Consort with thee, Death is to mee as Life;
So forcible within my heart I feel   955
The Bond of Nature draw me to my own,
My own in thee, for what thou art is mine;
Our State cannot be sever'd, we are one,
One Flesh; to lose thee were to lose myself.
    So *Adam,* and thus *Eve* to him repli'd.   960
O glorious trial of exceeding Love,
Illustrious evidence, example high!
Ingaging me to emulate, but short
Of thy perfection, how shall I attain,
Adam, from whose dear side I boast me sprung,   965
And gladly of our Union hear thee speak,

One Heart, one Soul in both; whereof good proof
This day affords, declaring thee resolv'd,
Rather than Death or aught than Death more dread
Shall separate us, linkt in Love so dear,   970
To undergo with mee one Guilt, one Crime,
If any be, of tasting this fair Fruit,
Whose virtue, for of good still good proceeds,
Direct, or by occasion hath presented
This happy trial of thy Love, which else   975
So eminently never had been known.
Were it I thought Death menac't would ensue
This my attempt, I would sustain alone
The worst, and not persuade thee, rather die
Deserted, than oblige thee with a fact   980
Pernicious to thy Peace, chiefly assur'd
Remarkably so late of thy so true,
So faithful Love unequall'd; but I feel
Far otherwise th' event, not Death, but Life
Augmented, op'n'd Eyes, new Hopes, new Joys,   985
Taste so Divine, that what of sweet before
Hath toucht my sense, flat seems to this, and harsh.
On my experience, *Adam,* freely taste,
And fear of Death deliver to the Winds.
   So saying, she embrac'd him, and for joy   990
Tenderly wept, much won that he his Love
Had so ennobl'd, as of choice to incur
Divine displeasure for her sake, or Death.
In recompense (for such compliance bad
Such recompense best merits) from the bough   995
She gave him of that fair enticing Fruit
With liberal hand: he scrupl'd not to eat
Against his better knowledge, not deceiv'd,
But fondly overcome with Female charm.
Earth trembl'd from her entrails, as again   1000
In pangs, and Nature gave a second groan,
Sky low'r'd, and muttering Thunder, some sad drops
Wept at completing of the mortal Sin
Original; while *Adam* took no thought,
Eating his fill, nor *Eve* to iterate   1005
Her former trespass fear'd, the more to soothe
Him with her lov'd society, that now
As with new Wine intoxicated both
They swim in mirth, and fancy that they feel
Divinity within them breeding wings   1010
Wherewith to scorn the Earth: but that false Fruit
Far other operation first display'd,
Carnal desire inflaming, hee on *Eve*
Began to cast lascivious Eyes, she him
As wantonly repaid; in Lust they burn: 1015
Till *Adam* thus 'gan *Eve* to dalliance move.

Eve, now I see thou art exact of taste,
And elegant, of Sapience no small part,
Since to each meaning savour we apply,
And Palate call judicious; I the praise   1020
Yield thee, so well this day thou hast purvey'd.
Much pleasure we have lost, while we abstain'd
From this delightful Fruit, nor known till now
True relish, tasting; if such pleasure be
In things to us forbidden, it might be wish'd,   1025
For this one Tree had been forbidden ten.
But come, so well refresh't, now let us play,
As meet is, after such delicious Fare;
For never did thy Beauty since the day
I saw thee first and wedded thee, adorn'd   1030
With all perfections, so inflame my sense
With ardor to enjoy thee, fairer now
Than ever, bounty of this virtuous Tree.
    So said he, and forbore not glance or toy
Of amorous intent, well understood   1035
Of *Eve,* whose Eye darted contagious Fire.
Her hand he seiz'd, and to a shady bank,
Thick overhead with verdant roof imbowr'd
He led her nothing loath; Flow'rs were the Couch,
Pansies, and Violets, and Asphodel,   1040
And Hyacinth, Earth's freshest softest lap.
There they thir fill of Love and Love's disport
Took largely, of thir mutual guilt the Seal,
The solace of thir sin, till dewy sleep
Oppress'd them, wearied with their amorous play.   1045
Soon as the force of that fallacious Fruit,
That with exhilarating vapour bland
About thir spirits had play'd, and immost powers
Made err, was now exhal'd, and grosser sleep
Bred of unkindly fumes, with conscious dreams   1050
Encumber'd, now had left them, up they rose
As from unrest, and each the other viewing,
Soon found thir Eyes how op'n'd, and thir minds
How dark'n'd; innocence, that as a veil
Had shadow'd them from knowing ill, was gone,   1055
Just confidence, and native righteousness,
And honour from about them, naked left
To guilty shame: hee cover'd, but his Robe
Uncover'd more. So rose the *Danite* strong
Herculean Samson from the Harlot-lap   1060
Of *Philistean Dalilah,* and wak'd
Shorn of his strength, They destitute and bare
Of all thir virtue: silent, and in face
Confounded long they sat, as struck'n mute,
Till *Adam,* though not less than *Eve* abasht,   1065
At length gave utterance to these words constrain'd.

O *Eve,* in evil hour thou didst give ear
To that false Worm, of whomsoever taught
To counterfeit Man's voice, true in our Fall,
False in our promis'd Rising; since our Eyes   1070
Op'n'd we find indeed, and find we know
Both Good and Evil, Good lost, and Evil got,
Bad Fruit of Knowledge, if this be to know,
Which leaves us naked thus, of Honour void,
Of Innocence, of Faith, of Purity,   1075
Our wonted Ornaments now soil'd and stain'd,
And in our Faces evident the signs
Of foul concupiscence; whence evil store;
Even shame, the last of evils; of the first
Be sure then. How shall I behold the face   1080
Henceforth of God or Angel, erst with joy
And rapture so oft beheld? those heav'nly shapes
Will dazzle now this earthly, with thir blaze
Insufferably bright. O might I here
In solitude live savage, in some glade   1085
Obscur'd, where highest Woods impenetrable
To Star of Sun-light, spread thir umbrage broad,
And brown as Evening: Cover me ye Pines,
Ye Cedars, with innumerable boughs
Hide me, where I may never see them more.   1090
But let us now, as in bad plight, devise
What best may for the present serve to hide
The Parts of each from other, that seem most
To shame obnoxious, and unseemliest seen,
Some Tree whose broad smooth Leaves together sew'd,   1095
And girded on our loins, may cover round
Those middle parts, that this new comer, Shame,
There sit not, and reproach us as unclean.
   So counsell'd hee, and both together went
Into the thickest Wood, there soon they chose   1100
The Figtree, not that kind for Fruit renown'd,
But such as at this day to *Indians* known
In *Malabar* or *Decan* spreads her Arms
Branching so broad and long, that in the ground
The bended Twigs take root, and Daughters grow   1105
About the Mother Tree, a Pillar'd shade
High overarch't, and echoing Walks between;
They gather'd, broad as *Amazonian* Targe,
Shelters in cool, and tends his pasturing Herds
At Loopholes cut through thickest shade: Those Leaves   1110
They gather'd, broad as *Amazonian* Targe,
And with what skill they had, together sew'd,
To gird thir waist, vain Covering if to hide
Thir guilt and dreaded shame; O how unlike

1103 *Malabar or Decan*: parts of India.   1111 *Amazonian Targe*: shield or target.

To that first naked Glory. Such of late 1115
Columbus found th' *American* so girt
With feather'd Cincture, naked else and wild
Among the Trees on Isles and woody Shores.
Thus, fenc't, and as they thought, thir shame in part
Cover'd, but not at rest or ease of Mind, 1120
They sat them down to weep, nor only Tears
Rain'd at thir Eyes, but high Winds worse within
Began to rise, high Passions, Anger, Hate,
Mistrust, Suspicion, Discord, and shook sore
Thir inward State of Mind, calm Region once 1125
And full of Peace, now, toss't and turbulent:
For Understanding rul'd not, and the Will
Heard not her lore, both in subjection now
To sensual Appetite, who from beneath
Usurping over sovran Reason claim'd 1130
Superior sway: From thus distemper'd breast,
Adam, estrang'd in look and alter'd style,
Speech intermitted thus to *Eve* renew'd.
    Would thou hadst heark'n'd to my words, and stay'd
With me, as I besought thee, when that strange 1135
Desire of wand'ring this unhappy Morn,
I know not whence possess'd thee; we had then
Remain'd still happy, not as now, despoil'd
Of all our good, sham'd, naked, miserable.
Let none henceforth seek needless cause to approve 1140
The Faith they owe; when earnestly they seek
Such proof, conclude, they then begin to fail.
    To whom soon mov'd with touch of blame thus *Eve.*
What words have pass't thy Lips, *Adam* severe,
Imput'st thou that to my default, or will 1145
Of wand'ring, as thou call'st it, which who knows
But might as ill have happ'n'd thou being by,
Or to thyself perhaps: hadst thou been there,
Or here th' attempt, thou couldst not have discern'd
Fraud in the Serpent, speaking as he spake; 1150
No ground of enmity between us known,
Why hee should mean me ill, or seek to harm.
Was I to have never parted from thy side?
As good have grown there still a lifeless Rib.
Being as I am, why didst not thou the Head 1155
Command me absolutely not to go,
Going into such danger as thou said'st?
Too facile then thou didst not much gainsay,
Nay, didst permit, approve, and fair dismiss.
Hadst thou been firm and fixt in thy dissent, 1160
Neither had I transgress'd, nor thou with mee.
    To whom then first incenst *Adam* repli'd.
Is this the Love, is this the recompense
Of mine to thee, ingrateful *Eve,* exprest

Immutable when thou wert lost, not I,   1165
Who might have liv'd and joy'd immortal bliss,
Yet willingly chose rather Death with thee:
And am I now upbraided, as the cause
Of thy transgressing? not enough severe,
It seems, in thy restraint: what could I more?   1170
I warn'd thee, I admonish'd thee, foretold
The danger, and the lurking Enemy
That lay in wait; beyond this had been force,
And force upon free Will hath here no place.
But confidence then bore thee on, secure   1175
Either to meet no danger, or to find
Matter of glorious trial; and perhaps
I also err'd in overmuch admiring
What seem'd in thee so perfet, that I thought
No evil durst attempt thee, but I rue   1180
That error now, which is become my crime,
And thou th' accuser. Thus it shall befall
Him who to worth in Women overtrusting
Lets her Will rule; restraint she will not brook,
And left to herself, if evil thence ensue,   1185
Shee first his weak indulgence will accuse.
   Thus they in mutual accusation spent
The fruitless hours, but neither self-condemning,
And of thir vain contést appear'd no end.

The End of the Ninth Book

[The Son descends to judge the transgressors and after
pronouncing judgment clothes them "in pity." Sin and
Death build a bridge from Hell to Earth, and Satan
returns to Pandemonium. Adam and Eve debate the meaning of "death" and pray for peace. Their prayer reaches
Heaven, where the Son intercedes for them. God accepts
it, but sends the archangel Michael to expel them from
paradise. Before doing so, Michael reveals to Adam a
vision of the history of the chosen race, including the
incarnation of the Son, the death, resurrection, and ascen-
sion. Adam is shocked by the visions of disease and war
but is comforted by the revelation of Christ's redemption
and the final defeat of Satan. Michael and Adam then
descend from their hill to Eve.]

BOOK XII

We may no longer stay: go, waken *Eve;*
Her also I with gentle Dreams have calm'd   595
Portending good, and all her spirits compos'd
To meek submission: thou at season fit
Let her with thee partake what thou hast heard,
Chiefly what may concern her Faith to know,
The great deliverance by her Seed to come   600

(For by the Woman's Seed) on all Mankind.
That ye may live, which will be many days,
Both in one Faith unanimous though sad,
With cause for evils past, yet much more cheer'd
With mediation on the happy end.   605
 He ended, and they both descend the Hill;
Descended, *Adam* to the Bow'r where *Eve*
Lay sleeping ran before, but found her wak't;
And thus with words not sad she him receiv'd.
 Whence thou return'st, and whither went'st, I know;   610
For God is also in sleep, and Dreams advise,
Which he hath sent propitious, some great good
Presaging, since with sorrow and heart's distress
Wearied I fell asleep: but now lead on;
In mee is no delay; with thee to go,   615
Is to stay here; without thee here to stay,
Is to go hence unwilling; thou to mee
Art all things under Heav'n, all places thou,
Who for my wilful crime art banisht hence.
This further consolation yet secure   620
I carry hence; though all by mee is lost,
Such favour I unworthy am voutsaf't,
By mee the Promis'd Seed shall all restore.
 So spake our Mother *Eve,* and *Adam* heard
Well pleas'd, but answer'd not; for now too nigh   625
Th' Archangel stood, and from the other Hill
To thir fixt Station, all in bright array
The Cherubim descended; on the ground
Gliding meteorous, as Ev'ning Mist
Ris'n from a River o'er the marish glides,   630
And gathers ground fast at the Labourer's heel
Homeward returning. High in Front advanc't,
The brandisht Sword of God before them blaz'd
Fierce as a Comet; which with torrid heat,
And vapour as the *Libyan* Air adust,   635
Began to parch that temperate Clime; whereat
In either hand the hast'ning Angel caught
Our ling'ring Parents, and to th' Eastern Gate
Led them direct, and down the Cliff as fast
To the subjected Plain; then disappear'd.   640
They looking back, all th' Eastern side beheld
Of Paradise, so late thir happy seat,
Wav'd over by that flaming Brand, the Gate
With dreadful Faces throng'd and fiery Arms:
Some natural tears they dropp'd, but wip'd them soon;   645
The World was all before them, where to choose
Thir place of rest, and Providence thir guide:
They hand in hand with wand'ring steps and slow,
Through *Eden* took thir solitary way.
                              The End

WILLIAM WORDSWORTH

Although *The Prelude* is autobiographical, Wordsworth conceived of personal history as a worthy subject for epic treatment. He does not invoke muses or use obvious elements of epic machinery, but he echoes *Paradise Lost* frequently and maintains a high decorum throughout. His aim is to explore the limits of the imagination, which involves a combination of lyric and heroic modes. Rather than personify Olympian muses, for example, he personifies nature as the source of inspiration, beginning with the little "breeze" that blesses the poet and subsequently tracing throughout the poem the relations between imagination and nature. Imagination becomes his mode of grace; prophets are those who make living contact with "nature's secondary grace." It is nature's ways to man that he "justifies"; men achieve liberty and moral awareness only through contact with nature. The central antagonist of the poem is not a great Adversary but the poet's own "unnatural" self and the unnatural, urbanized complexity that stifles him in London and diverts the French Revolution from its true aims. The "fable," or plot, is the growth of his mind through imagination and the restoration of imagination after it has been "impaired."

But the parallels with *Paradise Lost,* numerous as they are, should not be extended too far. Wordsworth considered *The Prelude* merely a preface to "some philosophic song / Of Truth" fitted "to the Orphean lyre" (I. 229) that was to follow. By the early 1800's the time had passed when he could employ traditional epic machinery without feeling ill at ease; perhaps more important, the common body of beliefs necessary to a communal epic had been undermined. Consequently, the echoes of epic technique serve as much for contrast as for an indication of the spirit and meaning of the poem. Wordsworth does not pretend that his responses are Everyman's. His immediate audience is personal rather than national. *The Prelude* is partly conversation, partly confession. It is epic in proportion, ambition, and often in style; but it also contains hints of the unheroic wanderer.

Included here are parts of the first and the last books, which set the problems the poet is to examine and the solutions at which he arrives. Many things that impair the imagination described in intervening books can be inferred from the concluding passages.

FROM THE PRELUDE

Book First
INTRODUCTION—CHILDHOOD AND SCHOOL-TIME

Oh there is blessing in this gentle breeze,
A visitant that while it fans my cheek
Doth seem half-conscious of the joy it brings
From the green fields, and from yon azure sky.
Whate'er its mission, the soft breeze can come   5
To none more grateful than to me; escaped
From the vast city, where I long had pined
A discontented sojourner: now free,
Free as a bird to settle where I will.
What dwelling shall receive me? in what vale   10
Shall be my harbour? underneath what grove

Shall I take up my home? and what clear stream
Shall with its murmur lull me into rest?
The earth is all before me. With a heart
Joyous, nor scared at its own liberty,   15
I look about; and should the chosen guide
Be nothing better than a wandering cloud,
I cannot miss my way. I breathe again!
Trances of thought and mountings of the mind
Come fast upon me: it is shaken off,   20
That burthen of my own unnatural self,
The heavy weight of many a weary day
Not mine, and such as were not made for me.
Long months of peace (if such bold word accord
With any promises of human life),   25
Long months of ease and undisturbed delight
Are mine in prospect; whither shall I turn,
By road or pathway, or through trackless field,
Up hill or down, or shall some floating thing
Upon the river point me out my course?   30

    Dear Liberty! Yet what would it avail
But for a gift that consecrates the joy?
For I, methought, while the sweet breath of heaven
Was blowing on my body, felt within
A correspondent breeze, that gently moved   35
With quickening virtue, but is now become
A tempest, a redundant energy,
Vexing its own creation. Thanks to both,
And their congenial powers, that, while they join
In breaking up a long-continued frost,   40
Bring with them vernal promises, the hope
Of active days urged on by flying hours,—
Days of sweet leisure, taxed with patient thought
Abstruse, nor wanting punctual service high,
Matins and vespers of harmonious verse!   45
    Thus far, O Friend! did I, not used to make
A present joy the matter of a song,
Pour forth that day my soul in measured strains
That would not be forgotten, and are here
Recorded: to the open fields I told   50
A prophecy: poetic numbers came
Spontaneously to clothe in priestly robe
A renovated spirit singled out,
Such hope was mine, for holy services.
My own voice cheered me, and, far more, the mind's   55

---

16 *chosen guide*: the echo of the ending of *Paradise Lost* (XII. 646) in "The earth is all before me" (line 14) together with the words "guide" and "wandering" (lines 16–17) suggests that Wordsworth consciously contrasts his "wandering cloud" as guide with Adam and Eve's "Providence thir guide," although Adam and Eve "with wandering steps and slow" leave Eden, and Wordsworth "cannot miss" his way to it. The priestly role of the poet and the "renovated spirit singled out" of lines 50–56 are clearly Miltonic.

Internal echo of the imperfect sound;
To both I listened, drawing from them both
A cheerful confidence in things to come.

. . . .

    Fair seed-time had my soul, and I grew up
Fostered alike by beauty and by fear:
Much favoured in my birth-place, and no less
In that belovèd Vale to which erelong
We were transplanted; there were we let loose   305
For sports of wider range. Ere I had told
Ten birth-days, when among the mountain slopes
Frost, and the breath of frosty wind, had snapped
The last autumnal crocus, 't was my joy
With store of springes o'er my shoulder hung   310
To range the open heights where woodcocks run
Along the smooth green turf. Through half the night,
Scudding away from snare to snare, I plied
That anxious visitation;—moon and stars
Were shining o'er my head. I was alone,   315
And seemed to be a trouble to the peace
That dwelt among them. Sometimes it befell
In these night wanderings, that a strong desire
O'erpowered my better reason, and the bird
Which was the captive of another's toil   320
Became my prey; and when the deed was done
I heard among the solitary hills
Low breathings coming after me, and sounds
Of undistinguishable motion, steps
Almost as silent as the turf they trod.   325

    Nor less, when spring had warmed the cultured Vale,
Moved we as plunderers where the mother-bird
Had in high places built her lodge; though mean
Our object and inglorious, yet the end
Was not ignoble. Oh! when I have hung   330
Above the raven's nest, by knots of grass
And half-inch fissures in the slippery rock
But ill sustained, and almost (so it seemed)
Suspended by the blast that blew amain,
Shouldering the naked crag, oh, at that time   335
While on the perilous ridge I hung alone,
With what strange utterance did the loud dry wind
Blow through my ear! the sky seemed not a sky
Of earth—and with what motion moved the clouds!

    Dust as we are, the immortal spirit grows   340
Like harmony in music; there is a dark
Inscrutable workmanship that reconciles
Discordant elements, makes them cling together
In one society. How strange, that all

The terrors, pains, and early miseries,   345
Regrets, vexations, lassitudes interfused
Within my mind, should e'er have borne a part,
And that a needful part, in making up
The calm existence that is mine when I
Am worthy of myself! Praise to the end!   350
Thanks to the means which Nature deigned to employ;
Whether her fearless visitings, or those
That came with soft alarm, like hurtless light
Opening the peaceful clouds; or she would use
Severer interventions, ministry   355
More palpable, as best might suit her aim.

   One summer evening (led by her) I found
A little boat tied to a willow tree
Within a rocky cove, its usual home.
Straight I unloosed her chain, and stepping in   360
Pushed from the shore. It was an act of stealth
And troubled pleasure, nor without the voice
Of mountain-echoes did my boat move on;
Leaving behind her still, on either side,
Small circles glittering idly in the moon,   365
Until they melted all into one track
Of sparkling light. But now, like one who rows,
Proud of his skill, to reach a chosen point
With an unswerving line, I fixed my view
Upon the summit of a craggy ridge,   370
The horizon's utmost boundary; far above
Was nothing but the stars and the grey sky.
She was an elfin pinnace; lustily
I dipped my oars into the silent lake,
And, as I rose upon the stroke, my boat   375
Went heaving through the water like a swan;
When, from behind that craggy steep till then
The horizon's bound, a huge peak, black and huge,
As if with voluntary power instinct,
Upreared its head. I struck and struck again,   380
And growing still in stature the grim shape
Towered up between me and the stars, and still,
For so it seemed, with purpose of its own
And measured motion like a living thing,
Strode after me. With trembling oars I turned,   385
And through the silent water stole my way
Back to the covert of the willow tree;
There in her mooring-place I left my bark,—
And through the meadows homeward went, in grave
And serious mood; but after I had seen   390
That spectacle, for many days, my brain
Worked with a dim and undetermined sense
Of unknown modes of being; o'er my thoughts

There hung a darkness, call it solitude
Or blank desertion. No familiar shapes
Remained, no pleasant images of trees,   395
Of sea or sky, no colours of green fields;
But huge and mighty forms, that do not live
Like living men, moved slowly through the mind
By day, and were a trouble to my dreams.   400

   Wisdom and Spirit of the universe!
Thou Soul that art the eternity of thought
That givest to forms and images a breath
And everlasting motion, not in vain
By day or star-light thus from my first dawn   405
Of childhood didst thou intertwine for me
The passions that build up our human soul;
Not with the mean and vulgar works of man,
But with high objects, with enduring things—
With life and nature—purifying thus   410
The elements of feeling and of thought,
And sanctifying, by such discipline,
Both pain and fear, until we recognise
A grandeur in the beatings of the heart.

. . . .

BOOK TWELFTH
IMAGINATION AND TASTE, HOW IMPAIRED AND RESTORED

. . . .

   There are in our existence spots of time,
That with distinct pre-eminence retain
A renovating virtue, whence—depressed   210
By false opinion and contentious thought,
Or aught of heavier or more deadly weight,
In trivial occupations, and the round
Of ordinary intercourse—our minds
Are nourished and invisibly repaired;   215
A virtue, by which pleasure is enhanced,
That penetrates, enables us to mount,
When high, more high, and lifts us up when fallen.
This efficacious spirit chiefly lurks
Among those passages of life that give   220
Profoundest knowledge to what point, and how,
The mind is lord and master—outward sense
The obedient servant of her will. Such moments
Are scattered everywhere, taking their date
From our first childhood. I remember well,   225
That once, while yet my inexperienced hand
Could scarcely hold a bridle, with proud hopes
I mounted, and we journeyed towards the hills:
An ancient servant of my father's house

Was with me, my encourager and guide: 230
We had not travelled long, ere some mischance
Disjoined me from my comrade; and, through fear
Dismounting, down the rough and stony moor
I led my horse, and, stumbling on, at length
Came to a bottom, where in former times 235
A murderer had been hung in iron chains.
The gibbet-mast had mouldered down, the bones
And iron case were gone; but on the turf,
Hard by, soon after that fell deed was wrought,
Some unknown hand had carved the murderer's name. 240
The monumental letters were inscribed
In times long past; but still, from year to year
By superstition of the neighbourhood,
The grass is cleared away, and to this hour
The characters are fresh and visible: 245
A casual glance had shown them, and I fled,
Faltering and faint, and ignorant of the road:
Then, reascending the bare common, saw
A naked pool that lay beneath the hills,
The beacon on the summit, and, more near, 250
A girl, who bore a pitcher on her head,
And seemed with difficult steps to force her way
Against the blowing wind. It was, in truth,
An ordinary sight; but I should need
Colours and words that are unknown to man, 255
To paint the visionary dreariness
Which, while I looked all round for my lost guide,
Invested moorland waste and naked pool,
The beacon crowning the long eminence,
The female and her garments vexed and tossed 260
By the strong wind. When, in the blessèd hours
Of early love, the loved one at my side,
I roamed, in daily presence of this scene,
Upon the naked pool and dreary crags,
And on the melancholy beacon, fell 265
A spirit of pleasure and youth's golden gleam;
And think ye not with radiance more sublime
For these remembrances, and for the power
They had left behind? So feeling comes in aid
Of feeling, and diversity of strength 270
Attends us, if but once we have been strong.
Oh! mystery of man, from what a depth
Proceed thy honours. I am lost, but see
In simple childhood something of the base
On which thy greatness stands; but this I feel, 275
That from thyself it comes, that thou must give,
Else never canst receive. The days gone by
Return upon me almost from the dawn
Of life: the hiding-places of man's power

Open; I would approach them, but they close.   280
I see by glimpses now; when age comes on,
May scarcely see at all; and I would give,
While yet we may, as far as words can give,
Substance and life to what I feel, enshrining,
Such is my hope, the spirit of the Past   285
For future restoration.

. . . .

BOOK FOURTEENTH
CONCLUSION

In one of those excursions (may they ne'er
Fade from remembrance!) through the Northern tracts
Of Cambria ranging with a youthful friend,
I left Bethgelert's huts at couching-time,
And westward took my way, to see the sun   5
Rise, from the top of Snowdon. To the door
Of a rude cottage at the mountain's base
We came, and roused the shepherd who attends
The adventurous stranger's steps, a trusty guide;
Then, cheered by short refreshment, sallied forth.   10

    It was a close, warm, breezeless summer night,
Wan, dull, and glaring, with a dripping fog
Low-hung and thick that covered all the sky;
But, undiscouraged, we began to climb
The mountain-side. The mist soon girt us round,   15
And, after ordinary travellers' talk
With our conductor, pensively we sank
Each into commerce with his private thoughts:
Thus did we breast the ascent, and by myself
Was nothing either seen or heard that checked   20
Those musings or diverted, save that once
The shepherd's lurcher, who, among the crags,
Had to his joy unearthed a hedgehog, teased
His coiled-up prey with barkings turbulent.
This small adventure, for even such it seemed   25
In that wild place and at the dead of night,
Being over and forgotten, on we wound
In silence as before. With forehead bent
Earthward, as if in opposition set
Against an enemy, I panted up   30
With eager pace, and no less eager thoughts.
Thus might we wear a midnight hour away,
Ascending at loose distance each from each,
And I, as chanced, the foremost of the band;
When at my feet the ground appeared to brighten,   35
And with a step or two seemed brighter still;
Nor was time given to ask or learn the cause,

For instantly a light upon the turf
Fell like a flash, and lo! as I looked up
The Moon hung naked in a firmament   40
Of azure without cloud, and at my feet
Rested a silent sea of hoary mist.
A hundred hills their dusky backs upheaved
All over this still ocean; and beyond,
Far, far beyond, the solid vapours stretched,   45
In headlands, tongues, and promontory shapes,
Into the main Atlantic, that appeared
To dwindle, and give up his majesty,
Usurped upon far as the sight could reach.
Not so the ethereal vault; encroachment none   50
Was there, nor loss; only the inferior stars
Had disappeared, or shed a fainter light
In the clear presence of the full-orbed Moon,
Who, from her sovereign elevation, gazed
Upon the billowy ocean, as it lay   55
All meek and silent, save that through a rift—
Not distant from the shore whereon we stood,
A fixed, abysmal, gloomy, breathing-place—
Mounted the roar of waters, torrents, streams
Innumerable, roaring with one voice!   60
Heard over earth and sea, and, in that hour,
For so it seemed, felt by the starry heavens.
   When into air had partially dissolved
That vision, given to spirits of the night
And three chance human wanderers, in calm thought   65
Reflected, it appeared to me the type
Of majestic intellect, its acts
And its possessions, what it has and craves,
What in itself it is, and would become:
There I beheld the emblem of a mind   70
That feeds upon infinity, that broods
Over the dark abyss, intent to hear
Its voices issuing forth to silent light
In one continuous stream; a mind sustained
By recognitions of transcendent power,   75
In sense conducting to ideal form,
In soul of more than mortal privilege.
One function, above all, of such a mind
Had Nature shadowed there, by putting forth,
'Mid circumstances awful and sublime,   80
That mutual dominations which she loves
To exert upon the face of outward things,
So moulded, joined, abstracted, so endowed
With interchangeable supremacy,
That men, least sensitive, see, hear, perceive,   85
And cannot choose but feel. The power, which all
Acknowledge when thus moved, which Nature thus

To bodily sense exhibits is the express
Resemblance of that glorious faculty
That higher minds bear with them as their own.   90
This is the very spirit in which they deal
With the whole compass of the universe:
They from their native selves can send abroad
Kindred mutations; for themselves create
A like existence; and, whene'er it dawns   95
Created for them, catch it, or are caught
By its inevitable mastery,
Like angels stopped upon the wing by sound
Of harmony from Heaven's remotest spheres.
Them the enduring and the transient both   100
Serve to exalt; they build up greatest things
From least suggestions; ever on the watch,
Willing to work and to be wrought upon,
They need not extraordinary calls
To rouse them; in a world of life they live,   105
By sensible impressions not enthralled,
But by their quickening impulse made more prompt
To hold fit converse with the spiritual world,
And with the generations of mankind
Spread over time, past, present, and to come,   110
Age after age, till Time shall be no more.

Romance

Introduction

In our times the word "romance" is inevitably associated with love. Not, of course, with *any* kind of love (as no one is likely to think, for instance, of married love in a romantic connection, perhaps least of all married persons) but rather with that highly special kind of premarital affliction that in its more advanced stages deprives its victims of sleep, appetite, and other prerequisites of sentient life. In medieval times, however, "romance" at first had little to do with love: it was used primarily to distinguish from Latin works those written in the vernacular languages of France, Spain, and Italy—the "Romance languages." Because the vernacular works of greatest popularity were, in fact, "romances," the term gradually lost its linguistic significance and became the name of the literary genre.

The English metrical romances of the thirteenth and fourteenth centuries were verse stories, usually of considerable length, depicting the adventures of wandering knights ("knights errant") who set forth from castle and court impelled by love, religious faith, or chivalric gallantry. The origin of these stories appears to lie in the old Celtic myths and rituals of Ireland, Wales, Brittany, Cornwall, and western Scotland. Tales based on these myths and rituals were preserved by oral tradition and subsequently fashioned into French romances by Breton minstrels of the twelfth century, thus supplanting the older *chansons de geste,* or "songs of great deeds." At this stage, the chivalric spirit and aristocratic values seem to have been incorporated into the tales, the old gods and goddesses of the Celtic myths being demoted to knights and ladies who still retained traces of their former status.

It is impossible to be sure precisely what the original rituals and myths consisted of, but from existing early romances it can be inferred that they had much in common with vegetation rituals practiced and dramatized in myth by most primitive agricultural societies. Typical ritual sequences involving mortification, purgation, revitalization, and celebration centered in the death of the old year and the birth of the new, the resurrection of the old king in the form of a young one, the triumph of life over death, light over darkness, summer over winter, fertility over sterility. Obviously related to such lore is the recurrent motif in medieval romance of a young knight's journey to a land tyrannized by an oppressor (dragon, giant, or enemy forces) or lying under some kind of blighting curse. Often the king of the land ("Fisher King," "Maimed King") is incapacitated by old age or a wound associated with sexual impotence, like the thigh wound of Adonis in Greek mythology, and the king's physical debilities are the "cause" of the blight upon the land or of the life-suppressing influence of the dragon or curse. The young knight may restore the land to fertility and the king to health by killing the dragon, in a battle suggesting the victory of summer over winter, and marrying the king's daughter, in a symbolic union of sky god with earth goddess. A similar happy ending may result from the knight's utterance of the "right" words—perhaps a question about the king's illness, the "bleeding lance" in his chambers, or the grail carried by his servants—which lift the curse much as Oedipus' solution to the riddle of the Sphinx lifted the curse from Thebes and his identification of himself as the "wound" or "disease" blighting Thebes lifted the later curse.

Thus, elements of nature such as seasonal and daily cycles become recurrent features of romance. Gawain must wait a year, "each season in turn succeeding the other," before making his journey into the wintry region of the Green Knight. The Ancient Mariner offends a wintry Polar Spirit and, in a reversal of symbolic values, is becalmed under a searing sun in an oceanic wasteland, finally achieving an order of recovery under the aegis of the moon. Chrétien de Troyes' Perceval, a child of nature, begins his adventures in the springtime, passes through a period of spiritual backwardness during the winter, and achieves enlightenment in the spring. Behind this seasonal and daily cycle lies the archetypic pattern of *withdrawal-transformation-return,* which normally incorporates a death-and-rebirth motif associated with the rhythms of nature. Thus we have the sun declining into a bloody sunset (to "go west" used to be a common metaphor for dying), withdrawing from the visible world into darkness, and reappearing the next morning in a different part of the sky, miraculously transformed, reborn, "risen." So the abundant life of summer dies through the autumn, "withdraws" underground during winter ("wynter rasure," as Malory puts it, "dothe allway arace and deface grene summer"), but is reborn with the spring.

The *quest,* a ubiquitous structural element in romance, presupposes this pattern of withdrawal-transformation-return: the knight withdraws from courtly society into the isolation of nature, where he undergoes various tests, is transformed in character and status, and finally returns to the court as an initiate fully qualified to sit at the Round Table or to serve Gloriana. Normally the death-and-rebirth motif is involved in the quest, as it is in Chrétien's *The Knight of the Cart,* where Lancelot makes the "otherworld jouney" to the castle of death to recover the "captured" Guinevere. Lancelot is more successful than Orpheus, who glances back and hence loses Eurydice in the Greek myth; however, in the lay of *Sir Orfeo,* where the Greek land of the dead becomes a medieval castle in "a fair country" and Hades becomes the King of Fairy, the

Anglicized Orpheus successfully rescues his Queen, Dame Herodis, from the fairyland of death. Sometimes the otherworld journey of the romance hero carries Christian overtones of the Harrowing of Hell, that is, of Christ's journey to release the captive souls of those condemned to hell since the Fall of Adam and Eve. In *The Turk and Gawain,* for example, Gawain crosses by boat to the Isle of Man (Lancelot employed an equally traditional but more painful method in rescuing Guinevere, crossing a river by a "sword bridge"), where, aided by the Turk—a "stalwortht knight" enchanted into the form of a dwarf with the gift of invisibility—he triumphs over the oppressive king and releases many captive men and women. The same Harrowing of Hell theme takes a more sophisticated and allegorical form in the final cantos of the first book of *The Faerie Queene.*

Not all otherworld journeys are successful, however: in Malory's *Balin, or the Knight with Two Swords* the well-intentioned but cursed hero makes two otherworld journeys, both of which end in disaster. In modern literature the otherworld journey with Harrowing of Hell overtones is not easily come by, though it forms one of the underlying themes of Conrad's prose romance *Heart of Darkness,* in which Marlow withdraws from European society into the hellish otherworld of the Congo in his quest for the "damned soul" of Kurtz, cannot release Kurtz from his inner "horror" but is himself initiated into the knowledge of evil, and returns to Europe transformed by his experiences. Harrowings of Hell more often appear in secular guise in the "Western," the most popular form of naive romance today, in which a standard plot features the cowboy hero making a perilous journey to the almost inaccessible mountain hideout of the outlaws and managing to release their hostages. In *Victory* Conrad inverts the "harrowing" pattern by having the satanic Mr. Jones and his cohorts journey across water to the island retreat of Heyst (rhymes with Christ).

Whereas the journey of the epic hero is normally one-directional (despite the concentric pattern of "Dante's" movement), the hero of romance goes out and back again, perfecting a circular figure in space that is, internally, a perfecting of character (the romantic equivalent to the "vertical quest" of epic). In medieval romances, character is tested in terms of Christian and chivalric virtues, and the hero's difficulties in the face of competing social, ethical, and religious imperatives are the thematic center of the work. In *Tristan and Iseult,* for instance, Tristan is torn between the necessity of honoring his feudal and chivalric obligations to King Mark and that of maintaining his courtly love allegiance to Iseult. Here, the competing values arise from the same chivalric system, as they do in *Gawain and the Green Knight,* whose hero is tested in both chastity and courtesy as well as in knightly courage. But in Chrétien's *Perceval* the competition is essentially between values arising from two different systems, the chivalric and the religious, as we find the hero (a prototype of Spenser's Redcross Knight as well as Milton's Samson) graduating from heroic action to Christian understanding, from uncouth warrior to "God's fool." In some cases, the competition of value systems may prove poetically unmanageable, as seems to be the case in Chrétien's *Knight of the Cart,* left unfinished perhaps because Chrétien had written himself into a corner by figuring Lancelot as Christ in a Harrowing of Hell plot but also as the worldly cuckolder of Arthur. In Malory's *Tale of the Sangreal* Lancelot's duality of character turns his story in a tragic direction. He appears to succeed in his quest of the Holy Grail, actually entering the room in which it stands; but when he attempts to approach it, a great heat is generated, which causes him to collapse, and he never again sees the Grail. That he sees it at all is an index of his knightly and religious excellence, but his inability to approach it is an index of his spiritual imperfection, his remaining tied to an earthly and dishonorable love for Queen Guinevere. Lancelot's son Galahad, however, is perfect in all respects and is thus granted not only the sight of the Grail but a drink from it and a vision of Christ.

Even in romances that do not feature the quest, the withdrawal-transformation-return pattern is prominent. In one romance motif a royal child is withdrawn from his proper society through theft, abandonment, or protective hiding, is raised in a distant land, and later returns in disguise, performs some great deed, and claims his kingdom. This is the case with the young Arthur and the Welsh hero Llew Llawgyffes; it forms the entire plot of *King Horn* and *Havelok the Dane* and one strand of the plot of Shakespeare's *Cymbeline*. The motif is still going strong as late as *Wuthering Heights,* where it is given malign dimensions in Heathcliff's withdrawal into the "wilderness" of America and his return to claim the Heights and Thrushcross Grange. Another version of the withdrawal-transformation-return pattern is the tale of the lovely lady bewitched into a mysterious, deathlike sleep, as in the story of the Sleeping Beauty treated by Scott in *The Bridal of Triermain,* or turned into an ugly hag, as in Chaucer's *Wife of Bath's Tale,* and subsequently restored to life and beauty through the ministrations of a handsome knight. In inverted form this motif appears in *The Lady of Shalott* as Lancelot unwittingly causes the Lady's fatal "awakening." Still another version of the pattern appears in tales of a knight who, after being wooed and won by a fairy lady (as the Ancient Mariner is "won" by the lady Death-in-Life and Keats's knight by *la belle dame sans merci*), withdraws with her into the delights or torments of fairyland but upon breaking some fairy taboo is compelled to return to reality. In the medieval *Partenay,* for instance, the hero breaks the taboo against spying upon his fairy lady on Saturdays and discovers that she is a serpent from the waist down. Forgiven the first time, he offends a second and is expelled. Keats's *Lamia* is a late working of the same theme, and literature generally, not to mention the cinema and television, is well stocked with sinuous and sensuous *femmes fatales* luring into their coils a host of errant young men who suffer bewitchment before returning to their blonde, blue-eyed, and apparently non-reptilian sweethearts.

Epic and romance both have a close relation to myth. In epic we not only find the poet claiming close contact to the gods by invoking their assistance in his high endeavor, but we encounter in the poem itself what Pope calls "supernatural machinery," that is, the gods, goddesses, and tutelary spirits who hover over the field of human action guarding, assisting, and influencing their favorites (and thus bearing the same relation to the characters *in* the poem as the Muse or quasi-deity to the poet writing it). This supernatural machinery of epic derives either from the Greek pantheon, as in Homer and Virgil, or from the Christian, as in Dante and Milton. In medieval romance, however, we find not gods but characters and animals that are often anthropomorphized forces of nature. Thus the Green Knight is not a god but an incarnation of nature's vitality and regenerative powers, precisely what we should expect if, in Dylan Thomas' phrase, "the force that through the green fuse drives the flower" were to become quasi-human. Robin Hood, who inhabits Sherwood Forest and goes by the title "King of the May," looks suspiciously like a vegetation god reduced to human proportions. In early stories Gawain, like the Irish hero Cuchulain, reveals his earlier role as a sun god not only in his golden hair and gleaming armor but also in the fact that his strength waxes until noon and then wanes toward evening. The further we get from the original myths and rituals from which romance arose, the less the characters betray elements of nature behind their ordinary humanity. In *Gawain and the Green Knight* the pagan myth and ritual aspects of the hero and his opponent have already become submerged under a heavy surface of Christian values; yet still visible behind the overt theme of the Christian knight subjected to tests of manners and virtue is the primitive problem of man negotiating as best he can with the mysterious forces of nature. When the Christian element has become entirely dominant, as in the story of Spenser's Redcross Knight, we still find the major task of the hero to be that of conquering a dragon who allegorically represents "fallen nature." Even *The Ancient Mariner,* which by no means derives from pagan myth and ritual, presents no less than *Gawain and the Green Knight* man's problems in dealing with a world of nature fraught with sacred and mysterious forces.

If romance has "outward" associations with myth and ritual, so it has "inward" associations with dream, the gods of the sky seeming to coalesce with the gods of the psyche to form characters somehow outside or above ordinary reality. This outward-inward fusion in romance perhaps explains why the genre is so often regarded as the special province of the marvelous and mysterious, since in myth and ritual man engages the mysteries of nature and in dream the mysteries of his own mind. Like the dream-narrative, the romance-narrative is characterized by a lack of adequate motivation, by unexpected transfers of identity, by extreme cases of coincidence, and by an abeyance of normal laws of nature (dislocations of time and place and cause and effect) and a dissolution of the barrier between reality and fantasy. We encounter witches and ogres, dwarfs, giants, dragons, lovely damsels and shining heroes, magicians, seers, trees with the capacity of speech, swords fated to deal the "dolorous stroke," men gifted with invulnerability or cursed with powerlessness: in short, a world in which imagination "bodies forth the forms of things unknown," in which fear and desire automatically conjure up their objective correlatives, and anything is possible.

The analogy with dream extends to the romance having multiple levels of significance, both "manifest" and "latent" content. Though most romances appear to present fantasy and adventure for their sheer entertainment value as "story," we are often aware of dimensions of meaning not accounted for by the literal level of the narrative. This may mean that we are reading formal allegory, as in the *Roman de la Rose,* in much of Malory, in Tasso's *Jerusalem Delivered,* or in *The Faerie Queene.* Or it may mean that we have become conscious of mythic elements not entirely buried in a romance whose surface concerns are other than mythic, as in *Sir Gawain and the Green Knight.* In the earliest medieval romances, the tale itself is paramount; the poet is the transmitter of traditional material not of his own making, and his principal burden is to remain faithful to the narrative details of the "original" as he knows it. Hence, unlike the epic poet, the romantic teller rarely intrudes his presence into his tale, not even to invoke aid in the telling of it. When the narrative so dominates the narrator, the tale is not supplied with meaning but is instinct with it, and the telling of it is like a verbal enactment of a ritual, each phase of which must be done exactly as in the past because it holds special, perhaps sacred, meanings of which even the narrator is not fully aware. This domination of narrator by his own narrative, producing a captive speaker if not a captive audience, takes a later form in the device of the manuscript found in a bottle or secret desk drawer and transmitted by the finder, and it achieves its finest literary fulfilment in *The Ancient Mariner,* where the "hero" is compelled to tell his tale in an endless ritual of confession and penance.

Again, we note that the impulses underlying the formulations of the dream narrative—the extremes of dread and desire, which give us the nightmare and the wish-fulfilment dream respectively—produce analogous categories of romance. When we encounter handsome knights who successfully fend off the assaults of lovely and lecherous females without tainting their souls, unhorse villainous "black knights" without a scratch, and inhale the fumes of countless dragons without getting lung cancer, we are clearly in the world of wish-fulfilment, where all charms are impervious to the touch of cold philosophy, a world purified (as other literary worlds are purified, each for its own kind of intensity) to the point where right literally makes might and moral power becomes physical power, as with the "magic" of Prospero in Shakespeare's *The Tempest.* At the other extreme, in the category of nightmare, are romances like *The Tale of Balin,* whose hero's every good intention is intercepted and perversely translated into disaster; *Wuthering Heights,* where a bleak, tormented landscape fittingly reflects the demonic nature of Heathcliff—"an unreclaimed creature, without refinement, without cultivation: an arid wilderness of furze and whinstone...a fierce, pitiless, wolfish man"; or *Heart of Darkness,* where Marlow's progress into the interior of the Congo is a descent into nightmare, hell, and the primordial past. Normally the elements of nightmare and wish-fulfilment are both present, the hero fighting his way through various forces of oppression to a gratifying conclusion.

In the "wish-fulfilment romance," the external movement of the hero on his quest—his erratic, wandering course—mirrors his internal condition in that although he is "obliged" by moral considerations, religious zeal, or the imperatives of duty and chivalry to perform well, freedom of choice is constantly present. He is "finding his way" within as well as without, and the progress of his quest through a material landscape, marked as it is by repeated trials, is a projected disclosure of his spiritual landscape. In "nightmare romance," on the other hand, the hero's actions arise less from obligation than compulsion. The free play of impulse and idea gives way to rigidity and repetitiveness in heroes fated, cursed, doomed, bewitched, obsessed, "seized" from without or within. Kurtz cannot conquer the "heavy, mute spell of the wilderness" nor can Balin cease delivering the "dolorous stroke" any more than the Ancient Mariner can leave untold his tale of horror. Thus, whereas the central feature of the wish-fulfilment form is usually the free-ranging quest, that of the nightmare form is the prison. This may be a real dungeon, as in Byron's *The Prisoner of Chillon;* the "dark tower" to which Childe Roland came; Poe's House of Usher; the gloomy forests and ruined castles where the good fall into the clutches of the evil in Gothic romances like those of Mrs. Radcliffe; the Congo jungle; or the harrowing machine of Kafka's "In the Penal Colony." When captivity is figured in a prison of some material form, the quest turns static, becoming a struggle to escape or a helpless anguish, and the romantic hero is reduced from a doer of deeds to a victim. If we do find a questing or at least a physically unrestrained hero in nightmare romance, the prison will often be internalized as an *idée fixe* that holds the mind captive, as with Heathcliff or Ahab. The hero's external freedom of movement itself may be a version of imprisonment, because like the Byronic hero and the Ancient Mariner he may be an example of the fate of the Wandering Jew or Cain, the man condemned to move forever with a full cargo of inexpiable guilt.

Unlike the novel, characterization in the romance is normally at a minimum, the tendency being to distribute the inner qualities of personality outward in a process analogous to the displacement techniques of dream. This is obvious enough in allegorical characters like Spenser's Sir Guyon and Tasso's Godfrey, who are externalizations of "Temperance" and "Understanding" respectively. Here we have characterization by synecdoche, in which the psychological part not merely stands for but literally becomes the whole person. The uncompleted plan of *The Faerie Queene* was originally to fragment the character of the ideal man into the individual qualities of Holiness, Temperance, Chastity, Courtesy, and so on and to transform the fragments into the synecdochic "wholes" of the Redcross Knight, Sir Guyon, Britomart, Sir Calidore, and so on, with Prince Arthur, the "complete man," threading his way through the adventures of the various heroes as a thematic reminder that the ultimate moral goal is a synthesis of virtues and as a formal reminder that Spenser's artistic goal is a unity of parts. However, even in romances not dominated by a sustained allegorical intent, an extreme subjective intensity creates a suggestion of allegory, of characters and actions being projections of interior forces, as in the suggestion of an *id-ego-superego* psychomachy underlying the interpersonal tensions of Heathcliff, Catherine, and Linton in *Wuthering Heights*.

Another quasi-allegorical way of distributing inner qualities outward is the use of various "alter-ego" devices in which certain potentialities of the hero are represented in other characters. Whereas the novelist normally deals in "rounded" characters like Tom Jones or Frederick Henry, who are complex in that their social, political, historical, emotional, and intellectual dimensions are given full play, the writer of romance deals in comparatively "flat," or simplified, characters who are isolated from society, politics, and history, whose intellectual and emotional range is highly limited, and whose conduct is highly stylized. Because characters in the novel are presented as complex, they have a built-in capacity to develop that is usually lacking in the characters of romance, whose external "scene" may alter radically from episode to episode but who are themselves "on rails." In romances devoid of thematic content, like the Western romance and much of Gothic romance, the surface adventures of an unchanging and largely insentient hero constitute the total literary reality, which thus serves as escapist entertainment. In romances of greater literary sophistication, the hero may seem quite as uncomplicated as his naive counterpart, but this is because his complexity, his capacity to be other than he appears, is present not in himself but outside himself. The hero's ride through a fully described winter wasteland may do outside duty for an inner, novelistic exploration of his bleakness of mind and feeling; the disappearance of a trusted adviser may suggest the hero's break with conscience; a change of apparel or a journey across water may signal a transformation of identity.

This same principle of characterization accounts also for the puzzling recurrence of "doubles" in romance—characters who are all but identical, like

Chaucer's Palamoun and Arcite, Malory's Balin and Balan, Shakespeare's Demetrius and Lysander, Poe's two William Wilsons, and Conrad's ship captain and Leggett. In many instances, such doubles reflect the tendency of romance to develop through parallels and contrasts a highly symmetrical literary form of which *The Knight's Tale* is a perfect example. This is at least part of the function of such "nominal" doubles as Iseult of Ireland and Iseult of Brittany, Reynild and Rymenhild (the rival females in *King Horn*), and Shem and Shaun in *Finnegan's Wake*. But in many cases character-doubling is also an "alter-ego" device to suggest a composite personality fraught with internal division, as the morality play peoples the stage with representatives of the hero's internal division or as Lear's daughters and Gloucester's sons externally reflect their fathers' divided personalities. Stevenson achieves the same effect by collapsing two "different" characters into one identity in *Dr. Jekyll and Mr. Hyde*. The sense of inner division is heightened by the manipulation of the two characters into some kind of open conflict in which the hero may, like Balin and William Wilson, kill the "better self" in an act symbolic of moral suicide, or he may, like the ship captain in Conrad's "The Secret Sharer," come to terms with the "other self" through vicarious experience, recognition, and subsequent banishment. What is at stake in such works is the integrity of the personality, and the "quest" becomes a displaced descent into the unconscious, the "night journey" of the soul, which may lead to reintegration of self or total loss of identity.

As we might expect, these recurrent themes, structural methods, and character types are reflected in the narrative manner and language of romance. As a play like Shakespeare's *The Tempest* should remind us, romance may sometimes appear in dramatic form; but normally the worlds of Camelot and fairyland resist the here-and-now immediacy of drama. Purely imaginary realms or metaphors of internal reality, they are too remote from surface realism to be presented directly. Hence, whereas drama gives us characters like Hamlet standing before us saying "I am" (first-person pronoun, present-tense verb), romance gives us a storyteller using third-person pronouns and either past or "timeless" present-tense verb (("He was" or "He is"): "A gentle knight *was* pricking on the plaine" or "It *is* an ancient Mariner/And he stoppeth one of three." The distance of the past allows for mythic enlargement of the hero, and the "timeless" present allows dreamlike qualities to permeate the action. In either case, the connective links of the narrative are set beyond ordinary causation.

For instance, in the quotations about the ancient mariner, the two lines are held together by the loose conjunction "and," which is typical of romance as a whole. Tragedy holds its story together by a plot based on probability; it specializes in conjunctions of cause and effect: "*Because A* happens, *B* happens, and *therefore C* and *D*. But romance plots are usually *episodic*. The events are strung out in loose sequence along the line of the quest and connected by means of additive or incremental conjunctions indicating sequence rather than cause: "*A* happens *and then B, then C*." Since the unity of romance does not arise from tightly knit plots, it is usually achieved by paralleling actions, balancing and contrasting characters, and playing variations on themes. This accounts for the high degree of stylization and structural patterning that we mentioned earlier.

Perhaps the most distinctive grammatical feature of romance is its use, not necessarily in fact but in imaginative effect, of the subjunctive mood. The subjunctive is an "if-mood," as befits a world of fantasy and "illogical" connections of the secret-sharer kind; and though it may appear in all three tenses—"It might have been," "If it now were," "It may yet be"—the things and events it refers to are really outside time. Thus although the statement "A gentle knight was pricking on the plaine" seems to assert a fact, the Redcross Knight did not, does not, and will not take the fabulous allegorical journey depicted by Spenser. Of course all literature is hypothetical in this sense, but some works, like the realistic novel and satire, *appear* to assert the here-and-now existence of their worlds, to say not *"If* this were" but "This is or was," or like epic, "Long ago in Troy (or Rome or Eden) these events occurred." Camelot, fairyland, and the dark tower of Roland are perennially remote—and for that reason perennially present, too. Coleridge's ancient mariner is not a turn-of-the-nineteenth-century seaman but an ancient wanderer with a message from "beyond the land," beyond time and place. If we trace the lady of Shalott back through the centuries to the "times" of King Arthur, we find her atemporal—neither more immediate nor more remote from us than from Tennyson's contemporaries and in fact a symbol of an art that demands indirection and expires upon looking directly out the window at nature.

These grammatical and formal qualities of romance give us a stable vantage point from which to view its evolutionary changes. They remain more or less constant among numerous mutations of the form. To begin with, romance achieved literary form partly as a development from the older epic poem. Later, after the metrical alliterative romances gave way to the prose romances of the sixteenth century (like those of Robert Greene and Sir Philip Sidney), it prepared the way for the novel (in French, *roman*), which used many of the same narrative techniques and often the traveling quest of the hero but anchored them in circumstantial (and often bourgeois) realism. In the late seventeenth and early eighteenth centuries the major function of romance was to supply fuel for parody and burlesque, its form and conventions (along with those of epic) providing material for such mock-heroic works as *Hudibras* and *The Dunciad*. With the Celtic "revival" of the later eighteenth century, straightforward romance came back strongly in works like Gray's "The Bard" and Macpherson's "translations" of *Ossian,* and in "Gothic" horror stories that converted the never-never land of romance into nightmarish settings. The quality of romance during this period was unimpressive compared to that of novels like *Moll Flanders, Pamela, Tom Jones,* and *Tristram Shandy.* But in the nineteenth century the genre achieved considerable prominence in Coleridge's *Ancient Mariner, Christabel,* and *Kubla Khan,* Keats's *Endymion. The Eve of St. Agnes,* and *Lamia,* Tennyson's *Idylls of the King,* Browning's *Childe Roland,* and various works of William Morris, to mention only a few. Though the novel was the dominant nineteenth-century narrative form, it by no means substituted for or superseded prose romance, as the works of Hawthorne, Melville, Poe, Emily Brontë, and Scott indicate.

In the twentieth century, romance (like post-romanticism) has been absorbed into new currents, but its changes are again transmutations rather than essential reconstitutions. An encyclopedic work like Joyce's *Finnegan's Wake,* despite its documentary realism and the drabness of Earwicker's foreground story, clearly owes a good deal to romance, in its cyclical form, its "night journey" into the unconscious, its identifications of H. C. Earwicker with Tristram, and its use of Anna Livia Plurabelle's rivering "quest" of Father Ocean as a structural principle. One of Conrad's first novels, written in collaboration with Ford Maddox Hueffer, was entitled *Romance,* and his subsequent fiction retains generic if not titular associations with the form. Romance has exerted an influence on the drama, as in Yeats's *On Baile's Strand,* and on the narrative poem, as in Eliot's "mock-romance" *The Waste Land.* Thomas Mann in *The Holy Sinner* and J. R. R. Tolkien in his trilogy *The Lord of the Rings* have written full-fledged romances on the medieval pattern. It is true that much twentieth-century literature, especially prose fiction, is less "in" the romance tradition than "in reaction" to it, specializing in the representational and realistic and turning to fantasy as a means of satirizing the familiar rather than confronting the unknown. In asphalt wastelands, the dragons come in eight-cylinder models and the black knights carry switchblades. Nevertheless, if nature has been largely stripped of the marvelous, except in science fiction and in some westerns, the mind itself, Hopkins reminds us, "has mountains...no-man-fathomed," and man's continuing confrontation of its mysteries still demands a form capable of pursuing motives past the threshold of rationality.

EDMUND SPENSER

According to Spenser's introductory letter to Ralegh, written while the first three books of the poem were going through the press, *The Faerie Queene* was to have been four times as long as it is. The first twelve books were to deal with the twelve private virtues of the good man, the second twelve with the corresponding public virtues of the good governor. Spenser actually completed six books and a few cantos of a seventh. These six books present us with the adventures of (I) the Redcross Knight, who represents Holiness, (II) Sir Guyon, or Temperance, (III) Britomart, or Chastity, (IV) Cambell and Triamond, or Friendship, (V) Sir Artegall, or Justice, and (VI) Sir Calidore, or Courtesy. From the letter to Ralegh, we learn that these knights are all sent forth from the court of Gloriana, Queen of Fairyland (Queen Elizabeth I), one every day during the twelve days of her annual feast. Now and again throughout the poem, Prince Arthur, the perfect knight who embodies all the virtues separately represented by the other knights and who is himself wandering in search of Gloriana, appears briefly to take part in the adventures of the other knights, usually acting as rescuer, as when he frees the Redcross Knight from Orgoglio in Book I. Thus the center of Spenser's fictional world is the court of Gloriana, which is both alpha and omega, point of departure for the twelve knights and final goal of Prince Arthur. This, then, like the journey of Chaucer's pilgrims to Canterbury, is the "framing story" of *The Faerie Queene,* and each book of the poem tells its individual tale centering on one of the knights.

Book I presents us with the tale of a knight, his lady, and their experiences in a hazardous world. At the literal level of the poem, we follow the external adventures of the Redcross Knight as he encounters dragons, magicians, deceptively beautiful witches, giants, and even men who are trees. The basic story is simple: Una journeys to Gloriana's court to request the services of a knight to help free her royal parents, imprisoned by a dragon. A "clownish," that is, rustic, young man offers himself for the task, is first turned down, but is finally accepted when it is found that the armor Una has brought with her fits him perfectly. They depart for the land of Una's parents, are separated, undergo various adventures, are rejoined, and are eventually betrothed to one another after the knight has slain the dragon and released her parents.

Spenser, however, is less interested in telling an exciting story than in developing what he calls his "continued Allegory, or darke conceit"—the sustained metaphoric association of the surface story with an underlying level of religious and moral meaning. Spenser's allegory is not a simple, one-for-one equation between character and abstract moral virtue, between action and religious idea. Though he identifies the Redcross Knight as "Holiness," the knight is sometimes more and sometimes less than that—more, for instance, when he is battling the dragon in Canto XI, less when he becomes lustfully enamored of the false Fidessa (Duessa). The allegory is sufficiently flexible and manifold in meaning that the Redcross Knight can represent mankind, England, English Protestantism, and the religious and moral impulse that seeks fulfilment in holiness. His mission is to conquer godlessness in all its forms, especially within himself, in order to become genuinely united with Una, who primarily represents spiritual truth but is also associated at various times with Christian faith, the English church, The Virgin, and chaste love. Una's royal parents, who

> had of yore
> Their scepters stretcht from East to Westerne shore,
> And all the world in their subjection held;
> Till that infernal feend with foule uprore
> Forwasted all their land, and them expeld...   (I.i.5)

are Adam and Eve after the Fall, the former King and Queen of Eden; and the "infernal feend," who takes the form of the dragon conquered by the knight in Canto XI, is Satan, the serpent in the Garden of Eden, the Enemy of man whose seductions caused Adam and Eve to be expelled from their paradisal kingdom and put in bondage (original sin) to himself. In seeking to free Una's parents, then, the Redcross Knight acquires another meaning, his mission being associated with Christ's as an attempt to redeem fallen mankind from captivity in sin. His three-day battle with the dragon parallels Christ's "harrowing of hell"—that is, according to medieval theology, Christ's descent into hell or Limbo during the three days between His burial and His resurrection to free the souls of all who had lived since the Fall. During his fight with the dragon, the Redcross Knight is sustained first by the Well of Life, then by the Tree of Life, these representing the two sacraments accepted by the Protestants— baptism and communion.

Because of the complexity and occasional abstruseness of Spenser's "darke conceit," readers are sometimes counseled to attend to the story and disregard the allegorical import, which is rather like reading Swift's *A Modest Proposal* for the logic and disregarding the satire. Reading *The Faerie Queene* for the narrative alone is not only inadvisable but impossible. In the first place, it should become immediately apparent that the primary qualities of "story"— suspense, rapid pace, lively dialogue, straightforward development—are simply not there. If the story "unfolds," it does so out of a luxuriant richness of descriptive detail, with great deliberateness and meditative lingering, so that the poem is less the narration of a story than the filling out of a pattern comprising juxtapositions and oppositions of characters, actions, and themes. For instance, after the Redcross Knight and Una are separated in Canto II, the adventures of one parallel the adventures of the other—Truth (Una) being without a temporal champion or institution of holiness (Redcross) and the potential church or militant temporal force being without Truth. Such contrasts and parallels are often separated by a considerable number of lines. The density and richness of Spenser's poetic method lies in its massive and extended cross references, which unfold a stock of ironies not evident in local passages alone.

The connection of parts can often be made only on the allegorical level. The definition of "Error," for instance, whom only a person of superhuman literal-mindedness could accept as a natural beast fittingly named, ultimately involves the definition of the entire pilgrimage of Truth and Holiness toward their final union, which constitutes the defeat of duplicity and false institutions. Thus if one of the major themes of Book I is the confusion of appearance and reality—a confusion that usually reflects on the knight's degree of spiritual awareness—the book is itself an "appearance" demanding an effort by the reader to unmask it. It is in this sense of the continual interplay of surface and emergent meaning that the often used term "dreamlike" applies to Spenser's poem. Identities tend to melt into one another before the distinctions between them are sharpened by the exposure of their dialectical opposition, as Duessa helps define Fidessa, and as Archimago, the arch image-magician, ultimately helps define the errant Una as the single truth. (It was perhaps in his blocking out of ironically related systems that Spenser offered Milton the most fruitful structural help for *Paradise Lost*.) Thus the narrative, like dream-narratives, contains elements of both irrationality and precision. If it were only irrational, we could dismiss it; if its surface were only precise, we could accept it literally. But the combination of the two requires that we search beyond the literal level for the symbolic that will impart meaning and coherence to the apparently irrational.

from THE FAERIE QUEENE

A Letter of the Authors

Expounding His Whole Intention in the Course of This Worke: Which for That It Giveth Great Light to the Reader, for the Better Understanding Is Hereunto Annexed

To the Right noble, and Valorous, Sir Walter Raleigh knight, Lo. Wardein of the Stanneryes, and her Majesties liefetenaunt of the County of Cornewayll

Sir knowing how doubtfully all Allegories may be construed, and this booke of mine, which I have entituled the *Faery Queene*, being a continued Allegory, or darke conceit, I have thought good aswell for avoyding of gealous opinions and misconstructions, as also for your better light in reading thereof, (being so by you commanded,) to discover unto you the general intention and meaning, which in the whole course thereof I have fashioned, without expressing of any particular purposes or by-accidents therein occasioned. The generall end therefore of all the booke is to fashion a gentleman or noble person in vertuous and gentle discipline: Which for that I conceived shoulde be most plausible and pleasing, being coloured with an historicall fiction, the which the most part of men delight to read, rather for variety of matter, then for profite of the ensample: I chose the historye of King Arthure, as most fitte for the excellency of his person, being made famous by many mens former workes, and also furthest from the daunger of envy, and suspition of present time. In which I have followed all the antique Poets historicall, first Homere, who in the Persons of Agamemnon and Ulysses hath ensampled a good governour and a vertuous man, the one in his *Ilias,* the other in his *Odysseis:* then Virgil, whose like intention was to doe in the person of Aeneas: after him Ariosto comprised them both in his Orlando: and lately Tasso dissevered them againe, and formed both parts in two persons, namely that part which they in Philosophy call Ethice, or vertues of a private man, coloured in his Rinaldo: The other named Politice in his Godfredo. By ensample of which excellente Poets, I labour to pourtraict in Arthure, before he was king, the image of a brave knight, perfected in the twelve private morall vertues, as Aristotle hath devised, the which is the purpose of these first twelve bookes: which if I finde to be well accepted, I may be perhaps encouraged, to frame the other part of polliticke vertues in his person, after that hee came to be king. To some I know this Methode will seeme displeasaunt, which had rather have good discipline delivered plainly in way of precepts, or sermoned at large, as they use, then thus clowdily enwrapped in Allegoricall devises. But such, me seeme, should be satisfide with the use of these dayes, seeing all things accounted by their showes, and nothing esteemed of, that is not delightfull and pleasing to commune sence. For this cause is Xenophon preferred before Plato, for that the one in the exquisite depth of his judgement, formed a Commune welth such as it should be,* but the other in the person of Cyrus and the Persians fashioned a government such as might best be: So much more profitable and gratious is doctrine by ensample, then by rule. So have I laboured to doe in the person of Arthure: whome I conceive after his long education by Timon, to whom he was by Merlin delivered to be brought up, so soone as he was borne of the Lady Igrayne, to have seene in a dream or vision the Faery Queen, with whose excellent beauty ravished, he awaking resolved to seeke her out, and so being by Merlin armed, and by Timon thoroughly instructed, he went to seeke her forth in Faerye land. In that Faery Queene I meane glory in my generall intention, but in my particular I conceive the most excellent and glorious person of our soveraine the Queene, and her kingdome in Faery land. And yet in some places els, I doe otherwise shadow her. For considering she beareth two persons, the one of a most royall Queene or Empresse, the other of a most vertuous and beautifull Lady, this latter part in some places I doe express in Belphoebe, fashioning her name according to your owne excellent conceipt of Cynthia, (Phoebe and Cynthia being both names of Diana.) So in the person of Prince Arthure I sette forth magnificence in particular, which vertue for that (according to Aristotle and the rest) it is the perfection of all the rest, and conteineth in it them all, therefore in the whole course I mention the deedes of Arthure applyable to that vertue, which I write of in that booke. But of the xii. other vertues, I make xii. other knights the patrones, for the more variety of the history. Of which these three bookes contayn three, The first of the knight of the Redcrosse, in whome I express Holynes: The seconde of Sir Guyon, in whome I sette forth Temperaunce: The third of Britomartis a Lady knight, in whome I picture Chastity. But because the beginning of the whole worke seemeth abrupte and as depending upon other antecedents, it needs that ye know the occasion of these three knights severall adventures. For the Methode of a Poet historical is not such, as of an Historiographer. For an His-

---

* Spenser refers to Plato's *Republic* and Xenophon's *Cyropaedia.*

toriographer discourseth of affayres orderly as they were donne, accounting as well the times as the actions, but a Poet thrusteth into the middest, even where it most concerneth him, and there recoursing to the thinges forepaste, and divining of thinges to come, maketh a pleasing Analysis of all. The beginning therefore of my history, if it were to be told by an Historiographer, should be the twelfth booke, which is the last, where I devise that the Faery Queene kept her Annuall feaste xii. dayes, uppon which xii. severall dayes, the occasions of the xii. severall adventures hapned, which being undertaken by xii. severall knights, are in these xii books severally handled and discoursed. The first was this. In the beginning of the feast, there presented him selfe a tall clownishe younge man, who falling before the Queen of Faeries desired a boone (as the manner then was) which during that feast she might not refuse: which was that hee might have the atchievement of any adventure, which during that feaste should happen, that being graunted, he rested him on the floore, unfitte through his rusticity for a better place. Soone after entred a faire Ladye in mourning weedes, riding on a white Asse, with a dwarfe behind her leading a warlike steed, that bore the Armes of a knight, and his speare in the dwarfes hand. Shee falling before the Queene of Faeries, complayned that her father and mother an ancient King and Queene, had bene by an huge dragon many years shut up in a brasen Castle, who thence suffred them not to yssew: and therefore besought the Faery Queene to assygne her some one of her knights to take on him that exployt. Presently that clownish person upstarting, desired that adventure: whereat the Queene much wondering, and the Lady much gainesaying, yet he earnestly importuned his desire. In the end the Lady told him that unlesse that armour which she brought, would serve him (that is the armour of a Christian man specified by Saint Paul v. Ephes.) that he could not succeed in that enterprise, which being forthwith put upon him with dewe furnitures thereunto, he seemed the goodliest man in al that company, and was well liked of the Lady. And eftesoones taking on him knighthood, and mounting on that straunge Courser, he went forth with her on that adventure: where beginneth the first booke, vz.

A gentle knight was pricking on the playne. &c.

The second day ther came in a Palmer bearing an Infant with bloody hands, whose Parents he complained to have bene slayn by an Enchaunteresse called Acrasia: and therfore craved of the Faery Queene, to appoint him some knight, to performe that adventure, which being assigned to Sir Guyon, he presently went forth with that same Palmer: which is the beginning of the second booke and the whole subject thereof. The third day there came in, a Groome who complained before the Faery Queene, that a vile Enchaunter called Busirane had in hand a most faire Lady called Amoretta, whom he kept in most grievous torment, because she would not yield him the pleasure of her body. Whereupon Sir Scudamour the lover of that Lady presently tooke on him that adventure. But being unable to performe it by reason of the hard Enchauntments, after long sorrow, in the end met with Britomartis, who succoured him, and reskewed his love.

But by occasion hereof, many other adventures are intermedled, but rather as Accidents, then intendments. As the love of Britomart, the overthrow of Marinell, the misery of Florimell, the vertuousnes of Belphoebe, the lasciviousnes of Hellenora, and many the like.

Thus much Sir, I have briefly overronne to direct your understanding to the wel-head of the History, that from thence gathering the whole intention of the conceit, ye may as in a handfull gripe al the discourse, which otherwise may happily seeme tedious and confused. So humbly craving the continuaunce of your honorable favour towards me, and th'eternall establishment of your happines, I humbly take leave.

23. January, 1589
Yours most humbly affectionate.
ED. SPENSER.

from BOOK I

1

formerly

      Lo I the man, whose Muse whilome° did maske,
        As time her taught, in lowly Shepheards weeds,
      Am now enforst a far unfitter taske,
        For trumpets sterne to chaunge mine Oaten reeds,
        And sing of Knights and Ladies gentle deeds;   5
      Whose prayses having slept in silence long,

appoints

      Me, all too meane, the sacred Muse areeds°
        To blazon broad emongst her learned throng:
      Fierce warres and faithful loves shall moralize my song.

2

      Helpe then, O holy Virgin chiefe of nine,   10
        Thy weaker Novice to performe thy will,
      Lay forth out of thine everlasting scryne
        The antique rolles, which there lye hidden still,
        Of Faerie knights and fairest Tanaquill,
      Whom that most noble Briton Prince so long   15
      Sought through the world, and suffered so much ill,
        That I must rue his undeservéd wrong:
      O helpe thou my weake wit, and sharpen my dull tong.

3

      And thou most dreaded impe of highest Jove,
        Faire Venus sonne, that with thy cruell dart   20

shoot

      At that good knight so cunningly didst rove,°
        That glorious fire it kindled in his hart,

ebony

      Lay now thy deadly Heben° bow apart,
        And with thy mother milde come to mine ayde:

Mars

      Come both, and with you bring triumphant Mart,°   25
        In loves and gentle jollities arrayd,
      After his murdrous spoiles and bloudy rage allayd.

---

2 *Shepheards weeds*: shepherds' attire, emblematic of the pastoral poet. Spenser had written *The Shepheardes Calendar* earlier. 4 *For trumpets...reeds*: i.e., to switch from pastoral poetry, whose emblem is the shepherd's pipe (made of "oaten reed"), to heroic poetry, whose emblem is the trumpet. 10 *chiefe of nine*: Clio, the Muse of history. 12 *scryne*: cabinet for papers. 14 *Tanaquill*: Gloriana (Queen Elizabeth). 15 *Briton Prince*: Prince Arthur. 19 *dreaded impe*: Cupid.

4

And with them eke, O Goddesse heavenly bright,
  Mirrour of grace and Majestie divine,
  Great Lady of the greatest Isle, whose light   30
  Like Phoebus lampe throughout the world doth shine,
  Shed thy faire beames into my feeble eyne,
lowly   And raise my thoughts too humble and too vile,°
  To thinke of that true glorious type of thine,
  The argument of mine afflicted stile: 35
The which to heare, vouchsafe, O dearest dred a-while.

Canto I

The Patron of true Holinesse,
  Foule Errour doth defeate:
Hypocrisie him to entrappe,
  Doth to his home entreate.

1

cantering   A gentle Knight was pricking° on the plaine,
  Ycladd in mightie armes and silver shielde,
  Wherein old dints of deepe wounds did remaine,
  The cruell markes of many a bloudy fielde;
  Yet armes till that time did he never wield: 5
  His angry steede did chide his foming bitt,
  As much disdayning to the curbe to yield:
manly   Full jolly° knight he seemd, and faire did sitt,
jousts As one for knightly giusts° and fierce encounters fitt.

2

But on his brest a bloudie Crosse he bore,   10
  The deare remembrance of his dying Lord,
  For whose sweete sake that glorious badge he wore,
  And dead as living ever him adored:
  Upon his shield the like was also scored,
  For soveraine hope, which in his helpe he had: 15
  Right faithfull true he was in deede and word,
serious   But of his cheere did seeme too solemne sad;°
dreaded Yet nothing did he dread, but ever was ydrad.°

3

bound   Upon a great adventure he was bond,°
  That greatest Gloriana to him gave,   20
  That greatest Glorious Queene of Faerie lond,
  To winne him worship, and her grace to have,
  Which of all earthly things he most did crave;
yearn   And ever as he rode, his hart did earne°
powers To prove his puissance° in battell brave   25
  Upon his foe, and his new force to learne;
Upon his foe, a Dragon horrible and stearne.

4

A lovely Ladie rode him faire beside,
  Upon a lowly Asse more white then snow,
  Yet she much whiter, but the same did hide   30

folded Under a vele, that wimpled° was full low,
  And over all a blacke stole she did throw,
  As one that inly mournd: so was she sad,
  And heavie sat upon her palfrey slow:
  Seeméd in heart some hidden care she had,   35
And by her in a line a milke white lambe she lad.

5

So pure an innocent, as that same lambe,
  She was in life and every vertuous lore,
  And by descent from Royall lynage came
  Of ancient Kings and Queenes, that had of yore   40
  Their scepters stretcht from East to Westerne shore,
  And all the world in their subjection held;
  Till that infernall feend with foule uprore
  Forwasted all their land, and them expeld:
Whom to avenge, she had this Knight from far compeld.   45

6

Behind her farre away a Dwarfe did lag,
  That lasie seemd in being ever last,
  Or wearied with bearing of her bag
  Of needments at his backe. Thus as they past,
  The day with cloudes was suddeine overcast,   50
  And angry Jove an hideous storme of raine
sweetheart (earth) Did poure into his Lemans° lap so fast,
man...cover That every wight° to shrowd° it did constrain,
also And this faire couple eke° to shroud themselves were fain.

7

Enforst to seeke some covert nigh at hand,   55
  A shadie grove not far away they spide,
  That promist ayde the tempest to withstand:
  Whose loftie trees yclad with sommers pride,
  Did spred so broad, that heavens light did hide,
penetrable Not perceable° with power of any starre: 60
  And all within were pathes and alleies wide,
  With footing worne, and leading inward farre:
Faire harbour that them seemes; so in they entred arre.

8

And foorth they passe, with pleasure forward led,
  Joying to heare the birdes sweete harmony,   65
  Which therein shrouded from the tempest dred,
  Seemd in their song to scorne the cruell sky.
  Much can they prayse the trees so straight and hy,
  The sayling Pine, the Cedar proud and tall,

The vine-prop Elme, the Poplar never dry,   70
   The builder Oake, sole king of forrests all,
The Aspine good for staves, the Cypresse funerall.

9

reward   The Laurell, meed° of mightie Conquerours
   And Poets sage, the Firre that weepeth still,
   The Willow worne of forlorne Paramours,   75
   The Eugh obedient to the benders will,
   The Birch for shaftes, the Sallow for the mill,
   The Mirrhe sweete bleeding in the bitter wound,
   The warlike Beech, the Ash for nothing ill,
   The fruitfull Olive, and the Platane round,   80
The carver Holme, the Maple seeldom inward sound.

10

Led with delight, they thus beguile the way,
   Untill the blustring storme is overblowne;
thinking   When weening° to returne, whence they did stray,
   They cannot finde that path, which first was showne, 85
   But wander too and fro in wayes unknowne,
   Furthest from end then, when they neerest weene,
   That makes them doubt, their wits be not their owne:
   So many pathes, so many turnings seene,
That which of them to take, in diverse doubt they been. 90

11

At last resolving forward still to fare,
   Till that some end they finde or in or out,
   That path they take, that beaten seemd most bare,
out of   And like to lead the labyrinth about;°
   Which when by tract they hunted had throughout,   95
   At length it brought them to a hollow cave,
   Amid the thickest woods. The Champion stout
forthwith   Eftsoones° dismounted from his courser brave,
And to the Dwarfe a while his needlesse spere he gave.

12

"Be well aware," quoth then that Ladie milde,   100
   "Least suddaine mischiefe ye too rash provoke:
   The danger hid, the place unknowne and wilde,
   Breedes dreadfull doubts: Oft fire is without smoke,
   And perill without show: therefore your stroke
   Sir knight with-hold, till further triall made."   105
   "Ah Ladie," said he, "shame were to revoke
   The forward footing for an hidden shade:
Vertue gives her selfe light, through darkenesse for to
   wade."

13

"Yea but," quoth she, "the perill of this place
know   I better wot° then you, though now too late   110

To wish you backe returne with foule disgrace,
Yet wisedome warnes, whilest foot is in the gate,
To stay the steppe, ere forcéd to retrate.
This is the wandring wood, this Errours den,
A monster vile, whom God and man does hate: 115
advise   Therefore I read° beware." "Fly fly," quoth then
The fearefull Dwarfe: "this is no place for living men."

14

But full of fire and greedy hardiment,
The youthfull knight could not for ought be staide,
But forth unto the darksome hole he went, 120
And lookéd in: his glistring armor made
A litle glooming light, much like a shade,
By which he saw the ugly monster plaine,
Halfe like a serpent horribly displaide,
But th' other halfe did womans shape retaine, 125
Most lothsom, filthie, foule, and full of vile disdaine.

15

And as she lay upon the durtie ground,
Her huge long taile her den all overspred,
folds   Yet was in knots and many boughtes° upwound,
Pointed with mortall sting. Of her there bred 130
A thousand yong ones, which she dayly fed,
Sucking upon her poisonous dugs, eachone
Of sundry shapes, yet all ill favoréd:
strange   Soone as that uncouth° light upon them shone,
Into her mouth they crept, and suddain all were gone. 135

16

Their dam upstart, out of her den effraide,
And rushéd forth, hurling her hideous taile
About her curséd head, whose folds displaid
entwining   Were stretcht now forth at length without entraile.°
She lookt about, and seeing one in mayle 140
Arméd to point, sought backe to turne againe;
evil   For light she hated as the deadly bale,°
Ay wont in desert darknesse to remaine,
Where plaine none might her see, nor she see any plaine.

17

Which when the valiant Elfe perceived, he lept 145
As Lyon fierce upon the flying pray,
cutting   And with his trenchand° blade her boldly kept
From turning backe, and forcéd her to stay:
Therewith enraged she loudly gan to bray,
And turning fierce, her speckled taile advaunst, 150
Threatning her angry sting, him to dismay:
upraised   Who nought aghast, his mightie hand enhaunst:°
The stroke down from her head unto her shoulder glaunst.

18

Much daunted with that dint, her sence was dazd,
   Yet kindling rage, her selfe she gathered round,   155
   And all attonce her beastly body raizd
   With doubled forces high above the ground:

then
   Tho° wrapping up her wrethéd sterne arownd,
   Lept fierce upon his shield, and her huge traine
   All suddenly about his body wound,   160
   That hand or foot to stirre he strove in vaine:
God helpe the man so wrapt in Errours endlesse traine.

19

His Lady sad to see his sore constraint,
   Cride out, "Now now Sir knight, shew what ye bee,
   Add faith unto your force, and be not faint: 165
   Strangle her, else she sure will strangle thee."
   That when he heard, in great perplexitie,
   His gall did grate for griefe and high disdaine,
   And knitting all his force got one hand free,
   Wherewith he grypt her gorge with so great paine,   170
That soone to loose her wicked bands did her constraine.

20

Therewith she spewd out of her filthy maw
   A floud of poyson horrible and blacke,
   Full of great lumpes of flesh and gobbets raw,
   Which stunck so vildly, that it forst him slacke   175
   His grasping hold, and from her turne him backe:
   Her vomit full of bookes and papers was,
   With loathly frogs and toades, which eyes did lacke,
   And creeping sought way in the weedy gras:

vomit
Her filthy parbreake° all the place defiléd has.   180

21

As when old father Nilus gins to swell
   With timely pride above the Aegyptian vale,
   His fattie waves do fertile slime outwell,
   And overflow each plaine and lowly dale:

subside
   But when his later spring gins to avale,°   185
   Huge heapes of mudd he leaves, wherein there breed
   Ten thousand kindes of creatures, partly male
   And partly female of his fruitfull seed;

see
Such ugly monstrous shapes elswhere may no man reed.°

22

The same so sore annoyéd has the knight,   190
   That welnigh chokéd with the deadly stinke,
   His forces faile, ne can no longer fight.
   Whose corage when the feend perceived to shrinke,
   She pouréd forth out of her hellish sinke
   Her fruitfull curséd spawne of serpents small,   195

Deforméd monsters, fowle, and blacke as inke,
Which swarming all about his legs did crall,
And him encombred sore, but could not hurt at all.

23

wane

As gentle Shepheard in sweete even-tide,
When ruddy Phoebus gins to welke° in west,   200
High on an hill, his flocke to vewen wide,
Markes which do byte their hasty supper best;
A cloud of combrous gnattes do him molest,
All striving to infixe their feeble stings,
That from their noyance he no where can rest,   205

rustic

But with his clownish° hands their tender wings
He brusheth oft, and oft doth mar their murmurings.

24

beset

Thus ill bestedd,° and fearfull more of shame,
Then of the certaine perill he stood in,
Halfe furious unto his foe he came,   210
Resolved in minde all suddenly to win,

cease

Or soone to lose, before he once would lin;°
And strooke at her with more then manly force,
That from her body full of filthie sin
He raft her hatefull head without remorse;   215
A streame of cole black bloud forth gushéd from her corse.

25

Her scattred brood, soone as their Parent deare
They saw so rudely falling to the ground,
Groning full deadly, all with troublous feare,
Gathred themselves about her body round,   220
Weening their wonted entrance to have found
At her wide mouth: but being there withstood
They flockéd all about her bleeding wound,
And suckéd up their dying mothers blood,
Making her death their life, and eke her hurt their good.   225

26

That detestable sight him much amazde,
To see th' unkindly Impes of heaven accurst,
Devoure their dam; on whom while so he gazd,
Having all satisfide their bloudy thurst,
Their bellies swolne he saw with fulnesse burst,   230
And bowels gushing forth: well worthy end
Of such as drunke her life, the which them nurst;
Now needeth him no lenger labour spend,
His foes have slaine themselves, with whom he should
    contend.

27

His Ladie seeing all, that chaunst, from farre   235
Approacht in hast to greet his victorie,

Christian armor

And said, "Faire knight, borne under happy starre,
  Who see your vanquisht foes before you lye;
  Well worthy be you of that Armorie,°
  Wherein ye have great glory wonne this day,   240
  And prooved your strength on a strong enimie,
  Your first adventure: many such I pray,
And henceforth ever wish, that like succeed it may."

28

Then mounted he upon his Steede againe,
  And with the Lady backward sought to wend;   245
  That path he kept, which beaten was most plaine,
  Ne ever would to any by-way bend,
  But still did follow one unto the end,
  The which at last out of the wood them brought.
  So forward on his way (with God to frend)   250
  He passéd forth, and new adventure sought;
Long way he travelléd, before he heard of ought.

29

clothes

At length they chaunst to meet upon the way
  An aged Sire, in long blacke weedes° yclad,
  His feete all bare, his beard all hoarie gray,   255
  And by his belt his booke he hanging had;
  Sober he seemde, and very sagely sad,
  And to the ground his eyes were lowly bent,
  Simple in shew, and voyde of malice bad,
  And all the way he prayéd, as he went,   260
And often knockt his brest, as one that did repent.

30

bowing
replied

simple
telling

meddle

He faire the knight saluted, louting° low,
  Who faire him quited,° as that courteous was:
  And after askéd him, if he did know
  Of straunge adventures, which abroad did pas.   265
  "Ah my deare Sonne," quoth he, "how should, alas,
  Silly° old man, that lives in hidden cell,
  Bidding° his beades all day for his trespas,
  Tydings of warre and worldly trouble tell?
With holy father sits not with such things to mell.°   270

31

"But if of daunger which hereby doth dwell,
  And homebred evill ye desire to heare,
  Of a straunge man I can you tidings tell,
  That wasteth all this countrey farre and neare."
  "Of such," said he, "I chiefly do inquere,   275
  And shall you well reward to shew the place,
  In which that wicked wight his dayes doth weare:
  For to all knighthood it is foule disgrace,
That such a cursed creature lives so long space."

32

"Far hence," quoth he, "in wastfull wildernesse   280
  His dwelling is, by which no living wight
  May ever passe, but thorough great distresse."
  "Now," sayd the Lady, "draweth toward night,

late   And well I wote, that of your later° fight
  Ye all forwearied be: for what so strong,   285
  But wanting rest will also want of might?
  The Sunne that measures heaven all day long,

rest At night doth baite° his steedes the Ocean waves emong.

33

"Then with the Sunne take Sir, your timely rest,
  And with new day new worke at once begin: 290
  Untroubled night they say gives counsell best."
  "Right well Sir knight ye have adviséd bin,"
  Quoth then that aged man; "the way to win
  Is wisely to advise: now day is spent;

lodging   Therefore with me ye may take up your In°   295
  For this same night." The knight was well content:
So with that godly father to his home they went.

34

A little lowly Hermitage it was,
  Downe in a dale, hard by a forests side,
  Far from resort of people, that did pas   300
apart   In travell to and froe: a little wyde°
built   There was an holy Chappell edifyde,°
  Wherein the Hermite dewly wont to say
  His holy things each morne and eventyde:
  Thereby a Christall streame did gently play,   305
Which from a sacred fountaine welléd forth alway.

35

Arrivéd there, the little house they fill,
  Ne looke for entertainement, where none was:
  Rest is their feast, and all things at their will;
  The noblest mind the best contentment has.   310
  With faire discourse the evening so they pas:
  For that old man of pleasing wordes had store,
  And well could file his tongue as smooth as glas;
  He told of Saintes and Popes, and evermore
He strowd an *Ave-Mary* after and before.   315

36

The drouping Night thus creepeth on them fast,
  And the sad humour loading their eye liddes,
  As messenger of Morpheus on them cast
  Sweet slombring deaw, the which to sleepe them biddes.
leads   Unto their lodgings then his guestes he riddes:°   320
  Where when all drownd in deadly sleepe he findes,

He to his study goes, and there amiddes
His Magick bookes and artes of sundry kindes,
He seekes out mighty charmes, to trouble sleepy mindes.

37

Then choosing out few wordes most horrible   325.
(Let none them read), thereof did verses frame,
With which and other spelles like terrible,
He bade awake blacke Plutoes griesly Dame,
And cursèd heaven, and spake reprochfull shame
Of highest God, the Lord of life and light;   330
A bold bad man, that dared to call by name
Great Gorgon, Prince of darknesse and dead night,
At which Cocytus quakes, and Styx is put to flight.

38

And forth he cald out of deepe darknesse dred
Legions of Sprights, the which like little flyes   335
Fluttring about his ever damnèd hed,
A-waite whereto their service he applyes,
frighten   To aide his friends, or fray° his enimies:
Of those he chose out two, the falsest twoo,
And fittest for to forge true-seeming lyes;   340
The one of them he gave a message too,
The other by him selfe staide other worke to doo.

39

dispersed   He making speedy way through spersèd° ayre,
And through the world of waters wide and deepe,
To Morpheus house doth hastily repaire.   345
Amid the bowels of the earth full steepe,
And low, where dawning day doth never peepe,
His dwelling is; there Tethys his wet bed
Doth ever wash, and Cynthia still doth steepe
In silver deaw his ever-drouping hed,   350
Whiles sad Night over him her mantle black doth spred.

40

Whose double gates he findeth lockèd fast,
The one faire framed of burnisht Yvory,
The other all with silver overcast;
And wakefull dogges before them farre do lye,   355
Watching to banish Care their enimy,
Who oft is wont to trouble gentle Sleepe.
By them the Sprite doth passe in quietly,
And unto Morpheus comes, whom drownèd deepe
notice   In drowsie fit he findes: of nothing he takes keepe.°   360

---

328 *Dame*: Proserpine. 333 *Cocytus...Styx*: rivers in hell. 348 *Tethys*: wife of Ocean.
349 *Cynthia*: goddess of the moon, also called Diana.

41

And more, to lulle him in his slumber soft,
   A trickling streame from high rocke tumbling downe
   And ever-drizling raine upon the loft,
   Mixt with a murmuring winde, much like the sowne

swoon
   Of swarming Bees, did cast him in a swowne:°   365
   No other noyse, nor peoples troublous cryes,

always
   As still° are wont t'annoy the walléd towne,
   Might there be heard: but carelesse Quiet lyes,
Wrapt in eternall silence farre from enemyes.

42

The messenger approching to him spake,   370
   But his wast wordes returnd to him in vaine:
   So sound he slept, that nought mought him awake.
   Then rudely he him thrust, and pusht with paine,
   Whereat he gan to stretch: but he againe
   Shooke him so hard, that forced him to speake.   375
   As one then in a dreame, whose dryer braine
   Is tost with troubled sights and fancies weake,
He mumbled soft, but would not all his silence breake.

43

The Sprite then gan more boldly him to wake,
   And threatned unto him the dreaded name   380
   Of Hecate: whereat he gan to quake,
   And lifting up his lumpish head, with blame
   Halfe angry askéd him, for what he came.
   "Hither," quoth he, "me Archimago sent,
   He that the stubborne Sprites can wisely tame,   385
   He bids thee to him send for his intent

senses
A fit false dreame, that can delude the sleepers sent."°

44

The God obayde, and calling forth straight way

delusive
   A diverse° dreame out of his prison darke,
   Delivered it to him, and downe did lay   390

anxieties
   His heavie head, devoide of carefull carke,°
   Whose sences all were straight benumbd and starke.
   He backe returning by the Yvorie dore,
   Remounted up as light as chearefull Larke,
   And on his litle winges the dreame he bore   395
In hast unto his Lord, where he him left afore.

45

Who all this while with charmes and hidden artes,
   Had made a Lady of that other Spright,
   And framed of liquid ayre her tender partes

---

376 *dryer braine*: the waking portions of his brain, associated with dryness as sleepiness is associated with excessive moisture. 381 *Hecate*: queen of Hades. 393 *Yvorie dore*: Delusive dreams enter through the ivory door, true ones through the gate of horn.

So lively, and so like in all mens sight,⠀⠀⠀⠀⠀⠀⠀⠀400
That weaker sence it could have ravisht quight
The maker selfe for all his wondrous witt,
Was nigh beguiléd with so goodly sight:
Her all in white he clad, and over it
Cast a blacke stole, most like to seeme for Una fit.⠀⠀405

46

Now when that ydle dreame was to him brought
Unto that Elfin knight he bad him fly,
Where he slept soundly void of evill thought
And with false shewes abuse his fantasy,
in the way⠀⠀⠀⠀In sort as° he him schooléd privily:⠀⠀⠀⠀⠀⠀410
And that new creature borne without her dew
Full of the makers guile, with usage sly
He taught to imitate that Lady trew,
Whose semblance she did carrie under feignéd hew.

47

Thus well instructed, to their worke they hast⠀⠀⠀⠀415
And comming where the knight in slomber lay
The one upon his hardy head him plast,
And made him dreame of loves and lustfull play
That nigh his manly hart did melt away,
Bathéd in wanton blis and wicked joy:⠀⠀⠀⠀⠀⠀⠀420
Then seeméd him his Lady by him lay,
complained...cupid⠀⠀And to him playnd,° how that false wingéd boy°
Her chast hart had subdewd, to learne Dame pleasures toy.

48

And she her selfe of beautie soveraigne Queene
Fair Venus seemde unto his bed to bring⠀⠀⠀⠀⠀⠀425
believe⠀⠀⠀⠀Her, whom he waking evermore did weene°
ever⠀⠀⠀⠀To be the chastest flowre, that ay° did spring
On earthly braunch, the daughter of a king,
lover⠀⠀⠀⠀Now a loose Leman° to vile service bound:
And eke the Graces seeméd all to sing,⠀⠀⠀⠀⠀⠀⠀430
Hymen iô Hymen, dauncing all around,
Whilst freshest Flora her with Yvie girlond crownd.

49

In this great passion of unwonted lust,
Or wonted feare of doing ought amis,
He started up, as seeming to mistrust⠀⠀⠀⠀⠀⠀⠀435
Some secret ill, or hidden foe of his:
Lo there before his face his Lady is,
Under blake stole hyding her bayted hooke,
And as halfe blushing offred him to kis,
With gentle blandishment and lovely looke,⠀⠀⠀⠀⠀440
Most like that virgin true, which for her knight him took.

---

431 *Hymen:* god of marriage.

50

<table>
<tr><td>manner</td><td>All cleane dismayd too see so uncouth sight,
  And halfe enragéd at her shamelesse guise,°
  He thought have slaine her in his fierce despight:
  But hasty heat tempring with sufferance wise,
  He stayde his hand, and gan himselfe advise
  To prove his sense, and tempt her faignéd truth.</td><td></td></tr>
<tr><td>fashion
then did...pity</td><td> Wringing her hands in wemens pitteous wise,°
  Tho can° she weepe, to stirre up gentle ruth,°
Both for her noble bloud, and for her tender youth.</td><td></td></tr>
</table>

445

450

51

And said, "Ah Sir, my liege Lord and my love,
  Shall I accuse the hidden cruell fate,
  And mightie causes wrought in heaven above,
subdue   Or the blind God, that doth me thus amate,°
  For hopéd love to winne me certaine hate?   455
  Yet thus perforce he bids me do, or die.
  Die is my dew: yet rew my wretched state
  You, whom my hard avenging destinie
Hath made judge of my life or death indifferently.

52

"Your owne deare sake forst me at first to leave   460
  My Fathers kingdome," There she stopt with teares;
  Her swollen hart her speach seemd to bereave,
  And then againe begun, "My weaker yeares
  Captived to fortune and frayle worldly feares,
  Fly to your faith for succour and sure ayde: 465
  Let me not dye in languor and long teares.
  "Why Dame," quoth he, "what hath ye thus dismayd?
What frayes ye, that were wont to comfort me affrayd?"

53

dire   "Love of your selfe," she said, "and deare° constraint
  Lets me not sleepe, but wast the wearie night   470
  In secret anguish and unpittied plaint,
  Whiles you in carelesse sleepe are drownéd quight."
  Her doubtfull words made that redoubted knight
  Suspect her truth: yet since no untruth he knew,
  Her fawning love with foule disdainefull spight   475
disgrace   He would not shend,° but said, "Deare dame I rew,
That for my sake unknowne such griefe unto you grew.

54

"Assure your selfe, it fell not all to ground;
  For all so deare as life is to my hart,
  I deeme your love, and hold me to you bound;   480
  Ne let vaine feares procure your needlesse smart,
  Where cause is none, but to your rest depart."

cease   Not all content, yet seemd she to appease°
                          Her mournefull plaintes, beguiléd of her art,
                          And fed with words, that could not chuse but please,   485
                       So slyding softly forth, she turnd as to her ease.

                                         55
                       Long after lay he musing at her mood,
                          Much grieved to thinke that gentle Dame so light,
                          For whose defence he was to shed his blood.
                          At last dull wearinesse of former fight   490
spirit   Having yrockt a sleepe his irkesome spright,°
                          That troublous dreame gan freshly tosse his braine,
                          With bowres, and beds, and Ladies deare delight:
                          But when he saw his labour all was vaine,
                       With that misforméd spright he backe returnd againe.   495

                                      CANTO II

                          The guilefull great Enchaunter parts
                             The Redcrosse Knight from Truth:
                          Into whose stead faire falshood steps,
                             And workes him wofull ruth.

                                          1
                       By this the Northerne wagoner had set
                          His sevenfold teme behind the stedfast starre,
                          That was in Ocean waves yet never wet,
                          But firme is fixt, and sendeth light from farre
                          To all, that in the wide deepe wandring arre.   5
the cock   And chearefull Chaunticlere° with his note shrill
                          Had warnéd once, that Phoebus fiery carre
                          In hast was climbing up the Easterne hill,
                       Full envious that night so long his roome did fill.

                                          2
                       When those accurséd messengers of hell,   10
                          That feigning dreame, and that faire-forgéd Spright
                          Came to their wicked maister, and gan tell
unsuccessful   Their bootelesse° paines, and ill succeeding night:
                          Who all in rage to see his skilfull might
                          Deluded so, gan threaten hellish paine   15
                          And sad Prosérpines wrath, them to affright.
                          But when he saw his threatning was but vaine,
                       He cast about, and searcht his balefull bookes againe.

                                          3
forthwith   Eftsoones° he tooke that miscreated faire,
                          And that false other Spright, on whom he spred   20
                          A seeming body of the subtile aire,

---

1–2 *By this...starre*: By this time the Big Dipper had set behind the North Star.

Like a young Squire, in loves and lusty-hed
His wanton dayes that ever loosely led,
Without regard of armes and dreaded fight:
Those two he tooke, and in a secret bed,   25
misleading   Covered with darknesse and misdeeming° night,
Them both together laid, to joy in vaine delight.

4

Forthwith he runnes with feignéd faithfull hast
Unto his guest, who after troublous sights
And dreames, gan now to take more sound repast,   30
Whom suddenly he wakes with fearefull frights,
As one aghast with feends or damnéd sprights,
And to him cals, "Rise rise unhappy Swaine,
That here wex old in sleepe, whiles wicked wights
Have knit themselves in Venus shamefull chaine;   35
Come see, where your false Lady doth her honour staine."

5

All in amaze he suddenly up start
With sword in hand, and with the old man went;
Who soone him brought into a secret part,
mingled   Where that false couple were full closely ment°   40
In wanton lust and lewd embracément:
Which when he saw, he burnt with gealous fire,
blinded   The eye of reason was with rage yblent,°
And would have slaine them in his furious ire,
But hardly was restreinéd of that aged sire.   45

6

Returning to his bed in torment great,
And bitter anguish of his guiltie sight,
He could not rest, but did his stout heart eat,
And wast his inward gall with deepe despight,
Yrkesome of life, and too long lingring night.   50
At last faire Hesperus in highest skie
Had spent his lampe, and brought forth dawning light
Then up he rose, and clad him hastily;
The Dwarfe him brought his steed: so both away do fly.

7

Now when the rosy-fingred Morning faire,   55
Weary of aged Tithones saffron bed,
Had spred her purple robe through deawy aire,
the sun   And the high hils Titan° discoveréd,
The royall virgin shooke off drowsy-hed,
And rising forth out of her baser bowre,   60
Lookt for her knight, who far away was fled,

---

51 *Hesperus*: the evening star. 56 *Tithones*: husband of Aurora, goddess of dawn.

situation

And for her Dwarfe, that wont to wait each houre;
Then gan she waile and weepe, to see that woefull stowre.°

8

And after him she rode with so much speede
  As her slow beast could make; but all in vaine: 65
For him so far had borne his light-foot steede,
Prickéd with wrath and fiery fierce disdaine,
That him to follow was but fruitlesse paine;
Yet she her weary limbes would never rest,
But every hill and dale, each wood and plaine   70
Did search, sore grievéd in her gentle brest,
He so ungently left her, whom she lovéd best.

9

But subtill Archimago, when his guests
  He saw divided into double parts.
  And Una wandring in woods and forrests,   75
Th' end of his drift, he praisd his divelish arts
That had such might over true meaning harts;
Yet rests not so, but other meanes doth make,
How he may worke unto her further smarts:
For her he hated as the hissing snake,   80
And in her many troubles did most pleasure take.

10

He then devisde himselfe how to disguise;
  For by his mightie science he could take
  As many formes and shapes in seeming wise,
As ever Proteus to himselfe could make: 85
Sometime a fowle, sometime a fish in lake,
Now like a foxe, now like a dragon fell,
That of himselfe he oft for feare would quake,
And oft would flie away. O who can tell
The hidden power of herbes, and might of Magicke spell?   90

11

But now seemde best, the person to put on
  Of that good knight, his late beguiléd guest:
  In mighty armes he was yclad anon,
And silver shield: upon his coward brest
A bloudy crosse, and on his craven crest   95
A bounch of haires discolourd diversly:

manly

Full jolly° knight he seemde, and well addrest,
And when he sate upon his courser free,
Saint George himself ye would have deeméd him to be.

12

But he the knight, whose semblaunt he did beare,   100
  The true Saint George was wandred far away,

---

76 *end of his drift*: object of his design.

Still flying from his thoughts and gealous feare;
Will was his guide, and griefe led him astray.
At last him chaunst to meete upon the way

Saracen   A faithlesse Sarazin° all armed to point,   105
In whose great shield was writ with letters gay

"without faith"   Sans foy:° full large of limbe and every joint
He was, and caréd not for God or man a point.

13

He had a faire companion of his way,
A goodly Lady clad in scarlot red,   110

ornamented . . . value Purfled° with gold and pearle of rich assay,°
And like a Persian mitre on her hed

brooches   She wore, with crownes and owches° garnishéd,
The which her lavish lovers to her gave;
Her wanton palfrey all was overspred   115
With tinsell trappings, woven like a wave,
Whose bridle rung with golden bels and bosses brave.

14

With faire disport and courting dalliaunce
She intertainde her lover all the way:
But when she saw the knight his speare advaunce,   120
She soone left off her mirth and wanton play,
And bad her knight addresse him to the fray:

pranced   His foe was nigh at hand. He prickt° with pride
And hope to winne his Ladies heart that day,
Forth spurréd fast: adowne his coursers side   125
The red bloud trickling staind the way, as he did ride.

15

The knight of the Redcrosse when him he spide,
Spurring so hote with rage dispiteous,
Gan fairely couch his speare, and towards ride:

fierce   Soone meete they both, both fell° and furious,   130
That daunted with their forces hideous,
Their steeds do stagger, and amazéd stand,
And eke themselves too rudely rigorous,
Astonied with the stroke of their owne hand,
Do backe rebut, and each to other yeeldeth land.   135

16

As when two rams stird with ambitious pride,
Fight for the rule of the rich fleecéd flocke,
Their hornéd fronts so fierce on either side
Do meete, that with the terrour of the shocke

stone   Astonied both, stand sencelesse as a blocke,°   140
Forgetfull of the hanging victory:
So stood these twaine, unmovéd as a rocke,
Both staring fierce, and holding idely
The broken reliques of their former cruelty.

17

The Sarazin sore daunted with the buffe   145
   Snatcheth his sword, and fiercely to him flies;
requites   Who well it wards, and quyteth° cuff with cuff:
   Each others equall puissaunce envies,
   And through their iron sides with cruell spies
   Does seeke to perce: repining courage yields   150
   No foote to toe. The flashing fier flies
   As from a forge out of their burning shields,
And streames of purple bloud new dies the verdant fields.

18

"Curse on that Crosse," quoth then the Sarazin,
stroke   "That keepes thy body from the bitter fit;°   155
   Dead long ygoe I wote thou haddest bin,
   Had not that charme from thee forwarnéd it:
   But yet I warne thee now assuréd sitt,
   And hide thy head." Therewith upon his crest
   With rigour so outrageous he smitt,   160
   That a large share it hewd out of the rest,
And glauncing downe his shield, from blame him fairely
delivered   blest.°

19

Who thereat wondrous wroth, the sleeping spark
   Of native vertue gan eftsoones revive,
   And at his haughtie helmet making mark,   165
   So hugely stroke, that it the steele did rive,
   And cleft his head. He tumbling downe alive,
   With bloudy mouth his mother earth did kis,
   Greeting his grave: his grudging ghost did strive
   With the fraile flesh; at last it flitted is,   170
Whither the soules do fly of men, that live amis.

20

The Lady when she saw her champion fall,
   Like the old ruines of a broken towre,
   Staid not to waile his woefull funerall,
   But from him fled away with all her powre;   175
scurry   Who after her as hastily gan scowre,°
   Bidding the Dwarfe with him to bring away
   The Sarazins shield, signe of the conqueroure.
   Her soone he overtooke, and bad to stay,
For present cause was none of dread her to dismay.   180

21

She turning backe with ruefull countenaunce,
   Cride, "Mercy mercy Sir vouchsafe to show
innocent   On silly° Dame, subject to hard mischaunce,
   And to your mighty will." Her humblesse low

In so ritch weedes and seeming glorious show,   185
Did much emmove his stout heroicke heart,
And said, "Deare dame, your suddein overthrow
Much rueth me; but now put feare apart,
And tell, both who ye be, and who that tooke your part."

22

Melting in teares, then gan she thus lament;   190
"The wretched woman, whom unhappy howre
Hath now made thrall to your commandément,
Before that angry heavens list to lowre,
And fortune false betraide me to your powre
Was (O what now availeth that I was!)   195
Borne the sole daughter of an Emperour,
He that the wide West under his rule has,
And high hath set his throne, where Tiberis doth pas.

23

"He in the first flowre of my freshest age,
heir   Betrothéd me unto the onely haire°   200
Of a most mighty kind, most rich and sage;
Was never Prince so faithfull and so faire,
Was never Prince so meeke and debonaire;
But ere my hopéd day of spousall shone,
My dearest Lord fell from high honours staire,   205
foes   Into the hands of his accursed fone,°
And cruelly was slaine, that shall I ever mone.

24

"His blessed body spoild of lively breath,
Was afterward, I know not how, convaid
And fro me hid: of whose most innocent death   210
When tidings came to me unhappy maid,
O how great sorrow my šad soule assaid.
Then forth I went his woefull corse to find,
And many yeares throughout the world I straid,
A virgin widow, whose deepe wounded mind   215
With love, long time did languish as the striken hind.

25

"At last it chauncéd this proud Sarazin
To meete me wandring, who perforce me led
With him away, but yet could never win
The Fort, that Ladies hold in soveraigne dread.   220
There lies he now with foule dishonour dead,
Who whiles he livde, was calléd proud Sans foy,
The eldest of three brethren, all three bred
Of one bad sire, whose youngest is Sans joy,
"without law"   And twixt them both was borne the bloudy bold Sans loy.°   225

---

198 *Tiberis*: Tiber River, in Rome.

26

"In this sad plight, friendlesse, unfortunate,

   Now miserable I Fidessa° dwell,
   Craving of you in pitty of my state,
   To do none ill, if please ye not do well."
   He in great passion all this while did dwell,   230
   More busying his quicke eyes, her face to view,
   Then his dull eares, to heare what she did tell;
   And said, "Faire Lady hart of flint would rew
The underservéd woes and sorrowes, which ye shew.

27

"Henceforth in safe assuraunce may ye rest,   235
   Having both found a new friend you to aid,
   And lost an old foe, that did you molest:
   Better new friend then an old foe is said."
   With chaunge of cheare the seeming simple maid
   Let fall her eyen, as shamefast to the earth,   240
   And yeelding soft, in that she nought gain-said,
   So forth they rode, he feining seemely merth,
And she coy lookes: so dainty they say maketh derth.

28

Long time they thus together traveiléd,
   Till weary of their way, they came at last,   245
   Where grew two goodly trees, that faire did spred
   Their armes abroad, with gray mosse overcast,
   And their greene leaves trembling with every blast,
   Made a calme shadow far in compasse round:
   The fearefull Shepheard often there aghast   250
   Under them never sat, ne wont there sound
His mery oaten pipe, but shund th' unlucky ground.

29

But this good knight soone as he them can spie,
   For the coole shade him thither hastly got:
   For golden Phoebus now ymounted hie,   255
   From fiery wheeles of his faire chariot
   Hurléd his beame so scorching cruell hot,
   That living creature mote it not abide;
   And his new Lady it enduréd not.
   There they alight, in hope themselves to hide   260
From the fierce heat, and rest their weary limbs a tide.

30

Faire seemely pleasaunce each to other makes,
   With goodly purposes there as they sit:
   And in his falséd fancy he her takes
   To be the fairest wight, that livéd yit;   265
   Which to expresse, he bends his gentle wit,

And thinking of those braunches greene to frame
A girlond for her dainty forehead fit,
He pluckt a bough; out of whose rift there came
Small drops of gory bloud, that trickled downe the same.   270

31

Therewith a piteous yelling voyce was heard,
  Crying, "O spare with guilty hands to teare
confined   My tender sides in this rough rynd embard,°
  But fly, ah fly far hence away, for feare
  Least to you hap, that happened to me heare,   275
  And to this wretched Lady, my deare love,
  O too deare love, love bought with death too deare."
raise   Astond he stood, and up his haire did hove°
And with that suddein horror could no member move.

32

At last whenas the dreadfull passion   280
  Was overpast, and manhood well awake,
  Yet musing at the straunge occasion,
  And doubting much his sence, he thus bespake;
  "What voyce of damnéd Ghost from Limbo lake,
  Or guilefule spright wandring in empty aire,   285
  Both which fraile men do oftentimes mistake,
fearful   Sends to my doubtfull° eares these speaches rare,
And ruefull plaints, me bidding guiltlesse bloud to spare?"

33

Then groning deepe, "Nor damned Ghost," quoth he,
  "Nor guilefull sprite to thee these wordes doth speake,   290
"Doubt"   But once a man Fradubio,° now a tree,
  Wretched man, wretched tree; whose nature weake,
  A cruell witch her curséd will to wreake,
  Hath thus transformed, and plast in open plaines,
the North Wind   Where Boreas° doth blow full bitter bleake,   295
  And scorching Sunne does dry my secret vaines:
For though a tree I seeme, yet cold and heat me paines."

34

"Say on Fradubio then, or man, or tree,"
  Quoth then the knight, "by whose mischievous arts
  Art thou misshapéd thus, as now I see?   300
  He oft finds med'cine, who his griefe imparts;
  But double griefs afflict concealing harts,
  As raging flames who striveth to suppresse."
  "The author then," said he, "of all my smarts,
  Is one Duessa a false sorceresse,   305
That many errant knights hath brought to wretchednesse.

---

284 *Limbo*: region bordering hell where lost spirits reside.

35

"In prime of youthly yeares, when corage hot
The fire of love and joy of chevalree
First kindled in my brest, it was my lot
To love this gentle Lady, whom ye see,   310
Now not a Lady, but a seeming tree;
With whom as once I rode accompanyde,
Me chauncéd of a knight encountred bee,
That had a like faire Lady by his syde,
Like a faire Lady, but did fowle Duessa hyde.   315

36

proclaim   "Whose forgéd beauty he did take in hand,°
All other Dames to have exceeded farre;
I in defence of mine did likewise stand,
Mine, that did then shine as the Morning starre:
So both to battell fierce arraungéd arre,   320
In which his harder fortune was to fall
hazard   Under my speare: such is the dye° of warre:
prize of war   His Lady left as a prise martiall,°
Did yield her comely person, to be at my call.

37

"So doubly loved of Ladies unlike faire,   325
Th' one seeming such, the other such indeede,
One day in doubt I cast for to compare,
which one   Whether° in beauties glorie did exceede;
A Rosy girlond was the victors meede:
Both seemde to win, and both seemde won to bee,   330
So hard the discord was to be agreede.
Fraelissa was as faire, as faire mote bee,
And ever false Duessa seemde as faire as shee.

38

"The wicked witch now seeing all this while
The doubtfull ballaunce equally to sway,   335
What not by right, she cast to win by guile,
And by her hellish science raised streight way
A foggy mist, that overcast the day,
And a dull blast, that breathing on her face,
Dimmed her former beauties shining ray,   340
And with foule ugly forme did her disgrace:
Then was she faire alone, when none was faire in place.

39

"Then cride she out, 'Fye, fye, deforméd wight,
Whose borrowed beautie now appeareth plaine
To have before bewitchéd all mens sight;   345
O leave her soone, or let her soone be slaine.'
Her lothly visage viewing with disdaine,
Eftsoones I thought her such, as she me told,

And would have kild her; but with faignéd paine,
The false witch did my wrathfull hand withhold;   350
treelike form   So left her, where she now is turnd to trëen mould.°

40

"Thens forth I tooke Duessa for my Dame,
ignorantly   And in the witch unweeting° joyd long time,
knew   Ne ever wist°, but that she was the same,
Till on a day (that day is every Prime,   355
When Witches wont do penance for their crime)
I chaunst to see her in her proper hew,
Bathing her selfe in origane and thyme:
A filthy foule old woman I did vew,
That ever to have toucht her, I did deadly rew.   360

41

"Her neather partes misshapen, monstruous,
Were hidd in water, that I could not see,
But they did seeme more foule and hideous,
Then womans shape man would beleeve to bee.
Thens forth from her most beastly companie   365
I gan refraine, in minde to slip away,
Soone as appeard safe opportunitie:
For danger great, if not assured decay
I saw before mines eyes, if I were knowne to stray.

42

"The divelish hag by chaunges of my cheare   370
Perceived my thought, and drownd in sleepie night,
With wicked herbes and ointments did besmeare
My bodie all, through charmes and magicke might,
That all my senses were bereavéd quight:
Then brought she me into this desert waste,   375
pitched   And by my wretched lovers side me pight,°
Where now enclosed in wooden wals full faste,
Banisht from living wights, our wearie dayes we waste."

43

"But how long time," said then the Elfin knight,
"Are you in this misforméd house to dwell?"   380
"We may not chaunge," quoth he, "this evil plight,
Till we be bathéd in a living well;
That is the terme prescribéd by the spell."
"O how," said he, "mote I that well out find,
well-being   That may restore you to your wonted well?"°   385
"Time and sufiséd fates to former kynd
Shall us restore, none else from hence may us unbynd."

44

called   The false Duessa, now Fidessa hight,°
Heard how in vaine Fradubio did lament,

355 *Prime*: when the new moon first appears.

And knew well all was true. But the good knight   390
Full of sad feare and ghastly dreriment,
When all this speech the living tree had spent,
The bleeding bough did thrust into the ground,
That from the bloud he might be innocent,
And with fresh clay did close the wooden wound: 395
Then turning to his Lady, dead with feare her found.

45

Her seeming dead he found with feignéd feare,
As all unweeting of that well she knew,
And paynd himself with busie care to reare
Her out of carelesse swowne. Her eylids blew   400
And dimméd sight with pale and deadly hew
At last she up gan lift: with trembling cheare
Her up he tooke, too simple and too trew,
And oft her kist. At length all passéd feare,
He set her on her steede, and forward forth did beare.   405

[In Cantos III–X, the adventures of the Redcrosse Knight
and Una, who have been separated by the crafty Archimago,
continue. Taken by "Fidessa" (actually Duessa) to the House
of Pride, the Redcrosse Knight fights and conquers Sans joy
(Melancholy), but is captured by Orgoglio (Pride). Una,
meanwhile, encounters the perfect knight, Prince Arthur, who
is in quest of Gloriana, and persuades him to help the Redcrosse Knight escape from Orgoglio. Prince Arthur kills
Orgoglio and exposes "Fidessa" as actually Duessa, an ugly,
misshapen creature. Reunited, the Redcrosse Knight and Una
continue on their journey, only to have the knight yield to
Despair and nearly commit suicide. Una rescues him and leads
him to the House of Holiness, where he overcomes his weak-
nesses (primarily lust, pride, and despair) and takes the
sacraments, after which he is granted a vision of heaven and
the assurance that he will become Saint George, patron saint
of England. First, however, he must encounter the "old
Dragon," Satan. Their three-day battle is described in Canto
XI.]

Canto XI

The knight with that old Dragon fights
  Two days incessantly:
The third him overthrowes, and gayns
  Most glorious victory.

1

High time now gan it wex for Una fayre
  To thinke of those her captive Parents deare,
And their forwasted kingdom to repayre:
Whereto whenas they now approched neare,
With hartie wordes her knight she gan to cheare,   5
And in her modest maner thus bespake:

"Deare knight, as deare as ever knight was deare,
That all these sorrowes suffer for my sake,
High heven behold the tedious toyle ye for me take!

2

"Now are we come unto my native soyle, 10
And to the place where all our perilles dwell;
Here haunts that feend, and does his dayly spoyle;
Therefore, henceforth, bee at your keeping well,
And ever ready for your foeman fell:
The sparke of noble corage now awake, 15
And strive your excellent selfe to excell:
That shall ye evermore renowmed make
Above all knights on earth, that batteill undertake."

3

And pointing forth, "Lo! yonder is," (said she)
"The brasen towre, in which my parents deare 20
For dread of that huge feend emprisond be;
Whom I from far see on the walles appeare,
Whose sight my feeble soule doth greatly cheare:
And on the top of all I do espye
The watchman wayting tydings glad to heare; 25
That, (O my Parents!) might I happily
Unto you bring, to ease you of your misery!"

4

With that they heard a roaring hideous sownd,
That all the ayre with terror filled wyde,
almost And seemd uneath° to shake the stedfast ground. 30
Eftsoones that dreadful Dragon they espide,
Where stretcht he lay upon the sunny side
Of a great hill, himselfe like a great hill.
But all so soone, as he from far descride
Those glistring armes, that heaven with light did fill, 35
unto He roused himselfe full blith, and hastned them untill.°

5

go apart Then bad the knight his Lady yede aloofe,°
And to an hill her selfe with draw aside,
trial From whence she might behold that battailles proof°
And eke be safe from daunger far descryde: 40
She him obayd, and turned a little wyde.
Now O thou sacred Muse, most learned Dame,
Fair ympe of *Phœbus,* and his aged bride,
The Nourse of time, and everlasting fame,
That warlike hands ennoblest with immortall name; 45

---

42 *Muse*: Clio, Muse of history. 43 *bride*: Mnemosyne, or Memory.

6

O gently come into my feeble brest,
    Come gently, but not with that mighty rage,
    Wherewith the martiall troupes thou doest infest,
    And harts of great Heroës doest enrage,
    That nought their kindled courage may aswage,   50
    Soone as thy dreadfull trompe begins to sownd;
    The God of warre with his fiers equipage
    Thou doest awake, sleepe never he so sownd,
And scared nations doest with horrour sterne astownd.

7

musical strain   Faire Goddess lay that furious fit° aside,   55
    Till I of warres and bloudy *Mars* do sing,
    And Briton fields with Sarazin bloud bedyde,
    Twixt that great faery Queene and Paynim king,
    That with their horrour heaven and earth did ring,
    A worke of labour long, and endlesse prayse: 60
    But now a while let downe that haughtie string,
    And to my tunes thy second tenor rayse,
That I this man of God his godly armes may blaze.

8

By this the dreadfull Beast drew night to hand,
    Halfe flying, and halfe footing in his hast,   65
    That with his largenesse measured much land,
    And made wide shadow under his huge wast;
    As mountaine doth the valley overcast.
    Approching nigh, he reared high afore
    His body monstrous, horrible, and vast,   70
    Which to increase his wondrous greatnesse more,
Was swolne with wrath, and poyson, and with bloudy gore.

9

And over all with brasen scales was armd,
close-laid   Like plated cote of steele, so couched neare°
body   That nought mote perce; ne might his corse° bee harmd   75
    With dint of swerd, nor push of pointed speare:
    Which as an Eagle, seeing pray appeare,
shaped   His aery plumes doth rouze, full rudely dight;°
    So shaked he, that horror was to heare:
    For as the clashing of an Armor bright,   80
Such noyse his rouzed scales did send unto the knight.

10

His flaggy winges, when forth he did display,
    Were like two sayles, in which the hollow wynd
    Is gathered full, and worketh speedy way:

---

52 *God of warre*: Mars. 56–9 *Till I...did ring*: Refers to a future episode in *The Faerie Queene* that never got written.

feathers   And eke the pennes,° that did his pineons bynd,   85
    Were like mayne-yardes with flying canvas lynd;
    With which whenas him list the ayre to beat,
    And there by force unwonted passage fynd,
    The cloudes before him fledd for terror great,
And all the hevens stood still amazed with his threat.   90

11

His huge long tayle, wownd up in hundred foldes,
    Does overspred his long bras-scaly back,
coils   Whose wreathed boughtes° when ever he unfoldes,
    And thick entangled knots adown does slack,
    Bespotted as with shieldes of red and blacke,   95
    It sweepeth all the land behind him farre,
    And of three furlongs does but litle lacke;
    And at the point two stinges in fixed arre,
Both deadly sharp, that sharpest steele exceeden farre.

12

But stinges and sharpest steele did far exceed   100
    The sharpnesse of his cruel rending clawes:
    Dead was it sure, as sure as death in deed,
    What ever thing does touch his ravenous pawes,
    Or what within his reach he ever drawes.
    But his most hideous head my tongue to tell   105
    Does tremble; for his deepe devouring jawes
    Wyde gaped, like the griesly mouth of hell,
prey   Through which into his darke abysse all ravin° fell.

13

And, that more wondrous was, in either jaw
    Threeranckes of yron teeth enraunged were,   110
    In which yett trickling blood, and gobbets raw,
    Of late devoured bodies did appeare,
    That sight thereof bredd cold congealed feare;
    Which to increase, and all atonce to kill,
    A cloud of smoothering smoke, and sulphure seare,   115
    Out of his stinking gorge forth steemed still,
That all the ayre about with smoke and stench did fill.

14

His blazing eyes, like two bright shining shieldes,
    Did burne with wrath, and sparkled living fyre:
    As two broad Beacons, sett in open fieldes,   120
    Send forth their flames far off to every shyre,
    And warning give that enimies conspyre
    With fire and sword the region to invade:
    So flam'd his eyne with rage and rancorous yre;
    But far within, as in a hollow glade,   125
Those glaring lampes were sett that made a dreadfull shade.

15

So dreadfully he towardes him did pas,
   Forelifting up a-loft his speckled brest,
   And often bounding on the brused gras,
   As for great joyance of his newcome guest.   130
   Eftsoones he gan advance his haughty crest,
chafed   As chauffed° Bore his bristles doth upreare;
   And shoke his scales to battaile ready drest,
   That made the Redcrosse knight nigh quake for feare,
As bidding bold defyaunce to his foeman neare.   135

16

The knight gan fayrely couch his steady speare,
   And fiersely ran at him with rigorous might:
   The pointed steele, arriving rudely theare,
   His harder hyde would nether perce nor bight,
   But, glauncing by, foorth passed forward right.   140
jolted   Yet sore amoved° with so puissaunt push,
   The wrathfull beast about him turned light,
   And him so rudely, passing by, did brush
With his long tayle, that horse and man to ground did rush.

17

Both horse and man up lightly rose againe,   145
   And fresh encounter towardes him addrest;
   But th' ydle stroke yet backe recoyld in vaine,
   And found no place his deadly point to rest.
   Exceeding rage enflamed the furious Beast,
defiance   To be avenged of so great despight;°   150
   For never felt his imperceable brest
   So wondrous force from hand of living wight;
Yet had he prov'd the powre of many a puissant knight.

18

Then, with his waving wings displayed wyde,
   Himself up high he lifted from the ground,   155
   And with strong flight did forcibly divyde
   The yielding ayre, which nigh too feeble found
   Her flitting parts, and element unsound,
   To beare so great a weight: he, cutting way
   With his broad sayles, about him soared round;   160
diving   At last, low stouping° with unweldy sway,
Snatcht up both horse and man, to beare them quite away.

19

lying below   Long he them bore above the subject° plaine,
made of yew   So far as Ewghen° bow a shaft may send,
   Till struggling strong did him at last constraine   165
   To let them downe before his fightes end:
wild   As hagard° hauke, presuming to contend
fit   With hardie fowle, above his hable° might,

His wearie pounces all in vaine doth spend,
    To trusse the pray too heavie for his flight;   170
Which comming downe to ground, does free it selfe by fight.

20

dispossessed   He so disseized° of his gryping grosse,
piercing   The knight his thrillant° speare againe assayd
    In his bras-plated body to embosse,
    And three mens strength unto the stroke he layd;   175
    Wherewith the stiffe beame quaked, as affrayd,
    And glauncing from his scaly necke, did glyde
    Close under his left wing, then broad displayd.
    The percing steele there wrought a wound full wyde,
That with the uncouth smart the Monster lowdly cryde.   180

21

He cryde, as raging seas are wont to rore,
    When wintry storme his wrathfull wreck does threat,
    The rolling billowes beat the ragged shore,
    As they the earth would shoulder from her seat,
    And greedie gulfe does gape, as he would eat   185
    His neighbour element in his revenge:
    Then gin the blustring breathren boldly threat,
    To move the world from off his stedfast henge,
And boystrous battell make, each other to avenge.

22

The steely head stuck fast still in his flesh,   190
    Till with his cruell clawes he snatcht the wood,
    And quite a sunder broke. Forth flowed fresh
    A gushing river of blacke gory blood,
    That drowned all the land whereon he stood;
    The streame thereof would drive a water-mill: 195
    Trebly augmented was his furious mood
    With bitter sence of his deepe rooted ill,
That flames of fire he threw forth from his large nosethril.

23

His hideous tayle then hurled he about,
    And therewith all enwrapt the nimble thyes   200
    Of his froth-fomy steed, whose courage stout
    Striving to loose the knott that fast him tyes,
entangles   Himselfe in streighter bandes too rash implyes,°
    That to the ground he is perforce constraynd
    To throw his ryder; who can quickly ryse   205
defiled   From off the earth, with durty blood distaynd,
For that reprochfull fall right fowly he disdaynd;

24

And fercely tooke his trenchand blade in hand,
    With which he stroke so furious and so fell,

That nothing seemd the puissaunce could withstand: 210
   Upon his crest the hardned yron fell,
   But his more hardned crest was armd so well,
   That deeper dint therein it would not make;
   Yet so extremely did the buffe him quell,
   That from thenceforth he shund the like to take,   215
But when he saw them come he did them still forsake.

25

The knight was wroth to see his stroke beguyld,
   And smot againe with more outrageous might;
   But backe againe the sparcling steele recoyld,
   And left not any marke where it did light,   220
struck   As if in Adamant rocke it had beene pight.°
   The beast, impatient of his smarting wound
   And of so fierce and forcible despight,
mount   Thought with his winges to stye° above the ground;
But his late wounded wing unserviceable found.   225

26

Then full of griefe and anguish vehement,
   He lowdly brayd, that like was never heard;
   And from his wide devouring oven sent
   A flake of fire, that flashing in his beard
   Him all amazd, and almost made afeard: 230
singed   The scorching flame sore swinged° all his face,
   And through his armour all his body seard,
plight   That he could not endure so cruell cace,°
But thought his armes to leave, and helmet to unlace.

27

Hercules Not that great Champion° of the antique world,   235
   Whom famous Poetes verse so much doth vaunt,
   And hath for twelve huge labours high extold,
   So many furies and sharpe fits did haunt,
   When him the poysoned garment did enchaunt,
   When Centaures blood and bloody verses charmd;   240
   As did this knight twelve thousand dolours daunt,
   Whom fyrie steele now burnt, that erst him armd;
That erst him goodly armd, now most of all him harmd.

28

burnt   Faynt, wearie, sore, emboyled, grieved, brent,°
   With heat, toyle, wounds, armes, smart, and inward fire,   245
   That never man such mischiefes did torment:
   Death better were; death did he oft desire
   But death will never come when needes require.
   Whom so dismayd when that his foe beheld,
   He cast to suffer him no more respire,   250
tail   But gan his sturdy sterne° about to weld,
And him so strongly stroke, that to the ground him feld.

29

It fortuned, (as fayre it then befell)
  Behynd his backe, unweeting, where he stood,
  Of auncient time there was a springing well,   255
  From which fast trickled forth a silver flood,
  Full of great vertues, and for med'cine good:
  Whylome, before that cursed Dragon got
  That happy land, and all with innocent blood
was called Defyld those sacred waves, it rightly hot°   260
The well of life, ne yet his vertues had forgot:

30

For unto life the dead it could restore,
  And guilt of sinfull crimes cleane wash away;
  Those that with sicknesse were infected sore
  It could recure; and aged long decay   265
  Renew, as one were borne that very day.
  Both Silo this, and Jordan, did excell,
  And th' English Bath, and eke the German Spau:
  Ne can Cephise, nor Hebrus, match this well:
Into the same the knight back overthrowen fell.   270

31

Now gan the golden Phœbus for to steepe
  His fierie face in billowes of the west,
  And his faint steedes watred in Ocean deepe,
daily Whiles from their journall° labours they did rest;
cast When that infernall Monster, having kest°   275
  His wearie foe into that living well,
  Gan high advaunce his broad discoloured brest
  Above his wonted pitch, with countenance fell,
And clapt his yron wings as victor he did dwell.

32

Which when his pensive Lady saw from farre,   280
  Great woe and sorrow did her soule assay,
thinking As weening° that the sad end of the warre;
  And gan to highest God entirely pray
  That feared chaunce from her to turne away:
  With folded hands, and knees full lowly bent,   285
  All night shee watcht, ne once adowne would lay
  Her dainty limbs in her sad dreriment,
But praying still did wake, and waking did lament.

33

The morrow next gan earely to appeare,
  That Titan rose to runne his daily race;   290
  But earely, ere the morrow next gan reare

---

267 *Silo*: Siloam, a pool in the Bible with healing powers. Following are famous rivers and watering places.

Out of the sea faire Titans deawy face,
Up rose the gentle virgin from her place,
And looked all about, if she might spy
Her loved knight to move his manly pace: 295
fear for   For she had great doubt of° his safety,
Since late she saw him fall before his enimy.

34

At last she saw where he upstarted brave
Out of the well, wherein he drenched lay:
As Eagle fresh out of the Ocean wave,   300
Where he hath left his plumes all hoary gray,
And deckt himselfe with feathers youthly gay,
young hawk   Like Eyas hauke° up mounts unto the skies,
His newly budded pineons to assay,
And marveiles at himselfe, still as he flies: 305
So new this new-borne knight to battell new did rise.

35

Whom when the damned feend so fresh did spy,
No wonder if he wondred at the sight,
And doubted, whether his late enemy
It were, or other new supplied knight.   310
He, now to prove his late renewed might,
High brandishing his bright deaw-burning blade,
Upon his crested scalpe so sore did smite,
That to the scull a yawning wound it made:
The deadly dint his dulled senses all dismaid.   315

36

know   I wote° not, whether the revenging steele
Were hardned with that holy water dew,
Wherein he fell, or sharper edge did feele,
Or his baptized hands now greater grew;
Or other secret vertue did ensew;   320
Else never could the force of fleshly arme,
become stained Ne molten mettall in his bloud embrew:°
moment   For till that stownd° could never wight him harme,
By subtilty, nor slight, nor might, nor mighty charme.

37

The cruell wound enraged him so sore,   325
That loud he yelded for exceeding paine;
As hundred ramping Lyons seem'd to rore,
Whom ravenous hunger did thereto constraine:
Then gan he tosse aloft his stretched traine,
And therewith scourge that buxome aire so sore,   330
desirous   That to his force to yeelden it was faine;°
nothing   Ne ought° his sturdie strokes might stand afore,
That high trees overthrew, and rocks in peeces tore.

38

The same advauncing high above his head,
　With sharpe intended sting so rude him smot,　　　　335
　That to the earth him drove, as stricken dead,
called him alive　Ne living wight would have him life behot:°
　The mortall sting his angry needle shot
　Quite through his shield, and in his shoulder seasd,
　Where fast it stucke, ne would there out be got:　　340
　The griefe thereof him wondrous sore diseasd,
Ne might his ranckling paine with patience be appeasd.

39

But yet more mindfull of his honour deare,
　Then of the grievous smart, which him did wring,
　From loathed soile he can him lightly reare,　　　　345
　And strove to loose the farre infixed sting:
　Which when in vaine he tryde with struggeling,
　Inflam'd with wrath, his raging blade he heft,
　And strooke so strongly, that the knotty string
　Of his huge taile he quite a sunder cleft,　　　　350
Five joynts thereof he hewd, and but the stump him left.

40

Hart cannot thinke, what outrage, and what cryes,
hurled forth　With foule enfouldred° smoake and flashing fire,
　The hell-bred beast threw forth unto the skyes,
　That all was covered with darknesse dire:　　　　355
　Then fraught with rancour, and engorged ire,
　He cast at once him to avenge for all,
　And gathering up himselfe out of the mire,
　With his uneven wings did fiercely fall
Upon his sunne-bright shield, and gript it fast withall.　360

41

Much was the man encombred with his hold,
　In feare to lose his weapons in his paw,
talons　Ne wist yett how his talaunts° to unfold;
　Nor harder was from Cerberus greedy jaw
　To plucke a bone, then from his cruell claw　　　365
take　To reave° by strength the griped gage away:
　Thrise he assayd it from his foote to draw,
　And thrise in vaine to draw it did assay;
was useless　It booted nought° to thinke to robbe him of his pray.

42

Tho, when he saw no power might prevaile,　　　　370
　His trusty sword he cald to his last aid,
　Wherewith he fiersly did his foe assaile,
　And double blowes about him stoutly laid,
　That glauncing fire out of the yron plaid,

As sparkles from the Andvile use to fly,   375
When heavy hammers on the wedge are swaid:
Therewith at last he forst him to unty
One of his grasping feete, him to defend thereby.

43

The other foote, fast fixed on his shield,
Whenas no strength nor stroks mote him constraine   380
To loose, ne yet the warlike pledge to yield,
He smott thereat with all his might and maine,
such   That nought so° wondrous puissaunce might sustaine:
Upon the joint the lucky steele did light,
And made such way that hewd it quite in twaine;   385
diminished   The paw yett missed not his minisht° might,
placed   But hong still on the shield, as it at first was pight.°

44

For griefe thereof and divelish despight,
From his infernall fournace forth he threw
Huge flames that dimmed all the hevens light,   390
Enrold in duskish smoke and brimstone blew:
As burning Aetna from his boyling stew
Doth belch out flames, and rockes in peeces broke,
And ragged ribs of mountaines molten new,
Enwrapt in coleblacke clowds and filthy smoke,   395
That at the land with stench and heven with horror choke.

45

The heate whereof, and harmefull pestilence
annoyed   So sore him noyd,° that forst him to retire
A little backward for his best defence,
To save his body from the scorching fire,   400
breathe forth Which he from hellish entrailes did expire.°
It chaunst, (eternall God that chaunce did guide)
As he recoiled backeward, in the mire,
His nigh foreweried feeble feet did slide,
And downe he fell, with dread of shame sore terrifide.   405

46

There grew a goodly tree him faire beside,
Loaden with fruit and apples rosy redd,
As they in pure vermilion had been dide,
observable   Whereof great vertues over-all were redd;°
For happy life to all which thereon fedd,   410
And life eke everlasting did befall:
place   Great God it planted in that blessed stedd°
With his Almighty hand, and did it call
The tree of life, the crime of our first fathers fall.

---

414 *the crime*: Adam's fall "brought death into this world," as Milton says; thus man loses
the Tree of Life.

47

In all the world like was not to be fownd,   415
   Save in that soile, where all good things did grow,
   And freely sprong out of the fruitfull grownd,
   As incorrupted Nature did them sow,
   Till that dredd Dragon all did overthrow.
   Another like faire tree eke grew thereby,   420

forthwith   Whereof whoso did eat, eftsoones° did know
   Both good and ill. O mournfull memory!

caused   That tree through one man's fault hath doen° us all to dy.

48

From that first tree forth flowd, as from a well,

powerfully healing A trickling streame of Balme, most soveraine°   425
   And dainty deare, which on the ground still fell,
   And overflowed all the fertile plaine,
   As it had deawed bene with timely raine:
   Life and long health that gracious ointment gave,
   And deadly wounds could heale, and reare againe   430
   The sencelesse corse appointed for the grave:
Into that same he fell, which did from death him save.

49

For nigh thereto the ever damned Beast
   Durst not approch, for he was deadly made,
   And al that life preserved did detest;   435
   Yet he it oft adventur'd to invade.
   By this the drouping day-light gan to fade,
   And yield his rowme to sad succeeding night,
   Who with her sable mantle gan to shade
   The face of earth and wayes of living wight,   440
And high her burning torch set up in heaven bright.

50

When gentle Una saw the second fall
   Of her deare knight, who, weary of long fight
   And faint through losse of blood, moov'd not at all,
   But lay, as in a dreame of deepe delight,   445
   Besmeard with pretious Balme, whose vertuous might
   Did heale his woundes, and scorching heat alay;
   Againe she stricken was with sore affright,
   And for his safetie gan devoutly pray,

noxious   And watch the noyous° night, and wait for joyous day.   450

51

The joyous day gan early to appeare;
   And fayre Aurora from the deawy bed
   Of aged Tithone gan herselfe to reare

---

420 *Another...Tree*: the Tree of the Knowledge of Good and Evil, of whose fruit Adam and Eve ate. 452 *Aurora*: goddess of dawn. 453 *Tithone*: Aurore's "aged" husband.

With rosy cheekes, for shame as blushing red:
  Her golden locks for hast were loosely shed   455
  About her eares, when Una her did marke
  Clymbe to her charet, all with flowers spred,
  From heven high to chace the chearelesse darke;
With mery note her lowd salutes the mounting larke.

52

Then freshly up arose the doughty knight,   460
  All healed of his hurts and woundes wide,
  And did himselfe to battaile ready dight;
  Whose early foe awaiting him beside
  To have devourd, so soone as day he spyde,
  When now he saw himselfe so freshly reare,   465
  As if late fight had nought him damnifyde,
  He woxe dismaid, and gan his fate to feare:
Nathlesse with wonted rage he him advaunced neare.

53

And in his first encounter, gaping wyde,
  He thought attonce him to have swallowd quight,   470
  And rusht upon him with outragious pryde;
  Who him rencountring fierce, as hauke in flight,
  Perforce rebutted backe. The weapon bright,
  Taking advantage of his open jaw,
  Ran through his mouth with so importune might,   475
  That deepe emperst his darksom hollow maw,
And, back retyrd, his life blood forth with all did draw.

54

So downe he fell, and forth his life did breath,
  That vanisht into smoke and cloudes swift;
  So downe he fell, that th' earth him underneath   480
  Did grone, as feeble so great load to lift;
  So downe he fell, as an huge rocky clift,
  Whose false foundacion waves have washt away,
force...torn   With dreadfull poyse° is from the mayneland rift,°
  And rolling downe great Neptune doth dismay: 485
So downe he fell, and like an heaped mountaine lay.

55

The knight him selfe even trembled at his fall,
  So huge and horrible a masse it seemd;
  And his deare Lady, that beheld it all,
misjudged   Durst not approch for dread which she misdeemd;°   490
  But yet at last, whenas the direfull feend
  She saw not stirre, off-shaking vaine affright
  She nigher drew, and saw that joyous end:
  Then God she praysd, and thankt her faithfull knight,
That had atchievde so great a conquest by his might.   495

Canto XII

Faire Una to the Redcrosse knight
Betrouthed is with joy:
Though false Duessa it to barre
Her false sleights doe imploy.

1

Behold I see the haven nigh at hand,
   To which I meane my wearie course to bend;
sail   Vere the maine shete,° and beare up with the land,
known The which afore is fairely to be kend,°
   And seemeth safe from stormes, that may offend;   5
   There this faire virgin wearie of her way
   Must landed be, now at her journeyes end:
   There eke my feeble barke a while may stay,
Till merry wind and weather call her thence away.

2

Scarsely had *Phœbus* in the glooming East   10
   Yet harnessed his firie-footed teeme,
   Ne reard above the earth his flaming creast,
   When the last deadly smoke aloft did steeme,
   That signe of last outbreathed life did seeme,
   Unto the watchman on the castle wall;   15
   Who thereby dead that balefull Beast did deeme,
   And to his Lord and Ladie lowd gan call,
To tell, how he had seene the Dragons fatall fall.

3

Uprose with hastie joy, and feeble speed
   That aged Sire, the Lord of all that land,   20
   And looked forth, to weet, if true indeede
   Those tydings were, as he did understand,
   Which whenas true by tryall he out fond,
   He had to open wyde his brazen gate,
   Which long time had bene shut, and out of hond   25
   Proclaymed joy and peace through all his state;
recently oppressed For dead now was their foe, which them forrayed late.°

4

Then gan triumphant Trompets sound on hie,
   That sent to heaven the ecchoed report
   Of their new joy, and happie victorie   30
wrong Gainst him, that had them long opprest with tort°
   And fast imprisoned in sieged fort.
   Then all the people, as in solemne feast,
   To him assembled with one full consort,
   Rejoycing at the fall of that great beast,   35
From whose eternall bondage now they were releast.

5

Forth came that auncient Lord, and aged Queene,
Arayd in antique robes downe to the grownd,
grave   And sad° habiliments right well beseene:
A noble crew about them waited rownd   40
Of sage and sober peres, all gravely gownd;
Whom far before did march a goodly band
to make ring   Of tall young men, all hable armes to sownd;°
But now they laurell braunches bore in hand,
Glad signe of victory and peace in all their land.   45

6

Unto that doughtie Conquerour they came,
And him before themselves prostrating low,
Their Lord and Patrone loud did him proclame,
And at his feet their lawrell boughes did throw.
Soone after them, all dauncing on a row,   50
dressed   The comely virgins came, with girlands dight,°
As fresh as flowres in medow greene doe grow
When morning deaw upon their leaves doth light;
And in their handes sweet Timbrels all upheld on hight.

7

And them before the fry of children yong   55
Their wanton sportes and childish mirth did play,
And to the Maydens sownding tymbrels song
In well attuned notes a joyous lay,
And made delightfull musick all the way,
Untill they came where that faire virgin stood: 60
As fayre Diana in fresh sommers day
ranged   Beholdes her nymphes enraung'd° in shady wood,
Some wrestle, some do run, some bathe in christall flood.

8

So she beheld those maydens meriment
With chearefull vew; who when to her they came,   65
Themselves to ground with gratious humblesse bent,
And her adored by honorable name,
Lifting to heaven her everlasting fame:
Then on her head they set a girland greene,
And crownéd her twixt earnest and twixt game;   70
attractive   Who in her selfe-resemblance well beseene,°
appearance   Did seeme such, as she was, a goodly maiden Queene.

9

mob   And after all, the raskall many° ran,
Heapéd together in rude rablement,
To see the face of that victorious man: 75
Whom all admired, as from heaven sent,
And gazd upon with gaping wonderment.

But when they came, where that dead Dragon lay,
Stretcht on the ground in monstrous large extent,
senseless   The sight with idle° feare did them dismay,   80
Ne durst approach him nigh, to touch, or once assay.

10

Some feard, and fled; some feard and well it faynd;
One that would wiser seeme, then all the rest,
Warnd him not touch, for yet perhaps remaynd
Some lingring life within his hollow brest,   85
Or in his wombe might lurke some hidden nest
Of many Dragonets, his fruitfull seed;
Another said, that in his eyes did rest
Yet sparckling fire, and bad thereof take heed;
Another said, he saw him move his eyes indeed.   90

11

One mother, when as her foolehardie chyld
Did come too neare, and with his talants play,
Halfe dead through feare, her litle babe revyld,
female friends   And to her gossips° gan in counsell say;
"How can I tell, but that his talants may   95
Yet scratch my sonne, or rend his tender hand?"
So diversly themselves in vaine they fray;
Whiles some more bold, to measure him nigh stand,
To prove how many acres he did spread of land.

12

Thus flockéd all the folke him round about,   100
The whiles that hoarie king, with all his traine,
Being arrivéd, where that champion stout
defeat   After his foes defeasance° did remaine,
Him goodly greetes, and faire does entertaine,
With princely gifts of yvorie and gold,   105
And thousand thankes him yeelds for all his paine.
Then when his daughter deare he does behold,
Her dearely doth imbrace, and kisseth manifold.

13

And after to his Pallace he them brings,
oboes   With shaumes,° and trompets, and with Clarions sweet;   110
And all the way the joyous people sings,
And with their garments strowes the pavéd street:
Whence mounting up, they find purveyance meet
Of all, that royall Princes court became,
And all the floore was underneath their feet   115
Bespred with costly scarlot of great name,
On which they lowly sit, and fitting purpose frame.

14

conduct   What needs me tell their feast and goodly guize,°
In which was nothing riotous nor vaine?

What needs of daintie dishes to devize,   120
Of comely services, or courtly trayne?
My narrow leaves cannot in them containe
The large discourse of royall Princes state.
Yet was their manner then but bare and plaine:
For th' antique world excesse and pride did hate;   125
Such proud luxurious pompe is swollen up but late.

15

Then when with meates and drinkes of every kinde
    Their fervent appetites they quenchéd had,
    That auncient Lord gan fit occasion finde,
    Of straunge adventures, and of perils sad,   130
    Which in his travell him befallen had,
    For to demaund of his renowméd guest:
    Who then with utt'rance grave, and count'nance sad,
    From point to point, as is before exprest,
Discourst his voyage long, according his request.   135

16

Great pleasure mixt with pittifull regard,
feel   That godly King and Queene did passionate,°
    Whiles they his pittifull adventures heard,
    That oft they did lament his lucklesse state,
    And often blame the too importune fate,   140
    That heapd on him so many wrathfull wreakes:
    For never gentle knight, as he of late,
    So tosséd was in fortunes cruell freakes;
And all the while salt teares bedeawd the hearers cheaks.

17

Then said that royall Pere in sober wise: 145
    "Deare Sonne, great beene the evils, which ye bore
    From first to last in your late enterprise,
know not   That I note,° whether prayse, or pitty more:
    For never living man, I weene, so sore
    In sea of deadly daungers was distrest;   150
    But since now safe ye seiséd have the shore,
    And well arrivéd are (high God be blest),
Let us devize of ease and everlasting rest."

18

"Ah dearest Lord," said then that doughy knight,
    "Of ease or rest I may not yet devize;   155
    For by the faith, which I to armes have plight,
    I bounden am streight after this emprize,
    As that your daughter can ye well advize,
    Backe to returne to that great Faerie Queene,
    And her to serve six yeares in warlike wize,   160
sorrow   Gainst that proud Paynim king, that workes her teene:°
Therefore I ought crave pardon, till I there have beene."

19

"Unhappie falles that hard necessitie,"
  Quoth he, "the troubler of my happie peace,
  And vowéd foe of my felicitie;
  Ne I against the same can justly preace:°   165
  But since that band° ye cannot now release,
  Nor doen undo (for vowes may not be vaine),
  Soone as the terme of those six yeares shall cease,
  Ye then shall hither backe returne againe,   170
The marriage to accomplish vowd betwixt you twain.

press (argue) — line 165
bond (promise) — line 166

20

"Which for my part I covet to performe,
  In sort as through the world I did proclame,
  That who so kild that monster most deforme,
  And him in hardy battaile overcame,   175
  Should have mine onely daughter to his Dame,
  And of my kingdome heire apparaunt bee:
  Therefore since now to thee perteines the same,
  By dew desert of noble chevalree,
Both daughter and eke kingdome, lo I yield to thee."   180

21

Then forth he calléd that his daughter faire,
  The fairest Un' his onely daughter deare,
  His onely daughter, and his onely heyre;
  Who forth proceeding with sad° sober cheare,
  As bright as doth the morning starre appeare   185
  Out of the East, with flaming lockes bedight,°
  To tell that dawning day is drawing neare,
  And to the world does bring long wishéd light;
So faire and fresh that Lady shewd her selfe in sight.

grave — line 184
bedecked — line 186

22

So faire and fresh, as freshest flowre in May;   190
  For she had layd her mournefull stole aside,
  And widow-like sad wimple throwne away,
  Wherewith her heavenly beautie she did hide,
  Whiles on her wearie journey she did ride;
  And on her now a garment she did weare,   195
  All lilly white, withoutten spot, or pride,°
  That seemed like silke and silver woven neare,°
But neither silke nor silver therein did appeare.

decoration — line 196
close — line 197

23

The blazing brightnesse of her beauties beame,
  And glorious light of her sunshyny face   200
  To tell, were as to strive against the streame.
  My ragged rimes are all too rude and bace,
  Her heavenly lineaments for to enchace.°
  Ne wonder; for her owne deare lovéd knight,

adorn — line 203

All were she dayly with himselfe in place,   205
  Did wonder much at her celestiall sight:
Oft had he seene her faire, but never so faire dight.

24

dressed   So fairely dight,° when she in presence came,
  She to her Sire made humble reverence,
  And bowéd low, that her right well became,   210
  And added grace unto her excellence:
  Who with great wisdome, and grave eloquence
  Thus gan to say. But eare he thus had said,
  With flying speede, and seeming great pretence,
  Came running in, much like a man dismaid,   215
A Messenger with letters, which his message said.

25

All in the open hall amazéd stood,
unexpected At suddeinnesse of that unwarie° sight,
  And wondred at his breathlesse hastie mood.
  But he for nought would stay his passage right   220
  Till fast before the king he did alight;
  Where falling flat, great humblesse he did make,
placed   And kist the ground, whereon his foot was pight;°
  Then to his hands that writ he did betake,
Which he disclosing, red thus, as the paper spake.   225

26

"To thee, most mighty king of Eden faire,
  Her greeting sends in these sad lines addrest,
  The wofull daughter, and forsaken heire
  Of that great Emperour of all the West;
  And bids thee be advizéd for the best,   230
  Ere thou thy daughter linck in holy band
  Of wedlocke to that new unknowen guest:
  For he already plighted his right hand
Unto another love, and to another land.

27

"To me sad mayd, or rather widow sad,   235
  He was affiauncéd long time before,
  And sacred pledges he both gave, and had,
  False erraunt knight, infamous, and forswore:
  Witnesse the burning Altars, which he swore,
  And guiltie heavens of his bold perjury,   240
  Which though he hath polluted oft of yore,
  Yet I to them for judgement just do fly,
And them conjure t' avenge this shamefull injury.

28

"Therefore since mine he is, or free or bond,
  Or false or trew, or living or else dead,   245

Withhold, O soveraine Prince, your hasty hond
advise　　From knitting league with him, I you aread;°
think　　　Ne weene° my right with strength adowne to tread,
Through weakenesse of my widowhed, or woe:
For truth is strong, her rightfull cause to plead,　　　　250
And shall find friends, if need requireth soe,
So bids thee well to fare, Thy neither friend, nor foe, Fidessa."

29

When he these bitter byting words had red,
The tydings straunge did him abashéd make,
That still he sate long time astonishéd　　　　255
As in great muse, ne word to creature spake.
At last his solemne silence thus he brake,
With doubtfull eyes fast fixéd on his guest:
"Redoubted knight, that for mine onely sake
Thy life and honour late adventurest,　　　　260
Let nought be hid from me, that ought to be exprest.

30

"What meane these bloudy vowes, and idle threats,
Throwne out from womanish impatient mind?
What heavens? what altars? what enragéd heates
Here heapéd up with termes of love unkind,　　　　265
My conscience cleare with guilty bands would bind?
High God be witnesse, that I guiltlesse ame.
But if your selfe, Sir knight, ye faultie find,
Or wrappéd be in loves of former Dame,
With crime do not it cover, but disclose the same."　　　　270

31

To whom the Redcrosse knight this answere sent,
"My Lord, my King, be nought hereat dismayd,
Till well ye wote by grave intendiment,
What woman, and wherefore doth me upbrayd
With breach of love, and loyaltie betrayd.　　　　275
It was in my mishaps, as hitherward
I lately traveild, that unwares I strayd
Out of my way, through perils straunge and hard;
That day should faile me, ere I had them all declard.

32

"There did I find, or rather I was found　　　　280
Of this false woman, that Fidessa hight,
Fidessa hight the falsest Dame on ground,
Most false Duessa, royall richly dight,
That easie was t' invegle weaker sight:
Who by her wicked arts, and wylie skill,　　　　285
Too false and strong for earthly skill or might,
Unwares me wrought unto her wicked will,
And to my foe betrayd, when least I fearéd ill."

33

Then steppéd forth the goodly royall Mayd,
 And on the ground her selfe prostrating low,   290
 With sober countenaunce thus to him sayd:
 "O pardon me, my soveraigne Lord, to show
 The secret treasons, which of late I know
 To have bene wroght by that false sorceresse.
 She onely she it is, that earst did throw   295
 This gentle knight into so great distresse,
That death him did awaite in dayly wretchednesse.

34

"And now it seemes, that she subornéd hath
 This craftie messenger with letters vaine,
harm To worke new woe and improvided scath;°   300
 By breaking of the band betwixt us twaine;
treachery Wherein she uséd hath the practicke paine°
 Of this false footman, clokt with simplenesse,
 Whom if ye please for to discover plaine,
 Ye shall him Archimago find, I ghesse,   305
The falsest man alive; who tries shall find no lesse."

35

The king was greatly movéd at her speach,
freighted And all with suddein indignation fraight,°
bade Bad° on that Messenger rude hands to reach.
 Eftsoones the Gard, which on his state did wait,   310
deceiver Attacht that faitor° false, and bound him strait:
 Who seeming sorely chtraufféd at his band,
 As chainéd Beare, whom cruell dogs do bait,
 With idle force did faine them to withstand,
And often semblaunce made to scape out of their hand.   315

36

But they him layd full low in dungeon deepe,
 And bound him hand and foote with yron chains.
 And with continuall watch did warely keepe;
 Who then would thinke, that by his subtile trains
 He could escape fowle death or deadly paines?   320
 Thus when that Princes wrath was pacifide,
banns He gan renew the late forbidden banes,°
 And to the knight his daughter deare he tyde,
With sacred rites and vowes for ever to abyde.

37

His owne two hands the holy knots did knit,   325
 That none but death for ever can devide;
 His owne two hands, for such a turne most fit,
sacramental The housling° fire did kindle and provide,
 And holy water thereon sprinckled wide;
torch At which the bushy Teade° a groome did light,   330

And sacred lampe in secret chamber hide,
Where it should not be quenchéd day nor night,
For feare of evill fates, but burnen ever bright.

38

Then gan they sprinckle all the posts with wine,
And made great feast to solemnize that day;   335
They all perfumde with frankencense divine,
And precious odours fetcht from far away,
That all the house did sweat with great aray:
And all the while sweete Musicke did apply
Her curious skill, the warbling notes to play,   340
To drive away the dull Melancholy;
The whiles one sung a song of love and jollity.

39

During the which there was an heavenly noise
Heard sound through all the Pallace pleasantly,
Like as it had bene many an Angels voice,   345
Singing before th' eternall majesty,
threefold Trinity   In their trinall triplicities° on hye;
Yet wist no creature, whence that heavenly sweet
Proceeded, yet each one felt secretly
proper   Himselfe thereby reft of his sences meet,°   350
spirit   And ravishéd with rare impression in his sprite.°

40

Great joy was made that day of young and old,
And solemne feast proclaimd throughout the land,
That their exceeding merth may not be told:
Suffice it heare by signes to understand   355
The usuall joyes at knitting of loves band.
Thrise happy man the knight himselfe did hold,
Possesséd of his Ladies hart and hand,
And ever, when his eye did her behold,
His heart did seeme to melt in pleasures manifold.   360

41

Her joyous presence and sweet company
In full content he there did long enjoy,
Ne wicked envie, ne vile gealosy
His deare delights were able to annoy:
Yet swimming in that sea of blisfull joy,   365
He nought forgot, how he whilome had sworne,
In case he could that monstrous beast destroy,
Unto his Farie Queene backe to returne:
The which he shortly did, and Una left to mourne.

42

Now strike your sailes ye jolly Mariners,   370
anchorage   For we be come unto a quiet rode,°

Where we must land some of our passengers,
And light this wearie vessell of her lode.
Here she a while may make her safe abode,
Till she repairéd have her tackles spent,   *375*
And wants supplide. And then againe abroad
On the long voyage whereto she is bent:
Well may she speede and fairely finish her intent.

SAMUEL TAYLOR COLERIDGE *(1772–1834)*

"The Rime of the Ancient Mariner" first appeared, along with the fragmentary "Christabel" and "Kubla Khan," in 1798 as Coleridge's contribution to *Lyrical Ballads,* a collection of poems by him and Wordsworth. Their aim, as Coleridge says in *Biographia Literaria* (Chapter XIV), was for each poet to deal with a different kind of subject matter. Wordsworth was "to give the charm of novelty to things of every day," whereas Coleridge was to treat "persons and characters supernatural, or at least romantic; yet so as to transfer from our inward nature a human interest and a semblance of truth sufficient to procure for these shadows of imagination that willing suspension of disbelief for the moment, which constitutes poetic faith." As the title of their collection suggests, most of the poems in it had some connection to the ballad.

It is a question whether to consider "The Ancient Mariner" as ballad or as romance since it has features of both. It employs the traditional ballad stanza of four lines—alternating tetrameters and trimeters in a rhyme scheme of *abcb*—although it sometimes expands this to five- and six-line stanzas. The poem is balladic also in its use of incremental repetition and its occasional wrenching of accent, as in *countrée,* both of which give it the singing or chanting quality common to the folk ballad. Its use of archaic spellings here and there— Coleridge eliminated many of these after the first edition, where, for instance, the spelling is "Ancyent Marinere"—suggests the ballad but also Spenserian romance. The poem is of course far longer than ordinary ballads, although perhaps not as long or involved as the average romance. Its narrative technique, its use of the "framing story" of the Mariner's encounter with the Wedding-Guest, is a popular device of romance; but more important is the fact that unlike most ballads, "The Ancient Mariner" is a complex, ambiguous poem charged with symbolism and governed by a profound moral seriousness. It takes its narrative structure from the erratic sea-voyage of the Mariner, which, though not actually a quest, is like the "perilous journey" of quest-romance in that the hero enters a supernatural realm where he is initiated into mysteries of life and death, his character is tested, and his identity is transformed. Analogous structural devices are the descent to the underworld, here the South Pole, and the passage across water to the "castle marvelous" of medieval romance, which takes the form here of the Ship of Death and Death-in-Life. This pattern of withdrawal-and-return, the movement away from and back to the harmonious society, here represented by the wedding group, is typical of romance. And the poem takes its thematic structure from the "crime-suffering-catharsis-rebirth" pattern prominent in many romances, as in Book I of *The Faerie Queene,* where the Redcross Knight sins through misdirection of faith and finally despair, suffers imprisonment and wounds, undergoes the penitential catharsis of religous discipline, and is reborn as Saint George. So the Mariner passes from criminal to tale-teller, committing his crime against the sanctity of communal Nature, suffering his nightmarish excommunication from life, gradually being purged of his guilt, and rejoining the community of the living as one still stigmatized yet given miraculous communicative powers. At another symbolic level, "The Ancient Mariner," like Tennyson's "The Lady of Shalott," is a complex metaphor dealing with the poet's relations to art, imagination, and life.

THE RIME OF THE ANCIENT MARINER

PART THE FIRST

An ancient Mariner meeteth three Gallants bidden to a wedding feast, and detaineth one.

It is an ancient Mariner,
And he stoppeth one of three.
"By thy long grey beard and glittering eye,
Now wherefore stopp'st thou me?

The Bridegroom's doors are opened wide,   5
And I am next of kin;
The guests are met, the feast is set:
May'st hear the merry din."

He holds him with his skinny hand,
"There was a ship," quoth he.   10
"Hold off! unhand me, greybeard loon!"
Eftsoons his hand dropt he.

The Wedding-Guest is spellbound by the eye of the old sea-faring man, and constrained to hear his tale.

He holds him with his glittering eye—
The Wedding-Guest stood still,
And listens like a three years' child: 15
The Mariner hath his will.

The Wedding-Guest sat on a stone:
He cannot choose but hear;
And thus spake on that ancient man,
The bright-eyed Mariner.   20

"The ship was cheered, the harbour cleared,
Merrily did we drop
Below the kirk, below the hill,
Below the lighthouse top.

The Mariner tells how the ship sailed southward with a good wind and fair weather, till it reached the line.

The Sun came up upon the left,   25
Out of the sea came he!
And he shone bright, and on the right
Went down into the sea.

Higher and higher every day,
Till over the mast at noon—"   30

The Wedding-Guest heareth the bridal music; but the Mariner continueth his tale.

The Wedding-Guest here beat his breast,
For he heard the loud bassoon.

The Bride hath paced into the hall,

Red as a rose is she;
Nodding their heads before her goes   35
The merry minstrelsy.

The Wedding-Guest he beat his breast,
Yet he cannot choose but hear;
And thus spake on that ancient man,
The bright-eyed Mariner.   40

The ship drawn by
a storm toward the
South Pole.

"And now the storm-blast came, and he
Was tyrannous and strong:
He struck with his o'ertaking wings,
And chased us south along.

With sloping masts and dipping prow,   45
As who pursued with yell and blow
Still treads the shadow of his foe
And forward bends his head,
The ship drove fast, loud roared the blast,
And southward aye we fled.   50

And now there came both mist and snow
And it grew wondrous cold:
And ice, mast-high, came floating by,
As green as emerald.

The land of ice,
and of fearful
sounds, where no
living thing was
to be seen.

And through the drifts the snowy clifts   55
Did send a dismal sheen:
Nor shapes of men nor beasts we ken—
The ice was all between.

The ice was here, the ice was there,
The ice was all around:·   60
It cracked and growled, and roared and howled,
Like noises in a swound!

Till a great sea-bird,
called the Alba-
tross, came through
the snow-fog, and
was received with
great joy and
hospitality.

At length did cross an Albatross:
Thorough the fog it came;
As if it had been a Christian soul,   65
We hailed it in God's name.

It ate the food it ne'er had eat,
And round and round it flew.
The ice did split with a thunder-fit;
The helmsman steered us through!   70

And lo! the
Albatross proveth a
bird of good omen,
and followeth the
ship as it returned
northward through
fog and floating
ice.

And a good south wind sprung up behind;
The Albatross did follow,
And every day, for food or play,
Came to the mariners' hollo!

In mist or cloud, on mast or shroud,   75
It perched for vespers nine;
Whiles all the night, through fog-smoke white,
Glimmered the white moonshine."

The ancient Mariner inhospitably killeth the pious bird of good omen.

"God save thee, ancient Mariner!
From the fiends that plague thee thus!—   80
Why look'st thou so?"—"With my crossbow
I shot the Albatross.

PART THE SECOND

"The Sun now rose upon the right:
Out of the sea came he,
Still hid in mist, and on the left   85
Went down into the sea.

And the good south wind still blew behind,
But no sweet bird did follow,
Nor any day for food or play
Came to the mariners' hollo!   90

His shipmates cry out against the ancient Mariner for killing the bird of good luck.

And I had done a hellish thing,
And it would work 'em woe:
For all averred, I had killed the bird
That made the breeze to blow.
Ah wretch! said they, the bird to slay,   95
That made the breeze to blow!

But when the fog cleared off, they justify the same, and thus make themselves accomplices in the crime.

Nor dim nor red, like God's own head,
The glorious Sun uprist:
Then all averred, I had killed the bird
That brought the fog and mist.   100
'Twas right, said they, such birds to slay,
That bring the fog and mist.

The fair breeze continues; the ship enters the Pacific Ocean and sails northward, even till it reaches the Line.

The fair breeze blew, the white foam flew,
The furrow followed free;
We were the first that ever burst   105
Into that silent sea.

The ship hath been suddenly becalmed.

Down dropt the breeze, the sails dropt down,
'Twas sad as sad could be;
And we did speak only to break
The silence of the sea!   110

All in a hot and copper sky,
The bloody Sun, at noon,
Right up above the mast did stand,
No bigger than the Moon.

Day after day, day after day,   115
We stuck, nor breath nor motion;
As idle as a painted ship
Upon a painted ocean.

And the Albatross
begins to be
avenged.

Water, water, everywhere,
And all the boards did shrink;   120
Water, water, everywhere,
Nor any drop to drink.

The very deep did rot: O Christ!
That ever this should be!
Yea, slimy things did crawl with legs   125
Upon the slimy sea.

About, about, in reel and rout
The death-fires danced at night;
The water, like a witch's oils,
Burnt green, and blue, and white.   130

And some in dreams assurèd were

A Spirit had fol-
lowed them; one of
the invisible in-
habitants of this
planet, neither de-
parted souls nor

Of the Spirit that plagued us so;
Nine fathom deep he had followed us
From the land of mist and snow.

angels; concerning whom the learned Jew, Josephus, and the Platonic Constantinopolitan, Michael
Psellus, may be consulted. They are very numerous, and there is no climate or element without one
or more.

And every tongue, through utter drought,   135
Was withered at the root;
We could not speak, no more than if
We had been choked with soot.

The shipmates, in
their sore distress,
would fain throw
the whole guilt on
the ancient Mar-
iner: in sign
whereof they hang
the dead sea-bird
round his neck.

Ah! well-a-day! what evil looks
Had I from old and young!   140
Instead of the cross, the Albatross
About my neck was hung.

PART THE THIRD

"There passed a weary time. Each throat
Was parched, and glazed each eye.
A weary time! a weary time!   145

The ancient
Mariner beholdeth
a sign in the ele-
ment afar off.

How glazed each weary eye!
When looking westward, I beheld
A something in the sky.

At first it seemed a little speck,
And then it seemed a mist;   150

It moved and moved, and took at last
A certain shape, I wist.

A speck, a mist, a shape, I wist!
And still it neared and neared:
As if it dodged a watersprite,   155
It plunged and tacked and veered.

At its nearer
approach it seemeth
him to be a ship;
and at a dear ran-
som he freeth his
speech from the
bonds of thirst.

With throats unslaked, with black lips baked,
We could not laugh nor wail;
Through utter drought all dumb we stood!
I bit my arm, I sucked the blood,   160
And cried, A sail! a sail!

With throats unslaked, with black lips baked,
Agape they heard me call:

A flash of joy;

Gramercy! they for joy did grin,
And all at once their breath drew in,   165
As they were drinking all.

And horror follows.
For can it be a ship
that comes onward
without wind or
tide?

See! See! (I cried) she tacks no more!
Hither to work us weal;
Without a breeze, without a tide,
She steadies with upright keel!   170

The western wave was all a-flame.
The day was well-nigh done!
Almost upon the western wave
Rested the broad bright Sun;
When that strange shape drove suddenly   175
Betwixt us and the Sun.

It seemeth him but
the skeleton of a
ship.

And straight the Sun was flecked with bars,
(Heaven's Mother send us grace!)
As if through a dungeon-grate he peered
With broad and burning face.   180

Alas! (thought I, and my heart beat loud)
How fast she nears and nears!
Are those her sails that glance in the Sun,
Like restless gossameres!

And its ribs are
seen as bars on the
face of the setting
Sun. The Spectre-
Woman and her
Death-mate, and
no other on board
the skeleton ship.

Are those her ribs through which the Sun   185
Did peer, as through a grate?
And is that Woman all her crew?
Is that a Death? and are there two?
Is Death that woman's mate?

Like vessel, like
crew!

Her lips were red, her looks were free,   190
Her locks were yellow as gold:

Her skin was as white as leprosy,
The Nightmare Life-in-Death was she,
Who thicks man's blood with cold.

Death and Life-in-
Death have diced
for the ship's crew,
and she (the latter)
winneth the ancient
Mariner.

The naked hulk alongside came   195
And the twain were casting dice;
"The game is done! I've won, I've won!"
Quoth she, and whistles thrice.

No twilight within
the courts of the
Sun.

The Sun's rim dips; the stars rush out:
At one stride comes the dark;   200
With far-head whisper, o'er the sea,
Off shot the spectre-bark.

We listened and looked sideways up!
Fear at my heart, as at a cup,
My life-blood seemed to sip!   205
The stars were dim, and thick the night,
The steersman's face by his lamp gleamed white;
From the sails the dew did drip—

At the rising of the
Moon,

Till clomb above the eastern bar
The hornèd Moon, with one bright star   210
Within the nether tip.

One after another,

One after one, by the star-dogged Moon,
Too quick for groan or sigh,
Each turned his face with a ghastly pang,
And cursed me with his eye.   215

His shipmates drop
down dead;

Four times fifty living men,
(And I heard nor sigh nor groan)
With heavy thump, a lifeless lump,
They dropped down one by one.

But Life-in-Death
begins her work
on the ancient
Mariner.

The souls did from their bodies fly,—   220
They fled to bliss or woe!
And every soul, it passed me by,
Like the whizz of my crossbow!"

Part The Fourth

The Wedding-Guest
feareth that a spirit
is talking to him;

"I fear thee, ancient Mariner!
I fear thy skinny hand!   225
And thou art long, and lank, and brown,
As is the ribbed sea-sand.

I fear thee and thy glittering eye,
And thy skinny hand. so brown"—

But the ancient
Mariner assureth
him of his bodily
life, and proceedeth

"Fear not, fear not, thou Wedding-Guest!   230
This body dropt not down.

to relate his hor-
rible penance.
Alone, alone, all, all alone,
Alone on a wide wide sea!
And never a saint took pity on
My soul in agony.   235

He despiseth the
creatures of the
calm.
The many men, so beautiful!
And they all dead did lie:
And a thousand thousand slimy things
Lived on; and so did I.

And envieth that
they should live,
and so many lie
dead.
I looked upon the rotting sea,   240
And drew my eyes away;
I looked upon the rotting deck,
And there the dead men lay.

I looked to Heaven, and tried to pray;
But or ever a prayer had gusht,   245
A wicked whisper came, and made
My heart as dry as dust.

I closed my lids, and kept them close,
And the balls like pulses beat;
For the sky and the sea, and the sea and the sky,   250
Lay like a load on my weary eye,
And the dead were at my feet.

But the curse
liveth for him in
the eye of the
dead men.
The cold sweat melted from their limbs,
Nor rot nor reek did they;
The look with which they looked on me   255
Had never passed away.

An orphan's curse would drag to hell
A spirit from on high;
But oh! more horrible than that
Is a curse in a dead man's eye!   260
Seven days, seven nights, I saw that curse,
And yet I could not die.

In his loneliness
and fixedness he
yearneth towards
the journeying
Moon, and the Stars
that still sojourn,
yet still move on-
ward; and every-
where the blue sky
belongs to them,
and is their ap-
pointed rest, and
their native country
and their own natu-
ral homes, which they
enter unannounced,
as lords that are certainly expected and yet there is a silent joy at their arrival.
The moving Moon went up the sky,
And nowhere did abide:
Softly she was going up,   265
And a star or two beside—

Her beams bemocked the sultry main,
Like April hoar-frost spread;
But where the ship's huge shadow lay,
The charmèd water burnt alway   270
A still and awful red.

By the light of the
Moon he beholdeth
God's creatures of
the great calm.

Beyond the shadow of the ship,
I watched the water-snakes:
They moved in tracks of shining white,
And when they reared, the elfish light   275
Fell off in hoary flakes.

Within the shadow of the ship
I watched their rich attire:
Blue, glossy green, and velvet black,
They coiled and swam; and every track   280
Was a flash of golden fire.

Their beauty and
their happiness.

O happy living things! no tongue
Their beauty might declare:
A spring of love gushed from my heart,

He blesseth them
in his heart.

And I blessed them unaware: 285
Sure my kind saint took pity on me,
And I blessed them unaware.

The spell begins to
break.

The selfsame moment I could pray;
And from my neck so free
The Albatross fell off, and sank   290
Like lead into the sea.

Part The Fifth

'O sleep! it is a gentle thing,
Beloved from pole to pole!
To Mary Queen the praise be given!
She sent the gentle sleep from Heaven,   295
That slid into my soul.

By grace of the
holy Mother, the
ancient Mariner is
refreshed with rain.

The silly buckets on the deck,
That had so long remained,
I dreamt that they were filled with dew;
And when I awoke, it rained.   300

My lips were wet, my throat was cold,
My garments all were dank;
Sure I had drunken in my dreams,
And still my body drank.

I moved, and could not feel my limbs: 305
I was so light—almost
I thought that I had died in sleep,
And was a blessèd ghost.

He heareth sounds
and seeth strange
sights and commo-
tions in the sky
and the element.

And soon I heard a roaring wind:
It did not come anear;   310

297 *silly*: useless.

But with its sound it shook the sails,
That were so thin and sere.

The upper air burst into life!
And a hundred fire-flags sheen,
To and fro they were hurried about! 315
And to and fro, and in and out,
The wan stars danced between.

And the coming wind did roar more loud,
And the sails did sigh like sedge;
And the rain poured down from one black cloud; 320
The Moon was at its edge.

The thick black cloud was cleft, and still
The Moon was at its side:
Like waters shot from some high crag,
The lightning fell with never a jag, 325
A river steep and wide.

The loud wind never reached the ship,
Yet now the ship moved on!
Beneath the lightning and the Moon
The dead men gave a groan. 330

The bodies of the ship's crew are inspired, and the ship moves on;

They groaned, they stirred, they all uprose,
Nor spake, nor moved their eyes;
It had been strange, even in a dream,
To have seen those dead men rise.

The helmsman steered, the ship moved on; 335
Yet never a breeze up blew;
The mariners all 'gan work the ropes,
Where they were wont to do;
They raised their limbs like lifeless tools—
We were a ghastly crew. 340

The body of my brother's son
Stood by me, knee to knee:
The body and I pulled at one rope,
But he said nought to me."

"I fear thee, ancient Mariner!" 345
"Be calm, thou Wedding-Guest!

But not by the souls of the men, nor by daemons of earth or middle air, but by a blessed troop of angelic spirits, sent down by the invocation of the guardian saint.

'Twas not those souls that fled in pain,
Which to their corses came again,
But a troop of spirits blest:

For when it dawned—they dropt their arms, 350
And clustered round the mast;

314 *sheen*: shone.

Sweet sounds rose slowly through their mouths,
And from their bodies passed.

Around, around, flew each sweet sound,
Then darted to the Sun;   355
Slowly the sounds came back again,
Now mixed, now one by one.

Sometimes a-dropping from the sky
I heard the skylark sing;
Sometimes all little birds that are,   360
How they seemed to fill the sea and air
With their sweet jargoning!

And now 'twas like all instruments,
Now like a lonely flute;
And now it is an angel's song,   365
That makes the Heavens be mute.

It ceased; yet still the sails made on
A pleasant noise till noon,
A noise like of a hidden brook
In the leafy month of June,   370
That to the sleeping woods all night
Singeth a quiet tune.

Till noon we quietly sailed on,
Yet never a breeze did breathe:
Slowly and smoothly went the ship,   375
Moved onward from beneath.

The lonesome Spirit from the South Pole carries on the ship as far as the Line, in obedience to the angelic troop, but still requireth vengeance.

Under the keel nine fathom deep,
From the land of mist and snow,
The Spirit slid: and it was he
That made the ship to go.   380
The sails at noon left off their tune,
And the ship stood still also.

The Sun, right up above the mast,
Had fixed her to the ocean:
But in a minute she 'gan stir,   385
With a short uneasy motion—
Backwards and forwards half her length
With a short uneasy motion.

Then, like a pawing horse let go,
She made a sudden bound: 390
It flung the blood into my head,
And I fell down in a swound.

The Polar Spirit's
fellow daemons, the
invisible inhabitants
of the element,
take part in his
wrong; and two of
them relate, one to
the other, that
penance long and
heavy for the
ancient Mariner
hath been accorded
to the Polar Spirit,
who returneth
southward.

How long in that same fit I lay,
I have not to declare;
But ere my living life returned,   395
I heard and in my soul discerned
Two voices in the air.
'Is it he?' quoth one, 'Is this the man?
By Him who died on cross,
With his cruel bow he laid full low   400
The harmless Albatross.

The Spirit who bideth by himself
In the land of mist and snow,
He loved the bird that loved the man
Who shot him with his bow.'   405

The other was a softer voice,
As soft as honeydew:
Quoth he, 'The man hath penance done,
And penance more will do.'

PART THE SIXTH

FIRST VOICE
" 'But tell me, tell me! speak again,   410
Thy soft response renewing—
What makes that ship drive on so fast?
What is the ocean doing?'

SECOND VOICE
'Still as a slave before his lord,
The Ocean hath no blast;   415
His great bright eye most silently
Up to the Moon is cast—

If he may know which way to go;
For she guides him smooth or grim.
See, brother, see! how graciously   420
She looketh down on him.'

FIRST VOICE
The Mariner hath
been cast into a
trance; for the angelic
power causeth the
vessel to drive
northward faster
than human life
could endure.
'But why drives on that ship so fast,
Without or wave or wind?'

SECOND VOICE
'The air is cut away before,
And closes from behind.   425

Fly, brother, fly! more high, more high!
Or we shall be belated:

> For slow and slow that ship will go,
> When the Mariner's trance is abated.'

The supernatural
motion is retarded;
the Mariner
awakes, and his
penance begins
anew.

> I woke, and we were sailing on   430
> As in a gentle weather:
> 'Twas night, calm night, the Moon was high;
> The dead men stood together.

> All stood together on the deck,
> For a charnel-dungeon fitter: 435
> All fixed on me their stony eyes,
> That in the Moon did glitter.

> The pang, the curse, with which they died,
> Had never passed away:
> I could not draw my eyes from theirs,   440
> Nor turn them up to pray.

The curse is finally
expiated.

> And now this spell was snapt: once more
> I viewed the ocean green,
> And looked far forth, yet little saw
> Of what had else been seen—   445

> Like one that on a lonesome road
> Doth walk in fear and dread,
> And having once turned round walks on,
> And turns no more his head;
> Because he knows a frightful fiend   450
> Doth close behind him tread.

> But soon there breathed a wind on me,
> Nor sound nor motion made:
> Its path was not upon the sea,
> In ripple or in shade.   455

> It raised my hair, it fanned my cheek
> Like a meadow-gale of spring—
> It mingled strangely with my fears,
> Yet it felt like a welcoming.

> Swiftly, swiftly flew the ship,   460
> Yet she sailed softly too:
> Sweetly, sweetly blew the breeze—
> On me alone it blew.

And the ancient
Mariner beholdeth
his native country.

> Oh! dream of joy! is this indeed
> The lighthouse top I see?   465
> Is this the hill? is this the kirk?
> Is this mine own countree?

We drifted o'er the harbour-bar,
And I with sobs did pray—
O let me be awake, my God!   470
Or let me sleep alway.

The harbour-bay was clear as glass,
So smoothly was it strewn!
And on the bay the moonlight lay,
And the shadow of the Moon.   475

The rock shone bright, the kirk no less,
That stands above the rock:
The moonlight steeped in silentness
The steady weathercock.

And the bay was white with silent light,   480
Till rising from the same,
Full many shapes, that shadows were,
In crimson colours came.

The angelic spirits leave the dead bodies, and appear in their own forms of light.

A little distance from the prow
Those crimson shadows were: 485
I turned my eyes upon the deck—
O, Christ! what saw I there!

Each corse lay flat, lifeless and flat,
And, by the holy rood!
A man all light, a seraph-man,   490
On every corse there stood.

This seraph-band, each waved his hand:
It was a heavenly sight!
They stood as signals to the land,
Each one a lovely light;   495

This seraph-band, each waved his hand,
No voice did they impart—
No voice; but oh! the silence sank
Like music on my heart.

But soon I heard the dash of oars,   500
I heard the Pilot's cheer;
My head was turned perforce away,
And I saw a boat appear.

The Pilot and the Pilot's boy,   505
I heard them coming fast:
Dear Lord in Heaven! it was a joy
That dead men could not blast.

I saw a third—I heard his voice:
It is the Hermit good!
He singeth loud his godly hymns   510
That he makes in the wood.
He'll shrieve my soul, he'll wash away
The Albatross's blood.

PART THE SEVENTH

The Hermit of the Wood

"This Hermit good lives in that wood
Which slopes down to the sea.   515
How loudly his sweet voice he rears!
He loves to talk with the marineres
That come from a far countree.

He kneels at morn, and noon, and eve—
He hath a cushion plump: 520
It is the moss that wholly hides
The rotted old oak-stump.

The skiff-boat neared: I heard them talk,
'Why this is strange, I trow!
Where are those lights so many and fair,   525
That signal made but now?'

Approacheth the ship with wonder.

'Strange, by faith!' the Hermit said—
'And they answered not our cheer!
The planks look warped! and see those sails,
How thin they are and sere!   530
I never saw aught like to them,
Unless perchance it were
Brown skeletons of leaves that lag
My forest-brook along;
When the ivy-tod is heavy with snow,   535
And the owlet whoops to the wolf below,
That eats the she-wolf's young.'

'Dear Lord! it hath a fiendish look—'
(The Pilot made reply)
'I am a-feared'—'Push on, push on!'   540
Said the Hermit cheerily.

The boat came closer to the ship,
But I nor spake nor stirred;
The boat came close beneath the ship,
And straight a sound was heard.   545

Under the water it rumbled on,
Still louder and more dread:

The ship suddenly sinketh.

It reached the ship, it split the bay;
The ship went down like lead.

Stunned by that loud and deadful sound,   550
Which sky and ocean smote,
Like one that hath been seven days drowned
My body lay afloat;

The ancient Mariner is saved in the Pilot's boat.

But swift as dreams, myself I found
Within the Pilot's boat.   555

Upon the whirl, where sank the ship,
The boat spun round and round;
And all was still, save that the hill
Was telling of the sound.

I moved my lips—the Pilot shrieked   560
And fell down in a fit;
The holy Hermit raised his eyes,
And prayed where he did sit.

I took the oars: the Pilot's boy,
Who now doth crazy go,   565
Laughed loud and long, and all the while
His eyes went to and fro.
'Ha! ha!' quoth he, 'full plain I see,
The Devil knows how to row.'

And now, all in my own countree,   570
I stood on the firm land!
The Hermit stepped forth from the boat,
And scarcely he could stand.

The ancient Mariner earnestly entreateth the Hermit to shrive him; and the penance of life falls on him.

'O shrieve me, shrieve me, holy man!'
The Hermit crossed his brow.   575
'Say quick,' quoth he, 'I bid thee say—
What manner of man are thou?'

Forthwith this frame of mine was wrenched
With a woeful agony,
Which forced me to begin my tale;   580
And then it left me free.

And ever and anon throughout his future life an agony constraineth him to travel from land to land,

Since then, at an uncertain hour,
That agony returns:
And till my ghastly tale is told,
This heart within me burns.   585

I pass, like night, from land to land;
I have strange power of speech;
That moment that his face I see,
I know the man that must hear me:
To him my tale I teach.   590

What loud uproar bursts from that door!
The wedding-guests are there:
But in the garden-bower the Bride
And Bride-maids singing are:
And hark the little vesper bell,   595
Which biddeth me to prayer!

O Wedding-Guest! this soul hath been
Alone on a wide wide sea:
So lonely 'twas, that God Himself
Scarce seemèd there to be.   600

O sweeter than the marriage-feast,
'Tis sweeter far to me,
To walk together to the kirk
With a goodly company!—

To walk together to the kirk,   605
And all together pray,
While each to his great Father bends,
Old men, and babes, and loving friends,
And youths and maidens gay!

And to teach, by his own example, love and reverence to all things that God made and loveth.

Farewell, farewell! but this I tell   610
To thee, thou Wedding-Guest!
He prayeth well, who loveth well
Both man and bird and beast.

He prayeth best, who loveth best
All things both great and small;   615
For the dear God who loveth us,
He made and loveth all."

The Mariner, whose eye is bright,
Whose beard with age is hoar,
Is gone: and now the Wedding-Guest   620
Turned from the Bridegroom's door.

He went like one that hath been stunned,
And is of sense forlorn:
A sadder and a wiser man,
He rose the morrow morn.   625

JOHN KEATS *(1795–1821)*

The narrative framework of "The Eve of St. Agnes" is rather sketchy. The "scene," or background of the action, is the Romeo and Juliet situation in which the feuding of the young lovers' families prevents their meeting and marrying. The central action encompassed by this scene is derived from a popular legend according to which a young and virtuous girl who follows a prescribed ritual on St. Agnes' Eve—going to bed without eating, speaking, or looking behind her—may be granted a visionary glimpse of her true love and future husband. Thus the principal event of the poem, depicted in stanzas 26 to 37, where Madeline falls asleep, dreams, and finally awakens, is the conventional dream-vision of both romance in general and of Keatsian romance and quasi-romance in particular (*Endymion*, "Isabella," "Lamia," "La Belle Dame Sans Merci"). In most of Keats's poems, the dream-vision, which is associated with the pull of the imagination away from the world of fact and reason, is somehow shattered. The imagination "cannot cheat so well / As she is famed to do" ("Nightingale Ode"); the touch of "cold philosophy" intrudes ("Lamia"); and the speaker or hero awakes to find himself "on the cold hill's side" of a dreary reality ("La Belle Dame"). Here, however, the wish-fulfilment dream of romance achieves a somewhat ambiguous triumph. Although Madeline responds with distress at learning that "this is no dream" (stanza 37), still the dream-vision of romantic union imposes itself on waking reality as the lovers steal away from the castle. Their fearfulness, the difficulty of negotiating the dark stairway, the threat of the bloodhound, and the groaning hinges of the door are all an index of the resistance reality offers to wish-fulfilment; the ambiguity of the dream's success is betokened by that of the storm, which assists their flight and yet remains a threat.

THE EVE OF ST. AGNES

1

St. Agnes' Eve—Ah, bitter chill it was!
The owl, for all his feathers, was a-cold;
The hare limped trembling through the frozen grass,
And silent was the flock in woolly fold:
Numb were the Beadsman's fingers, while he told   5
His rosary, and while his frosted breath,
Like pious incense from a censer old,
Seemed taking flight for heaven, without a death,
Past the sweet Virgin's picture, while his prayer he saith.

2

His prayer he saith, this patient, holy man;   10
Then takes his lamp, and riseth from his knees,
And back returneth, meagre, barefoot, wan,
Along the chapel aisle by slow degrees:
The sculptured dead, on each side, seem to freeze,
Emprisoned in black, purgatorial rails: 15
Knights, ladies, praying in dumb orat'ries,
He passeth by; and his weak spirit fails
To think how they may ache in icy hoods and mails.

---

1 *St. Agnes' Eve*: January 21. The night before is traditionally considered the coldest of the year. 16 *dumb orat'ries*: small chapels that are "dumb" because the knights and ladies are sculptures. 18 *To think*: upon thinking.

3

Northward he turneth through a little door,
And scarce three steps, ere Music's golden tongue   20
Flattered to tears this aged man and poor;
But no—already had his death-bell rung:
The joys of all his life were said and sung:
His was harsh penance on St. Agnes' Eve:
Another way he went, and soon among   25
Rough ashes sat he for his soul's reprieve,
And all night kept awake, for sinners' sake to grieve.

4

That ancient Beadsman heard the prelude soft;
And so it chanced, for many a door was wide,
From hurry to and fro. Soon, up aloft,   30
The silver, snarling trumpets 'gan to chide:
The level chambers, ready with their pride,
Were glowing to receive a thousand guests:
The carved angels, ever eager-eyed,
Stared, where upon their heads the cornice rests,   35
With hair blown back, and wings put crosswise on their breasts.

5

At length burst in the argent revelry,
With plume, tiara, and all rich array,
Numerous as shadows haunting faerily
The brain, new-stuffed, in youth, with triumphs gay   40
Of old romance. These let us wish away,
And turn, sole-thoughted, to one Lady there,
Whose heart had brooded, all that wintry day,
On love, and winged St. Agnes' saintly care,
As she had heard old dames full many times declare.   45

6

They told her how, upon St. Agnes' Eve,
Young virgins might have visions of delight,
And soft adorings from their loves receive
Upon the honeyed middle of the night,
If ceremonies due they did aright;   50
As, supperless to bed they must retire,
And couch supine their beauties, lily white;
Nor look behind, nor sideways, but require
Of Heaven with upward eyes for all that they desire.

7

Full of this whim was thoughtful Madeline: 55
The music, yearning like a God in pain,
She scarcely heard: her maiden eyes divine,
Fixed on the floor, saw many a sweeping train

---

21 *Flattered*: charmed.

Pass by—she heeded not at all: in vain
Came many a tiptoe, amorous cavalier,   60
And back retired; not cooled by high disdain,
But she saw not: her heart was otherwhere,
She sighed for Agnes' dreams, the sweetest of the year.

8

She danced along with vague, regardless eyes,
Anxious her lips, her breathing quick and short: 65
The hallowed hour was near at hand: she sighs
Amid the timbrels, and the thronged resort
Of whisperers in anger, or in sport;
'Mid looks of love, defiance, hate, and scorn,
Hoodwinked with faery fancy; all amort,   70
Save to St. Agnes and her lambs unshorn,
And all the bliss to be before to-morrow morn.

9

So, purposing each moment to retire,
She lingered still. Meantime, across the moors,
Had come young Porphyro, with heart on fire   75
For Madeline. Beside the portal doors,
Buttressed from moonlight, stands he, and implores
All saints to give him sight of Madeline,
But for one moment in the tedious hours,
That he might gaze and worship all unseen;   80
Perchance speak, kneel, touch, kiss—in sooth such things have been.

10

He ventures in: let no buzzed whisper tell:
All eyes be muffled, or a hundred swords
Will storm his heart, Love's fev'rous citadel:
For him, those chambers held barbarian hordes,   85
Hyena foemen, and hot-blooded lords,
Whose very dogs would execrations howl
Against his lineage: not one breast affords
Him any mercy, in that mansion foul,
Save one old beldame, weak in body and in soul.   90

11

Ah, happy chance! the agéd creature came,
Shuffling along with ivory-headed wand,
To where he stood, hid from the torch's flame,
Behind a broad hall-pillar, far beyond
The sound of merriment and chorus bland: 95
He startled her; but soon she knew his face,
And grasped his fingers in her palsied hand,
Saying, "Mercy, Porphyro! hie thee from this place;
They are all here to-night, the whole bloodthirsty race!

---

70 *amort*: as though dead.

12

"Get hence! get hence! there's dwarfish Hildebrand;   100
He had a fever late, and in the fit
He cursèd thee and thine, both house and land:
Then there's that old Lord Maurice, not a whit
More tame for his gray hairs—Alas me! flit!
Flit like a ghost away."—"Ah, Gossip dear,   105
We're safe enough; here in this armchair sit,
And tell me how"—"Good saints! not here, not here;
Follow me, child, or else these stones will be thy bier."

13

He followed through a lowly archèd way,
Brushing the cobwebs with his lofty plume;   110
And as she muttered, "Well-a—well-a-day!"
He found him in a little moonlight room,
Pale, latticed, chill, and silent as a tomb.
"Now tell me where is Madeline," said he,
"Oh tell me, Angela, by the holy loom   115
Which none but secret sisterhood may see,
When they St. Agnes' wool are weaving piously."

14

"St. Agnes! Ah! it is St. Agnes' Eve—
Yet men will murder upon holy days:
Thou must hold water in a witch's sieve,   120
And be liege-lord of all the elves and fays,
To venture so: it fills me with amaze
To see thee, Porphyro!—St. Agnes' Eve!
God's help! my lady fair the conjurer plays
This very night: good angels her deceive!   125
But let me laugh awhile, I've mickle time to grieve."

15

Feebly she laugheth in the languid moon,
While Porphyro upon her face doth look,
Like puzzled urchin on an agèd crone
Who keepeth closed a wond'rous riddlebook,   130
As spectacled she sits in chimney nook.
But soon his eyes grew brilliant, when she told
His lady's purpose, and he scarce could brook
Tears, at the thought of those enchantments cold,
And Madeline asleep in lap of legends old.   135

16

Sudden a thought came like a full-blown rose,
Flushing his brow, and in his pained heart

---

105 *Gossip*: god mother. 117 *St. Agnes' wool*: On the anniversary of the martyrdom of
St. Agnes, two lambs were blessed while the Agnus Dei (Lamb of God) was sung. Afterwards, the lambs were shorn and their wool woven into cloth by the nuns. 124 *conjurer
plays*: i.e., by following the ritual for young ladies on St. Agnes' Eve, Madeline hopes to
"conjure" a vision of her lover.

Made purple riot: then doth he propose
A stratagem, that makes the beldame start:
"A cruel man and impious thou art: 140
Sweet lady, let her pray, and sleep, and dream
Alone with her good angels, far apart
From wicked men like thee. Go, go! I deem
Thou canst not surely be the same that thou didst seem."

17

"I will not harm her, by all saints I swear,"   145
Quoth Porphyro: "O may I ne'er find grace
When my weak voice shall whisper its last prayer,
If one of her soft ringlets I displace,
Or look with ruffian passion in her face:
Good Angela, believe me by these tears;   150
Or I will, even in a moment's space,
Awake, with horrid shout, my foemen's ears,
And beard them, though they be more fanged than wolves and bears."

18

"Ah! why wilt thou affright a feeble soul?
A poor, weak, palsy-stricken, churchyard thing,   155
Whose passing-bell may ere the midnight toll;
Whose prayers for thee, each morn and evening,
Were never missed." Thus plaining, doth she bring
A gentler speech from burning Porphyro;
So woful, and of such deep sorrowing,   160
That Angela gives promise she will do
Whatever he shall wish, betide her weal or woe.

19

Which was, to lead him, in close secrecy,
Even to Madeline's chamber, and there hide
Him in a closet, of such privacy   165
That he might see her beauty unespied,
And win perhaps that night a peerless bride,
While legioned faeries paced the coverlet,
And pale enchantment held her sleepy-eyed.
Never on such a night have lovers met,   170
Since Merlin paid his Demon all the monstrous debt.

20

"It shall be as thou wishest," said the Dame:
"All cates and dainties shall be stored there
Quickly on this feast-night: by the tambor frame
Her own lute thou wilt see: no time to spare,   175
For I am slow and feeble, and scarce dare

---

171 *Merlin...Demon*: the magician Merlin, son of a demon, was imprisoned in a rock by
Vivien, who used the magic he had taught her. 173 *cates*: delicate foods. 174 *Tambor
frame*: an embroidery frame.

On such a catering trust my dizzy head.
Wait here, my child, with patience; kneel in prayer
The while: Ah! thou must needs the lady wed,
Or may I never leave my grave among the dead." 180

21

So saying, she hobbled off with busy fear.
The lover's endless minutes slowly passed;
The Dame returned, and whispered in his ear
To follow her; with aged eyes aghast
From fright of dim espial. Safe at last, 185
Through many a dusky gallery, they gain
The maiden's chamber, silken, hushed and chaste;
Where Porphyro took covert, pleased amain.
His poor guide hurried back with agues in her brain.

22

Her faltering hand upon the balustrade, 190
Old Angela was feeling for the stair,
When Madeline, St. Agnes' charmed maid,
Rose, like a missioned spirit, unaware:
With silver taper's light, and pious care,
She turned, and down the aged gossip led 195
To a safe level matting. Now prepare,
Young Porphyro, for gazing on that bed;
She comes, she comes again, like ring-dove frayed and fled.

23

Out went the taper as she hurried in;
Its little smoke, in pallid moonshine, died: 200
She closed the door, she panted, all akin
To spirits of the air, and visions wide:
No uttered syllable, or, woe betide!
But to her heart, her heart was voluble,
Paining with eloquence her balmy side; 205
As though a tongueless nightingale should swell
Her throat in vain, and die, heart-stifled, in her dell.

24

A casement high and triple-arched there was,
All garlanded with carven imag'ries
Of fruits, and flowers, and bunches of knotgrass, 210
And diamonded with panes of quaint device,
Innumerable of stains and splendid dyes,
As are the tiger-moth's deep-damasked wings;
And in the midst, 'mong thousand heraldries,
And twilight saints, and dim emblazonings, 215
A shielded scutcheon blushed with blood of queens and kings.

188 *amain*: greatly. 198 *frayed*: afraid.

25

Full on this casement shone the wintry moon,
And threw warm gules on Madeline's fair breast,
As down she knelt for heaven's grace and boon;
Rose-bloom fell on her hands, together pressed,   220
And on her silver cross soft amethyst,
And on her hair a glory, like a saint:
She seemed a splendid angel, newly dressed,
Save wings, for heaven:—Porphyro grew faint:
She knelt, so pure a thing, so free from mortal taint.   225

26

Anon his heart revives: her vespers done,
Of all its wreathéd pearls her hair she frees;
Unclasps her warméd jewels one by one;
Loosens her fragrant bodice; by degrees
Her rich attire creeps rustling to her knees: 230
Half-hidden, like a mermaid in seaweed,
Pensive awhile she dreams awake, and sees,
In fancy, fair St. Agnes in her bed,
But dares not look behind, or all the charm is fled.

27

Soon, trembling in her soft and chilly nest,   235
In sort of wakeful swoon, perplexed she lay,
Until the poppied warmth of sleep oppressed
Her soothéd limbs, and soul fatigued away;
Flown, like a thought, until the morrow-day;
Blissfully havened both from joy and pain;   240
Clasped like a missal where swart Paynims pray;
Blinded alike from sunshine and from rain,
As though a rose should shut, and be a bud again.

28

Stol'n to this paradise, and so entranced,
Porphyro gazed upon her empty dress,   245
And listened to her breathing, if it chanced
To wake into a slumberous tenderness;
Which when he heard, that minute did he bless,
And breath'd himself: then from the closet crept,
Noiseless as fear in a wide wilderness,   250
And over the hush'd carpet, silent, stept,
And 'tween the curtains peep'd, where, lo!—how fast she slept.

29

Then by the bed-side, where the faded moon
Made a dim, silver twilight, soft he set
A table, and, half anguish'd, threw thereon   255

---

218 *gules*: red.   236 *perplexed*: half asleep.   241 *missal*: prayer book; *swart*: black;
Paynims: pagans.

A cloth of woven crimson, gold, and jet:—
O for some drowsy Morphean amulet!
The boisterous, midnight, festive clarion,
The kettle-drum, and far heard clarinet,
Affray his ears, though but in dying tone:—   260
The hall door shuts again, and all the noise is gone.

30

And still she slept an azure-lidded sleep,
In blanched linen, smooth, and lavendered,
While he from forth the closet brought a heap
Of candied apple, quince, and plum, and gourd;   265
With jellies soother than the creamy curd,
And lucent syrops, tinct with cinnamon;
Manna and dates, in argosy transferred
From Fez; and spiced dainties, every one,
From silken Samarcand to cedared Lebanon.   270

31

These delicates he heaped with glowing hand
On golden dishes and in baskets bright
Of wreathed silver: sumptuous they stand
In the retired quiet of the night,
Filling the chilly room with perfume light.—   275
"And now, my love, my seraph fair, awake!
Thou art my heaven, and I thine eremite:
Open thine eyes, for meek St. Agnes' sake,
Or I shall drowse beside thee, so my soul doth ache."

32

Thus whispering, his warm, unnerved arm   280
Sank in her pillow. Shaded was her dream
By the dusk curtains:—'twas a midnight charm
Impossible to melt as iced stream:
The lustrous salvers in the moonlight gleam;
Broad golden fringe upon the carpet lies: 285
It seemed he never, never could redeem
From such a steadfast spell his lady's eyes;
So mused awhile, entoiled in woofed phantasies.

33

Awakening up, he took her hollow lute,—
Tumultuous,—and, in chords that tenderest be,   290
He played an ancient ditty, long since mute,
In Provence called "La belle dame sans mercy:"
Close to her ear touching the melody;—
Wherewith disturbed, she uttered a soft moan:

---

257 Morphean amulet: a charm of the god of dreams. *266 soother*: smoother. *277 eremite*: worshiper.

He ceased—she panted quick—and suddenly   295
Her blue affrayed eyes wide open shone:
Upon his knees he sank, pale as smooth-sculptured stone.

34
Her eyes were open, but she still beheld,
Now wide awake, the vision of her sleep:
There was a painful change, that night expelled   300
The blisses of her dream so pure and deep
At which fair Madeline began to weep,
And moan forth witless words with many a sigh;
While still her gaze on Porphyro would keep;
Who knelt, with joined hands and piteous eye,   305
Fearing to move or speak, she looked so dreamingly.

35
"Ah, Porphyro!" said she, "but even now
Thy voice was at sweet tremble in mine ear,
Made tuneable with every sweetest vow;
And those sad eyes were spiritual and clear: 310
How changed thou art! how pallid, chill, and drear!
Give me that voice again, my Porphyro,
Those looks immortal, those complainings dear!
Oh leave me not in this eternal woe,
For if thou diest, my Love, I know not where to go."   315

36
Beyond a mortal man impassioned far
At these voluptuous accents, he arose,
Ethereal, flushed, and like a throbbing star
Seen mid the sapphire heaven's deep repose;
Into her dream he melted, as the rose   320
Blendeth its odor with the violet,—
Solution sweet: meantime the frost-wind blows
Like Love's alarum, pattering the sharp sleet
Against the window-panes; St. Agnes' moon hath set.

37
'Tis dark: quick pattereth the flaw-blown sleet: 325
"This is no dream, my bride, my Madeline!"
'Tis dark: the icéd gusts still rave and beat:
"No dream, alas! alas! and woe is mine!
Porphyro will leave me here to fade and pine.—
Cruel! what traitor could thee hither bring?   330
I curse not, for my heart is lost in thine,
Though thou forsakest a deceivéd thing;—
A dove forlorn and lost with sick unprunéd wing."

---

325 *flaw-blown*: windblown.

38

"My Madeline! sweet dreamer! lovely bride!
Say, may I be for aye thy vassal blest?   335
Thy beauty's shield, heart-shaped and vermeil dyed?
Ah, silver shrine, here will I take my rest
After so many hours of toil and quest,
A famished pilgrim,—saved by miracle.
Though I have found, I will not rob thy nest   340
Saving of the sweet self; if thou think'st well
To trust, fair Madeline, to no rude infidel.

39

"Hark! 'tis an elfin-storm from faery land,
Of haggard seeming, but a boon indeed:
Arise—arise! the morning is at hand,   345
The bloated wassailers will never heed:—
Let us away, my love, with happy speed;
There are no ears to hear, or eyes to see,—
Drowned all in Rhenish and the sleepy mead:
Awake! arise! my love, and fearless be,   350
For o'er the southern moors I have a home for thee."

40

She hurried at his words, beset with fears,
For there were sleeping dragons all around,
At glaring watch, perhaps, with ready spears—
Down the wide stairs a darkling way they found.—   355
In all the house was heard no human sound.
A chain-drooped lamp was flickering by each door;
The arras, rich with horseman, hawk, and hound,
Fluttered in the besieging wind's uproar;
And the long carpets rose along the gusty floor.   360

41

They glide, like phantoms, into the wide hall;
Like phantoms, to the iron porch they glide;
Where lay the porter, in uneasy sprawl,
With a huge empty flagon by his side:
The wakeful bloodhound rose, and shook his hide,   365
But his sagacious eye an inmate owns:
By one, and one, the bolts full easy slide:—
The chains lie silent on the footworn stones;—
The key turns, and the door upon its hinges groans.

42

And they are gone: ay, ages long ago   370
These lovers fled away into the storm.
That night the baron dreamt of many a woe,
And all his warrior-guests, with shade and form

---

344 *haggard*: wild. 346 *bloated wassailers*: drunken revelers. 366 *But...owns*: i.e., the
dog recognizes Madeline as one of the household.

Of witch, and demon, and large coffin-worm
Were long be-nightmared. Angela the old   375
Died palsy-twitched, with meager face deform;
The beadsman, after thousand avés told,
For aye unsought for slept among his ashes cold.

ALFRED, LORD TENNYSON *(1809–1892)*

The Lady of Shalott is a highly compressed romance. Lacking the range and
variety of poems like *The Faerie Queene* or *Sir Gawain and the Green Knight,*
it seems like a single episode isolated from a larger romantic context but
perfectly self-contained. The elaborate narrative trappings of earlier romances
—exhaustive nature descriptions, prolonged dialogues, all the patient detail of
scene and action—have been reduced in size and grandeur yet remain pro-
portionate to the length and complexity of the poem. The old familiar elements
of the romantic world are here—King Arthur's court at Camelot, Sir Lancelot
on his war-horse, a fairy lady imprisoned in a tower, not by a dragon but by
a curse. However, the order and perspective in which the events of the poem
appear are inverted. Normally, the romantic hero sets forth, like Gawain or
the Redcross Knight, from the social world of the court and passes into the
world of nature where his adventures are conducted in comparative isolation.
In *The Lady of Shalott,* however, the Lady starts her quest at the end rather
than at the beginning of the poem, and she journeys to rather than from the
court, passing from isolation to society, from fantasy to reality. The combat
between the hero and an antagonist, which plays a central role in the action
of romance, takes the form here of a thematic opposition between the solitary
world of the imagination (associated with art, timelessness, dream, night) and
the public world of fact and reality (associated with life, time, mortality, day).

THE LADY OF SHALOTT

PART 1

On either side the river lie
Long fields of barley and of rye,
That clothe the wold and meet the sky;
And thro' the field the road runs by
    To many-towered Camelot;   5
And up and down the people go,
Gazing where the lilies blow
Round an island there below,
    The island of Shalott.

Willows whiten, aspens quiver,   10
Little breezes dusk and shiver
Thro' the wave that runs for ever
By the island in the river
    Flowing down to Camelot.
Four gray walls, and four gray towers,   15

---

377 *avés: Ave Marias* ("Hail Marys").
3 *wold*: plains. 5 *Camelot*: King Arthur's castle.

Overlook a space of flowers,
And the silent isle imbowers
     The Lady of Shalott.

By the margin, willow-veiled,
Slide the heavy barges trailed   20
By slow horses; and unhailed
The shallop flitteth silken-sailed
     Skimming down to Camelot:
But who hath seen her wave her hand?
Or at the casement seen her stand?   25
Or is she known in all the land,
     The Lady of Shalott?

Only reapers, reaping early
In among the bearded barley,
Hear a song that echoes cheerly   30
From the river winding clearly,
     Down to towered Camelot;
And by the moon the reaper weary,
Piling sheaves in uplands airy,
Listening, whispers " 'Tis the fairy   35
     Lady of Shalott."

Part 2

There she weaves by night and day
A magic web with colors gay.
She has heard a whisper say,
A curse is on her if she stay   40
     To look down to Camelot.
She knows not what the curse may be,
And so she weaveth steadily,
And little other care hath she,
     The Lady of Shalott.   45

And moving thro' a mirror clear
That hangs before her all the year,
Shadows of the world appear.
There she sees the highway near
     Winding down to Camelot;   50
There the river eddy whirls,
And there the surly village-churls,
And the red cloaks of market girls,
     Pass onward from Shalott.

Sometimes a troop of damsels glad,   55
An abbot on an ambling pad,
Sometimes a curly shepherd-lad,
Or long-haired page in crimson clad,
     Goes by to towered Camelot;
And sometimes thro' the mirror blue   60

The knights come riding two and two:
She hath no loyal knight and true,
      The Lady of Shalott.

But in her web she still delights
To weave the mirror's magic sights,   65
For often thro' the silent nights
A funeral, with plumes and lights
      And music, went to Camelot;
Or when the moon was overhead,
Came two young lovers lately wed: 70
"I am half-sick of shadows," said
      The Lady of Shalott.

PART 3

A bow-shot from her bower-eaves,
He rode between the barley-sheaves,
The sun came dazzling thro' the leaves,   75
And flamed upon the brazen greaves
      Of bold Sir Lancelot.
A redcross knight for ever kneeled
To a lady in his shield,
That sparkled on the yellow field,   80
      Beside remote Shalott.

The gemmy bridle glittered free,
Like to some branch of stars we see
Hung in the golden Galaxy.
The bridle bells rang merrily   85
      As he rode down to Camelot;
And from his blazoned baldric slung
A mighty silver bugle hung,
And as he rode his armor rung,
      Beside remote Shalott.   90

All in the blue unclouded weather
Thick-jewelled shone the saddle-leather,
The helmet and the helmet-feather
Burned like one burning flame together,
      As he rode down to Camelot;   95
As often thro' the purple night,
Below the starry clusters bright,
Some bearded meteor, trailing light,
      Moves over still Shalott.

His broad clear brow in sunlight glowed;   100
On burnished hooves his war-horse trode;
From underneath his helmet flowed
His coal-black curls as on he rode,
      As he rode down to Camelot.
From the bank and from the river   105
He flashed into the crystal mirror,

"Tirra lirra," by the river
  Sang Sir Lancelot.

She left the web, she left the loom,
She made three paces thro' the room,   110
She saw the water-lily bloom,
She saw the helmet and plume,
  She looked down to Camelot.
Out flew the web and floated wide;
The mirror cracked from side to side;   115
"The curse is come upon me," cried
  The Lady of Shalott.

PART 4

In the stormy east-wind straining,
The pale yellow woods were waning,
The broad stream in his banks complaining, 120
Heavily the low sky raining
  Over towered Camelot;
Down she came and found a boat
Beneath a willow left afloat,
And round about the prow she wrote   125
  The Lady of Shalott.

And down the river's dim expanse—
Like some bold seër in a trance,
Seeing all his own mischance—
With a glassy countenance   130
  Did she look to Camelot.
And at the closing of the day
She loosed the chain, and down she lay;
The broad stream bore her far away,
  The Lady of Shalott.   135

Lying, robed in snowy white
That loosely flew to left and right—
The leaves upon her falling light—
Thro' the noises of the night
  She floated down to Camelot: 140
And as the boat-head wound along
The willowy hills and fields among,
They heard her singing her last song,
  The Lady of Shalott.

Heard a carol, mournful, holy,   145
Chanted loudly, chanted lowly,
Till her blood was frozen slowly,
And her eyes were darkened wholly,
  Turned to towered Camelot.
For ere she reached upon the tide 150
The first house by the water-side,

Singing in her song she died,
> The Lady of Shalott.

Under tower and balcony,
By garden-wall and gallery,   155
A gleaming shape she floated by,
Dead-pale between the houses high,
> Silent into Camelot.
Out upon the wharfs they came,
Knight and burgher, lord and dame,   160
And round the prow they read her name,
> *The Lady of Shalott.*

Who is this? and what is here?
And in the lighted palace near
Died the sound of royal cheer;   165
And they crossed themselves for fear,
> All the knights at Camelot:
But Lancelot mused a little space;
He said, "She has a lovely face;
God in his mercy lend her grace,   170
> The Lady of Shalott."

ROBERT BROWNING *(1812–1899)*

Written in one day during January 1852, "Childe Roland," Browning said, "came upon me as a kind of dream." No doubt it comes upon most readers as a kind of dream too, a nightmarish dream full of meanings difficult to pin down. In later life, Browning said that he had been "conscious of no allegorical intention in writing it," but its general significance, he agreed, might be summarized in the statement, "He that endureth to the end shall be saved." But to what "end" has the hero endured, what does "saved" mean in the context of the poem, and why has Browning drawn on the age of chivalry to formulate that meaning? Such a handy moral platitude hardly seems to do justice to the intense suggestiveness of the work, and even if it were more or less accurate we should still feel dissatisfied, acutely conscious that the "moral" ignores all that is important in the immediate poetic experience—not only the tone and imagery but such concrete details as the identity of the "hoary cripple" and the nature and function of the Dark Tower itself. Despite Browning's demurrer, the poem has been subjected to a variety of allegorical readings, apparently on the assumption that the speaker's words in line 167—"solve it, you!"— are a direct challenge to the reader's ingenuity.

Unquestionably, the poem *is* enigmatic, and it does invite some kind of critical translation, though we may doubt that there is any allegorical "key" that will bring all its meanings into systematic alignment. Not as a solution, then, but as a critical basis for interpretive refinements, the following generic information should be helpful to the student. "Childe Roland" belongs to a form of quest romance featuring the "otherworld journey"—a medieval form whose central motifs are the passage of the knight (here a "childe," or one of gentle birth, sometimes a candidate for knighthood) through a wasteland ("that ominous tract"), his crossing of a body of water (stanzas 19–21), and his arrival at the "Dolorous Tower" (stanza 31). The Tower is the abode of a tyrant associated variously with Death, or Satan, who holds certain people in captivity, normally including a lovely damsel and often a wounded nobleman. The wandering knight, having been treated hospitably by them, agrees for the sake of the nobleman and his daughter to challenge the tyrant—perhaps by blowing a horn to call him forth—in hopes of freeing them. The knight normally triumphs and is given sovereignty over the otherworld as well as the hand of the damsel (though he may defer his rewards, as in the Breton lay *Sir Degare*). If he is defeated, as in *Balin,* his death may be a futile climax to a wasted and misdirected life.

CHILDE ROLAND TO THE DARK TOWER CAME*

1

My first thought was, he lied in every word,
   That hoary cripple, with malicious eye
   Askance to watch the working of his lie
On mine, and mouth scarce able to afford
Suppression of the glee, that pursed and scored   5
   Its edge, at one more victim gained thereby.

2

What else should he be set for, with his staff?
   What, save to waylay with his lies, ensnare
   All travellers who might find him posted there,
And ask the road? I guessed what skull-like laugh   10
Would break, what crutch 'gin write my epitaph
   For pastime in the dusty thoroughfare,

3

If at his counsel I should turn aside
   Into that ominous tract which, all agree,
   Hides the Dark Tower. Yet acquiescingly   15
I did turn as he pointed: neither pride
Nor hope rekindling at the end descried,
   So much as gladness that some end might be.

4

For, what with my whole world-wide wandering,
   What with my search drawn out thro' years, my hope   20
   Dwindled into a ghost not fit to cope
With that obstreperous joy success would bring,—
I hardly tried now to rebuke the spring
   My heart made, finding failure in its scope.

5

As when a sick man very near to death   25
   Seems dead indeed, and feels begin and end

---

* See Edgar's song in *King Lear,* III. iv. 187–190.

The tears and takes the farewell of each friend,
And hears one bid the other go, draw breath
Freelier outside, ("since all is o'er, he saith,
    "And the blow fallen no grieving can amend;")   30

6

While some discuss if near the other graves
    Be room enough for this, and when a day
    Suits best for carrying the corpse away,
With care about the banners, scarves and staves:
And still the man hears all, and only craves   35
    He may not shame such tender love and stay.

7

Thus, I had so long suffered in this quest,
    Heard failure prophesied so oft, been writ
    So many times among "The Band"—to wit,
The knights who to the Dark Tower's search addressed   40
Their steps—that just to fail as they, seemed best,
    And all the doubt was now—should I be fit?

8

So, quiet as despair, I turned from him,
    That hateful cripple, out of his highway
    Into the path he pointed. All the day   45
Had been a dreary one at best, and dim
Was settling to its close, yet shot one grim
    Red leer to see the plain catch its estray.

9

For mark! no sooner was I fairly found
    Pledged to the plain, after a pace or two,   50
    Than, pausing to throw backward a last view
O'er the safe road, 't was gone; grey plain all round:
Nothing but plain to the horizon's bound.
    I might go on; nought else remained to do.

10

So, on I went. I think I never saw   55
Such starved ignoble nature; nothing throve:
    For flowers—as well expect a cedar grove!
But cockle, spurge, according to their law
Might propagate their kind, with none to awe,
    You 'd think; a burr had been a treasure-trove.   60

11

No! penury, inertness and grimace,
    In some strange sort, were the land's portion. "See

---

48 *estray*: a stray (the speaker).

"Or shut your eyes," said Nature peevishly,
  "It nothing skills: I cannot help my case:
  " 'T is the Last Judgment's fire must cure this place,   65
  "Calcine its clods and set my prisoners free."

12

If there pushed any ragged thistle-stalk
  Above its mates, the head was chopped; the bents
  Were jealous else. What made those holes and rents
In the dock's harsh swarth leaves, bruised as to baulk   70
All hope of greenness? 't is a brute must walk
  Pashing their life out, with a brute's intents.

13

As for the grass, it grew as scant as hair
  In leprosy; thin dry blades pricked the mud
  Which underneath looked kneaded up with blood.   75
One stiff blind horse, his every bone a-stare,
Stood stupefied, however he came there:
  Thrust out past service from the devil's stud!

14

Alive? he might be dead for aught I know,
  With that red gaunt and colloped neck a-strain,   80
  And shut eyes underneath the rusty mane;
Seldom went such grotesqueness with such woe;
I never saw a brute I hated so;
  He must be wicked to deserve such pain.

15

I shut my eyes and turned them on my heart.   85
  As a man calls for wine before he fights,
  I asked one draught of earlier, happier sights,
Ere fitly I could hope to play my part.
Think first, fight afterwards—the soldier's art:
  One taste of the old time sets all to rights.   90

16

Not it! I fancied Cuthbert's reddening face
  Beneath its garniture of curly gold,
  Dear fellow, till I almost felt him fold
An arm in mine to fix me to the place,
That way he used. Alas, one night's disgrace!   95
Out went my heart's new fire and left it cold.

17

Giles then, the soul of honour—there he stands
  Frank as ten years ago when knighted first.
  What honest man should dare (he said) he durst.
Good—but the scene shifts—faugh! what hangman hands   100

66 *Calcine*: burn to powder.

Pin to his breast a parchment? His own bands
  Read it. Poor traitor, spit upon and curst!

18

Better this present than a past like that;
  Back therefore to my darkening path again!
  No sound, no sight as far as eye could strain.   105
Will the night send a howlet or a bat?
I asked: when something on the dismal flat
  Came to arrest my thoughts and change their train.

19

A sudden little river crossed my path
  As unexpected as a serpent comes.   110
  No sluggish tide congenial to the glooms;
This, as it frothed by, might have been a bath
For the fiend's glowing hoof—to see the wrath
  Of its black eddy bespate with flakes and spumes.

20

So petty yet so spiteful! All along,   115
  Low scrubby alders kneeled down over it;
  Drenched willows flung them headlong in a fit
Of mute despair, a suicidal throng:
The river which had done them all the wrong,
  Whate'er that was, rolled by, deterred no whit.   120

21

Which, while I forded,—good saints, how I feared
  To set my foot upon a dead man's cheek,
  Each step, or feel the spear I thrust to seek
For hollows, tangled in his hair or beard!
—It may have been a water-rat I speared,   125
  But, ugh! it sounded like a baby's shriek.

22

Glad was I when I reached the other bank.
  Now for a better country. Vain presage!
  Who were the strugglers, what war did they wage,
Whose savage trample thus could pad the dank
Soil to a plash? Toads in a poisoned tank,   130
  Or wild cats in a red-hot iron cage—

23

The fight must so have seemed in that fell cirque.
  What penned them there, with all the plain to choose?
  No footprint leading to that horrid mews,
None out of it. Mad brewage set to work   135
Their brains, no doubt, like galley slaves the Turk
  Pits for his pastime, Christians against Jews.

---

106 *howlet*: owl.   114 *bespate*: bespattered.   133 *cirque*: arena.   135 *mews*: enclosure.

24

And more than that—a furlong on—why, there!
   What bad use was that engine for, that wheel,   140
   Or brake, not wheel—that harrow fit to reel
Men's bodies out like silk? with all the air
Of Tophet's tool, on earth left unaware,
   Or brought to sharpen its rusty teeth of steel.

25

Then came a bit of stubbed ground, once a wood,   145
   Next a marsh, it would seem, and now mere earth
   Desperate and done with; (so a fool finds mirth,
Makes a thing and then mars it, till his mood
Changes and off he goes!) within a rood—
   Bog, clay and rubble, sand and stark black dearth.   150

26

Now blotches rankling, colored gay and grim,
   Now patches where some leanness of the soil's
   Broke into moss or substances like boils;
Then came some palsied oak, a cleft in him
Like a distorted mouth that splits its rim   155
   Gaping at death, and dies while it recoils.

27

And just as far as ever from the end!
   Naught in the distance but the evening, naught
   To point my footstep further! At the thought,
A great black bird, Apollyon's bosom friend,   160
Sailed past, nor beat his wide wing dragon-penned
   That brushed my cap—perchance the guide I sought.

28

For, looking up, aware I somehow grew,
   'Spite of the dusk, the plain had given place
   All round to mountains—with such name to grace   165
Mere ugly heights and heaps now stolen in view.
How thus they had surprised me—solve it, you!
   How to get from them was no clearer case.

29

Yet half I seemed to recognize some trick
   Of mischief happened to me, God knows when—   170
   In a bad dream perhaps. Here ended, then,
Progress this way. When, in the very nick
Of giving up, one time more, came a click
   As when a trap shuts—you're inside the den!

---

141 *brake*: machine for crushing flax or hemp, hence a device of torture.   143 *Tophet's*:
Hell's.   160 *Apollyon's*: the devil's.

30

Burningly it came on me all at once,   175
   This was the place! those two hills on the right,
   Crouched like two bulls locked horn in horn in fight;
While to the left, a tall scalped mountain...Dunce,
Dotard, a-dozing at the very nonce,
   After a life spent training for the sight!   180

31

What in the midst lay but the Tower itself?
   The round squat turret, blind as the fool's heart,
   Built of brown stone, without a counterpart
In the whole world. The tempest's mocking elf
Points to the shipman thus the unseen shelf   185
   He strikes on, only when the timbers start.

32

Not see? because of night perhaps?—why, day
   Came back again for that! before it left,
   The dying sunset kindled through a cleft:
The hills, like giants at a hunting, lay,   190
Chin upon hand, to see the game at bay—
   "Now stab and end the creature—to the heft!"

33

Not hear? when noise was everywhere! it tolled
   Increasing like a bell. Names in my ears
   Of all the lost adventurers my peers—   195
How such a one was strong, and such was bold,
And such was fortunate, yet each of old
   Lost, lost! one moment knelled the woe of years.

34

There they stood, ranged along the hillsides, met
   To view the last of me, a living frame   200
   For one more picture! in a sheet of flame
I saw them and I knew them all. And yet
Dauntless the slug-horn to my lips I set,
   And blew. *"Childe Roland to the Dark Tower came."*

Satire

Introduction

That satire is a literary form rather than a collection of various modes of verbal attack is not overly obvious at first glance. The Latin *satura* means a mixture of different things, in particular a dish of assorted fruits and perhaps grain; most words associated with satire, even by satirists themselves, like "farragoes," "hodgepodge," "medley," "mishmash," and "olio," suggest that it has the unity of a pot of stew. Its formal integrity seems even further compromised by its refusal to stand apart: we find it infiltrating the novel (as in Thomas Peacock's *Nightmare Abbey*), drama (Marston's *The Malcontent*), pastoral (Gay's *Shepherd's Week*), romance (Butler's *Hudibras*), lyric (Blake's "London"), and other genres. At best it would seem a flexible form, at worst an amorphous one.

We can get some clues about the motives behind satire from satirists, who are readier than most poets to explain why they have chosen their particular literary form. The Roman poet Juvenal, for instance, devotes the first of his sixteen satires to it, concluding that he writes satire because, given the current state of Rome and the world generally, he finds it impossible not to:

> Such fulsome objects meeting everywhere,
> 'Tis hard to write, but harder to forbear.
> To view so lewd a town, and to refrain,
> What hoops of iron could my spleen contain!

Ben Jonson echoes this sentiment: "Who is so patient of this impious world, / That he can check his spirit, or rein his tongue?" Certainly not Jonson himself, who adds:

> I'll strip the ragged follies of the time
> Naked as at their birth:...
> ...and with a whip of steel
> Print wounding lashes in their iron ribs.

The satirist's motive for writing thus appears to be the personal gratification of unleashing destructive impulses in print, a kind of symbolic murder—the Art of Poisoning, one critic called it, or at least, as Jonson suggests, a linguistic whipping, with the stress on the whipper's pleasure.

But whipping is normally a punishment, and however privately gratifying punishment may be to the punisher it is usually justified as being in the public interest. John Dryden, for instance, argues that lampooning (direct satire of an individual), although not perhaps a pleasant species of writing, is nevertheless permissible when the victim has become "a public nuisance." In fact, Dryden says, " 'Tis an action of virtue, to make examples of vicious men." Thus Alexander Pope, who if Dryden is right must have piled up a treasury of spiritual merits, can claim that the satirist is "To Virtue only and her friends a friend," a claim seconded by his friend Jonathan Swift, who said that satire is the product of "a public spirit, prompting men of genius to mend the world as far as they are able." The satirist now appears to have a divided personality as both private agent and public conscience. Juvenal's famous phrase *saeva indignatio* ("savage indignation") perhaps suggests this division, *saeva* implying the personal hostility vented in attack, *indignatio* the suprapersonal moral consciousness that puts the attack in the public interest.

But if satire manages to incorporate both private hostility and public morality, we should expect a certain tension between them and a predominance of one or the other in individual works. The literary form of morality is the sermon, moralizing governed by a corrective intention; the literary form of hostility is invective, denunciation governed by a destructive intention. Neither of these in its pure form is properly satire; they are the upper and lower boundaries or vanishing points of satire, the points where the energy of satire escapes when the tension between hostility and morality fails.

Invective—railing, vilifying, denouncing, berating, name-calling—is personal, offering a release of indignation, hatred, or anger immediately, explosively. The sermon is essentially impersonal, the speaker acting not in his own behalf but as the mouthpiece of gods, church, morality in general. The railer wants the verbal equivalent of physical destruction for his victims, offering corrosive without corrective; the sermoner wants their moral reformation, thus featuring corrective without corrosive, which is perhaps why the sermon is associated with somnolence no less than reverence.

The sermon, despite obvious drawbacks, exercises a strong magnetic attraction upon satire, many works tending to pass through the elusive ironies of satire toward the earnest, straightforward appeals of moralizing. Wyatt's "Epistle to John Poins" moves from the fictional ironies of the old country-mouse town-mouse story to a final section in which Wyatt prays for an aching conscience on the part of those who have abandoned virtue. Robert Burns, after some deft deflations of the "rigidly righteous" in his "Address to the Unco Guid," abruptly exchanges his stiletto for a cross:

> Who made the heart, 'tis He alone
> Decidedly can try us;

> He knows each chord, its various tone,
>   Each spring, its various bias:
> Then at the balance, let's be mute,
>   We never can adjust it:
> What's done we partly may compute
>   But know not what's resisted.

Leaving judgment to God, however, is not likely to appeal to satirists, nor are they content for long with the straightforwardness of sermonizing, which as Swift says is "to bawl one day in seven against the lawfulness of those methods most in use toward the pursuit of greatness, riches and pleasure, which are the constant practice of all men alive on the other six." Without some corrosive to make the patient sit up and take notice, the corrective medicine of sermon is difficult to administer.

Satire thus inclines more to invective than to pure moralizing. A good example is Kent's speech to Oswald in *King Lear*. According to Kent, Oswald is

a knave, a rascal, an eater of broken meats; a base, proud, shallow, beggarly, three-suited, hundred-pound, filthy worsted-stocking knave; a lily-livered, action-taking knave; a whoreson, glass-gazing, super-serviceable, finical rogue; one-trunk-inheriting slave; one that wouldst be a bawd in way of good service, and art nothing but the composition of a knave, beggar, coward, pandar, and the son and heir of a mongrel bitch.

Kent's catalog of accusations is a mixture of high- and low-grade invective. Calling Oswald an "action-taking knave," for instance, meaning that he prefers the courtroom to the dueling-yard as a scene of combat, is wittier than calling him simply "a knave, beggar, coward, pandar." "How easy it is," Dryden observed, "to call rogue and villain, and that wittily! But how hard to make a man appear a fool, a blockhead, or a knave, without using any of those opprobrious terms!" True enough, but true also that the curse, especially when it rises like Kent's into a bellclapping, polysyllabic malediction, is infinitely pleasing to the human ear, as long as it falls upon someone else, which is why we go on reading satire that descends to invective long after we have put down that which rises to sermoning. Invective alone is not genuine satire, but in its aim of destroying its victim's surface identity and exposing his real identity (Kent, for instance, rubbing out the pseudo-Oswald and giving us the real one in all his baseness, proudness, shallowness, etc.) we can discern the characteristic assumption of satire (that appearances are deluding) and the characteristic goal of satire (to strip away pretensions, hypocrisies, phoniness).

Satire, then, can be thought of as operating between the poles of sermon and invective, combining corrosive and corrective power. Its corrosive power is contained in irony, which is, briefly, the art of meaning more than one says. There are various sorts of irony—tragic, comic, Socratic, cosmic, romantic, and so on—satiric irony being the irony of attack, distinguished from invective in that it seeks not to destroy but to diminish. At least, that would appear to be the distinction between Kent's ferocious abuse of Oswald and Byron's precise, rather quiet couplet on Wordsworth:

> We learn from Horace, "Homer sometimes sleeps;"
> We feel without him—Wordsworth sometimes wakes.

This example shows clearly that destruction need not be by demolition; caught in satire's ironic focus, the object of attack may simply diminish to the vanishing point. The ironist walks softly and carries a cane-sword.

The various types of satiric irony—understatement, inversions of praise and blame, satiric catalogs, allegory, false logic, and others—are less immediately important than their underlying strategy. The indirectness, often even elusiveness, of the satirist's statements implies his trust in the reader's intelligence; the writer and the reader are thus brought into alliance as insiders sharing a joke unavailable to the less shrewd. Again, the fact that he passes up a direct frontal attack in favor of obliqueness implies the satirist's superiority to what he attacks. Pope's unfailing politeness, his air of imperturbable urbanity, suggest that however devastating his satire may be, he has far more power in reserve than he has needed or shown. In the "Epistle to Dr. Arbuthnot," for instance, notice how he annihilates "Sporus" (Lord Hervey) by having "Arbuthnot" tell him that there is no need for him to bring out his *real* satiric weapons:

> ARBUTHNOT. What? that thing of silk,
> Sporus, that mere white curd of ass's milk?
> Satire or sense, alas! can Sporus feel?
> Who breaks a butterfly upon a wheel?

Two passages from *Don Juan* can be instructive in this regard. Here is one from the dedication, in which Byron addresses the "intellectual eunuch Castlereagh," the most prominent politician in England at the time:

> Cold-blooded, smooth-faced, placid miscreant!
> Dabbling its sleek young hands in Erin's gore,
> And thus for wider carnage taught to pant,
> Transferr'd to gorge upon a sister shore,
> The vulgarest tool that Tyranny could want,
> With just enough of talent, and no more,
> To lengthen fetters by another fixed,
> And offer poison long already mixed.

Here, especially at the opening, Byron's own indignation gets in the way of effective satire, triggering the verbal equivalent of an apoplectic seizure. Purely personal hostility must be mixed with a degree of impersonality, if only to keep the attack from degenerating into wild haymakers. Contrast the effect on Southey of this passage, in which Byron, while commenting upon his tendency to digress in *Don Juan,* is reminded of the French word *longeurs* (long, boring passages in a work):

> I know that what our neighbors call "longeurs"
> (We've not so good a *word,* but have the *thing,*
> In that complete perfection which insures
> An epic from Bob Southey every spring),
> Form not the true temptation which allures
> The reader....

The pure hatred of the lines on Castlereagh gives way here to amused contempt, explosive self-expression to casual comment. Part of the success lies in the fact that Southey does not even merit being the principal subject of the stanza: Byron polishes him off in parenthesis.

As these examples would suggest, satiric corrosives act primarily on the object under attack—Southey, Lord Hervey, Wordsworth. But the acid of irony often eats its way through the immediate victim, dissolves logical boundaries, and bathes everything in sight. (The churchmen who helped keep Moliere's *Tartuffe* off the stage because they felt it attacked genuine piety as well as religious hypocrisy may have been bad critics, but their instincts were essentially sound.) This keeps satirists constantly busy writing apologies (like the one Swift added to *A Tale of a Tub* claiming that it was not Religion and Learning but corruptions of them at which he aimed) and explanations that seek to confine their satire to a given subject, while their audiences, grown hyperalert to irony, nod and smile in unbelieving agreement.

Satiric corrective, on the other hand, aims less at the object under attack than at the reader. Proving Thomas Shadwell perfectly qualified to be monarch of poetic dullness, as Dryden does in *Mac Flecknoe,* is not designed to make Shadwell less dull in the future. What is corrected is not Shadwell but our opinion of him, which presumably drifts from approval to contempt. Correction is involved in another sense also, because as readers we must "correct for" the distortion and overstatement of satire. Science, for instance, neither is nor was in Swift's time the crackpot cult we encounter in Book III of *Gulliver's Travels.* Still, in "correcting for" we may find ourselves "corrected," too, our rejection of a satiric extreme leaving us with a more complex or balanced view than we had to begin with ("Science is not *this* absurd, but it's not as rational as I originally assumed, either").

Relatively uncomplicated irony leaves us in little doubt as to what position we are asked to take. In probing serious moral issues, however, satiric irony is sometimes difficult to come to terms with. In the "Digression concerning Madness" in *A Tale of a Tub,* for instance, Swift's subject is the friction between appearances and reality: apparent greatness harbors inner corruption; the world's conquerors, philosophers, and theologians are prompted not by nobility, courage, industry, and intelligence but by an inner madness whose vapors have settled in one or another part of their bodies. Then Swift speaks of the man who practices the "noble art" of accepting surface appearances:

And he, whose fortunes and dispositions have placed him in a convenient station to enjoy the fruits of this noble art; he that can, with Epicurus, content his ideas with the films and images that fly off upon his senses from the superficies of things; such a man, truly wise, creams off nature, leaving the sour and the dregs for philosophy and reason to lap up. This is the sublime and refined point of felicity, called, the possession of being well deceived; the serene peaceful state, of being a fool among knaves.

Lining oneself up with those who are fools among knaves is not especially appealing, but what is the alternative? Only that of lapping up, with philosophy and reason, "the sour and dregs" of nature, the inner corruption of things that wear outwardly an attractive dress. Evidently one must be either deceived or in despair; and the reader may well feel like dismissing the whole matter on the grounds that Swift is simply attacking everything. But the point is that his use of satiric irony has made a complacent reading of the passage impossible; the reader is compelled to explore the issues for himself in an attempt to find a tenable position. To the satiric vision, the inertia of complacency is intolerable. The whip of irony is laid across the reader's intellect not with punitive violence but with a light flicking motion designed to keep the brain moving—even to induce a little intellectual skipping and dancing.

I.   The Grammar of Satire   Given the aim of moral correction, satire becomes consciously rhetorical, an instrument of persuasion. Persuasion seeks to promote communion of belief through the evaporation of differences; its object, in grammatical terms, is to transform "I-you" into "we" relationships. Satire, of course, involves not only an "I-you" or "speaker-reader" dimension but also an "it," or object of attack. Sometimes the "you" may be identical to the "it," the satire attacking its audience, but normally, as persuasion, satire aims to enlist the audience in its own cause. The lyric poet may address himself to no one, merely putting words into the air, and the narrative poet of epic or romance may address an indefinite audience of no particular time or place; but the satirist speaks directly to his contemporaries, making certain assertions and demands. Although individual satires may transcend their time and place, satire itself is the most topical of genres. Its dominant grammatical tense, therefore, is the present, and its verbal mood the indicative. Whereas romance, for instance, deals primarily in the subjunctive mood, creating an "if"-world of desire or dread (a Camelot of Arthur, a Dark Tower of Childe Roland), the present indicative of satire locks onto current realities. Romance says "If this were," satire "This is."

Satire's present indicative follows naturally from the fact that you can attack and correct only the present. The only meaningful attack upon the future or the past is upon present opinions of them. Works like *Brave New World* or *1984* that seem to be in the future tense are actually in a disguised present tense, their future an extrapolation of present realities; both attack not the future but present notions, among other things, of progress. So too with grammatical mood: satiric fantasies like *Gulliver's Travels* that appear subjunctive are warped or ironic forms of the indicative, either presenting a caricature of This Is or negatively asserting This Is by means of This Is Not. In Book I of *Gulliver's Travels* Lilliput's vices are usually caricatures of England's, and its virtues are merely arrows pointing to England's vices. Even specific uses of the subjunctive lead by contrast back to the present indicative. Take the opening of Rochester's *A Satire against Mankind:*

> <u>Were I</u> (who to my cost already am
> One of those strange prodigious creatures, Man)
> A spirit free, to choose for my own share
> What case of flesh and blood <u>I pleased</u> to wear,
> <u>I'd be</u> a dog, a monkey, or a bear
> Or any thing but that vain animal
> <u>Who is</u> so proud of being rational.

The hypothetical *were's* and *would's* set up possibilities that are significant only because they bear on the real, existent "is-ness" of the proudly rational creature.

The past has special prominence in satire, however—as an aid to rather than an object of attack. It is often argued that satirists are basically conservative, resisting innovation, change, progress, sticking to established forms and beliefs.

True enough, no doubt, but it is also true that one who intends to move the earth needs a place to stand, an outside platform of values to give leverage to his attack. Assaulting the world because it falls short of *his* standards risks making him merely presumptuous—a radical or a cynic. It is sounder strategy to play the public spokesman measuring civilization against its own best achievements. This lines up the satirist with traditional values, so that from the reader's standpoint he becomes more attractive as a practitioner of affirmative debunking. Satirists, in short, use what they can, their genre being what it is, and their use of the past as ideal may no more indicate their personal beliefs than their use of geographical ideals ("England can't measure up to France" or "City life is corrupt compared to the country") or ideals quite outside space and time ("Everything falls short of Utopia").

In satire, then, all tenses reinforce the present and all moods the indicative. But the indicative, we should add, contains an implicit imperative mood, the moral imperative that by indictment demands reformation: "You don't measure up" necessarily implies the imperative, "Measure up!" As we have indicated, however, this imperative is often less a "Measure up!" directed at the "it" of attack than a "Measure!" directed at the "you"-audience, a demand to the audience to judge more accurately the nature of the "it." Here again, satire combines invective with sermon, the present indicative immediacy and assertiveness of the first with the implicit moral imperative of the second.

Satire's present indicative differs from the present indicative of most documentary fiction, which also seeks to represent What Is. Satire "goes after" the world, it "corrodes," "acts upon," "diminishes" its protagonists, whether they are persons like Shadwell or ideas like progress or vices like hypocrisy. Satire has no "heroes," no centers of sympathy, only focal points of disapproval. And to corrode, act upon, or diminish its protagonists, satire presents them as actively imposing upon the world their corruptive natures: the Shadwells are *riding high,* even a Goddess of Dulness *reigns,* and hypocrisy *envelops* everything. Realistic fiction, on the contrary, is for the most part spiritually in the passive rather than the active voice. Naturalistic novels like Hemingway's *A Farewell to Arms* or Hardy's *Tess of the D'Urbervilles* do not represent unsympathetic protagonists acting but sympathetic protagonists being acted upon. The Tesses are ridden down and the Catherines killed. Another way of putting it is to say that in order to make its protagonists objects of attack, satire makes them subjects of action; they are in the nominative case, whereas the protagonists of naturalistic fiction are in the objective case, where they are done unto.

II. Satiric Forms: Direct Satire As implied earlier, satire, being a "mixture," does not lend itself to neat formal divisions or categories, but we can distinguish three main kinds of satire—"direct," "indirect," and "parody." (These may interpenetrate each other so that a given satire involves elements of all, but the object of discussing forms is not to put labels on individual poems but to understand the convergence in a particular poem of qualities that might otherwise go unnoticed.)

Direct satire is the simplest and most eclectic of the three since in it the author delivers his attack as a commentary or discourse in the first person, as an "I." The essence of this kind of satire is informality and an air of improvisation; thus a great many direct satires are labeled "epistles," suggesting the offhandedness of the personal letter, or "essays," the word retaining something of its original meaning of "an attempt." Some examples of direct satire are Hall's Satire II, Donne's Satire III, Rochester's "Satire against Mankind," Pope's *Moral Essays,* Johnson's "Vanity of Human Wishes," and Philip Wylie's *Generation of Vipers.*

Direct satire has several advantages. For one thing, the first-person delivery imparts immediacy to the poem: the speaker is, as it were, here before us, talking directly to us, and so, having been buttonholed, we listen. Also, it lends credibility to the poem: a "real" person is voicing his opinions and feelings, and therefore we cannot dismiss the satire as "just a fiction" or "mere art." Actually, of course, the "credibility game" is a convention quite as much as the happy ending of comedy or the "walkdown" of the Western, some of the art of satire being its attempt to persuade us that it is not art at all. (Even in fraternal hazing during initiations the ridicule is made to look as real as possible, the fact that it is intended partly as sport being concealed until it is over.) Again, the use of first-person address offers great scope and range of attack without forfeiting economy. Rochester's "Satire against Mankind," though its heaviest barrages are aimed at man's pride in reason, sprays shot over the whole terrain of human pretension. This free-ranging attack can be managed in only 224 lines because with no plots to develop, scenes to start, or characters to portray, all Rochester need do is begin talking.

We said "Rochester" in the last sentence, and because of the first-person address readers often assume that the "I" of direct satire is the author. Normally, however, the "I" is the author's invention, a character, persona, or "speaker" distinct from himself. No one is likely to equate Swift with the speaker of *A Modest Proposal,* the humanitarian economist who proposes that the Irish fatten up and market their children as an antidote for famine and poverty; but even the "P" who seems to stand for Pope in his "Epistle to Dr. Arbuthnot" is a fictional character with no more reality outside his poem than Romeo has outside *Romeo and Juliet.* And just as Romeo is what he is because Shakespeare is writing tragedy, so Pope's "P" or Rochester's "I" is what he is because these authors are writing satire. The conventions of satire do not provide for gentleness, love, humility, or mercy any more than the conventions of football provide for javelins. Because satirists are persistently accused of "crimes" committed by their "speakers," we apparently need to remind ourselves that whatever his motive in choosing a particular mask figure, persona, or speaker, the satirist practices an art at one remove from the sort of name-calling punishable by libel laws.

III. Indirect Satire   Direct satire occurs when the author discourses as an "I." *Indirect* satire, however, is presented as a fiction or story in which there are at least the rudiments of a plot, characters, and dialogue. We have already stressed a fictional aspect of direct satire in noting that the author adopts the role of satiric speaker and hence becomes a character in a fictional situation. Direct satire employing dialogue, like Pope's "Epistle to Dr. Arbuthnot" and Rochester's "Satire against Mankind," moves even further toward fiction. Works like Swift's *A Modest Proposal* and *An Argument against Abolishing Christianity,* in which we find a vividly characterized speaker talking in the first person but *not* delivering a satiric commentary—in fact, unaware that he is even involved in a satire—lie somewhere between direct and indirect satire.

Indirect satire, then, features not a "speaker" but a "narrator," the person who tells the story or presents the scene. Our consciousness of his presence may vary considerably depending on how distinctly he is characterized. In Betjeman's "In Westminster Abbey" and Burns's "Holy Willie's Prayer," we are entirely unaware of the narrator since we are in immediate contact with the fictional characters themselves, the nameless Englishwoman and Holy Willie, whose prayers we overhear. We are more conscious of the narrators of Hardy's "In Church" and Dryden's "Mac Flecknoe": they are "there," it is their voices we hear, but aside from selecting the material to present, they do not interpret the fiction for us, do not comment upon what is happening, and hence remain comparatively shadowy. In *Hudibras* and *Don Juan,* however, the narrator is not only conspicuous but obtrusive. His tone of voice colors the story, and he frequently interrupts the story to make satiric observations about the characters or about people and issues in actual life. In all the foregoing examples, the narrator stands outside his story; but sometimes, as in *Tristram Shandy* and *Gulliver's Travels,* he tells a story in which he is also a participant.

Direct satire exerts a certain gravitational pull upon indirect satire. The reader of *Don Juan,* for instance, can hardly help noticing how frequently the narrator interrupts his story to engage in direct satire of other poems and poets, especially Byron's favorite target Southey:

> But let me to my story: I must own,
> If I have any fault, it is digression—
> Leaving my people to proceed alone,
> While I soliloquize beyond expression;
> But these are my addresses from the throne,
> Which put off business to the ensuing session:
> Forgetting each omission is a loss to
> The world, not quite so great as Ariosto.

This tendency to digress from indirect to direct satire becomes one of the organizing structural principles of Swift's *A Tale of a Tub,* in which the satiric allegory of Peter, Jack, and Martin is regularly broken up by formal sections entitled "Digressions" (one of them "A Digression in Praise of Digressions"), each devoted to satiric commentary. In *The Dunciad* the story of the events in the court of Dulness—the crowning of Cibber and the spread of the goddess' dominion over England—is skeletal at best; the real flesh of the satire is the direct lampooning of individual poets and the state of modern letters. Sterne's *Tristram Shandy,* which uses both comedy and satire, is notorious for its digressions; Book III of *Gulliver's Travels* is dominated by direct satire as the plot becomes highly episodic and digressive and Gulliver repeatedly slips out of fictional character to become Swift's mouthpiece.

As this would suggest, satire in fictional form—in the form of epic, romance, novel, short story—often seems a caricature of fiction. The indirect satirist has little interest in shaping coherent sequences of action or in constructing tightly knit plots on the Aristotelean model. Nor is he concerned to create fully rounded characters with the kind of social and psychological reality that we expect from the novelist. His characters are not persons but personifications. Shadwell in Dryden's "Mac Flecknoe" is not a human being but an incarnation of poetic nonsense, a huge face bulging with blankness and shrouded in the vapors of idiocy. Sir Hudibras is a distillation of the absurdities and corruptions of logic, rhetoric, mathematics, philosophy, and especially Puritanism—an enormously inflated bluenose. King Cibber in the first book of *The Dunciad* is not a writer but a grotesque series of metamorphosing objects, a plagiarizing worm feeding on old books, a cerebral bowling ball overbiased by dullness, a log worshiped by hundreds of croaking literary toads.

Satiric characterization, in short, is reductive instead of inclusive: it focuses upon certain characteristics of people and then magnifies and distorts them until they become the total reality. The Yahoos of Gulliver's fourth journey are not creatures with certain bestial qualities but Bestiality itself. If the vanity of youthful beauty took a human form, it would be Belinda; if sanctimoniousness could pray and chauvinism orate, they would produce Holy Willie's prayer and a speech beginning "next to of course god america i." Indirect satire thus is easily accommodated to allegory and perhaps especially to the "beast fable," in which human qualities are attributed to animal characters, as in Chaucer's "Nun's Priest's Tale," Wyatt's first epistle to Poins, and Johnson's "Fable of the Vultures."

This magnifying and distorting quality of satiric characterization not only helps diminish the person or thing attacked but lends permanence to the satire. We cannot hope to read *Hudibras* as Butler's contemporaries did, taking a sly pleasure in recognizing oblique allusions to actual events and people. The political allegory in *Gulliver's Travels* is for most modern readers merely an extraneous annoyance requiring them to keep an index finger poised over the footnotes. But if the satirist has truly caught the essence of an absurdity, his satire rises above the obscurely topical and becomes good for all time. Swift's scientists at the Grand Academy of Lagado, who have discovered that words are symbols distinct from their referents and who therefore seek a purer form of communication through the objects they carry about in sacks, may seem only fantastic exaggerations of an eighteenth-century linguistic view stemming from Bacon and Hobbes—until we encounter the twentieth-century philosophy of logical positivism. Colley Cibber and Thomas Shadwell have appropriately enough dropped into the dead-letter file of literary history, but as King Colley and King Shadwell they are enduring symbols of a poetic dullness from which, alas, no age is exempt.

IV.   Parody   Parody is a type of irony, and satiric parody is an imitation that ridicules its model through deliberate incongruity. A railer might say, for instance, that baseball pitchers on the mound are absurdly self-conscious posturers. A direct satirist might liken their pre-pitch preparations to a debutante at her dressing table. A parodist like Jonathan Winters, however, dons a baseball uniform, leans away from the television camera, rubs an imaginary baseball, squints into the camera, shakes off a sign, hitches up his sleeve, rubs the ball some more, twitches his cap brim, shifts a plug of tobacco to his other cheek, rubs the ball some more, squints again, shakes off another sign, wipes his forehead, rubs the ball again, and then, in a final act of rubbing the ball, suddenly throws up his hands and looks down in mock horror at what is now, presumably, a coverless baseball unraveling in the dust. The incongruity consists in a disproportion between manner and matter. So Pope in *The Rape of the Lock* imitates the style, structure, and conventions of the heroic mode to depict not a major crisis in the Trojan War as *The Iliad* does, or man's primal fall from innocence as *Paradise Lost* does, but the snipping off of a lock of girl's hair.

The effect of such disproportion is to further trivialize an already insignificant subject, but it is also to imply a certain pomposity about the heroic mode itself. Swift's *A Modest Proposal* marshalls an impressive amount of fact and logic and shapes it into a consecutive argument in the best tradition of the persuasive essay. As a result, he indicts not merely the modest proposer and those he stands for but, through imitation, a literary form (and the rhetoric and logic it relies on) that can lend an-air of plausibility to what is morally insane.

One of the reasons satire seems formless, we said earlier, is that it appears in so many different forms—romance, novel, pastoral, epic, and so on. In such cases, however, it is not merely that the satiric spirit has taken up residence in a normally nonsatiric container; instead, in the process of imitating these genres and while giving the appearance of inhabiting them, satire has actually absorbed them, converting them to its own substance. A satiric novel or pastoral, this would suggest, no longer *is* a novel or pastoral, or if it is, it is so in the same sense that a salmon in the digestive tract of a shark is still a salmon. Satiric novels, like those of Thomas Love Peacock, tend to be parodies of novels, satiric pastorals parodies of pastoral. This is acknowledged with respect to the epic genre; hence we have "mock-epic"—not an epic, but a satiric form. But perhaps we need to think also of "mock-essay," as in *A Modest Proposal;* "mock-elegy," as in Swift's "A Satirical Elegy"; "mock-romance," as in *Hudibras* and *Don Quixote* and *The Waste Land;* "mock-song," as in "The Love Song of J. Alfred Prufrock"; "mock-tragedy," as in A. E. Housman's *Fragment of a Greek Tragedy;* and so on. If so, it becomes all the more necessary for us to understand the traditional values, conventions, and techniques of various genres in order to see how they have been warped into satiric shapes. *The Rape of the Lock* is enjoyable in itself, but without some knowledge of its epic forerunners, most of the poem's significance would be lost. For a minor instance, consider the passage that occurs just as the lock is about to be snipped:

> Ev'n then, before the fatal engine closed,
> A wretched sylph too fondly interposed;
> Fate urged the shears, and cut the sylph in twain,
> (But airy substance soon unites again).

Though impressive in its immediate context, this passage becomes much richer in the light of Milton's lines recording the encounter of Satan and the archangel Michael during the war in heaven (*Paradise Lost,* Book VI):

> [Michael's sword] met
> The sword of *Satan* with steep force to smite
> Descending, and in half cut sheer, nor stay'd,
> But with swift wheel reverse, deep entering shear'd
> All his right side; then *Satan* first knew pain,
> And writh'd him to and fro convolv'd; so sore
> The griding sword with discontinuous wound
> Pass'd through him, but th' Ethereal substance clos'd
> Not long divisible, and from the gash
> A stream of Nectarous humor issuing flow'd
> Sanguine, such as Celestial Spirits may bleed,
> And all his Armor stain'd erewhile so bright.

Or consider how the closing line of Swift's "mock-elegy" on Marlborough (p. 487)—"Turned to that dirt from whence he sprung"—depends upon our knowledge of the standard elegiac metaphor about "dust unto dust," which receives a mordant literalness in Swift's substitution of "dirt" for "dust."

Satire's most natural form, then, seems to be "mock-form," or parody, just as its most natural kind of meaning seems to be irony, or "mock-meaning." Indirect satire, as we observed, tends to pervert the normal interests of narrative fiction in ways (digression, abstraction, distortion) that suggest parody, and direct satire is given to a scatter-gun attack that forgoes style and form in the cause of straight truth undoctored by art. An element of antiform and mock-art is recurrent in satire. In this regard, satire is literature ridiculing itself, a kind of open-ended literary criticism generated by and within literature that not only attacks specific works and modes but raises basic issues about literary art in general—the relation of form to content, for instance. If the content of *The Rape of the Lock,* the world of Belinda and the Baron, rattles about inside its epic form like a marble in a suit of armor, does that mean that form and content are easily separable? Or does it mean that a form like the epic dictates a certain content and that only when you arbitrarily disengage the most mechanical aspects of that form and yoke it by force to an alien content do you get the sort of friction we find in Pope's poem? Or again, the notion of poetic autonomy, or the poem as its own context of meaning, is implicitly disputed by a genre in which extravagant allusiveness is fully meaningful only in the light of outside information like prior poems or historical incidents.

Parody is of course not confined merely to literary forms and modes but can be directed toward virtually anything, from astronomical investigations of lunar phenomena—as when Samuel Butler's scientists discover an elephant on the moon that is actually a mouse in the barrel of their telescope—to the protean nature of political forms—as when George Orwell's animals in *Animal Farm* overthrow the totalitarian regime of Farmer Jones and thus achieve the freedom to be victimized by one of their own making. All forms, it seems, are vulnerable to the satiric vision. Indeed, given its basic reliance upon irony, which announces only what it does *not* mean and hence opens up endless mazes of potential inference, satire at its most intense makes everything suspect. All meanings become mirages, all manners seem mannerism, all forms arbitrary and unreal. Here we encounter, as at the end of *The Dunciad,* a world gradually disappearing into the dark night of stupidity, from which we awaken, like Prufrock, into a world of stultifying triviality in which we drown. But the satirist only apparently leaves us drowning. His creation of a world of total repellence is possible only as an inversion of a world of total appeal, the dark night of stupidity being meaningful only in contrast to a daylight of intelligence as night is meaningful only in contrast to day. He does not draw any blueprints for the ideal, but some conception of it lies behind his satire, and he compels us to envisage it for ourselves.

GEOFFREY CHAUCER

In *The Canterbury Tales* Chaucer follows a popular medieval and early Renaissance practice of presenting a number of different stories as parts of a single "framing tale" that unifies them. The framing tale here begins with the pilgrim

Chaucer arriving on a spring evening at the Tabard Inn in Southwark, at the southern end of London Bridge. There he meets a company of pilgrims who intend the following morning to journey on horseback to the shrine at Canterbury Cathedral (about fifty-five miles from London) commemorating the martyr Archbishop Thomas à Becket, murdered in 1170 by followers of Henry II and canonized three years later. At supper, the Host—the tavern keeper, Harry Bailly—proposes that as a way of passing the time on their pilgrimmage each pilgrim tell four stories, two going and two coming back. The Host agrees to go along with them to act as moderator and to pick the winning storyteller, who upon their return to the Tabard Inn will be rewarded with a supper paid for by the others. The next morning they set out. They draw lots to see who will tell his story first, and the Knight wins. This marks the conclusion of what is called the "General Prologue," in which Chaucer has not only set up his framing tale but also described and characterized in brief sketches each of the pilgrims—32 in all, counting the Host, the pilgrim Chaucer, and the Canon's Yeoman, who catches up with them along the way. Had Chaucer stuck to his original scheme, each pilgrim telling 4 stories, there would have been about 120 tales. As it is, there are 24 tales plus the General Prologue, and two of these, the Cook's and the Squire's, are unfinished. Between each tale are "links," which develop the framing tale begun in the General Prologue by presenting exchanges and sometimes arguments between certain pilgrims.

Many literary genres popular during the medieval period are represented in Chaucer's collection of tales: the *fabliau,* a verse story about lower-class persons in humorous and often obscene predicaments (Miller's, Reeve's, Cook's, and Shipman's tales); the romance on the "loathly lady" theme (Wife of Bath's tale) and the oriental romance (Squire's tale); the moral exemplum, a cautionary tale illustrating the dangers of indiscretion and vice (Friar's and Pardoner's tales); the saint's legend or "life" (Second Nun's tale); the burlesque or mock-romance (tale of Sir Topas); the Miracle of the Virgin story (Prioress' tale); the medieval "tragedy" (Monk's tale); and the beast fable (Nun's Priest's tale).

The medieval pardoner was an agent of the Church empowered to grant indulgences of sins to persons donating money or goods to a charitable enterprise. These indulgences were supposed to be freely given, not sold, and to be efficacious only if the sins to which they applied were confessed and sincerely repented. Normally, pardoners were not allowed to preach, only to explain their mission and function; ideally, but not normally, they conducted themselves with decency, sobriety, and piety. In Chaucer's time "pardoning" was a profitable business, and hence a great many con-men with phony credentials roamed England, fleecing the timorous and gullible through the sale of fake relics, which were thought by the pious to have miraculous powers, and indulgences.

As a member of this spiritual protection-racket, Chaucer's Pardoner is the con-man par excellence. In the General Prologue we learn that the Pardoner is a *eunuchus ex nativitate,* a eunuch from birth, that the relics he is carrying are phony, that he is an eminently successful pitchman, and that he is riding along with the Summoner, disguising his eunuchry (though the pilgrim Chaucer easily sees through him) by adopting the role of a gay young blade singing a song called "Come hither, love, to me." That he is with the Summoner is highly ironic, because as the representative of the Archdeacon, the Summoner is an agent of justice, the one man who ought to be putting the Pardoner in jail. Instead, these two avatars of the Church are guzzling ale and singing a concupiscent song as they ride to the shrine of the "holy blessed martyr" at Canterbury Cathedral. Our next brief glimpse of the Pardoner comes when he interrupts the Wife of Bath, who is about to tell her tale, by registering his hearty approval of her willful defiance of divine prohibitions. Then we come to the Pardoner's own prologue and tale, which are immediately preceded by the "link" or transitional passages connecting them with the tale just told by the Physician. The Host—the master of ceremonies for the tale-telling—after lamenting over the Physician's sad narrative, in which a father murders his chaste daughter to prevent her from becoming the object of a corrupt judge's lust, calls upon the Pardoner to alleviate his sadness with "a funny story." At this point our selection begins.

The Pardoner's prologue is a remarkable self-exposé. What should be a confession penitently delivered becomes perverted (as everything associated with the Pardoner is) into an impenitent vaunting of rascality. It should be noted that although the Pardoner freely acknowledges the most damning of sins, the one thing he does not mention, and has in fact made every effort to conceal, is his eunuchry. It is this that gives special point to the Pardoner's anger when the Host returns his devastating refusal to the Pardoner's playful offer of pardons at the conclusion of his tale. The Pardoner's physical sterility, his inability to beget children, is symbolic of his spiritual sterility, his failure to beget good deeds, to make virtue multiply. Although he assures prospective purchasers that the holy bone placed in a well will make "cattle multiply" and that whoever puts on "this mitten" shall have "multiplying of his grain," the Pardoner's relics are quite as sterile as he himself. What really multiplies under his loving care is money, for in him the Word of God that once called forth the miracle of Creation has degenerated into the sly rhetoric that calls forth cash in return for hollow promises.

The tale itself takes the form of a carefully organized sermon. It begins with a point-by-point, perfectly orthodox indictment of sins—drunkenness, gluttony, gambling, and blasphemy—each indictment documented by "authorities" and abbreviated exemplums drawn from Biblical and classical history. Then it moves into the tale proper, the exemplum of the three rioters who seek and find Death, which embodies each of the four sins previously inveighed against and serves as a full-scale illustration of the theme the Pardoner always preaches and personally ignores: Greed is the root of all evil.

The satiric irony of *The Pardoner's Tale* cuts in all directions. The Pardoner's own contempt for his yokel audiences is less of a reproof to them than are the self-designing, hypocritical techniques he employs to appeal to their own self-interest and hypocrisy. Master of deception that he is, the Pardoner is mastered by self-deception in feeling that he is exempt from the ironic fate of the three rioters, who could not understand that death in the Christian scheme of things is not someone you encounter outside but something you engender inside. Through the Pardoner, of course, the whole medieval practice of "pardoning" and the general debasement of spiritual values are attacked. But like all great satiric characters, the Pardoner transcends the local conditions of his age to become representative of self-defeating duplicity in all periods.

Introduction to the Pardoner's Tale*

. . . .

good friend	'Thou beel amy, thou Pardoner,' he sayde,
amusing tale; jest	'Telle us som myrthe or japes right anon.'
	'It shal be doon,' quod he, 'by Seint Ronyon! 320
loaf	But first,' quod he, 'heere at this ale-stake
	I wol bothe drynke, and eten of a cake.'
	But right anon thise gentils gonne to crye,
ribald jest	'Nay, lat hym telle us of no ribaudye!
learn	Telle us som moral thyng, that we may leere 325
wisdom	Som wit, and thanne wol we gladly heere.'
	'I graunte, ywis,' quod he, 'but I moot thynke
respectable	Upon som honest thyng while that I drynke.'

THE PARDONER'S PROLOGUE

Heere Folweth the Prologe of the Pardoners Tale

Radix malorum est Cupiditas. Ad Thimotheum, 6°.

Sirs	'Lordynges,' quod he, 'in chirches whan I preche,
	I peyne me to han an hauteyn speche, 330
sonorously	And rynge it out as round as gooth a belle,
know	For I kan al by rote that I telle.
text	My theme is alwey oon, and evere was—
	Radix malorum est Cupiditas.
declare	First I pronounce whennes that I come, 335
	And thanne my bulles shewe I, alle and some.
	Oure lige lordes seel on my patente,
	That shewe I first, my body to warente,
cleric	That no man be so boold, ne preest ne clerk,
from	Me to destourbe of Cristes hooly werk. 340
	And after that thanne telle I forth my tales;
	Bulles of popes and of cardynales,
	Of patriarkes and bishopes I shewe,
	And in Latyn I speke a wordes fewe,
	To saffron with my predicacioun, 345
	And for to stire hem to devocioun.
glass cases	Thanne shewe I forth my longe cristal stones,
rags	Ycrammed ful of cloutes and of bones,—
suppose; all	Relikes been they, as wenen they echoon.
brass	Thanne have I in latoun a sholder-boon 350
	Which that was of an hooly Jewes sheep.

---

* From *The Canterbury Tales* by Geoffrey Chaucer. Edited by A. C. Cawley. Everyman's Library. Reprinted by permission of E. P. Dutton & Co., Inc. and J. M. Dent & Sons Ltd.

---

321 *ale-stake*: See I. 667.   323 But immediately the gentlefolk cried out.   327 Certainly I will...but I must think.   330 I take pains to speak loudly.   334 1 Tim. vi. 10: 'The love of money is the root of all evil.'   336 I show my papal mandates, one and all.   337–38 First I show our liege lord's (i.e. bishop's) seal on my licence to sell indulgences, in order to protect myself.   345 To flavour my sermon with.   350–51 Divination by means of the shoulder-bone of a sheep is referred to in the *Parson's Tale*, X. 1585. The "holy Jew" may be Jacob.

note	"Goode men," I seye, "taak of my wordes keep;
washed	If that this boon be wasshe in any welle,
	If cow, or calf, or sheep, or oxe swelle
	That any worm hath ete, or worm ystonge, 355
its	Taak water of that welle and wassh his tonge,
restored to health	And it is hool anon; and forthermoore,
pustules	Of pokkes and of scabbe, and every soore
	Shal every sheep be hool that of this welle
also	Drynketh a draughte. Taak kep eek what I telle: 360
	If that the good-man that the beestes oweth
week; crows	Wol every wyke, er that the cok hym croweth,
	Fastynge, drynken of this welle a draughte,
that (same); ancestors	As thilke hooly Jew oure eldres taughte,
stock	His beestes and his stoor shal multiplie. 365
cures	And, sires, also it heeleth jalousie;
fallen into	For though a man be falle in jalous rage,
	Lat maken with this water his potage,
mistrust	And nevere shal he moore his wyf mystriste,
	Though he the soothe of hir defaute wiste, 370
although	Al had she taken prestes two or thre.
glove	Heere is a miteyn eek, that ye may se.
	He that his hand wol putte in this mitayn,
	He shal have multipliyng of his grayn,
	Whan he hath sowen, be it whete or otes, 375
groats	So that he offre pens, or elles grotes.
	Goode men and wommen, o thyng warne I yow:
person	If any wight be in this chirche now
	That hath doon synne horrible, that he
shriven	Dar nat, for shame, of it yshryven be, 380
	Or any womman, be she yong or old,
cuckold	That hath ymaad hir housbonde cokewold,
	Swich folk shal have no power ne no grace
	To offren to my relikes in this place.
	And whoso fyndeth hym out of swich blame, 385
	He wol come up and offre in Goddes name,
absolve	And I assoille him by the auctoritee
	Which that by bulle ygraunted was to me."
trick	By this gaude have I wonne, yeer by yeer,
since	An hundred mark sith I was pardoner. 390
	I stonde lyk a clerk in my pulpet,
ignorant; seated	And whan the lewed peple is doun yset,
	I preche so as ye han herd bifoore,
idle tales	And telle an hundred false japes moore.
	Thanne peyne I me to strecche forth the nekke, 395
nod	And est and west upon the peple I bekke,
barn	As dooth a dowve sittynge on a berne.
eagerly	Myne handes and my tonge goon so yerne
industry	That it is joye to se my bisynesse.

---

355 That has eaten any worm, or that any worm has stung. 361 If the master of the house who owns the beasts. 368 Have his soup made with this water. 370 Though he knew the truth about her misdemeanour. 390 *mark*: coin worth two-thirds of a pound.

wickedness	Of avarice and of swich cursednesse	400
generous	Is al my prechyng, for to make hem free	
give; especially	To yeven hir pens, and namely unto me.	
	For myn entente is nat but for to wynne,	
not at all	And nothyng for correccioun of synne.	
buried	I rekke nevere, whan that they been beryed,	405
	Though that hir soules goon a-blakeberyed!	
certainly; sermon	For certes, many a predicacioun	
comes	Comth ofte tyme of yvel entencioun;	
	Som for plesance of folk and flaterye,	
	To been avaunced by ypocrisye,	410
	And som for veyne glorie, and som for hate.	
	For whan I dar noon oother weyes debate,	
sharply	Thanne wol I stynge hym with my tonge smerte	
escape	In prechyng, so that he shal nat asterte	
slandered	To been defamed falsly, if that he	415
	Hath trespased to my bretheren or to me.	
individual	For though I telle noght his propre name,	
	Men shal wel knowe that it is the same,	
	By signes, and by othere circumstances.	
	Thus quyte I folk that doon us displesances;	420
pretence	Thus spitte I out my venym under hewe	
	Of hoolynesse, to semen hooly and trewe.	
describe	But shortly myn entente I wol devyse:	
covetousness	I preche of no thyng but for coveityse.	
	Therfore my theme is yet, and evere was,	425
	Radix malorum est Cupiditas.	
	Thus kan I preche agayn that same vice	
practice	Which that I use, and that is avarice.	
	But though myself be gilty in that synne,	
cease	Yet kan I maken oother folk to twynne	430
	From avarice, and soore to repente.	
	But that is nat my principal entente;	
	I preche nothyng but for coveitise.	
	Of this mateere it oghte ynogh suffise.	
	Thanne telle I hem ensamples many oon	435
	Of olde stories longe tyme agoon.	
	For lewed peple loven tales olde;	
relate; keep in mind	Swiche thynges kan they wel reporte and holde.	
suppose	What, trowe ye, that whiles I may preche,	
by my teaching	And wynne gold and silver for I teche,	440
poverty; voluntarily	That I wol lyve in poverte wilfully?	
thought of	Nay, nay, I thoghte it nevere, trewely!	
	For I wol preche and begge in sondry landes;	

---

403 Is only to gain money. 406 Go a-blackberrying, i.e., go to blazes. 409 One for the purpose of pleasing and flattering folk. 411 *som* (twice): another. 412 When I dare quarrel in no other way, i.e., when I dare not quarrel openly. 413 *hym*: i.e., someone whom the Pardoner hates. 420 Thus I pay back people who offend us. 434 i.e., enough has been said about my motives for preaching. 435 *ensamples*: moral tales used by preachers to illustrate their sermons.

I wol nat do no labour with myne handes,
Ne make baskettes, and lyve therby,   445
in idleness   By cause I wal nat beggen ydelly.
imitate   I wol noon of the apostles countrefete;
wool   I wol have moneie, wolle, chese, and whete,
Al were it yeven of the povereste page,
Or of the povereste wydwe in a village,   450
although; die   Al sholde hir children sterve for famyne.
juice   Nay, I wol drynke licour of the vyne,
And have a joly wenche in every toun.
But herkneth, lordynges, in conclusioun:
desire   Youre likyng is that I shal telle a tale.   455
Now have I dronke a draughte of corny ale,
By God, I hope I shal yow telle a thyng
That shal by reson been at youre likyng.
For though myself be a ful vicious man,
A moral tale yet I yow telle kan,   460
win (money)   Which I am wont to preche for to wynne.
Now hoold youre pees! my tale I wol bigynne.'

THE PARDONER'S TALE

Heere Bigynneth the Pardoners Tale

once   In Flaundres whilom was a compaignye
practiced   Of yonge folk that haunteden folye,
As riot, hasard, stywes, and tavernes,   465
where; guitars   Where as with harpes, lutes, and gyternes,
They daunce and pleyen at dees bothe day and nyght,
And eten also and drynken over hir myght,
Thurgh which they doon the devel sacrifise
Withinne that develes temple, in cursed wise,   470
excess; unnatural   By superfluytee abhomynable.
Hir othes been so grete and so dampnable
terrible   That it is grisly for to heere hem swere.
tear to pieces   Oure blissed Lordes body they totere,—
it seemed to them   Hem thoughte that Jewes rente hym noght ynough;   475
laughed   And ech of hem at otheres synne lough.
And right anon thanne comen tombesteres
Fetys and smale, and yonge frutesteres,
sellers of wafer-cakes Syngeres with harpes, baudes, wafereres,
very   Whiche been the verray develes officeres   480
To kyndle and blowe the fyr of lecherye,
attached   That is annexed unto glotonye.
The hooly writ take I to my witnesse

---

445 A reference to Paul the Hermit, who plied the trade of basketmaker. 449 Although it were given by the poorest servant. 456 *corny*: tasting strongly of corn or malt. 458 That shall in consequence be to your liking. 465 Such as riotous living, gambling, brothels. 474 The reference is to swearing by the parts of Christ's body (e.g., 651). 477–78 And then straightway came graceful and slender dancing girls and young fruit-sellers. 483–84 Eph. v. 18.

lechery	That luxurie is in wyn and dronkenesse.
unnaturally	Lo, how that dronken Looth, unkyndely, 485
	Lay by his doghtres two, unwityngly;
knew not	So dronke he was, he nyste what he wroghte.
Herod	Herodes, whoso wel the stories soghte,
	Whan he of wyn was repleet at his feeste,
command	Right at his owene table he yaf his heeste 490
slay	To sleen the Baptist John, full giltelees.
Seneca	Senec seith a good word douteless;
	He seith he kan no difference fynde
	Bitwix a man that is out of his mynde
drunk	And a man which that is dronkelewe, 495
	But that woodnesse, yfallen in a shrewe,
lasts	Persevereth lenger than dooth dronkenesse.
wickedness	O glotonye, ful of cursednesse!
ruin	O cause first of oure confusioun!
origin	O original of oure dampnacioun, 500
redeemed	Til Crist hadde boght us with his blood agayn!
	Lo, how deere, shortly for to sayn,
	Aboght was thilke cursed vileynye!
corrupted	Corrupt was al this world for glotonye.
	Adam oure fader, and his wyf also, 505
	Fro Paradys to labour and to wo
	Were dryven for that vice, it is no drede.
	For whil that Adam fasted, as I rede,
	He was in Paradys; and whan that he
forbidden	Eet of the fruyt deffended on the tree, 510
	Anon he was out cast to wo and peyne.
	O glotonye, on thee wel oghte us pleyne!
if a man knew	O, wiste a man how manye maladyes
follow from	Folwen of excesse and of glotonyes,
temperate	He wolde been the moore mesurable 515
	Of his diete, sittynge at his table.
	Allas! the shorte throte, the tendre mouth,
	Maketh that est and west and north and south,
	In erthe, in eir, in water, men to swynke
	To gete a glotoun deyntee mete and drynke! 520
	Of this matiere, o Paul, wel kanstow trete:
	'Mete unto wombe, and wombe eek unto mete,
	Shal God destroyen bothe,' as Paulus seith.
	Allas! a foul thyng is it, by my feith,
	To seye this word, and fouler is the dede, 525
red (wine)	Whan man so drynketh of the white and rede
privy	That of his throte he maketh his pryvee,

---

485 Gen. xix. 30–36.   488 As anyone could see who consulted the histories carefully.   496 Except that madness, when it has befallen a wretched creature.   502–503 In short, how dearly paid for was that execrable wickedness.   512 We have good reason to complain against you. 517 The short-lived pleasure of swallowing, the delicate mouth.   518–19 *Maketh that...* *men to swynke*: causes men to toil.   522–23 1 Cor. vi. 13: "Meats for the belly, and the belly for meats: but God shall destroy both it and them."

Thurgh thilke cursed superfluitee.

sorrowfully   The apostel wepyng seith ful pitously,

'Ther walken manye of whiche yow toold have I—   530

I seye it now wepyng, with pitous voys—

That they been enemys of Cristes croys,

belly   Of whiche the ende is deeth, wombe is hir god!'

stomach   O wombe! O bely! O stynkyng cod,

filled full   Fulfilled of dong and of corrupcioun!   535

sound   At either ende of thee foul is the soun.

How greet labour and cost is thee to fynde!

Thise cookes, how they stampe, and streyne, and grynde,

And turnen substaunce into accident,

To fulfille al thy likerous talent!   540

Out of the harde bones knokke they

The mary, for they caste noght awey

sweetly   That may go thurgh the golet softe and swoote.

spices   Of spicerie of leef, and bark, and roote

Shal been his sauce ymaked by delit,   545

To make hym yet a newer appetit.

But, certes, he that haunteth swiche delices

those   Is deed, whil that he lyveth in tho vices.

A lecherous thyng is wyn, and dronkenesse

strife   Is ful of stryvyng and of wrecchednesse.   550

drunken   O dronke man, disfigured is thy face,

Sour is thy breeth, foul artow to embrace,

And thurgh thy dronke nose semeth the soun

As though thou seydest ay 'Sampsoun, Sampsoun!'

And yet, God woot, Sampsoun drank nevere no wyn.   555

stuck   Thou fallest as it were a styked swyn;

sense of decency   Thy tonge is lost, and al thyn honeste cure;

tomb   For dronkenesse is verray sepulture

wisdom   Of mannes wit and his discrecioun.

In whom that drynke hath dominacioun   560

secret; doubt   He kan no conseil kepe, it is no drede.

Now kepe yow fro the white and fro the rede,

And namely fro the white wyn of Lepe,

for sale; Cheapside   That is to selle in Fysshstrete or in Chepe.

secretly   This wyn of Spaigne crepeth subtilly   565

into; near   In othere wynes, growynge faste by,

530–33 Phil. iii. 18–19: "For many walk, of whom I have told you often, and now tell you even weeping, that they are the enemies of the cross of Christ: Whose end is destruction, whose god is their belly."   537 What a great labour and cost it is to provide for you.   538 How they pound (in a mortar) and strain (through a sieve).   539 *substaunce* and *accident*: philosophical terms for (*a*) the real essence of a thing and (*b*) its external form. 'To turn substance into accident' therefore means in this context 'to turn food, the true purpose of which is to sustain the body, into a means of tickling the palate.'   540 To gratify your dainty appetite.   545–46 His sauce shall be delightfully made, to give him a still sharper appetite. (*his* and *hym* are used indefinitely.)   547 He who makes a practice of such pleasures (1 Tim. v. 6).   563 *namely*: especially; *Lepe*: town in Spain, near Cadiz.   565ff. A humorous allusion to the vintner's illicit practice of mixing the cheaper (and stronger) wines of Spain with the dearer wines of France.

Of which ther ryseth swich fumositee
That whan a man hath dronken draughtes thre,
And weneth that he be at hoom in Chepe,
He is in Spaigne, right at the toune of Lepe,—   570
Nat at the Rochele, ne at Burdeux toun;

then   And thanne wol he seye 'Sampsoun, Sampsoun!'
  But herkneth, lordynges, o word, I yow preye,

most notable records   That alle the sovereyn actes, dar I seye,
Of victories in the Olde Testament,   575

true   Thurgh verray God, that is omnipotent,
Were doon in abstinence and in preyere.

look at; learn   Looketh the Bible, and ther ye may it leere.

behold   Looke, Attilla, the grete conquerour,
Deyde in his sleep, with shame and dishonour,   580
Bledynge ay at his nose in dronkenesse.
A capitayn sholde lyve in sobrenesse.

consider   And over al this, avyseth yow right wel
What was comaunded unto Lamuel—
Nat Samuel, but Lamuel, seye I—   585

read   Redeth the Bible, and fynde it expresly
Of wyn-yevyng to hem that han justise.
Namoore of this, for it may wel suffise.
  And now that I have spoken of glotonye,

forbid gambling   Now wol I yow deffenden hasardrye.   590
lies   Hasard is verray mooder of lesynges,
perjury   And of deceite, and cursed forswerynges,
blasphemy   Blaspheme of Crist, manslaughtre, and wast also
property; furthermore   Of catel and of tyme; and forthermo,
reproach   It is repreeve and contrarie of honour   595
gambler   For to ben holde a commune hasardour.
rank   And ever the hyer he is of estaat,
considered abandoned   The moore is he yholden desolaat.
practices   If that a prynce useth hasardrye,
In alle governaunce and policye   600
He is, as by commune opinioun,
Yholde the lasse in reputacioun.
  Stil boun, that was a wys embassadour,
Was sent to Corynthe, in ful greet honour,

Lacedaemon   Fro Lacidomye, to make hire alliaunce.   605
And whan he cam, hym happede, par chaunce,
That alle the gretteste that were of that lond,

found   Pleyynge atte hasard he hem fond.
For which, as soone as it myghte be,
He stal hym hoom agayn to his contree,   610

reputation   And seyde, 'Ther wol I nat lese my name,
dishonor   Ne I wol nat take on me so greet defame,
Yow for to allie unto none hasardours.

---

567 *fumositee*: See V. 358.   586–87 And find the explicit statement about the giving of wine to those who have the administration of justice (Prov. xxxi 4–6).   600 In all government and political affairs.   606 It happened to him, by chance.

	Sendeth othere wise embassadours;	
I would rather	For, by my trouthe, me were levere dye	615
	Than I yow sholde to hasardours allye.	
	For ye, that been so glorious in honours,	
	Shul nat allyen yow with hasardous	
treaty	As by my wyl, ne as by my tretee.'	
	This wise philosophre, thus seyde hee.	620

> Looke eek that to the kyng Demetrius

Parthians The kyng of Parthes, as the book seith us,
Sente him a paire of dees of gold in scorn,
previously For he hadde used hasard ther-biforn;
For which he heeld his glorie or his renoun 625
repute At no value or reputacioun.
Lordes may fynden oother maner pley
Honest ynough to dryve the day awey.

> Now wol I speke of othes false and grete

treat (of them) A word or two, as olde bookes trete. 630
unnatural Gret sweryng is a thyng abhominable,
reprehensible And fals sweryng is yet moore reprevable.
altogether The heighe God forbad sweryng at al,
Witnesse on Mathew; but in special
Jeremiah Of sweryng seith the hooly Jeremye, 635
truly 'Thou shalt swere sooth thyne othes, and nat lye,
judgment And swere in doom, and eek in rightwisnesse';
wicked thing But ydel sweryng is a cursednesse.
Bihoold and se that in the firste table
commandments Of heighe Goddes heestes honurable, 640
Hou that the seconde heeste of hym is this:
vain 'Take nat my name in ydel or amys.'
sooner Lo, rather he forbedeth swich sweryng
Than homycide or many a cursed thyng;
I seye that, as by ordre, thus it stondeth; 645
This knoweth, that his heestes understondeth,
How that the seconde heeste of God is that.
furthermore; bluntly And forther over, I wol thee telle al plat,
depart That vengeance shal nat parten from his hous
That of his othes is to outrageous. 650
'By Goddes precious herte,' and 'By his nayles,'
And 'By the blood of Crist that is in Hayles,
Sevene is my chaunce, and thyn is cynk and treye!'
'By Goddes armes, if thou falsly pleye,
This daggere shal thurghout thyn herte go!' 655
This fruyt cometh of the bicched bones two,
perjury Forsweryng, ire, falsnesse, homycide.

---

634 Matt. v. 36. 636–37 Jer. iv. 2. 639 i.e., in the first five commandments. 641 The second commandment according to the Vulgate numbering, but the third in the A.V. 645–46 Thus, I say, is the order in which the commandments stand; those who understand His commandments know this. 652 The Abbey of Hailes in Gloucestershire, where the monks displayed a phial containing what was believed to be some of Christ's blood. 653 The allusion is to the game of hazard. 656 *bicched bones*: cursed bones, i.e., dice.

	Now, for the love of Crist, that for us dyde,
forgo	Lete youre othes, bothe grete and smale.
	But sires, now wol I telle forth my tale.	660
profligates	Thise riotoures thre of whiche I telle,
	Longe erst er prime rong of any belle,
seated	Were set hem in a taverne for to drynke,
	And as they sat, they herde a belle clynke
(which) was; its	Biforn a cors, was caried to his grave.	665
	That oon of hem gan callen to his knave:
	'Go bet,' quod he, 'and axe redily
by	What cors is this that passeth heer forby;
	And looke that thou reporte his name weel.'
	'Sire,' quod this boy, 'it nedeth never-a-deel;	670
	It was me toold er ye cam heer two houres.
(by God), indeed	He was, pardee, an old felawe of youres;
	And sodeynly he was yslayn to-nyght,
very drunk	Fordronke, as he sat on his bench upright.
privy; call	Ther cam a privee theef, men clepeth Deeth,	675
	That in this contree al the peple sleeth,
in two	And with his spere he smoot his herte atwo,
more	And wente his wey withouten wordes mo.
during this plague	He hath a thousand slayn this pestilence.
	And, maister, er ye come in his presence,	680
	Me thynketh that it were necessarie
	For to be war of swich an adversarie.
	Beth redy for to meete hym everemoore;
mother	Thus taughte me my dame; I sey namoore.'
the innkeeper	'By seinte Marie!' seyde this taverner	685
truth	'The child seith sooth, for he hath slayn this yeer,
	Henne over a mile, withinne a greet village,
servant	Bothe man and womman, child, and hyne, and page;
	I trowe his habitacioun be there.
forewarned	To been avysed greet wysdom it were,	690
	Er that he dide a man a dishonour.'
	'Ye, Goddes armes!' quod this riotour,
	'Is it swich peril with hym forto meete?
	I shal hym seke by wey and eek by strete,
a vow; worthy	I make avow to Goddes digne bones!	695
of one mind	Herkneth, felawes, we thre been al ones;
to	Lat ech of us holde up his hand til oother,
	And ech of us bicomen otheres brother,
	And we wol sleen this false traytour Deeth.
	He shal be slayn, he that so manye sleeth,	700
	By Goddes dignitee, er it be nyght!'
together; troth	Togidres han thise thre hir trouthes plight
	To lyve and dyen ech of hem for oother,

---

662 Long before any bell rang for prime (the canonical office sung at sunrise). 666 One of them called out to his servant. 667 Go as quickly as you can...and ask at once. 670 It isn't at all necessary. 687 Over a mile from here.

born	As though he were his owene ybore brother.
frenzy	And up they stirte, al dronken in this rage, 705
	And forth they goon towardes that village
before	Of which the taverner hadde spoke biforn.
	And many a grisly ooth thanne han they sworn,
torn to pieces	And Cristes blessed body al torente—
die; catch	Deeth shal be deed, if that they may hym hente! 710
	Whan they han goon nat fully half a mile,
stepped	Right as they wolde han troden over a stile,
poor	An oold man and a povre with hem mette.
greeted	This olde man ful mekely hem grette,
keep you	And seyde thus, 'Now, lordes, God yow see!' 715
	The proudeste of thise riotoures three
	Answerde agayn, 'What, carl, with sory grace!
wrapped up	Why artow al forwrapped save thy face?
do you live	Why lyvestow so longe in so greet age?
looked; face	This olde man gan looke in his visage, 720
	And seyde thus: 'For I ne kan nat fynde
India	A man, though that I walked into Ynde,
	Neither in citee ne in no village,
exchange	That wolde chaunge his youthe for myn age;
must; have	And therfore moot I han myn age stille, 725
	As longe tyme as it is Goddes wille.
	Ne Deeth, allas! ne wol nat han my lyf.
wretch	Thus walke I, lyk a restelees kaityf,
	And on the ground, which is my moodres gate,
	I knokke with my staf, bothe erly and late, 730
dear mother	And seye "Leeve mooder, leet me in!
	Lo how I vanysshe, flessh, and blood, and skyn!
	Allas! whan shul my bones been at reste?
	Mooder, with yow wolde I chaunge my cheste
been	That in my chambre longe tyme hath be, 735
	Ye, for an heyre clowt to wrappe in me!"
	But yet to me she wol nat do that grace,
withered	For which ful pale and welked is my face.
	But, sires, to yow it is no curteisye
	To speken to an old man vileynye, 740
unless	But he trespasse in word, or elles in dede.
	In Hooly Writ ye may yourself wel rede:
	"Agayns an oold man, hoor upon his heed,
advice	Ye sholde arise;" wherfore I yeve yow reed,
	Ne dooth unto an oold man noon harm now, 745
	Namoore than that ye wolde men did to yow
	In age, if that ye so longe abyde.
	And God be with yow, where ye go or ryde!

---

717 *carl*: fellow; *with sory grace*: bad luck to you! 734–36 i.e., he is willing to exchange the chest containing all his worldly goods for a shroud of hair-cloth to wrap himself in. 740 To speak rudely to an old man. 743–44 Lev. xix. 32: "Thou shalt rise up before the hoary head, and honour the face of the old man." 748 Whether you walk or ride, i.e., in all circumstances.

where	I moot go thider as I have to go.'
	'Nay, olde cherl, by God, thou shalt nat so,' 750
at once	Seyde this oother hasardour anon;
depart; easily	'Thou partest nat so lightly, by Seint John!
that (same)	Thou spak right now of thilke traytour Deeth,
	That in this contree alle oure freendes sleeth.
promise: spy	Have heer my trouthe, as thou art his espye, 755
pay for	Telle where he is, or thou shalt it abye,
	By God, and by the hooly sacrement!
	For soothly thou art oon of his assent
	To sleen us yonge folk, thou false theef!'
desirous	'Now, sires,' quod he, 'if that yow be so leef 760
	To fynde Deeth, turne up this croked wey,
faith	For in that grove I lafte hym, by my fey,
	Under a tree, and there he wole abyde;
	Noght for youre boost he wole him no thyng hyde.
	Se ye that ook? Right there ye shal hym fynde. 765
redeemed	God save yow, that boghte agayn mankynde,
	And yow amende!' Thus seyde this olde man;
each	And everich of thise riotoures ran
	Til he cam to that tree, and ther they founde
	Of floryns fyne of gold ycoyned rounde 770
	Wel ny an eighte busshels, as hem thoughte.
	No lenger thanne after Deeth they soughte,
	But ech of hem so glad was of that sighte,
	For that the floryns been so faire and brighte,
	That doun they sette hem by this precious hoord. 775
	The worste of hem, he spak the firste word.
note	'Bretheren,' quod he, 'taak kep what that I seye;
jest	My wit is greet, though that I bourde and pleye.
	This tresor hath Fortune unto us yiven,
jollity	In myrthe and jolitee oure lyf to lyven, 780
	And lightly as it comth, so wol we spende.
would have supposed	Ey! Goddes precious dignitee! who wende
fortune	To-day that we sholde han so fair a grace?
	But myghte this gold be caried fro this place
else	Hoom to myn hous, or elles unto youres— 785
know	For wel ye woot that al this gold is oures—
	Thanne were we in heigh felicitee.
	But trewely, by daye it may nat bee.
violent	Men wolde seyn that we were theves stronge,
have us hanged	And for oure owene tresor doon us honge. 790
	This tresor moste ycaried be by nyghte
craftily as possible	As wisely and as slyly as it myghte.
advise; lots	Wherfore I rede that cut among us alle
drawn	Be drawe, and lat se wher the cut wol falle;

---

758 For truly you are in conspiracy with him.   764 He will not hide himself at all for your boasting.   770–71 Very nearly eight bushels, it seemed to them, of fine gold florins coined round.   781 And as easily as it came, so will we spend it.

	And he that hath the cut with herte blithe	795
quickly	Shal renne to the town, and that ful swithe,	
	And brynge us breed and wyn ful prively.	
guard secretly	And two of us shul kepen subtilly	
	This tresor wel; and if he wol nat tarie,	
	Whan it is nyght, we wol this tresor carie,	800
	By oon assent, where as us thynketh best.'	
	That oon of hem the cut broghte in his fest,	
	And bad hem drawe, and looke where it wol falle;	
	And it fil on the yongeste of hem alle,	
	And forth toward the toun he wente anon.	805
as	And also soone as that he was gon,	
	That oon of hem spak thus unto that oother:	
	'Thow knowest wel thou art my sworen brother;	
advantage	Thy profit wol I telle thee anon.	
	Thou woost wel that oure felawe is agon,	810
	And heere is gold, and that ful greet plentee,	
divided	That shal departed been among us thre.	
nevertheless; plan	But nathelees, if I kan shape it so	
	That it departed were among us two,	
	Hadde I nat doon a freendes torn to thee?'	815
know not	That oother answerde, 'I noot hou that may be.	
two	He woot wel that the gold is with us tweye;	
	What shal we doon? What shal we to hym seye?'	
a secret; scoundrel	'Shal it be conseil?' seyde the firste shrewe,	
	'And I shal tellen in a wordes fewe	820
	What we shal doon, and brynge it wel aboute.'	
promise	'I graunte,' quod that oother, 'out of doute,	
betray	That, by my trouthe, I wol thee nat biwreye.'	
know	'Now,' quod the firste, 'thou woost wel we be tweye,	
	And two of us shul strenger be than oon.	825
seated	Looke whan that he is set, that right anoon	
	Arys as though thou woldest with hym pleye,	
pierce	And I shal ryve hym thurgh the sydes tweye	
	Whil that thou strogelest with hym as in game,	
	And with thy daggere looke thou do the same;	830
	And thanne shal al this gold departed be,	
between	My deere freend, bitwixen me and thee.	
desires	Thanne may we bothe oure lustes all fulfille,	
	And pleye at dees right at oure owene wille.'	
	And thus acorded been thise shrewes tweye	835
	To sleen the thridde, as ye han herd me seye.	
	This yongeste, which that wente to the toun,	
turns over and over	Ful ofte in herte he rolleth up and doun	
	The beautee of thise floryns newe and brighte.	
if only I could	'O Lord!' quod he, 'if so were that I myghte	840
	Have al this tresor to myself allone,	
	Ther is no man that lyveth under the trone	

---

801 With one accord, to where it seems best to us. 821 And bring it about successfully.

Of God that sholde lyve so murye as I!'
And atte laste the feend, oure enemy,

buy   Putte in his thought that he sholde poyson beye,   845
With which he myghte sleen his felawes tweye;
For-why the feend foond hym in swich lyvynge
That he hadde leve him to sorwe brynge.
For this was outrely his fulle entente,
To sleen hem bothe, and nevere to repente.   850
And forth he gooth, no lenger wolde he tarie,

apothecary   Into the toun, unto a pothecarie,
And preyde hym that he hym wolde selle

kill   Som poyson, that he myghte his rattes quelle;
yard   And eek ther was a polcat in his hawe,   855
capons; killed   That, as he seyde, his capouns hadde yslawe,
And fayn he wolde wreke hym, if he myghte,

annoyed   On vermyn that destroyed hym by nyghte.
The pothecarie answerde, 'And thou shalt have
A thyng that, also God my soule save,   860
In al this world ther is no creature,

concoction   That eten or dronken hath of this confiture
Noght but the montance of a corn of whete,
That he ne shal his lif anon forlete;

die   Ye, sterve he shal, and that in lasse while   865
Than thou wolt goon a paas nat but a mile,
This poysoun is so strong and violent.'

taken   This cursed man hath in his hond yhent
afterwards   This poysoun in a box, and sith he ran
Into the nexte strete unto a man,   870
And borwed of hym large botelles thre;
And in the two his poyson poured he;
The thridde he kepte clene for his drynke.
For al the nyght he shoop hym for to swynke

In cariynge of the gold out of that place.   875
bad luck to him   And whan this riotour, with sory grace,
Hadde filled with wyn his grete botels thre,
To his felawes agayn repaireth he.

preach   What nedeth it to sermone of it moore?
planned   For right as they hadde cast his deeth bifoore,   880
Right so they han hym slayn, and that anon.
And whan that this was doon, thus spak that oon:
'Now lat us sitte and drynke, and make us merie,
And afterward we wol his body berie.'
And with that word it happed hym, par cas,   885
To take the botel ther the poyson was,
And drank, and yaf his felawe drynke also,

847–48 Because the fiend found him living such a life that he had permission to bring him to sorrow. 857 And he would gladly avenge himself. 860 God save my soul. 863–64 No bigger amount than a grain of wheat, who shall not give up his life immediately. 866 Than it would take you to trot a mile. 874–75 He planned to toil at carrying the gold. 885 It happened to him, by chance.

For which anon they storven bothe two.
    But certes, I suppose that Avycen
Wroot nevere in no canon, ne in no fen,   890

symptoms   Mo wonder signes of empoisonyng
Than hadde thise wrecches two, er hir endyng.
Thus ended been thise homycides two,
And eek the false empoysonere also.
    O cursed synne of alle cursednesse!   895

treacherous   O traytours homycide, O wikkednesse!
lechery; gambling O glotonye, luxurie, and hasardrye!
vile language   Thou blasphemour of Crist with vileynye
from habit   And othes grete, of usage and of pride!
    Allas! mankynde, how may it bitide   900
That to thy creatour, which that the wroghte,
redeemed   And with his precious herte-blood thee boghte,
ungrateful   Thou art so fals and so unkynde, allas?
    Now, goode men, God foryeve yow youre trespas,
keep   And ware yow fro the synne of avarice!   905
cure   Myn hooly pardoun may yow alle warice,
So that ye offre nobles or sterlynges,
Or elles silver broches, spoones, rynges.
bow   Boweth youre heed under this hooly bulle!
wool   Cometh up, ye wyves, offreth of youre wolle!   910
Youre names I entre heer in my rolle anon;
go   Into the blisse of hevene shul ye gon.
absolve   I yow assoille, by myn heigh power,
Yow that wol offre, as clene and eek as cleer
As ye were born.—And lo, sires, thus I preche.   915
physician   And Jhesu Crist, that is oure soules leche,
So graunte yow his pardoun to receyve,
For that is best; I wol yow nat deceyve.
    But, sires, o word forgat I in my tale:
bag   I have relikes and pardoun in my male,   920
excellent   As faire as any man in Engelond,
Whiche were me yeven by the popes hond.
If any of yow wole, of devocion,
Offren, and han myn absolucion,
Com forth anon, and kneleth heere adoun,   925
And mekely receyveth my pardoun;
Or elles taketh pardoun as ye wende,
Al newe and fressh at every miles ende,
again and again So that ye offren, alwey newe and newe,
Nobles or pens, whiche that be goode and trewe.   930
everyone   It is an honour to everich that is heer
competent   That ye mowe have a suffisant pardoneer
T'assoille yow, in contree as ye ryde,

---

889 *Avycen*: Avicenna, the eleventh-century Arab physician, whose celebrated treatise on medicine, known as the "Book of the Canon in Medicine," was divided into "fens," or chapters. 895 O most accursed of all sins! 907 Provided you offer gold and silver coins. 915 The Pardoner now addresses his fellow pilgrims.

because of accidents For aventures whiche that may bityde.
Paraventure ther may fallen oon or two 935
in two Doun of his hors, and breke his nekke atwo.
Looke which a seuretee is it to yow alle
come by chance That I am in youre felaweshipe yfalle,
high and low That may assoille yow, bothe moore and lasse,
Whan that the soule shal fro the body passe. 940
advise I rede that oure Hoost heere shal bigynne,
For he is moost envoluped in synne.
Com forth, sire Hoost, and offre first anon,
And thou shalt kisse the relikes everychon,
Ye, for a grote! Unbokele anon thy purs.' 945
may I have 'Nay, nay!' quod he, 'thanne have I Cristes curs!
Lat be,' quod he, 'it shal nat be, so theech!
Thou woldest make me kisse thyn olde breech,
And swere it were a relyk of a seint,
stained Though it were with thy fundement depeint! 950
found But, by the croys which that Seint Eleyne fond,
testicles I wolde I hadde thy coillons in myn hond
holy things In stide of relikes or of seintuarie.
Lat kutte hem of, I wol thee helpe hem carie;
enshrined They shul be shryned in an hogges toord!' 955
  This Pardoner answerde nat a word;
So wrooth he was, no word ne wolde he seye.
  'Now,' quod oure Hoost, 'I wol no lenger pleye
With thee, ne with noon oother angry man.'
But right anon the worthy Knyght bigan, 960
laughed Whan that he saugh that al the peple lough,
quite 'Namoore of this, for it is right ynough!
cheerful Sire Pardoner, be glad and myrie of cheere;
And ye, sire Hoost, that been to me so deere,
I prey yow that ye kisse the Pardoner. 965
nearer And Pardoner, I prey thee, drawe thee neer,
did (before) And, as we diden, lat us laughe and pleye.'
Anon they kiste, and ryden forth hir weye.
Heere Is Ended the Pardoners Tale

SIR THOMAS WYATT *(1503–1542)*

The verse epistle is a popular satiric form combining the relaxed informality of a personal letter with the disciplined expressiveness of poetry. From the satirist's standpoint, its advantages arise from the fact that it places the reader in the position of eavesdropper rather than audience. Audiences must be entertained or instructed, but eavesdropping, as everyone knows, is its own reward; hence anything additional—wit, irony, humor, style—is a distinct bonus. The satirist is thus able to make points obliquely, without the burden of a direct bid for approval. Moreover, truth and plain-dealing are built into the epistolary form, are therefore "not labored at nor spun." Exaggeration and misrepresentation

---

937 See what a safeguard it is. 947 As I hope to prosper. 951 A reference to the finding of the Cross by St. Helen, the mother of Constantine.

are hardly to be expected of a man writing to a friend, so what he attacks must surely deserve attacking. And finally, because the satiric letter-writer has been caught off guard, he cannot be expected to be on his best behavior. What in public speech would seem ill-natured and immoderate is only natural when a man does not know anyone is listening; thus the satirist gets around the rules of attack without breaking them.

Wyatt's epistle here illustrates the ease with which pastoral accommodates itself to satire, for in it he uses a world of rustic simplicity to gain satiric leverage against the sophisticated but morally slippery world of the court. Wyatt had good cause to know precisely how slippery that world was, since during a lifetime of excellent and loyal service to Henry VIII he was twice imprisoned, at least once because of trumped-up charges.

EPISTLE TO JOHN POINS: OF THE COURTIER'S LIFE

Mine own John Poynz, since ye delight to know
The cause why that homeward I me draw,
And flee the press of courts where so they go,

Rather then to live thrall, under the awe
Of lordly looks, wrappid within my cloak,   5
To will and lust learning to set a law;

It is not for because I scorn or moke
The power of them, to whom fortune hath lent
Charge over us, of Right, to strike the stroke:

But true it is that I have always meant   10
Less to esteem them then the common sort,
Of outward things that judge in their intent,

Without regard what doth inward resort.
I grant sometime that of glory the fire
Doth touch my heart: me list not to report   15

Blame by honour and honour to desire.
But how may I this honour now attain
That cannot dye the colour black a liar?

My Poynz, I cannot frame me tune to feign,
To cloak the truth for praise without desert,   20
Of them that list all vice for to retain.

I cannot honour them that sets their part
With Venus and Bacchus all their life long;
Nor hold my peace of them although I smart.

I cannot crouch nor kneel to do so great a wrong,   25
To worship them, like god on earth alone,
That are as wolves these silly lambs among.

I cannot with my words complain and moan,
And suffer nought; nor smart without complaint,
Nor turn the word that from my mouth is gone.   30

---

3 *press*: throngs. 6 *set a law*: restrain, govern. 7 *moke*: mock. 27 *silly*: simple, foolish.
30 *turn...gone*: go back on what I have said.

I cannot speak and look like a saint,
Use wiles for wit and make deceit a pleasure,
And call craft counsel, for profit still to paint.

I cannot wrest the law to fill the coffer
With innocent blood to feed myself fat,   35
And do most hurt where most help I offer.

I am not he that can allow the state
Of high Caesar and damn Cato to die,
That with his death did scape out of the gate

From Caesar's hands (if Livy do not lie)   40
And would not live where liberty was lost:
So did his heart the common weal apply.

I am not he such eloquence to boast,
To make the crow singing as the swan,
Nor call the lion of coward beasts the most   45

That cannot take a mouse as the cat can:
And he that dithe for hunger of the gold
Call him Alexander; and say that Pan

Passeth Apollo in music manyfold;
Praise Sir Topas for a noble tale,   50
And scorn the story that the knight told.

Praise him for counsel that is drunk of ale;
Grin when he laugheth that beareth all the sway,
Frown when he frowneth and groan when he is pale;

On other's lust to hand both night and day: 55
None of these points would ever frame in me;
My wit is nought—I cannot learn the way.

And much the less of things that greater be,
That asken help of colours of devise
To join the mean with each extremity,   60

With the nearest virtue to cloak alway the vice:
And as to purpose likewise it shall fall,
To press the virtue that it may not rise;

As drunkenness good fellowship to call;
The friendly foe with his double face—   65
Say he is gentle and courtois therewithal;

---

37 *allow*: acknowledge, accept. 47 *dithe*: dieth. 49 *Passeth*: surpasseth; *manyfold*: many
times over. 50 *Sir Topas*: "The Tale of Sir Topas" in Chaucer's *Canterbury Tales.* 51
story...told: "The Knight's Tale," *Canterbury Tales.* 53 *sway*: power. 59 *asken*: require;
colours of devise: emblems of deceit. 60–63 *To join...rise*: Wyatt's wordplay on "vice"
makes these lines confusing. Virtue is conceived of here in the Aristotelean sense as the
mean or point of moderation between two extremes of vice. Wyatt puns on "vice" by
suggesting that the extremes of vice constitute a "vise," which when activated by the forces
of flattery and deceit, presses in on the virtuous mean, crushing vices and virtue together.
Hence, in flattery and deceit, vices are labeled virtues, as "drunkenness" in line 64 is
labeled "good fellowship" and genuine virtue is "depressed" and "may not rise." 66
courtois: courteous.

And say that favell hath a goodly grace
In eloquence; and cruelty to name
Zeal of justice and change in time and place;

And he that sufferth offence without blame   70
Call him pitiful; and him true and plain
That raileth reckless to every man's shame.

Say he is rude that cannot lie and feign;
The lecher a lover; and tyranny
To be the right of a prince's reign.   75

I cannot, I. No, no, it will not be.
This is the cause that I could never yet
Hang on their sleeves that way as thou mayest see

A chip of chaunce more then a pound of wit.
This maketh me at home to hunt and to hawk   80
And in foul weder at my book to sit,

In frost and snow then with my bow to stalk.
No man doth mark whereso I ride or go.
In lusty leas at liberty I walk

And of these news I feel nor weal nor woe,   85
Sauf that a clog doth hang yet at my heel:
No force for that, for it is ordered so,

That I may leap both hedge and dike full well.
I am not now in France to judge the wine,
With saffry sauce the delicates to feel;   90

Nor yet in Spain, where one must him incline
Rather then to be, outwardly to seem.
I meddle not with wits that be so fine;

Nor Flanders cheer letteth not my sight to deem
Of black and white, nor taketh my wit away   95
With beastliness, they beasts do so esteem;

Nor I am not where Christ is given in prey
For money, poison and traison, at Rome—
A common practice used night and day:

But here I am in Kent and Christendom   100
Among the muses where I read and rhyme;
Where if thou list, my Poynz, for to come,
Thou shalt be judge how I do spend my time.

JOSEPH HALL *(1574–1656)*

Although we sometimes speak of the "golden age" of Elizabethan England,
the Elizabethan satirists called it an "iron age," the last and least of the four

---

67 *favell*: flattery. 73 *rude*: crude, untutored. 77 *cause*: reason. 79 *chaunce*: chance. 81
weder: weather. 85 *these news*: presumably the news which his friend Poins (Poynz)
has sent him from the court. 86 *sauf*: save, except; *clog*: hindrance (may refer to Wyatt's
having been placed in the custody of his father after his release from prison in 1536. The
reasons for Wyatt's imprisonment are not known). 90 *saffry*: savoury. 94 *letteth*:
hindereth; *deem*: judge.

ages of civilization, and they looked back with pastoral nostalgia to the Golden Age of Saturn. In a fallen world, poetry is sometimes regarded as a form of compensation, a way of giving fictional grandeur to unlovely realities. But Hall sees no such merit in the work of his poetic contemporaries, and to account for the present literary squalor he feels obliged to recast the old myth of the Muses.

SATIRE II from *VIRGIDEMIAE* (1597)

Whilom the sisters nine were vestal maids,
And held their temple in the secret shades
Of fair Parnassus, that two-headed hill
Whose ancient fame the southern world did fill,
And in the stead of their eternal flame   5
Was the cool stream that took his endless name
From out the fertile hoof of winged steed:
There did they sit and do their holy deed
That pleased both heaven and earth, till that of late—
Whom should I fault? or the most righteous fate?   10
Or heaven, or men, or fiends, or ought beside
That ever made that foul mischance betide?—
Some of the sisters in securer shades
Deflowered were;
And ever since disdaining sacred shame   15
Done ought that might their heavenly stock defame.
Now is Parnassus turned to the stews,
And on bay-stalks the wanton myrtle grows.
Cithaeron hill's become a brothel bed,
And Pyrene sweet turned to a poisoned head   20
Of coal-black puddle, whose infectious stain
Corrupteth all the lowly fruitful plain.
Their modest stole, to garish looser weed
Decked with love-favours, their late whoredoms' meed,
And where they wont sip of the simple flood   25
Now toss they bowls of Bacchus' boiling blood.
I marveled much with doubtful jealousy

---

1 *Whilom*: formerly; *sisters nine*: the nine Muses. 3 *Parnassus*: mountain ridge northwest of Athens where the muses sometimes congregated, regarded as the seat of music and poetry; *two-headed*: perhaps because, according to the historian Herodotus, two enormous crags broke off and crushed the Persian forces in 480 B.C. 6 *stream*: Hippocrene spring. 7 *fertile...steed*: the winged horse Pegasus had created the Hippocrene spring for the muses by stamping his hoof on the earth. 8 *do...deed*: The muses had various activities: entertaining the gods with song, dance, and poetry; judging musical contests; prophesying; dispensing the arts of healing, etc. Probably what is meant here is their function of inspiring poets. 15 *Done ought*: have done nothing (to inspire modern poets). 16 *stews*: brothels. 17 *bay-stalks*: conquerors and triumphant poets were crowned with bay leaves; *wanton myrtle*: the myrtle was sacred to Aphrodite, goddess of love. 18 *Cithaeron hill*: Cithaeron, the brother of Helicon, murdered his father and was himself killed with his brother when he attempted to murder Helicon. They were both turned into mountains. Hall seems to have confused Mount Cithaeron, which was harsh and wild, with Mount Helicon, which was the home of Apollo and the muses and the site of the Hippocrene spring. 20 *Pyrene*: the Pirene spring near Corinth. 23 *weed*: garment. 24 *meed*: pay, reward (perhaps "mead," connecting with what follows). 25 *wont*: were wont to. 26 *Bacchus*: Roman name for Dionysus, the Greek god of wine, revelry, regeneration.

Whence came such litters of new poetry?
Methought I feared, lest the horse-hoofed well
His native banks did proudly over-swell   30
In some late discontent, thence to ensue
Such wondrous rabblements of rhymesters new.
But since, I saw it painted on fame's wings:
The Muses to be woxen wantonings.
Each bush, each bank, and each base apple-squire   35
Can serve to sate their beastly lewd desire.
Ye bastard poets, see your pedigree:
From common trulls, and loathesome brothelry.

JOHN DONNE

Donne's Satire III assumes a quasi-dramatic form in that the speaker addresses
an unnamed listener on the subject of religion and the poem has a kind of plot.
Although the poem looks at first as though it will turn into sectarian propaganda,
which might impoverish it as satire, the speaker, we gather further on, is not
so much defending a sectarian pass as opening avenues for the pursuit of
genuine faith, which remains undefined. It is typical of satire that rather than
supply answers, it prefers to clear the field of popular pseudo-answers, leaving
the reader to find his own solutions in the knowledge that they are not easily
come by. Part of Donne's technique is to provide a running contrast between
the easy and the difficult, the limited and the embracing—in brief, between the
material and the spiritual. Thus he sets in diminished perspective the easy
physical courage required to battle nations, climates, or duelists—compared to
combating the Devil, the world, and the flesh, where hard and uncertain
victories are won; ridicules the sectarians and their casual liaisons with faith;
and sets the limitations of secular and ecclesiastical power beside that of God.
The "plot" of the satire takes the form of a sustained metaphor dealing with
courtship, marriage, and wedded fidelity. The courtship theme, centering on
the question "What will you dare for love of me?" dominates the first 32 lines;
the question of a suitable bride dominates lines 33–43; the question of finding
such a bride dominates lines 43–88; and, the wedding having taken place, the
question of marital fidelity—with the underlying idea of "What God hath
joined, let no man put asunder"—dominates the remainder of the poem.

SATIRE III, RELIGION

Kind pity chokes my spleen; brave scorn forbids
Those tears to issue which swell my eyelids;
I must not laugh, nor weep sins, and be wise,
Can railing then cure these worn maladies?
Is not our mistress, fair Religion,   5
As worthy of all our souls' devotion,
As virtue was to the first blinded age?

---

28 *litters*: rubbish. 29 *horse-hoofed well*: the Hippocrene spring (see note to line 7). 33
But since: but since then. 34 *The...wantonings*: i.e., the Muses have become wantons.
35 *apple-squire*: pimp and gigolo.
7 *blinded age*: the pagan age, when the light of Christianity had not yet been seen.

Are not heaven's joys as valiant to assuage
Lusts, as earth's honor was to them? Alas,
As we do them in means, shall they surpass   10
Us in the end, and shall thy father's spirit
Meet blind philosophers in heaven, whose merit
Of strict life may be imputed faith, and hear
Thee, whom he taught so easy ways and near
To follow, damned? O, if thou dar'st, fear this;   15
This fear great courage and high valor is.
Dar'st thou aid mutinous Dutch, and dar'st thou lay
Thee in ships, wooden sepulchers, a prey
To leaders' rage, to storms, to shot, to dearth?
Dar'st thou dive seas and dungeons of the earth?   20
Hast thou courageous fire to thaw the ice
Of frozen North discoveries? and thrice
Colder than salamanders, like divine
Children in the oven, fires of Spain, and the line,
Whose countries limbecks to our bodies be,   25
Canst thou for gain bear? And must every he
Which cries not, "Goddess!" to thy mistress, draw,
Or eat thy poisonous words? Courage of straw!
O desperate coward, wilt thou seem bold, and
To thy foes and his (who made thee to stand   30
Sentinel in his world's garrison) thus yield,
And for forbidden wars, leave th' appointed field?
Know thy foes: The foul Devil (whom thou
Strivest to please) for hate, not love, would allow
Thee fain his whole realm to be quit; and as   35
The world's all parts wither away and pass,
So the world's self, thy other loved foe, is
In her decrepit wane, and thou, loving this,
Dost love a withered and worn strumpet; last,
Flesh (itself's death) and joys which flesh can taste,   40
Thou lovest; and thy fair goodly soul, which doth
Give this flesh power to taste joy, thou dost loathe.
Seek true religion. O, where? Mirreus,
Thinking her unhoused here, and fled from us,
Seeks her at Rome; there, because he doth know   45
That she was there a thousand years ago.
He loves her rags so, as we here obey

---

9 *earth's honor*: i.e., honor here on earth, reputation, the desire for which kept lust in check among pagan men just as desire for "heaven's joys" should do for modern men. 12 *blind...heaven*: pagan philosophers like Plato and Aristotle whose "strict life," virtuous enough to have been the product of "faith," was no doubt rewarded by heaven. 17 *mutinous Dutch*: Englishmen could volunteer to fight with the Dutch against the Spanish. 23–24 *Colder...line*: salamanders were thought able to live in fire, like the "divine children," Mesach, Shadrach, and Abednego, who lived through the fiery furnace in Daniel 3:19–27. So men, "for gain," will endure the tormenting heat of Spanish territories and "the line" (the equator). 25 *limbecs*: alembics; apparatus used by alchemists in distilling. 27 *draw*: draw his blade, i.e., fight a duel. 30 *his*: God's. 33 *thy foes*: i.e., the Devil, the world (line 37), and the flesh (line 40). 43 *Mirreus*: imaginary character representing a Roman Catholic.

The statecloth where the Prince sat yesterday.
Crantz to such brave loves will not be enthralled,
But loves her only, who at Geneva is called   50
Religion—plain, simple, sullen, young,
Contemptuous, yet unhandsome; as among
Lecherous humors, there is one that judges
No wenches wholesome but coarse country drudges.
Graius stays still at home here, and because   55
Some preachers, vile ambitious bawds, and laws
Still new, like fashions, bid him think that she
Which dwells with us, is only perfect, he
Embraceth her whom his Godfathers will
Tender to him, being tender, as wards still   60
Take such wives as their guardians offer, or
Pay values. Careless Phrygius doth abhor
All, because all cannot be good, as one
Knowing some women whores, dares marry none.
Graccus loves all as one, and thinks that so   65
As women do in divers countries go
In divers habits, yet are still one kind,
So doth, so is religion; and this blind-
ness too much light breeds; but unmoved thou
Of force must one, and forced but one allow;   70
And the right; ask thy father which is she,
Let him ask his; though truth and falsehood be
Near twins, yet truth a little elder is;
Be busy to seek her, believe me this,
He's not of none, nor worst, that seeks the best.   75
To adore, or scorn an image, or protest,
May all be bad; doubt wisely; in strange way
To stand inquiring right, is not to stray;
To sleep, or run wrong, is. On a huge hill,
Cragged and steep, Truth stands, and he that will   80
Reach her, about must, and about must go,
And what the hill's suddenness resists, win so;
Yet strive so, that before age, death's twilight,
Thy soul rest, for none can work in that night.
To will implies delay, therefore now do.   85
Hard deeds, the body's pains; hard knowledge too
The mind's endeavors reach, and mysteries

---

49 *Crantz*: imaginary character representing a Puritan. 55 *Graius*: imaginary character representing a traditionalist, one who accepts the going faith, not for its truth but because it is sanctioned by the state, his "Godfather." 62 *Pay values*: if one took a wife other than that recommended by his guardian, he "paid values" or forfeited a certain sum; *Phrygius*: imaginary character representing a skeptic. 65 *Graccus*: imaginary character representing a Universalist. 68–69 *this blindness...breeds*: to accept all religions equally without seeing differences is blindness too. 75 *He's...best*: i.e., the man who seeks the best faith cannot be of no faith, an unbeliever, nor of the worst faith, a bad believer. 85 *To will implies delay*: good intentions unacted on are merely procrastination. 86–87 *Hard deeds...reach*: as difficult actions require physical effort, so profound knowledge can be obtained only by intellectual effort.

Are like the sun, dazzling, yet plain to all eyes.
Keep the truth which thou hast found; men do not stand
In so ill case here, that God hath with his hand   90
Signed king's blank charters to kill whom they hate,
Nor are they vicars, but hangmen to fate.
Fool and wretch, wilt thou let thy soul be tied
To man's laws, by which she shall not be tried
At the last day? O, will it then boot thee   95
To say a Philip, or a Gregory,
A Harry, or a Martin taught thee this?
Is not this excuse for mere contraries
Equally strong? Cannot both sides say so?
That thou mayest rightly obey power, her bounds know;   100
Those passed, her nature and name is changed; to be
Then humble to her is idolatry.
As streams are, power is; those blest flowers that dwell
At the rough stream's calm head, thrive and do well,
But having left their roots, and themselves given   105
To the stream's tyrannous rage, alas, are driven
Through mills, and rocks, and woods, and at last, almost
Consumed in going, in the sea are lost.
So perish souls, which more choose men's unjust
Power from God claimed, than God himself to trust.   110

WILLIAM CARTWRIGHT *(1611–1643)*

Neoplatonist works like Castiglione's *Il Cortegiano* (The Courtier) emphasized that the body is but the suit of flesh worn by the soul and physical beauty is an external manifestation of inner virtue. The ladder of love, therefore, should lead from these external irrelevancies upward to a conjunction of souls (love-looks, it was held, pierced through the eye straight to the soul, but compare *A Midsummer Night's Dream*) and finally to the heights of a disinterested contemplation of pure virtue; or, as Cartwright puts it, "from sex to soul, from soul to thought." Cartwright himself had written about love in the platonic vein earlier; hence, perhaps, the amusing air here of the disgruntled renegade glancing back at sour and unnourishing grapes.

NO PLATONIQUE LOVE (pub. 1651)

Tell me no more of minds embracing minds,
   And hearts exchanged for hearts;
That spirits spirits meet, as winds do winds,
   And mix their subtlest parts;

89–92 *men do not stand...hangmen to fate*: the human condition on earth is not *this* bad, namely, that the laws of kings and Popes are of absolute authority; rather, kings and Popes are here to serve God's justice, not their own. 96–97 *Philip*: Philip II of Spain; *Gregory*: the name of several Popes; *Harry*: Henry VIII of England; *Martin*: Martin Luther. 100–102 *That thou...is idolatry*: to obey authority rightly, learn the limits of authority, for when these limits have been exceeded (as when a king or churchman demands more than he should) then authority is no longer authority, and to continue obeying it is senseless idolatry.

That two unbodied essences may kiss,   5
And then, like angels, twist and feel one bliss.

I was that silly thing that once was wrought
    To practice this thin love;
I climbed from sex to soul, from soul to thought;
    But thinking there to move,   10
Headlong I rolled from thought to soul, and then
From soul I lighted at the sex again.

As some strict down-looked men pretend to fast,
    Who yet in closets eat;
So lovers who profess they spirits taste,   15
    Feed yet on grosser meat;
I know they boast they souls to souls convey,
Howe'er they meet, the body is the way.

Come, I will undeceive thee, they that tread
    Those vain aërial ways,   20
Are like young heirs and alchemists misled
    To waste their wealth and days,
For searching thus to be forever rich,
They only find a medicine for the itch.

SAMUEL BUTLER *(1612–1680)*

Samuel Butler was ideally equipped to be a satirist. He was skeptical of novelty, distrustful of religion, dubious about philosophical pretensions, contemptuous of empirical science, and disdainful of sentiment. But Puritanism he detested particularly. Thus in *Hudibras* he embodies the absurdities of the Presbyterians in his anti-hero, a Cromwellian colonel and Justice of the Peace as well as pseudo-chivalric knight, and those of the Independents in Ralpho, the knight's squire, with whom he engages in an endless intellectual combat over religious issues. Part I of the poem was published in 1662, Parts II and III following in 1664 and 1678. In Part I, Hudibras and Ralpho journey to a "western" town where they attempt to stop the sport of bear-baiting. After an initial success in which they imprison their opponents, the tables are turned, and they wind up in jail. Hudibras, meanwhile, takes a fancy to a widow and her property (not in that order), and Parts II and III detail his futile efforts to win her hand and land.

Part I was highly popular with the Royalists and Charles II, who had been restored to the throne in 1660, after the Interregnum of Cromwell, from which drab period Butler's poem emerges with all the energy of a repressed Id. Parts II and III, however, were less successful. In them the structure of the poem sags; passages of stinging wit begin to succumb to descriptive *longeurs;* and dramatic focus is diffused as Butler takes on an increasing number of antagonists.

Like Chaucer's *Tale of Sir Topas, Hudibras* is a mock-heroic romance; but whereas Sir Topas is bathed in a rather genial irony, Hudibras is the object of

---

21 *alchemists:* the chemists of the Middle Ages and Renaissance, whose chief aims were to change base metals into gold and to discover the elixir of perpetual youth.

a Juvenalian *saeva indignatio*. Chaucer seeks to prompt a smile, Butler a sneer. Presenting his satire as a pseudo-romance, Butler ridicules both the Puritans and the heroic form and spirit as well. Instead of a chivalric knight-errant setting forth on a quest to redress grievances, we have Sir Hudibras, the arrant Puritan meddler setting out to suppress the popular sport of bear-baiting, thus instead of freeing the people from a monster, freeing the monster from the people. Fantastic in form, the poem nevertheless implies a cynically realistic vision in terms of which the romantic metaphor of human experience—of man idealized as noble, heroic, altruistic—is merely a pathetic and phony attempt to dignify a debased reality. In the canto presented here, in which we find an epic inventory of Sir Hudibras' intellectual and spiritual weapons prior to his sallying forth, the skewer of satire runs through the Puritans to make a shish kebab of contemporary linguists, logicians, rhetoricians, mathematicians, philosophers, theologians, and sectarians. "Beknighted" self-aggrandizement, though most grotesquely obvious in Puritans, is nevertheless universal.

HUDIBRAS

from Part I, Canto I (1663)

THE ARGUMENT* OF THE FIRST CANTO

Sir Hudibras his passing worth,
The manner how he sallied forth:
His arms and equipage are shown;
His horse's virtues, and his own.
The adventure of the bear and fiddle,
Is sung, but breaks off in the middle.

CANTO 1

When civil fury first grew high,
And men fell out, they knew not why,
When hard words, jealousies, and fears
Set folks together by the ears,
And made them fight, like mad or drunk,   5
For dame religion as for punk;
Whose honesty they all durst swear for,
Though not a man of them knew wherefore:
When gospel-trumpeter, surrounded
With long-eared rout, to battle sounded,   10
And pulpit, drum ecclesiastic,
Was beat with fist, instead of a stick;
Then did Sir Knight abandon dwelling,
And out he rode a-coloneling.
    A wight he was whose very sight would   15
Entitle him Mirror of Knighthood;
That never bent his stubborn knee

---

* *Argument*: synopsis, summary.

---

1 *When...high*: When the Civil War began (1642).   6 *punk*: prostitutes.   9 *gospel-trumpeter*: Puritan—perhaps Cromwell here.   14 *a-coloneling*: as a colonel.   15 *wight*: man.

To anything but chivalry,
Nor put up blow, but that which laid
Right worshipful on shoulder blade: 20
Chief of domestic knights, and errant,
Either for chartel or for warrant:
Great on the bench, great in the saddle,
That could as well bind o'er, as swaddle.
Mighty he was at both of these,   25
And styled of war as well as peace.
So some rats of amphibious nature
Are either for the land or water.
But here our authors make a doubt,
Whether he were more wise or stout.   30
Some hold the one, and some the other;
But howsoe'er they make a pother,
The difference was so small, his brain
Outweighed his rage but half a grain;
Which made some take him for a tool   35
That knaves do work with, called a fool,
And offer to lay wagers that
As Montaigne, playing with his cat,
Complains she thought him but an ass,
Much more she would Sir Hudibras.   40
(For that's the name our valiant knight
To all his challenges did write.)
But they're mistaken very much,
'Tis plain enough he was no such.
We grant, although he had much wit,   45
He was very shy of using it,
As being loath to wear it out,
And therefore bore it not about,
Unless on holidays, or so,
As men their best apparel do.   50
Beside, 'tis known he could speak Greek
As naturally as pigs squeak:
That Latin was no more difficile,
Than to a blackbird 'tis to whistle.
Being rich in both, he never scanted   55
His bounty unto such as wanted;
But much of either would afford
To many that had not one word.
For Hebrew roots, although th' are found

---

19 *put up*: endured, suffered, would accept. 20 *worshipful...blade*: i.e., the touch on the shoulders that was received by a man being knighted. 21 *errant*: wandering—a knight-errant in medieval times wandered in search of adventures in which he could display his prowess or redress wrongs. 22 *chartel*: cartel, a letter of challenge to individual combat. 23 *on the bench*: i.e., as a judge. 24 *bind o'er*: to put under legal bond to appear at a specified time and place, as at a law court; *swaddle*: bind up (as in swaddling clothes) or beat. 30 *stout*: brave. 38 *Montaigne*: (1533–1592; French essayist). In his *Apology for Raymond Sebond* Montaigne considered it debatable whether he played with his cat or his cat played with him. 59 *Hebrew roots*: grammatical roots (bases) of Hebrew words.

To flourish most in barren ground,   60
He had such plenty as sufficed
To make some think him circumcised;
And truly so, perhaps, he was,
'Tis many a pious Christian's case.
   He was in logic a great critic,   65
Profoundly skilled in analytic.
He could distinguish, and divide
A hair 'twixt south and southwest side;
On either which he would dispute,
Confute, change hands, and still confute.   70
He'd undertake to prove, by force
Of argument, a man's no horse.
He'd prove a buzzard is no fowl,
And that a lord may be an owl,
A calf an alderman, a goose a justice,   75
And rooks, committee-men and trustees;
He'd run in debt by disputation,
And pay with ratiocination.
All this by syllogism true,
In mood and figure, he would do.   80
   For rhetoric, he could not ope
His mouth but out there flew a trope:
And when he happened to break off
In the middle of his speech, or cough,
He had hard words ready to show why,   85
And tell what rules he did it by.
Else, when with greatest art he spoke,
You'd think he talked like other folk,
For all a rhetorician's rules
Teach nothing but to name his tools.   90
His ordinary rate of speech
In loftiness of sound was rich;
A Babylonish, dialect,
Which learnéd pedants much affect.
It was a parti-coloured dress   95
Of patched and piebald languages:
'Twas English cut on Greek and Latin,
Like fustian heretofore on satin.
It had an odd promiscuous tone,
As if he had talked three parts in one.   100
Which made some think, when he did gabble,
They had heard three labourers of Babel;
Or Cerberus himself pronounce
A leash of languages at once.
This he as volubly would vent   105

---

80 *mood and figure*: terms in logic.   82 *trope*: figure of speech.   85 *hard words*: complex, difficult words   95–96 *It...languages*: words from various languages mingled in his speech. 98 *fustian...satin*: fustian (a coarse material) lined with satin.   103 *Cerberus*: the three-headed dog that guards the gates of Hell.

As if his stock would ne'er be spent.
And truly, to support that charge,
He had supplies as vast and large.
For he could coin or counterfeit
New words with little or no wit: 110
Words so debased and hard, no stone
Was hard enough to touch them on.
And when with hasty noise he spoke 'em,
The ignorant for current took 'em.
That had the orator who once   115
Did fill his mouth with pebble stones
When he harangued, but known his phrase,
He would have used no other ways.
   In mathematics he was greater
Than Tycho Brahe, or Erra Pater: 120
For he, by geometric scale,
Could take the size of pots of ale;
Resolve, by sines and tangents straight,
If bread or butter wanted weight;
And wisely tell what hour o' the day   125
The clock doth strike, by algebra.
   Beside, he was a shrewd philosopher,
And had read every text and gloss over:
Whate'er the crabbed'st author hath,
He understood by implicit faith;   130
Whatever sceptic could inquire for;
For every "why" he had a "wherefore";
Knew more than forty of them do,
As far as words and terms could go.
All which he understood by rote,   135
And, as occasion served, would quote:
No matter whether right or wrong:
They might be either said or sung.
His notions fitted things so well,
That which was which he could not tell;   140
But oftentimes mistook the one
For the other, as great clerks have done.
He could reduce all things to acts,
And knew their natures by abstracts;
Where entity and quiddity,   145
The ghosts of defunct bodies fly;
Where truth in person does appear,
Like words congealed in northern air.
He knew what's what, and that's as high

---

112 *touch*: test. Touchstone, a flintlike stone, was formerly used to test the purity of gold or silver by the streak left on it when it was rubbed with the metal. 115 *orator*: Demosthenes (c.385–322 B.C.; Greek orator) supposedly perfected his delivery by speaking with pebbles in his mouth. 120 *Brahe*: (1546–1601; Danish mathematician and astronomer); *Pater*: pseudonym of William Lilly (1602–1681), an English astrologer influential with some Puritans. 129 *crabbed'st*: most difficult and abstruse.

As metaphysic wit can fly.   150
In school-divinity as able
As he that hight irrefragable;
Profound in all the nominal
And real ways, beyond them all;
And, with as delicate a hand,   155
Could twist as tough a rope of sand;
And weave fine cobwebs, fit for skull
That's empty when the moon is full;
Such as take lodgings in a head
That's to be let unfurnishéd.   160
He could raise scruples dark and nice,
And after solve 'em in a trice;
As if divinity had catched
The itch, of purpose to be scratched;
Or, like a mountebank, did wound   165
And stab herself with doubts profound,
Only to show with how small pain
The sores of faith are cured again;
Although by woeful proof we find
They always leave a scar behind.   170
He knew the seat of Paradise,
Could tell in what degree it lies:
And, as he was disposed, could prove it,
Below the moon, or else above it.
What Adam dreamt of when his bride   175
Came from her closet in his side:
Whether the Devil tempted her
By a High-Dutch interpreter:
If either of them had a navel;
Who first made music malleable: 180
Whether the serpent, at the fall,
Had cloven feet, or none at all.
All this without a gloss or comment,
He would unriddle in a moment,
In proper terms, such as men smatter   185
When they throw out and miss the matter.
    For his religion, it was fit
To match his learning and his wit:
'Twas Presbyterian true blue,
For he was of that stubborn crew   190

---

152 *hight irrefragable*: (was) called unanswerable, irrefutable; i.e., Alexander of Hales, a medieval English theologian and philosopher who was called, for his skill in argument, "Doctor Irrefragabilis." 153 *nominal*: refers to one school of medieval philosophy, nominalism, which maintains that universals (abstract, general terms) are merely words or names and do not represent existent realities; only actual physical particulars are real. 154 *real*: refers to the other school of medieval philosophy, realism, which maintains that universals have an equal, sometimes superior, reality to actual physical particulars. 161 *nice*: unusually subtle, difficult to discern. 172 *degree*: as in latitude and longitude; he could pinpoint the location of Paradise. 178 *High-Dutch*: dialect of Dutch. 179 *If...novel*: It was believed by some theologians that Adam and Eve had no navels.

Of errant saints, whom all men grant
To be the true church militant:
Such as do build their faith upon
The holy text of pike and gun;
Decide all controversies by   195
Infallible artillery;
And prove their doctrine orthodox
By apostolic blows and knocks;
Call fire, and sword, and desolation,
A godly-thorough Reformation,   200
Which always must be carried on,
And still be doing, never done:
As if religion were intended
For nothing else but to be mended.
A sect, whose chief devotion lies   205
In odd perverse antipathies;
In falling out with that or this,
And finding somewhat still amiss:
More peevish, cross, and splenetic,
Than dog distract, or monkey sick: 210
That with more care keep holiday
The wrong, than others the right way:
Compound for sins they are inclined to
By damning those they have no mind to;
Still so perverse and opposite,   215
As if they worshipped God for spite,
The self-same thing they will abhor
One way, and long another for.
Free-will they one way disavow,
Another, nothing else allow.   220
All piety consists therein
In them, in other men all sin.
Rather than fail, they will defy
That which they love most tenderly,
Quarrel with minced pies, and disparage   225
Their best and dearest friend, plum-porridge.
Fat pig and goose itself oppose,
And blaspheme custard through the nose.
The apostles of this fierce religion,
Like Mahomet's, were ass and widgeon,   230
To whom our knight, by fast instinct
Of wit and temper, was so linked
As if hypocrisy and nonsense
Had got the advowson of his conscience.
   Thus was he gifted and accoutered,   235
We mean on the inside, not the outward:
That next of all we shall discuss;...

---

230 *Mahomet*: Mohammed (570–632; Arabian prophet who founded the Mohammedan religion); *widgeon*: type of fresh-water duck.   234 *advowson*: the right to appoint someone to a vacant post in the Church of England.

JOHN DRYDEN *(1631–1700)*

Thomas Shadwell (c. 1640–1692), the "true-blue-Protestant poet" of the sub-title, was a poet, playwright, and one-time friend of Dryden's. Like many seventeenth-century poets, he was self-designated as the literary heir of Ben Jonson, whose merits as a comic playwright and poet Shadwell proclaimed publicly and persistently over a period of years, against Dryden's objections. Apparently, Dryden finally wearied of objecting and decided to demolish. In 1678 the death of an Irish priest and poetaster, Richard Flecknoe, who had a well-earned reputation as a "lackwit," offered Dryden the opportunity to cast Shadwell in the role of Mac Flecknoe ("son of Flecknoe") and to dramatize the coronation ceremony at the end of which the regal mantle of the King of Nonsense falls from Flecknoe's shoulders to Shadwell's. Although written in 1678, the poem was not published (though it was circulated in manuscript) until 1682, a few months after the appearance of Shadwell's *The Medal of John Bayes,* a scurrilous attack on Dryden's earlier satire *The Medal.*

The "heroic couplet" used by almost all Restoration and early eighteenth-century poets is an ideal instrument for satiric dissecting. It lends itself to concise and logical precision, to an epigrammatic incisiveness, and when governed by the mock-heroic spirit as in this poem, to a devastating reversal of effect as the first line soars aloft and the second shoots it down:

> Sh—— alone, of all my sons, is he
> Who stands confirmed in full stupidity.

This damning statement rendered in the accents of praise is typical of the satiric technique throughout. Dryden never stoops to invective or outright denunciation but remains aloof, politely distant, manipulating everything indirectly through the fiction of Flecknoe and yet counteracting the civility of the style with the insipidity of its subject.

MAC FLECKNOE (1682)

Or, A Satire Upon The True-Blue-Protestant Poet T. S.

All human things are subject to decay,
And when fate summons, monarchs must obey.
This Flecknoe found, who, like Augustus, young
Was called to empire, and had governed long;
In prose and verse, was owned, without dispute,   5
Through all the realms of Nonsense, absolute.
This agéd prince, now flourishing in peace,
And blest with issue of a large increase;
Worn out with business, did at length debate
To settle the succession of the state;   10
And, pond'ring which of all his sons was fit
To reign, and wage immortal war with wit,
Cried: " 'Tis resolved; for nature pleads that he
Should only rule, who most resembles me:
Sh—— alone my perfect image bears,   15
Mature in dulness from his tender years;

---

3 *Augustus* (caesar): (63 B.C. – A.D. 14; first Roman emperor, 27 B.C. – A.D. 14.) 8 *issue...increase*: many children. 12 *wit*: intelligence.

Sh—— alone, of all my sons, is he
Who stands confirmed in full stupidity.
The rest to some faint meaning make pretense,
But Sh—— never deviates into sense.   20
Some beams of wit on other souls may fall,
Strike through, and make a lucid interval;
But Sh——'s genuine night admits no ray,
His rising fogs prevail upon the day:
Besides, his goodly fabric fills the eye,   25
And seems designed for thoughtless majesty:
Thoughtless as monarch oaks that shade the plain,
And, spread in solemn state, supinely reign.
Heywood and Shirley were but types of thee,
Thou last great prophet of tautology: 30
Even I, a dunce of more renown than they,
Was sent before but to prepare thy way;
And, coarsely clad in Norwich drugget, came
To teach the nations in thy greater name.
My warbling lute, the lute I whilom strung,   35
When to King John of Portugal I sung,
Was but the prelude to that glorious day,
When thou on silver Thames didst cut thy way,
With well-timed oars before the royal barge,
Swelled with the pride of thy celestial charge;   40
And big with hymn, commander of an host,
The like was ne'er in Epsom blankets tossed.
Methinks I see the new Arion sail,
The lute still trembling underneath thy nail.
At thy well-sharpened thumb from shore to shore   45
The treble squeaks for fear, the basses roar;
Echoes from Pissing Alley Sh—— call,
And Sh—— they resound from Aston Hall.
About thy boat the little fishes throng,
As at the morning toast that floats along.   50
Sometimes, as prince of thy harmonious band,
Thou wield'st thy papers in thy threshing hand.
St. André's feet ne'er kept more equal time,
Not ev'n the feet of thy own *Psyche's* rime;
Though they in number as in sense excel;   55
So just, so like tautology, they fell
That, pale with envy, Singleton forswore

---

25 *goodly...eye*: Shadwell was fat. 29 *Heywood*: Thomas Heywood (c. 1570–1641),
English dramatist; *Shirley*: James Shirley (1596–1666), English dramatist. Both men were
prolific writers. 33 *Norwich drugget*: coarse woolen cloth. (Shadwell was born in Norfolk,
near Norwich.) 35 *whilom*: formerly (an archaic word in Dryden's day). 36 *King...
Portugal*: John IV (1605–1656), said to have been Flecknoe's patron. 42 *Epsom blankets*:
some reference to Shadwell's comedy, *Epsom Wells,* seems intended. 43 *Arion*: half-
legendary Greek musician and poet. Shadwell was proud of his musical talents. 48 *Aston
Hall*: obscure reference. 53 *St. André('s)*: a well-known French dancing master. 54
Psyche's rhyme: refers to Shadwell's verse-opera *Psyche* (1675). 57–59 *Singleton...
Villerius*: refers to the musician and singer, John Singleton, who took the part of Villerius
in the first English opera, *The Siege of Rhodes* (1656), by Sir William D'Avenant (1606–
1668), Villerius had been ridiculed for fighting with lute and sword.

The lute and sword which he in triumph bore,
And vowed he n'er would act Villerius more."
Here stopped the good old sire, and wept for joy   60
In silent raptures of the hopeful boy.
All arguments, but most his plays, persuade
That for anointed dullness he was made.
    Close to the walls which fair Augusta bind,
(The fair Augusta much to fears inclined,)   65
An ancient fabric raised to inform the sight,
There stood of yore, and Barbican it hight:
A watchtower once; but now, so fate ordains,
Of all the pile an empty name remains.
From its old ruins brothel-houses rise,   70
Scenes of lewd loves, and of polluted joys,
Where their vast courts the mother-strumpets keep,
And, undisturbed by watch, in silence sleep.
Near these a Nursery erects its head,
Where queens are formed, and future heroes bred;   75
Where unfledged actors learn to laugh and cry,
Where infant punks their tender voices try,
And little Maximins the gods defy.
Great Fletcher never treads in buskins here,
Nor greater Jonson dares in socks appear;   80
But gentle Simkin just reception finds
Amidst this monument of vanished minds;
Pure clinches the suburbian muse affords,
And Panton waging harmless war with words.
Here Flecknoe, as a place to fame well known,   85
Ambitiously designed his Sh——'s throne.
For ancient Dekker prophesied long since
That in this pile should reign a mighty prince,
Born for a scourge of wit and flail of sense,
To whom true dullness should some *Psyches* owe,   90
But worlds of *Misers* from his pen should flow;
Humourists and hypocrites it should produce,
Whole Raymond families and tribes of Bruce.
    Now empress fame had published the renown
Of Sh——'s coronation through the town.   95
Roused by report of fame, the nations meet,
From near Bunhill and distant Watling Street.

---

64 *Augusta*: the name given ancient London by the Romans. 67 *Barbican it hight*: Barbican
it is called (a watchtower once stood at Barbican in North London). 74 *Nursery*: a training
school for novice actors. 77 *punks*: harlots. 78 *Maximins*: the hero of Dryden's play
Tyrannic Love (1669). 79 *Fletcher*: John Fletcher (1579–1625), English dramatist; *buskins*:
high shoes worn by actors in ancient tragedies. 80 *Jonson*: Ben Jonson (c. 1573–1637),
English poet and dramatist; *socks*: low shoes worn by actors in ancient comedies. 81
Simkin: *The Humors of Simkin,* a low farce. 83 *clinches*: puns. 84 *Panton*: Thomas
Panton, a "wit." 87 *Dekker*: Thomas Dekker (c. 1572–1632), English poet, dramatist, and
pamphleteer. 91–93 *Misers...Humourists...Raymond...Bruce*: *The Miser* (1672), *The
Humourists* (1671), and *The Virtuoso* (1676)—plays by Shadwell; Raymond, a character in
The Humourists; Bruce in *The Virtuoso*. 97 *Bunhill...Watling Street*: well-known places
in London.

No Persian carpets spread the imperial way,
But scattered limbs of mangled poets lay;
From dusty shops neglected authors come,   100
Martyrs of pies and relics of the bum.
Much Heywood, Shirley, Ogleby there lay,
But loads of Sh—— almost chocked the way.
Bilked stationers for yeomen stood prepared,
And Herringman was captain of the guard.   105
The hoary prince in majesty appeared,
High on a throne of his own labours reared.
At his right hand our young Ascanius sat,
Rome's other hope and pillar of the state.
His brows thick fogs, instead of glories, grace,   110
And lambent dullness played around his face.
As Hannibal did to the altars come,
Sworn by his sire a mortal foe to Rome;
So Sh—— swore, nor should his vow be vain,
That he till death true dullness would maintain;   115
And, in his father's right and realm's defence,
Ne'er to have peace with wit nor truce with sense.
The king himself the sacred unction made,
As king by office and as priest by trade.
In his sinister hand, instead of ball,   120
He placed a mighty mug of potent ale;
Love's Kingdom to his right he did convey,
At once his sceptre and his rule of sway;
Whose righteous lore the prince had practised young,
And from whose loins recorded *Psyche* sprung.   125
His temples, last, with poppies were o'erspread,
That nodding seemed to consecrate his head.
Just at that point of time, if fame not lie,
On his left hand twelve reverend owls did fly.
So Romulus, 'tis sung, by Tiber's brook,   130
Presage of sway from twice six vultures took.
Th' admiring throng loud acclamations make,
And omens of the future empire take.
The sire then shook the honors of his head,
And from his brow damps of oblivion shed   135
Full on the filial dullness: long he stood,
Repelling from his breast the raging god;
At length burst out in this prophetic mood:
    "Heavens bless my son, from Ireland let him reign
To far Barbadoes on the western main;   140
Of his dominion may no end be known,

101 *Martyrs…bum*: pages torn from worthless books were placed under pies or used as toilet paper. 102 *Ogleby*: John Ogleby (1600–1676), English translator of Homer and Virgil. 105 *Herringman*: Henry Herringman, Dryden's first publisher. 108 *Ascanius*: son of Aeneas in Virgil's *Aeneid* (here, Shadwell). 112 *Hannibal*: (247–c. 183 B.C.) Carthaginian general whose father made him swear eternal hatred of Rome. 120 *sinister*: left. 122 *Love's Kingdom*: play by Flecknoe (published in 1664). 129–30 *On…Romulus*: Romulus' proposal for a site for Rome was accepted because he saw twelve vultures whereas Remus saw only six. 130 *Tiber*: river running past Rome.

And greater than his father's be his throne;
Beyond *Love's Kingdom* let him stretch his pen!"
He paused, and all the people cried, "Amen."
Then thus continued he: "My son, advance   145
Still in new impudence, new ignorance.
Success let others teach, learn thou from me
Pangs without birth, and fruitless industry.
Let *Virtuosos* in five years be writ;
Yet not one thought accuse thy toil of wit.   150
Let gentle George in triumph tread the stage,
Make Dorimant betray, and Loveit rage;
Let Cully, Cockwood, Fopling, charm the pit,
And in their folly show the writer's wit.
Yet still thy fools shall stand in thy defense,   155
And justify their author's want of sense.
Let 'em be all by thy own model made
Of dullness, and desire no foreign aid;
That they to future ages may be known,
Not copies drawn, but issue of thy own.   160
Nay, let thy men of wit too be the same,
All full of thee, and differing but in name.
But let no alien S—dl—y interpose,
To lard with wit thy hungry *Epsom* prose.
And when false flowers or rhetoric thou wouldst cull,   165
Trust nature, do not labor to be dull;
But write thy best, and top; and, in each line,
Sir Formal's oratory will be thine.
Sir Formal, though unsought, attends thy quill,
And does thy northern dedications fill.   170
Nor let false friends seduce thy mind to fame,
By arrogating Jonson's hostile name.
Let father Flecknoe fire thy mind with praise,
And uncle Ogleby thy envy raise.
Thou art my blood, where Jonson has no part: 175
What share have we in nature, or in art?
Where did his wit on learning fix a brand,
And rail at arts he did not understand?
Where made he love in Prince Nicander's vein,
Or swept the dust in *Psyche's* humble strain?   180
Where sold he bargains, "whip-stitch, kiss my arse,"
Promised a play and dwindled to a farce?

147–50 *learn...wit*: Shadwell had apologized for writing hastily, but Dryden suggests that he wrote *The Virtuoso* slowly, carefully, and badly. 151 *George*: George Etherege, popular contemporary dramatist. The names that follow are of characters, mostly humorous ones, in his plays. 163–64 *S–dl–y, Epsom*: Charles Sedley, from whom Shadwell borrowed in *Epsom Wells*. 168 *Sir Formal*('s): Sir Formal Trifle, a character in Shadwell's *The Virtuoso*. 170 *northern dedications*: to the Duke of Newcastle, a northern peer. 172 *arrogating...name*: Shadwell professed himself a disciple of Ben Jonson and affected Jonson's rough speech and manner; *hostile*: because Jonson's work is vastly superior to Shadwell's. 179 *Nicander's vein*: the stilted speech of Nicander, a character in Shadwell's *Psyche*. 181 *sold he bargains*: gave he coarse replies—such as that immediately following —to innocent questions.

When did his muse from Fletcher scenes purloin,
As thou whole Etherege dost transfuse to thine?
But so transfused, as oils on water flow,   185
His always floats above, thine sinks below.
This is thy province, this thy wondrous way,
New humors to invent for each new play:
This is that boasted bias of thy mind,
By which one way, to dullness, 'tis inclined;   190
Which makes thy writings lean on one side still,
And, in all changes, that way bends thy will.
Nor let thy mountain belly make pretense
Of likeness; thine's a tympany of sense.
A tun of main in thy large bulk is writ,   195
But sure thou 'rt but a kilderkin of wit.
Like mine thy gentle numbers feebly creep,
Thy tragic muse gives smiles, thy comic sleep.
With whate'er gall thou sett'st thyself to write,
Thy inoffensive satires never bite.   200
In thy felonious heart, though venom lies,
It does but touch thy Irish pen, and dies.
Thy genius calls thee not to purchase fame
In keen iambics, but mild anagram:
Leave writing plays, and choose for thy command   205
Some peaceful province in Acrostic Land.
There thou mayst wings display and altars raise,
And torture one poor word ten thousand ways.
Or if thou wouldst thy diff'rent talents suit,
Set thy own songs, and sing them to thy lute."   210
He said, but his last words were scarcely heard,
For Bruce and Longvil had a *trap* prepar'd,
And down they sent the yet declaiming bard.
Sinking he left his drugget robe behind,
Borne upwards by a subterranean wind.   215
The mantle fell to the young prophet's part,
With double portion of his father's art.

JOHN WILMOT, EARL OF ROCHESTER *(1647–1680)*

All creation, according to the Stoics, was formed from a pre-existent "Something," but Rochester, with mordant metaphysical skepticism, prefers to enthrone the "Great Negative" as the true sustaining power of the universe and

---

189–92 *This...will*: Dryden parodies four lines from Shadwell's Epilogue to *The Humourists*:
  A humour is the bias of the mind,
  By which with violence 'tis one way inclined:
  It makes our actions lean on one side still,
  And in all changes that way bends the will.
196 *kilderkin*: small barrel (contrasted with *tun*).   207 *wings, altars*: poems were sometimes written so that their appearance on the page suggested the form of objects such as these. 212 *Bruce and Longvil*: characters in Shadwell's *The Virtuoso* who prepared a trap door through which Sir Formal drops, still talking.

human affairs. Virtue, thought, politicians, fools, ministers, gratitude, the promises of kings, and the vows of whores are all illusory "somethings" begotten upon and longing for a return to the womb of Nothing. Platonism, with its conception of material unreality issuing from and returning to intellectual reality, is here given a shrewd, ironic twist, for the origin of everything now becomes an inconceivable universal idea, an intellectual essence rarefied out of existence.

In "Upon Nothing," Rochester satirizes everything; in his "Satire against Mankind," he is more temperate. His real object of attack, however, is less mankind than man's complacent faith in the infallibility of reason. Rochester would agree with Swift that man is not "the rational animal" but "the animal with the capacity of reason." The dialogue form—the introduction of a second speaker in the person of the parson—is a neat gambit allowing Rochester to parody his opposition and then to score points off his own parody. But it also allows him to damn reason without qualification up to line 46, then to "ground" the reader's annoyance at his extremism by setting up an equally extreme counterposition that he can then use both as an object of ridicule and as an opportunity to make a reasonable concession (I am not against reason itself, only against false reason) that really paves the way to an even more extreme and sweeping indictment of man than was originally the case. Thus with an air of sweet reasonableness itself, Rochester gives a generous inch to take an unguarded mile.

Rochester was a notorious rake and cynic in the court of Charles II, a debauchee whose deathbed conversion to the Church made his life a kind of biographical morality play for the pious and perhaps a tragedy for the cynics.

UPON NOTHING

Nothing! thou elder brother even to shade,
That hadst a being ere the world was made
And, well fixed, art alone of ending not afraid.

Ere time and place were, time and place were not,
When primitive Nothing something straight begot,   5
Then all proceeded from the great united...What?

Something, the general attribute of all,
Severed from thee, its sole original,
Into thy boundless self must undistinguished fall.

Yet Something did thy mighty power command,   10
And from thy fruitful emptiness's hand
Snatched men, beasts, birds, fire, air and land.

Matter, the wicked'st offspring of thy race,
By form assisted, flew from thy embrace,
And rebel light obscured thy reverend dusky face.   15

With form and matter, time and place did join
Body, thy foe, with thee did leagues combine,
To spoil thy peaceful realm and ruin all thy line.

But turncoat time assists the foe in vain
And, bribed by thee, assists thy short-lived reign.   20
And to thy hungry womb drives back thy slaves again.

Though mysteries are barred from laic eyes,
And the Divine alone, with warrant, pries
Into thy bosom, where the truth in private lies,

Yet this of thee tne wise may freely say: 25
Thou from virtuous nothing tak'st away,
And to be part with thee the wicked wisely pray.

Great Negative, how vainly would the wise
Inquire, define, distinguish, teach, devise,
Didst thou not stand to point their dull philosophies?   30

Is or *is not*, the two great ends of fate,
And *true* or *false*, the subject of debate,
That perfect or destroy the vast designs of fate,

When they have racked the politician's breast,
Within thy bosom most securely rest,   35
And, when reduced to thee, are least unsafe and best.

But, Nothing, why does Something still permit
That sacred monarchs should at council sit
With persons highly thought at best for nothing fit,

Whilst weighty Something modestly abstains   40
From princes' coffers and from statesmen's brains,
And nothing there like stately Nothing reigns?

Nothing, who dwell'st with fools in grave disguise,
For whom they reverend shapes and forms devise—
Lawn sleeves, and furs, and gowns—when they like thee look wise.   45

French truth, Dutch prowess, British policy,
Hibernian learning, Scotch civility,
Spaniards' dispatch, Danes' wit, are mainly seen in thee.

The great man's gratitude to his best friend,
Kings' promises, whores' vows: towards thee they bend,   50
Flow swiftly into thee, and in thee ever end.

A SATIRE AGAINST MANKIND

Were I (who to my cost already am
One of those strange prodigious creatures, Man)
A spirit free, to choose for my own share
What case of flesh and blood I pleased to wear,
I'd be a dog, a monkey, or a bear,   5
Or any thing but that vain animal
Who is so proud of being rational.
The senses are too gross, and he'll contrive
A sixth, to contradict the other five;
And before certain instinct, will prefer   10

Reason, which fifty times for one does err.
Reason, an *ignis fatuus* in the mind,
Which leaving light of nature, sense, behind,
Pathless and dang' rous wandring ways it takes,
Through errors, fenny bogs, and thorny brakes,   15
Whilst the misguided follower climbs with pain
Mountains of whimsies, heaped in his own brain,
Stumbling from thought to thought, falls headlong down
Into doubt's boundless sea, where like to drown,
Books bear him up awhile, and makes him try   20
To swim with bladders of philosophy,
In hopes still t'oretake th' escaping light,
The vapour dances in his dazzled sight,
Till spent, it leaves him to eternal night.
Then old age and experience, hand in hand,   25
Lead him to death, and make him understand
After a search so painful, and so long,
That all his life he has been in the wrong:
Huddled in dirt the reas'ning engine lies,
Who was so proud, so witty, and so wise.   30
Pride drew him in, as cheats their bubbles catch,
And makes him venture—to be made a wretch.
His wisdom did his happiness destroy,
Aiming to know what world he should enjoy,
And wit was his vain frivolous pretence   35
Of pleasing others, at his own expense;
For wits are treated just like common whores,
First they're enjoyed, and then kicked out of doors,
The pleasure past, a threatning doubt remains
That frights th'enjoyer with succeeding pains: 40
Women and men of wit are dang'rous tools
And ever fatal to admiring fools.
Pleasure allures, and when the fops escape,
'Tis not that they're beloved, but fortunate,
And therefore what they fear, at least they hate.   45
   But now methinks some formal band, and beard,
Takes me to task: Come on, Sir, I'm prepared.
   Then by your favour, anything that's writ
Against this gibeing jingling knack called wit
Likes me abundantly, but you take care   50
Upon this point, not to be too severe.
Perhaps my muse were fitter for this part,
For I profess I can be very smart
On wit, which I abhor with all my heart.
I long to lash it in some sharp essay,   55

---

29 *engine*: The "new philosophy" associated with Descartes and, especially for Rochester, Hobbes was frequently taken to imply that man was nothing more than a complicated mechanism. 31 *cheats their bubbles*: The modern equivalent would be "con-men their pigeons." 40 *succeeding pains*: i.e., of venereal diseases. 46 *band*: the Geneva band worn by parsons at the time. 50 *Likes me*: "I like."

But your grand indiscretion bids me stay
And turns my tide of ink another way.
What rage ferments in your degen'rate mind
To make you rail at reason and mankind?
Blessed glorious Man! to whom alone kind Heaven   60
An everlasting soul has freely given;
Whom his great Maker took such care to make
That from himself he did the image take,
And this fair frame, in shining reason dressed,
To dignify his nature above beast.   65
Reason, by whose aspiring influence
We take a flight beyond material sense,
Dive into mysteries, then soaring, pierce
The flaming limits of the universe,
Search Heaven and Hell, find out what's acted there,   70
And give the world true grounds of hope and fear.
   Hold, mighty man, I cry—all this we know
From the pathetic pen of Ingello,
From Patrick's *Pilgrim*, Sibbes' soliloquies,
And 'tis this very reason I despise.   75
This supernatural gift that makes a mite
Think he is the image of the infinite,
Comparing his short life, void of all rest,
To the Eternal and the ever blessed.
This busy, puzzling stirrer up of doubt   80
That frames deep mysteries, then finds 'em out;
Filling with frantic crowds of thinking fools
Those reverend Bedlams, colleges, and schools,
Borne on whose wings, each heavy sot can pierce
The limits of the boundless universe.   85
So charming ointments make an old witch fly
And bear a crippled carcass through the sky.
'Tis this exalted power whose business lies
In nonsense and impossibilities.
This made a whimsical philosopher,   90
Before the spacious world, his tub prefer,
And we have modern cloistered coxcombs who
Retire to think, cause they have naught to do.
But thoughts are given for action's government,
Where action ceases, thought's impertinent.   95
Our sphere of action is life's happiness,
And he who thinks beyond, thinks like an ass.
Thus, whilst 'gainst false reas'ning I inveigh,
I own right reason, which I would obey:

---

73 *pathetic...Ingello*: Nathaniel Ingelo (c. 1621–1683) published in 1660 an allegorical romance, *Bentivolio and Urania,* which was "pathetic" in the sense of being emotionally overwrought as well as inept. 74 *Patrick's* Pilgrim, *Sibbes' soliloquies*: Simon Patrick's *The Parable of the Pilgrim* was a religious allegory published in 1664. Richard Sibbes (1577–1635), a Puritan, wrote many religious works, although none of them was specifically titled "soliloquies." 99 *own*: recognize, acknowledge.

That reason that distinguishes by sense,   100
And gives us rules of good and ill from thence,
That bounds desires with a reforming will
To keep 'em more in vigour, not to kill.
Your reason hinders, mine helps t'enjoy,
Renewing appetites yours would destroy.   105
My reason is my friend, yours is a cheat;
Hunger calls out, my reason bids me eat;
Perversely yours your appetite does mock,
This asks for food, that answers "What's a-clock?"
This plain distinction, Sir, your doubt secures,   110
'Tis not true reason I despise, but yours.
Thus I think reason righted; but for man,
I'll ne'er recant—defend him if you can.
For all his pride and his philosophy,
'Tis evident, beasts are in their degree   115
As wise at least, and better far than he.
Those creatures are the wisest who attain
By surest means the ends at which they aim.
If therefore Jowler finds and kills his hares
Better than Meres supplies committee chairs,   120
Though one's a statesman, th'other but a hound,
Jowler, in justice, would be wiser found.
You see how far man's wisdom here extends.
Look next, if human nature makes amends,
Whose principles most gen'rous are and just,   125
And to whose morals you would sooner trust.
Be judge yourself, I'll bring it to the test:
Which is the basest creature, man or beast?
Birds feed on birds, beasts on each other prey,
But savage man alone does man betray.   130
Pressed by necessity, they kill for food;
Man undoes man to do himself no good.
With teeth and claws by nature armed they hunt
Nature's allowances, to supply their want;
But man, with smiles, embraces, friendships, praise,   135
Unhumanely his fellow's life betrays,
With voluntary pains works his distress,
Not through necessity but wantonness.
For hunger or for love, they fight or tear,
Whilst wretched man is still in arms for fear;   140
For fear he arms and is of arms afraid,
By fear, to fear, successively betrayed;
Base fear, the source whence his best passions came;
His boasted honor and his dear bought fame;

---

100 *sense*: the senses, instinct. 105 *appetites*: used both in the modern sense, as a desire for food, and in the older sense, as referring to desire in general, passions. 112 *I...righted*: "I have established the proper nature and functions of reason, thus giving reason its due, though I seemed earlier to disparage it." 115 *in their degree*: at their level in the hierarchy of things. 120 *Meres*: Sir Thomas Meres (1635–1715; Commissioner for the Admiralty, 1679–1684).

That lust of power, to which he's such a slave,   145
And for the which alone he dares be brave;
To which his various projects are designed
Which makes him gen'rous, affable, and kind;
For which he takes such pains to be thought wise,
And screws his actions in a forced disguise,   150
Leading a tedious life in misery
Under laborious, mean hypocrisy.
Look to the bottom of his vast design
Wherein man's wisdom, power, and glory join:
The good he acts, the ill he does endure,   155
'Tis all for fear, to make himself secure.
Merely for safety, after fame we thirst,
For all men would be cowards if they durst.
And honesty's against all common sense,
Men must be knaves, 'tis their own defence.   160
Mankind's dishonest, if you think it fair
Amongst known cheats to play upon the square,
You'll be undone...
Nor can weak truth your reputation save;
The knaves will all agree to call you knave.   165
Wronged shall he live, insulted o'er, oppressed,
Who dares be less a villain than the rest.
Thus, Sir, you see what human nature craves:
Most men are cowards, all men should be knaves.
The difference lies, as far as I can see,   170
Not in the thing itself, but the degree;
And all the subject matter of debate
Is only who's a knave of the first rate?
    All this with indignation have I hurled
At the pretending part of the proud world,   175
Who swollen with selfish vanity devise
False freedoms, holy cheats, and formal lies
Over their fellow slaves to tyrannize.
    But if in court so just a man there be
(In court, a just man?—yet unknown to me)   180
Who does his needful flattery direct,
Not to oppress and ruin but protect,
Since flattery, which way so ever laid,
Is still a tax on that unhappy trade.
If so upright a statesman you can find,   185
Whose passions bend to his unbiased mind,
Who does his arts and policies apply
To raise his country, not his family;
Nor while his pride, owned avarice withstands,
Receives aureal bribes from friends' corrupted hands.   190
    Is there a churchman who on God relies?

---

157 *Merely*: entirely, wholly.   174–224 In some early editions of the poem this concluding section was distinguished from the foregoing and labeled "Postscript" or "An Addition to the Satire against Mankind."   184 *that...trade*: the "trade" of the courtier.   189–90 *Nor ...hands*: The text of these lines is corrupt.

Whose life his faith and doctrine justifies?
Not one blown up with vain prelatic pride
Who for reproof of sins does man deride;
Whose envious heart with his obstreperous saucy eloquence   195
Dares chide at kings and rail at men of sense;
Who from his pulpit vents more peevish lies,
More bitter railings, scandals, calumnies,
Than at a gossiping are thrown about
When the good wives get drunk and then fall out.   200
None of that sensual tribe whose talents lie
In avarice, pride, sloth, and gluttony;
Who hunt good livings but abhor good lives;
Whose lust exalted, to that height arrives
They act adultery with their own wives,   205
And ere a score of years completed be,
Can from the lofty pulpit proudly see
Half a large parish their own progeny.
   Nor doting B—— who would be adored
For domineering at the council board: 210
A greater fop, in business at fourscore,
Fonder of serious toys, affected more
Than the gay glittering fool at twenty proves
With all his noise, his tawdry clothes and loves.
   But a meek humble man of modest sense   215
Who, preaching peace, does practice continence;
Whose pious life's a proof he does believe
Mysterious truths which no man can conceive.
If upon earth there dwell such godlike men,
I'll here recant my paradox to them,   220
Adore those shrines of virtue, homage pay,
And with the rabble world their laws obey.
If such there are, yet grant me this at least:
Man differs more from man, than man from beast.

JONATHAN SWIFT *(1667–1745)*

Although Swift's greatest satires were written in prose, his satiric verse is also notable. "A Description of the Morning" exemplifies the fact that one of the conventions in the art of satire is apparent artlessness. Under Swift's unobtrusive control, the poem appears to move with the disinterested neutrality of a camera over the London street scene, thus giving the reader not a satiric attack, but merely (or so it would seem) a reproduction of "what is." His "Satirical Elegy," on the other hand, is a direct attack on an individual—a lampoon. John Churchill, First Duke of Marlborough (1650–1722) and an ancestor of Sir Winston Churchill, was a great English militarist but roundly hated by

---

209 *B——*: The identity of "B" remains uncertain.

Swift and other Tories because of the harmful influence that they felt he and his wife exerted on Queen Anne.

A DESCRIPTION OF THE MORNING

Now hardly here and there an hackney-coach
Appearing, showed the ruddy morn's approach.
Now Betty from her master's bed had flown,
And softly stole to discompose her own;
The slip-shod 'prentice from his master's door   5
Had pared the dirt, and sprinkled round the floor.
Now Moll had whirled her mop with dexterous airs,
Prepared to scrub the entry and the stairs.
The youth with broomy stumps began to trace
The kennel-edge, where wheels had worn the place.   10
The small-coal man was heard with cadence deep,
Till drowned in shriller notes of chimney-sweep:
Duns at his lordship's gate began to meet;
And brickdust Moll had screamed through half the street.
The turnkey now his flock returning sees,   15
Duly let out a-nights to steal for fees:
The watchful bailiffs take their silent stands,
And schoolboys lag with satchels in their hands.

A SATIRICAL ELEGY ON THE DEATH OF A LATE
FAMOUS GENERAL, 1722

His Grace! impossible! what dead!
Of old age too, and in his bed!
And could that Mighty Warrior fall?
And so inglorious, after all!
Well, since he's gone, no matter how,   5
The last loud trump must wake him now:
And, trust me, as the noise grows stronger,
He'd wish to sleep a little longer.
And could he be indeed so old
As by the news-papers we're told?   10
Threescore, I think, is pretty high;
'Twas time in conscience he should die.
This world he cumbered long enough;
He burnt his candle to the snuff;
And that's the reason, some folks think,   15
He left behind so great a stink.

Behold his funeral appears,
Nor widow's sighs, nor orphan's tears,
Wont at such times each heart to pierce,
Attend the progress of his hearse.   20

---

13 *Duns*: creditors. 15 *turnkey*: jailer.

But what of that, his friends may say,
He had those honors in his day.
True to his profit and his pride,
He made them weep before he died.

Come hither, all ye empty things,   25
Ye bubbles raised by breath of Kings;
Who float upon the tide of state,
Come hither, and behold your fate.
Let pride be taught by this rebuke,
How very mean a thing's a Duke;   30
From all his ill-got honors flung,
Turned to that dirt from whence he sprung.

ALEXANDER POPE

The Rape of the Lock is based on an actual incident. Lord Petre, the "Baron,"
did cut off one of Miss (as we would say instead of "Mrs.") Fermor's locks.
At the request of John Caryll, Pope wrote and published in 1712 a two-canto
version of the poem in an attempt to ease tensions that had arisen between
the families involved in the incident. In 1714, he expanded the two cantos to
the present five, mainly by adding the "machinery" of the sylphs, gnomes, and
so on, which he gallantly explains to Miss Fermor in his prefatory letter.

    The Rape of the Lock is the most famous example in English of the mock-
heroic form so congenial to Restoration and Augustan satirists (see, for example,
Butler's *Hudibras,* Dryden's *Mac Flecknoe,* Swift's *Battle of the Books,* and
Pope's *The Dunciad*). The mock-heroic thrives on incongruity and disproportion, its normal technique being to present us with an elephant of form giving
birth to a flea of content. The result in all mock-heroic poems, probably, is
that the values attached to elephant and flea, both of which, taken separately,
have their appropriate place and value in the hierarchy of things, are simultaneously diminished by their disjunctive interaction. However, this mutual
debasement of form and content can be handled in various ways. It can be
emphasized, as it is in *Hudibras,* in which the values implied by the heroic
vision—order, ceremony, chivalry, nobility, and so on—suffer as much satiric
diminution as those of the Puritans who are represented in the knightly
Hudibras. On the other hand, this mutual debasement can be weighted in
either direction. In the *Tale of Sir Topas,* for instance, the satire, though
gentle on the whole, takes a somewhat greater toll of the metrical romance form
than it does of the bourgeois knight and what he represents. In *The Rape of
the Lock,* the reverse is the case, the heroic form and vision being presented,
like Lear, as "more sinned against than sinning." It is not, in other words,
that the heroic is an absurd idealizing of human experience, but that human
experience—this particular incident and the conduct it engenders—is absurdly
inadequate to the ideal implicit in the heroic. "Absurd" is perhaps too strong
a word to apply to *The Rape of the Lock,* since Pope's satire, like Chaucer's,
evokes the tolerant amusement of the Horatian, not, like Butler's, the bitter
contempt of the Juvenalian. He prefers to rally than to rail and as a result the
trivial is invested with a good deal of charm and vivacity.

THE RAPE OF THE LOCK (1712–1714)

An Heroi-Comical Poem

Nolueram, Belinda, tuos violare capillos;
Sed juvat, hoc precibus me tribuisse tuis.—MARTIAL*

To Mrs. Arabella Fermor

Madam,—It will be in vain to deny that I have some regard for this piece, since I dedicate it to you. Yet you may bear me witness, it was intended only to divert a few young ladies, who have good sense and good humor enough to laugh not only at their sex's little unguarded follies, but at their own. But as it was communicated with the air of a secret, it soon found its way into the world. An imperfect copy having been offered to a bookseller, you had the good nature for my sake to consent to the publication of one more correct: this I was forced to before I had executed half my design, for the machinery was entirely wanting to complete it.

The machinery, Madam, is a term invented by the critics, to signify that part which the deities, angels, or daemons are made to act in a poem: for the ancient poets are in one respect like many modern ladies: let an action be never so trivial in itself, they always make it appear of the utmost importance. These machines I determined to raise on a very new and odd foundation, the Rosicrucian doctrine of spirits.

I know how disagreeable it is to make use of hard words before a lady; but 'tis so much the concern of a poet to have his works understood, and particularly by your sex, that you must give me leave to explain two or three difficult terms.

The Rosicrucians are a people I must bring you acquainted with. The best account I know of them is in a French book called *Le Comte de Gabalis*,† which, both in its title and size is so like a novel that many of the fair sex have read it for one by mistake. According to these gentlemen, the four elements are inhabited by spirits, which they call sylphs, gnomes, nymphs and salamanders. The gnomes, or daemons of earth, delight in mischief; but the sylphs, whose habitation is in the air, are the best-conditioned creatures imaginable. For they say, any mortals may enjoy the most intimate familiarities with these gentle spirits, upon a condition very easy to all true adepts, an inviolate preservation of chastity.

As to the following cantos, all the passages of them are as fabulous as the vision at the beginning, or the transformation at the end; (except the loss of your hair, which I always mention with reverence). The human persons are as fictitious as the airy ones; and the character of Belinda, as it is now managed, resembles you in nothing but in beauty.

If this poem had as many graces as there are in your person, or in your mind, yet I could never hope it should pass through the world half so uncensured as you have done. But let its fortune be what it will, mine is happy enough, to have given me this occasion of assuring you that I am, with the truest esteem, Madam, your most obedient, humble servant,

A. POPE

---

* *Nolueram...tuis*: "I was reluctant, Belinda, to violate your locks, but I am glad to have granted this to your prayers" (Martial, *Epigrams,* XII, 86).
† *Le Comte de Gabalis*: by Montfaucon de Villars.

CANTO 1

What dire offense from amorous causes springs,
What mighty contests rise from trivial things,
I sing—This verse to CARYLL, Muse! is due:
This, even Belinda may vouchsafe to view:
Slight is the subject, but not so the praise,   5
If she inspire, and he approve my lays.
   Say what strange motive, goddess! could compel
A well-bred lord t' assault a gentle belle?
O say what stranger cause, yet unexplored,
Could make a gentle belle reject a lord?   10
In tasks so bold, can little men engage,
And in soft bosoms dwells such mighty rage?
   Sol through white curtains shot a timorous ray,
And oped those eyes that must eclipse the day:
Now lap-dogs give themselves the rousing shake,   15
And sleepless lovers, just at twelve, awake:
Thrice rung the bell, the slipper knocked the ground,
And the pressed watch returned a silver sound.
Belinda still her downy pillow pressed,
Her guardian sylph prolonged the balmy rest: 20
'Twas he had summoned to her silent bed
The morning dream that hovered o'er her head;
A youth more glittering than a birth-night beau,
(That even in slumber caused her cheek to glow)
Seemed to her ear his winning lips to lay,   25
And thus in whispers said, or seemed to say.
   "Fairest of mortals, thou distinguished care
Of thousand bright inhabitants of air!
If e'er one vision touched thy infant thought,
Of all the nurse and all the priest have taught;   30
Of airy elves by moonlight shadows seen,
The silver token, and the circled green,
Or virgins visited by angel powers,
With golden crowns and wreaths of heavenly flowers;
Hear and believe! thy own importance know,   35
Nor bound thy narrow views to things below.
Some secret truths, from learnèd pride concealed,
To maids alone and children are revealed:
What though no credit doubting wits may give?
The fair and innocent shall still believe.   40
Know, then, unnumbered spirits round thee fly,
The light militia of the lower sky:
These, though unseen, are ever on the wing,
Hang o'er the box, and hover round the Ring.
Think what an equipage thou hast in air,   45

---

3 *Caryll*: see headnote above. 11 *little men*: Lord Petre was short. 32 *silver token*: silver coin that fairies were supposed to leave; *circled green*: grass marked by a fairy ring. 44 *the box*: theater box; *the Ring*: carriage-drive in Hyde Park.

And view with scorn two pages and a chair.
As now your own, our beings were of old,
And once inclosed in woman's beauteous mold;
Thence, by a soft transition, we repair
From earthly vehicles to these of air.   50
Think not, when woman's transient breath is fled,
That all her vanities at once are dead;
Succeeding vanities she still regards,
And though she plays no more, o'erlooks the cards.
Her joy in gilded chariots, when alive,   55
And love of omber, after death survive.
For when the fair in all their pride expire,
To their first elements their souls retire:
The sprites of fiery termagants in flame
Mount up, and take a salamander's name.   60
Soft yielding minds to water glide away,
And sip, with nymphs, their elemental tea.
The graver prude sinks downward to a gnome,
In search of mischief still on earth to roam.
The light coquettes in sylphs aloft repair,   65
And sport and flutter in the fields of air.
   "Know farther yet; whoever fair and chaste
Rejects mankind, is by some sylph embraced:
For spirits, freed from mortal laws, with ease
Assume what sexes and what shapes they please.   70
What guards the purity of melting maids,
In courtly balls, and midnight masquerades,
Safe from the treacherous friend, the daring spark,
The glance by day, the whisper in the dark,
When kind occasion prompts their warm desires,   75
When music softens, and when dancing fires?
'Tis but their sylph, the wise celestials know,
Though honor is the word with men below.
   "Some nymphs there are, too conscious of their face,
For life predestined to the gnomes' embrace.   80
These swell their prospects and exalt their pride,
When offers are disdained, and love denied:
Then gay ideas crowd the vacant brain,
While peers, and dukes, and all their sweeping train,
And garters, stars, and coronets appear,   85
And in soft sounds, 'Your Grace' salutes their ear.
'Tis these that early taint the female soul,
Instruct the eyes of young coquettes to roll,
Teach infant cheeks a bidden blush to know,
And little hearts to flutter at a beau.   90

---

46 *chair*: sedan chair. 56 *omber*: a card game of Spanish origin (*hombre;* "man"). 73
spark: fop, dandy. 75 *kind occasion*: propitious moment. 81 *prospects*: hopes, expectations. 85 *garters*: worn by knights of the Garter; *stars*: worn by Knights of the Garter,
of the Thistle, and of the Bath. 89 *bidden blush*: blush produced artificially, by rouge
or by pinching the cheeks.

"Oft when the world imagine women stray,
The sylphs through mystic mazes guide their way,
Through all the giddy circle they pursue,
And old impertinence expel by new.
What tender maid but must a victim fall   95
To one man's treat, but for another's ball?
When Florio speaks, what virgin could withstand,
If gentle Damon did not squeeze her hand?
With varying vanities, from every part,
They shift the moving toyshop of their heart;   100
When wigs with wigs, with sword-knots sword-knots strive,
Beaux banish beaux, and coaches coaches drive.
This erring mortals levity may call,
Oh blind to truth! the sylphs contrive it all.
   "Of these am I, who thy protection claim,   105
A watchful sprite, and Ariel is my name.
Late, as I ranged the crystal wilds of air,
In the clear mirror of thy ruling star
I saw, alas! some dread event impend,
Ere to the main this morning sun descend,   110
But heaven reveals not what, or how, or where:
Warned by the sylph, oh pious maid, beware!
This to disclose is all thy guardian can:
Beware of all, but most beware of man!"
   He said; when Shock, who thought she slept too long,   115
Leaped up, and waked his mistress with his tongue.
'Twas then, Belinda, if report say true,
Thy eyes first opened on a billet-doux;
Wounds, charms, and ardors, were no sooner read,
But all the vision vanished from thy head.   120
   And now, unveiled, the toilet stands displayed,
Each silver vase in mystic order laid.
First, robed in white, the nymph intent adores,
With head uncovered, the cosmetic powers.
A heavenly image in the glass appears,   125
To that she bends, to that her eye she rears;
Th' inferior priestess, at her altar's side,
Trembling, begins the sacred rites of pride.
Unnumbered treasures ope at once, and here
The various offerings of the world appear;   130
From each she nicely culls with curious toil,
And decks the goddess with the glittering spoil.
This casket India's glowing gems unlocks,
And all Arabia breathes from yonder box.
The tortoise here and elephant unite,   135

---

96 *treat*: entertainment with refreshments served. 97, 98 *Florio, Damon*: rival suitors
101 *sword-knots*: ribbons attached to the hilts of swords. 110 *main*: sea. 115 *shock*:
a type of lapdog, often a poodle, with hair clipped short in places. 118 *billet-doux*: love
letter. 121 *toilet*: toilet table. 127 *inferior priestess*: Belinda's maid, Betty. 131 *nicely . . .
toil*: fastidiously selects with careful diligence.

Transformed to combs, the speckled and the white.
Here files of pins extend their shining rows,
Puffs, powders, patches, Bibles, billet-doux.
Now awful beauty puts on all its arms;
The fair each moment rises in her charms,   140
Repairs her smiles, awakens every grace,
And calls forth all the wonders of her face;
Sees by degrees a purer blush arise,
And keener lightnings quicken in her eyes.
The busy sylphs surround their darling care,   145
These set the head, and those divide the hair,
Some fold the sleeve, while others plait the gown;
And Betty's praised for labors not her own.

Canto 2

Not with more glories, in th' ethereal plain,
The sun first rises o'er the purpled main,
Than, issuing forth, the rival of his beams
Launched on the bosom of the silver Thames.
Fair nymphs, and well-dressed youths around her shone,   5
But every eye was fixed on her alone.
On her white breast a sparkling cross she wore,
Which Jews might kiss, and infidels adore.
Her lively looks a sprightly mind disclose,
Quick as her eyes, and as unfixed as those: 10
Favors to none, to all she smiles extends;
Oft she rejects, but never once offends.
Bright as the sun, her eyes the gazers strike,
And, like the sun, they shine on all alike.
Yet graceful ease, and sweetness void of pride,   15
Might hide her faults, if belles had faults to hide:
If to her share some female errors fall,
Look on her face, and you'll forget 'em all.
   This nymph, to the destruction of mankind,
Nourished two locks, which graceful hung behind   20
In equal curls, and well conspired to deck
With shining ringlets the smooth ivory neck.
Love in these labyrinths his slaves detains,
And mighty hearts are held in slender chains.
With hairy springes we the birds betray,   25
Slight lines of hair surprise the finny prey,
Fair tresses man's imperial race ensnare,
And beauty draws us with a single hair.
   Th' adventurous baron the bright locks admired;
He saw, he wished, and to the prize aspired.   30

---

138 *patches*: small pieces of black silk or court plaster applied to the faces of fashionable
ladies to create "beauty marks." 143 *purer blush*: i.e., as she applies rouge to her cheeks.
3 *rival*: Belinda. 4 *Launched...Thames*: boarded a barge for Hampton Court, a royal
palace upriver from London. 25 *springes*: traps, snares. 26 *finny prey*: fish.

Resolved to win, he meditates the way,
By force to ravish, or by fraud betray;
For when success a lover's toils attends,
Few ask, if fraud or force attained his ends.
   For this, ere Phoebus rose, he had implored   35
Propitious Heaven, and every power adored,
But chiefly Love—to Love an altar built,
Of twelve vast French romances, neatly gilt.
There lay three garters, half a pair of gloves;
And all the trophies of his former loves;   40
With tender billet-doux he lights the pyre,
And breathes three amorous sighs to raise the fire.
Then prostrate falls, and begs with ardent eyes
Soon to obtain, and long possess the prize:
The powers gave ear, and granted half his prayer,   45
The rest, the winds dispersed in empty air.
   But now secure the painted vessel glides,
The sunbeams trembling on the floating tides:
While melting music steals upon the sky,
And softened sounds along the waters die;   50
Smooth flow the waves, the zephyrs gently play,
Belinda smiled, and all the world was gay.
All but the sylph—with careful thoughts oppressed,
Th' impending woe sat heavy on his breast.
He summons straight his denizens of air;   55
The lucid squadrons round the sails repair:
Soft o'er the shrouds aërial whispers breathe,
That seemed but zephyrs to the train beneath.
Some to the sun their insect-wings unfold,
Waft on the breeze, or sink in clouds of gold;   60
Transparent forms, too fine for mortal sight,
Their fluid bodies half dissolved in light.
Loose to the wind their airy garments flew,
Thin glittering textures of the filmy dew,
Dipped in the richest tincture of the skies,   65
Where light disports in ever-mingling dyes,
While every beam new transient colors flings,
Colors that change whene'er they wave their wings.
Amid the circle, on the gilded mast,
Superior by the head, was Ariel placed;   70
His purple pinions opening to the sun,
He raised his azure wand, and thus begun.
   "Ye sylphs and sylphids, to your chief give ear,
Fays, fairies, genii, elves, and daemons, hear!
Ye know the spheres and various tasks assigned   75
By laws eternal to th' aërial kind.
Some in the fields of purest ether play,

---

35 *Phoebus*: the sun. 38 *romances*: novels. 45 *granted...prayer*: see IV, 1.80. 56 *repair*: gather. 73 *sylphids*: young sylphs.

And bask and whiten in the blaze of day.
Some guide the course of wandering orbs on high,
Or roll the planets through the boundless sky.   80
Some less refined, beneath the moon's pale light,
Pursue the stars that shoot athwart the night,
Or suck the mists in grosser air below,
Or dip their pinions in the painted bow,
Or brew fierce tempests on the wintry main,   85
Or o'er the glebe distil the kindly rain.
Others on earth o'er human race preside,
Watch all their ways, and all their actions guide:
Of these the chief the care of nations own,
And guard with arms divine the British throne.   90
  "Our humbler province is to tend the fair,
Not a less pleasing, though less glorious care;
To save the powder from too rude a gale,
Nor let the imprisoned essences exhale;
To draw fresh colors from the vernal flowers;   95
To steal from rainbows ere they drop in showers
A brighter wash; to curl their waving hairs,
Assist their blushes, and inspire their airs;
Nay oft, in dreams, invention we bestow,
To change a flounce, or add a furbelow.   100
  "This day, black omens threat the brightest fair
That e'er deserved a watchful spirit's care;
Some dire disaster, or by force, or slight;
But what, or where, the Fates have wrapped in night.
Whether the nymph shall break Diana's law,   105
Or some frail china jar receive a flaw;
Or stain her honor, or her new brocade;
Forget her prayers, or miss a masquerade;
Or lose her heart, or necklace, at a ball;
Or whether Heaven has doomed that Shock must fall.   110
Haste, then, ye spirits! to your charge repair:
The fluttering fan be Zephyretta's care;
The drops to thee, Brillante, we consign;
And, Momentilla, let the watch be thine;
Do thou, Crispissa, tend her favorite lock;   115
Ariel himself shall be the guard of Shock.
  "To fifty chosen sylphs, of special note,
We trust th' important charge, the petticoat:
Oft have we known that sevenfold fence to fail,
Though stiff with hoops, and armed with ribs of whale;   120
Form a strong line about the silver bound,
And guard the wide circumference around.
  "Whatever spirit, careless of his charge,
His post neglects, or leaves the fair at large,
Shall feel sharp vengeance soon o'ertake his sins,   125

---

86 *glebe*: field. 105 *Diana's law*: chastity. 113 *drops*: earrings.

Be stopped in vials, or transfixed with pins;
Or plunged in lakes of bitter washes lie,
Or wedged whole ages in a bodkin's eye:
Gums and pomatums shall his flight restrain,
While clogged he beats his silken wings in vain;   130
Or alum styptics with contracting power
Shrink his thin essence like a rivelled flower:
Or, as Ixion fixed, the wretch shall feel
The giddy motion of the whirling mill,
In fumes of burning chocolate shall glow,   135
And tremble at the sea that froths below!"
   He spoke; the spirits from the sails descend;
Some, orb in orb, around the nymph extend;
Some thrid the mazy ringlets of her hair;
Some hang upon the pendants of her ear: 140
With beating hearts the dire event they wait,
Anxious, and trembling for the birth of Fate.

Canto 3

Close by those meads, for ever crowned with flowers,
Where Thames with pride surveys his rising towers,
There stands a structure of majestic frame,
Which from the neighboring Hampton takes its name.
Here Britain's statesmen oft the fall foredoom   5
Of foreign tyrants, and of nymphs at home;
Here thou, great ANNA! whom three realms obey,
Dost sometimes counsel take—and sometimes tea.
   Hither the heroes and the nymphs resort,
To taste awhile the pleasures of a court;   10
In various talk th' instructive hours they passed,
Who gave the ball, or paid the visit last;
One speaks the glory of the British Queen,
And one describes a charming Indian screen;
A third interprets motions, looks, and eyes;   15
At every word a reputation dies.
Snuff, or the fan, supply each pause of chat,
With singing, laughing, ogling, *and all that*.
   Meanwhile, declining from the noon of day,
The sun obliquely shoots his burning ray;   20
The hungry judges soon the sentence sign,
And wretches hang that jurymen may dine;
The merchant from th' exchange returns in peace,
And the long labors of the toilet cease.
Belinda now, whom thirst of fame invites,   25

---

128 *bodkin('s)*: a blunt needle with a large eye. 129 *Gums and pomatums*: perfumed ointments. 132 *rivelled*: shriveled. 133 *Ixion*: In Greek mythology, Ixion, for attempting to seduce Hera, was condemned by Zeus to be bound to a fiery wheel that rolled endlessly through the sky. 139 *thrid*: thread.
7 *great Anna*: (1665–1714; queen of England, 1702–1714). 23 *exchange*: London stock exchange.

Burns to encounter two adventurous knights,
At omber singly to decide their doom;
And swells her breast with conquests yet to come.
Straight the three bands prepare in arms to join,
Each band the number of the sacred nine.   30
Soon as she spreads her hand, th' aërial guard
Descend, and sit on each important card:
First Ariel perched upon a Matadore,
Then each, according to the rank they bore;
For sylphs, yet mindful of their ancient race,   35
Are, as when women, wondrous fond of place.
   Behold, four Kings in majesty revered,
With hoary whiskers and a forky beard;
And four fair Queens whose hands sustain a flower,
Th' expressive emblem of their softer power;   40
Four Knaves in garbs succinct, a trusty band,
Caps on their heads, and halberts in their hand;
And particolored troops, a shining train,
Draw forth to combat on the velvet plain.
   The skilful nymph reviews her force with care: 45
"Let Spades be trumps!" she said, and trumps they were.
   Now move to war her sable Matadores,
In show like leaders of the swarthy Moors.
Spadillio first, unconquerable lord!
Led off two captive trumps, and swept the board.   50
As many more Manillio forced to yield,
And marched a victor from the verdant field.
Him Basto followed, but his fate more hard
Gained but one trump and one plebeian card.
With his broad saber next, a chief in years,   55
The hoary Majesty of Spades appears,
Puts forth one manly leg, to sight revealed,
The rest, his many-colored robe concealed.
The rebel Knave, who dares his prince engage,
Proves the just victim of his royal rage.   60
Even mighty Pam, that kings and queens o'erthrew
And mowed down armies in the fights of Lu,
Sad chance of war! now destitute of aid,
Falls undistinguished by the victor Spade!
   Thus far both armies to Belinda yield;   65
Now to the baron fate inclines the field.
His warlike Amazon her host invades,
Th' imperial consort of the crown of Spades.
The Club's black tyrant first her victim died,

---

29 *in...join*: i.e., as epic heroes join arms in personal combat. 30 *sacred nine*: number of
cards dealt to each player. 33 *Matadore*: The three highest cards in omber were called
matadors. 36 *place*: high social station, distinction. 42 *halberts*: weapons that were a
combination of battle-ax and spear. 49 *Spadillio*: ace of spades, a "matador," see note
on line 33. 51 *Manillio*: deuce of spades, a "matador." 53 *Basto*: ace of clubs, a
"matador." 54 *Plebeian*: low card. 61 *Pam*: Jack of clubs, the highest card in the game
of Lu (line 62).

Spite of his haughty mien, and barbarous pride: 70
What boots the regal circle on his head,
His giant limbs, in state unwieldy spread;
That long behind he trails his pompous robe,
And, of all monarchs, only grasps the globe?
   The baron now his Diamonds pours apace; 75
Th' embroidered King who shows but half his face,
And his refulgent Queen, with powers combined
Of broken troops an easy conquest find.
Clubs, Diamonds, Hearts, in wild disorder seen,
With throngs promiscuous strow the level green. 80
Thus when dispersed a routed army runs,
Of Asia's troops, and Afric's sable sons,
With like confusion different nations fly,
Of various habit, and of various dye,
The pierced battalions disunited fall, 85
In heaps on heaps; one fate o'erwhelms them all.
   The Knave of Diamonds tries his wily arts,
And wins (oh shameful chance!) the Queen of Hearts.
At this, the blood the virgin's cheek forsook,
A livid paleness spreads o'er all her look; 90
She sees, and trembles at th' approaching ill,
Just in the jaws of ruin, and codille.
And now (as oft in some distempered state)
On one nice trick depends the general fate.
An Ace of Hearts steps forth: the King unseen 95
Lurked in her hand, and mourned his captive Queen:
He springs to vengeance with an eager pace,
And falls like thunder on the prostrate Ace.
The nymph exulting fills with shouts the sky;
The walls, the woods, and long canals reply. 100
   Oh thoughtless mortals! ever blind to fate,
Too soon dejected, and too soon elate.
Sudden, these honors shall be snatched away,
And cursed for ever this victorious day.
   For lo! the board with cups and spoons is crowned, 105
The berries crackle, and the mill turns round;
On shining altars of Japan they raise
The silver lamp; the fiery spirits blaze:
From silver spouts the grateful liquors glide,
While China's earth receives the smoking tide: 110
At once they gratify their scent and taste,
And frequent cups prolong the rich repast.
Straight hover round the fair her airy band;
Some, as she sipped, the fuming liquor fanned,
Some o'er her lap their careful plumes displayed, 115

71 *boots*: use, serves, i.e., what good is.... 80 *strow*: strew. 84 *habit*: apparel; *dye*: color. 92 *codille*: defeat. The loser in omber was said to be given codille. 95 *King*: of hearts, a higher card than the Baron's ace. 106 *berries*: coffee beans; *mill*: coffee grinder. 107 *Shining...Japan*: lacquered tables. 110 *China's earth*: China cups.

Trembling, and conscious of the rich brocade.
Coffee (which makes the politician wise,
And see through all things with his half-shut eyes)
Sent up in vapors to the baron's brain
New stratagems, the radiant lock to gain.   120
Ah cease, rash youth! desist ere 'tis too late,
Fear the just gods, and think of Scylla's fate!
Changed to a bird, and sent to flit in air,
She dearly pays for Nisus' injured hair!
 But when to mischief mortals bend their will,   125
How soon they find fit instruments of ill!
Just then, Clarissa drew with tempting grace
A two-edged weapon from her shining case:
So ladies in romance assist their knight,
Present the spear, and arm him for the fight.   130
He takes the gift with reverence and extends
The little engine on his fingers' ends;
This just behind Belinda's neck he spread,
As o'er the fragrant steams she bends her head.
Swift to the lock a thousand sprites repair,   135
A thousand wings, by turns, blow back the hair;
And thrice they twitched the diamond in her ear;
Thrice she looked back, and thrice the foe drew near.
Just in that instant, anxious Ariel sought
The close recesses of the virgin's thought;   140
As on the nosegay in her breast reclined,
He watched th' ideas rising in her mind,
Sudden he viewed, in spite of all her art,
An earthly lover lurking at her heart.
Amazed, confused, he found his power expired,   145
Resigned to fate, and with a sigh retired.
 The peer now spreads the glittering forfex wide,
T' inclose the lock; now joins it, to divide.
Even then, before the fatal engine closed,
A wretched sylph too fondly interposed;   150
Fate urged the shears, and cut the sylph in twain,
(But airy substance soon unites again)
The meeting points the sacred hair dissever
From the fair head, for ever, and for ever!
 Then flashed the living lightning from her eyes,   155
And screams of horror rend th' affrighted skies.
Not louder shrieks to pitying Heaven are cast,
When husbands or when lap-dogs breathe their last;
Or when rich China vessels fallen from high,
In glittering dust and painted fragments lie!   160
 "Let wreaths of triumph now my temples twine"

122–24 *Scylla...Nisus'*: Scylla was turned into a bird for cutting from the hair of her
father, King Nisus of Megara, the famous bright lock on which his life and throne depended
and giving it to her lover, and her father's enemy, Minos of Crete.   147 *forfex*: scissors.
152 *But...unites again*: see *Paradise Lost*, VI, 330ff.

(The victor cried) "the glorious prize is mine!
While fish in streams, or birds delight in air,
Or in a coach and six the British fair,
As long as *Atalantis* shall be read,   165
Or the small pillow grace a lady's bed,
While visits shall be paid on solemn days,
When numerous wax lights in bright order blaze,
While nymphs take treats, or assignations give,
So long my honor, name, and praise shall live!   170
What time would spare, from steel receives its date,
And monuments, like men, submit to fate!
Steel could the labor of the gods destroy,
And strike to dust th' imperial towers of Troy;
Steel could the works of mortal pride confound,   175
And hew triumphal arches to the ground.
What wonder then, fair nymph! thy hairs should feel
The conquering force of unresisted steel?"

Canto 4

But anxious cares the pensive nymph oppressed,
And secret passions labored in her breast.
Not youthful kings in battle seized alive,
Not scornful virgins who their charms survive,
Not ardent lovers robbed of all their bliss,   5
Not ancient ladies when refused a kiss,
Not tyrants fierce that unrepenting die,
Not Cynthia when her manteau's pinned awry,
E'er felt such rage, resentment, and despair,
As thou, sad virgin! for thy ravished hair.   10
   For, that sad moment, when the sylphs withdrew,
And Ariel weeping from Belinda flew,
Umbriel, a dusky, melancholy sprite,
As ever sullied the fair face of light,
Down to the central earth, his proper scene,   15
Repaired to search the gloomy Cave of Spleen.
   Swift on his sooty pinions flits the gnome,
And in a vapor reached the dismal dome.
No cheerful breeze this sullen regions knows,
The dreaded east is all the wind that blows.   20
   Here in a grotto, sheltered close from air,

---

165 *Atalantis*: *Secret Memoirs and Manners of Several Persons of Quality, of Both Sexes. From the New Atalantis, an Island in the Mediterranean* (1709), by Mary de la Rivière Manley (c. 1663–1724; English playwright, novelist, and pamphleteer), in which under the guise of fiction, the scandalous affairs in the contemporary world of fashion were depicted. 168 *wax lights*: carried by the attendants of a lady on her visits. 171 *from...date*: i.e., steel destroys.
8 *Cynthia*: Diana, goddess of chastity; *manteau*: upper garment, cloak or mantle. 13ff. The journey to the underworld is a common feature of epic poetry. 16 *Spleen*: depression, low spirits, sometimes called "vapors" (see lines 18, 59)—a fashionable malady among eighteenth-century ladies, thought to result from exposure to damp climate. 20 *dreaded...blows*: The east wind was thought conducive to spleen.

And screened in shades from day's detested glare,
She sighs for ever on her pensive bed,
Pain at her side, and Megrim at her head.
    Two handmaids wait the throne: alike in place,   25
But differing far in figure and in face.
Here stood Ill-nature like an ancient maid,
Her wrinkled form in black and white arrayed;
With store of prayers, for mornings, nights, and noons,
Her hand is filled; her bosom with lampoons.   30
    There Affectation, with a sickly mien,
Shows in her cheek the roses of eighteen,
Practiced to lisp, and hang the head aside,
Faints into airs, and languishes with pride,
On the rich quilt sinks with becoming woe,   35
Wrapped in a gown, for sickness, and for show.
The fair ones feel such maladies as these,
When each new night dress gives a new disease.
    A constant vapor o'er the palace flies;
Strange phantoms rising as the mists arise;   40
Dreadful, as hermit's dreams in haunted shades,
Or bright, as visions of expiring maids.
Now glaring fiends, and snakes on rolling spires,
Pale specters, gaping tombs, and purple fires:
Now lakes of liquid gold, Elysian scenes,   45
And crystal domes, and angels in machines.
    Unnumbered throngs on every side are seen
Of bodies changed to various forms by Spleen.
Here living teapots stand, one arm held out,
One bent; the handle this, and that the spout: 50
A pipkin there, like Homer's tripod walks;
Here sighs a jar, and there a goose pie talks;
Men prove with child, as powerful fancy works,
And maids turned bottles, call aloud for corks.
    Safe passed the gnome through this fantastic band,   55
A branch of healing spleenwort in his hand.
Then thus addressed the power: "Hail, wayward Queen!
Who rule the sex to fifty from fifteen:
Parent of vapors, and of female wit,
Who give th' hysteric or poetic fit,   60
On various tempers act by various ways,
Make some take physic, others scribble plays;
Who cause the proud their visits to delay,
And send the godly in a pet to pray.
A nymph there is, that all thy power disdains,   65
And thousands more in equal mirth maintains.
But oh! if e'er thy gnome could spoil a grace,

---

24 *Megrim*: migraine headache. 30 *lampoons*: malicious personal satires. 43–46 *fiends...
machines*: the kind of hallucinations spleen might cause. 51 *pipkin*: small earthenware pot;
Homer's tripod: see Homer's epic *Iliad*, XVIII, 368ff. 56 *spleenwort*: thought to be a
remedy for spleen (see note to line 16). 64 *pet*: bad mood.

Or raise a pimple on a beauteous face,
Like citron waters matrons' cheeks inflame,
Or change complexions at a losing game; 70
If e'er with airy horns I planted heads,
Or rumpled petticoats, or tumbled beds,
Or caused suspicion when no soul was rude,
Or discomposed the headdress of a prude,
Or e'er to costive lap dog gave disease, 75
Which not the tears of brightest eyes could ease:
Hear me, and touch Belinda with chagrin,
That single act gives half the world the spleen."
    The Goddess with a discontented air
Seems to reject him, though she grants his prayer. 80
A wondrous bag with both her hands she binds,
Like that where once Ulysses held the winds;
There she collects the force of female lungs,
Sighs, sobs, and passions, and the war of tongues.
A vial next she fills with fainting fears, 85
Soft sorrows, melting griefs, and flowing tears.
The gnome rejoicing bears her gifts away,
Spreads his black wings, and slowly mounts to day.
    Sunk in Thalestris' arms the nymph he found,
Her eyes dejected and her hair unbound. 90
Full o'er their heads the swelling bag he rent,
And all the furies issued at the vent.
Belinda burns with more than mortal ire,
And fierce Thalestris fans the rising fire.
"O wretched maid!" she spread her hands, and cried, 95
(While Hampton's echoes, "Wretched maid!" replied)
"Was it for this you took such constant care
The bodkin, comb, and essence to prepare?
For this your locks in paper durance bound,
For this with torturing irons wreathed around? 100
For this with fillets strained your tender head,
And bravely bore the double loads of lead?
Gods! shall the ravisher display your hair,
While the fops envy and the ladies stare!
Honor forbid! at whose unrivaled shrine 105
Ease, pleasure, virtue, all our sex resign.
Methinks already I your tears survey,
Already hear the horrid things they say,
Already see you a degraded toast,
And all your honor in a whisper lost! 110
How shall I, then, your helpless fame defend?

---

69 *citron waters*: brandy flavored with citron or lemon peel. 71 *horns...heads*: i.e., I deceived husbands into thinking their wives were unfaithful. 75 *costive*: constipated. 82 *Ulysses...winds*: see Homer's *Odyssey*, X, 19ff. 89 *Thalestris*: a companion of Belinda. 99 *in...durance*: i.e., in curl papers (fastened with strips of lead—see *irons*, line 100, *lead*, line 102. 101 *fillets*: bands. 109 *toast*: person toasted, whose health is drunk (here, who is the subject of an ironic toast).

'Twill then be infamy to seem your friend!
And shall this prize, th' inestimable prize,
Exposed through crystal to the gazing eyes,
And heightened by the diamond's circling rays,   115
On that rapacious hand for ever blaze?
Sooner shall grass in Hyde Park Circus grow,
And wits take lodgings in the sound of Bow;
Sooner let earth, air, sea, to chaos fall,
Men, monkeys, lap dogs, parrots, perish all!"   120
    She said; then raging to Sir Plume repairs,
And bids her beau demand the precious hairs:
(Sir Plume of amber snuffbox justly vain,
And the nice conduct of a clouded cane)
With earnest eyes, and round unthinking face,   125
He first the snuffbox opened, then the case,
And thus broke out—"My Lord, why, what the devil?
Z—ds! damn the lock! 'fore God, you must be civil!
Plague on't! 'tis past a jest—nay prithee, pox!
Give her the hair"—he spoke, and rapped his box.   130
"It grieves me much" (replied the peer again)
"Who speaks so well should ever speak in vain,
But by this lock, this sacred lock I swear,
(Which never more shall join its parted hair;
Which never more its honors shall renew,   135
Clipped from the lovely head where late it grew)
That while my nostrils draw the vital air,
This hand, which won it, shall for ever wear."
He spoke, and speaking, in proud triumph spread
The long-contended honors of her head.   140
    But Umbriel, hateful gnome! forbears not so;
He breaks the vial whence the sorrows flow.
Then see! the nymph in beauteous grief appears,
Her eyes half-languishing, half-drowned in tears;
On her heaved bosom hung her drooping head,   145
Which, with a sigh, she raised; and thus she said:
    "For ever cursed be this detested day,
Which snatched my best, my favorite curl away!
Happy! ah ten times happy had I been,
If Hampton Court these eyes had never seen!   150
Yet am I not the first mistaken maid,
By love of courts to numerous ills betrayed.
Oh had I rather unadmired remained
In some lone isle, or distant northern land;
Where the gilt chariot never marks the way,   155
Where none learn omber, none e'er taste bohea!

114–16 *Exposed...blaze*: Presumably the Baron intends to enshrine the lock under the
crystal of his jewelled watch. 117 *Sooner...grow*: the grass in Hyde Park (see note to I.
44 above) is worn by the constant carriage traffic. 118 *sound of Bow*: within hearing of
the bells at St. Mary le Bow (Bowchurch) in Cheapside, the commercial section of London.
124 *conduct*: manner of carrying. 156 *bohea*: a kind of black tea.

There kept my charms concealed from mortal eye,
Like roses that in deserts bloom and die.
What moved my mind with youthful lords to roam?
Oh had I stayed, and said my prayers at home!   160
'Twas this, the morning omens seemed to tell:
Thrice from my trembling hand the patchbox fell;
The tottering china shook without a wind,
Nay, Poll sat mute, and Shock was most unkind!
A sylph too warned me of the threats of fate,   165
In mystic visions, now believed too late!
See the poor remnants of these slighted hairs!
My hands shall rend what even thy rapine spares:
These in two sable ringlets taught to break,
Once gave new beauties to the snowy neck;   170
The sister-lock now sits uncouth, alone,
And in its fellow's fate foresees its own;
Uncurled it hangs, the fatal shears demands,
And tempts, once more, thy sacrilegious hands.
Oh hadst thou, cruel! been content to seize   175
Hairs less in sight, or any hairs but these!"

CANTO 5

She said: the pitying audience melt in tears.
But fate and love had stopped the baron's ears.
In vain Thalestris with reproach assails,
For who can move when fair Belinda fails?
Not half so fixed the Trojan could remain,   5
While Anna begged and Dido raged in vain.
Then grave Clarissa graceful waved her fan;
Silence ensued, and thus the nymph began.
    "Say, why are beauties praised and honored most,
The wise man's passion, and the vain man's toast?   10
Why decked with all that land and sea afford,
Why angels called, and angel-like adored?
Why round our coaches crowd the white-gloved beaux,
Why bows the side-box from its immost rows?
How vain are all these glories, all our pains,   15
Unless good sense preserve what beauty gains:
That men may say, when we the front-box grace,
'Behold the first in virtue as in face!'
Oh! if to dance all night, and dress all day,
Charmed the smallpox, or chased old age away;   20
Who would not scorn what housewife's cares produce,
Or who would learn one earthly thing of use?
To patch, nay ogle, might become a saint,

---

169 *break*: disengage.
5–6 *Not...vain*: Anna, on behalf of her sister Dido, begged the Trojan Aeneas to remain
in Carthage, but he refused—in Virgil's *Aeneid*, IV. 9–34 *Say why...soul*: Clarissa's speech
here parodies Sarpedon's battlefield exhortation to Glaucus in Book XII of *The Iliad*.
14, 17 *side-box, front-box*: theater boxes. 23 *patch*: see note to I. 138 above. To apply
patches.

Nor could it sure be such a sin to paint.
But since, alas! frail beauty must decay, 25
Curled or uncurled, since locks will turn to grey;
Since painted, or not painted, all shall fade,
And she who scorns a man, must die a maid;
What then remains, but well our power to use,
And keep good-humor still whate'er we lose? 30
And trust me, dear! good-humor can prevail,
When airs, and flights, and screams, and scolding fail.
Beauties in vain their pretty eyes may roll;
Charms strike the sight, but merit wins the soul."
   So spoke the dame, but no applause ensued; 35
Belinda frowned, Thalestris called her prude.
"To arms, to arms!" the fierce virago cries,
And swift as lightning to the combat flies.
All side in parties, and begin th' attack:
Fans clap, silks rustle, and tough whalebones crack; 40
Heroes' and heroines' shouts confusedly rise,
And bass, and treble voices strike the skies.
No common weapons in their hands are found,
Like gods they fight, nor dread a mortal wound.
   So when bold Homer makes the gods engage, 45
And heavenly breasts with human passions rage;
'Gainst Pallas, Mars; Latona, Hermes arms;
And all Olympus rings with lond alarms:
Jove's thunder roars, Heaven trembles all around,
Blue Neptune storms, the bellowing deeps resound: 50
Earth shakes her nodding towers, the ground gives way,
And the pale ghosts start at the flash of day!
   Triumphant Umbriel on a sconce's height
Clapped his glad wings, and sate to view the fight:
Propped on their bodkin spears, the sprites survey 55
The growing combat, or assist the fray.
   While through the press enraged Thalestris flies,
And scatters death around from both her eyes,
A beau and witling perished in the throng,
One died in metaphor, and one in song. 60
"O cruel nymph! a living death I bear,"
Cried Dapperwit, and sunk beside his chair.
A mournful glance Sir Fopling upwards cast,
"Those eyes are made so killing"—was his last.
Thus on Maeander's flowery margin lies 65
Th' expiring swan, and as he sings he dies.
   When bold Sir Plume had drawn Clarissa down,
Chloe stepped in, and killed him with a frown;

---

24 *paint*: use rouge, beauty aids. 32 *airs*: affected behavior. 37 *virago*: Amazon, female warrior. 45 *So...engage*: as in *The Iliad*, XX. 62 *Dapperwit*: a fop in William Wycherley's comedy, *Love in a Wood* (1671). 63 *Sir Fopling* (Flutter): main character in George Etherege's comedy, *The Man of Mode* (1676). 64 "*Those...killing*": from a song in *Camilla* (London, 1706), a popular opera by Marc Antonio Bononcini.

She smiled to see the doughty hero slain,
But, at her smile, the beau revived again.   70
   Now Jove suspends his golden scales in air,
Weighs the men's wits against the lady's hair;
The doubtful beam long nods from side to side;
At length the wits mount up, the hairs subside.
   See fierce Belinda on the baron flies,   75
With more than usual lightning in her eyes:
Nor feared the chief th' unequal fight to try,
Who sought no more than on his foe to die.
But this bold lord with manly strength endued,
She with one finger and a thumb subdued: 80
Just where the breath of life his nostrils drew,
A charge of snuff the wily virgin threw;
The gnomes direct, to every atom just,
The pungent grains of titillating dust.
Sudden, with starting tears each eye o'erflows,   85
And the high dome re-echoes to his nose.
   "Now meet thy fate," incensed Belinda cried,
And drew a deadly bodkin from her side.
(The same, his ancient personage to deck,
Her great-great-grandsire wore about his neck,   90
In three seal rings; which after, melted down,
Formed a vast buckle for his widow's gown:
Her infant grandame's whistle next it grew,
The bells she jingled, and the whistle blew;
Then in a bodkin graced her mother's hairs,   95
Which long she wore, and now Belinda wears.)
   "Boast not my fall" (he cried) "insulting foe!
Thou by some other shalt be laid as low.
Nor think, to die dejects my lofty mind:
All that I dread is leaving you behind!   100
Rather than so, ah let me still survive,
And burn in Cupid's flames—but burn alive."
   "Restore the lock!" she cries; and all around
"Restore the lock!" the vaulted roofs rebound.
Not fierce Othello in so loud a strain   105
Roared for the handkerchief that caused his pain.
But see how oft ambitious aims are crossed,
And chiefs contend till all the prize is lost!
The lock, obtained with guilt, and kept with pain,
In every place is sought, but sought in vain: 110
With such a prize no mortal must be blest,
So Heaven decrees! with Heaven who can contest?
   Some thought it mounted to the lunar sphere,
Since all things lost on earth are treasured there.
There heroes' wits are kept in ponderous vases,   115

---

71 *scales*: i.e., of justice.   91 *seal rings*: rings used as seals to authenticate letters, documents, etc.   105–106 *Othello...handkerchief*: see Shakespeare's *Othello*, IV. i. 38–46.

And beaux' in snuff-boxes and tweezer-cases.
There broken vows, and deathbed alms are found,
And lovers' hearts with ends of riband bound,
The courtier's promises, and sick man's prayers,
The smiles of harlots, and the tears of heirs,   120
Cages for gnats, and chains to yoke a flea,
Dried butterflies, and tomes of casuistry.
 But trust the Muse—she saw it upward rise,
Though marked by none but quick, poetic eyes:
(So Rome's great founder to the heavens withdrew,   125
To Proculus alone confessed in view)
A sudden star, it shot through liquid air,
And drew behind a radiant trail of hair.
Not Berenice's lock first rose so bright,
The heavens bespangling with disheveled light.   130
The sylphs behold it kindling as it flies,
And pleased pursue its progress through the skies.
 This the beau monde shall from the Mall survey,
And hail with music its propitious ray.
This the blest lover shall for Venus take,   135
And send up vows from Rosamonda's lake.
This Partridge soon shall view in cloudless skies,
When next he looks through Galileo's eyes;
And hence th' egregious wizard shall foredoom
The fate of Louis, and the fall of Rome.   140
 Then cease, bright nymph! to mourn thy ravished hair,
Which adds new glory to the shining sphere!
Not all the tresses that fair head can boast
Shall draw such envy as the lock you lost.
For, after all the murders of your eye,   145
When, after millions slain, yourself shall die;
When those fair suns shall set, as set they must,
And all those tresses shall be laid in dust;
This lock, the Muse shall consecrate to fame,
And 'midst the stars inscribe Belinda's name.   150

Pope's "Advertisement" below indicates the circumstances that gave rise to the *Epistle to Dr. Arbuthnot*. The two attacks upon him to which he refers appeared in 1733 and were authored by Lady Mary Wortley Montagu ("Sappho") and Lord Hervey ("Sporus"). These attacks, combined with the

---

125–26 *Rome's...view*: According to Livy (Book XVI), Romulus, the founder of Rome, was transported to heaven by the blasts of a thunderstorm. Proculus claimed to have seen Romulus in a vision. 129 *Berenice's lock*: According to legend, Berenice (third century B.C.; Egyptian princess) gave a lock of her hair to the gods in order that her husband might return safely from the wars. The lock was transformed into a constellation. 133 *beau monde*: world of fashion; *the Mall*: fashionable promenade in St. James's Park. 136 *Rosamonda's lake*: also in St. James's Park. 137 *Partridge*: John Partridge (1644–1715), English astrologer who had predicted each year the downfall of the Pope and the King of France. He was satirized by Swift in the Partridge-Bickerstaff papers. 138 *Galileo's eyes*: the telescope. 140 *fate of Louis*: refers to Partridge's predictions of Louis' downfall (see note to line 137).

fact that his old friend Arbuthnot, who was dying, had recently encouraged him to continue his denunciations of vice, spurred Pope to write a poem that is both a satire and a defense of satire. The "Pope" presented here is a man of candor and good will in a world of deceit and vindictiveness who is driven at last by the interminable, buzzing assaults of his enemies to forego his habitual tolerance and "flap" them. The dialogue form allows Pope to enhance his own character by virtue of his close friendship with Arbuthnot and to further demolish Lord Hervey by having even Arbuthnot, presented throughout as the image of forbearance, rise up in wrath and ridicule at the mention of "Sporus' " name (lines 305–308).

EPISTLE TO DR. ARBUTHNOT (1735)

Advertisement

This paper is a sort of bill of complaint, begun many years since, and drawn up by snatches, as the several occasions offered. I had no thoughts of publishing it, till it pleased some persons of rank and fortune (the authors of *Verses to the Imitator of Horace,* and of an *Epistle to a Doctor of Divinity from a Nobleman at Hampton Court*) to attack, in a very extraordinary manner, not only my writings (of which, being public, the public is judge), but my person, morals, and family, whereof, to those who know me not, a truer information may be requisite. Being divided between the necessity to say something of myself, and my own laziness to undertake so awkward a task, I thought it the shortest way to put the last hand to this Epistle. If it have anything pleasing, it will be that by which I am most desirous to please, the truth and the sentiment; and if anything offensive, it will be only to those I am least sorry to offend, the vicious or the ungenerous.

Many will know their own pictures in it, there being not a circumstance but what is true; but I have, for the most part, spared their names, and they may escape being laughed at, if they please.

I would have some of them know, it was owing to the request of the learned and candid friend to whom it is inscribed, that I make not as free use of theirs as they have done of mine. However, I shall have this advantage, and honor, on my side, that whereas, by their proceeding, any abuse may be directed at any man, no injury can possibly be done by mine, since a nameless character can never be found out, but by its truth and likeness.—POPE

> **P.** Shut, shut the door, good John! fatigued, I said,
> Tie up the knocker, say I'm sick, I'm dead.
> The Dog Star rages! nay 'tis past a doubt,
> All Bedlam, or Parnassus, is let out:
> Fire in each eye, and papers in each hand, 5
> They rave, recite, and madden round the land.
> What walls can guard me, or what shades can hide?
> They pierce my thickets, through my grot they glide,

---

1 *John*: Pope's servant, John Serle. 3 *Dog Star*: the heat of the "dog days," when Syrius rises with the sun, is supposed to make men go mad—hence "Bedlam" of line 4, Bedlam being Bethlehem Hospital for the insane. 4 *Parnassus*: mountain in Greece sacred to Apollo and the Muses—hence here, "poets." 8 *grot*: Pope had constructed an elaborate grotto at his Twickenham estate, the "Twit'nam" of line 21.

By land, by water, they renew the charge,
They stop the chariot, and they board the barge.   10
No place is sacred, not the church is free,
Even Sunday shines no sabbath-day to me:
Then from the Mint walks forth the man of rhyme,
Happy! to catch me, just at dinner-time.
    Is there a parson, much bemused in beer,   15
A maudlin poetess, a rhyming peer,
A clerk, foredoomed his father's soul to cross,
Who pens a stanza, when he should engross?
Is there, who, locked from ink and paper, scrawls
With desperate charcoal round his darkened walls?   20
All fly to Twit'nam, and in humble strain
Apply to me, to keep them mad or vain.
Arthur, whose giddy son neglects the laws,
Imputes to me and my damned works the cause:
Poor Cornus sees his frantic wife elope,   25
And curses wit, and poetry, and Pope.
    Friend to my life! (which did not you prolong,
The world had wanted many an idle song)
What drop or nostrum can this plague remove?
Or which must end me, a fool's wrath or love?   30
A dire dilemma! either way I'm sped,
If foes, they write, if friends, they read me dead.
Seized and tied down to judge, how wretched I!
Who can't be silent, and who will not lie:
To laugh, were want of goodness and of grace,   35
And to be grave, exceeds all power of face.
I sit with sad civility, I read
With honest anguish, and an aching head;
And drop at last, but in unwilling ears,
This saving counsel, "Keep your piece nine years."   40
    "Nine years!" cries he, who, high in Drury Lane,
Lulled by soft zephyrs through the broken pane,
Rhymes ere he wakes, and prints before Term ends,
Obliged by hunger, and request of friends:
"The piece, you think, is incorrect? why, take it,   45
I'm all submission; what you'd have it, make it."
    Three things another's modest wishes bound,
My friendship, and a prologue, and ten pound.
    Pitholeon sends to me: "You know his Grace,
I want a patron; ask him for a place."   50
Pitholeon libelled me—"But here's a letter

---

13 *Mint*: area in London where debtors and criminals could not be arrested. 23 *Arthur*: Arthur Moore, whose son had used, against Pope's desire, some of Pope's lines in a play. 40 *Keep...nine years*: In his *Ars Poetica*, Horace advised would-be poets to put their manuscripts aside for nine years before deciding whether they should be published. 41 *Drury Lane*: disreputable area of London near one of the theaters. 43 *Term*: when the courts were in session. 49 *Pitholeon*: "A foolish poet of Rhodes, who pretended much to Greek" (Pope's note); here, Leonard Welsted, who had slandered Pope.

Informs you, Sir, 'twas when he knew no better.
Dare you refuse him? Curll invites to dine,
He'll write a journal, or he'll turn divine."
Bless me! a packet. " 'Tis a stranger sues,   55
A virgin tragedy, an orphan Muse."
If I dislike it, "Furies, death and rage!"
If I approve, "Commend it to the stage."
There (thank my stars) my whole commission ends,
The players and I are, luckily, no friends.   60
Fired that the house reject him, " 'Sdeath! I'll print it,
And shame the fools—Your interest, Sir, with Lintot."
Lintot, dull rogue! will think your price too much:
"Not, Sir, if you revise it, and retouch."
All my demurs but double his attacks;   65
At last he whispers, "Do; and we go snacks."
Glad of a quarrel, straight I clap the door,
"Sir, let me see your works and you no more."
    'Tis sung, when Midas' ears began to spring,
(Midas, a sacred person and a king),   70
His very minister who spied them first,
(Some say his queen) was forced to speak, or burst.
And is not mine, my friend, a sorer case,
When every coxcomb perks them in my face?
    A. Good friend, forbear! you deal in dangerous things. 75
I'd never name queens, ministers, or kings;
Keep close to ears, and those let asses prick,
'Tis nothing—— **P.** Nothing? if they bite and kick?
Out with it, DUNCIAD! let the secret pass,
That secret to each fool, that he's an ass: 80
The truth once told (and wherefore should we lie?)
The Queen of Midas slept, and so may I.
    You think this cruel? Take it for a rule,
No creature smarts so little as a fool.
Let peals of laughter, Codrus! round thee break,   85
Thou unconcerned canst hear the mighty crack:
Pit, box, and gallery in convulsions hurled,
Thou standst unshook amidst a bursting world.
Who shames a scribbler? break one cobweb through,
He spins the slight, self-pleasing thread anew: 90
Destroy his fib or sophistry, in vain,
The creature's at his dirty work again,
Throned in the center of his thin designs,
Proud of a vast extent of flimsy lines!
Whom have I hurt? has poet yet, or peer,   95
Lost the arched eyebrow, or Parnassian sneer?
And has not Colley still his lord, and whore?

---

53 *Curll*: Edmund Curll, disreputable publisher.   54 *He'll write...divine*: i.e., he will slander Pope in the *London Journal* or, as Welsted did, write a theological book.   62 *Lintot*: Bernard Lintot, who published much of Pope's work   66 *go snacks*: split the profits—and expenses.   97 *Colley*: Colley Cibber, hero of *The Dunciad*.

His butchers Henley, his Freemasons Moore?
Does not one table Bavius still admit?
Still to one bishop Philips seem a wit?   100
Still Sappho—— **A.** Hold! for God's sake—you'll offend,
No names—be calm—learn prudence of a friend:
I too could write, and I am twice as tall;
But foes like these—— **P.** One flatterer's worse than all.
Of all mad creatures, if the learned are right,   105
It is the slaver kills, and not the bite.
A fool quite angry is quite innocent:
Alas! 'tis ten times worse when they repent.
  One dedicates in high heroic prose,
And ridicules beyond a hundred foes: 110
One from all Grub Street will my fame defend,
And, more abusive, calls himself my friend.
This prints my letters, that expects a bribe,
And others roar aloud, "Subscribe, subscribe."
  There are, who to my person pay their court: 115
I cough like Horace, and, though lean, am short,
Ammon's great son one shoulder had too high,
Such Ovid's nose, and "Sir! you have an eye"—
Go on, obliging creatures, make me see
All that disgraced my betters, met in me.   120
Say for my comfort, languishing in bed,
"Just so immortal Maro held his head":
And when I die, be sure you let me know
Great Homer died three thousand years ago.
  Why did I write? what sin to me unknown   125
Dipped me in ink, my parents', or my own?
As yet a child, nor yet a fool to fame,
I lisped in numbers, for the numbers came.
I left no calling for this idle trade,
No duty broke, no father disobeyed.   130
The Muse but served to ease some friend, not wife,
To help me through this long disease, my life,
To second, ARBUTHNOT! thy art and care,
And teach the being you preserved, to bear.
  But why then publish? Granville the polite,   135
And knowing Walsh, would tell me I could write;
Well-natured Garth inflamed with early praise;
And Congreve loved, and Swift endured my lays;
The courtly Talbot, Somers, Sheffield read,
Even mitred Rochester would nod the head,   140

---

98 *Henley*: John Henley, known as "Orator" Henley, was an eccentric preacher whose elocution was admired by the lower classes. 99 *Bavius*: insipid Roman poet ridiculed by Virgil in *Eclogues III*. 100 *Philips*: Ambrose Philips, a writer of pastoral poetry. 101 *Sappho*: Lady Mary Wortley Montagu. 111 *Grub Street*: area in which hack writers lived. 117 *Ammon's great son*: Alexander the Great. 122 *Maro*: Virgil. 135–139 *Granville...Sheffield*: English authors and public figures who encouraged Pope as a poet. 140 *Rochester*: Francis Atterbury, Bishop of Rochester.

And St. John's self (great Dryden's friend before)
With open arms received one poet more.
Happy my studies, when by these approved!
Happier their author, when by these beloved!
From these the world will judge of men and books,   145
Not from the Burnets, Oldmixons, and Cookes.
    Soft were my numbers; who could take offense
While pure description held the place of sense?
Like gentle Fanny's was my flowery theme,
A painted mistress, or a purling stream.   150
Yet then did Gildon draw his venal quill;
I wished the man a dinner, and sat still.
Yet then did Dennis rave in furious fret;
I never answered—I was not in debt.
If want provoked, or madness made them print,   155
I waged no war with Bedlam or the Mint.
    Did some more sober critic come abroad;
If wrong, I smiled; if right, I kissed the rod.
Pains, reading, study, are their just pretense,
And all they want is spirit, taste, and sense.   160
Commas and points they set exactly right,
And 'twere a sin to rob them of their mite.
Yet ne'er one sprig of laurel graced these ribalds,
From slashing Bentley down to piddling Tibbalds:
Each wight, who reads not, and but scans and spells,   165
Each word-catcher, that lives on syllables,
Even such small critics some regard may claim,
Preserved in Milton's or in Shakespeare's name.
Pretty! in amber to observe the forms
Of hairs, or straws, or dirt, or grubs, or worms!   170
The things, we know, are neither rich nor rare,
But wonder how the devil they got there.
    Were others angry: I excused them too;
Well might they rage, I gave them but their due.
A man's true merit 'tis not hard to find;   175
But each man's secret standard in his mind,
That casting-weight pride adds to emptiness,
This, who can gratify? for who can guess?
The bard whom pilfered Pastorals renown,
Who turns a Persian tale for half-a-crown,   180
Just writes to make his barrenness appear,
And strains, from hard-bound brains, eight lines a year;
He, who still wanting, though he lives on theft,
Steals much, spends little, yet has nothing left:

---

141 *St. John's self*: Henry St. John, Viscount Bolingbroke. 146 *Burnets, Oldmixons, and Cookes*: "Authors of secret and scandalous history" (Pope's note). 149 *Fanny's*: Lord Hervey, the "Sporus" of lines 305–33 below. 151 *Gildon*: minor poet, critic and dramatist who had attacked Pope. 153 *Dennis*: John Dennis, prominent critic and an old enemy of Pope's. 164 *Bentley*: Richard Bentley, classical scholar, editor of Homer and Milton; *Tibbalds*: Lewis Theobald (rhymes with "ribald"), Elizabethan scholar and editor of Shakespeare who had attacked Pope's edition of Shakespeare and hence became the first hero of *The Dunciad*.

And he, who now to sense, now nonsense leaning, 185
Means not, but blunders round about a meaning:
And he, whose fustian's so sublimely bad,
It is not poetry, but prose run mad:
All these, my modest satire bade translate,
And owned that nine such poets made a Tate. 190
How did they fume, and stamp, and roar, and chafe!
And swear, not Addison himself was safe.
  Peace to all such! but were there one whose fires
True genius kindles, and fair fame inspires;
Blest with each talent and each art to please, 195
And born to write, converse, and live with ease:
Should such a man, too fond to rule alone,
Bear, like the Turk, no brother near the throne,
View him with scornful, yet with jealous eyes,
And hate for arts that caused himself to rise; 200
Damn with faint praise, assent with civil leer,
And, without sneering, teach the rest to sneer;
Willing to wound, and yet afraid to strike,
Just hint a fault, and hesitate dislike;
Alike reserved to blame, or to commend, 205
A timorous foe, and a suspicious friend;
Dreading even fools, by flatterers besieged,
And so obliging, that he ne'er obliged;
Like Cato, give his little senate laws,
And sit attentive to his own applause; 210
While wits and Templars every sentence raise,
And wonder with a foolish face of praise—
Who but must laugh, if such a man there be?
Who would not weep, if Atticus were he?
  What though my name stood rubric on the walls, 215
Or plastered posts, with claps, in capitals?
Or smoking forth, a hundred hawkers' load,
On wings of winds came flying all abroad?
I sought no homage from the race that write;
I kept, like Asian monarchs, from their sight: 220
Poems I heeded (now be-rhymed so long)
No more than thou, great George! a birthday song.
I ne'er with wits or witlings passed my days,
To spread about the itch of verse and praise;
Nor like a puppy, daggled through the town, 225
To fetch and carry sing-song up and down;
Not at rehearsals sweat, and mouthed, and cried,
With handkerchief and orange at my side;
But sick of fops, and poetry, and prate,

190 *Tate*: Nahum Tate, poet laureate (1692–1715). 193–214 "Atticus" refers here to Joseph Addison. The historical Atticus was a rich patron and a friend of Cicero. 209 *Cato...laws*: Addison had written *Cato*, a popular tragedy. Addison often held court at Button's Coffee House and decreed laws of taste for his circle of admirers. 211 *Templars*: law students at the Inns of Court. 215 *rubric*: Titles of new books were often publicized in red letters. 216 *claps*: posters.

To Bufo left the whole Castalian state.   230
   Proud as Apollo on his forkèd hill,
Sate full-blown Bufo, puffed by every quill;
Fed with soft dedication all day long,
Horace and he went hand in hand in song.
His library (where busts of poets dead   235
And a true Pindar stood without a head)
Received of wits an undistinguished race,
Who first his judgment asked, and then a place:
Much they extolled his pictures, much his seat,
And flattered every day, and some days eat: 240
Till grown more frugal in his riper days,
He paid some bards with port, and some with praise;
To some a dry rehearsal was assigned,
And others (harder still) he paid in kind.
Dryden alone (what wonder?) came not nigh,   245
Dryden alone escaped this judging eye:
But still the great have kindness in reserve,
He helped to bury whom he helped to starve.
   May some choice patron bless each grey goose quill!
May every Bavius have his Bufo still!   250
So when a statesman wants a day's defense,
Or envy holds a whole week's war with sense,
Or simple pride for flattery makes demands,
May dunce by dunce be whistled off my hands!
Blessed be the great! for those they take away,   255
And those they left me; for they left me GAY;
Left me to see neglected genius bloom,
Neglected die, and tell it on his tomb:
Of all thy blameless life the sole return
My verse, and QUEENSBERRY weeping o'er thy urn!   260
   Oh let me live my own, and die so too!
(To live and die is all I have to do:)
Maintain a poet's dignity and ease,
And see what friends, and read what books I please:
Above a patron, though I condescend   265
Sometimes to call a minister my friend.
I was not born for courts or great affairs:
I pay my debts, believe, and say my prayers;
Can sleep without a poem in my head,
Nor know, if Dennis be alive or dead.   270
   Why am I asked what next shall see the light?
Heavens! was I born for nothing but to write?
Has life no joys for me? or (to be grave)
Have I no friend to serve, no soul to save?
"I found him close with Swift"—"Indeed? no doubt,"   275
(Cries prating Balbus) "something will come out."

---

230 *Bufo*: probably Lord Halifax but also any tasteless patron. 256 *Gay*: John Gay, close friend of Pope, author of *The Beggar's Opera*. 260 *Queensberry*: The Duke and Duchess of Queensberry befriended and supported John Gay during the closing years of his life.

'Tis all in vain, deny it as I will.
"No, such a genius never can lie still";
And then for mine obligingly mistakes
The first lampoon Sir Will. or Bubo makes.   280
Poor guiltless I! and can I choose but smile,
When every coxcomb knows me by my style?
 Cursed be the verse, how well soe'er it flow,
That tends to make one worthy man my foe,
Give virtue scandal, innocence a fear,   285
Or from the soft-eyed virgin steal a tear!
But he who hurts a harmless neighbor's peace,
Insults fallen worth, or beauty in distress,
Who loves a lie, lame slander helps about,
Who writes a libel, or who copies out: 290
That fop, whose pride affects a patron's name,
Yet absent, wounds an author's honest fame:
Who can your merit selfishly approve,
And show the sense of it without the love;
Who has the vanity to call you friend,   295
Yet wants the honor, injured, to defend;
Who tells whate'er you think, whate'er you say,
And if he lie not, must at least betray:
Who to the dean, and silver bell can swear,
And sees at Canons what was never there;   300
Who reads, but with a lust to misapply,
Make satire a lampoon, and fiction, lie.
A lash like mine no honest man shall dread,
But all such babbling blockheads in his stead.
 Let Sporus tremble—— **A.** What? that thing of silk,   305
Sporus, that mere white curd of ass's milk?
Satire or sense, alas! can Sporus feel?
Who breaks a butterfly upon a wheel?
 P. Yet let me flap this bug with gilded wings,
This painted child of dirt, that stinks and stings: 310
Whose buzz the witty and the fair annoys,
Yet wit ne'er tastes, and beauty ne'er enjoys:
So well-bred spaniels civilly delight
In mumbling of the game they dare not bite.
Eternal smiles his emptiness betray,   315
As shallow streams run dimpling all the way.
Whether in florid impotence he speaks,
And, as the prompter breathes, the puppet squeaks;
Or at the ear of Eve, familiar toad,
Half froth, half venom, spits himself abroad,   320
In puns, or politics, or tales, or lies,

---

280 *Sir Will.*: Sir William Yonge, Whig politician; *Bubo*: George Bubb Dodington, Whig patron. 300 *Canons*: sumptuous estate of the Duke of Chandos, whose ostentation Pope had been accused of ridiculing in his *Epistle to the Earl of Burlington.* 305 *Sporus*: Lord Hervey.

Or spite, or smut, or rhymes, or blasphemies.
His wit all see-saw, between that and this,
Now high, now low, now master up, now miss,
And he himself one vile antithesis.   325
Amphibious thing! that acting either part,
The trifling head, or the corrupted heart,
Fop at the toilet, flatterer at the board,
Now trips a lady, and now struts a lord.
Eve's tempter thus the Rabbins have expressed,   330
A cherub's face, a reptile all the rest;
Beauty that shocks you, parts that none will trust,
Wit that can creep, and pride that licks the dust.
   Not fortune's worshiper, nor fashion's fool,
Not lucre's madman, nor ambition's tool,   335
Not proud, nor servile; be one poet's praise,
That, if he pleased, he pleased by manly ways:
That flattery, even to kings, he held a shame,
And thought a lie in verse or prose the same.
That not in fancy's maze he wandered long,   340
But stooped to truth, and moralized his song:
That not for fame, but virtue's better end,
He stood the furious foe, the timid friend,
The damning critic, half-approving wit,
The coxcomb hit, or fearing to be hit;   345
Laughed at the loss of friends he never had,
The dull, the proud, the wicked, and the mad;
The distant threats of vengeance on his head,
The blow unfelt, the tear he never shed;
The tale revived, the lie so oft o'erthrown,   350
The imputed trash, and dullness not his own;
The morals blackened when the writings 'scape,
The libelled person, and the pictured shape;
Abuse, on all he loved, or loved him, spread,
A friend in exile, or a father, dead;   355
The whisper, that to greatness still too near,
Perhaps, yet vibrates on his sovereign's ear—
Welcome for thee, fair Virtue! all the past:
For thee, fair Virtue! welcome even the last!
   A. But why insult the poor, affront the great?   360
   P. A knave's a knave, to me, in every state:
Alike my scorn, if he succeed or fail,
Sporus at court, or Japhet in a jail,
A hireling scribbler, or a hireling peer,
Knight of the post corrupt, or of the shire;   365
If on a pillory, or near a throne,
He gain his prince's ear, or lose his own.
   Yet soft by nature, more a dupe than wit,

---

341 *Stooped*: a falcon's dive for its prey is called "stooping." 363 *Japhet*: Japhet Crook, a forger who was punished by life imprisonment and the loss of his ears.

Sappho can tell you how this man was bit:
This dreaded satirist Dennis will confess   370
Foe to his pride, but friend to his distress:
So humble, he has knocked at Tibbald's door,
Has drunk with Cibber, nay, has rimed for Moore.
Full ten years slandered, did he once reply?
Three thousand suns went down on Welsted's lie   375
To please a mistress one aspersed his life;
He lashed him not, but let her be his wife:
Let Budgell charge low Grub Street on his quill,
And write whate'er he pleased, except his will;
Let the two Curlls of town and court abuse   380
His father, mother, body, soul, and Muse.
Yet why? that father held it for a rule,
It was a sin to call our neighbor fool:
That harmless mother thought no wife a whore:
Hear this, and spare his family, James Moore!   385
Unspotted names, and memorable long,
If there be force in virtue, or in song.
   Of gentle blood (part shed in honor's cause,
While yet in Britain honor had applause)
Each parent sprung— **A.** What fortune, pray?   390
   P.   Their own;
And better got than Bestia's from the throne.
Born to no pride, inheriting no strife,
Nor marrying discord in a noble wife,
Stranger to civil and religious rage,   395
The good man walked innoxious through his age.
No courts he saw, no suits would ever try,
Nor dared an oath, nor hazarded a lie.
Unlearn'd, he knew no schoolman's subtle art,
No language but the language of the heart.   400
By nature honest, by experience wise,
Healthy by temp'rance and by exercise;
His life, though long, to sickness passed unknown,
His death was instant and without a groan.
Oh grant me thus to live, and thus to die!   405
Who sprung from kings shall know less joy than I.
   O friend! may each domestic bliss be thine!
Be no unpleasing melancholy mine:
Me, let the tender office long engage
To rock the cradle of reposing age,   410
With lenient arts extend a mother's breath,
Make languor smile, and smooth the bed of death;

---

378 *Budgell*: Eustace Budgell, who had attacked Pope, was accused of forging a will.
380 *Two Curlls*: i.e., the bookseller and Lord Hervey. 392 *Bestia's*: L. Calpurnius Bestia,
Roman proconsul charged with taking bribes from Rome's enemies; here probably the
Duke of Marlborough, whose wealth came from "the throne," that is, through the favors of
Queen Anne. 398 *dared an oath*: Pope's father, a Catholic, refused to take the Oaths of
Allegiance and Supremacy as well as the oath denying the Pope.

Explore the thought, explain the asking eye,
And keep a while one parent from the sky!
On cares like these if length of days attend,   415
May Heav'n, to bless those days, preserve my friend,
Preserve him social, cheerful, and serene,
And just as rich as when he served a queen.
A. Whether that blessing be denied or giv'n,
Thus far was right;—the rest belongs to Heav'n.   420

The Dunciad was begun by Pope as a retaliatory attack upon Lewis Theobald, a Shakespearean editor who had published an edition entitled *Shakespeare Restored: or a Specimen of the Many Errors as Well Committed as Unamended by Mr. Pope in his Late Edition of this Poet.* Theobald was much the better Shakespearean editor, but Pope was an incomparably better poet; combining poetic talent with asperity, in which he and Theobald were about equal, Pope set about writing a mock-heroic poem that he originally intended to call *The Progress of Dulness* and in which Theobald was to reign supreme as the King of Dulness. Pope published the poem, as *The Dunciad,* in 1728; revised and republished it in 1729; added Book IV in 1742; and in 1743 revised all four books and published the whole for the last time. In this final version, the long reign of Theobald as King of Dulness came to an end, Pope substituting for him an actor, dramatist, theatrical manager, and poetaster named Colley Cibber. As poet laureate (since 1730) in a century in which the English genius for misbestowing that honor was in fullest flower, Cibber was superbly qualified to reign as Theobald's successor.

Like *Mac Flecknoe, The Dunciad* reinforces its mock-heroic form and style by centering its action in the ritual of coronation. The "disproportion game" that Pope played so deftly in *The Rape of the Lock* is continued in *The Dunciad,* but the techniques Pope used in the earlier poem, although repeated here, are also complicated. They are repeated in that we again find the characters and their conduct trivialized by the heroic lens through which they are viewed. But Pope complicates this technique by allowing the heroic lens to create a certain magnitude also in the objects on which it focuses. Maynard Mack gives an excellent analysis of this function of the epic-heroic in the poem when he says:

...the epic vehicle is gradually made throughout the poem to enlarge and give a status of serious menace to all this ludicrous activity. Here the epic circumstance of a presiding goddess proved invaluable. Partly ludicrous herself, she could also become the locus of inexhaustible negation behind the movements of her trivial puppets; her force could be associated humorously, but also seriously, with the powerful names of Chaos, Night, Anti-Christ, and with perversions of favourite order symbols like the sun, monarchy, and gravitation. Here, too, the epic backgrounds as supplied by Milton could be drawn in. Mr. C. S. Lewis has remarked of *Paradise Lost* that "only those will fully understand it who see that it might have been a comic poem" [*A Preface to Paradise Lost* (1942), p. 93]. *The Dunciad* is one realization of that might-have-been. Over and above the flow of Miltonic echoes and allusions, or the structural resemblances like Cibber's (or Theobald's) Pisgah-vision [Book III] based on Adam's, or the clustered names of dunces like those of Milton's devils, thick as the leaves that strew bad books in Grubstreet—*The Dunciad* is a version of Milton's theme in being the story of an uncreating Logos. As the poem progresses, our sense of this increases through the calling in of more and more powerful associations by the epic vehicle. The activities of the duncal associations by the epic vehicle. The activities of the duncal associations more and more equated with religious anti-values, culminating in the passage on the Eucharist quoted earlier [Book IV, 549–62]. The metaphor of the coronation of the king-dunce moves always closer to and then flows into the metaphor of the Day of the Lord, the descent of the anti-Messiah, the uncreating Word. Meantime, symbols which have formerly been ludicrous—insects, for instance, or sleep—are given by this expansion in the epic vehicle a more sombre cast. The dunces thicken and become less individual, more anonymous, expressive of blind inertia—bees in swarm, or locusts blackening the land. Sleep becomes tied up with its baser physical manifestations, with drunkenness, with deception, with ignorance, with neglect of obligation and finally with death. This is the sleep which *is* death, we realize, a *Narrendämmerung,* the twilight of the moral will. And yet, because of the ambivalence of the mock-heroic metaphor, Pope can keep to the end the tension between all these creatures as comic and ridiculous, and their destructive potentiality in being so. Certainly two of the finest puns in any poetry are those with which he continues to exploit this tension at the very end of the poem, when Dulness finally *yawns* and Nature *nods.**

from THE DUNCIAD

Book I

ARGUMENT

The Proposition, the Invocation, and the Inscription. Then the original of the great empire of Dulness, and cause of the continuance thereof. The College of the goddess in the City, with her private Academy for Poets in particular; the governors of it, and the four Cardinal Virtues. Then the poem hastes into the midst of things, presenting her, on the evening of a Lord Mayor's day, revolving the long succession of her sons, and the glories past and to come. She fixes her eye on Bays to be the instrument of that great event which is the subject of the poem. He is described pensive among his books, giving up the cause, and apprehending the period of her empire. After debating whether to betake himself to the Church, or to gaming, or to party-writing, he raises an altar of proper books, and (making first his solemn prayer and declaration) purposes thereon to sacrifice all his unsuccessful writings. As the pile is kindled, the goddess, beholding the flame from her seat, flies and puts it out, by casting upon it the poem of Thulè. *She forthwith reveals herself to him, transports him to her temple, unfolds her arts, and initiates him into her mysteries; then denouncing the death of Eusden the Poet Laureate, anoints him, carries him to court, and proclaims him successor.*

Book I

The mighty Mother, and her Son, who brings
The Smithfield muses to the ear of kings,

---

* Maynard Mack, " 'Wit and Poetry and Pope': Some Observations on his Imagery," in *Pope and His Contemporaries: Essays Presented to George Sherburn* (Clarendon Press, 1949), pp. 20–40. Reprinted by permission of the author.

---

1 *Mother...Son*: the goddess Dulness and Colley Cibber. 2 *Smithfield muses*: Smithfield was the marketplace where Bartholomew Fair was held each year. Cibber's plays are thus associated with the inferior dramatic productions that were part of the Fair.

I sing. Say you, her instruments the great!
Call'd to this work by Dulness, Jove, and Fate:
You by whose care, in vain decry'd and curst, 5
Still Dunce the second reigns like Dunce the first;
Say how the goddess bade Britannia sleep,
And pour'd her spirit o'er the land and deep.
In eldest time, ere mortals writ or read,
Ere Pallas issu'd from the Thund'rer's head, 10
Dulness o'er all possess'd her ancient right,
Daughter of Chaos and eternal Night:
Fate in their dotage this fair idiot gave,
Gross as her sire, and as her mother grave,
Laborious, heavy, busy, bold, and blind, 15
She rul'd, in native anarchy, the mind.
Still her old empire to restore she tries,
For, born a goddess, Dulness never dies.
O Thou! whatever title please thine ear,
Dean, Drapier, Bickerstaff, or Gulliver! 20
Whether thou choose Cervantes' serious air,
Or laugh and shake in Rab'lais' easy chair,
Or praise the court, or magnify mankind,
Or thy griev'd country's copper chains unbind;
From thy Boeotia thro' her pow'r retires, 25
Mourn not, my SWIFT, at aught our realm acquires.
Here pleas'd behold her mighty wings outspread
To hatch a new Saturnian age of lead.
Close to those walls where Folly holds her throne,
And laughs to think Monroe would take her down, 30
Where o'er the gates, by his fam'd father's hand,
Great Cibber's brazen, brainless brothers stand;
One cell there is, conceal'd from vulgar eye,
The Cave of Poverty and Poetry.
Keen, hollow winds howl thro' the bleak recess, 35
Emblem of music caus'd by emptiness.
Hence bards, like Proteus long in vain tied down,
Escape in monsters, and amaze the town.
Hence miscellanies spring, the weekly boast

---

10 *Pallas...Thund'rer's head*: Pallas Athena, goddess of wisdom and truth, who was born from the forehead of Zeus. 19 *Thou*: Jonathan Swift, Dean of St. Patrick's in Dublin, who wrote *The Drapier's Letters*, used the pseudonym of "Isaac Bickerstaff" in a satire against an astrologist, and wrote *Gulliver's Travels*. 21 *Cervantes*: author of *Don Quixote*. 22 *Rab'lais'*: Francois Rabelais (1494–1553), French satirist and humorist. 24 *copper chains*: In *The Drapier's Letters* Swift satirized W. Wood, who had received a patent from the English to mint copper coins in Ireland. 25 *Boeotia*: Like Ireland in Swift's time, Boeotia was associated in ancient Greece with illiteracy and stupidity. 28 *Saturnian... lead*: In Roman mythology the age of Saturn was golden. After it came ages of silver, bronze, and iron, each more degenerate than its predecessor. "In the chemical language," Pope says, "Saturn is lead." 29–30 *Close...down*: Bethlehem Hospital (Bedlam), an asylum for the insane, whose chief physician at this time was Dr. James Monroe. 32 *brothers*: two statues of lunatics fashioned by Cibber's father and placed over the entrance to Bethlehem Hospital. 37 *Proteus*: In classical mythology, a sea god who had the power of assuming different shapes. If tied down and held until he had run through all his changes and reassumed his own form, he was compelled to answer questions.

Of Curll's chaste press, and Lintot's rubric post: 40
Hence hymning Tyburn's elegiac lines,
Hence Journals, Medleys, Merc'ries, Magazines;
Sepulchral lies, our holy walls to grace,
And New-year Odes, and all the Grub-street race.
    In clouded majesty here Dulness shone;   45
Four guardian virtues, round, support her throne:
Fierce champion Fortitude, that knows no fears
Of hisses, blows, or want, or loss of ears:
Calm Temperance, whose blessings those partake
Who hunger, and who thirst for scribbling sake: 50
Prudence, whose glass presents th' approaching jail:
Poetic Justice, with her lifted scale,
Where, in nice balance, truth with gold she weighs,
And solid pudding against empty praise.
    Here she beholds the chaos dark and deep,   55
Where nameless somethings in their causes sleep,
Till genial Jacob, or a warm third day,
Call forth each mass, a poem, or a play:
How hints, like spawn, scarce quick in embryo lie,
How new-born nonsense first is taught to cry,   60
Maggots half-form'd in rhyme exactly meet,
And learn to crawl upon poetic feet.
Here one poor word an hundred clenches makes,
And ductile dulness new maeanders takes;
There motley images her fancy strike,   65
Figures ill pair'd, and similes unlike.
She sees a mob of metaphors advance,
Pleas'd with the madness of the mazy dance;
How Tragedy and Comedy embrace;
How Farce and Epic get a jumbled race;   70
How Time himself stands still at her command,
Realms shift their place, and Ocean turns to land.
Here gay description Egypt glads with show'rs,
Or gives to Zembla fruits, to Barca flow'rs:
Glitt'ring with ice here hoary hills are seen,   75
There painted valleys of eternal green;
In cold December fragrant chaplets blow,
And heavy harvests nod beneath the snow.
    All these and more the cloud-compelling Queen
Beholds thro' fogs, that magnify the scene.   80
She, tinsell'd o'er in robes of varying hues,
With self-applause her wild creation views;

---

40 *Curll*: Edmund Curll (1675–1747), who often published obscene material; *Lintot*:
Barnaby Bernard Lintot (1675–1736), publisher who advertised books with the "post."
41 *Tyburn*: where criminals were executed. 44 *New-year Odes*: As poet-laureate, Cibber's
duties included writing an ode to the New Year to be sung at court; *Grub-street race*: hack
writers who lived on Grub Street in London. 57 *Jacob*: Jacob Tonson (1656–1736), a
publisher; *third day*: playwrights were given the money taken in on the third day of
performances of a new play. 63 *clenches*: puns. 69–72 *How Tragedy...land*: refers to
the violations of the dramatic unities of action, place, and time in current plays. 74 *Barca*:
a desert area in Libya.

Sees momentary monsters rise and fall,
And with her own fools-colours gilds them all,
   'T was on the day when * * rich and grave,   85
Like Cimon, triumph'd both on land and wave:
(Pomps without guilt, of bloodless swords and maces,
Glad chains, warm furs, broad banners, and broad faces)
Now night descending, the proud scene was o'er,
But liv'd, in Settle's numbers, one day more.   90
Now may'rs and shrieves all hush'd and satiate lay,
Yet ate, in dreams, the custard of the day;
While pensive poets painful vigils keep,
Sleepless themselves, to give their readers sleep.
Much to the mindful Queen the feast recalls   95
What City swans once sung within the walls;
Much she revolves their arts, their ancient praise,
And sure succession down from Heywood's days.
She saw, with joy, the line immortal run,
Each sire imprest, and glaring in his son: 100
So watchful Bruin forms, with plastic care,
Each growing lump, and brings it to a bear.
She saw old Prynne in restless Daniel shine,
And Eusden eke out Blackmore's endless line;
She saw slow Philips creep like Tate's poor page,   105
And all the mighty mad in Dennis rage.
   In each she marks her image full exprest,
But chief in Bays's monster-breeding breast:
Bays, form'd by nature stage and town to bless,
And act, and be, a coxcomb with success.   110
Dulness, with transport eyes the lively dunce,
Remembering she herself was pertness once.
Now (shame to fortune!) an ill run at play
Blank'd his bold visage, and a thin third day:
Swearing and supperless the hero sate,   115
Blasphem'd his gods, the dice, and damn'd his fate;
Then gnaw'd his pen, then dash'd it on the ground,
Sinking from thought to thought, a vast profound!
Plung'd for his sense, but found no bottom there;

---

85 *when* * *: earlier editions read "when Thorold." Sir George Thorold was Lord Mayor of London in 1720. 86 *Cimon*: Greek commander (fifth century B.C.) who won battles on land and sea over the Persians. 90 *Settle's numbers*: Elkanah Settle (1648–1724), as City Poet, wrote the script for the pageants performed on Lord Mayor's Day. 91 *shrieves*: sheriffs. 98 *Heywood*: evidently Thomas Heywood, a seventeenth-century dramatist who also wrote scripts for the Lord Mayor's Day pageants. 103 *Prynne*: William Prynne (1600–1669), pilloried for writing *Histriomastix*, 1633; *Daniel*: Daniel Defoe (1661–1731), pilloried for writing *The Shortest Way with the Dissenters,* 1702. 104 *Eusden*: the Rev. Laurence Eusden (1688–1730), poet laureate from 1718 to 1730; *Blackmore*: Sir Richard Blackmore (1665–1729), wrote a number of dull and lengthy poems. 105 *Philips*: Ambrose Philips (1675–1749), a minor poet who composed slowly; *Tate*: Nahum Tate (1652–1715), poet laureate from 1692 to 1715. 108 *Bays's*: i.e., Cibber, who as poet laureate wears the crown of bay leaves. 113 *play*: gambling. White's, a club Cibber belonged to, was notorious for gambling. 118 *profound*: depth, i.e., bathos. Rather than rising to sublimity Cibber sinks to bathos.

Yet wrote and flounder'd on in mere despair.   120
Round him much embryo, much abortion lay,
Much future ode, and abdicated play;
Nonsense precipitate, like running lead,
That slipp'd thro' cracks and ziz-zags of the head;
All that on Folly Frenzy could beget,   125
Fruits of dull heat, and sooterkins of wit.
Next, o'er his books his eyes began to roll,
In pleasing memory of all he stole,
How here he sipp'd, how there he plunder'd snug,
And suck'd all o'er, like an industrious bug.   130
Here lay poor Fletcher's half-eat scenes, and here
The frippery of crucify'd Moliere;
There hapless Shakespear, yet of Tibbald sore,
Wish'd he had blotted for himself before.
The rest on out-side merit but presume,   135
Or serve (like other fools) to fill a room;
Such with their shelves as due proportion hold,
Or their fond parents drest in red and gold;
Or where the pictures for the page atone,
And Quarles is sav'd by beauties not his own.   140
Here swells the shelf with Ogilby the great;
There, stamp'd with arms, Newcastle shines complete:
Here all his suff'ring brotherhood retire,
And 'scape the martyrdom of jakes and fire:
A Gothic library! of Greece and Rome   145
Well purg'd, and worthy Settle, Banks, and Broome.
  But, high above, more solid learning shone,
The classics of an age that heard of none;
There Caxton slept, with Wynkyn at his side,
One clasp'd in wood, and one in strong cowhide;   150
There, sav'd by spice, like mummies, many a year,

---

120 *mere*: complete, total. 122 *abdicated*: unfinished. 126 *sooterkins*: small animals similar
to rats, which according to a joke of the time, were born to Dutch women as a result
of their habit of warming themselves in winter by sitting with their petticoats over small
stoves. 131 *Fletcher*: John Fletcher (1579–1625), Jacobean dramatist. 133 *There...sore*:
Lewis Theobald (1688–1744) published in 1726 *Shakespeare restored; or, a Specimen of
the many Errors as well committed as unamended by Mr Pope, in his late Edition of this
Poet*. 134 *Wish'd...blott'd*: Shakespeare's contemporary, Ben Jonson, said that when
the actors praised Shakespeare to him by saying that he never blotted (corrected) a line,
"My answer hath been, 'Would he had blotted a thousand.'" Pope's point is that had
Shakespeare foreseen how Theobald would "correct" his plays, Shakespeare would have
been quick to correct them himself. 135 *out-side merit*: i.e., the book covers; *but*: only.
137 *Such...hold*: those books whose merit is in their being the right size to fill out the
bookshelf. 139 *pictures...atone*: those books whose handsome illustrations make up for
deficient writing. 140 *Quarles*: Francis Quarles' book *Emblems* (1635), in which verses
accompany and explain symbolic pictures. 141 *Ogilby the great*: John Ogilby (1600–1676)
translated Homer and Virgil; the translations appeared in large folio texts. 142 *Newcastle*:
Margaret Cavendish, Duchess of Newcastle (1624–1674), a prolific writer. 144 *jakes*: toilet.
145 *Gothic*: a synonym for *barbarous* in Pope's time. 146 *Settle*: see note to line 90 above;
Banks: John Banks, Restoration dramatist; *Broome*: Richard Brome, a Jacobean dramatist.
149 *Caxton*: William Caxton (1422?–1491), the first English printer; *Wynkyn*: Wynkyn de
Worde (d. 1534), an early printer.

Dry Bodies of Divinity appear;
De Lyra there a dreadful front extends,
And here the groaning shelves Philemon bends.
   Of these twelve volumes, twelve of amplest size,   155
Redeem'd from tapers and defrauded pies,
Inspir'd he seizes; these an altar raise;
An hecatomb of pure unsully'd lays
That altar crowns; a folio common-place
Founds the whole pile, of all his works the base;   160
Quartos, octavos, shape the less'ning pyre;
A twisted Birth-day Ode completes the spire.
   Then he: "Great tamer of all human art!
First in my care, and ever at my heart;
Dulness! whose good old cause I yet defend,   165
With whom my muse began, with whom shall end,
E'er since Sir Fopling's periwig was praise,
To the last honours of the butt and bays:
O thou! of bus'ness the directing soul!
To this our head like bias to the bowl,   170
Which, as more pond'rous, made its aim more true,
Obliquely waddling to the mark in view:
O! ever gracious to perplex'd mankind,
Still spread a healing mist before the mind;
And, lest we err by wit's wild dancing light,   175
Secure us kindly in our native night.
Or, if to wit a coxcomb make pretence,
Guard the sure barrier between that and sense;
Or quite unravel all the reas'ning thread,
And hang some curious cobweb in its stead!   180
As, forc'd from wind-guns, lead itself can fly,
And pond'rous slugs cut swiftly thro' the sky;
As clocks to weight their nimble motion owe,
The wheels above urg'd by the load below:
Me emptiness and dulness could inspire,   185
And were my elasticity and fire.
Some daemon stole my pen (forgive th' offence)
And once betray'd me into common sense:
Else all my prose and verse were much the same;
This, prose on stilts, that, poetry fall'n lame.   190

153 *De Lyra*: Nicholas de Lyra (d. 1340), author. 154 *Philemon*: Philemon Holland (1552–1637), a prolific translator of Greek and Latin classics. 156 *defrauded pies*: Pages from old books were sometimes used to line piepans; that, Pope suggests, would have been highly appropriate in the present case. 158 *unsully'd*: untouched, unread. 159 *folio common-place*: a large notebook in which Cibber recorded his own ideas as well as copied passages from other writers. 167 *Sir Fopling's periwig*: In the performances of *Love's Last Shift*, his first play, Cibber acted the role of Sir Fopling, wearing a huge wig. 168 *butt and bays*: the barrel (butt) of wine given annually to the poet laureate, and his bay-leaf crown. 170 *To...bowl*: Dulness unbalances the brain as a bias or weight does a bowling ball. 181 *wind-guns*: air-guns. 188 *And once...sense*: i.e., when Cibber wrote *The Careless Husband*, a play that Pope thought well of.

Did on the stage my fops appear confin'd?
My life gave ampler lessons to mankind.
Did the dead letter unsuccessful prove?
The brisk example never fail'd to move.
Yet sure had Heav'n decreed to save the state,   195
Heav'n had decreed these works a longer date.
Could Troy be sav'd by any single hand,
This grey-goose weapon must have made her stand.
What can I now? my Fletcher cast aside,
Take up the Bible, once my better guide?   200
Or tread the path by vent'rous heroes trod,
This box my thunder, this right hand my god?
Or chair'd at White's amidst the doctors sit,
Teach oaths to gamesters, and to nobles wit?
Or bidst thou rather party to embrace?   205
(A friend to party thou, and all her race;
'T is the same rope at diff'rent ends they twist;
To dulness Ridpath is as dear as Mist.)
Shall I, like Curtius, desp'rate in my zeal,
O'er head and ears plunge for the commonweal?   210
Or rob Rome's ancient geese of all their glories,
And cackling save the monarchy of Tories?
Hold—to the Minister I more incline;
To serve his cause, O Queen! is serving thine.
And see! thy very Gazetteers give o'er,   215
Ev'n Ralph repents, and Henley writes no more.
What then remains? Ourself. Still, still remain
Cibberian forehead, and Cibberian brain.
This brazen brightness, to th' squire so dear;
This polish'd hardness, that reflects the peer: 220
This arch absurd, that wit and fool delights;
This mess, toss'd up of Hockley-hole and Whites;
Where dukes and butchers join to wreathe my crown,
At once the bear and fiddle of the town.
    "O born in sin, and forth in folly brought;   225
Works damn'd, or to be damn'd! (your father's fault)

---

197 *Troy*: i.e., London. 198 *grey-goose weapon*: his quill pen. 200 *Take up...guide*: Cibber's father wanted him to be a clergyman. 203 *White's*: See note to line 113 above; *doctors*: men so well studied in the art of gambling that "doctoring" the dice is a common practice. 205 *Or bidst...embrace*: i.e., or do you prefer political parties—Whig or Tory? 208 *Ridpath*: George Ridpath (d. 1726), author of a Whig newspaper; *Mist*: Nathaniel Mist (d. 1737), owner of a Tory newspaper. 211 *Rome's ancient geese*: The geese whose warning cackles enabled Manlius to repulse an attack on Rome by the Gauls in 390 B.C. 213 *the Minister*: Sir Robert Walpole. 215 *Gazetteers*: *The Daily Gazetteer,* written by hacks, was controlled by Walpole's Whig government. With Walpole's loss of office early in 1742, the paper's extreme partisanship of the Whigs diminished considerably. 216 *Ralph*: James Ralph (1705–1762), an American who wrote first for the *Gazetteer,* then, "repenting," for *The Champion,* an opposition paper; *Henley*: John Henley (1692–1756), a clergyman-journalist who supported Walpole. 222 *Hockley-hole*: Hockley-in-the-Hole, a "sporting" center in London for bear-baiting, dog-fights, and the like. 224 *bear and fiddle*: i.e., the object of public baiting and the would-be entertainer.

Go, purify'd by flames ascend the sky,
My better and more Christian progeny!
Unstain'd, untouch'd, and yet in maiden sheets,
While all your smutty sisters walk the streets.   230
Ye shall not beg, like gratis-given Bland,
Sent with a pass, and vagrant thro' the land;
Not sail with Ward, to ape-and-monkey climes,
Where vile mundungus trucks for viler rhymes:
Not sulphur-tipt, emblaze an ale-house fire;   235
Not wrap up oranges, to pelt your sire!
O! pass more innocent, in infant state,
To the mild Limbo of our Father Tate:
Or peaceably forgot, at once be blest
In Shadwell's bosom with eternal rest!   240
Soon to that mass of nonsense to return,
Where things destroy'd are swept to things unborn."
    With that, a tear (portentous sign of grace!)
Stole from the master of the sev'nfold face;
And thrice he lifted high the birth-day brand,   245
And thrice he dropt it from his quiv'ring hand;
Then lights the structure, with averted eyes:
The rolling smoke involves the sacrifice.
The op'ning clouds disclose each work by turns:
Now flames the Cid, and now Perolla burns;   250
Great Caesar roars, and hisses in the fires;
King John in silence modestly expires;
No merit now the dear Nonjuror claims,
Moliere's old stubble in a moment flames.
Tears gush'd again, as from pale Priam's eyes   255
When the last blaze sent Ilion to the skies.
    Rous'd by the light, old Dulness heav'd the head,
Then snatch'd a sheet of *Thulè* from her bed;
Sudden she flies, and whelms it o'er the pyre;
Down sink the flames, and with a hiss expire.   260
    Her ample presence fills up all the place;
A veil of frogs dilates her awful face:
Great in her charms! as when on shrieves and may'rs

---

228 *My better...progeny*: i.e., better and more Christian than Cibber's actual son, Theophilus, and daughter, Charlotte, whose immorality was notorious. 231 *Bland*: Henry Bland (d. 1746), a writer for the government newspaper, *Daily Courant*, which was distributed postage-free ("gratis-given"). 233 *Ward*: Edward Ward (1667–1731), poetaster and journalist whose works, Pope says, "are yearly sold into the plantations," i.e., the "ape-and-monkey climes." 234 *mundungus*: poor-grade tobacco. 236 *oranges...sire*: Oranges were sold in the theaters and, like tomatoes today, often used to "pelt" vile actors like Cibber. 240 *Shadwell*: Thomas Shadwell (1642?–1692), dramatist satirized by Dryden in *Mac Flecknoe*. 248 *involves*: encloses, envelopes. 250 *the Cid*: Cibber's *Ximena: or The Heroic Daughter* (1712), which was based on Corneille's *Le Cid* (1636); *Perolla*: Cibber's *Perolla and Isidora* (1705). 251 *Great Caesar*: Cibber's *Caesar in Egypt* (1724). 252 *King John*: Cibber's *Papal Tyranny* (1735), based on Shakespeare's *King John*; it was never performed publicly, hence "in silence modestly expires." 253 *Nonjuror*: play by Cibber (1717) based on Molière's *Tartuffe* (1669). 255 *Priam*: king of Troy ("Ilion"). 258 *Thulè*: tiresome poem by Ambrose Philips (1675–1749). It is used here as a wet blanket.

She looks, and breathes herself into their airs.
She bids him wait her to her sacred dome: 265
Well pleas'd he enter'd, and confess'd his home.
So spirits ending their terrestrial race
Ascend, and recognize their native place.
This the Great Mother dearer held than all
The clubs of Quidnuncs, or her own Guildhall: 270
Here stood her opium, here she nurs'd her owls,
And here she plann'd th' imperial seat of fools.
    Here to her chosen all her works she shows;
Prose swell'd to verse, verse loit'ring into prose:
How random thoughts now meaning chance to find,   275
Now leave all memory of sense behind;
How prologues into prefaces decay,
And these to notes are fritter'd quite away;
How index-learning turns no student pale,
Yet holds the eel of science by the tail;   280
How, with less reading than makes felons 'scape,
Less human genius than God gives an ape,
Small thanks to France, and none to Rome or Greece,
A vast, vamp'd, future, old, reviv'd, new piece,
'Twixt Plautus, Fletcher, Shakespear, and Corneille,   285
Can make a Cibber, Tibbald, or Ozell.
    The goddess then, o'er his anointed head,
With mystic words, the sacred opium shed.
And lo! her bird (a monster of a fowl,
Something betwixt a Heideggre and owl)   290
Perch'd on his crown. "All hail! and hail again,
My son: the promis'd land expects thy reign.
Know, Eusden thirsts no more for sack or praise;
He sleeps among the dull of ancient days;
Safe, where no critics damn, no duns molest,   295
Where wretched Withers, Ward, and Gildon rest,
And high-born Howard, more majestic sire,
With Fool of Quality completes the quire.
Thou, Cibber! thou, his laurel shalt support,
Folly, my son, has still a friend at court.   300
Lift up your gates, ye princes, see him come!
Sound, sound, ye viols; be the cat-call dumb!

---

270 *Quidnuncs*: political club-members so called because they continually asked "Quid nunc?" i.e., "What now, what's the latest news?"; *her own Guildhall*: Dulness is associated with businessmen in the City of London, not with the Court. 280 *science*: knowledge. 286 *Ozell*: John Ozell (d. 1743), a prolific translator. 290 *Heideggre*: John Heidegger, who managed the opera house in the Haymarket, was notoriously ugly. 293 *Eusden*: Laurence Eusden (1648–1730), a minor poet. 296 *Withers*: George Withers (1588–1667), a minor poet and pamphleteer; *Ward*: See note to line 233 above; *Gildon*: Charles Gildon (1665–1724), a writer who had criticized Pope. 297 *Howard*: Edward Howard, Restoration poet and playwright whose long poem, *The British Princes,* was often referred to contemptuously. 298 *Fool of Quality*: Lord Hervey, whom Pope had satirized as "Sporus" in his *Epistle to Dr. Arbuthnot*. Hervey died just before the final version of *The Dunciad* was published. 299 *his*: i.e., Eusden's. 302 *cat-call*: squeaking instrument often used in theaters to show disapproval.

Bring, bring the madding bay, the drunken vine;
The creeping, dirty, courtly ivy join.
And thou! his aid-de-camp, lead on my sons,   305
Light-arm'd with points, antitheses, and puns.
Let Bawdry, Billingsgate, my daughters dear,
Support his front, and Oaths bring up the rear:
And under his, and under Archer's wing,
Gaming and Grub-street skulk behind the King.   310
      "O! when shall rise a monarch all our own,
And I, a nursing-mother, rock the throne;
'Twixt prince and people close the curtain draw,
Shade him from light, and cover him from law;
Fatten the courtier, starve the learned band,   315
And suckle armies, and dry-nurse the land:
Till senates nod to lullabies divine,
And all be sleep, as at an ode of thine."
      She ceas'd. Then swells the Chapel-Royal throat:
"God save King Cibber!" mounts in ev'ry note.   320
Familiar White's, "God save King Colley!" cries;
"God save King Colley!" Drury-lane replies:
To Needham's quick the voice triumphal rode,
But pious Needham dropt the name of God;
Back to the Devil the last echoes roll,   325
And "Coll!" each butcher roars at Hockley-hole.
      So when Jove's block descended from on high
(As sings thy great forefather Ogilby)
Loud thunder to its bottom shook the bog,
And the hoarse nation croak'd, "God save King Log!"   330

[In Book I the Goddess of Dulness chooses Colley Cibber to become King of the
empire of Dulness. In Book II his coronation takes place amid great celebration and
games. In Book III he falls asleep, dreams of the past and present progress of
Dulness, and envisions its future triumph over all. Pope's "Argument" (synopsis) of
Book IV is presented below, with those portions which we have omitted appearing
within brackets.]

Book IV

ARGUMENT

    The poet being, in this book, to declare the completion of the
prophecies mentioned at the end of the former, makes a new invocation;

---

305 *thou!*: Lord Hervey. Pope carried this couplet over from earlier editions, apparently
forgetting that Hervey was now officially dead.   307 *Billingsgate*: London fishmarket notorious for vulgar language.   309 *Archer*: Thomas Archer (d. 1743), Groom Porter to George
I and George II; as such, he was in charge of gambling and card playing at Court.   322
Drury-lane: London theater of which Cibber was one of the managers.   324 *pious Needham*:
Mother Needham, a procuress notorious for her foul language.   325 *the Devil*: Pope com-
ments, "The Devil tavern in Fleet Street, where these odes are usually rehearsed before they
are performed at Court."   326 *Hockley-hole*: See note to line 222 above.   327 *Jove's block*:
an allusion to the story of how Jupiter, when asked by frogs to supply them with a king,
dropped a log among them.   328 *Ogilby*: See note to line 141 above. The story about
"Jove's block" appearing in Aesop's *Fables* was paraphrased in verse by Ogilby in 1651.

as the greater poets are wont, when some high and worthy matter is to be sung. He shows the goddess coming in her majesty to destroy order and science, and to substitute the kingdom of the dull upon earth: how she leads captive the sciences, and silences the Muses; and what they be who succeed in their stead. All her children, by a wonderful attraction, are drawn about her; and bear along with them divers others, who promote her empire by connivance, weak resistance, or discouragement of arts; such as halfwits, tasteless admirers, vain pretenders, the flatterers of dunces, or the patrons of them. All these crowd round her; one of them offering to approach her, is driven back by a rival, but she commends and encourages both. [The first who speak in form are the geniuses of the schools, who assure her of their care to advance her cause by confining youth to words, and keeping them out of the way of real knowledge. Their address, and her gracious answer; with her charge to them and the universities. The universities appear by their proper deputies, and assure her that the same method is observed in the progress of education. The speech of Aristarchus on this subject. They are driven off by a band of young gentlemen returned from travel with their tutors; one of whom delivers to the goddess, in a polite oration, an account of the whole conduct and fruits of their travels; presenting to her at the same time a young nobleman perfectly accomplished. She receives him graciously, and endues him with the happy quality of want of shame. She sees loitering about her a number of indolent persons abandoning all business and duty, and dying with laziness: to these approaches the antiquary, Annius, entreating her to make them virtuosos, and assign them over to him; but Mummius, another antiquary, complaining of his fraudulent proceeding, she finds a method to reconcile their difference. Then enter a troop of people fantastically adorned, offering her strange and exotic presents: amongst them, one stands forth, and demands justice on another who had deprived him of one of the greatest curiosities in nature; but he justifies himself so well that the goddess gives them both her approbation. She recommends to them to find proper employment for the indolents before mentioned, in the study of butterflies, shells, birds'-nests, moss, &c., but with particular caution not to proceed beyond trifles, to any useful or extensive views of nature, or of the Author of Nature. Against the last of these apprehensions, she is secured by a hearty address from the minute philosophers and freethinkers, one of whom speaks in the name of the rest. The youth thus instructed and principled, are delivered to her in a body, by the hands of Silenus; and then admitted to taste the cup of the Magus, her high priest, which causes a total oblivion of all obligations, divine, civil, moral, or rational. To these her adepts she sends priests, attendants, and comforters, of various kinds;] confers on them orders and degrees; and then dismissing them with a speech, confirming to each his privileges, and telling what she expects from each, concludes with a yawn of extraordinary virtue: the progress and effects whereof on all orders of men, and the consummation of all, in the restoration of Night and Chaos, conclude the poem.

Book IV

Yet, yet a moment, one dim ray of light
Indulge, dread chaos, and eternal night!
Of darkness visible so much be lent,
As half to show, half veil, the deep intent.
Ye powers! whose mysteries restored I sing,   5

To whom time bears me on his rapid wing,
Suspend a while your force inertly strong,
Then take at once the poet and the song.
   Now flamed the Dog Star's unpropitious ray,
Smote every brain, and withered every bay;   10
Sick was the sun, the owl forsook his bower,
The moon-struck prophet felt the madding hour:
Then rose the seed of chaos, and of night,
To blot out order, and extinguish light,
Of dull and venal a new world to mold,   15
And bring Saturnian days of lead and gold.
   She mounts the throne: her head a cloud concealed,
In broad effulgence all below revealed;
('Tis thus aspiring Dulness ever shines)
Soft on her lap her laureate son reclines.   20
   Beneath her footstool, science groans in chains,
And wit dreads exile, penalties, and pains.
There foamed rebellious logic, gagged and bound,
There, stripped, fair rhetoric languished on the ground;
His blunted arms by sophistry are borne,   25
And shameless Billingsgate her robes adorn.
Morality, by her false guardians drawn,
Chicane in furs, and casuistry in lawn,
Gasps, as they straiten at each end the cord,
And dies, when Dulness gives her Page the word.   30
Mad Máthesis alone was unconfined,
Too mad for mere material chains to bind,
Now to pure space lifts her ecstatic stare,
Now running round the circle finds it square.
But held in tenfold bonds the Muses lie,   35
Watched both by envy's and by flattery's eye:
There to her heart sad tragedy addressed
The dagger wont to pierce the tyrant's breast;
But sober history restrained her rage,
And promised venegeance on a barbarous age.   40
There sunk Thalia, nerveless, cold, and dead,
Had not her sister satire held her head;
Nor couldst thou, Chesterfield! a tear refuse,
Thou weptst, and with thee wept each gentle Muse.
   When lo! a harlot form soft sliding by,   45
With mincing step, small voice, and languid eye:
Foreign her air, her robe's discordant pride

---

20 *laureate son*: Colley Cibber.   26 *Billingsgate*: foul language; so called because of the London fishmarket of that name.   28 *Chicane...lawn*: Judges wore furs, bishops lawn sleeves.   30 *Page*: Sir Francis Page (1661?–1741), notorious as the "hanging judge."   31–34 *Mad Máthesis...square*: glances at "mad" mathematical speculations about space and matter and at such ambitious mathematicians as Hobbes who persisted in trying to square the circle.   41 *Thalia*: muse of comedy.   43 *Chesterfield*: Lord Chesterfield had opposed the Stage Licensing Act of 1737, which was considered an attack on theatrical liberties. 45 *harlot form*: Italian opera, often ridiculed during this period.

In patch-work fluttering, and her head aside:
By singing peers upheld on either hand,
She tripped and laughed, too pretty much to stand;   50
Cast on the prostrate Nine a scornful look,
Then thus in quaint recitativo spoke.
    "O Cara! Cara! silence all that train:
Joy to great chaos! let division reign:
Chromatic tortures soon shall drive them hence,   55
Break all their nerves, and fritter all their sense:
One trill shall harmonize joy, grief, and rage,
Wake the dull church, and lull the ranting stage;
To the same notes thy sons shall hum, or snore,
And all thy yawning daughters cry, 'Encore.'   60
Another Phoebus, thy own Phoebus, reigns,
Joys in my jigs, and dances in my chains.
But soon, ah soon, rebellion will commence,
If music meanly borrows aid from sense.
Strong in new arms, lo! Giant Handel stands,   65
Like bold Briareus, with a hundred hands;
To stir, to rouse, to shake the soul he comes,
And Jove's own thunders follow Mars's drums.
Arrest him, empress; or you sleep no more——"
She heard, and drove him to th' Hibernian shore.   70
    And now had fame's posterior trumpet blown,
And all the nations summoned to the throne.
The young, the old, who feel her inward sway,
One instinct seizes, and transports away.
None need a guide, by sure attraction led,   75
And strong impulsive gravity of head:
None want a place, for all their center found,
Hung to the goddess and cohered around.
Not closer, orb in orb, conglobed are seen
The buzzing bees about their dusky queen.   80
    The gathering number, at it moves along,
Involves a vast involuntary throng,
Who gently drawn, and struggling less and less,
Roll in her vortex, and her power confess.
Not those alone who passive own her laws,   85
But who, weak rebels, more advance her cause.
Whate'er of dunce in college or in town
Sneers at another, in toupee or gown;
Whate'er of mongrel no one class admits,
A wit with dunces, and a dunce with wits.   90
    Nor absent they, no members of her state,
Who pay her homage in her sons, the great;
Who, false to Phoebus, bow the knee to Baal;

---

51 *Nine*: the nine muses.   53 *"O Cara! Cara!"*: "O beloved! beloved!" (Italian).   54
division: a pun on the technical musical term.   65 *Handel*: famous contemporary composer
of *The Messiah*.   77 *want*: lack.   93 *Phoebus, Baal*: Phoebus Apollo, Greek god of poetry
and of the sun. Baal, among the ancient Semitic people, was a sun god, hence a false god.

Or impious, preach his word without a call.
Patrons, who sneak from living worth to dead,   95
Withhold the pension, and set up the head;
Or vest dull flattery in the sacred gown;
Or give from fool to fool the laurel crown.
And (last and worst) with all the cant of wit,
Without the soul, the Muse's hypocrite.   100
    There marched the bard and blockhead, side by side,
Who rhymed for hire, and patronized for pride.
Narcissus, praised with all a parson's power,
Looked a white lily sunk beneath a shower.
There moved Montalto with superior air;   105
His stretched-out arm displayed a volume fair;
Courtiers and patriots in two ranks divide,
Through both he passed, and bowed from side to side:
But as in graceful act, with awful eye
Composed he stood, bold Benson thrust him by: 110
On two, unequal crutches propped he came,
Milton's on this, on that one Johnston's name.
The decent knight retired with sober rage,
Withdrew his hand, and closed the pompous page.
But (happy for him as the times went then)   115
Appeared Apollo's mayor and aldermen,
On whom three hundred gold-capped youths await,
To lug the ponderous volume off in state.
    When Dulness, smiling—"Thus revive the wits!
But murder first, and mince them all to bits;   120
As erst Medea (cruel, so to save!)
A new edition of old Æson gave;
Let standard authors, thus, like trophies borne,
Appear more glorious as more hacked and torn.
And you, my critics! in the chequered shade,   125
Admire new light through holes yourselves have made.
    "Leave not a foot of verse, a foot of stone,
A page, a grave, that they can call their own;
But spread, my sons, your glory thin or thick,
On passive paper, or on solid brick.   130
So by each bard an alderman shall sit,
A heavy lord shall hang at every wit,
And while on fame's triumphal car they ride,
Some slave of mine be pinioned to their side."

....

96 *Withhold...head*: i.e., refuse a living poet a stipend in favor of commissioning busts of dead poets. 98 *laurel crown*: the laureateship. 103 *Narcissus*: the pale-complexioned Lord Hervey, the "Sporus" of the *Epistle to Dr. Arbuthnot*. 105 *Montalto*: Sir Thomas Hanmer, the Shakespearean editor, noted for his pomposity. 110 *Benson*: William Benson, who had a monument to Milton raised in Westminster Abbey and commissioned a bust of Arthur Johnston, a Scot who had translated the Psalms into Latin verse. 121–24 *As erst Medea ...torn*: Emending and "correcting" the works of famous authors like Shakespeare are likened to Medea's cutting of Aeson's throat to restore his youth.

Next, bidding all draw near on bended knees,   565
The queen confers her titles and degrees.
Her children first of more distinguished sort,
Who study Shakespeare at the Inns of Court,
Impale a glow worm, or *vertú* profess,
Shine in the dignity of F.R.S.   570
Some, deep Freemasons, join the silent race
Worthy to fill Pythagoras' place:
Some botanists, or florists at the least,
Or issue members of an annual feast.
Nor past the meanest unregarded, one   575
Rose a Gregorian, one a Gormogon.
The last, not least in honor or applause,
Isis and Cam made doctors of her laws.
    Then, blessing all, "Go, children of my care!
To practice now from theory repair.   580
All my commands are easy, short, and full:
My sons! be proud, be selfish, and be dull.
Guard my prerogative, assert my throne:
This nod confirms each privilege your own.
The cap and switch be sacred to his grace;   585
With staff and pumps the marquis lead the race;
From stage to stage the licensed earl may run,
Paired with his fellow-charioteer, the sun;
The learnèd baron butterflies design,
Or draw to silk Arachne's subtile line;   590
The judge to dance his brother sergeant call;
The senator at cricket urge the ball;
The bishop stow (pontific luxury!)
An hundred souls of turkeys in a pie;
The sturdy squire to Gallic masters stoop,   595
And drown his lands and manors in a soup.
Others import yet nobler arts from France,
Teach kings to fiddle, and make senates dance.
Perhaps more high some daring son may soar,
Proud to my list to add one monarch more;   600
And nobly conscious, princes are but things
Born for first ministers, as slaves for kings,
Tyrant supreme! shall three estates command,
And make one mighty Dunciad of the land!"
    More she had spoke, but yawned—All Nature nods: 605

568 *Inns of Court*: law schools. 569 *vertú*: an interest in the fine arts. 570 *F.R.S.*: Fellow
of the Royal Society. 572 *Pythagoras'*: the Greek philosopher (sixth century B.C.) who
formed secret societies. 576 *Gregorian...Gormogon*: names given members of contemporary secret societies. 578 *Isis and Cam*: Oxford and Cambridge universities. 580 *To
practice...repair*: The omitted portions of Book IV could be said to deal with theoretical
discussions about inculcating dullness in men and institutions; now the Goddess of Dulness
urges her disciples to go forth and practice what they have preached. 598 *Teach...dance*:
i.e., make Parliament dance to the king's tune as obediently as the French must do in their
absolute monarchy. Much of this paragraph, especially lines 595ff., ridicules the English
tendency to imitate French fashions and practices.

What mortal can resist the yawn of gods?
Churches and chapels instantly it reached;
(St. James's first, for leaden Gilbert preached)
Then catched the schools; the hall scarce kept awake;
The convocation gaped, but could not speak: 610
Lost was the nation's sense, nor could be found,
While the long solemn unison went round:
Wide, and more wide, it spred o'er all the realm;
Even Palinurus nodded at the helm:
The vapor mild o'er each committee crept;   615
Unfinished treaties in each office slept;
And chiefless armies dozed out the campaign;
And navies yawned for orders on the main.
   O Muse! relate (for you can tell alone,
Wits have short memories, and dunces none),   620
Relate, who first, who last resigned to rest;
Whose heads she partly, whose completely blessed;
What charms could faction, what ambition lull,
The venal quiet, and entrance the dull;
Till drowned was sense, and shame, and right, and wrong—   625
O sing, and hush the nations with thy song!
   In vain, in vain—the all-composing hour
Resistless falls: the Muse obeys the power.
She comes! she comes! the sable throne behold
Of night primeval, and of chaos old!   630
Before her, fancy's gilded clouds decay,
And all its varying rainbows die away.
Wit shoots in vain its momentary fires,
The meteor drops, and in a flash expires.
As one by one, at dread Medea's strain,   635
The sickening stars fade off th' ethereal plain;
As Argus' eyes by Hermes' wand oppressed,
Closed one by one to everlasting rest;
Thus at her felt approach, and secret might,
Art after art goes out, and all is night.   640
See skulking truth to her old cavern fled,
Mountains of casuistry heaped o'er her head!
Philosophy, that leaned on Heaven before,
Shrinks to her second cause, and is no more.
Physic of metaphysic begs defense,   645
And metaphysic calls for aid on sense!
See mystery to mathematics fly!

---

608 *Gilbert*: Dr. John Gilbert, later Archbishop of York. 614 *Palinurus*: the pilot of Aeneas' fleet, who fell into the ocean while asleep at the helm; here, he stands for Sir Robert Walpole, the Prime Minister, who is asleep at the helm of government. 628 *the power*: the sleep-inducing power of the mighty yawn (see line 605), which prevents the Muse from inspiring the narrator further. 635 *Medea's strain*: great sorceress in classical mythology. 637 *As Argus'...oppressed*: Hermes' music lulled asleep all the 100 eyes of Argus Panoptes ("all-seeing"), who had been assigned by Hera to guard Io. 641 *truth... cavern*: Democritus had claimed that truth was concealed at the bottom of a well until he pulled her out.

In vain! they gaze, turn giddy, rave, and die.
Religion blushing veils her sacred fires,
And unawares morality expires. 650
For public flame, nor private, dares to shine;
Nor human spark is left, nor glimpse divine!
Lo! thy dread empire, Chaos! is restored;
Light dies before thy uncreating word:
Thy hand, great Anarch! lets the curtain fall; 655
And universal darkness buries all.

WILLIAM BLAKE *(1757–1827)*

Blake's satire in *The Marriage of Heaven and Hell* operates like the "infernal method" of printing, which employs corrosives to melt "apparent surfaces away, and display the infinite which was hid." The "apparent surfaces" subjected to Blake's corrosives here are primarily the notions of heaven and hell, good and evil, foisted on men by contemporary religious dogma, but the acid of his satire spills over and eats its way into all forms of "reason" that would impose prudential restraints on and thereby pervert the natural functioning of energy, imagination, and impulse. Destroying "apparent surfaces" is, however, only half of Blake's satiric purpose, for once the surfaces are destroyed, the "infinite" that they concealed must be liberated. Satiric destruction and creation are thus in accord with the central dialectical premise of the satire itself, that "Without Contraries is no progression. Attraction and Repulsion, Reason and Energy, Love and Hate, are necessary to Human existence." Blake destroys the three errors and creates the three "Contraries" stated in the section called "The Voice of the Devil." The conventional terms used by Milton in *Paradise Lost*—"Angels & God," "Devils & Hell," "good and evil"—he retains, but he inverts their values and redefines them. The angels and God are delimiting forces associated with Reason and expressing themselves in prohibitions; the devils and hell are liberating forces associated with Imagination and expressing themselves in desires; "Good is the passive that obeys Reason, Evil is the active springing from Energy." The first "Memorable Fancy" leads to the "Proverbs of Hell," which are introduced by Blake with the dead-pan irony characteristic of Swift—Blake acting the role of Gulliver reporting from Hell. In a series of brilliant, gnomic oracles, Blake thus reveals the "infinite" of "infernal wisdom" lying behind the "apparent surfaces" that stultify the normal view of the demonic. In the second "Memorable Fancy" Blake demolishes the "ghost in the machine" idea, the radical separation of soul and body and the denigration of the latter common to Christian theology and rational philosophy, and constructs through allegory the proper relationship between the two—one in which, as Yeats says, "the body is not bruised to pleasure soul." Deceived by religion and philosophy, man has nearly shut the "doors of perception," which are the bodily senses; but by opening them to the creative imagination, by freeing the "Prolific" from the tyranny of the "Devouring," man could gain access to the "infinite." In the third "Memorable Fancy" Blake delivers a withering blast of ridicule at the conventional notion of hell as a materialistic torture chamber populated by pitchfork-wielding devils. This notion is a

---

654 *uncreating word*: opposite of the creating word of God: "Let there be light."

"phantasy" that can be seen only if one dons, with the help of an "angel," the ideological spectacles of education, religion and reason. This hell, like God and heaven, angels and devils, is a creation of the human mind externalized. But the creations foisted upon man by conventional religion are distorted ones, the products of a repressive reason rather than an emancipating imagination. The conventional view, which seeks to spiritualize man by degrading the body, inevitably brutalizes man instead, as Blake demonstrates by imposing upon the angel his own "phantasy" in the form of a Swiftian vision of man as Yahoo.

THE MARRIAGE OF HEAVEN AND HELL

THE ARGUMENT

Rintrah roars & shakes his fires in the burden'd air;
Hungry clouds swag on the deep.

Once meek, and in a perilous path,
The just man kept his course along
The vale of death.   5
Roses are planted where thorns grow,
And on the barren heath
Sing the honey bees.

Then the perilous path was planted,
And a river and a spring   10
On every cliff and tomb,
And on the bleached bones
Red clay brought forth;

Till the villain left the paths of ease,
To walk in perilous paths, and drive   15
The just man into barren climes.

Now the sneaking serpent walks
In mild humility,
And the just man rages in the wilds
Where lions roam.   20
Rintrah roars and shakes his fires in the burdened air;
Hungry clouds swag on the deep.

As a new heaven is begun, and it is now thirty-three years since its advent, the Eternal Hell revives. And lo! Swedenborg is the Angel sitting at the tomb:*

---

* Emanuel Swedenborg (1688–1772), the Swedish visionary, had prophesied that the Last Judgment would occur in 1757, the year Blake was born. The "new heaven" ushered in by his own birth, Blake suggests, naturally requires a revival of "Eternal Hell," which he is about to present in this poem.

---

1 *Rintrah*: the "just man" of lines 4, 16, and 19, whose "meekness" (line 3) turns to wrath when he encounters the perversion of values represented by the "villain" and "sneaking serpent" of lines 14 and 17.   2 *swag*: portmanteau word combining "sway" and "wag."   5 *vale of death*: earthly existence.   13 *Red clay*: i.e., Adam, which means in Hebrew literally "red clay."

his writings are the linen clothes folded up. Now is the dominion of Edom, and the return of Adam into Paradise; see Isaiah xxxiv and xxxv Chap.*

Without Contraries is no progression. Attraction and Repulsion, Reason and Energy, Love and Hate, are necessary to Human existence.

From these contraries spring what the religious call Good and Evil. Good is the passive that obeys Reason. Evil is the active springing from Energy.

Good is Heaven. Evil is Hell.

THE VOICE OF THE DEVIL

All Bibles or sacred codes have been the causes of the following Errors:

1. That Man has two real existing principles; Viz: a Body and a Soul.

2. That Energy, called Evil, is alone from the Body; and that Reason, called Good, is alone from the Soul.

3. That God will torment Man in Eternity for following his Energies.

But the following Contraries to these are True:

1. Man has no Body distinct from his Soul; for that called Body is a portion of Soul discerned by the five Senses, the chief inlets of Soul in this age.

2. Energy is the only life, and is from the Body; and Reason is the bound or outward circumference of Energy.

3. Energy is Eternal Delight.

Those who restrain desire do so because theirs is weak enough to be restrained; and the restrainer or Reason usurps its place and governs the unwilling.

And being restrained, it by degrees becomes passive, till it is only the shadow of desire.

The history of this is written in *Paradise Lost*,† and the Governor or Reason is called Messiah.

And the original Archangel, or possessor of the command of the heavenly host, is call'd the Devil or Satan, and his children are call'd Sin & Death.

But in the Book of Job, Milton's Messiah is call'd Satan.

For this history has been adopted by both parties.

It indeed appear'd to Reason as if Desire was cast out; but the Devil's account is, that the Messiah fell, & formed a heaven of what he stole from the Abyss.

This is shewn in the Gospel, where he prays to the Father to send the comforter, or Desire, that Reason may have Ideas to build on; the Jehovah of the Bible being no other than he who dwells in flaming fire.

Know that after Christ's death, he became Jehovah.

But in Milton, the Father is Destiny, the Son a Ratio of the five senses, & the Holy-ghost Vacuum!

NOTE: The reason Milton wrote in fetters when he wrote of Angels & God, and at liberty when of Devils & Hell, is because he was a true Poet and of the Devil's party without knowing it.

A MEMORABLE FANCY

As I was walking among the fires of hell, delighted with the enjoyments of Genius, which to Angels look like torment and insanity, I collected some of their

* In these chapters Isaiah predicts the destruction of the heavens and earth, which will be followed by the restoration of a paradise for the redeemed.

† Blake's unorthodox interpretation of Milton's epic in the following paragraphs turns Milton's Christian cosmology, in effect, upside down.

Proverbs; thinking that as the sayings used in a nation mark its character, so the Proverbs of Hell show the nature of Infernal wisdom better than any description of buildings or garments.

When I came home: on the abyss of the five senses, where a flat sided steep frowns over the present world, I saw a mighty Devil folded in black clouds, hovering on the sides of the rock: with corroding fires* he wrote the following sentence now perceived by the minds of men, & read by them on earth:

> How do you know but ev'ry Bird that cuts the airy way,
> Is an immense world of delight, clos'd by your senses five?

PROVERBS OF HELL

In seed time learn, in harvest teach, in winter enjoy.

Drive your cart and your plow over the bones of the dead.

The road of excess leads to the palace of wisdom.

Prudence is a rich, ugly old maid courted by Incapacity.

He who desires but acts not, breeds pestilence.

The cut worm forgives the plow.

Dip him in the river who loves water.

A fool sees not the same tree that a wise man sees.

He whose face gives no light, shall never become a star.

Eternity is in love with the productions of time.

The busy bee has no time for sorrow.

The hours of folly are measured by the clock; but of wisdom, no clock can measure.

All wholesome food is caught without a net or a trap.

Bring out number, weight, and measure in a year of dearth.

No bird soars too high, if he soars with his own wings.

A dead body revenges not injuries.

The most sublime act is to set another before you.

If the fool would persist in his folly he would become wise.

Folly is the cloak of knavery.

Shame is Pride's cloak.

Prisons are built with stones of Law, Brothels with bricks of Religion.

The pride of the peacock is the glory of God.

The lust of the goat is the bounty of God.

The wrath of the lion is the wisdom of God.

The nakedness of woman is the work of God.

Excess of sorrow laughs. Excess of joy weeps.

The roaring of lions, the howling of wolves, the raging of the stormy sea, and the destructive sword are portions of eternity, too great for the eye of man.

The fox condemns the trap, not himself.

Joys impregnate. Sorrows bring forth.

Let man wear the fell of the lion, woman the fleece of the sheep.

The bird a nest, the spider a web, man friendship.

The selfish, smiling fool, and the sullen, frowning fool shall be both thought wise, that they may be a rod.

---

* The Devil's proverbs are etched with "corrosives" in the same manner Blake etched the text of this poem.

What is now proved was once only imagined.

The rat, the mouse, the fox, the rabbit watch the roots; the lion, the tiger, the horse, the elephant watch the fruits.

The cistern contains: the fountain overflows.

One thought fills immensity.

Always be ready to speak your mind, and a base man will avoid you.

Everything possible to be believed is an image of truth.

The eagle never lost so much time as when he submitted to learn of the crow.

The fox provides for himself, but God provides for the lion.

Think in the morning. Act in the noon. Eat in the evening. Sleep in the night.

He who has suffered you to impose on him, knows you.

As the plow follows words, so God rewards prayers.

The tygers of wrath are wiser than the horses of instruction.

Expect poison from the standing water.

You never know what is enough unless you know what is more than enough.

Listen to the fool's reproach! it is a kingly title!

The eyes of fire, the nostrils of air, the mouth of water, the beard of earth.

The weak in courage is strong in cunning.

The apple tree never asks the beech how he shall grow; nor the lion, the horse, how he shall take his prey.

The thankful receiver bears a plentiful harvest.

If others had not been foolish, we should be so.

The soul of sweet delight can never be defil'd.

When thou seest an Eagle, thou seest a portion of Genius; lift up thy head!

As the caterpiller chooses the fairest leaves to lay her eggs on, so the priest lays his curse on the fairest joys.

To create a little flower is the labour of ages.

Damn braces. Bless relaxes.

The best wine is the oldest, the best water the newest.

Prayers plow not! Praises reap not!

Joys laugh not! Sorrows weep not!

The head Sublime, the heart Pathos, the genitals Beauty, the hands & feet Proportion.

As the air to a bird or the sea to a fish, so is contempt to the contemptible.

The crow wish'd every thing was black, the owl that every thing was white.

Exuberance is Beauty.

If the lion was advised by the fox, he would be cunning.

Improvement makes strait roads; but the crooked roads without Improvement are roads of Genius.

Sooner murder an infant in its cradle than nurse unacted desires.

Where man is not, nature is barren.

Truth can never be told so as to be understood, and not be believ'd.

Enough! or Too much.

The ancient Poets animated all sensible objects with Gods or Geniuses, calling them by the names and adorning them with the properties of woods, rivers, mountains, lakes, cities, nations, and whatever their enlarged & numerous senses could perceive.

And particularly they studied the genius of each city & country, placing it under its mental deity;

Till a system was formed, which some took advantage of, & enslav'd the vulgar by attempting to realize or abstract the mental deities from their objects: thus began Priesthood;

Choosing forms of worship from poetic tales.

And at length they pronounc'd that the Gods had order'd such things.

Thus men forgot that All deities reside in the human breast.

A MEMORABLE FANCY

The Prophets Isaiah and Ezekiel dined with me, and I asked them how they dared so roundly to assert that God spoke to them; and whether they did not think at the time that they would be misunderstood, & so be the cause of imposition.

Isaiah answer'd: "I saw no God, nor heard any, in a finite organical perception; but my senses discov'd the infinite in everything, and as I was then perswaded, & remain confirm'd, that the voice of honest indignation is the voice of God, I cared not for consequences, but wrote."

Then I asked: "does a firm perswasion that a thing is so, make it so?"

He replied: "All poets believe that it does, & in ages of imagination this firm perswasion removed mountains; but many are not capable of a firm perswasion of any thing."

Then Ezekiel said: "The philosophy of the east taught the first principles of human perception: some nations held one principle for the origin, and some another: we of Israel taught that the Poetic Genius (as you now call it) was the first principle and all the others merely derivative, which was the cause of our despising the Priests & Philosophers of other countries, and prophecying that all Gods would at last be proved to originate in ours & to be the tributaries of the Poetic Genius; it was this that our great poet, King David, desired so fervently & invokes so pathetic'ly, saying by this he conquers enemies & governs kingdoms; and we so loved our God, that we cursed in his name all the deities of surounding nations, and asserted that they had rebelled: from these opinions the vulgar came to think that all nations would at last be subject to the jews."

"This," said he, "like all firm perswasions, is come to pass; for all nations believe the jews' code and worship the jews' god, and what greater subjection can be?"

I heard this with some wonder, & must confess my own conviction. After dinner I ask'd Isaiah to favour the world with his lost works; he said none of equal value was lost. Ezekiel said the same of his.

I also asked Isaiah what made him go naked and barefoot three years? he answer'd: "the same that made our friend Diogenes, the Grecian."

I then asked Ezekiel why he eat dung, & lay so long on his right & left side? he answer'd, "the desire of raising other men into a perception of the infinite: this the North American tribes practise, & is he honest who resists his genius or conscience only for the sake of present ease or gratification?"

The ancient tradition that the world will be consumed in fire at the end of six thousand years is true, as I have heard from Hell.

For the cherub with his flaming sword is hereby commanded to leave his guard at tree of life; and when he does, the whole creation will be consumed and appear infinite and holy, whereas it now appears finite & corrupt.

This will come to pass by an improvement of sensual enjoyment.

But first the notion that man has a body distinct from his soul is to be expunged; this I shall do by printing in the infernal method, by corrosives, which in Hell are salutary and medicinal, melting apparent surfaces away, and displaying the infinite which was hid.

If the doors of perception were cleansed every thing would appear to man as it is, infinite.

For man has closed himself up, till he sees all things thro' narrow chinks of his cavern.

A Memorable Fancy

I was in a Printing house in Hell, & saw the method in which knowledge is transmitted from generation to generation.

In the first chamber was a Dragon-Man, clearing away the rubbish from a cave's mouth; within, a number of Dragons were hollowing the cave.

In the second chamber was a Viper folding round the rock & the cave, and others adorning it with gold, silver and precious stones.

In the third chamber was an Eagle with wings and feathers of air: he caused the inside of the cave to be infinite; around were numbers of Eagle-like men who built palaces in the immense cliffs.

In the fourth chamber were Lions of flaming fire, raging around & melting the metals into living fluids.

In the fifth chamber were Unnam'd forms, which cast the metals into the expanse.

There they were receiv'd by Men who occupied the sixth chamber, and took the forms of books & were arranged in libraries.

The Giants* who formed this world into its sensual existence, and now seem to live in it in chains, are in truth the causes of its life & the sources of all activity; but the chains are the cunning of weak and tame minds which have power to resist energy; according to the proverb, the weak in courage is strong in cunning.

Thus one portion of being is the Prolific, the other the Devouring: to the Devourer it seems as if the producer was in his chains; but it is not so, he only takes portions of existence and fancies that the whole.

But the Prolific would cease to be Prolific unless the Devourer, as a sea, received the excess of his delights.

Some will say: "Is not God alone the Prolific?" I answer: "God only Acts & Is, in existing beings or Men."

These two classes of men are always upon earth, & they should be enemies: whoever tries to reconcile them seeks to destroy existence.

Religion is an endeavour to reconcile the two.

Note: Jesus Christ did not wish to unite, but to separate them, as in the Parable of sheep and goats! & he says: "I came not to send Peace, but a Sword."

Messiah or Satan or Tempter was formerly thought to be one of the Antediluvians who are our Energies.

A Memorable Fancy

An Angel came to me and said: "O pitiable foolish young man! O horrible! O dreadful state! consider the hot burning dungeon thou art preparing for thyself to all eternity, to which thou art going in such career."

---

* The Giants are man's five senses.

I said: "Perhaps you will be willing to shew me my eternal lot, & we will contemplate together upon it, and see whether your lot or mine is most desirable."

So he took me thro' a stable & thro' a church & down into the church vault, at the end of which was a mill: thro' the mill we went, and came to a cave:* down the winding cavern we groped our tedious way, till a void boundless as a nether sky appear'd beneath us, & we held by the roots of trees and hung over this immensity; but I said: "if you please, we will commit ourselves to this void, and see whether providence is here also: if you will not, I will": but he answer'd: "do not presume, O young man, but as we here remain, behold thy lot which will soon appear when the darkness passes away."

So I remain'd with him, sitting in the twisted root of an oak; he was suspended in a fungus, which hung with the head downward into the deep.

By degrees we beheld the infinite Abyss, fiery as the smoke of a burning city; beneath us, at an immense distance, was the sun, black but shining; round it were fiery tracks on which revolv'd vast spiders, crawling after their prey, which flew, or rather swum, in the infinite deep, in the most terrific shapes of animals sprung from corruption; & the air was full of them, & Seem'd composed of them: these are Devils, and are called Powers of the air. I now asked my companion which was my eternal lot? he said: "between the black & white spiders."

But now, from between the black & white spiders, a cloud and fire burst and rolled thro' the deep, black'ning all beneath, so that the nether deep grew black as a sea, & rolled with a terrible noise; beneath us was nothing now to be seen but a black tempest, till looking east between the clouds & the waves, we saw a cataract of blood mixed with fire, and not many stones' throw from us appear'd and sunk again the scaly fold of a monstrous serpent; at last, to the east, distant about three degrees, appear'd a fiery crest above the waves; slowly it reared like a ridge of golden rocks, till we discover'd two globes of crimson fire, from which the sea fled away in clouds of smoke; and now we saw it was the head of Leviathan; his forehead was divided into streaks of green & purple like those on a tyger's forehead: soon we saw his mouth & red gills hang just above the raging foam, tinging the black deep with beams of blood, advancing toward us with all the fury of a spiritual existence.

My friend the Angel climb'd up from his station into the mill: I remain'd alone; & then this appearance was no more, but I found myself sitting on a pleasant bank beside a river by moonlight, hearing a harper, who sung to the harp; & his theme was: "The man who never alters his opinion is like standing water, & breeds reptiles of the mind."

But I arose and sought for the mill, & there I found my Angel, who, surprised, asked me how I escaped?

I answer'd "All that we saw was owing to your metaphysics; for when you ran away, I found myself on a bank by moonlight hearing a harper. But now we have seen my eternal lot, shall I shew you yours?" he laugh'd at my proposal; but I by force suddenly caught him in my arms, & flew westerly thro' the night, till we were elevated above the earth's shadow; then I flung myself with him directly into the body of the sun; here I clothed myself in white, & taking in

---

* The "stable" "church" and "mill" represent contemporary education ("horses of instruction"), religion, and reason.

my hand Swedenborg's volumes, sunk from the glorious clime, and passed all the planets till we came to saturn: here I stay'd to rest, & then leap'd into the void between saturn & the fixed stars.

"Here," said I, "is your lot, in this space—if space it may be call'd. Soon we saw the stable and the church, & I took him to the altar and open'd the Bible, and lo! it was a deep pit, into which I descended, driving the Angel before me; soon we saw seven houses of brick; one we enter'd; in it were a number of monkeys, baboons, & all of that species, chain'd by the middle, grinning and snatching at one another, but withheld by the shortness of their chains: however, I saw that they sometimes grew numerous, and then the weak were caught by the strong, and with a grinning aspect, first coupled with, & then devour'd, by plucking off first one limb and then another, till the body was left a helpless trunk; this, after grinning & kissing it with seeming fondness, they devour'd too; and here & there I saw one savourily picking the flesh off his own tail; as the stench terribly annoy'd us both, we went into the mill, & I in my hand brought the skeleton of a body, which in the mill was Aristotle's Analytics.

So the Angel said: "thy phantasy has imposed upon me, & thou oughtest to be ashamed."

I answer'd "we impose on one another, & it is but lost time to converse with you whose works are only Analytics."

Opposition is true friendship.

I have always found that Angels have the vanity to speak of themselves as the only wise; this they do with a confident insolence sprouting from systematic reasoning.

Thus Swedenborg boasts that what he writes is new: tho' it is only the Contents or Index of already publish'd books.

A man carried a monkey about for a shew, & because he was a little wiser than the monkey, grew vain, and conceiv'd himself as much wiser than seven men. It is so with Swedenborg: he shews the folly of churches, & exposes hypocrites, till he imagines that all are religious, & himself the single one on earth that ever broke a net.

Now hear a plain fact: Swedenborg has not written one new truth. Now hear another: he has written all the old falsehoods.

And now hear the reason. He conversed with Angels who are all religious, & conversed not with Devils who all hate religion, for he was incapable thro' his conceited notions.

Thus Swedenborg's writings are a recapitulation of all superficial opinions, and an analysis of the more sublime—but no further.

Have now another plain fact. Any man of mechanical talents may, from the writings of Paracelsus or Jacob Behmen, produce ten thousand volumes of equal value with Swedenborg's, and from those of Dante or Shakespear an infinite number.

But when he has done this, let him not say that he knows better than his master, for he only holds a candle in sunshine.

A MEMORABLE FANCY

Once I saw a Devil in a flame of fire, who arose before an Angel that sat on a cloud, and the Devil utter'd these words:

"The worship of God is: Honouring his gifts in other men, each according to his genius, and loving the greatest men best: those who envy or calumniate great men hate God; for there is no other God."

The Angel hearing this became almost blue; but mastering himself he grew yellow, & at last white, pink, & smiling, and then replied:

"Thou Idolater! is not God One? & is not he visible in Jesus Christ? and has not Jesus Christ given his sanction to the law of ten commandments? and are not all other men fools, sinners, & nothings?"

The Devil answer'd: "bray a fool in a morter with wheat, yet shall not his folly be beaten out of him; if Jesus Christ is the greatest man, you ought to love him in the greatest degree; now hear how he has given his sanction to the law of ten commandments: did he not mock at the sabbath and so mock the sabbath's God? murder those who were murder'd because of him? turn away the law from the woman taken in adultery? steal the labor of others to support him? bear false witness when he omitted making a defence before Pilate? covet when he pray'd for his disciples, and when he bid them shake off the dust of their feet against such as refused to lodge them? I tell you, no virtue can exist without breaking these ten commandments. Jesus was all virtue, and acted from impulse, not from rules."

When he had so spoken, I beheld the Angel, who stretched out his arms, embracing the flame of fire, & he was consumed and arose as Elijah.

NOTE: This Angel, who is now become a Devil, is my particular friend; we often read the Bible together in its infernal or diabolical sense, which the world shall have whether they will or no.

One Law for the Lion & Ox is Oppression.

ROBERT BURNS *(1759–1796)*

Burns's satiric poems here differ in tone and technique. The "Address to the Unco Guid" moves from ironic attack to direct moral exhortation, a movement paralleled by Burns's abandonment of the Scottish dialect of the first six stanzas for the rather stiff formality of pulpit English in the last two. This tendency toward a final moral generalization that shifts the poem from the concrete to the abstract, from dramatic implication to direct statement, is suppressed in "Holy Willie's Prayer," and the result is a release of satiric energy. This poem takes the form of a dramatic monologue in which we follow the self-protective maneuverings of Holy Willie's prayer to a God who looks very much like Holy Willie. To paraphrase Oscar Levant, Burns has stripped away the false hypocrisy of the public Willie to expose the real hypocrisy of the private Willie.

ADDRESS TO THE UNCO GUID, OR THE RIGIDLY RIGHTEOUS

> *My son, these maxims make a rule,*
> *An' lump them ay thegither;*
> *The* Rigid Righteous *is a fool,*
> *The* Rigid Wise *anither:*
> *The* Cleanest corn *that e'er was dight**

---

* *corn...dight:* grain that ever was winnowed.

May hae some pyles o' caff† in;
So ne'er a fellow-creature slight
For random fits o' daffin.‡
SOLOMON (Eccles. vii, 16.)§

O ye, wha are sae guid yoursel,
    Sae pious and sae holy,
Ye've nought to do but mark and tell
    Your neebours' fauts and folly;
Whase life is like a weel-gaun mill,   5
    Supplied wi' store o' water;
The heapet happer's ebbing still,
    An' still the clap plays clatter!

Hear me, ye venerable core,
    As counsel for poor mortals   10
That frequent pass douce Wisdom's door
    For glaikit Folly's portals;
I for their thoughtless, careless sakes
    Would here propone defences—
Their donsie tricks, their black mistakes,   15
    Their failings and mischances.

Ye see your state wi' theirs compared,
    And shudder at the niffer;
But cast a moment's fair regard,
    What makes the mighty differ?   20
Discount what scant occasion gave,
    That purity ye pride in,
And (what's aft mair than a' the lave)
    Your better art o' hidin.

Think, when your castigated pulse   25
    Gies now and then a wallop,
What ragings must his veins convulse
    That still eternal gallop:
Wi' wind and tide fair i' your tail,
    Right on ye scud your sea-way;   30
But in the teeth o' baith to sail,
    It makes an unco leeway.

See Social Life and Glee sit down,
    All joyous and unthinking,
Till, quite transmugrified, they're grown   35

---

† *pyles o' caff:* grains of chaff.
‡ *daffin:* folly.
§ "Be not righteous over much; neither make thyself over wise: why shouldest thou destroy thyself?"

---

5 *weel-gaun:* well-going. 7 *happer:* hopper (into which the grain is poured). 8 *clap:* clapper—device that jiggles the hopper. 9 *core:* company. 11 *douce:* grave, prudent. 12 *glaikit:* thoughtless. 14 *propone:* propose. 15 *donsie:* unlucky. 18 *niffer:* exchange. 23 *lave:* rest. 32 *unco:* very great.

Debauchery and Drinking:
  Oh, would they stay to calculate
Th' eternal consequences;
  Or—your more dreaded hell to state—
Damnation of expenses!   40

Ye high, exalted, virtuous dames,
  Tied up in godly laces,
Before ye gie poor Frailty names,
  Suppose a change o' cases:
A dear-loved lad, convenience snug,   45
  A treach'rous inclination—
But, let me whisper i' your lug,
  Ye're aiblins nae temptation.

Then gently scan your brother man,
  Still gentler sister woman;   50
Tho' they may gang a kennin wrang,
  To step aside is human:
One point must still be greatly dark,
  The moving *why* they do it;
And just as lamely can ye mark   55
  How far perhaps they rue it.

Who made the heart, 'tis He alone
  Decidedly can try us;
He knows each chord, its various tone,
  Each spring, its various bias: 60
Then at the balance, let's be mute,
  We never can adjust it;
What's done we partly may compute,
  But know not what's resisted.

HOLY WILLIE'S PRAYER

And send the godly in a pet to pray.

Pope.*

ARGUMENT

Holy Willie† was a rather oldish bachelor elder, in the parish of Mauchline, and much and justly famed for that polemical chattering which ends in tippling orthodoxy, and for that spiritualised bawdry which refines to liquorish devotion. In a sessional process with a gentleman in Mauchline—a Mr. Gavin Hamilton—Holy Willie and his priest, Father Auld, after full hearing in the Presbytery of Ayr,‡ came off but second best,

---

* *Pope:* "The Rape of the Lock," IV. 64.
† *Holy Willie:* William Fisher (1737–1809), an elder in the parish church at Mauchline.
‡ *Presbytery of Ayr:* a court composed of Presbyterian ministers and elders representing the congregations within the county of Ayr (southwestern Scotland); the court met at Mauchline, near where Burns was born.

---

47 *lug*: ear. 48 *aiblins*: perhaps. 51 *kennin*: little.

owing partly to the oratorical powers of Mr. Robert Aiken, Mr. Hamilton's counsel; but chiefly to Mr. Hamilton's being one of the most irreproachable and truly respectable characters in the country. On losing his process, the muse overheard him at his devotions as follows:

O Thou that in the Heavens does dwell,
Wha, as it pleases best Thysel,
Sends ane to Heaven an' ten to Hell
  A' for Thy glory,
And no for onie guid or ill   5
  They've done before Thee!

I bless and praise Thy matchless might,
When thousands Thou hast left in night,
That I am here before Thy sight,
  For gifts an' grace   10
A burning and a shining light
  To a' this place.

What was I, or my generation,
That I should get sic exaltation?
I, wha deserved most just damnation   15
  For broken laws
Sax thousand years ere my creation,
  Thro' Adam's cause!

When from my mither's womb I fell,
Thou might hae plunged me deep in hell,   20
To gnash my gooms, and weep, and wail
  In burning lakes,
Whare damnéd devils roar and yell,
  Chained to their stakes.

Yet I am here, a chosen sample,   25
To show Thy grace is great and ample:
I'm here a pillar o' Thy temple,
  Strong as a rock
A guide, a buckler, and example
  To a' Thy flock.   30

But yet, O Lord! confess I must;
At times I'm fashed wi' fleshly lust;
An' sometimes, too, in warldly trust,
  Vile self gets in;
But Thou remembers we are dust,   35
  Defiled wi' sin.

O Lord! yestreen, Thou kens, wi' Meg—
Thy pardon I sincerely beg—

---

2 *Thysel*: Thyself.   5 *onie guid*: any good.   14 *sic*: such.   17 *Sax...creation*: It was formerly held that the Fall of Adam and Eve occurred about six thousand years earlier. 29 *buckler*: a small round shield. Here, it means "defender."   32 *fashed*: troubled, disturbed. 37 *kens*: knowest.

Oh may 't ne're be a living plague
    To my dishonour!
An' I'll ne'er lift a lawless leg   40
    Again upon her.

Besides, I farther maun avow—
Wi' Leezie's lass, three times, I trow—
But, Lord, that Friday I was fou,   45
    When I cam near her,
Or else, Thou kens, Thy servant true
    Wad never steer her.

Maybe Thou lets this fleshly thorn
Buffet Thy servant e'en and morn,   50
Lest he owre proud and high should turn
    That he's sae gifted:
If sae, Thy han' maun e'en be borne
    Until Thou lift it.

Lord, bless Thy chosen in this place,   55
For here Thou has a chosen race!
But God confound their stubborn face
    An' blast their name,
Wha bring Thy elders to disgrace
    An' open shame!   60

Lord, mind Gau'n Hamilton's deserts:
He drinks, an' swears, an' plays at cartes,
Yet has sae monie takin arts
    Wi' great and sma',
Frae God's ain priest the people's hearts   65
    He steals awa.

And when we chastened him therefore,
Thou kens how he bred sic a splore,
And set the warld in a roar
    O' laughin at us: 70
Curse Thou his basket and his store,
    Kail an' potatoes!

Lord, hear my earnest cry and prayer,
Against that Presbytery of Ayr!
Thy strong right hand, Lord, mak it bare   75
    Upo' their heads!
Lord, visit them, an' dinna spare,
    For their misdeeds!

O Lord, my God! that glib-tongued Aiken,
My vera heart and flesh are quakin,   80
To think how we stood sweatin, shakin,

---

43 *maun*: must. 45 *fou*: full (of liquor). 48 *steer*: disturb. 51 *owre*: over(ly). 63 *takin*: charming. 68 *splore*: fuss, row. 72 *kail*: a kind of cabbage. 75 *bare*: bear down, strike.

An' pished wi' dread,
While he, wi' hingin lip an' snakin,
    Held up his head.

Lord, in Thy day o' vengeance try him!   85
Lord, visit him wha did employ him!
And pass not in Thy mercy by them,
    Nor hear their prayer,
But for Thy people's sake destroy them,
    An' dinna spare!   90

But, Lord, remember me and mine
Wi' mercies temporal and divine,
That I for grace an' gear may shine
    Excelled by nane;
And a' the glory shall be Thine—   95
    Amen, Amen!

GEORGE GORDON, LORD BYRON

Popularly imagined as a super-romantic, indistinguishable from the "Byronic hero" and hence from the demonic, mysterious, and cursed, Byron was actually as much neoclassic as Romantic. In an age in which poets prided themselves upon liberating poetic feeling and expression from the bonds of eighteenth-century reason and verse forms, Byron as a young man stood out as the writer of *English Bards and Scotch Reviewers,* a formal verse satire in heroic couplets that damned, among others, the Lakists (Wordsworth, Coleridge, Southey) and held up Pope as the model of poetic excellence. Although he went on to write lyrics and a quasi-romance (*Childe Harold's Pilgrimage*), he distinguished himself, not in the literary forms most popular among the romantics—song, reflective lyric, ode, ballad—but in satires like *Beppo, The Vision of Judgment,* and *Don Juan.* In the drama, when everyone else was turning to Elizabethan-Jacobean models (Wordsworth's *The Borderers,* Coleridge's *Remorse,* Keats's *Otho the Great,* Shelley's *The Cenci*), Byron, like his neoclassic predecessors, sought the compression, balance, and order of classical Greek tragedy.

    Don Juan is ostensibly a mock-epic poem—"My poem's epic, and is meant to be / Divided in twelve books"—but it is less mock-epic than mock-romance, a comic-satiric version of the Renaissance Italian romances of Pulci, Ariosto, and Tasso. His hero derives from the old Spanish legend of the dashing, heroically licentious, demonic lover whose exploits had been dramatized by Tirso de Molina, Molière, Goldoni, and Mozart. *Don Juan* was never finished, but as it is, in sixteen cantos, it is one of the longest English poems. Like the Italian romances, it employs the *ottava rima* verse form, an eight-line stanza rhyming *abababcc,* which provided Byron with six lines in which to maneuver in a relaxed, conversational tone toward a final couplet that rises to dramatic climax, turns on comic irony, or exploits satiric deflation. The Italian romance had always been a loose poetic form, episodic in action and diffuse in dramatic focus, substituting for plot coherence a great variety of incident and a swiftness of pace. Its multiple narratives were so complex and rambling, its numerous

---

82 *pished*: pissed. 83 *snakin*: sneering. 93 *gear*: goods.

characters appeared and disappeared so randomly, that the reader needed a program and map to keep track of everything. Something like this is also true of Byron's poem, not, however, because the narrative is complex but because the act of narration is complex, because the narrator continually intrudes his presence into the story in the digressive manner of Sterne's *Tristram Shandy* and Swift's *A Tale of a Tub*. Here again we have Byron as both romantic and neoclassicist. Since these digressions repeatedly interrupt, divert, and nearly destroy the poem's pretensions to epic form, they attack restrictive literary forms in general—which sounds typically romantic. The digressions seem romantic also because they invariably individualize the narrator, giving us the personal accents of the poet's voice rather than the impersonal tones of the traditional epic poet in his role as spokesman for the Muses, the nation, or God. However, since the digressions reveal the poet in the act of literary creation and since that act is presented as one of pure improvisation governed by whimsy, they also constitute a satire on the cherished romantic views about the dignity of the poetic imagination. And that should remind us that those "personal accents" are the accents not of Byron, but of his comic-satiric speaker, whose volatility of mind and mood may be unique but whose role as *persona* is in the eighteenth-century tradition.

from DON JUAN (Canto III)

78

And now they were diverted by their suite,
    Dwarfs, dancing girls, black eunuchs, and a poet,
Which made their new establishment complete;
    The last was of great fame, and liked to show it;   620
His verses rarely wanted their due feet;
    And for his theme—he seldom sung below it,
He being paid to satirize or flatter,
As the Psalm says, "inditing a good matter."

79

He praised the present, and abused the past,   625
    Reversing the good custom of old days,
An Eastern anti-jacobin at last
    He turned, preferring pudding to *no* praise—
For some few years his lot had been o'ercast
    By his seeming independent in his lays,   630
But now he sung the Sultan and the Pasha—
With truth like Southey, and with verse like Crashaw.

---

617 *they*: i.e., Haidée (rhymes with "tidy") and Don Juan (rhymes with "true one"). After a shipwreck, Don Juan was found on the shore of one of the smaller Greek islands by Haidée, the daughter of Lambro, a rich Greek pirate who controls the island. Haidée and Juan carry on a love affair while Lambro is at sea. After a false report of his death, Lambro returns unrecognized to find a large feast in process. He enters his castle; then the scene shifts to Haidée and Juan, who are being entertained elsewhere in the castle. 618 *a poet*: The poet is Southey, poet laureate at the time and one of Byron's favorite targets of satire (see, e.g., Byron's *The Vision of Judgment*). 624 *"inditing...matter"*: See Psalm 45:1. 627 *anti-jacobin*: an opponent of radical ideas, as Southey, like Coleridge and Wordsworth, had become. 632 *Crashaw*: seventeenth-century poet whose verse Byron regarded as contemptible.

80

He was a man who had seen many changes,
    And always changed as true as any needle;
His polar star being one which rather ranges,   635
    And not the fixed—he knew the way to wheedle:
So vile he 'scaped the doom which oft avenges;
    And being fluent (save indeed when fee'd ill),
He lied with such a fervor of intention—
There was no doubt he earn'd his laureate pension.   640

81

But he had genius,—when a turncoat has it,
    The *Vates irritabilis* takes care
That without notice few full moons shall pass it;
    Even good men like to make the public stare:—
But to my subject—let me see—what was it?   645
    Oh—the third canto—and the pretty pair—
Their loves, and feasts, and house, and dress, and mode
    Of living in their insular abode.

82

Their poet, a sad trimmer, but no less
    In company a very pleasant fellow,   650
Had been the favorite of full many a mess
    Of men, and made them speeches when half mellow;
And though his meaning they could rarely guess,
    Yet still they deigned to hiccup or to bellow
The glorious meed of popular applause,   655
Of which the first ne'er knows the second cause.

83

But now being lifted into high society,
    And having picked up several odds and ends
Of free thoughts in his travels, for variety,
    He deemed, being in a lone isle, among friends,   660
That without any danger of a riot, he
    Might for long lying make himself amends;
And singing as he sung in his warm youth,
Agree to a short armistice with truth.

84

He had travelled 'mongst the Arabs, Turks, and Franks,   665
    And knew the self-loves of the different nations;
And having lived with people of all ranks,
    Had something ready upon most occasions—
Which got him a few presents and some thanks.
    He varied with some skill his adulations;   670
To "do at Rome as Romans do," a piece

---

642 *Vates irritabilis*: irritable poet-prophet (see Horace, *Epistles*, II. 2. 102).   649 *trimmer*: one who changes his opinions, policies, etc. to suit the occasion.   671 *"do...do"*: St. Augustine, *Epistles*, 36, 14.

Of conduct was which he observed in Greece.

85

Thus, usually, when he was asked to sing,
　He gave the different nations something national;
'Twas all the same to him—"God save the king,"   675
　Or *"Ca ira,"* according to the fashion all:
His muse made increment of anything,
　From the high lyric down to the low rational:
If Pindar sang horse-races, what should hinder
Himself from being as pliable as Pindar?   680

86

In France, for instance, he would write a chanson;
　In England a six canto quarto tale;
In Spain he'd make a ballad or romance on
　The last war—much the same in Portugal;
In Germany, the Pegasus he'd prance on   685
　Would be old Goethe's—(see what says De Staël);
In Italy he'd ape the "Trecentisti;
In Greece, he'd sing some sort of hymn like this t' ye:

1

The isles of Greece, the isles of Greece!
　Where burning Sappho loved and sung,   690
Where grew the arts of war and peace,
　Where Delos rose, and Phœbus sprung!
Eternal summer gilds them yet,
But all, except their sun, is set.

2

The Scian and the Teian muse,   695
　The hero's harp, the lover's lute,
Have found the fame your shores refuse;
　Their place of birth alone is mute
To sounds which echo further west
Than your sires' "Islands of the Blest."   700

3

The mountains look on Marathon—
　And Marathon looks on the sea;
And musing there an hour alone,
　I dreamed that Greece might still be free;
For standing on the Persians' grave,   705
I could not deem myself a slave.

---

676 *"Ca ira"*: "it will succeed"—a song of the French Revolutionists. 679 *Pindar*: Greek
lyric poet (c. 522–433 B.C.). 681 *chanson*: song written in a simple style. 685 *Pegasus*: in
Greek mythology, a winged horse. 686 *Goethe's...De Staël*: Madame de Staël, Baronne
de Staël-Holstein (1766–1817; French writer), had recently claimed that Goethe represented
the entire literature of Germany. 687 *"Trecentisti"*: writers in the fourteenth-century
Italian Style. 695 *Scian*: Homer, of the island of Scio; *Teian*: Anacreon, of Teos, Asia
Minor. 700 *"Islands...Blest"*: mythical islands in the "Western Ocean" supposed to be
the abode of the happy dead (see Hesiod's *Works and Days,* 169). 701 *Marathon*: where,
in 490 B.C., the invading Persians were defeated by the Greek army commanded by Miltiades.

4

A king sate on the rocky brow
  Which looks o'er sea-born Salamis;
And ships, by thousands, lay below,
  And men in nations;—all were his!   710
He counted them at break of day—
And when the sun set where were they?

5

And where are they? and where art thou,
  My country? On thy voiceless shore
The heroic lay is tuneless now—   715
  The heroic bosom beats no more!
And must thy lyre, so long divine,
Degenerate into hands like mine?

6

'Tis something, in the dearth of fame,
  Though linked among a fettered race,
To feel at least a patriot's shame,   720
  Even as I sing, suffuse my face;
For what is left the poet here?
For Greeks a blush—for Greece a tear.

7

Must *we* but weep o'er days more blest?   725
  Must *we* but blush?—Our fathers bled.
Earth! render back from out thy breast
  A remnant of our Spartan dead!
Of the three hundred grant but three,
To make a new Thermopylæ!   730

8

What, silent still? and silent all?
  Ah! no;—the voices of the dead
Sound like a distant torrent's fall,
  And answer, "Let one living head,
But one arise,—we come, we come!"   735
'Tis but the living who are dumb.

9

In vain—in vain; strike other chords;
  Fill high the cup with Samian wine!
Leave battles to the Turkish hordes,
  And shed the blood of Scio's vine!   740
Hark, rising to the ignoble call—
How answers each bold Bacchanal!

10

You have the Pyrrhic dance as yet;
  Where is the Pyrrhic phalanx gone?

---

708 *Salamis*: where, in 480 B.C., the Greeks won a decisive naval victory over the fleet of
Xerxes, King of Persia.   730 *Thermopylae*: mountain pass where, in 480 B.C., 300 Spartans
fought literally to the last man in a courageous attempt to hold back the invading Persians.
738 *Samian*: from Samos, an island near Scio (line 740).   743 *Pyrric dance*: ancient war
dance.   744 *Pyrric phalanx*: military formation used by Pyrrhus (third-century B.C. Greek
general and King of Epirus).

Of two such lessons, why forget   745
   The nobler and the manlier one?
You have the letters Cadmus gave—
Think ye he meant them for a slave?

11

Fill high the bowl with Samian wine!
   We will not think of themes like these!   750
It made Anacreon's song divine:
   He served—but served Polycrates—
A tyrant; but our masters then
Were still, at least, our countrymen.

12

The tyrant of the Chersonese   755
   Was freedom's best and bravest friend;
That tyrant was Miltiades!
   Oh! that the present hour would lend
Another despot of the kind!
Such chains as his were sure to bind.   760

13

Fill high the bowl with Samian wine!
   On Suli's rock, and Parga's shore,
Exists the remnant of a line
   Such as the Doric mothers bore;
And there, perhaps, some seed is sown,   765
The Heracleidan blood might own.

14

Trust not for freedom to the Franks—
   They have a king who buys and sells;
In native swords, and native ranks,
   The only hope of courage dwells;   770
But Turkish force, and Latin fraud,
Would break your shield, however broad.

15

Fill high the bowl with Samian wine!
   Our virgins dance beneath the shade—
I see their glorious black eyes shine;   775
   But gazing on each glowing maid,
My own the burning tear-drop laves,
To think such breasts must suckle slaves.

16

Place me on Sunium's marbled steep,
   Where nothing, save the waves and I,   780
May hear our mutual murmurs sweep;

---

747 *Cadmus*: legendary inventor of the alphabet. 752 *Polycrates*: Tyrant (King) of Samos, at whose court Anacreon lived for awhile. 757 *Miltiades*: sixth-century B.C. Athenian general who founded a colony in the Thracian Chersonese and ruled tyrannically. Byron has perhaps confused him with another Miltiades (see note to line 701). 762–66 *On...own*: the Albanians, who had fought off the Turks at various times; *Heracleidan* pertains to Heracles (Hercules). 767 *Franks*: in the Near East, a name given to western Europeans.

There, swan-like, let me sing and die:
A land of slaves shall ne'er be mine—
Dash down yon cup of Samian wine!

87

Thus sung, or would, or could, or should have sung,   785
   The modern Greek, in tolerable verse;
If not like Orpheus quite, when Greece was young,
   Yet in these times he might have done much worse:
His strain displayed some feeling—right or wrong;
   And feeling, in a poet, is the source   790
Of others' feeling; but they are such liars,
And take all colors—like the hands of dyers.

88

But words are things, and a small drop of ink,
   Falling like dew, upon a thought, produces
That which makes thousands, perhaps millions, think;   795
   'Tis strange, the shortest letter which man uses
Instead of speech, may form a lasting link
   Of ages; to what straits old Time reduces
Frail man, when paper—even a rag like this,
Survives himself, his tomb, and all that's his!   800

89

And when his bones are dust, his grave a blank,
   His station, generation, even his nation,
Become a thing, or nothing, save to rank
   In chronological commemoration,
Some dull MS. oblivion long has sank,   805
   Or graven stone found in a barrack's station
In digging the foundation of a closet,
May turn his name up, as a rare deposit.

90

And glory long has made the sages smile;
   'Tis something, nothing, words, illusion, wind—   810
Depending more upon the historian's style
   Than on the name a person leaves behind:
Troy owes to Homer what whist owes to Hoyle:
   The present century was growing blind
To the great Marlborough's skill in giving knocks,   815
Until his late Life by Archdeacon Coxe.

91

Milton's the prince of poets—so we say;
   A little heavy, but no less divine:
An independent being in his day—
   Learn'd, pious, temperate in love and wine;   820

---

813 *Hoyle*: Edmond Hoyle wrote a book on the card game of whist (1742). 816 *Coxe*: William Coxe, Archdeacon of Wiltshire, helped revive the fame of John Churchill, Duke of Marlborough (1650–1722; English general) by publishing Marlborough's *Memoirs* in 1817–1819.

But, his life falling into Johnson's way,
   We're told this great high priest of all the Nine
Was whipt at college—a harsh sire—odd spouse,
For the first Mrs. Milton left his house.

92

All these are, *certes*, entertaining facts,   825
   Like Shakespeare's stealing deer, Lord Bacon's bribes;
Like Titus' youth, and Caesar's earliest acts;
   Like Burns (whom Doctor Currie well describes);
Like Cromwell's pranks;—but although truth exacts
   These amiable descriptions from the scribes,   830
As most essential to their hero's story,
They do not much contribute to his glory.

93

All are not moralists, like Southey, when
   He prated to the world of "Pantisocracy;"
Or Wordsworth unexcised, unhired, who then   835
   Seasoned his pedlar poems with Democracy;
Or Coleridge, long before his flighty pen
   Let to the *Morning Post* its aristocracy;
When he and Southey, following the same path,
Espoused two partners (milliners of Bath).   840

94

Such names at present cut a convict figure,
   The very Botany Bay in moral geography;
Their loyal treason, renegado rigor,
   Are good manure for their more bare biography.
Wordsworth's last quarto, by the way, is bigger   845
   Than any since the birthday of typography;
A drowsy frowsy poem, called the *"Excursion,"*
Writ in a manner which is my aversion

95

He there builds up a formidable dyke
   Between his own and others' intellect;   850
But Wordsworth's poem, and his followers, like
   Joanna Southcote's Shiloh, and her sect,

---

821 *his...way*: Johnson included a rather unsympathetic biography of Milton in his *Lives of the English Poets* (1779–1780). 822 *Nine:* the nine Muses. 827 *Titus'...acts*: The youth of Titus Vespasianus (Roman Emperor, 79–81), like that of Julius Caesar and Robert Burns (line 828), was noted for its dissoluteness. 828 *Currie*: Dr. James Currie wrote a *Life of Robert Burns* (1800). 829 *Cromwell's pranks*: Cromwell was supposed to have robbed orchards as a youth. 834 *"Pantisocracy"*: the plan of Southey and Coleridge for an ideal commonwealth to be established in America. 835 *unexcised*: Wordsworth held a sinecure position as distributor of stamps. 838 *Morning Post*: In 1798 Coleridge, no longer full of revolutionary ardor, began writing political articles for the *Morning Post*, a liberal newspaper. 840 *two partners*: Edith and Sarah Fricker. 842 *Botany Bay*: English convict colony in New South Wales, Australia. 852 *Joanna Southcote*: popular religious fanatic who predicted in 1813, when she was over 60, that in 1814 she would give birth to a new Messiah.

Are things which in this century don't strike
    The public mind—so few are the elect;
And the new births of both their stale virginities   855
Have proved but dropsies, taken for divinities.

96

But let me to my story: I must own,
    If I have any fault, it is digression—
Leaving my people to proceed alone,
    While I soliloquize beyond expression;   860
But these are my addresses from the throne,
    Which put off business to the ensuring session:
Forgetting each omission is a loss to
The world, not quite so great as Ariosto.

97

I know that what our neighbors call *"longueurs"*   865
    (We've not so good a *word*, but have the *thing*,
In that complete perfection which insures
    An epic from Bob Southey every spring),
Form not the true temptation which allures
    The reader; but 'twould not be hard to bring   870
Some fine examples of the *epopée*,
To prove its grand ingredient is *ennui*.

98

We learn from Horace, "Homer sometimes sleeps;"
    We feel without him,—Wordsworth sometimes wakes,—
To show with what complacency he creeps,   875
    With his dear *"Waggoners,"* around his lakes.
He wishes for "a boat" to sail the deeps—
    Of Ocean?—No, of air; and then he makes
Another outcry for "a little boat,"
And drivels seas to set it well afloat.   880

99

If he must fain sweep o'er the ethereal plain,
    And Pegasus runs restive in his "Waggon,"
Could he not beg the loan of Charles's Wain?
    Or pray Medea for a single dragon?
Or if, too classic for his vulgar brain,   885
    He feared his neck to venture such a nag on,
And he must needs mount nearer to the moon,
Could not the blockhead ask for a balloon?

---

856 *dropsies:* Instead of giving birth to a Messiah in 1814 (see previous note), Miss Southcote died of dropsy in that year.   864 *Ariosto:* (1474–1533; Italian romantic poet, author of *Orlando Furioso*).   865 *"longeurs"*: long, dull, wearisome passages.   871 *epopée*: epic. 873 *Horace:* in *Ars Poetica* ("Art of Poetry"), 359.   883 *Charles's Wain:* i.e., Charles's Wagon, the constellation that we call the Great Bear or the Big Dipper.   884 *Medea:* Medea used a chariot pulled by dragons or winged serpents.

100

"Pedlars," and "Boats," and "Waggons!" Oh! ye shades
  Of Pope and Dryden, are we come to this?   890
That trash of such sort not alone evades
  Contempt, but from the bathos' vast abyss
Floats scumlike uppermost, and these Jack Cades
  Of sense and song above your graves may hiss—
The "little boatman" and his "Peter Bell"   895
Can sneer at him who drew "Achitophel"!

101

T' our tale.—The feast was over, the slaves gone,
  The dwarfs and dancing girls had all retired;
The Arab lore and Poet's song were done,
  And every sound of revelry expired;   900
The lady and her lover, left alone,
  The rosy flood of Twilight's sky admired;—
Ave Maria! o'er the earth and sea,
That heavenliest hour of Heaven is worthiest thee!

102

Ave Maria! blessèd be the hour!   905
  The time, the clime, the spot, where I so oft
Have felt that moment in its fullest power
  Sink o'er the earth so beautiful and soft,
While swung the deep bell in the distant tower,
  Or the faint dying day-hymn stole aloft,   910
And not a breath crept through the rosy air,
And yet the forest leaves seemed stirred with prayer.

103

Ave Maria! 'tis the hour of prayer!
  Ave Maria! 'tis the hour of Love!
Ave Maria! may our spirits dare   915
  Look up to thine and to thy Son's above!
Ave Maria! oh that face so fair!
  Those downcast eyes beneath the Almighty Dove—
What though 'tis but a pictured image?—strike—
That painting is no idol,—'tis too like.   920

104

Some kinder casuists are pleased to say,
  In nameless print—that I have no devotion;
But set those persons down with me to pray,
  And you shall see who has the properest notion
Of getting into Heaven the shortest way;   925
  My altars are the mountains and the Ocean,

---

893 *Jack Cade*: a commoner who pretended to be a nobleman while leading an uprising
against Henry VI in 1450. See Shakespeare's *2 Henry VI*, Act IV. 896 *"Achitophel"*: refers
to Dryden's *Absalom and Achitophel* (1681). 921 *casuists*: practicers of subtle and specious
logic.

Earth, air, stars,—all that springs from the great Whole,
Who hath produced, and will receive the Soul.

105

Sweet Hour of Twilight!—in the solitude
    Of the pine forest, and the silent shore   930
Which bounds Ravenna's immemorial wood,
    Rooted where once the Adrian wave flowed o'er,
To where the last Caesarean fortress stood,
    Evergreen forest! which Boccaccio's lore
And Dryden's lay made haunted ground to me,   935
How have I loved the twilight hour and thee!

106

The shrill cicalas, people of the pine,
    Making their summer lives one ceaseless song,
Were the sole echoes, save my steed's and mine,
    And vesper bell's that rose the boughs along;   940
The spectre huntsman of Onesti's line,
    His hell-dogs, and their chase, and the fair throng
Which learned from this example not to fly
From a true lover,—shadowed my mind's eye.

107

Oh, Hesperus! thou bringest all good things—   945
    Home to the weary, to the hungry cheer,
To the young bird the parent's brooding wings,
    The welcome stall to the o'erlabored steer;
Whate'er of peace about our hearthstone clings,
    What'er our household gods protect of dear,   950
Are gathered round us by thy look of rest;
Thou bring'st the child, too, to the mother's breast.

108

Soft hour! which wakes the wish and melts the heart
    Of those who sail the seas, on the first day
When they from their sweet friends are torn apart;   955
    Or fills with love the pilgrim on his way
As the far bell of vesper makes him start,
    Seeming to weep the dying day's decay;
Is this a fancy which our reason scorns?
Ah! surely nothing dies but something mourns!   960

109

When Nero perished by the justest doom
    Which ever the destroyer yet destroyed,

935 *Dryden's lay: Theodore and Honoria,* a poem by Dryden based on a story in Boccaccio's *Decameron.* 936 *How...thee*: Byron spent a good deal of time at Ravenna, Italy, while writing this third canto. 937 *cicalas*: locusts. 941 *Onesti's*: "Onesti" was the family name of Boccaccio's hero; "Theodore" was the name of Dryden's hero. The story tells how Honoria, a pitiless lady beloved by Onesti, finally accepts Onesti after she has seen the spirit of another merciless woman pursued by a spectre huntsman and his "hell-dogs."

Amidst the roar of liberated Rome,
  Of nations freed, and the world overjoyed,
Some hands unseen strewed flowers upon his tomb: 965
  Perhaps the weakness of a heart not void
Of feeling for some kindness done, when power
Had left the wretch an uncorrupted hour.

110

But I'm digressing; what on earth has Nero,
  Or any such like sovereign buffoons,   970
To do with the transactions of my hero,
  More than such madmen's fellow man—the moon's?
Sure my invention must be down at zero,
  And I grown one of many "wooden spoons"
Of verse (the name with which we Cantabs please   975
To dub the last of honors in degrees).

111

I feel this tediousness will never do—
  'Tis being *too* epic, and I must cut down
(In copying) this long canto into two;
  They'll never find it out, unless I own,   980
The fact, excepting some experienced few;
  And then as an improvement 'twill be shown:
I'll prove that such the opinion of the critic is
From Aristotle *passim.*—See Ποιητικῆς.

ARTHUR HUGH CLOUGH *(1819–1861)*

The religious faith that Clough acquired in childhood was, like that of many Victorians, subjected to severe pressure by scientific challenges to Biblical authenticity. Clough became a skeptic, neither accepting nor rejecting belief. "The Latest Decalogue," with its dead-pan reformulation of the Mosaic code in terms of contemporary economic expediency, could serve as poetic epilogue to Swift's *Argument Against Abolishing Christianity.*

THE LATEST DECALOGUE

Thou shalt have one God only; who
Would be at the expense of two?
No graven images may be
Worshiped, except the currency.
Swear not at all; for, for thy curse   5
Thine enemy is none the worse.
At church on Sunday to attend
Will serve to keep the world thy friend.
Honor thy parents; that is, all
From whom advancement may befall.   10
Thou shalt not kill; but need'st not strive

---

975 *Cantabs:* Cantabrigians—i.e., Cambridge University men.   984 ποιηγικῆς: *Poetics.*

Officiously to keep alive.
Do not adultery commit;
Advantage rarely comes of it.
Thou shalt not steal; an empty feat,   15
When it's so lucrative to cheat.
Bear not false witness; let the lie
Have time on its own wings to fly.
Thou shalt not covet, but tradition
Approves all forms of competition.   20
The sum of all is, thou shalt love,
If anybody, God above:
At any rate shall never labor
More than thyself to love thy neighbor.

THOMAS HARDY *(1840–1928)*

Hardy's brief drama of the pride that goeth before a mirror ingeniously exploits the disparate perspectives of preacher, pupil, and reader. The inclusion of the pupil onlooker splits the scene into half-satire, half-pathos.

IN CHURCH*

"And now to God the Father," he ends,
And his voice thrills up to the topmost tiles:
Each listener chokes as he bows and bends,
And emotion pervades the crowded aisles.
Then the preacher glides to the vestry-door,   5
And shuts it, and thinks he is seen no more.

The door swings softly ajar meanwhile,
And a pupil of his in the Bible class,
Who adores him as one without gloss or guile,
Sees her idol stand with a satisfied smile   10
And re-enact at the vestry-glass
Each pulpit gesture in deft dumb-show
That had moved the congregation so.

JOHN MASEFIELD *(1878–   )*

Mock-heroic poems like *Mac Flecknoe* and *The Dunciad* exploit a continuous disproportion between style and content. "Cargoes" creates its disproportion by simple juxtaposition, the first two stanzas providing a destructive point of reference for the third.

CARGOES†

Quinquireme of Nineveh from distant Ophir,
Rowing home to haven in sunny Palestine,

* Reprinted from Collected Poems of Thomas Hardy by permission of the Estate, Macmillan & Co., Ltd., London, and The Macmillan Company of Canada Limited.
† Reprinted with permission of the publisher from *Collected Poems* by John Masefield. Copyright 1912 by The Macmillan Company, renewed 1940 by John Masefield.

With a cargo of ivory,
And apes and peacocks,
Sandalwood, cedarwood, and sweet white wine.   5

Stately Spanish galleon coming from the Isthmus,
Dipping through the Tropics by the palm-green shores,
With a cargo of diamonds,
Emeralds, amethysts,
Topazes, and cinnamon, and gold moidores.   10

Dirty British coaster with a salt-caked smoke-stack,
Butting through the Channel in the mad March days,
With a cargo of Tyne coal,
Road-rails, pig-lead,
Firewood, iron-ware, and cheap tin trays.   15

T. S. ELIOT *(1888–1965)*

Most of Eliot's early poetry—notably "Prufrock," "The Waste Land," and "The Hollow Men"—is satiric, featuring a modern world of diminished people in whom the unifying values of an earlier time (Classical Greece, for instance, or Renaissance Italy and England) have become dissociated, fragmented, or lost entirely. The Ideal as man's cultural past enters these poems in the form of allusions to myth, ritual, and literature, and stands as a poetic backdrop against which the Real, the immediate modern experience depicted, is trivialized by contrast. Eliot's irony is not bitterly Juvenalian but faintly melancholy; his tone is drily elegiac, reflecting regret at what man has lost by his cultural and spiritual "fall" and yet a kind of elegant derision at the fallen state itself.

"Prufrock" is indirect satire. Eliot does not flay the modern world with direct denunciation; he creates a fictional character whose dramatic monologue indirectly exposes that world and himself. Prufrock's love song, as the quotation from Dante suggests, cannot actually achieve the public status of song; it is "sung" only in the chambers of Prufrock's divided consciousness. Thus it hovers, like Prufrock himself, in the shadowy region "Between the motion / And the act" ("The Hollow Men"), less a song than a prolonged stutter in the mind. As he cannot really sing, so he cannot really act. Irresolute, he wanders in mind and body through the spiritual fog of London toward "the room" where, if he dared presume, he might "force the moment to its crisis" by proposing to the unnamed woman. One reason his song remains unsung is that his identity remains unformed because there is nothing beyond himself—in a world of marmalade and porcelain at one extreme and of "sawdust restaurants with oyster-shells" at the other—with which he can "identify" and thus structure a self. This inner incompleteness or self-division (the "you and I" of the opening line, for instance, are the contrary impulses of Prufrock's mind) reflects and perhaps helps create a fractionized outer world, a world of disconnected, dreary objects and of people whose spiritual disintegration is figured in their material fragmentation into "faces that you meet," "voices," "eyes," "arms," "fingers."

Thus Prufrock, intensely aware of the triviality and incoherence of this world, cannot define himself at all in modern terms, and yet in turning to the past for some kind of identity he finds only roles that are too big for him—John the Baptist, Lazarus, Hamlet—or else degrading—"an attendant lord,"

"an easy tool," "the Fool." He can call up a memory of imaginative vitality
once possessed, a memory of "mermaids singing" and "riding seaward on the
waves," but the only voices that "sing" to him are human, so that, unlike
Lazarus, he awakens from a spiritual dreamworld of death into an even more
deadly reality.

THE LOVE SONG OF J. ALFRED PRUFROCK*

*S'io credesse che mia risposta fosse
A persona che mai tornasse al mondo,
Questa fiamma staria senza piu scosse.
Ma perciocche giammai di questo fondo
Non torno vivo alcun, s'i'odo il vero,
Senza tema d'infamia ti rispondo.†*

Let us go then, you and I,
When the evening is spread out against the sky
Like a patient etherized upon a table;
Let us go, through certain half-deserted streets,
The muttering retreats   5
Of restless nights in one-night cheap hotels
And sawdust restaurants with oyster-shells:
Streets that follow like a tedious argument
Of insidious intent
To lead you to an overwhelming question. . . .   10
Oh, do not ask, "What is it?"
Let us go and make our visit.

In the room the women come and go
Talking of Michelangelo.

The yellow fog that rubs its back upon the window-panes,   15
The yellow smoke that rubs its muzzle on the window-panes
Licked its tongue into the corners of the evening,
Lingered upon the pools that stand in drains,
Let fall upon its back the soot that falls from chimneys,
Slipped by the terrace, made a sudden leap,   20
And seeing that it was a soft October night,
Curled once about the house, and fell asleep.

And indeed there will be time
For the yellow smoke that slides along the street,

* From *Collected Poems 1909–1962,* by T. S. Eliot, copyright, 1936, by Harcourt, Brace &
World Inc., © 1963, 1964, by T. S. Eliot. Reprinted by permission of Harcourt, Brace &
World, Inc., and Faber and Faber Ltd.

† *S'io...ti rispondo:* "If I thought I were replying to someone who would return to the
world, this flame would shake no more [i.e., I would speak no more]; but since no one
has ever returned from this place, if what I hear is true, I reply without fear of infamy."
In Dante's *Inferno,* canto xxvii, these lines are spoken by one of the shades, Guido da
Montefeltro, who has been asked to tell his story. The implication is that Prufrock's love
song, sung within the inferno of self, is equally shameful and confidential. 13 *the room:*
where the party is being held, Prufrock's destination. 23 *there will be time:* alludes to
Marvell's "To His Coy Mistress"—"Had we but world enough and time" etc. (see p. 127).

Rubbing its back upon the window-panes;   25
There will be time, there will be time
To prepare a face to meet the faces that you meet;
There will be time to murder and create,
And time for all the works and days of hands
That lift and drop a question on your plate;   30
Time for you and time for me,
And time yet for a hundred indecisions,
And for a hundred visions and revisions,
Before the taking of a toast and tea.

In the room the women come and go   35
Talking of Michelangelo.

And indeed there will be time
To wonder, "Do I dare?" and, "Do I dare?"
Time to turn back and descend the stair,
With a bald spot in the middle of my hair—   40
(They will say: "How his hair is growing thin!")
My morning coat, my collar mounting firmly to the chin,
My necktie rich and modest, but asserted by a simple pin—
(They will say: "But how his arms and legs are thin!")
Do I dare   45
Disturb the universe?
In a minute there is time

For decisions and revisions which a minute will reverse.
For I have known them all already, known them all:
Have known the evenings, mornings, afternoons,   50
I have measured out my life with coffee spoons;
I know the voices dying with a dying fall
Beneath the music from a farther room.
    So how should I presume?

And I have known the eyes already, known them all—   55
The eyes that fix you in a formulated phrase,
And when I am formulated, sprawling on a pin,
When I am pinned and wriggling on the wall,
Then how should I begin
To spit out all the butt-ends of my days and ways?   60
    And how should I presume?

And I have known the arms already, known them all—
Arms that are braceleted and white and bare
(But in the lamplight, downed with light brown hair!)
Is it perfume from a dress   65
That makes me so digress?
Arms that lie along a table, or wrap about a shawl,
    And should I then presume?
    And how should I begin?

---

52 *with a dying fall*: alludes to Shakespeare's *Twelfth Night,* I.i.4: "That strain again! It had a dying fall."

Shall I say, I have gone at dusk through narrow streets   70
And watched the smoke that rises from the pipes
Of lonely men in shirt-sleeves, leaning out of windows?...

I should have been a pair of ragged claws
Scuttling across the floors of silent seas.

And the afternoon, the evening, sleeps so peacefully!   75
Smoothed by long fingers,
Asleep...tired...or it malingers,
Stretched on the floor, here beside you and me.
Should I, after tea and cakes and ices,
Have the strength to force the moment to its crisis?   80
But though I have wept and fasted, wept and prayed,
Though I have seen my head (grown slightly bald) brought in upon a platter,

I am no prophet—and here's no great matter;
I have seen the moment of my greatness flicker,
And I have seen the eternal Footman hold my coat, and snicker,   85
And in short, I was afraid.

And would it have been worth it, after all,
After the cups, the marmalade, the tea,
Among the porcelain, among some talk of you and me,
Would it have been worth while,   90
To have bitten off the matter with a smile,
To have squeezed the universe into a ball
To roll it toward some overwhelming question,
To say: "I am Lazarus, come from the dead,
Come back to tell you all, I shall tell you all"—   95
If one, settling a pillow by her head,
    Should say: "That is not what I meant at all;
    That is not it, at all."

And would it have been worth it, after all,
Would it have been worth while,   100
After the sunsets and the dooryards and the sprinkled streets,
After the novels, after the teacups, after the skirts that trail along the floor—
And this, and so much more?—
It is impossible to say just what I mean!
But as if a magic lantern threw the nerves in patterns on a screen: 105
Would it have been worth while
If one, settling a pillow or throwing off a shawl,
And turning toward the window, should say:
    "That is not it at all,
    That is not what I meant, at all."   110

No! I am not Prince Hamlet, nor was meant to be;

---

82 *head...upon a platter*: alludes to John the Baptist, beheaded by king Herod, his head
carried in on a platter to gratify Queen Herodias. 85 *eternal Footman*: perhaps Death,
perhaps merely the personification of all footmen. 92 *a ball*: alludes to Marvell's "To His
Coy Mistress"—"Let us roll all our strength and all / Our sweetness up into a ball, And
tear our pleasures with rough strife / Through the iron gates of life."

Am an attendant lord, one that will do
To swell a progress, start a scene or two,
Advise the prince; no doubt, an easy tool,
Deferential, glad to be of use,   115
Politic, cautious, and meticulous;
Full of high sentence, but a bit obtuse;
At times, indeed, almost ridiculous—
Almost, at times, the Fool.

I grow old. . . . I grow old. . . .   120
I shall wear the bottoms of my trousers rolled.

Shall I part my hair behind? Do I dare to eat a peach?
I shall wear white flannel trousers, and walk upon the beach.
I have heard the mermaids singing, each to each.

I do not think that they will sing to me.   125

I have seen them riding seaward on the waves
Combing the white hair of the waves blown back
When the wind blows the water white and black.

We have lingered in the chambers of the sea
By sea-girls wreathed with seaweed red and brown   130
Till human voices wake us, and we drown.

E. E. CUMMINGS *(1894–1962)*

No amount of denunciation could so effectively perforate chauvinistic hypocrisy
as Cummings does merely by standing aside and allowing the speaker's *pro
patria* mouthings their own windy outlet. The satire takes its force not merely
from the self-parody of the speaker's words but also from the narrator's concluding comment, which brings the whole scene into visual focus and which,
in its flat, reportorial succinctness, provides a stylistic frame for those words.

NEXT TO OF COURSE GOD AMERICA I*

"next to of course god america i
love you land of the pilgrims' and so forth oh
say can you see by the dawn's early my
country 'tis of centuries come and go
and are no more what of it we should worry   5
in every language even deafanddumb
thy sons acclaim your glorious name by gorry
by jingo by gee by gosh by gum
why talk of beauty what could be more beaut-
iful than these heroic happy dead   10

---

113 *progress*: an official trip by royalty through the land. 117 *sentence*: in its older sense,
"maxims, aphorisms, opinions." 124 *mermaids singing*: alludes to Donne's "Song: Go and
Catch a Falling Star"—"Teach me to hear mermaids singing" etc. (see p. 35).

who rushed like lions to the roaring slaughter
they did not stop to think they died instead
then shall the voice of liberty be mute?"

He spoke. And drank rapidly a glass of water

JOHN BETJEMAN *(1906–   )*

Like Burns's "Holy Willie's Prayer," Betjeman's poem uses the dramatic monologue as an instrument of satire, both poems giving us direct access to the worshiper's devotions. The poem ridicules the hypocrisy of the British "establishment" in its religious, economic, and colonial aspects.

IN WESTMINSTER ABBEY*

Let me take this other glove off
   As the *vox humana* swells,
And the beauteous fields of Eden
   Bask beneath the Abbey bells.
Here, where England's statesmen lie,   5
Listen to a lady's cry.

Gracious Lord, oh bomb the Germans.
   Spare their women for Thy Sake,
And if that is not too easy
   We will pardon Thy Mistake.   10
But, gracious Lord, whate'er shall be,
Don't let anyone bomb me.

Keep our Empire undismembered
   Guide our Forces by Thy Hand,
Gallant blacks from far Jamaica,   15
   Honduras and Togoland;
Protect them Lord in all their fights,
And, even more, protect the whites.

Think of what our Nation stands for,
   Books from Boots' and country lanes,   20
Free speech, free passes, class distinction,
   Democracy and proper drains.
Lord, put beneath Thy special care
One-eighty-nine Cadogan Square.

Although dear Lord I am a sinner,   25
   I have done no major crime;
Now I'll come to Evening Service
   Whensoever I have time.
So, Lord, reserve for me a crown,
And do not let my shares go down.   30

---

* From *Slick But Not Streamlined* by John Betjeman. Reprinted by permission of the author.

2 *vox humana*: an organ stop that imitates the human voice. 20 *Boots'*: a lending-library system in England.

I will labour for Thy Kingdom,
   Help our lads to win the war,
Send white feathers to the cowards,
   Join the Women's Army Corps,
Then wash the Steps around Thy Throne   35
In the Eternal Safety Zone.

Now I feel a little better,
   What a treat to hear Thy Word,
Where the bones of leading statesmen,
   Have so often been interred.   40
And now, dear Lord, I cannot wait
Because I have a luncheon date.

                  1940

Appendix

The Nature of Literature: Critical Views

To define "literature" we must put it first into a general class and then distinguish it from all other members of that class. The first step is easy enough, since whatever else it may be, literature *is* verbal formulation, either oral or written. But distinguishing literature from other kinds of verbal formulation like philosophy, history, rhetoric, and ordinary speech is a different matter. We can begin by surveying some of the more persistent views of literature, drawing upon Meyer H. Abrams' observation in *The Mirror and the Lamp* that literary theories tend to fall into four categories depending upon which of four elements of art is stressed: (1) the *universe* or outside world that the poem reflects, represents, or imitates—"life"; (2) the *audience* to whom the poem is addressed; (3) the *poet* or writer; or (4) the *poem* itself. If the critic focuses upon the universe represented in the work, he is taking a MIMETIC view of literature; if upon the audience and the poem's effect, a PRAGMATIC view; if upon the poet who expresses himself in the poem, an EXPRESSIVE view; and if upon the poem itself, the literary object, an OBJECTIVE view. This is by no means the only way to classify critical theories—or, for that matter, critics; and no critic or theory would fall entirely and neatly within any one category. But it is a logical, reasonably simple scheme, and for our purposes of getting the lay of the critical land it ought to prove helpful.

I.   The Mimetic View: The Poem as Imitation   *Mimetic* comes from the Greek word *mimesis,* meaning "imitation." One of the earliest mimetic critics is Plato (427–347 B.C.), who in *The Republic* likens the painter to a man walking about with a mirror in which he reproduces the external world. Plato's famous rejection of artists from his ideal city stems in part from his view of art as mimesis, for what was alone fully real to Plato was the abstract world of Ideas or Universals; not particular chairs, tables, or horses but the perfect and enduring Idea of chair, table, or horse that is common to all members of each class. Since everything we see is but an imperfect version of the Idea of its class, and since artists imitate what we see, works of art are therefore twice removed from true Reality.

Like a good but original pupil, Aristotle (384–322 B.C.) shrewdly accepted the basic premise of his teacher but turned it to an entirely different use. In *The Poetics* he speaks of music, dancing, and literature as imitative arts. But unlike Plato he considers art not so much a copy of nature, a reproduction of external reality, as a representation of the humanly meaningful in nature. Thus he says that poetry is more philosophical than history because history records what actually happened—and actual human experience is chaotic and often illogical—whereas poetry removes the accidental from human experience in the process of giving it form and meaning. In this way, Aristotle takes an important step toward investing literature with the very qualities denied it by Plato—the universal and typical.

But the complete reversal of Plato's condemnation of mimetic art issued from his own metaphysical system in the hands of the Neo-Platonists, especially the philosopher Plotinus (A.D. 205?–270), who said that art should not be disparaged for imitating natural objects because it gives "no bare reproduction of the thing seen but goes back to the very Ideas from which Nature itself derives."

Partly as a consequence of using Platonism against Plato, the mimetic view of literature prevailed in classical times and indeed well into the eighteenth century. In the Renaissance it is perhaps most memorably recorded in Hamlet's remark to the players that the purpose of drama "both at the first and now, was and is, to hold, as 'twere, the mirror up to nature; to show virtue her own feature, scorn her own image, and the very age and body of the time his form and pressure." In 1774 Thomas Warton observed that literature has the "peculiar merit of faithfully recording the features of the times, and of preserving the most picturesque and expressive representation of manners." Despite the rise of Romanticism in the late eighteenth century and the shift of critical emphasis it occasioned, the mimetic view has by no means disappeared. The realistic and especially the naturalistic novels of the last eighty or so years have put considerable stress on the thing imitated—usually middle- or lower-class society—and on giving us "life as it really is." And today, if asked why they like a particular novel or short story, most readers would say something like: "Because it's so realistic. That's the way things actually are."

However, even the reader who gives his highest marks to a novel by saying "It's realistic" should be able to see the danger of assuming that realism is always a literary virtue. If it were, we should have to demote from the ranks of great literature such acknowledged masterpieces as *The Odyssey, The Divine Comedy, The Faerie Queene, The Tempest,* and *Paradise Lost,* in none of which is an overwhelming resemblance to any known time or place. Although poetry may be in some senses "a speaking picture," it is hardly a verbal photograph; that is true not only of heroic or fantastic modes of literature in which a deliberate distortion of reality is apparent but even of works that give every appearance of mirroring life, such as the documentary novel or realistic short story. In the first place, the poet lacks the objectivity needed to supply faithful reproductions of reality. His interests, moods, preferences, character—all his habits of mind and feeling—combine to make him less a mirror reflecting than a prism refracting life. In the second place, as Aristotle's distinction between poetry and history reminds us, life is chaotic and often confusing, whereas art is controlled and meaningful; thus even the most realistic of novels, for instance, is more an interpretation than a reproduction. Finally, we should remember that like any artist, the poet is limited by the medium he works in; his medium, language, is not an imitation of reality but a symbolic system by means of which man deals with reality. In a sense, languages are collective interpretations of reality, each one abstracting from reality what is relevant to the culture using it. The Eskimo language has a large variety of words to designate the different kinds and aspects of snow, as Polynesian has for coconuts and Arabic for camels. The poet trying to imitate the total reality of these objects in English obviously works under a handicap. He lacks the verbal tools to get at that reality, except by somewhat makeshift means; indeed, because he lacks them, he is not likely to be aware of that reality in the first place.

Apart from differences between particular languages, the nature of language itself imposes certain limitations upon the poet seeking to imitate reality. All discourse, for instance, has a linear dimension: written speech is spread out in space, and spoken speech in time. If what the poet seeks to imitate also has a linear dimension, this aspect of language may be helpful. Thus Pope's line on the Alexandrine can imitatively exploit its relationship to the linear shape and movement of a snake:

> A needless Alexandrine ends the song,
> That, like a wounded snake, drags its slow length along.

But much of what the poet imitates is not linear. Visual perceptions, moments of insight and feeling, occur instantaneously. Imitating in language a glimpse of a flying bird, the moment of "getting" a joke, or the sudden onset of pain inevitably falsifies the character of the experience by giving it a sense of duration that in reality it lacks. Such falsification occurs even in so brief a poem as Ezra Pound's "In a Station of the Metro," which imitates an act of imaginative association:

> The apparition of these faces in the crowd;
> Petals on a wet, black bough.*

Of course no one really expects literature to produce perfect reproductions of reality. Certainly poets themselves have felt no such obligation. Many of them would seem to agree with Theseus' claim in *A Midsummer Night's Dream* that poets operate with considerable freedom, not to say abandon:

> The poet's eye, in a fine frenzy rolling,
> Doth glance from heaven to earth, from earth to heaven;

---

* From *Personae* by Ezra Pound. Copyright 1926, 1954 by Ezra Pound. Reprinted by permission of the publishers, New Directions.

> And as imagination bodies forth
> The forms of things unknown, the poet's pen
> Turns them to shapes and gives to airy nothing
> A local habitation and a name.

And in *The Defense of Poesie* (c. 1583) Sir Philip Sidney reminds us that whereas other writers, such as philosophers, historians, or scientists, attempt to record facts and hence are tied to "nature" (reality),

...the poet, disdaining to be tied to any such subjection, doth grow in effect into another nature, in making things either better than nature bringeth forth, or, quite anew, forms such as never were in nature, as the heroes, demi-gods, cyclops, chimeras, furies, and such like; so as he goes hand in hand with nature, not enclosed within the narrow warrant of her gifts but freely ranging within the zodiac of his own wit.

This was the neoclassic position in general from the sixteenth to the nineteenth century—that art, although essentially mimetic, does not simply reproduce nature but makes things "either better than nature bringeth forth" (Arcadian landscapes, for instance, women of surpassing loveliness, heroes of extraordinary prowess) or "forms such as never were in nature" (gods and goddesses, fairies, dragons, and so on). Such a view, however, puts an obvious strain on the mimetic theory because if the purpose of art is to imitate nature, how can this be reconciled with the notion of improving upon or altogether transcending nature? "Improving upon" would appear to be merely a euphemism for "falsifying."

Much of the difficulty with mimetic theories stems from the fact that mimesis inevitably implies value judgments dependent on the degree of correspondence between the imitation and its subject. To judge the quality of an imitation we must compare it with its subject, as a portrait is compared with the person who sat for it. But if the subject is not available for comparison, as in the case of the *Mona Lisa,* what then? And if we discovered somehow that Leonardo's painting does not resemble the lady he was "imitating," would we feel obliged to grade it down? Even if we take "imitation" loosely, allowing for the transformation of nature by art—Homer's Polyphemus or Scylla, Aeschylus' Eumenides, Spenser's fairyland—the problem of comparison remains. As there is no model for any of these in nature, the artist presumably imitates a mental model, adopting, as Sidney and others suggest, a role analogous to that of God at the Creation. Unfortunately, the analogy is accurate, at least to the extent that the poetic mind is no less inscrutable than the divine. As a result, comparison is impossible.

One way of getting around this problem is to argue that by "imitation" we mean to stress not just the similarity but also the dissimilarity of literature and nature (reality). In other words, because it is an imitation, the poem is *not* what it imitates. Imitation from this standpoint would not be a passive copying of nature but a transformative process, a recreating of life through artificial means. As an artificial verbal structure the poem could enter into any of a variety of relationships to nature, ranging from close correspondence (e.g., *Robinson Crusoe, A Farewell to Arms, The Naked and the Dead*) to radical transformation (e.g., *The Divine Comedy, The Faerie Queene, Gulliver's*

Travels). We would want to insist, however, that no value judgments attach to imitation, that the fantastic, for instance, is not inferior to the realistic, only different. The trouble with this approach is that it distorts the usual meaning and implications of imitation: instead of "literature as mimesis," something like "literature as verbal artifice" would seem a more appropriate title for such a view.

Later on, we will suggest that literature's relation to reality can be regarded as metaphoric rather than mimetic, but for the moment we need to observe that critical theories can direct attention to the poem's "universe" without necessarily endorsing mimesis. Even if nature is not the model for literature, it can be both a source for the poet and a control for the reader. By "source" we mean that there could be no ballads about ravens or Spenserian knights "pricking on the plaine" unless there were real ravens and real knights and plains. Nature need not be limited merely to natural objects, of course: we could also have no fictional irresolution in Hamlet, courage in Satan, or love pangs in Troilus without real irresolution, courage, and love pangs in life. Which is not to say that the poet is confined to what nature or reality provides him but that he can take what is available in nature and transform it to suit his purposes. In the process, nature goes through the filter of fiction; its objects become pseudo-objects, or in Susanne Langer's phrase, "virtual" objects, "appearances." There is no danger that a still-life of fruit will start us salivating or that Oedipus' blinding will send us racing into the lobby to call an ambulance. An important aspect of "nature" in this broad sense is literature itself, which the poet may draw upon for inspiration (Chapman's translation of Homer being to Keats's sonnet what the nightingale is to his ode) or for content (e.g., the lines from Renaissance poems incorporated into *The Waste Land*). And we should want "nature" to include something even more indispensable—language—which the poet inherits or "comes into" in the same way he does his physical and cultural environment and which he also transforms "into something rich and strange."

As nature is a source for the poet, it is a "control" or standard of comparison for the reader. The statement that literature transforms nature, for instance, presupposes a knowledge of untransformed nature. This knowledge is "built in" when we are reading a contemporary poem because nature for the poet is at least roughly what it is for us. Chauvinism, political windiness, and the role of the glass of water in oratorical rituals are common knowledge, and hence E. E. Cummings' poem "next to of course god america i" (see p. 566) is immediately intelligible. Familiarity with modern English usage enables us to see that the poem's language is far from original, that every line except the last contains at least one rousing cliché; and our experience with real windbags—our awareness that not even the most inflated of them could compress so much nonsense so disconnectedly into one brief utterance—enables us to see that the poem is a satiric attack whose principal weapon is the intensification of the absurd.

Dealing with poets of the past, however, is another matter, especially if the only control one has is a knowledge of twentieth-century nature. There is an old story about the student who read *Hamlet* for the first time and said "It's full of clichés—like 'Something is rotten in the state of Denmark' and 'To be or not to be, that is the question.' " Any reader will exceed his quota of anachronistic boners unless he has some knowledge of literary history, which militates against misinterpretations by reconstructing as a control the nature available to poets of the past. Obviously, if the student is going to read poets of the past, a knowledge of the English language as it was used by them is a *sine qua non.* No one expects undergraduates to read *The Seafarer* in Anglo-Saxon any more, but Middle English has become nearly a foreign language to most twentieth-century readers, and even Shakespeare, though he falls technically within the scope of Modern English, requires heavy annotation for the student to grasp even the literal meaning of words like "favour," "commodity," "degree," and the like. An approach to literature as imitation demands that we know the raw materials that went into its making.

II.   The Pragmatic View: The Poem as Communication   The student may feel that of more immediate concern to him than the question "What does the poem imitate, discover, intensify, or transform?" is the question "Why should I study literature to begin with?" Answering that question, which is to say, trying to figure out what literature does for us or to us as its audience, brings us to the pragmatic view, which, like the mimetic, was first articulated in influential fashion by Plato and Aristotle. However, in discussing it further we can organize our remarks in terms of Horace's famous pronouncement in *The Art of Poetry* (c. 14 B.C.) that poetry profits (i.e., instructs) and pleases. For the sake of convenience, then, rather than descriptive accuracy, we can divide the effects of literature into instruction and pleasure, considering the poem in both cases as a communication but distinguishing between the communication of truth and the communication of emotion or feeling.

1. *The poem as a communication of truth.* Critics who regard literature as instructive usually have in mind other than merely factual information. Reading *Antigone, The Pardoner's Tale,* and *Wuthering Heights* can no doubt tell us something about Greek burial customs, medieval sermons, and nineteenth-century inheritance laws, but it is. unlikely that anyone would read these works to obtain such information, which is available elsewhere in more complete and authoritative form, or would feel that they stand or fall upon its accuracy. If factual accuracy were of cardinal importance, we should have to demote *The Winter's Tale,* for instance, because Shakespeare allows a shipwreck to occur in Bohemia, where, as Ben Jonson duly noted, "there is so Sea near by some 100 Miles," and *Paradise Lost* because Milton uses a Ptolemaic instead of a Copernican cosmology. But most readers feel that they can afford to give the poet a factual error here and there, and perhaps even a faulty cosmology, as long as they get something else out of the poem.

"Getting something out of" the poem, however, suggests a popular pragmatic view more often expressed by questions like "What's the moral of this poem? What's the author's message?" Such questions may sometimes reflect a legitimate concern about literary meanings, but usually they stem from a feeling that somewhere inside the poem, if one could just find it, is a lesson in living or a transistorized moral philosophy. This is the view of literature as a sugar-coated pill—a sour center of medicinal precepts well frosted over with pleasant episodes, stirring language, and fascinating characters. Or presumably that is what it should be. When it is not, when the sugar coating goes all the way to the center so that the pill becomes pure candy, then literature is regarded as degenerate or dissolute, its calorie-count entirely too high for the orthodox moral athlete.

The drawbacks of moral or message hunting are not hard to see, the immediate effect being to reduce the poem to a simple doctrinal statement that does scant justice to our literary experience. The "moral" of Hamlet's delay, his procrastination in taking revenge, becomes something like "A stitch in time saves nine," which substitutes the proverbial for the profound. Even worse, evaluation of works on this basis depends on how well the work squares with our own preconceptions about truth. What is not true becomes untrue, what is not moral, immoral. In extreme form, this leads to censorship, either by the individual who refuses to read poems expressing beliefs contrary to his own or by groups of people dedicated to the defense of some orthodoxy, usually of a religious or political sort. In the sixteenth and seventeenth centuries the moving spirit of censorship was Puritan and its special object of attention the theaters, which were regarded as centers of frivolity and moral corruption. In modern Russia, where political rather than moral censorship is dominant, the only works appropriate to an orthodox Communist audience appear to be those in which bands of radiantly happy peasants are pictured singing the "Internationale" as they pitch hay on the communal farm.

That is not to suggest that literature is devoid of meanings or truths; but regarding literature exclusively as a vehicle for the communication of truth runs the risk, oddly enough, of making it less meaningful than it actually is. What is disregarded, for one thing, is literary form. If a poem "says something" to us, it says it in a special way—so special that the manner of the saying becomes part of what is said. Discussion of this point can be taken up more appropriately when we come to the objective view of literature.

2. *The poem as a communication of feeling.* Following Horace's notion that literature instructs and pleases, let us now consider the PRAGMATIC view in terms of pleasure. In *Biographia Literaria,* Coleridge defined a poem as "that species of composition which is opposed to works of science by proposing for its *immediate* object pleasure, not truth." There is no reason why the receipt of truth may not be pleasurable, but most theorists associate pleasure with the feelings rather than with the mind. "The object of poetry," said J. S. Mill, "is confessedly to act upon the emotions," and this distinguishes poetry from science, he added, since science "addresses itself to the belief," not "the feelings." In acting upon the feelings, however, poetry may have various effects, two of which—stimulation and catharsis—have had particular prominence in literary theories.

One of the reasons Plato condemned literature, especially drama, is that it stimulates emotions that should be suppressed. He felt that tragedy, for instance, by exhibiting terrible crimes and great suffering, encourages men to be hysterical and womanish. A similar attitude underlies the programs of most censoring agencies; however, among its defenders, literature's stimulating effect is more often considered a mark of excellence. Thus in distinguishing the genuine poet from the mere rhymester, Pope says:

> 'Tis he, who gives my breast a thousand pains,
> Can make me feel each passion that he feigns;
> Enrage, compose, with more than magic art,
> With pity and with terror tear my heart.

As here, the emotional response to literature is often expressed in physiological terms. Emily Dickinson said, "If I feel physically as if the top of my head were taken off, I know this is poetry"; and Dylan Thomas noted that poetry is valuable to some people because it produces "a twanging at their tear ducts, or a prickling of the scalp, or a tickling of the spine, or tremors in what they hope is their heart."

If poetry is primarily a form of emotional excitation, then it must compete with a variety of other stimulants ranging from benzedrine to boxing matches. Why read Milton when martinis are available? One standard reply is that although liquor may be quicker, literature is better, its pleasure being of a nobler type. This is what Poe meant in *The Poetic Principle* when he said that "a poem deserves its title only inasmuch as it excites, by elevating the soul." A similar notion was expressed in about the first century A.D. by Longinus, whose epistolary manual *On the Sublime* explores the ways in which elevation of literary style produces elevation of response—"transport" or "ecstasy," emotions that transcend mere pleasure. To be "elevated" by poetry is not the same thing as getting "high" on martinis, primarily because the former is an aesthetic response. Thus Poe, an expert in both subjects, said, *"That* pleasure which is at once the most pure, the most elevating, and the most intense, is derived, I maintain, from the contemplation of the Beautiful."

The nature of the aesthetic experience—whether it is primarily emotional, attitudinal, elevating, organizing, and so on—has been variously argued, but there is pretty general agreement that it attends or results from "contemplation." Aestheticians speak of "disinterested" contemplation, of "detachment," "intransitive apprehension," and "aesthetic distance." Such terms do not imply that experiencing beauty is an act of frigid insensitivity but that it is an act divorced from practical considerations, "disinterested" being a far cry from "uninterested." Aesthetic contemplation thus presupposes an awareness of the fictional character of literary situations, the fact that they are appearances, not realities. We do not run away from a frightening mystery story or leap onto the stage to protect Desdemona against Othello (or at least only fictional characters like Fielding's Partridge do so). Similarly, aesthetic contemplation presupposes an awareness of the pragmatic "uselessness" of the art object. We cannot really "use" a sunset, a flower, a statue, portrait, or poem, though we can "misuse" them, as, for instance, if we played Beethoven's C Sharp Minor quartet as background music to promote table talk or treated Lawrence's *Women in Love* as a social document analogous to the Kinsey Report. Of course some art forms combine beauty and usefulness. A Grecian urn or a cathedral may be both beautiful and functional. If we consider the object aesthetically, however, we disregard its use: the urn might be ugly but highly serviceable, the cathedral beautiful but uninhabitable. As an aesthetic object the work of art is simply "there" to be contemplated, and because the impulse to use it is either irrelevant or psychically "blocked out," we see it more fully and intensely, from a greater variety of perspectives, than we do objects in real life. Calling art "useless," then, is merely a way of saying that from an aesthetic standpoint it is an end in itself, not a means to something else, and hence the pleasure derived from it is intransitive, remaining *with* the art object instead of carrying over to something else.

But art is not just one thing, or if it is, it is one thing with many facets and therefore hospitable to a variety of approaches. If we can "block out" the art object's use in order to see it aesthetically, so we can block out its aesthetic qualities in order to see its use. The intransitive aesthetic emotion, pleasure, or attitude may be selectively depressed in favor of a transitive emotion. Devotional music or hymns may stimulate emotions conducive to religious worship; martial music or poetry may stimulate patriotic sentiments; and social-protest novels may excite indignation and a clamor for reform. When, as in these examples, the function of the work predominates, when it has "useful" handles projecting from it too invitingly, it is likely to be of minor aesthetic importance. "The Star Spangled Banner" is not notable for its musical excellence nor does furniture-making rank high in the "arts"—in fact, here we differentiate between art and craft.

Yet even in the highest forms of art we may find an indirect inculcation of "right" emotions and attitudes. We cannot read Chaucer, Shakespeare, or Milton without undergoing in the process a subtle training of our feelings away from the sentimental and stock, the self-indulgent and over-simple, toward the discriminating, complex, and capacious. The feelings so trained are intransitive in that they, specifically, do not carry over directly into life, but the training itself is transitive, though not perhaps in any immediate sense. The student who has come to terms with Falstaff, for instance, who has resisted the too easy alternatives of warmly accepting or coldly rejecting that "huge hill of flesh," has surely undergone an experience that militates against emotional snap judgments in life. The student who has experienced the humor as well as the gravity of *Paradise Lost* should be disinclined in real life either to trivialize the grand or to aggrandize the trivial. Obviously one or two short-term investments in literary experience are not going to produce any large returns of emotional maturity. But a diversified and well-tended literary portfolio plays a significant part in keeping one's feelings both solvent and civilized.

Another pragmatic theory focusing upon emotional responses to literature descends from Aristotle, who said in *The Poetics* that tragedy arouses pity and fear in the beholders and effects a purgation (catharsis) of these emotions. In other words, Aristotle agreed with Plato that drama excites emotions, perhaps even emotions that might ordinarily be harmful; but he believed that it also purifies or sublimates these emotions so that pity and fear are not augmented but moderated. Precisely how this cathartic process works Aristotle did not say. In his *Politics* he spoke of music as a kind of homeopathic medicine, a "hair of the dog that bit you" remedy: people in states of ecstatic derangement are calmed not by soothing music, but paradoxically by highly impassioned music. So perhaps literary catharsis, as he conceived it, involves an exhaustion or moderation of emotion through vicarious experience, a "letting off of steam." Aesthetic distance would also seem relevant to catharsis: the emotions aroused, say, by Oedipus' blinding are mitigated by the awareness that this is a mimesis of blinding, not the real thing. And Aristotle's repeated stress upon coherence and unity of plot suggests that the perception of pattern, order, and form in the tragic action neutralizes the inchoate disorder of the emotional response; or, in Nietzschean terms, an Apollonian detachment and a Dionysian involvement become polarized.

Cathartic effects need not, of course, be limited to tragedy; literature in general has often been regarded as a lightning rod diverting potentially harmful impulses away from real life and grounding them in fiction. On this view, a pornographic novel acts not as an aphrodisiac but as a means of symbolic gratification, much as a football game is said not to spur aggression but to provide an outlet for it. There is no evidence that criminals are devoted readers of crime stories, as the Platonic view would seem to suggest, and if murder-mystery addicts are solid, law-abiding citizens we might argue that it is because their criminal tendencies have been discharged into fiction, all their murders acted out and worked off imaginatively. There is no easy way of gauging the validity of this theory, of course, since catharsis presumably takes place at an unconscious level. From the standpoint of social health, if the theory were true it would imply that the real danger to society is not books that provoke undesirable impulses but censors who would elminate such books. Clearly, however, a distinction in terms of literary merit is required; that is, one would argue that regarding sexual emotions, art becomes less an aphrodisiac and more a catharsis as the potentially pornographic is assimilated into aesthetic form. Borderline cases are inevitable, but Mickey Spillane and the photographs in *Playboy* are clearly at the opposite pole from James Joyce and Rubens. Problems are bound to arise when the reader cannot distinguish between sensual provocation and sensuous evocation; but this calls for a reform of the reader, not literature.

Before moving on to the expressive theory, we should note that the kind of criticism usually associated with an emphasis upon the emotional impact of art is "impressionistic criticism." The impressionistic critic attempts to express the felt qualities of literary works, thus presenting us, in Anatole France's phrase, with the "adventures of a sensitive soul among masterpieces." "Sensitive" is the key word here, the critic qualifying for his job as literary gourmet by virtue of a somewhat mysterious endowment of taste, sensibility, and cultivation. Adventures in taste, if conducted by someone like Walter Pater, may produce some genuine and penetrating literary insights. All too often, however, as attention swings from the poem to the critic, impressionism merely becomes synonymous with narcissism.

III.   The Expressive View: The Poem as Creation   Turning from the pragmatic to the expressive view is to turn from poetic effect to poetic cause. When Wordsworth calls poetry "the spontaneous overflow of powerful feeling," he emphasizes not the poem itself, the universe it imitates, or the audience it affects, but the act of poetic creation and the poet whose feelings are liberated by it. As citing Wordsworth would suggest, the expressive view came into its own with the rise of Romanticism, though there had been anticipations of it as far back as Longinus' claim that the "sublime" is the product of a poet with a great soul. On the whole, however, earlier criticism had given meager attention to the poet himself. According to one view, which had its origin in Plato's *Ion*, the poet was not responsible for his poems at all; he was inspired, possessed, seized by the *furor poeticus*, so that in the impassioned moments of "creation" he merely played the role of amanuensis to the gods or muses. Since poetry came not *from* but *through* him, the poet hardly qualified as a legitimate object of study. At best, he was, like the oracular priestess at Delphi, the vehicle of truths he did not himself understand; at worst, he was merely another madman. Countering this view, however, was one that put the poet in a better light by emphasizing his technical control over his work. Aristotle put little stock in the *furor poeticus* theory—his *Poetics* reads like a literary manual setting down rules-of-thumb on the proper construction of tragedies;

and Horace strictly subordinated inspiration to sound judgment, calling for diligent application of the file in revision and advising that rather than rush into print with the outpourings of genius, the poet confine his manuscript to his desk drawer for a decade before making it public.

Wordsworth's definition, with its "overflowing" metaphor, as opposed to the "mirror" metaphor common to mimetic theories, redirects attention from the external world passively reflected by the poet to the internal world of feeling actively expressed by (literally, "pressed forth from") the poet. Ill-adapted to drama, such a definition is particularly suited to lyric poetry; and lyric poetry had always been something of a stumbling block to the mimetic view, which along with the pragmatic, had dominated literary criticism since classical times. The Romantic movement itself was in some respects an "over-flow of powerful feeling," and what it overflowed were the dikes of neoclassicism. Not that neoclassic poetry was bereft of feeling (heroic drama, for instance, made a great point of "painting the passions"), but the feelings it expressed were either distanced from the poet through characterization, as in drama and epic, or controlled by decorum, as in pastoral elegies, or rendered obliquely through wit and irony, as in satire; whereas Romanticism released essentially lyric feelings having at least the *appearance* of the spontaneous and personal. Hence all the Romantics placed strong emphasis upon the artist, and especially upon his emotions and imagination: "I am certain of nothing," Keats said, "but the holiness of the heart's affections and the truth of the Imagination."

The expressive view has carried well into the twentieth century, to become articulated in various ways by such theorists as Benedetto Croce, R. G. Collingwood, and Suzanne Langer. For Croce, in his *Aesthetic* (1909), the creative process is alone significant. He equates "expression" with "intuition," and though he speaks of the indivisibility of expression and form, he neverthe-less discounts the formal embodiment of intuition in poems, paintings, statues, and so on as merely an external reproduction, necessary for communicative purposes but quite subordinate to the antecedent mental activity. Thus Croce can say that there is no difference between a shout of joy and "the expressive act (indeed all the five acts) of a regular tragedy." Similarly, in *The Principles of Art* (1938), Collingwood claims that "every utterance and every gesture that each one of us makes is a work of art." But there is obviously a world of difference between a shout or gesture of emotion and Keats's lines—

> My heart aches, and a drowsy numbness pains
> My sense, as though of hemlock I had drunk,
> Or emptied some dull opiate to the drains
> One minute past, and Lethe-wards had sunk.

The difference is between a symptomatic outburst of feeling and a disciplined, symbolic expression of feeling. A symptomatic utterance indicates the existence, at that time, of some emotion. But we may doubt that Keats was actually feeling an empathic combination of pain and joy when he wrote the above lines, just as we may doubt that there was a nightingale present at the time: the nightingale ode symbolizes, rather than signalizes, emotion. Nor must we assume that Kafka wrote *The Trial* in a fit of despair (in fact, he is reported to have read it aloud with great good humor) or that Shakespeare could scarcely stop laughing long enough to write the Falstaff scenes of *Henry IV*.

Even Wordsworth acknowledges that the poet expresses emotions "recollected in tranquillity," not pumping in the ventricles.

Poetic creation no doubt varies in character from poet to poet. From writers' accounts of their own experience it would seem that few proceed with the kind of highly conscious, inexorably logical detachment that Poe claims for himself in his essay on the composition of "The Raven." Nor do poems very often burst full-blown or even half-blown from opium-dreams, like Coleridge's abortive *Kubla Khan*. Frequently the process seems to begin with some seed or germ that inseminates the imagination; then a period of conscious work as possibilities are explored, adopted, discarded, modified; then, usually at some impasse, a period of unconscious work during which something jells, either wholly or in part; after which there is again the conscious labor of trying to fuse what "came" with what is needed. If the poet feels emotion while writing, it is most likely a prolonged state of tension punctuated by moments of depression when things are "wrong" and exultation when things are "right"; this whether he is writing tragedy or comedy, elegy or epithalamium. Contrary to Croce, words, rhythm, rhyme, stanzas, conventions, characters, scenes, plots, and so on are not merely means of communicating a preformed intuition: they are integral elements of the creative process itself, acting both to limit and to liberate poetic expression.

We have been assuming that in one way or another the poet expresses his feelings in the poem, though we hedged somewhat by saying that these feelings are presented, in lyric poems, with the "appearance" of the spontaneous and personal. That they are not really "spontaneous," directly transcribed from the heart, has already been noted; that they are not really "personal," directly giving us the poet's own feelings, needs mentioning. In *Feeling and Form* and *Problems of Art*, Suzanne Langer persuasively argues that what the poet expresses is not his own feelings but his insights into human feeling. That is obvious enough in drama or in quasi-dramatic forms like the novel, epic, or romance, where no one would attribute Iago's feelings to Shakespeare or the Pardoner's to Chaucer. But it is arguable that all literature, even the lyric, is dramatic since it involves the presentation at the very least of a character and an action, and perhaps also a scene. Arnold's lyric poem "Dover Beach," for instance, has a scene (a room with a window overlooking the English Channel), two characters (the speaker and his silent "love"), a physical action implied (her coming to the window), and a verbal action (the speaker's words, the poem itself). Here the poem takes place within a scene. In other poems, such as Auden's "Musée des Beaux Arts," scenes are present within the poem, which itself arises from an indeterminate setting; yet even in Auden's poem we have a character (the speaker) and a verbal action (the poem). If literature is always dramatic in this sense, the poet being distinct from the speaker, then all poets may be said not to project their feelings into, but to formulate feelings in, poetry.

There is probably no great disservice done "Dover Beach" if we read it under the impression that it embodies Arnold's own feelings about a general collapse of values, his impulse to substitute a magic circle of personal love and trust for the ebbing tide of public faith. But what is important from the standpoint of criticism is that the feelings attributed to Arnold are actually in the poem. Not that they are Arnold's but that they are part of "Dover Beach" is of primary significance. What we are concerned with here is the relation between literature and biography, between the poet and the man who is the poet. There is a natural temptation to allow the poet and the man to become fused in our imaginations, so that our feelings about the one influence our feelings about the other. A good deal of misdirected criticism grew up in the last century around Byron's poetry because critics, either enthused or repelled by the aura of mystery, adventure, and romance surrounding Byron himself, read their feelings about the man into their experience of the works. The same has been true in this century with Fitzgerald and Hemingway, whose novels would probably be less impressive to many readers if the writers were, say, part-time insurance salesmen and looked like Alfred Hitchcock. There are of course genuine reasons for admiring all three of these authors, but the fact that they were handsome or personable is not one of them. Naturally, it is gratifying if a great poet happens also to be a great or at least a likable man, but it is well to remember that what we read are poems, not men.

Confusing the man with the poet sometimes leads to the assumption that a poem expresses something that has actually happened in the man's life, and the reader may be inclined to feel that what is important is less the poem than the "sincerity" with which the poet rendered his experience. Some poems do seem to have a close relation to the author's experiences. Keats's sonnet "On First Looking Into Chapman's Homer" would certainly seem to result from Keats having looked into Chapman's Homer, his "Ode on a Grecian Urn" to result from his having contemplated a Grecian urn. Elegies usually stem from an event in the poet's life—the death of a friend; love sonnets are often addressed to the poet's mistress, and so on. What is significant, however, is not that the poet had a particular personal experience but that he converted it into a public experience that is the poem. Everyone has personal experiences; only poets transform them into art.

Poets also *discover* experience in the process of re-creating it poetically. As far as feeling is concerned, a poem may well reveal not what the poet actually felt but what upon imaginative re-examination he realizes he should have felt or wishes he had felt. An elegy on the death of an accomplished fellow poet, for instance, will not likely express that slight stir of pleasure, quickly suppressed, at the thought that a competitor has gone out of business. Moreover, the limitations of art require an abstraction from the fullness of any experience. Keats's sonnet on Chapman's Homer has no room for the feelings of momentary annoyance Keats may have felt when his reading was interrupted, for his feelings of hunger, sleepiness, headache, and so forth. All this does not mean that we should ignore biographical information but only that we should not approach it ingenuously or make it an end in itself. Trying to discover what copy of Chapman's Homer Keats read, where he read it and when, and in what frame of mind, may conceivably further our understanding of the poem; that is, something might turn up that would cause us to perceive in the poem meanings, values, and relations that we could not see before. What needs to be made certain, however, is that what we now see is actually there—that the deficiency was in our critical insight rather than in the poem's expressive power.

In such matters, the final authority about what the poem is or says must be the poem itself. Take, for instance, the debate over Wordsworth's little lyric "A Slumber Did My Spirit Seal":

A slumber did my spirit seal;
 I had no human fears:
She seemed a thing that could not feel
 The touch of earthly years.

No motion has she now, no force;
 She neither hears nor sees;
Rolled round in earth's diurnal course,
 With rocks, and stones, and trees.

One view holds that this poem is an elegiac lyric expressing sadness at the death of a young girl and a kind of numbed perplexity at the defeat of fancy by fact, of what "seemed" by what "is." However, a study of Wordsworth's life and thought discloses that he revered nature, attributing to it moral influences and healing powers and an immanent spiritual vitality with which man is intimately connected; in his poetry he sought to stress this sympathetic interdependence of man and nature, to discountenance the idea that nature is cut off from man—is something "out there," objective and alien. In the light of this information, then, we can revise our earlier view of the poem: it is an expression of solace instead of grief or puzzlement. The second stanza does not contrast with the first, it transcends it; an illusory kind of individual immortality is converted upward into a genuine immortality as the girl is absorbed into the timeless rhythms of nature.

But this would seem to be a case in which biographical information of one sort runs against the grain of the poem. The revised interpretation disregards the tone of the last stanza: the heavy, dirge-like rhythms, the lifelessness stressed by the repeated negatives ("no," "no," "neither," "nor"), the drabness of the objects chosen to represent nature ("rocks," "stones," "trees"). The result of these is an image not of joyous reunion with the collective life of nature but of death and isolation in a nature bleached of vitality and spiritual import, of imprisonment in an enormous graveyard rotating with objective, mechanical indifference. That this interpretation is at odds with the main current of Wordsworthian thought about nature only points out the resistances against which that current ran, and these are equally a part of Wordsworth's biography.

Emphasizing the autonomy of the poem leads us in the direction of objective theories of literature, but before taking that route we should mention briefly the relation of the poet to the neurotic. The ancient notion of the poet as possessed but only periodically so has its modern version in the view of the poet as neurotic, not quite insane but not quite sane either. Both views have the advantage of allowing society to accept or reject the poet when it wishes: if his truths are disconcerting, it is the mad side of his neurosis speaking; if they are comforting, it is the sane side. Freud considered the artist a man who, frustrated in his desires for power, riches, honor, or love, "turns away from reality and transfers all his interest, and all his libido too, onto the creation of his wishes in the life of phantasy." This turning from reality to the wish-fulfilments of daydream is a movement toward neurosis and psychosis. However, Freud observes, the artist finds the "way back to reality" by objectifying his fantasies in a socially approved form, making wish-fulfilment publicly available in literature. "Wish-fulfilment," from the standpoint either of poet or of audience, is not an ideal term. Although it might apply to romance, comedy, epic, and some novels, it is less relevant to tragedy, satire, "absurd" drama, existentialist fiction, and most realistic and naturalistic novels, which on the whole are nightmares of frustration, not dreams of fulfilment. No doubt there are poets who rather perversely wish to be frustrated, but it is a wish with less than universal appeal.

In "Art and Neurosis" Lionel Trilling points out that calling the poet neurotic does not account for his creative ability, which is a sign of health, not neurosis. Freud's view, which is grounded in the idea that those who can, do, and those who can't, daydream, takes too little note of the fact that the poet can and does do something: he writes poetry. Unlike other neurotics, he is not possessed by his neurosis but possesses it, masters it, transforms it into something quite unneurotic. Moreover, although the philistine elements of society view poets with a combination of contempt and fear, most societies have placed sufficient value on literature that practicing the poetic "vocation" may in itself bring power, riches, honor, or love. And finally, a blanket diagnosis can hardly do justice to so various a species as the poet, who ranges in character from the "well adjusted" to the near psychotic, who may be introverted or extroverted, Apollonian, Dionysiac, viscerotonic, somatotonic, or cerebrotonic, and perhaps worse. Poe was an alcoholic, Wilde a homosexual, Blake a visionary, Coleridge a pathological procrastinator and dope addict. But Chekhov and William Carlos Williams were doctors, Goethe a scientist, Sidney a soldier, courtier, and scholar, Donne a Dean of St. Paul's, Milton a secretary in the Council of State, and Wallace Stevens a lawyer and vice-president of a large insurance company—hardly failures in ordinary life thrown back upon literature as a form of compensatory fantasy. Perhaps the most that can be said is that inner frustrations and conflicts may motivate the poet (and the scientist, bank manager, or automobile salesman) and that some poems may be symbolic actions, strategies, or imaginative methods of dealing with such frustrations and conflicts. But the poem is more than just a symptom of inner tensions projected into words, an abbreviated case history, or a self-gratifying fantasy. It is a meaningful performance in language, the result of a creative process that demands intelligence, technical skill, knowledge, patience, and hard work. Rather than a flight from reality, the poem is a discovery of reality, a bodying forth of the forms of human experience and nature.

IV.   The Objective View: The Poem as Poem   If the poem is a discovery of reality, it is a way of knowing. It is also, as the OBJECTIVE view would stress, an object of knowledge, a thing in itself. The objective view came into its own with the "new criticism" of the twentieth century, which holds that a poem should be treated, in Eliot's phrase, "primarily as poetry and not another thing." In focusing upon what the poem imitates, what its effects are, or where it comes from and why, the previous theories tell us a great deal about the literary situation and process but do not answer the questions of primary interest to the objective critic: what are the properties of the poem itself, and what implications do these have for literary criticism?

Not until the nineteenth century does criticism begin to treat the poem "primarily as poetry and not another thing." Certain objective properties of the poem such as plot, meter, rhyme, imagery, and style had received sustained attention from Aristotle to Doctor Johnson. But these were significant because they contributed to poetry's work in the service of "another thing"—sociology or psychology (Aristotle's doctrine of catharsis); morality (promoting virtuous conduct through example and precept, as Sidney argues); religion (its "chief and principal" use being to celebrate God, Puttenham says); education in general (verse, Harington reminds us, being a great help to the memory); or merely diversion. What was "poetic" about poetry was its imaginative quality, its meter and rhyme, and its artful employment of language. Inside this "poetic" envelope was the "content"—the morality, religious truth, historical information, and so on—and it was this that justified poetry. In the nineteenth century, however, when Coleridge says that all the parts of a poem "mutually support and explain each other," this division between form and content begins to disappear. Instead of outer form and inner content, the poem has "organic form," in which the two interprenetrate. Form itself begins not merely to "contain" meaning but to "have" meaning. And because through the mutual support, proportion, and harmony of its parts, the poem achieves its own special unity and coherence, it must be studied in its own context, not in terms of philosophy, religion, politics, or "another thing."

Poe, who was greatly influenced by Coleridge, was a militant advocate of viewing the poem as poem. The argument that poetry's highest aim is to communicate truth he dismissed as "the heresy of *The Didactic*," rather like Mallarmé, who later asserted that "poetry is not written with ideas, it is written with words." Defending his position, Poe said:

We have taken it into our heads that to write a poem simply for the poem's sake, and to acknowledge such to have been our design, would be to confess ourselves radically wanting in the true Poetic dignity and force:—but the simple fact is, that, would we but permit ourselves to look into our own souls, we should immediately there discover that under the sun there neither exists nor *can* exist any work more thoroughly dignified—more supremely noble than this very poem—this poem *per se*—this poem which is a poem and nothing more—this poem written solely for the poem's sake.

From here it is not a great jump to the late nineteenth century and Pater, Wilde, Symonds, and Dowson, who fostered the "art for art's sake" movement in which literature was held to be quite indifferent to philosophy, politics, social issues, indeed life itself, the "aesthetic heresy" lying at the opposite extreme from Poe's "didactic heresy." The "art for art's sake" school has received a good many hard knocks from critics and readers because of its total divorce of literature from life. However, without endorsing the views of the Aesthetic Movement, we can acknowledge that the slogan "art for art's sake" makes a valid claim if we take it to mean that art has intrinsic worth and hence transcends its uses. That is not to say that literature has no uses analogous to those of discursive forms of writing like philosophy, science, rhetoric, and so on but rather that after we have stripped these away something still remains that is distinctively literary and valuable in its own right.

The "art for art's sake" movement and its carry-overs in the twentieth century are in part a reaction against the rise of science and the corresponding decline of interest in the humanities. Today the danger no longer appears to be that literature will seduce the unwary into a life of fantasy or rebellion, as Plato feared, but that it will merely be ignored in favor of more empirical demonstrations of truth in the sciences. Whereas critics like Sir Philip Sidney once praised poetry as a means of promoting moral and even heroic life, with the rise of science, laboratories rather than lyrics, facts rather than metaphors have seemed to offer the most effective means of dealing with reality and human conduct. Hence a desire on the part of literary apologists to remove literature from active competition with science, to give it an independent status to which the touchstones of science—objectivity, validity, reliability, prediction—are irrelevant. In accord with Poe's "didactic heresy," poetry is held to have no direct influence upon life—

> For poetry makes nothing happen: it survives
> In the valley of its saying where executives
> Would never want to tamper; it flows south
> From ranches of isolation and busy griefs,
> Raw towns that we believe and die in; it survives,
> A way of happening, a mouth. . . .*

—as Auden says in his "In Memory of W. B. Yeats." Hence poetry should avoid argument and meaning, in the sense in which discursive prose "means." Archibald MacLeish's poem "Ars Poetica" ("the art of poetry") has become a classic statement of this view:

> A poem should be palpable and mute
> As a globed fruit,
>
> Dumb
> As old medallions to the thumb,
>
> Silent as the sleeve-worn stone
> Of casement ledges where the moss has grown—
>
> A poem should be wordless
> As the flight of birds.
>
>   *
>
> A poem should be motionless in time
> As the moon climbs,
>
> Leaving, as the moon releases
> Twig by twig the night-entangled trees,
>
> Leaving, as the moon behind the winter leaves,
> Memory by memory the mind—
>
> A poem should be motionless in time
> As the moon climbs.
>
>   *
>
> A poem should be equal to:
> Not true.

For all the history of grief
An empty doorway and a maple leaf.

For love
The leaning grasses and two lights above the sea—

A poem should not mean
But be.*

Readers who adopt this point of view unquestionably have a valid point: many poems *are* closer to being self-contained, unique artifacts than they are to being logical discourse making statements about something. Even so, it is too extreme to say that poetry makes no statement at all. The concrete imagery of "Ars Poetica" itself reinforces a logical proposition, namely that a poem is mute and not designed to "mean" anything. If this proposition is to be taken at face value, the poem contradicts itself; if it is not, then the poem nevertheless implies a statement of some kind, perhaps a less extreme statement, such as: "Poems may not be totally devoid of statement, but sensory concreteness is what really counts." Extracting a proposition like this from the poem does an injustice to the full poetic reality, which both "says" and "is" more than this, but the point here is simply that the poem does say something.

But what the poem "says" it says in a special way. First, there is the large matter of poetic language, which most objective critics regard as radically different from the language of science—which is, ideally, mathematics—and from all other forms of propositional discourse. All the "new critics" in America —for example, John Crowe Ransom, Cleanth Brooks, Robert B. Heilman, Robert Penn Warren, Allen Tate, R. P. Blackmur—as well as their English counterparts—for example, I. A. Richards, William Empson, F. R. Leavis— have stressed the distinctive features of poetic language. In *The Burning Fountain* (1959) Philip Wheelwright systemizes these features philosophically and contrasts them with certain principles of what he calls "steno-language," that is, discursive language in its ideal form as a means of communication.

Wheelwright observes that in discursive language a symbol (word) is always distinct or distinguishable from its referent, the thing symbolized. The symbol "horse" has nothing about it, either visually or auditorily, that resembles or intrinsically suggests the animal that eats oats, just as the symbol "4" has nothing of "four-ness" about it. In the interests of communication, therefore, any other symbol would do as well as "horse"; we could call the animal "oat-eating quadruped," "nag," or even "xyz" so long as we agreed on the referent. In discursive language, symbols are self-effacing and, ideally, invisible because only their meaning, what they stand for or refer to, is important for communicative purposes. Discursive symbols, then, are rather like windows of clear glass through which we look to see their referents. In poetic language, however, symbols are like windows of colored glass: we look through them, but we cannot help being conscious of them and of the fact that their colors are imparted to their referents. The poetic symbol thus refers both beyond itself and to itself, and because it is "self-referring" no other symbol, despite the fact that it may have the same referent, can substitute for it. Take the second stanza of Marlowe's "The Passionate Shepherd to His Love":

> And we will sit upon the rocks
> Seeing the shepherds feed their flocks,
> By shallow rivers, to whose falls
> Melodious birds sing madrigals.

Self-reference is a quality of all the poetic symbols here insofar as they are *sounds,* not just indicators of meaning. As sounds, they act as units in a metrical pattern or serve the interests of rhyme, alliteration, assonance, consonance, and onomatopoeia. The symbols in the last line not only refer to music but are in themselves musical, containing an almost perfectly balanced pattern of sound and meter.

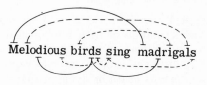

By paraphrase, we may be able to reproduce the literal meaning of this line; however, by breaking up its pattern of sound and rhythm, we will have destroyed what Langer calls its "import," which resides not in the meaning but in the *form* of the statement, in this particular choice and arrangement of poetic symbols.

Another ideal of discursive language is that each symbol should have one meaning only. Mathematics would obviously be in a bad way if the symbol "2" could mean both "two" and "three." Poetic symbols, however, may have multiple meanings, may be plurisignative or polysemous. When Desdemona denies that she has been unfaithful to Othello, he replies:

> O perjur'd woman! thou dost stone my heart,
> And makest me call what I intend to do
> A murder, which I thought a sacrifice.

"Stone" in the first line suggests "turn to stone" ("I am oblivious to your pleas for mercy and refuse to listen to any claims of innocence") but also "strike with stones" ("Your unfaithfulness hurts me as much as stoning my heart would"). An advocate of discursive language might regard this as communicative chaos, particularly because the two meanings are not only different but contradictory, one implying insensitivity, the other sensitivity. But ambiguity and paradox—always faults in discursive language, confusions of meaning that prevent our grasping the truth—may be in poetic language the only way of expressing the truth. Othello's emotional state *is* paradoxical, simultaneously embracing the callousness and stoniness of heart required for the act of murder and the anguish of heart involved in murdering the woman he loves.

Further, in discursive language a symbol should have a clear and precise meaning, vagueness of any sort being considered a defect. In poetic language, however, we may find what Wheelwright calls "soft focus." Most words have a degree of soft focus in that they not only "denote," or have literal meanings, but also "connote," or have emotional and qualitative associations. "Horse" and "steed" both denote that oat-eating quadruped, but their connotations are sufficiently different that we would never compel a knight in shining armor to suffer the indignity of riding merely a "horse." Poets, however, often employ words in ways that exploit their connotations and associations and minimize their denotations. In this stanza of Nashe's—

> Beauty is but a flower
> Which wrinkles will devour:
> Brightness falls from the air,
> Queens have died young and fair,
> Dust hath closed Helen's eye.
> I am sick, I must die.
> Lord, have mercy on us.

—the third line, "Brightness falls from the air," is an example of soft focus. We can easily supply the denotation of each symbol merely by looking it up in a dictionary, but the full import of the line extends into territories well beyond the reach either of dictionaries or of our own capacities of articulation. We can say that the line suggests death or dying in that "brightness" connotes brilliance, clarity, vitality, energy—qualities of life; that it suggests, through "falls," the primal Fall itself, which, as Milton says, "brought death into the world"; that in this context of human death it suggests a death of nature, of light, that first and sustaining product of the Creation, and hence the interdependence of man and nature; that it suggests the dying close of eyelids, which for the dying would present an image of a slow fall of light, a demise of vision and apprehension; and so on. It is obvious, however, that we are not dealing with a meaning that has clear outlines and a graspable form but with one that recedes dimly before us, eluding logical formulation yet remaining significant. And we should be careful to note that by "soft focus" we do not mean that the poet has written obscurely, that he has had a clear and exact idea in mind but has failed to give it clear and exact expression. When someone says "He's a nice guy," *that* is obscurity of expression, because apart from the fact that it is vaguely approving we do not have the least notion of what is meant—perhaps "He gave me a good grade, which I didn't deserve," perhaps "He contributed a million dollars to cancer research." With soft focus, on the other hand, the poet's expression is perfectly precise and perhaps the only one available for a meaning that has depth, subtlety, complexity, and profound significance.

In discursive language, the referent of any symbol should submit to classification either as a universal or as a particular, but not both. Universals are ordinarily represented by common names referring to classes of objects— "dog," "man," "house," and so on, whereas particulars are ordinarily represented either by proper names such as "Abraham Lincoln" or by particularized common names such as "this dog" or "the man in the red shirt standing by the widow." It would obviously be confusing in discursive communication if we used a proper name to mean not only one object but many. However, in poetic language we repeatedly encounter the "concrete universal," in which the single is also multiple, the particular also general. In *The Iliad*, for instance, Zeus admonishes the other Olympian deities not to interfere in the Trojan War or he will punish them; then he says, in Lattimore's translation:

> Let down out of the sky a cord of gold; lay hold of it
> all you who are gods and all who are goddesses, yet not
> even so can you drag down Zeus from the sky to the ground, not
> Zeus the high lord of counsel, though you try until you grow weary.

> Yet whenever I might strongly be minded to pull you,
> I could drag you up, earth and all and sea and all with you,
> then fetch the golden rope about the horn of Olympos
> and make it fast, so that all once more should dangle in mid air.

As supreme god, in other words, Zeus could, if he wanted, reabsorb all creation into himself, which means that he is a concrete universal—one god and yet all gods as well as all creation. Again, in the medieval lyric "Adam Lay I-Bowndyn" (page 111), the individual Adam who lies bound up as a result of taking the apple is particular and yet universal because he is all mankind. In fact, we associate Adam with mankind so automatically as to forget that the poem insists upon his individuality: "Fowre thowsand wynter / thowt he not to long." The poet is capitalizing upon the concrete universal, part of the tension of the poem being brought about by the paradoxical notion of one man existing in bondage for four thousand years without regarding it as a long time. Tension of this sort perhaps always exists between the concrete and the universal elements of literary symbols. Oedipus is a highly unique individual whose experience is rendered in concrete detail, yet the Oedipus experience has something in common with the experiences of other men, and once we notice this, whether in a Freudian sense or not, we recognize the universal in the particular, the "Oedipal" in Oedipus.

Finally, in discursive language a symbol should keep the same meaning throughout the course of a given argument or field of inquiry. In a given mathematical formula, the symbol "4" cannot mean "four" at one point and "six" at another, nor can this ambiguous meaning of "4" appear in mathematics as a whole, varying from mathematician to mathematician. But the meanings of poetic symbols are determined by the context in which they appear and hence may change as the context changes. This means that the referent of a given symbol may alter from poem to poem within poetry as a whole or even within a single poem. An example of the former case is the symbol "rose," which is associated with communion in Dante's *Paradiso*, with the infinitely desirable love of a lady in the medieval *Roman de la Rose*, with political dissension in Shakespeare's *Henry VI* plays, and with corrupted love in Blake's "The Sick Rose." An example of the latter case can be found in Othello's lines as he blows out the candle at Desdemona's bedside:

> Put out the light, and then put out the light:
> If I quench thee, thou flaming minister,
> I can again thy former light restore,
> Should I repent me: but once put out thy light,
> Thou cunning'st pattern of excelling nature,
> I know not where is that Promethean heat
> That can thy light relume.

The word "light" occurs five times in seven lines, its meaning shifting back and forth from "candle flame" to "life/spirit," the association of the two meanings in the one word ironically joining Desdemona and the candle in a union of innocence of which Othello is ignorantly "in the dark." Or again, in "The Falcon" (page 83), the symbol "faucon" in the opening refrain means (beyond the literal meaning of "bird," that is) "death as deprivation," whereas by the end of the poem, where the refrain is repeated, it has come to mean "death as redemption through Christ."

There are other distinctions between poetic and discursive symbols, but these should suffice to indicate the character of poetic meaning. Objective critics have repeatedly stressed that changing the form of a poetic expression also changes that which is expressed: a paraphrase, explanation, or commentary, however intelligent and thorough, cannot substitute for the poem itself. In other words, the poem *conveys* more than it says. When Pope, speaking of women, says,

> See how the world its veterans rewards!
> A youth of frolics, an old age of cards;
> Fair to no purpose, artful to no end,
> Young without lovers, old without a friend;
> A fop their passion, but their prize a sot;
> Alive, ridiculous, and dead, forgot!

it is not just what the speech "says" about women that interests and amuses us but also what it *implies* about the speaker's feelings and attitudes, the nervous coexistence of animus and restraint under the surface of literal statement. The speech conveys an uneasy resolution of contrary impulses: on the one hand, an intellectual detachment suggested by the regularity of the meter and rhyme, the artful placement of caesurae, the sustained pattern of antithesis, and the precision of the diction; on the other hand, an emotional involvement suggested by the meanings of the words themselves, their harshness ("fop," "sot," "ridiculous"), and also by their syntactic arrangement (the creation of irony through defeated expectation—"*but* their *prize*...a sot"), and by the way the speech moves from wit toward invective. We can roughly identify this tension between detachment and involvement in the speech and suggest what implies it, but we cannot *evoke* it as the speech itself does; something gets lost in the process of commentary or paraphrase, just as the humor of a joke gets lost in the explanation. This does not mean that criticism is futile, only that it is not poetry.

A major effect of poetic implication is to create a context in terms of which we read the poem. Actually, we have two contexts, one verbal, one dramatic. The meaning of any word is heavily dependent upon its verbal context, upon how it is "woven together" with other words. The word "spring," taken alone, could be a verb or one of several nouns; only when we surround it with other words does it acquire definitive meaning: "The spring is broken," "Spring is lovely," "It has spring in it," "Spring onto the chair," and so on. Similarly, only in the context of other lines and ultimately of the poem as a whole does a particular poetic expression take on full significance. "Beauty is truth, truth beauty," "My way of life / Is fallen into the sear, the yellow leaf," "How can we tell the dancer from the dance" in isolation may be true or false, absurd or profoundly suggestive, but put in their contexts of the "Ode on a Grecian Urn," *Macbeth*, and "Among School Children," where they are amplified, qualified, and intensified by the other parts of the poem, they acquire special significance.

In addition to building up an intricate and unique verbal context, a poem also builds up a dramatic context. In this connection the poem is less a verbal structure than a verbal action, action being the essence of drama (Greek *dran,* "to act"). Like words, actions are meaningful only in terms of their contexts, which are both external and internal. Take the case of a man raising both hands high above his head. If he is standing on a rostrum before a crowd of political partisans, we would interpret his action as a victory salute equivalent to "We shall win!" If he is standing in an alley before a gunman, we would read it as a sign of nonresistance, "Take it easy, I'm not going to try anything." The internal context is obviously more difficult to discern, our interpretation of it depending upon what "stylistic" clues we can pick up from the manner in which it is performed: the politician's hands may go up too hesitantly, slowly, or wearily to suggest real hope or confidence in his election; the victim of robbery may smile in such a way as to imply triumph, "Take my money—if you can find any!" The full meaning of the action is indeterminate, and the value we place upon it tentative, until we know as much as possible about its context.

What moves us, interests us, gives point and value to our experience of a poem is very often not entirely its purely verbal meanings but the dramatic context in which, as a verbal action, the poem occurs. Take, for instance, Hopkins' poem "Spring and Fall: To a Young Child":

> Márgarét, are you gríeving
> Over Goldengrove unleaving?
> Leáves, líke the things of man, you
> With your fresh thoughts care for, can you?
> Áh! ás the heart grows older
> It will come to such sights colder
> By and by, nor spare a sign
> Though worlds of wanwood leafmeal lie;
> And yet you wíll weep and know why.
> Now no matter, child, the name:
> Sórrow's spríngs áre the same.
> Nor mouth had, no nor mind, expressed
> What heart heard of, ghost guessed:
> It ís the blight man was born for,
> It is Margaret you mourn for.*

As a structure of verbal meanings, the poem is impressive primarily because of its development of the arboreal and seasonal images ("Goldengrove unleaving," "Leaves," "fresh," "grows," "colder," "wanwood leafmeal," "springs," "blight") as part of a central metaphor associating the rhythms of nature with those of human life and feeling. Margaret is the center of attention here, and the poem moves toward an explanation of her "grieving" as something beyond the reach of her thought or powers of expression, a grief resulting from her spiritual/emotional apprehension of her own imminent transition from spring to fall, from innocence to experience, from the sensitivity of childhood to the wintry indifference of adulthood. But the poem is more than an explanation conducted through imagery and metaphor; it is also an action by a character in a dramatic situation. The character is an older person, probably a man, speaking to a young girl, both situated in a pastoral scene; she is weeping, and the words he utters are a response to her youth, sorrow, tears, and the scene itself. Thus the words of the poem are "there" not only as words, images, metaphors, and symbols but as *choices* that the speaker makes and that therefore disclose to us his thoughts and feelings. The profound difference between his and the child's perspectives (and his awareness of the difference), his gentleness and sympathy toward her, and the pattern of his own evolving feelings— how his sorrow, generated by hers, moves out to encompass the whole human situation, not by "using" her plight as a springboard to abstract speculation, but by a process of expansion outward from the particular to the universal and then a fusion of both in a Margaret mourning the autumn of her own childhood and the "blight man was born for": this, and more, the poem conveys to us as an action fraught with implications. It is not just the poem's motives or strategies that give it significance, although we can interpret it along these lines as an attempt to promote communion and to tease consolation out of sorrow by universalizing the sources of sorrow: the "blight" is our common heritage; none of us suffers alone, not even Margaret. We should certainly recognize such a strategy or motive in the poem because it is by comparing it with other poems and statements having the same strategy in potential— for example, merely the phrase "Nobody lives forever"—that we can distinguish the special qualities of Hopkins' poem, discover its own "inscape," as Hopkins would say. But the point here is that what is important to our experience of the poem, what both governs and enriches our responses to it, is the dramatic context it implies. It is partly because of this context that we cannot rephrase or extract statements from the poem without loss, for the poem belongs "here," as an expression issuing from (and simultaneously creating) this particular character in this particular situation.

Speaking of a "central metaphor" in this poem should remind us of the centrality of metaphor in literature as a whole. Although a critical interest in metaphor goes at least as far back as Aristotle's *Poetics* and *Rhetoric,* objective criticism of the past thirty or so years has made it an object of intense study. Earlier, in discussing mimetic theories, we suggested that perhaps we get closer to the truth if we say that literature's relationship to reality is less mimetic than metaphoric. One of the reasons that the mimetic theory held the critical stage well into the eighteenth century but became increasingly subject to dispute since then is that "reality" itself has become increasingly subject to dispute since Locke, Berkeley, Kant, Hegel, and others. We have become more and more conscious that reality is not a ready-made "given" but the product of an interaction between the perceiving subject and the perceived object—that reality is a kind of vast reservoir of potentials, some of which become actualized at a particular occasion depending upon what mode of knowing is employed. The "reality" of a chair, for instance, is one thing if a man looks at it from a distance of ten feet, another thing if he looks at it through a microscope, and it would be still another thing if the human eye could see X rays or ultra-violet rays or infra-red rays. The major mode of knowing today is science: "Whatever can be known," Bertrand Russell has said, "can be known by means of science." But to say that the "real" reality of the chair is disclosed by scientific measurement—that the chair is so high, so wide, so thick, with so much mass and such and such a molecular structure, and so on—is merely to say that if we apply this particular mode of knowing to it, it obligingly gives us back this kind of "reality," different potentials in the object having been actualized by our method of investigation.

Lacking, then, a fixed and final reality "out there," mimetic reproduction becomes a dubious matter, as Plato was aware; hence the romantics for the most part discarded mimesis in favor of theories stressing the creative role of the imagination. What is central to the imagination, Coleridge argues, is its "esemplastic" power, which effects a synthesis, a "balance or reconciliation of opposite and discordant qualities." And T. S. Eliot has said that "when the poet's mind is perfectly equipped for his work, it is constantly amalgamating disparate experiences." A major way in which these balances, reconciliations, and amalgamations occur is through metaphor, which like mimesis, is based on comparison, similarity, likeness: "Snow is *like* tiny pieces of white paper," "The sun is *like* a ball of fire." (We can ignore Aristotle's grammatical distinction between metaphor and simile—that is, simile uses terms that state the comparison, such as "like," "as," "as if," whereas metaphor omits them—because the same mode of thought underlies both.) Unlike mimesis, however, metaphor does not imply a standard of valuation consequent upon the degree of likeness achieved: "A stone is like a boulder" is a poor metaphor because the degree of likeness is too great. On the other hand, "A stone is like a chicken" is a poor metaphor because the degree of unlikeness is too great. The value of a metaphor, it becomes apparent, lies neither in likeness nor in unlikeness but rather in its imaginative "life," its psychic energy, its power to vitalize consciousness by calling forth, as Shelley put it, "the before unapprehended relations of things."

We can divide metaphors into two types, *explicit* and *implicit*. In the explicit type, both of the compared items are present in the expression itself:

> O my Luve's like a red, red rose,
>
> Thou art my heaven, and I thine eremite,
>
> The atoms of Democritus
> And Newton's particles of light
> Are sands upon the Red Sea shore,
>
> Your Winter-garment of Repentance fling,
>
> God! giver of breath and bread;
> World's strand, sway of the sea.

A single underline indicates what I. A. Richards calls the "tenor" of the metaphor —that is, its subject, what is being clarified, explained, or illuminated by the comparison—and a double underline indicates the "vehicle" of the metaphor—that is, the clarifying, explaining, or illuminating image, which is normally more concrete and familiar than the tenor. In the *implicit* type of metaphor, on the other hand, only the vehicle is present in the expression, and therefore we have to infer what the tenor is. For instance, "The soldier snaked through the brush" contains an implicit metaphor in which the vehicle ("snaked") refers to a tenor that is not stated (manner of movement). We could convert this into an explicit metaphor simply by saying, "The soldier moved through the brush like a snake." This is an example of an implicit metaphor whose subject or tenor is easily identified. So too when Shakespeare says, "Poor soul, the center of my sinful earth," we readily infer that the vehicle ("sinful earth") refers to the unnamed tenor, body or flesh. When Shakespeare says in his next line, "Thrall to these rebel powers that thee array," we may not be precisely sure what the tenor of "rebel powers" is, but we have a pretty good notion that it is something on the order of "passions, worldly desires, sins." However, some poetic expressions present us with the vehicle of a metaphor whose tenor is extremely difficult to establish with any exactitude, though the metaphor is nevertheless charged with significance. For instance:

> Brightness falls from the air,
>
> Thou art a soul in bliss; but I am bound
> Upon a wheel of fire, that mine own tears
> Do scald like molten lead,
>
> Annihilating all that's made
> To a green thought in a green shade,

> Tyger! Tyger! burning bright
> In the forests of the night,
>
> We have lingered in the chambers of the sea
> By sea-girls wreathed with seaweed red and brown.

At this point some critics would contend that we have passed from metaphor to symbol, the distinction being that whereas the tenor of a metaphor can be expressed in nonmetaphoric terms, a symbol expresses a meaning that is otherwise inexpressible. This is an important point—certainly all the above examples are utterly untranslatable; however, we should prefer to subsume this conception of symbol under metaphor, regarding it as an extreme version of implicit metaphor in which the tenor has been collapsed into the vehicle.

What we are working toward is the notion that not just isolated words or parts of poems but poems themselves are metaphors. Perhaps we should note that the statement "Poems are metaphors" is itself metaphoric and therefore not the whole truth about poems. But it is a partial truth and one with fruitful consequences for a consideration of literature. For instance, it allows us to think of reality not as the object of poetic imitation, but as the tenor to which all literature refers metaphorically. Reality, then, is not the criterion by which we judge literature: it is a subject whose infinite variety is intensified and illuminated for us, however obliquely on occasion, by literature. Such a view tends to obviate the problem of belief. If the poem is a metaphor, it is not making a direct statement about reality or human affairs, even though it may appear to do so. We simply accept the fact that all metaphors have a built-in distortion as a condition of their being, because they are conceiving of one thing (tenor) in terms of something that it is not (vehicle). When Keats has Porphyro say to Madeline "Thou art my heaven," he asserts an identity between "thou" and "heaven" that is patently false. Metaphors, though they assert a relationship of identity between vehicle and tenor, are actually adjectival: the assertion "Madeline = heaven" means metaphorically "heavenly Madeline." Yet even if we acknowledge this adjectival character in Keats's metaphor—if it really means that Madeline and heaven have in common the qualities of desirability, ideality, and perhaps dubious availability —we should still say that the assertion is, if not patently false, merely a partial truth masquerading as a full truth. In this sense, all metaphors are partial perspectives claiming to be full perspectives. Man, Hamlet says, is "an angel," "a god," "the beauty of the world," and "the paragon of animals," but he is also "this quintessence of dust." None of these, taken alone, is the full truth. Hamlet is a man discontented with partial perspectives, and hence he runs through perhaps more metaphors than any other literary character, trying to encompass the full reality of the human condition only to discover that limited awareness is an inevitable feature of that condition and hence that such metaphors as "the readiness is all" must do duty for the "all" that he cannot achieve. If "nature loves to hide," as Heraclitus said, then metaphor is a major way of disclosing the hidden without plundering its hiding-place.

Considered in this light, literature becomes a vast vocabulary of metaphors, each offering a special view of some aspect of reality that it both imitates and creates—as an act of perception, the Gestaltists point out, distinguishes form from the miscellaneous stimuli received by the senses. Thus the various forms of literature impose order on given substances, sometimes reproducing fairly accurately what we have already learned to "see" and sometimes transforming it radically. How much a given work transforms reality is open to dispute. To the man who accepts a Ptolemaic universe, the cosmology of *Paradise Lost* would seem a reasonably close version of what is, whereas to Copernicans it would seem a radical transformation of what is in the interests of an invisible moral universe having a symbolic structure of light and dark, up and down. To someone who rejects the poem's Christian beliefs, the entire machinery of Gods, devils, and angels seems as "mythic" or symbolic as its physical cosmos, at best perhaps a kind of quasi-allegorical projection of psychic and moral forces into superhuman forms.

At one extreme on the scale of literary transformation, where there is a marked correspondence between poem and reality, we have imitative metaphors writ large, giving us the realism and naturalism of the documentary novel and short story, some drama, and some satire. At the other extreme (neither total likeness nor total unlikeness being possible), we have works of "high trans-formation" analogous to symbolic metaphors: romance, epic, symbolist lyric, and fantastic satire. It is possible, of course, for both extremes to appear in one form, as in some satire and pastoral. Pastorals often begin with a mythic Golden Age or dream world of some kind and then introduce into it some indigestible lump of reality, so that the two comment upon one another. Neither extreme, we repeat, should be automatically considered good or bad, better or worse, any more than we consider the view through a microscope better or worse than that through the eye alone. Poems of high transformation may cast intense imaginative light upon human experience by causing us to perceive fresh aspects of things and new relations between them. They may also cause us to make discoveries about the act of perception itself, in which we select the things we see and block out others, connect the present with the past, anticipate the future, smuggle into the experience certain social and personal attitudes, and so forth. At all points on the spectrum from fantasy to realism, the literary way of connecting verbal form to external universe—as opposed to the scientific, historical, or philosophical ways—takes into account the human instrument that sees and compares and interposes a style important in itself. Literature is thus a unique way of knowing and discovering likenesses, differing markedly from direct experience, abstract idea, or quanti-tative measurement. Its specialty is insight, its trademark style.

To sum up, the *expressive* dimension of literature is essentially the poet's stock of experience and social attitudes that causes him to organize his literary metaphor or formula in his particular Keatsian, Marvellian, Miltonic, or Shakespearean way—and also, no doubt, that makes him want to express himself to begin with. His special organization of general experience imparts coherence to his metaphor, just as the special organization of our arboreal experiences "creates" the tree we think we see. The *objective* dimension of literature is essentially the detached artifact that somehow both exists in its own right and yet refers to outer and inner phenomena. The *pragmatic* or communicative dimension involves the synchronization of the poet's and the audience's fund of experience and especially their fund of language, which comes loaded with centuries of experience. The poetic "world" is accepted as meaningful, not merely imaginary, because of a mutual agreement between poet and audience that things are indeed like this, or could be. The *mimetic* dimen-sion of literature lies in our realization that there is, in fact, a pre-literary something without which both poet and audience would fall silent. Thus a given work is like its author in some way, like its ambient universe, like some-thing in the audience, and since it is also a newly minted artifact, like nothing else in the world.

Index